Welsh
Founders of Pennsylvania.

WELSH FOUNDERS OF PENNSYLVANIA

By

THOMAS ALLEN GLENN

Two Volumes in One

CLEARFIELD

Originally published
Oxford, England, 1911-1913

Reprinted
Genealogical Publishing Company, Inc.
Baltimore, Maryland, 1970

Reprinted for
Clearfield Company, Inc. by
Genealogical Publishing Co., Inc.
Baltimore, Maryland
1991, 2000, 2001

Library of Congress Catalogue Card Number 75-112825
International Standard Book Number: 0-8063-0430-8

Made in the United States of America

Welsh Founders of Pennsylvania.

BY

THOMAS ALLEN GLENN.

VOL. I.

Oxford

[250 copies privately printed and the type distributed]

FOX, JONES AND COMPANY, KEMP HALL, HIGH STREET

1911

I DEDICATE THIS BOOK

TO

MY FRIEND

GEORGE H. EARLE, Jr.,

OF PHILADELPHIA.

Preface.

FIFTEEN YEARS ago I published, under the title "Merion in the Welsh Tract," an account of the settlement by Welshmen of Merion, Radnor, and Haverford, in Pennsylvania, with particular reference to the former township. Since then a long residence in Wales has afforded me opportunities of ascertaining the parentage and birth-places in the Principality of many more of those who, about the close of the seventeenth century, left their native hills to become Founders of the Commonwealth of Pennsylvania. I have also traced the lineage of some of these early colonists, and added much which it is hoped may prove of interest, and by way of verification, to several of those pedigrees which appeared in skeleton form in "Merion," and in "Gwynedd."

What has been gathered I here present to the public, trusting that this contribution to the history of my native State may be deemed of value, not only by the descendants of the Welsh pioneers, but also by those who may care to study the source from whence so many of Pennsylvania ancestry derive, at least in part, their marked abilities in the several professions, in finance, and in the successful management of great business enterprises.

Having the latter class especially in mind, I have prepared several charts showing the ancestry in all directions for a number of generations of a few of the first Welsh arrivals in the Province of Pennsylvania, or of their immediate forefathers. A glance at these charts[1] will show how descendants of several of the Welsh Founders derive

---

[1] Reference should be had to pedigrees xviii. and xix.

their blood from the ancient princely and noble families of Wales, the Plantagenets, and the great ruling families of England. It is, perhaps, of more than passing interest to know that in the comparatively small section of country represented by eastern Pennsylvania, there is a large number, perhaps the greatest number, of the posterity of the historic Norman houses of de Vere, de Bohun, de Clare, Mortimer, Holland, and of the Princes of North and South Wales. In addition to this, they are proven to have descended from all of the great Royal houses of Europe, and even from some of the Emperors of Rome. Up to the fourteenth century, indeed, there is hardly anyone who acted a great part in the world's history, in France, Spain, England, or Germany, who has not his lineal descendant in Pennsylvania. Here, also, noted for their attainments and honoured by their fellow citizens, are thousands who trace to Welshmen whose names, in the seventeenth and eighteenth centuries, were bye-words in every Cymric household. Considered as entirely removed from mere pride of race, this force must be reckoned with in the history of the world for centuries to come, and it gave to America no less a man than Abraham Lincoln, who, through his mother, whose characteristics he inherited, sprang from a Welshman of almost the same blood as the charts represent, and whose family removed from near Bala to Gwynedd, near Philadelphia, in 1698.

Great care has been exercised in the compilation of the pedigrees contained in the following pages, and nothing included which has not first been subjected to a severe critical test. The identity of individuals, so necessary in Welsh genealogies, in which, down to the eighteenth century, permanent surnames are infrequent, has been established by the comparison of signatures, the tenure of lands, or by local or family reference of which no reasonable doubt could be entertained. A few alliances appearing in the following pages will be found to vary from certain pedigrees heretofore accepted; but such departures from old genealogies have only been made after a patient investigation of the evidence, and are believed to be warranted by the facts. Citations to the authorities for all definite statements of importance are given.

It remains for me to express my thanks to all of those on both sides of the Atlantic who have so kindly assisted, in one way or another, in the preparation of this work. Of these I must first mention George H. Earle, Jr., Esq., of Philadelphia, to whom the inception of this volume is solely due, to whom it is dedicated, and whose editorial advice and personal interest has been untiring.

My hearty thanks are also due to Foster C. Griffith, Esq., of Trenton, N.J., John L. Cadwalader, Esq., of New York City, C. Morton Smith, Esq., of Philadelphia, Richard Y. Cook, Esq., of Philadelphia, Joseph H. Coates, Esq., of Philadelphia, Malcolm Lloyd, Esq., of Philadelphia, John W. Jordan, L.L.D., Historical Society of Pennsylvania, Edward Griffith, Esq., of Coedcymmer, Dolgelley, North Wales, Robert Jones, Esq., Probate Registry, St. Asaph, Henry A. Cleaver, Esq., Diocesan Registry, St. Asaph, North Wales, William M. Myddleton, Esq., of Lincoln, Philip H. Lawson, Esq., of Chester, and to the custodians of the National Library of Wales.

THOMAS ALLEN GLENN,

Meliden, Prestatyn,
    North Wales.

St. David's Day, 1911.

To the Reader.

UNTIL about the beginning of the eighteenth century few Welsh families possessed fixed surnames. John, son of William Howel, or William *ap*[1] (son of) Howel, would simply be known as *John Williams, John ap William*, or perhaps *John ap William Howel*. Supposing John Williams to have become the father of a boy named Hugh, the latter might call himself either *Hugh John, Hugh ap John, Hugh John William*, or *Hugh Jones*.

To make identification more certain, it was the custom in the fifteenth, sixteenth, and early part of the seventeenth centuries for Welshmen to describe themselves in official records by adding to their own given name those of a number of their ancestors. Thus, the sureties for the administrix of one Gruffydd ap Humphrey, of Llanfor, in 1590, are given in the Act Book at St. Asaph, as *Morgan John ap Res ap Tudor*, of Llandrillo, and *Gruffydd ap Howel ap David ap Rees [ap] David ap Rees*, of Llanfor, yeomen.

It was formerly the custom in Wales to designate individuals by epithets, such as *goch* (red), *ddu* (black), *llwyd* (grey), *gwyn* (white), *Vychan*, or *Fychan* (little), and often, in later days, some of these were retained by descendants as permanent surnames,—hence Gough, Lloyd, Gwyn and Wynn, Vaughan, etc. Some present day Welsh surnames are the results of contractions. Thus Prichard, from *ap Richard*, Bevan from *ab (ap) Evan*, Bowen from *ab (ap) Owen*, Price from *ap Rice*, or Rees (Rhys).

Daughters likewise assumed their father's given name as a surname, so that Jane, daughter of William Howel, would be called *Jane Howel*, or *Jane verch*[2] (daughter of) *Howel*, and it was not customary until after the beginning of the eighteenth century for women to change their names after marriage.

No attempt has been made to ensure absolute uniformity in the spelling of Welsh names in the following pages, and owing to the various spellings of the same names at different periods, and often at the same period, and in the same record, it would be quite impossible. The

---

[1] *AP*, in modern Welsh, *mab*, is also found in genealogies and records written *ab*; in a tenth century pedigree *map*.

[2] Verch, in modern Welsh *ferch*, is usually contracted *v.*, vch., or vz in records.

following brief explanation may be useful to the reader. *Gruffydd* is the same name as *Griffith*, and is so pronounced. In Welsh records of the sixteenth and seventeenth centuries, we find the form *Gruffyth*, the *u* being sounded like a thick English *i*. *Maredydd*, or *Meredydd*, is the English *Meredith*, and the name is so spelled in later Welsh documents. *Ieuan*, is another spelling of *Evan*, and in records is nearly always found contracted, and often written *Jeuan*. *Rees*, and *Res*, are the same as *Rhys*, which is, however, the most correct form. *Cadwalader* is also spelled *Cadwaladr*, and, as in most other cases, the spelling occurring in the record cited, or of the persons themselves, has been followed. The spelling of place-names has altered very much, even during the last half century. For instance, *Llanfor*, in Merionethshire, was formerly often written *Llanvawr*, and *Llanvor*. There is no *v* in the modern Welsh alphabet.

The student of Welsh genealogy will do well to remember that in Wales especially, the heirs to even very small estates were very frequently married at a *very* early age. Even so late as the seventeenth century, marriages of boys of from 14 to 16, to girls of 12 to 14, were quite common. This often makes the generations of the eldest line very short. It was also common to give two or more daughters, and sometimes two or more sons, the same name, which is occasionally confusing.

T. A. G.

Table of Contents.

PEDIGREE I.—Descendants of Marchweithian, lord of Isaled, and allied families: Aiken, Biddle, Cadwalader, Coates, Cook, Dickinson, Drexel, Earle, Erskine (descendants of David Lord Erskine and Frances Cadwalader), Foulke of Gwynedd, Ffoulke of Plâs Newydd, Francine, Gibbons, Humphrey, Jones (descendants of John ap Thomas of Llaithgwm), Kite, Leasher, Levering, Levick, Lloyd, McIlhenny, Maurice of Cae Môr, Means, Mitchell, Owen, Roberts, Roberts of Pencoyd, Rees of Fron Ween, Sellers, Troth, Thorne, Vaughan of Hendre Mawr, Wynn of Abercynllaith, Wynne of Bron Fadog, (Dr. Thomas Wynne), Yale of Plâs yn Yale, pp. 1-38; and *Chart*, facing p. 21.

PEDIGREE II.—Rees of Fron Ween, Penmaen. Families of Cook, Jones of Ciltalgarth, and Blockley, Rees, Roberts of Pencoyd, Merion, pp. 38-39.

PEDIGREE III.—Jones of Ciltalgarth and Blockley, Jones of Llaithgwm and Merion, Levick, p. 40.

PEDIGREE IV.—Vaughan of Llanwddyn, Abel, Davis, Ellis, Howel, Hughes, Humphrey (Humphreys), Jones, Maris, Morris, Mortimer of Coed Mawr and Pennsylvania, Scarlet, Smith, Thomas, Vaughan, pp. 41-48; and *Chart* facing p. 44.

PEDIGREE V.—Descendants of "Baron" Lewis Owen of Dolgelley, Vaughan of Hengwrt, and Tudder of Cefnrowen: Anwyl (and allied families), Coppock, Ellis, Evans, Griffith of Coedcymmer, Dolgelley, Jones, Lawson, Meyrick, Minshall, Owen of Caer Berllan, of Dolserey, of Garth Angharad, of Hengwrt, of Lewes (Delaware), of Maryland, of Swansea and of Carnarvon, Parry, Roberts of Dolgelley, Tudder of Dolgelley, Vaughan, pp. 48-61; and *Charts*, facing pp. 50, 52 and 60.

PEDIGREE VI.—David, or Davids, of Llanfor and Merion, p. 62.

PEDIGREE VII.—Thomas of Cefn Amwlch and Merion, p. 63.

PEDIGREE VIII.—Williams of Radnor, p. 63.

PEDIGREE IX.—Evans of Llanvachreth (Llanfachreth), Pennsylvania and Virginia, p. 64.

PEDIGREE X.—Jones of Bala, and Radnor, Pennsylvania, Evans, Rhys (Rees), p. 65.

PEDIGREE XI.—Lloyd of Llangower, Roberts of Llangower and Merion, p. 66.

PEDIGREE XII.—Humphreys, William (or Williams), Bala and Merion, p. 67.

PEDIGREE XIII.—Thomas of Bala and Merion, p. 67.

PEDIGREE XIV.—Rhydderch of Hirnant and Pennsylvania, p. 68.

PEDIGREE XV.—Morgan, Cadwalader, Evans of Gwynedd, Thomas, p. 69.

PEDIGREE XVI.—Wynn of Bryn yr Owen, Maryland and Pennsylvania, pp. 70, 71.

The Lands of Edward Jones and Company, in Merion, pp. 72-89.

PEDIGREE XVII.—Descendants of Ednowain Bendew, and allied families : Biddle, Borden, Cadwalader, Chew, Cook (pedigree of Capt. Thos. Cook, who removed from Earls Colne, Essex, to N. England, 1635), Erskine, Hare, Humphrey (Humphreys), Jones, Meredith, Rawle, Ringgold, Roberts of Pencoyd, Merion, Rowland, Streeper, Wister, Williams, Wynne (Dr. Thomas Wynne), pp. 90-107.

PEDIGREE XVIII.—Descendants of Rhirid Flaidd (the Wolf), "lord of Penllyn," and allied families : Earle (see Charts), Evans, Evan ap Edward, Fletcher, Hunter, John ap Edward, Edwards, Jones, Meyrick of Ucheldre, Morgan, Myddelton, Owen, Roberts, Vaughan of Llanuwchllyn, von Löhr, William ap Edward, Williams (and Royal descents), pp. 107-27 ; and *Charts*, facing pp. 116 and 124.

PEDIGREE XIX.—Descendants of the Princes of South Wales : Earle, Hunter, Iddings, Jones, Lewis, Morgan, von Löhr (van Leer). Wills, pp. 127-36.

PEDIGREE XX.—Descendants of Harry, of Machynlleth : Brinton, Eachus, Earle, Harry, McKim, Miller, Newlin, Potts (Royal descent of Owen of Machynlleth), pp. 136-38 ; and *Chart*, facing p. 138.

PEDIGREE XXI.—Lewis of Narberth : Banks, Earle, French, Hansell, Lewis, Meredith, Morris, p. 139.

PEDIGREE XXII.—Descendants of Cadwgan, lord of Nannau : Evans, Foulke of Gwynedd, Hugh, Pugh, John, Jones, Lloyd of Gydros, Morris, Pugh, Williams of Cae Fadog, pp. 140-42.

MANUSCRIPT PEDIGREES BROUGHT FROM WALES TO PENNSYLVANIA BY THE FIRST COLONISTS, viz., Evan ap Evan, 1698, John Hugh (Pugh), Hugh Meredith, Humphrey William, Robert Thomas, David Thomas, Edward Prees (Price), Rowland Ellis, John Roberts, and Edward Foulke, pp. 143-50.

PEDIGREE XXIII.—Davies of Trevor and Pennsylvania, p. 151.

WELSH FOUNDERS OF PENNSYLVANIA.—Genealogical Notes relating to nearly 300 families, in addition to many unmarried persons, who removed from Wales to Pennsylvania, principally between 1682 and 1700, representing a total of about 2,000 individuals of the first generation in the Province, bearing the surnames:

Andrews, Arthur, Bevan (Royal descent of John Bevan), Cadwalader, Cook, Cooper, Corbet (Chandler), Corne, David, Davis, Davies, Edward, Edwards, Ellis (Royal descent of Rowland Ellis), Evan, Evans, Foulke, Gibbons, Griffith, Griffiths, Hardyman, Harry, Haverd, Hayes, Hent, Howell, Hugh, Hughes, Humphrey, Humphreys, Iddings, James, Jarmon, Jenkins, John, Jones, Kinsey, Lewis (*sub* Ellis Lewis, gen. of Gillingham, Kibbee, Hovey, Conger), (*sub* William Lewis, gen. and arms from seal of; and Royal descent, through Henry, Earl of Somerset, of the late John T. Lewis of Phila., and families of Evans of Haverford, Hoffmann, Cuyler, and Hutchinson), Lloyd, Martin, Matthews, Meredith, Miles, Moore, Morgan, Morris, Mortimer, Oliver, Orme, Owen, Painter, Pardo, Parry, Peter (Peters), Philips, Powel, Price, Prichard, Pugh, Rees, Rhydderch, Rhytherrach, Rice, Richard, Richards, Rider, Robert, Roberts, Rothers, Rowland, Thomas, Tudor, Samuel, Samuels, Scourfield, Smith, Walker, Walter, Watkin (Watkins), Whelan (Isaac), William, Williams, Wisdom, Wynn, Wynne, pp. 152-219. *Chart*, facing p. 162.

PEDIGREE XXIV.—Hugh Roberts of Ciltalgarth and Merion, p. 220.

PEDIGREE XXV.—Humphrey, Iredell, Jones, Kirk, Tunis, Warner, Wynne, pp. 221-226.

PEDIGREE XXVI.—Lloyd of Penmaen and Merion, Families of Cotes of Cotes and Woodcote, Coates, Drexel, Henri, Howel, Jones, Kite, Neall, Oakford, Townsend, Tyson, pp. 226-233.

Errata and Addenda.

Page 2, line 31, after "*Wales*" read *and*.

Page 20, *n*. 1, for "*Grammer*" read *Grammar*.

Page 21, line 39, for "*Thomas Lord Erskine*" read *David Lord Erskine*.

Page 46, line 6, for "*Llwyndu*" read *Llwyn du*.

Page 46, foot note, line 2, for "*finals*" read *final s*.

Page 53, line 22, for "*1700*" read *1701*.

Page 53, line 23, for "*1785*" read *1703*.

Page 53. Humphrey Owen of Dolserey, b. 1694, m. Anne—, and had : (a) Robert, d. inft., (b) Robert, (c) David, b. 19 Nov., 1737 ; d. 19 June, 1763. David m. Anne— (b. 1741 ; d. 28 Oct., 1769), and had Humphrey Owen of Dolserey, Esq., who d. 15 Augt., 1826, aged 64. The latter married Elizabeth (d. 24 Dec., 1836, aged 54), and had David Owen of Cyfanedd fawr, Physician, b. 15 Jan., 1815 ; d. 17 Oct., 1843, and Ann Owen, who m. Thomas [? . . .] Stevens, and had Thomas James Stevens of Cyfanned Fawr, living 1875.

Page 58, line 28, for "*Wm. ap Robert*," read *Jno. ap Robert*.

Page 92, line 23, Iorwerth ap Rhirid did homage and fealty for his lands to Prince Edward (as Earl of Chester), at Flint, 22 April, 29 Edw. I. (1301); and was Baliff of the hundred of Englefield, 30-1 and 33-4 Edw. I. (Pat. Roll, 18 Edw. III., p. 1, memb. 23 ; Chester Chamb. Accts.).

Page 104, footnote, line 2, for "*Earle's Colne*" read *Earls Colne*.

Page 106, line 24, for "*ealty*" read *fealty*.

Page 109, line 23. A late reading gives this inscription as "Hic Iacet Madog Vachan" (Report of Royal Com. on Anct. Monuments, Montg.), which does not agree with other readings.

Page 110, line 38, for "*on an*" read *in an*.

Page 112, footnote 1, line 10, for "*Talacre*" read *Mostyn*, and line 15, for "*Talacre*" read *Mostyn*.

Page 116, line 5. The ped. of Wynne of Garth, by John Rhydderch (*circa* 1700), and others have been considered in this connection. The several obvious errors in these pedigrees confirm the conclusion, reached by evidences at hand, that J.W. of Garth with J.W. of Garth Llwyd have been confused by a copyist of Dwnn, or by Dwnn himself. It has been stated that Salusbury of Erbistock does not appear to have had access to Dwnn's pedigrees ; but this is mere surmise.

Page 126, line 34, for "*Catherine*" read *Catharine*.

Page 139, line 35, for "*Catherine*" read *Catharine*.

Page 148, line 24, Ellisa "Bynn" [?] was son of Ynyr ap Llewelyn ap Ynyr (Peniarth MS. 287, fo. 439-440).

Page 149, note 1, line 4, for "*descendant*" read *kinsman*.

Page 153, line 12, for "*1692*" read 1683.

Page 212, line 18, for "*bayvill*" read *Bayvill*.

XVI.

NOTES

NOTE to pages 4 and 5.—Cynwrig ap Llywarch of Carwedd Fynydd and Llyweni was dead before 22nd April, 1301, and was buried in Tremierchion Church. His effigy, representing him in the armour of the period, and cross-legged, formerly stood on the south side of the chancel; but is now in a recess on the north side of the Church, opposite to the south door. This effigy until recently was erroneously supposed to be that of Sir Robert Pounderling, who, according to tradition, was Constable of Dyserth Castle. Tremierchion Church is adjacent to Llyweni.

Cynwrig Fychan (or Vychan), son of the above Cynwrig ap Llywarch, did homage and fealty for his lands to Prince Edward (as Earl of Chester), at Flint Castle, 22nd April, 29 Edward I. (1301). He was one of the Council of Lord Reginald de Gray of Ruthin—*unus de consilio praedicti Reginaldi de Grey. . . . . cilicet Cynwricus Fychan.* (Patent Roll, 18 Edw. III., p. 1, memb. 23; Public Record Office; Owen, "A List of those who did Homage and Fealty to the First English Prince of Wales," No. 132—*Kenewrek Vaghan*, p. 8, and note 31 ; Wynne, "Hist. of Wales," apx., 376).

Einion ap Llywarch did homage and fealty for his lands with his brother, 22nd April, 1301. His name, as Yneny (Einion) Goch (i.e., Einion the Red), is next to that of his brother, Cynwrig Fychan, on the original roll (No. 133 of Owen's "List.")

Welsh Founders of Pennsylvania.

Pedigree I.

Marchweithian, lord of Isaled; "his lands were Carwedd Fynydd, Din Cadfael, Prees, Berain, Llyweni, Gwytherin, and many other townships in the Lordship of Isaled, as appears by the extent of the Lordship and Honour of Denbigh, made in the time of Edward III.," when Cynwrig Fychan, eighth in descent from Marchweithian, was living, and in possession of a part of his lands. Marchweithian's court (*llys*) was at Llyweni, near the town of Denbigh, and he was head of one of the Noble Tribes of Wales. It has been stated that Marchweithian flourished about the beginning of the eighth century, but the dates at which his descendants are known to have lived proves this to be wrong, and there is evidence to show that he was contemporary with Prince Gruffydd ap Cynan, who ruled in North Wales from 1080 to 1137, and that he fought beside that prince in the battle of Carno. [MS. ped. of John Thomas, of Llaithgwm, dated 1682; Cae Cyriog MS.; "History of Powys Fadog," iv., 101-2; Dwnn, ii., 83, 228, 332-3, 342-3.][1] Marchweithian was father of:

[1] For a description of Isaled, and further details concerning Marchweithian, see under "Roberts of Gwynedd," in vol. ii., of "Welsh Founders of Pennsylvania."

Marchwystl,[1] lord of Isaled [authorites cited *supra*], who was father of:

Ysdrwyth,[2] lord of Isaled [authorities cited *supra*], who was father of:

Tagno (or **Tangno**). [Authorities cited *supra*.] Tagno's house "was on the top of Fron Fawr," in the parish of Llannefydd; as no families seem to trace to Ysdrwyth through any son but Tagno, he is supposed to have been sole heir, and lord of all Isaled. Fron Fawr is now the name of a farm, a few miles from St. Asaph, on the road to Llannefydd. Tagno's sons divided their father's possessions between them.

> ISSUE:
> i. Ithel, the founder of Ithel's Chapel, now Llannefydd Parish Church, which he endowed with lands, and where he was buried under the High Altar.
> ii. Tyfod (or Tyfid), Farfsych, *of whom presently*.
> iii. Elidir, of Bryn y Neuadd.

Tyfod (or **Tyfid**) **Farfsych,**[3] of Carwedd Fynydd and Berain, in the parish of Llannefydd, Tre'r Twyssog and other lands in Henllan. He also held, as part of his share of his father's lands, a portion, if not all, of the parish of Cerrig y Druidion. He was father of:

Heilin Gloff, who is stated to have lived at Carwedd Fynydd. [Authorities cited *supra*.] He also held the lands of Berain, in Llannefydd, and lands in Henllan and Cerrig y Druidion. Heilin Gloff married Nest, daughter of Cadwgan ap Llywarch (or Llowarch) ap Bran, of Porthamel, lord of Cymwd Menai, in Anglesey. Llywarch ap Bran was head of one of the Fifteen Noble Tribes of Wales, a descendant of Rhodri Mawr, over-king of all

---

[1] This name, in the John Thomas pedigree, seems to be spelled Marchwystt, and in others, Marchwystle, &c.
[2] Variously spelled in different MSS.
[3] Spelled also Tivid, Tyvod, &c.

Wales, and lived towards the close of the reign of Gruffydd ap Cynan. The above alliance places him in the same generation as Marchweithian's grandson. Supposing, however, that Nest was a younger daughter, born when her father was somewhat advanced in years, the generations agree precisely, and this alliance, in any case, as well as those which follow, prove the correctness of the statement that Marchweithian was born about the middle of the eleventh century. Heilin Gloff was father of:

Llywarch (or Llowarch) ap Heilin, of Carwedd Fynydd, in the parish of Llannefydd. He also held lands about the town of Denbigh and elsewhere in Isaled, and was probably dead before 3 Edw. I. (1274-5). Llywarch married Gwenllian, daughter of Madog ap Rhirid Flaidd. [Authorities cited *supra.*] Rhirid Flaidd was an *uchelwr* and chief proprietor of Pennant Melangell, Montgomeryshire, and is styled *arglwydd* (lord) of Penllyn, but his interests in that cymwd were probably merely governmental, for although his great grandson had a grant of land there from Edward I., Rhirid's possessions were principally, if not altogether, elsewhere.

David, son of Urgeneth (or Gwrgene) Fleid (Flaidd) and brother of Rhirid Flaidd, is grantor in a deed to Baldwin (de Boulers), son of William, of Montgomery, dated between *circa* 1230-40, for certain parcels of land about Montgomery. Rhirid dwelt at Llys Celynyn, in the parish of Pennant Melangell, and died soon after his brother *Arthen*, in the first quarter of the thirteenth century. Einion, an uncle of Nest, fell at the siege of Dyserth Castle, in 1263, and her nephew, *Madog ap Iorwerth ap Madog ap Rhirid Flaidd*, received from Edward I. a grant of the lands of Penanthlu (or Pennantlliw), a township in the parish of Llanuwchllyn, Penllyn, at the close of the thirteenth century. [Add. MS. 14,886, fo. 91; 14,869, fos. 81b, 227b; Myddelton deeds at Chirk Castle; Extent of the "Commot of Penthlyn," *temp.* Edward I.]

ISSUE :
i. Cynwrig, *of whom presently.*
ii. Einion.

Cynwrig ap Llywarch. He held the lands of Carwedd Fynydd, Berain, and others near Denbigh, and elsewhere. [Authorities cited *supra.*] Cynwrig appears to have been a person of considerable standing in the community in which he lived, and seems to have held his lands partly from the king *in capite* and partly by knight's service from Henri de Lacy, who had been created lord of Rhuvoniog (including Isaled), thus supplanting Cynwrig's family. Under the designation of *Kenewvek Ab llawar* he is the fifth witness to the charter of " Henri de Lacy, Earl of Nicole (Lincoln), Constable of Chester, and lord of Rhos and Rhuvoniog," granted 3 Edward I. (1274-5) to Johan de la Chambre for two carucates of land in Llyweni, with liberties and freedom in the parts and forests adjacent,[1] and at a court held at Ruthin, on Tuesday, the Feast of St. Maur the Abbot, 25 Edward I. (15 January, 1296-7), he was one of the surities for Robert le Walker.[2]

Cynwrig ap Llywarch married Dyddgu, daughter of Cadwgan ap Ednyfed ap Cadwgan Ddu ap Llywarch Goch ap Llywarch of Llys Llywarch (or Llowarch), called Llywarch Holbwrch, Treasurer to Gruffydd ap Llewelyn ap Seisyllt, who was king of all Wales, and who died in 1063. The generations from Dyddgu to Llywarch Holbwrch, place the latter in the same generation as Marchweithian, thus further confirming the period at which the latter lived. Llys Llywarch (or Llowarch) (i.e. the court of Llywarch) was in the parish of Llannefydd, which formed part of Isaled, the cymwd over which Marchweithian was *arglwydd*, so it is necessary to explain that Llywarch was *arglwydd* of the cantref of Rhuvoniog

---

[1] Chambers MSS. Transcription of the Norman French of the original by J. Y. W. Lloyd, of Clochfaen, Esq., M.A., K.S.G.; made 1885.

[2] Ruthin Court Rolls, 25 Edw. I., No. 3, memb. 3, Public Record Office ; see also " The Court Rolls of the Lordship of Ruthin or Dyffryn=Clwyd, time of Edward I." in " Cymmrodorion Record Series," No. 2, 40·1.

(or Rhyfonioc), of which Isaled formed a part, prior, seemingly, to Marchweithian's appointment. The government of all Rhuvoniog, including Isaled, appears to have fallen into the hands of Henry de Lacy before the conquest of Wales by Edward I.

ISSUE:

i. Cynwrig Fychan (or Vychan), the eldest son[1], inherited the lands of Carwedd Fynydd and Berain, in the parish of Llannefydd, and others in Henllan, about Llyweni and elsewhere.[2] It is stated in one pedigree of this family that he lived at one time at Llys Llywarch (or Llowarch) in Llannefydd, which may have come to him from his mother's family, or have been acquired by purchase from her kinsfolk in the lifetime of his father. At a court held at Llannerch, near Denbigh, on Thursday in Whitsun Week, 22 Edward I., (June 10th, 1294), Cynwrig Fychan, then a young man, under the designation of *Kenw' Vagh^{a}n*, was attached because he depastured the lord's land without leave. The damages amounted to 6d., and he was quit.[3] He was living 8 Edward III. (1334), when he is named as a landholder in the "Extent of the Lordship and Honour of Denbigh"; he served with the English against the Scots, and was buried in Llannefydd Church where his effigy remains.[4]

ii. Einion, *of whom presently.*

Einion ap Cynwrig, second son of Cynwrig ap Llywarch of Carwedd Fynydd, and Berain, in the parish of Llannefydd, &c. [MS. ped. of John Thomas, of Llaithgwm, dated 1682; Cae Cyriog MS.; "History of Powys Fadog," iv., 102, *note* 1; 108; Harl. MS., 1971; MS. ped. of Edward

---

[1] Dwnn. ii., 228; "History of Powys Fadog," iv., 101-2.

[2] Extent of the Lordship and Honour of Denbigh, 8 Edw. III.

[3] Court of Llannerch, Ruthin Court Rolls, 22 Edw. I., Public Record Office; see also "Cymmrodorion Record Series," No. 2, 4. De Lacy's tenants holding by knight's fee, had usually rights of depasturage on the lord's land, for "all manner of beasts among all the glades of the forest," and "free pannage to all its swine of its own pale," likewise, "housebote and haybote in the forest of Llewenny," but leave must first be obtained.

[4] Cynwrig Fychan was ancestor to Rhys ap Maredydd, of Plas Iôlyn, in the parish of Yspytty Evan, Denbighshire, a Lancastrian captain, who, on Bosworth Field (1485) was entrusted by Henry VII. with the standard of England, after the former standard-bearer, Sir William Brandon, had been slain. The effigies of Rhys ap Maredydd, his wife, and his son, Sir Robert ap Rhys, Cross-bearer and Chaplain to Cardinal Wolsey, are to be seen in Yspytty Evan Church. Cadwaladr ap Robert ap Rhys was ancestor of the Price family of Rhiwlas, near Bala, and a MS. preserved in the library at Rhiwlas states that Rhys ap Maredydd slew Richard III. with his own hand. Grace, daughter, of Cadwaladr ap Robert, of Rhiwlas, married Watkin ap Edward, of Garth Llwyd, Llandderfel (died 1610-11), ancestor of John ap Edward, William ap Edward, and Evan ap Edward, early settlers in Merion, Pennsylvania. George H. Earle, Jr., of Philadelphia, is descended from this line. (See pedigree on another page). The Owen family, of Fron Goch and Merion, was also of this line, through intermarriage, by two descents (see "Roberts of Gwynedd," Vol. ii., "Welsh Founders of Pennsylvania.")

Rees,[1] Prees, or Price, Glenn's "Merion," 78.] He had for his share of his father's estates, lands in the parish of Cerrig y Druidion, Denbighshire, consisting, among others, of farms in the townships of Llaethwryd and Cwm Pen Aner. Einion, who lived in the reign of Edward III., removed to Cerrig y Druidion, where he died, and was buried.[2] His residence is supposed to have been Bryammer, in the township of Pen Cwm Aner, afterwards the home of his descendant, Evan Coch.

ISSUE :
i. Tudor ap Einion.
ii. Pill ap Einion. [Harl. MS., 1971.] He was ancestor of the Ffoulks of Plâs Newydd, Meriadoc.
iii. David ap Einion,[3] *of whom presently.*

David ap Einion, of the parish of Cerrig y Druidion. [MS. ped. of John Thomas, of Llaithgwm, dated 1682; Cae Cyriog MS.; "History of Powys Fadog," iv., 102, *note* 1, 108; MS. ped. of Edward Rees, or Prees, or Price, Glenn's "Merion," 78.] He had issue:

Evan Ddu (or Ieuan Ddu)[4], of the township of Cwm Pen Aner, in the parish of Cerrig y Druidion. [MS. ped. of John Thomas, of Llaithgwm, dated 1682; Cae Cyriog MS.; "History of Powys Fadog," iv., 102, *note* 1, 108; MS. ped. of Edward Rees, or Prees, or Price, Glenn's "Merion," 78.] He left issue:

i. Howel, who held many farms in Cerrig y Druidion, and left a great many descendants. [See Subsidy Rolls, cited *infra.*]
ii. Evan (otherwise Ieuan) Coch (Goch); *of whom presently.*

---

[1] NOTE. The MS. pedigree of Edward Rees (otherwise known as Edward Prees, or Price), who removed from near Bala to Merion, Pennsylvania, in 1682, which was compiled in Wales, at his request, sometime before 1700, states that Einion ap Cynwrig was the son of Cynwrig Vychan ap Cynwrig, instead of Cynwrig ap Llywarch [see copy of original pedigree in Glenn's "Merion," pp. 78-79.] This, however, does not agree with the Hafod Gynfor—Cae Môr pedigree in the Cae Cyriog MSS., that printed in "History of Powys Fadog," iv., 101, from Harl. MS. 1969, or the John Thomas pedigree of 1682, all of which state that Einion ap Cynwrig was the brother, not the son, of Cynwrig Fychan.

[2] Einion ap Cynwrig and his descendants were buried in the Church, or Churchyard, of Cerrig y Druidion.

[3] The order of birth of the sons of Einion ap Cynwrig, and of other generations, down to Thomas ap Hugh, cannot be precisely determined, and the numerals before the names of the children are, in this portion of the pedigree, rather for convenience sake, than to indicate priority of birth. At the same time, the issue have, in every case, been arranged, after careful investigation, according to their *probable* order.

[4] Black Evan, meaning black haired.

Pedigree I.

Evan Coch (or Goch), of the parish of Cerrig y Druidion. In the MS. pedigree of John Thomas, of Llaithgwm, dated 1682, this person is described as "Evan ap Coch of Bryammer, in the parish of Cerrig y Druidion and County Denbigh." In the Lay Subsidy Roll of 35 Hen. VIII. (1543), he is called "Ieuᵃn ap Coʒ," and "Ieuᵃn ap Koʒ," of the parish of Kerykedrudyon (Cerrig y Druidion); in the Cae Cyriog MSS. he appears as "Ieuan Goch, of Cwm Pen Aner, in the parish of Caer (Cerrig) y Drudion," and in Dwnn's Visitations of North Wales, ii., 254 (*col.* 2), he is mentioned as "Ieun côch o Gerrig y Drudion." In a pedigree in "History of Powys Fadog," vi., 446, he is called "of Garth Garmon." There can be no doubt whatever that the *ap* before *Coch* in the John Thomas pedigree and in the Subsidy Roll cited are superfluous. Coch, or Goch, means red, and applied to a person indicates red hair, or a florid complexion.

Evan Coch, under the designations of "Ieuᵃn ap Koʒ," and "Ieuᵃn ap Coʒ," is named in Lay Subsidy Roll, dated 12 Nov., 35 Hen. VIII. (1543), as grandfather of Rob'tus ap Gruff ap Ieuᵃn ap Koʒ (Coch), and Robt ap Tuder ap Ieuᵃn ap Coʒ (Coch), both of the parish of Cerrig y Druidion. [Lay Subsidy Roll, No. $\frac{220}{166}$, Denbighshire, under parish of Kerykedrudyon (Cerrig y Druidion). Pub. Rec. Office, London.]

Bryammer was an estate, now a farm, in the old township of Cwm Pen Aner, Cerrig y Druidion. According to tradition, the posterity of Evan Coch served under their kinsman, Rees (or Rhys) ap Maredydd, at Bosworth Field, in the army of Henry, Earl of Richmond, afterwards Henry VII.

Evan Coch married Gwenhwyfar, daughter of Thomas ap David Gam ap Cynwrig Llwyd ap Einion ap Goronwy Foel ap Cynwrig, descended from Marchudd ap Cynan, lord of Uwch Dulas. [MS. ped. of Edward Rees, or Prees, or Price; see Glenn's "Merion," 78; "History of Powys Fadog," v., 365.]

Issue:

i. Gruffydd (Griffith) ap |Evan Coch, of the parish of Cerrig y Druidion, who died prior to 12 Nov., 1543, leaving issue:
(*a*) Robert ap Gruffydd (otherwise Griffith) ap Evan Coch, whose daughter Catherine married Thomas Lloyd, of Gwern y Brychtwn, parish of Llandderfel, Penllyn, and

became ancestress to many Pennsylvanians[1]; (b) David ap Gruffydd ap Evan Coch, of Cerrig y Druidion. [Lay Subsidy Roll, Denbighshire, 35 Hen. VIII.

ii. Rees ap Evan Coch, *of whom presently.*

Rees ap Evan Coch, son of Evan (or Ieuan)[2] Coch, of the parish of Cerrig y Druidion. [MS. ped. of John Thomas, of Llaithgwm, dated 1682; Cae Cyriog MS.; "History of Powys Fadog," iv., 101-2, *note* 1, 108.]

ISSUE:

i. Tudor ap Rees, *of whom presently.*

ii. Evan (or Ieuan) ap Rees, of Cerrig y Druidion, who had issue, David ap Ieuan ap Rees, of the parish of "Kerrigidruidon" (Cerrig y Druidion), who died in or before 1590, and against the probate of whose will a caveat was entered by John ap David ap Ieuᵃn ap Res, son and heir of the said David ap Ieuan, 26 Augt., 1590. [Act Book $\frac{1584}{1593}$, Probate Registry, St. Asaph.]

Tudor ap Rees, (or Rhys), son of Rees ap Evan Coch, of the parish of Cerrig y Druidion. [MS. ped. of John Thomas, of Llaithgwm, dated 1682; Cae Cyriog MS.; "History of Powys Fadog," iv., 101-2, *note* 1, 108.]

---

[1] Thomas Lloyd was direct male ancestor of Edward Foulke, who removed to Gwynedd, Pennsylvania, 1698. [See Glenn's "Merion," 94-95.] Among the many descendants of this line are, J. Roberts Foulke, President of the Provident Trust Company, of Philadelphia, Hon. William Dudley Foulke, Richmond, Ind., Roland R., Walter L. and William G. Foulke, of Philadelphia, and Bayard Fish Foulke, and William Foulke, of New Rochelle, New York. For Foulke ped. see Jenkin's "Gwynedd,"32; Glenn's "Merion," 94-95; "Pedigree of Edward Foulke," chart and narrative, from MS. of T. A. Glenn, Library of Hist. Society of Pennsylvania.

Mary, the daughter of the above named Thomas Lloyd, of Gwern y Brychtwn, married Richard, of Tyddyn Tyfod, (now Tyddyn tyfiad) in the parish of Llanderfel, direct male ancestor to Richard Price, of Glanlloidiogin, Llanfor, whose will was proved at St. Asaph, 1686, and who was father of Edward Rees alias Prees or Price, who removed to Merion, Pennsylvania, 1682, Jane, wife of Cadwalader Morgan, and Hannah, wife of Rees John William, all of whom removed to Merion. Among the descendants of these lines, are Malcolm Lloyd, jr., of Philadelphia, Mrs. Henry T. Coates, Mrs. William M. Coates, Mrs. George M. Coates, Mrs. Norman M. Jones, of Philadelphia, the Ashbridge, Osborne, Troth, and Kite families. Richard Lloyd, b., 1713, son of Robert Lloyd, of Merion, and Lowry Jones, daughter of Rees John William (by Hannah, daughter of Richard Price, of Glanlloidiogin, parish of Llanfor), married, 1736, Hannah Sellers, of Darby, grand-daughter of Samuel Sellers, or Sellow, of Darby, and Ellen his wife, daughter of Henry Gibbons, of Derbyshire, England. The Gibbons' family was originally from Salop and of Welsh descent, the ancestors of those of the name found in Cheshire, Staffordshire, Derbyshire, and Warwickshire, being Richard and Edmund Gibbons sons of Gibbon ap Ithel, son of Ithel Fychan, who was slain at Whittington Castle, July, 1457. Samuel Sellers was born at Belper, in Derbyshire, and baptized at Duffield Church, 3 Feb., 1655, son of Thomas Sellers, son of Robert, son of Thomas, of Crich, died 1610, son of John, of Longston and Crich, died 1602-3, descended from William Sallowes or Sallow, of Stanton, Derbyshire, High Sheriff of Notts, died 1410, from Robert de Sallor, or Sallowes, time Henry II. Horace Wells Sellers, of Philadelphia, is a descendant. Other descendants of Rees John William, are Mrs. John R. Drexel (Alice G. Troth), Edward Troth, Samuel Troth, and Louis Stanwood Kite.

[2] Otherwise Rhys ap Ieuan, and so spelled in one pedigree.

Tudor ap Rees died before 12 Nov., 35 Hen. VIII. (1543). [Lay Subsidy Roll, No. $\frac{220}{188}$, Denbighshire, under parish of Kerykedrudyon (Cerrig y Druidion), in the hundred of Issalet (Isaled), Pub. Record Office, London.]

ISSUE:
i. Rees Coch ap Tudor, *of whom presently.*
ii. Margaret verch Tudor, living 12 Nov., 1543. Assessed in land and tenements, goods and cattle, in the parish of Cerrig y Druidion, 35 Hen. VIII. [Lay Subsidy Roll, cited *supra.*]

Rees Coch ap Tudor, son of Tudor ap Rees (or Rhys), of the parish of Cerrig y Druidion. [MS. ped. of John Thomas, of Llaithgwm, dated 1682; Cae Cyriog MS.; "History of Powys Fadog," iv., 101-2, *note* 1, 108.]

Rees Goch died before 41 Eliz. (1598-9)[1]. [Lay Subsidy Roll, Denbighshire, under Kerregydridion (Cerrig y Druidion), No. $\frac{220}{188}$, Pub. Rec. Office, London.]

Named as father of Evan ap Rees in probate of the will of Catherine verch Evan ap Rees, his granddaughter, 7 Oct., 1637. [Act Book $\frac{1687}{1670}$. Probate Registry, St. Asaph.]

ISSUE:
i. Evan ap Rees (or Rhys) Coch, *of whom presently.*
ii. Robert ap Rees, of Cerrig y Druidion. Administration of his goods granted to Jane verch Rytherch, his widow, 25 Jan., 1637. [Act Book $\frac{1687}{1670}$, Probate Registry, St. Asaph.]

Evan ap Rees Coch (or Goch) (written also Ieuan ap Rhys Goch), son of Rees Coch ap Tudor, of the parish of Cerrig y Druidion. [MS. ped. of John Thomas, of Llaithgwm, dated 1682; Cae Cyriog MS.; "History of Powys Fadog," iv., 101-2, *note* 1, 108.]

Evan . . . [Rees] ap Tuder, assessed in land in the parish of Kerregydridion (Cerrig y Druidion), Denbighshire, 41 Eliz. (1598-9). [Assessment of 2d. payment of the subsidy granted 39 and 40 Eliz. Lay Subsidy Roll, Denbighshire, 41 Eliz., No. $\frac{220}{188}$, Pub. Rec. Office, London.]

Ieuan ap Rees [Coch ap Tudor] is named in Lay Subsidy Roll for the hundred of Isalet, Denbighshire, under parish of Kerigydridion (Cerrig

---

[1] He is not mentioned in the Lay Subsidy Roll of 35 Hen. VIII. (1543), which would seem to indicate that he did not acquire landed property until after this date. The Roll, however, names only seven landholders, and it is probable that there were two assessments for this subsidy, and that the other roll is missing, which is often the case. I think, however, that Rees was the second son.

y Druidion), 3 Jac. I., (1605), as the father of David ap Ieuᵃn ap Rees, gentleman, and freeholder, and was then dead. [Lay Subsidy Roll, Denbighshire, 3 Jac. I., No. $\frac{220}{188}$, Pub. Rec. Office, London.]

ISSUE:

i. David ap Evan, of the parish of Cerrig y Druidion, gentleman, eldest son and heir. He succeeded to his father's estates in Cerrig y Druidion before 3 Jac. I., (1605); named in Lay Subsidy Roll, 3 Jac. I., (1605), under parish of Kerigydridion (Cerrig y Druidion) as David Ieuᵃn ap Rees, gentleman. [Lay Subsidy Roll, Denbighshire, No. $\frac{220}{188}$, Pub. Rec. Office, London.]

Named in Lay Subsidy Roll 18 Jac. I. (1620), under parish of Kerrigydrydion (Cerrig y Druidion), as David ap Evan. [Lay Subsidy Roll, Denbighshire, No. $\frac{220}{198}$, Pub. Rec. Office, London.] Also named as a landed proprietor in the parish of Kerigydridion (Cerrig y Druidion), Denbighshire, under the designation of David ap Evan, in the assessment of the 3rd subsidy granted 3 Car. I. (1627). [Lay Subsidy Roll, Denbighshire, No. $\frac{220}{190}$, Pub. Rec. Office, London.]

ii. Hugh ap Evan, *of whom presently*.

iii. Catherine verch Evan ap Rees. She died in the parish of Llanfor (Llanvawr), supposedly unmarried, 1637, leaving a will, proved 7 Oct., 1637. Administration of her goods granted to Thomas ap Hugh (her nephew) and Elize (Ellis) Morgan, executors. [Act Book $\frac{1637}{1670}$, Probate Registry, St. Asaph.]

Hugh ap Evan (or Ieuan), son of Evan ap Rees (or Rhys) Coch, of the parish of Cerrig y Druidion, Denbighshire. [MS. ped. of John Thomas, of Llaithgwm, dated 1682; Cae Cyriog MS.; "History of Powys Fadog," iv., 101-2, *note* 1, 108; will of Catherine verch Evan ap Rees, his sister, 7 Oct., 1637, cited *infra*.]

1620, 25 July. Hugh ap Ieuan, of Kerrig (Cerrig) y druidin, (Cerrig y Druidion) witnesses the will of Humffrey ap Robert Wynn (his kinsman), of the parish of Kerrig (Cerrig) y Druidion, Denbighshire; proved at St. Asaph, 10 Augt., 1620. [Register $\frac{1620}{1629}$, folio 53, Probate Registry, St. Asaph.]

ISSUE:

i. Thomas ap Hugh, *of whom presently*.
ii. Robert ap Hugh; removed to the parish of Llandderfel, where he died in 1638. Administration of his goods granted, 20 Oct., 1638, to his brother, Thomas ap Hugh, to the use of the children of deceased during their minority. (Two of these

Pedigree I.

children, Thomas Roberts and Elizabeth Roberts, are mentioned in the will of their uncle, Thomas ap Hugh, of Llaethgwm, dated 29 Dec., 1664, cited *infra*). [Act Book 1087/1870, Probate Registry, St. Asaph.]

iii. Owen ap Hugh, named in will of his brother, Thomas ap Hugh, of Llaethgwm, dated 29 Dec., 1664, who charges his estate with an annuity to be paid this Owen during the term of his natural life. His daughter, Elizabeth, married Thomas Andrews, and died in Pennsylvania. (See *infra*.)

iv. Humphrey ap Hugh, or Pugh (?).

v. Cadwalader ap Hugh, of Cerrig y Druidion.[1]

vi. Margaret, married Robert ap Evan Lloyd, of Cerrig y Druidion, ap John Gruffydd,[2] of Tir y Abbot, and had issue named hereafter. Administration of her goods, she dying a widow, granted, 12 March, 1639, to Evan Lloyd, of Tir y Abbot, and Thomas ap Hugh ap Ieuan, "her brother," then of Cerrig y Druidion, afterwards of Llaethgwm (Llaithgwm), Llandderfel.

[There may have been other children of Hugh ap Evan; perhaps a son, Hugh ap Hugh.]

Thomas ap Hugh, son of Hugh ap Evan (or Ieuan), was born in the parish of Cerrig y Druidion, Denbighshire. [MS. ped. of his son, John Thomas, or John ap Thomas, of Wern Fawr,[3] Llaithgwm, 1682, in MS. collection of the late J. J. Levick, M.D., of Philadelphia, now (1910) deposited in the Historical Society of Pennsylvania. Copies in possession of John L. Cadwalader, Esq., of New York

---

[1] He had a son named John Cadwalader, of Cerrig y Druidion, who is mentioned in a letter of Robert Vaughan, of Hendre Mawr, to his cousin in Pennsylvania, as his "uncle," i.e., his mother's first cousin. It should be observed here that in Wales at this period, the terms "uncle," and "nephew," unless employed in wills or some other legal document, did not always mean the same relationship as is now understood by these words. A parent's first cousin, as well as a parent's brother, was commonly referred to as "uncle," and the first cousin, once removed, frequently spoken of as "nephew."

[2] John Gruffydd (or Griffith), of Tir y Abbot, in the parish of Yspytty Evan, Denbighshire, was living, and taxed as a freeholder, 39—40 Eliz., and was son of Gruffydd ap Edward ap Hugh. This Gruffydd was living 1 Edw. VI., and his father, Edward ap Hugh, was dead before that year.

[3] The Cae Cyriog MS. pedigree, printed in the "Hist. of Powys Fadog" as cited, being that of his grandson, Edward Maurice, of Cae Môr, calls him "Thomas ab Hyw of Wern Fawr, co. Meirionydd." It was compiled sometime after 1709. Wern Fawr is a large farm, once called an estate, in the township of Llaithgwm, or Llaethgwm, formerly in the parish of Llandderfel, but now locally in that of Llanfor, although, for ecclesiastical purposes I believe it is still considered to be in the former parish. Llaithgwm Township also includes the farm and residence of the same name, adjoining Wern Fawr, and it has been stated that Thomas ap Hugh and his son, John Thomas, or John ap Thomas as he was sometimes called, held Llaithgwm House as well as Wern fawr. Whilst this may be so, the designation "of Llaethgwm" in the will of Thomas ap Hugh, it is clear, from several circumstances, refers to the township, and not to the property of the same name *in* the township.

City, and T. A. Glenn; see "An old Welsh Pedigree," "Pennsylvania Magazine of History and Biography," iv., (1880) 477; "History of Powys Fadog," iv., 101—2, note 1, 108; Cae Cyriog MS.]

1637, 7 Oct. Will of Catherine verch Evan ap Rees, of the parish of Llanvawr (Llanfor), deceased, proved, and administration of her goods granted to Thomas ap Hugh and Elize (Ellis) Morgan, executors. [Act Book $\frac{1687}{1670}$, Probate Registry, St. Asaph.][1] Catherine was aunt to Thomas ap Hugh; see *supra*.

1638, 20 Oct. Administration of the goods of Robert ap Hugh, of the parish of Llanthervell (Llandderfel), deceased, granted to Thomas ap Hugh, the brother of the said deceased, to the use and during the minority of the deceased's children. [Act Book $\frac{1687}{1670}$, Probate Registry, St. Asaph.]

1639, 12 March. Administration of the goods of Margaret verch Hugh ap Evan, widow, deceased, granted to Evan lloyd ap John Gruff. (Griffith,) grandfather of the children of deceased, and Thomas ap Hugh ap Evan, natural and legitimate brother of the deceased, to the use of Jane vch. Robt. ap Ieuan (Evan) lloyd, spin., Hugh ap Robt. ap Ieuan lloyd, Katherine vch. Robt. ap Ieuan lloyd, Evan ap Robt. ap Ieuan lloyd, et Lowri vch. Robt. ap Ieuan lloyd, natural and legitimate children of the said deceased, during their minority. Bond of Evan lloyd of Tir yr Abbat, in the county of Denbigh, yeoman, and Thomas ap Hugh ap Ieuan of Kerrig y druidion (Cerrig y Druidion) in the county of Denbigh, aforesaid. Same date. [Act Book $\frac{1687}{1670}$, Probate Registry, St. Asaph.]

Thomas ap Hugh must, therefore, have removed to Wern Fawr, in the township of Llaithgwm, in the parish of Llandderfel, after 1639. The distance from Cerrig y Druidion is about five miles.

1664, 29 Dec. Will of Thomas ap Hugh, of Llaethgwm (Llaithgwm) in the parish of Llanthervel (Llandderfel), in the Diocese of St. Asaph, in the county of Merioneth. Proved at St. Asaph, 4 April, 1666. [Recorded in Register $\frac{1644}{1666}$, folio 303; copy of original filed, Bundle for 1666.]

The testator gives and bequeaths unto his son Hugh Thomas (who had otherwise been provided for) the sum of six shillings. "I give, devise and bequeath unto my grandchild Sydney eldest Daughter of the said Hugh All my estate right title and interest of and to all that my messuage or tenement and lands . . . . . . called Tythyn y berth situate lyinge and being in Penmaen in the said Countie"[2] To her and her heirs and assigns for ever. He gives and bequeaths to his son John Thomas (who had previously been provided for) five pounds.

---

[1] This will cannot be found; only the record of probate in the Act Book cited appears to remain.

[2] In the township of Penmaen, parish of Llanfor. This farm, now called Berth, adjoins Fron Goch. Tythyn y berth means Pleasant, or Beautiful farm.

Pedigree I.

"I give Devise and bequeath unto my sonne Cadd^r. (Cadwalader) Thomas All my estate right title and interest wt'in and unto All that messuage or y tenement and Lands ...... called Keven y fedw situate and lyeing in Bettus (als) Kymin y Iskadwy (?) in the said Countie in as large and ample maner as Griffith Piers gent for the consideration of one hundred twentie and five poundes Current English money to him by mee payed did conveay the same in mortgage to me and my heires and assignes forever."[1]

The testator further gives and bequeaths "unto my Sonne in Law Gawen Vaughan and to my daughter Katherin his wiefe Five Shillings" (a settlement at marriage having been made).

He leaves bequests to Robert Vaughan, his grandchild, to be paid him at age of ten years, to Thomas Vaughan, his grandchild, to Dorothy and Elizabeth Vaughan,[2] his grandchildren, to his "Sonne in Law Maurice Edward and my Daughter Elizabeth his wief," to his "grandchild Edward Maurice their eldest Sonne," to be paid him at the age of ten years and to his grandchild Jane Maurice, daughter of the said Maurice Edward and Elizabeth his wife.

To his "daughter Elizabeth the younger fieftie poundes in money."

He charges his estate with an annuity to be paid to his (the testator's) brother Owen ap Hugh during his natural life.

Bequests to his nephew Thomas ap Robert, and neice Elizabeth verch Robert.

The testator charges his estate with the support of his "daughter Elizabeth the younger" until she be ten years old "and then pay her the legacie of Fieftie pounds."

Mentions marriage settlement with Rose "my now [second] wief," she to accept twenty pounds in lieu of dower at testator's decease, she having been otherwise provided for. He bequeaths her ten pounds additional, and household articles.

"I Doe Sowely nominate, constitute ordaine and appointe my said sonne Cadwalader Thomas to be sole Executor of this my last will and Testament."

"I Doe appointt my said two sonnes [in law] Gawen Vaughan and Maurice Edwards,[3] and my said sonnes Hugh Thomas and John Thomas to be Overseers of this my will."

Signed in full: Thomas ap Hugh.

Witnesses: Humffrey Pugh,[4] John Humphreys, Humphey Roberts.

Filed copy of original has endorsement: "I recd the original will," signed: Cadder Thomas.

Probate granted to "Cadwalader Thomas filio nati et l'timus," *i.e.*, natural and legitimate son, of said deceased, 4 April, 1666.

---

[1] Keven y fedw (Cefn y Bedw) is in the township of Bettws, or Llawr y Bettws in the parish of Llanfor.

[2] Elizabeth, daughter of Gawen Vaughan and Catherine his wife was baptized at Llanyckill (Llanycil) 25 May, 1663. [Transcript of Register in Diocesan Registry, St. Asaph.] Jane, her sister, was baptized at Llanyckill, 18 Feb., 1666, (1666—7.)

[3] Of Cae Môr. Written without the final *s supra*.

[4] He appears to have been the son of Hugh ap Evan, and brother to Thomas ap Hugh. Pugh is a contraction of *Ap Hugh*.

1666, 4 April. Bond, Cadwalader Thomas of Llaethgwm in the county of Merioneth, Gawen Vaughan of the parish of Llanyckill (Llanycil), and John Oliver, of Vaynol in the County of Flint, to the Lord Bishop of St. Asaph, setting forth that Thomas ap Hugh, of Llaethgwm in the parish of Llanddervel (Llandderfel), Diocese of St. Asaph, deceased, made his last will and testament in writing, and appointed the said bounden Cadwalader Thomas sole executor. That the said will by decree of Court is ordered to be delivered to the said executor by reason of divers lands and tenements therein mentioned as the only evidence he the said Cadwalader Thomas, hath to produce for the same. The above bounden persons undertake to hold the Lord Bishop and his officers harmless from loss or destruction of said will, and promise to deliver same up when demanded. Signed by all parties.[1] Witnesses: Samuell Matthrwey, Will: Roberts. [Filed. Bundle for 1666, Probate Registry, St. Asaph.]

1666, 30 March. Inventory of "ye goodes Cattell and Chatles" of Thomas ap Hugh, of the parish of Llanthervell (Llandderfel), deceased, appraised by Robert Thomas, Hugh David, Griffith ap Evan, and Hugh ap Will'm. Exhibited 4 April, 1666, by Cadwalader Thomas, son of the deceased. The live stock of the deceased consisted of 13 Horses, 6 Oxen, 20 Cows, 82 head of Cattle of various ages, and 300 Sheep.

Thomas ap Hugh died in March, (1666). The name of his first wife is unknown. He married, secondly, Rose———.

Issue by 1st wife:

i. Hugh Thomas, living 29 Dec., 1664; named in his father's will [2]

ii. John Thomas (called also John Thomas ap Hugh[3] and John ap Thomas), of the township of Llaethgwm, or Llaithgwm, parish of Llandderfel. He was High Constable for Penllyn. He joined the Society of Friends,[4] and, intending to remove with his family to Pennsylvania, died in Llaithgwm, 3 May, 1683. His will, executed in Wales, was proved at Philadelphia, because of his purchase of land in Pennsylvania.

1682, 9 Feb. Will of John Thomas, "of Llaethgwm [Llaithgwm] in the comott of Penllin, within the County of Merionyth, gentleman." Proved at Philadelphia, 1688. [Will Book A, folio 77, &c. Off. Reg. of Wills, Philadelphia. Original No. 41 of 1688, filed.]

---

[1] The signature of Cadwalader Thomas, attached to this document is identical with his signature on the marriage certificate of his brother-in-law, Robert Owen, of Fron Goch, 1678—9. Caddr, Cadder, &c., are contractions of Cadwaladr or Cadwalader, thus: Cad[wala]dr, or Cad[wala]der.

[2] He was perhaps the eldest son and heir, in which case he would have inherited any real property of his father, freehold or copyhold, not disposed of by the latter's will. It is possible, however, that Wern Fawr and other lands were entailed by a deed of trust, and that John Thomas inherited upon the death of Hugh without male issue.

[3] He is described as John Thomas ap Hugh of Llaythgwm, 1675; see Glenn's "Merion," 17.

[4] I should imagine that he did not identify himself fully with the Society of Friends, or Quakers, until in or after 1666, for in that year John Thomas is named as one of the Guardians of the Parish of Llandderfel, having, apparently, succeeded his father in that office, the latter being a strong Churchman. [Transcripts of Llandderfel Register, Diocesan Registry, St. Asaph.] He was sub-collector for Penllyn Isavon, 1663-4.

PEDIGREE I.   15

The testator leaves his lands in Pennsylvania to his sons, Thomas Jones, Robert John, Evan John, (Jones) and Cadwalader John. Mentions daughters Katharine, Mary, Sidney and "Elizabeth now wife of Rees Evan, of the township of Penmaen," and his wife Katharine. The Testator leaves bequests to ¼"my nephew John the younger son of my Brother Cadwalader Thomas;" "my nephew Thomas Cadwalader," and neices Katharine and Jane, "daughters of Cadwalader Thomas." He mentions "my Brother Cadwalader Thomas Late of Kiltalgarth[1] and now deceased," &c. A copy of the MS. pedigree of John Thomas, "of Llaithgwm, in the County of Merioneth, gent. 1682" cited *supra*, is appended to this genealogy. Katharine Robert (or Thomas) his widow, removed with her family, to Pennsylvania in 1683, and settled in Merion.[2] Her sons, and their descendants assumed the surname of Jones, see "Addenda" to this pedigree. [See also "John ap Thomas and his Friends" by J. J. Levick, M.D., "Pennsylvania Mag. of Hist. and Biog.," iv.; "Merion in the Welsh Tract," Glenn, 294 *et seq.*, and chart *infra*.]

iii. Cadwalader Thomas, *of whom presently*.
iv. Katherin, married Gawen Vaughan, of the parish of Llanycil, gentleman.
v. Elizabeth, married Maurice Edwards, of Cae Môr, gentleman. [Cae Cyriog MSS.; "Hist. Powys Fadog," iv., 108; Letters hereto appended.]

Issue by 2d wife:
vi. Elizabeth "the younger"; she is, perhaps, the Elizabeth Thomas who became the 2d wife of Humphrey ap Hugh, of Llwyn du, Esq.

Cadwalader Thomas ap Hugh, or Cadwalader Thomas, son of Thomas ap Hugh of Llaethgwm (Llaithgwm), parish of Llandderfel, Merionethshire.

1664, 29 Dec. Named as "my sonne Cadwalader Thomas" in will of his father, Thomas ap Hugh, of Llaethgwm (Llaithgwm), parish of Llandderfel, and appointed sole executor. Under said will he inherited a messuage tenement and lands called Keven y fedw, in the township of Bettws, in the parish of Llanfor, which his father had acquired as

---
[1] Ciltalgarth.
[2] John Thomas was twice married, his first wife being Ann Lloyd, buried at Llandderfel, 31 August, 1665, Elizabeth, a daughter by this marriage, did not come to Pennsylvania, but became the wife of Rees Evan, of Fron Ween, Penmaen, parish of Llanfor, before 1682 (see pedigree of Rees Evan, and particulars regarding his children, on another page). Sidney, one of the daughters of Rees Evan and Elizabeth, daughter of John Thomas, removed to Pennsylvania, and married Robert Roberts, of Pencoyd, Merion, in 1709 (see Glenn's "Merion," 105, but for *who*, tenth line from bottom of page, read *and*). Robert Roberts and Sydney, his wife, had six children. John the eldest, was ancestor of the Roberts family of Pencoyd, of whom the late George B. Roberts was President of the Pennsylvania Railroad Company. Phineas Roberts, another son, was ancestor to Richard Y Cook, of Philadelphia. For other descendants see Rees (Pedigree II.) and Wynne, in this volume, and in "Merion."

mortgage from one Piers Griffith.¹ [Will of Thomas ap Hugh, proved 4 April, 1666. Register $\frac{1642}{1666}$, folio 302 ; copy of original filed, Bundle for 1666, Probate Registry, St. Asaph.]

1666, 4 April. Will of Thomas ap Hugh, of Llaithgwm, deceased, proved by Cadwalader Thomas, natural and legitimate son of said deceased and the executor in said will named. Signs receipt for original will, (which by decree of Court, was delivered him), on copy of same. [Act Book $\frac{1637}{1676}$, Bundle for 1666 ; Register $\frac{1642}{1666}$, folio 302, Probate Registry, St. Asaph.]

1666, 4 April. Bond, Cadwalader Thomas, of Llaethgwm (Llaithgwm), *et al.*, in favour of the Lord Bishop of St. Asaph, *in re* estate of Thomas ap Hugh, late of Llaethgwm (Llaithgwm), deceased. [Bundle for 1666, Probate Registry, St. Asaph.]²

Shortly after his father's decease Cadawalader Thomas ap Hugh removed from Llaithgwm to the township of Ciltalgarth, in the adjoining parish of Llanfor. About this time he allied himself with the Society of Friends, and suffered severely during the persecution of the members of that religious body.

1674, 4 May. Cadwalader Thomas ap Hugh is named in a writ of commitment of members of the Society of Friends near Bala. [MS. Collection of the late J. J. Levick, M.D., of Philadelphia, consisting principally of papers of John ap Thomas, of Llaithgwm; see " Penna. Mag. of Hist. and Biog." iv. ; Glenn's " Merion," 17.]

1675, 16 May. Cadʳ. Thomas, of Ciltalgarth, is named in a list of those who unlawfully met together at Llwyn y Braner (Llwyn y Brain), in the parish of Llanvawr (Llanfor), dated as above. [MS. Collection of the late J. J. Levick, M.D. ; Glenn's " Merion," 17.]

1678, 6 March. Cadwalader Thomas a witness to bond of Owen Humphrey, of Llwyn du, in favour of Robert Owen, of Fron Goch, gentleman (brother of Ellen Owen, wife of Cadwalader Thomas), in re-marriage settlement made before marriage of said Robert Owen with Rebecca, daughter of said Owen Humphrey. [MSS. of Charles Morton Smith, Esq., of Philadelphia, Pennsylvania.]

1678-9, 11 March. Signs Marriage Certificate of his brother-in-law, Robert Owen, of Fron Goch, son of Owen ap Evan. [Original Certificate, in 1898, in possession of Mrs. Mary A. Haines, of Rosemont, Pennsylvania ; facsimile in collection of T. A. Glenn, and of Historical Society of Pennsylvania; see " Clovercroft Chronicles," and Glenn's " Merion," 125-6.]³

---

¹ Cadwalader Thomas does not appear to have retained Keven (or Kefn) y fedw very long. In 1679, one William Pierce, deceased, and who was probably son of Piers Griffith, the mortgagor above named, is described as late of this farm. See bond of Ellen Price, his widow, 20 May, 1679. [Probate Registry, St. Asaph, Bundle for 1679.]

² Copies at large of the more important documents *in re* estates of Cadwalader Thomas ap Hugh, Thomas ap Hugh, Robert ap Hugh, his brother, and other members of the family, are in the possession of John L. Cadwalader, Esq., of New York City, U.S.A.

³ The signatures of Thomas Cadwalader as signed on this certificate, and as attached to the bond *in re* the marriaged settlement, as above, have been compared with his signature on the official documents *in re* the estate of his father, Thomas ap Hugh, dated 1666, and found identical.

His descendant, the late Charles E. Cadwalader, of Philadelphia, says of Cadwalader Thomas ap Hugh : " His determined resistance and refusal to yield the dictates of his own conscience under a severe persecution, would appear to have cost him his life. As in the cases of Charles Lloyd, Thomas Lloyd, Robert Vaughan, Hugh Roberts, Robert Owen, and other members of the principal families of North Wales, he was made an example of a special prosecution by the Government. After repeated confiscations of his property and imprisonments, he was again arraigned and refusing to take the oaths, the Judges of the Circuit Court, by whom the commitment was made, had come to the extraordinary determination that the prosecution should be conducted under the statutes for High Treason and the writ *De Haeretico Comlurendo*, the penalties under the latter process not having been exercised since Queen Mary's time. They declared in open court that the sentence for a second refusal to take the prescribed oaths would be hanging and quartering as traitors for the men, and burning for the women. After a short interval Cadwalader Thomas was again brought into court and the oaths tendered him, and being again refused, though he made a 'solemn declaration of his allegiance to the King, and abhorrence of Popery,' he was remanded to close imprisonment and strictly kept as a felon or traitor, and during a very great frost was not allowed the benefit of a fireplace." It is said that a cold contracted at this time hastened his death. [MS. of the late Charles E. Cadwalader, M.D., in possession of T. A. Glenn.]

It does not appear that Cadwalader Thomas ever lived at Keven y fedw (Cefn y bedw) the property bequeathed him by his father.[1] He obtained on lease, after his father's decease, lands in the township of Ciltalgarth, adjacent to Llaithgwm. Upon his conviction as a recusant, his landlord, who was also his kinsman, commenced an action in ejectment against him, which, according to Besse's " Sufferings," was successful; but this is doubtful, as he appears to have maintained some holdings in Ciltalgarth, up to, or very near, the time of his death. After his last imprisonment, and, apparently, just before his decease, he went to live in the parish of Llandrillo, about eight miles from Ciltalgarth, where he also seems to have held lands, and where he died in or about the month of November, 1680.

Cadwalader Thomas ap Hugh married Ellin, or Ellen, Owen, daughter of Owen ap Evan, of Fron Goch.[2] [MS. Genealogy of Descendants of

---

[1] See note to p. 16.

[2] The marriage is supposed to have taken place after 16 May, 1675, presumably at the end of May or beginning of June of the same year, insomuch as in the official list of those persons who were fined for unlawfully meeting together in the house called Llwyn y Braner (now Llwyn y Brain) in the parish of Llanfor, Cadwalader Thomas is described as of the township of Ciltalgarth, whilst Ellen Owen appears three names lower down the list under that of her brother, Robert Owen "of vron goch" (Fron Goch), whereas married couples are entered in the list as " Hugh Roberts, and his wife of the same," &c. The late Howard Williams Lloyd, however, was under the impression that the marriage must have taken place earlier. As, however, Thomas Cadwalader was probably born in the early spring of 1675-6, and the youngest child, Elizabeth, in the autumn of 1680, and as possibly there may have been twins, I see no reason for altering my opinion, although, of course, the marriage may have been unknown to the informer, or to the Court Officers.

Evan Robert Lewis; original bound in "Some Records relating to Radnor and Merion Meeting," in MS. Colls. of the Genealogical Society of Pennsylvania, Library of Historical Society of Pennsylvania; and Records hereafter cited.] See Pedigree of Owen, in vol. ii., "Welsh Founders of Pennsylvania."

"Ellin, one of the daughters of the said Owen ab Evan died in Wales, but her son John Cadwalader lived and died in Philad^a." [MS. Genealogy, cited *supra*, in "Some Records relating to Radnor and Merion Meeting."] There are several copies of this Genealogy in existence. That here cited will be found in full in vol. ii. of "Welsh Founders of Pennsylvania."

1680, 9 Nov. Llandrillo, Merionethshire. Administration of the goods of Cadwallader Thomas ap Hugh, deceased, granted to John Owen,[1] brother of Ellena Owen, relict of the deceased, to the use of said Ellena Owen, and Thomas Cadwallader, Jane Cadwallader, Catherine Cadwallader, John Cadwallader and Elizabeth Cadwallader (sic), natural and legitimate children of said deceased. [Act Book $\frac{1677}{1686}$ folio 107, Probate Registry, St. Asaph.]

1680, 9 Nov. Bond, John Owen of Bala, in the County of Merioneth Robert Vaughan of Llanyckill in said County, and Rowland Owen of Llanfor in the same County, in favour of the Lord Bishop of St. Asaph.

For the good administration by "ye above bounden John Owen brother of Ellen Owen, wid. & Relict of Cadwallader (sic) Thomas ap Hugh late of Llandrillo in ye said Countye deced. of the goods rights and credits Cattle and Chattles of ye said Cadd^r Thomas ap Hugh" to the use of the said Ellen Owen & Thomas Cadwalader, Jane Cadwalader, Catherine Cadwalader, John Cadwalader, and Elizabeth Cadwalader, natural and lawful children of the said deceased. Signed by John Owen, Robert Vaughan, and Rowland Owen. Witnesses: Jo. Roberts, cl'ro., George Salusbury, Hen. Leishe (?), Tho. Harpur.

Endorsed: "Llandrillo 9 9 br. B. Admrâco Caddr. Thomas ap Hugh."

"Cōmo ad app'hēnd Robt. Wynne Brēū de Kerrig y Druidion et Joh' Jones, B. .... de Llanyckill." [Filed. Bundle for 1680, Probate Registry, St. Asaph.]

At the time of the death of Cadwalader Thomas ap Hugh, his brother, John ap Thomas, of Llaithgwm, and Robert Owen, the eldest brother of Ellen Owen, were members of the Society of Friends, and therefore could not administer because of their inability to take the prescribed oath. They had, also, because of their religious belief, been convicted of treasonable offences. John Owen and Rowland Owen did not join the Society of Friends.

---

[1] From researches in Wales, it appears that Owen ap Evan, of Fron Goch, had two sons other than those given in the genealogy of the Owen family, in "Merion," *viz.* Rowland and John, both younger than Robert. The date 1657, given "Merion," p. 123, as *about* the date of Robert Owen's birth is incorrect, as he was born several years earlier. See "Welsh Founders of Pennsylvania," vol. ii.

Pedigree I.

ISSUE:

i. Thomas Cadwalader, named as son of Cadwalader Thomas ap Hugh in above cited records, 9 Nov., 1680. and then a minor; called "my nephew Thomas Cadwalader," in will of John Thomas of Llaethgwm (Llaithgwm), dated 9 Feb., 1682 (1682-3), cited *supra*. In a letter, dated 1703, written by Robert Vaughan, son of Gawen Vaughan, the writer speaks of his cousin, Thomas Cadwalader, being on a visit to Dolobran, and being engaged in literary work there. He lived for a long time at Hendre Mawr. [MS. of the late Charles E. Cadwalader, M.D.] He died in Wales.[1]

ii. Jane, named in documents above cited, dated 9 Nov. 1680; "my nieces Katherine and Jane, daughters of Cadwalader Thomas," 9 Feb., 1682 (1682-3) cited *supra*.

iii. Catherine, named in documents above cited, dated 9 Nov., 1680, and in will of her uncle, John Thomas (or John ap Thomas), of Llaethgwm, 9 Feb., 1682 (1682-3) cited *supra*.

iv. John Cadwalader, *of whom presently*.

v. Elizabeth, named in documents cited *supra*, dated 9 Nov., 1680. I am inclined to suppose she died an infant before 9 Feb., 1682-3.

John Cadwalader, 2d son of Cadwalader Thomas ap Hugh, was born in the township of Ciltalgarth, in the parish of Llanfor, Merionethshire.

1680, 9 Nov. John Cadwalader named as second legitimate (and minor) son of Cadwalader Thomas ap Hugh, late of Llandrillo, County of Merioneth, deceased, in record of grant of Administration of the personal estate of said deceased to John Owen, brother of Ellen Owen, the widow of the said Cadwalader Thomas ap Hugh. [Act Book,$\frac{1677}{1688}$, folio 107, Probate Registry, St. Asaph.]

1680, 9 Nov. John Cadwalader named as second legitimate (and minor) son of Cadwalader Thomas ap Hugh, late of Llandrillo, deceased, in bond of John Owen, brother of Ellen Owen the widow of the said Cadwalader Thomas ap Hugh, *et al., in re* administration of the estate of the said deceased. [Filed. Bundle for 1680, Probate Registry, St. Asaph.]

1682, 9 Feb. Will of John Thomas of Llaethgwm, gentleman; proved 1688. "My nephew John the younger son of my Brother Cadwalder Thomas" [ap Hugh.] [Executed in Wales; proved in Philadelphia, Pennsylvania. Will Book A, folios 77-82, original No. 41 of 1688.]

---

[1] Robert Vaughan, of Hendre Mawr, Thomas Cadwalader, of Llanerch, and David Jones, of Kiltalgarth (Ciltalgarth), are witnesses to a bond dated 20 Dec., 1691, of John ap John, Dr. Thomas Wynne, and Hugh Roberts, and executed in Wales, concerning Pennsylvania lands. At this time Thomas Cadwalader is supposed to have been aged about 16 years and was, therefore, eligible as a witness. There is a place called Llanerch, about six or seven miles from Bala. [MSS. of Charles Morton Smith, Esq., of Philadelphia.]

John Cadwalader, at the age of thirteen, was sent to school in Pembrokeshire, where he remained under the care of members of the Society of Friends until 1697.[1]

1697, 19 March, (1st month). Certificate of Removal, John Cadwalader, a youth, from Pembrokeshire to Pennsylvania. It says of him : " We have known him since the age of thirteen, he hath the reputation of an apt scholar, and hath attained to as good a degree of learning as any at the school. His demeanour has been sober and innocent." It is said that at this time he was about nineteen years of age. [Radnor, (and Haverford and Merion) Monthly Meeting Records. Transcript in possession of the Historical Society of Pennsylvania ; original deposited in Friend's Library, Sixteenth Street below Race Street, Philadelphia, Pennsylvania.]

1703. Letter of Robert Vaughan, of Hendre Mawr, Merionethshire, to his cousin in Philadelphia, speaks of his "cousin Thomas Cadwalader" being on a visit to Dolobran and being "occupied there in the translation of an English work into Welsh, and refers to him as engaged in the administration of the family estate."

The late Dr. Charles E. Cadwalader, of Philadelphia, says :—
"Robert Vaughan was a relative of the family of John ap Thomas and seems to have acted as a guardian to the children of the latter's brother Cadwalader ap Thomas after their deaths ; " *viz.* after deaths of J. ap. T. and C. ap T.

Dr. Cadwalader further states that Robert Vaughan, of Hendre Mawr, refers in his letters to John Cadwalader, of Pennsylvania "as his cousin" and that he also mentions "a John Cadwalader of Cerig drydion [Cerrig y Druidion] as his uncle." The latter was the son of Cadwalader ap Hugh ap Evan, and first cousin to John Thomas, Cadwalader Thomas, and Katherin (or Catherine), the mother of Robert Vaughan, and was, therefore, " Uncle " (*viz.* a parent's first cousin) to Robert Vaughan, John Cadwalader, and the children of John Thomas.

Dr. Cadwalader, in 1894, informed the compiler that he had a number of letters written by Thomas Cadwalader, in Wales, to his brother, John Cadwalader, in Pennsylvania; also letters from Robert Vaughan, of Hendre Mawr, Merionethshire, to his "cousin John Cadwalader."

The MS. collection of the late J. J. Levick contains several letters from Edward Maurice, of Cae Môr, to his cousin Thomas Jones, of Merion, (son of John Thomas), and other correspondence with Robert Vaughan, of Hendre Mawr. Those from Edward Maurice are signed "your cousin Edward Maurice." One of these, dated 18th of 8mo., 1691, speaks of "cousin Robert Vaughan." There is also a draft of a letter, dated about 1708, addressed to "Loving cousin Robert Vaughan," in the handwriting of Thomas Jones, of Merion.

---

[1] The school in question was probably the Grammer School of Haverford-West, founded in 1612, and at the time considered one of the best schools in Wales. A number of boys from near Bala were, until recent years, sent to Pembrokeshire to be educated.

(To face page 21).

Heilin Gloff, of Carwedd Fynydd, from Marchweithian, lord of Isaled. = **Nest, dau. Cadwgan ap Llywarch ap Bran of Porthamel.**

- **Llywarch ap Heilin, of Carwedd Fynydd.** D. before 3 Edw. I., (1274).
  - **Cynwrig ap Llywarch of Carwedd Fynydd.** Wit. to Char. of Henry de Lacy to John de la Chambre, 3 Edw. I. (1274).
    - **Einion ap Cynwrig,** of the parish of Cerrig y Druidion, co. Denb. temp. Edw. II. and Edw. III.
      - **David ap Einion, of Cerrig y Druidion.**
        - **Evan Ddu, of Cerrig y Druidion.**
          - **Evan Coch, of Bryanmor,** twp. of Cwm Pen Aner, Cerrig y Druidion. = **Gwenhwyfar, dau. Thomas ap David Gam.** From Marchudd, lord of Isdulas, co. Denbigh.
            - **Rees ap Evan Coch, of Cerrig y Druidion.** = **Gruffydd ap Evan Coch, of Cerrig y Druidion.** D. before 12 Nov., 1543.
              - **Tudor ap Rees, of Cerrig y Druidion.** D. before 12 Nov., 1543. = **Evan ap Rees, of Cerrig y Druidion.**
                - **Rees Coch ap Tudor, of Cerrig y Druidion.** D. before 4 Eliz. (1598-9).
                  - **Evan ap Rees Coch, of Cerrig y Druidion.** Liv. 41 Eliz. (1598-9). = **Robert ap Rees, of Cerrig y Druidion.** Admon. 25 Jan. 1637.
                    - **David ap Evan, of Cerrig y Druidion, gentleman.** Liv. 3 Car. I. (1627). = **Hugh ap Evan, of Cerrig y Druidion.** Liv. 25 July, 1620.
                      - **Thomas ap Hugh, of Wern Fawr, Llandderfel.** Will proved at St. Asaph, 4 April 1666. = (2) Rose (a dau. Elizabeth, by 2d wf.)
                        - **Hugh Thomas.** Liv. 1664.
                          - Catherine, m. Gawen Vaughan, of Hendre Mawr.
                          - Elizabeth, m. Maurice Edwards, of Cae Môr.
          - **Tudor ap Einion.**
      - **Pill ap Einion.**

- **Gwenllian, dau. Madog ap Ithirid Flaidd,** of Pennant Melangell. Ithirid is styled lord of Penllyn, and d. circa 1207.
  - **Dyddgu, dau. Cadwgan ap Ednyfed.** From Llywarch Holbwrch, Treas. to Graffydd, Prince of Wales (d. 1063).

David Goch, of Penllech. Pension for life for gallant services to Edw. I., 12 Edw. II., 6 June (1319). Lessee of Manor of Neugoff, 1325. Crown tenant, 9 Nov. 1329. Did homage, 1344. Died Abbot of Bardsey Isle. = **Maud, dau. David Lloyd ap David ap Llewelyn.** From Owen Gwynedd, Prince of North Wales.

- **Ieuan Goch, of Penllech.** Liv. 26 Edw III. (1352) = **Efa, dau. Einion ap Celynin,** of Llwydiarth. Liv. 1340.
  - **Madog ap Ieuan, of Penllech.** Liv. after 1352. = **Ales, dau Ieuan ap Madog.** From Brochwel, Prince of Powys.
    - **Deikws Ddu, of Lleyn,** Captain under Henry of Bolingbroke. Forfeited 22 Rich II. (1398) = **Gwen. dau. Ieuan Ddu.** From Maelog. lord of Llechwedd Isaf.
      - **Einion ap Deikws.** D. before 1514. = **Morfydd, dau. Matw ap Llywarch.**
        - **Catherine, dau. Gruffydd ap Llewelyn ap Einion, ap David, ap Ieuan ap Einion.** David was the celebrated Constable of Harlech Castle, which he held for 7 years for the House of Lancaster, and he m. Margaret, dau. Robert Puleston, of Emral, Esq. = **Edward ap Evan, of Llanwddyn, co. Montg.** D. before 1513.
          - **Howel ap Einion, of Yspytty Evan.** Liv. 6 Hen. VI.
            - **Ellen, dau. Edward ap Evan.**
              - Gwerfyl, dau. David. of Llanrwst. (1st wife) = **Llewelyn ap David, of Llanrwst.**
                - ——dau.——; b. of half of Coed y Foel, Llanfor.
              - Robert ap Hugh, of Llandderfel. Admon. 20 Oct., 1838.

Rhys Wendot (or Gloff), s. Rhys Vychan, from "The Lord Rhys," Prince of So. Wales. Surrendered to the Earl of Hereford, 1283. D. in the Tower of London.

- **Madog Goch, of Lleyn, co. Carn.** Did homage for his lands to the King, at Carnarvon, 29, Edw. I., 28 April (1293).
  - **Trahaiarn Goch, of Lleyn,** of co. Carn. Lord of Cymytmaen, succeeded after 28 April, 1299.
    - **Cynwrig Fychan, of Llannefydd.** Deft. at Llannerch Court, 10 June, 1294. Liv. 8, Edw. III.
      - **Howel ap Cynwrig of Llannefydd.**
        - **Tudor ap Howel, of Llannefydd.**
          - **Einion ap Tudor, of Voelas, Yspytty Evan.** Liv. circa 1450.
            - **Dyddgu dau. Einion ap Tudor.**
              - Mali dau. Llewelyn ap Ieuan.
                - **Gruffydd ap Howel, of Yspytty Evan.** Liv. 12 Nov., 1543.
                  - **Lewis ap Gruffydd, of Yspytty Evan.** Liv. 1543. D. before 1601.
                    - Robert Lewis, of Yspytty Evan. Admon. 13 Mch., 1637, St. Asaph.
                      - **Evan Robert Lewis, of Llanfor and Llandderfel.** Bur. 28 Sept., 1668
                        - Owen ap Hugh. Liv.1664, 29 Dec.
                        - Humphrey ap Hugh. Liv. 1666.
                        - Cadwalader ap Hugh. of Cerrig y Druidion.
                        - Owen ap Evan, of Fron Goch, Llanfor, co. Mer., gentleman. D. before 6 Mar., 1678.

- **Cadwalader Thomas ap Hugh, of Cilualgarth,** at Llandrillo, Admon. 9 Nov., 1680. He was a friend and associate of William Penn. = **Ellen Owen,** Liv. 9 Nov. 1680.
  - **Thomas Cadwalader.** Under age, 9 Nov., 1680. Liv. 1710. D. in Wales.
  - Jane.
  - Catherine.
  - Elizabeth.
- **John Thomas, of Llaithgwm** gentleman. Will 9 Feb., 1683, proved at Philadelphia. 1686. D. at Llaithgwm. His sons assumed the surname of Jones.
- **Robert Owen, of Fron Goch. Rmvd to Penna, 1690.** J.P. Memb. Prov. Assembly. = **Rebecca, dau. Owen Humphrey, Esq , of Llwyp du, co. Mer., s. Humphrey ap Hugh, by Elizabeth, dau. John Puwell of Gadfa, and a descendant of Edward III.** (See ped. iv.)
- **John Cadwalader.** B. near Bala, co. Mer. Under age 9 Nov., 1680. Rmd. to Penna, 1698. D. in Philadelphia. = **Martha Jones.** B. 1679 in Bala.

- **Dr. Thomas Cadwalader,** of Philadelphia. D. near Trenton, N.J., 11 Nov. 1779 Surgeon General Continental Army. = **Hannah, dau. Thomas Lambert. Esq., of Trenton.** Mar. 18 June, 1738.
  - Anne, b. 1738. D. 1739.
  - Martha, b. 1739 ; mar. Capt. John Dagworthy.
  - Elizabeth Lloyd (1st wife). = **General John Cadwalader,** of Philadelphia. = **Williamina Boud.**
    - Anne, b. 1771. M. Robert Kemble.
    - Elizabeth, b. 1773 ; mar. Archibald McCall.
    - Maria, b. 1776; m. Samuel Ringgold.
    - **General Thomas Cadwalader,** m. Mary, dau. Colonel Clement Biddle.
      - David Erskine. Major 21st fus. Lt. Col Natal Carabineers. M. Anne Maria Spode.

The Cadwalader family is now represented by John Cadwalader, Esq., of Philadelphia; John I. Cadwalader, Esq., of New York, and Richard McCall Cadwalader of Philadelphia.

- Mary, m. 1731, Justice Samuel Dickinson.
  - Hannah, m. Samuel Morris.
  - Rebecca, m. Wm. Morris.

Thomas Americus, 3rd Baron Erskine.

John Cadwalader, 4th Baron Erskine, father of William Macnaghten, 5th Baron Erskine.

(Daughters.)

For detailed genealogy of this family see "Welsh Founders of Pennsylvania," vol. ii.

= Gwerfyl, dau. Maelgwn, lord of Maelienydd, co. Radnor.

= Tanglwyst, dau. Goronwy ap Einion. From Iestyn, Prince of Glamorgan.

= Gwerfyl, dau. Madog ap Meurig. From Elystan, Prince of Fferlis.

= Morfydd, dau. Madog Ddu. From Nefydd Hardd.

= Margaret, dau. Howel, lord of Rhos.

= Susanna, dau. and h. Maredydd ap Madog of Iâl.

Maredydd ap Tudor, of Voelas. Liv. 1450. Father of Rhys ap Maredydd capt. under Hen. VII. Standard-bearer at Bosworth Field.

= Llewelyn ap Ieuan, of Iâl. From Llewelyn Awdorchog, lord of Iâl.

John Thelwall, of Plas yn Ward, m. Ffelis, dau. John ap Rhys, by Alice, dau. and h. of Sir Walter Cooke, Knt.

David Thelwall, of Plas yn Ward, m. Tibot, dau. Jenkin de Weild, of Borasham.

Simon Thelwall, of Plas yn Ward, co. Denbigh, Esq. = Jauet Langford.

Richard Langford, Constable of Ruthin Castle. Receiver of Ruthin, 1431. s. John, L. Constable of R. and Steward of Vale of Clwyd.

Edward Langford, Constable of Ruthin Castle. D. 16 Hen. VI., m. Ellen, dau. John Dutton, of Dutton.

= Gwenllian, dau. Einion ap Ieuan Lloyd. From Bleddyn Lloyd, of Hafod nn Nos, Llangerniew.

Ellis ap Harri, of Yscelfiog.

Hugh ap Ellis ap Harri, of Yscelfiog, who had Alice, event. h. wio m. John Myddelton, of Gwaenynog, Esq. (d. 1598), and had William, who m. Catherine, dau. John Conway, Esq., of Bodrhyddlan, David, and other issue.

= Jane Lloyd. Liv. 13 Mar. 1687 (2d wife).

= Gainor ——. (2d wife) (A s., Robert, by Gainor, d.s.p.)

= Gainor John. Liv. 11 Mar. 1678, at Fron Goch.

Cadwalader ap Evan, of Coed y Foel, gentleman. (eld. s. and h.) Will proved at St. Asaph, 31 Jan., 1688.

John ap Evan.
Griffith ap Evan.
Evan Lloyd Evan.
Daughters.

Rowland Owen, of Fron Goch, gentleman. Will proved at St. Asaph, 7 Nov. 1717.

Evan Owen.

Dr. Edward Jones, of Bala, = Mary Wynne, co. Mer., son of John Lloyd. Liv. 27 May, 1782. Rmd. to Penn, 1692. Will proved at Philadelphia, 1738. J.P. and memb. of Prov. Assembly.

John Owen, of Bala, liv. 9 Nov., 1680.

Jane, m. Hugh Roberts, of Bala, gent.

Elizabeth.

Thomas, 3rd s. Dr. Edward Jones, had Alice, m. John von Knorr, and had Mary, m. John Lora, and had (1) Catherine, m. Count James Francine, of France, and had (a) Col. Louis R. Francine, grad. St. Cyr; mortally wounded at Gettysburg, 1863, Brevet Brig. Gen. (b) Albert (2) Sarah Ann, m. Thomas Hardy, s. Capt. Robt. Allen, and had Sarah Catherine, m. Edward Glenn (see infra.

Evan Owen, Justice Ct. Com. Pleas, Orphans Ct. City Ct., Master of Ct of Equity, Justice Ct. Chancery.

Owen Owen, b. 1690. = Anne, dau. John Wood, by High Sher. of Philadelphia, 1726; Coroner, 1729-1711. Jane, dau. John Bevan, Esq. of Treferig, co. Glam. desd. fr. Henry Somerset, 2d. Earl of Worcester, fr. Edward III

John Biddle = Sarah Owen.

John Owen, b. 1692. High Sheriff of co. Chester 1729-1741. Memb. Prov. Assembly, 1733-1748, Trustee of Loan Office of Penna.

Susanna, dau. Wm. Hudson, Mayor of Phila.

= Robert Owen, of Philadelphia, b. 1695.

John Ogden, s. David, of Middleton, co. Lanc.

= Hannah Owen, co. heiress.

= Joseph Wharton, Esq., of Walnut Grove.

Colonel Lambert Cadwalader, m. Mary McCall.

Mary, m. Philemon Dickinson.
Rebecca, m. Philemon Dickinson.

Margaret, m. Samuel Meredith.
Elizabeth, d. unm.

Col. Owen Biddle.
Col. Clement Biddle.

William Ogden (only child) served under Gen. Wayne at Stoney Point. D. 1818.

= Mary Piniard.

Robert Wharton, Col. 1st Penna Cavalry. Mayor of Philadelphia.

John Cadwalader. D. young.

Frances Cadwalader. 23 Mch., 1813.

D. = David Montagu, 2d Baron Erskine.

Hannah Ogden, m. Capt. William Duer, 1795, and had Mary Ann (only surv. dau.); m. Lewis W. Glenn, b. 1804 h. of Robert Owen, and of Thomas, 3rd son of Dr. Edward Jones.

Edward Morris Erskine, C.B., H.M. Envoy extraordinary and plenipotentiary to King of Hellenes, Brit. Min. at Stockholm, m. Caroline, dau. Robt. Hamilton Vaughan.

James Stuart, Baron Erskine in Bavaria. m. Wilhelmina, Countess Toerring Minucci, dau. Anton Joseph Clemens, Count Toerring Minucci, of Munich.

Jane Plumer, m. 1857, James Henry Callander, of Craigforth, and had (inter al.) Janey Sevilla, m. 1869, Archibald Campbell, bro. and h. apparent to the Duke of Argyll, who m. 1871, H.R.H. Princess Louise Caroline Alberta, dau. of Her Majesty Queen Victoria.

Lt. Col. T. A. Glenn, of Prestatyn, co. Flint, b. 1804 h. of Robert Owen, and of Thomas, 3rd son of Dr. Edward Jones.

Arddyn, dau. Ednowain ap Bradwen, lord of Talybont.

= Madog ap Ednowain Bendew, lord of Tegeingl. E. B. lived at Llys y Coed. Bodfari.

Arddyn, dau. Llewelyn, From Edwin, Prince of Tegeinge.

= Iorwerth ap Madog, of Yscelfiog and Bodfari.

Tibot, dau. Robert de Pulford, co. Ches. Liv. 1240.

= Rhirid ap Iorwerth, of Yscelfiog and Bodfari. Liv. circa 1240 to 1300.

Nest, dau. and h. of Iorwerth ap Grono ap Einion ap Seisayllt.

= Iorwerth ap Rhirid, of Yscelfiog and Bodfari.

Adles, dau. Ithel Vychan. lord of Mostyn, co. Flint.

= Roipert ap Iorwerth. Liv. 1339.

Angharad, dau. and b. of Madog Lloyd, of Bryn Cunallt.

= Cynric ap Roipert, of Yscelfiog and Bodfari. Bro. of Ithel Fychan, Archdeacon of Tegeingl, 1375-93.

——dau. and h. of Robin, bro. Robert, ancestor to the Wynns of Gwydir (liv. 1404) From Owain Gwynedd, Prince of North Wales

= Ithel Fychan, of Holt, Yscelfiog, and Bodfari.

Tanglwyst, dau. and h. of Gruffydd Lloyd.

= Cynric ap Ithel, of Yscelfiog and Bodfari. Liv. circa 1470.

Alice Thelwall, dau. Simon.
= Harri ap Cynrie (or Cynwrig), of Yscelfiog

Katherine, dau. and h. of Ithel ap Jenkin ap David ap Howel.
= John Wynne ap Harri, of Yscelfiog. D. before 1572.

Rees ap John Wynne, of Yscelfiog. Liv. 1592.

Grace Morgan, of Bodfari, Mar. 29 Oct., 1588.
= John ap Rees Wynne, of Yscelfiog. B. circa 1570.

Thomas ap John Wynne, of Yscelfiog. Bapt. 20 Dec. 1589. D. 1638-9.

Martha Buttall, of Wrexham (1st wife).
= Dr. Thomas Wynne, of Brouvadog, Yscelfiog co. Flint, Bapt. 20 July, 1627, Rmd. to Penna, 1682. Will proved at Philadelphia, 20 April, 1692. J.P., and memb. Prov. Assembly.

PEDIGREE I.

1718, 4 Oct. Will of Elizabeth Andrews, of Philadelphia, Pennsylvania, widow of Thomas Andrews, and daughter of Owen ap Hugh, brother of Thomas ap Hugh, of Wern Fawr, Llaithgwm: "Thomas Cadwalader,[1] son of cousin John Cadwalader"......" Cousin Robert Vaughan of Hendre Mawr, near Bala, Merionetshire"......"Cousin Thomas Jones of Merion (son of John Thomas of Llaithgwm, deceased) ......"Mary and Rebecca, daughters of said cousin John (Cadwalader). Executor: "Nephew Rees Prees," and "Cousins Robert Jones (son of John Thomas of Llaithgwm) and John Cadwalader, Trustees." [Proved at Philadelphia, 7 Jan., 1718-19. Will Book D, folio 112.]

1699, 26 Dec. (10th month). John Cadwalader and Martha, daughter of Dr. Edward Jones, of Merion, Philadelphia County, Pennsylvania, married at Merion Meeting.

John Cadwalader resided at first in Merion, but removed to Philadelphia.

1705, July. John Cadwalader admitted to the Freedom of the City of Philadelphia. Charles E. Cadwalader, M.D., states that at this time he inherited a considerable fortune from a kinsman in Wales.

John Cadwalader held many important Public Offices under the Provincial Government, and was one of the foremost citizens of Philadelphia of his day. See "Provincial Councillors of Pennsylvania," by Charles P. Keith, Esq., of Philadelphia, "Contemporary Biography," under "Cadwalader," in each of which will be found details regarding his descendants and their distinguished careers in public as well as in private life.

ISSUE:

i. Mary Cadwalader, married, as his 2d wife, Hon. Samuel Dickinson.
ii. Rebecca Cadwalader, married William Morris, Esq., of Barbadoes; settled in Trenton, New Jersey.
iii. Hannah Cadwalader, d. infant.
iv. Hannah Cadwalader, married Samuel Morris, Esq., of Philadelphia.
v. Letitia Cadwalader, d. infant.
vi. Thomas Cadwalader, M.D., married Hannah Lambert. His sons, General John Cadwalader and Colonel Lambert Cadwalader, served with great distinction in the American Revolution.[2] Frances, daughter of General John Cadwalader, married Thomas, Lord Erskine. For her descendants, see "The Peerage."

---

[1] This was Dr. Thomas Cadwalader, then a lad.

[2] Descendants include, John L. Cadwalader, of New York, John Cadwalader, of Philadelphia, and Richard M. Cadwalader, of Philadelpia, Mrs. S. Weir Mitchell, and Mrs. Henry J. Rowland. For a complete genealogy of the descendants of John Cadwalader, see Keith's "Provincial Councillors," and Moon's "Morris Genealogy."

PEDIGREE I.

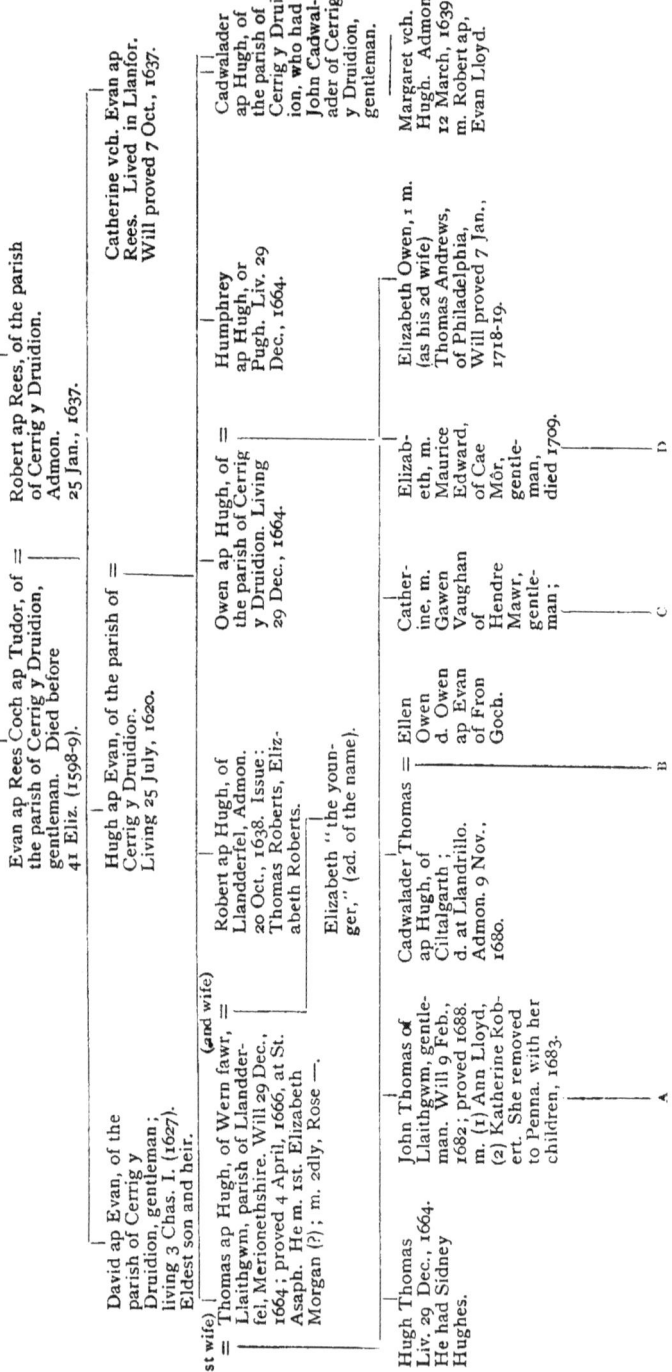

PEDIGREE I.

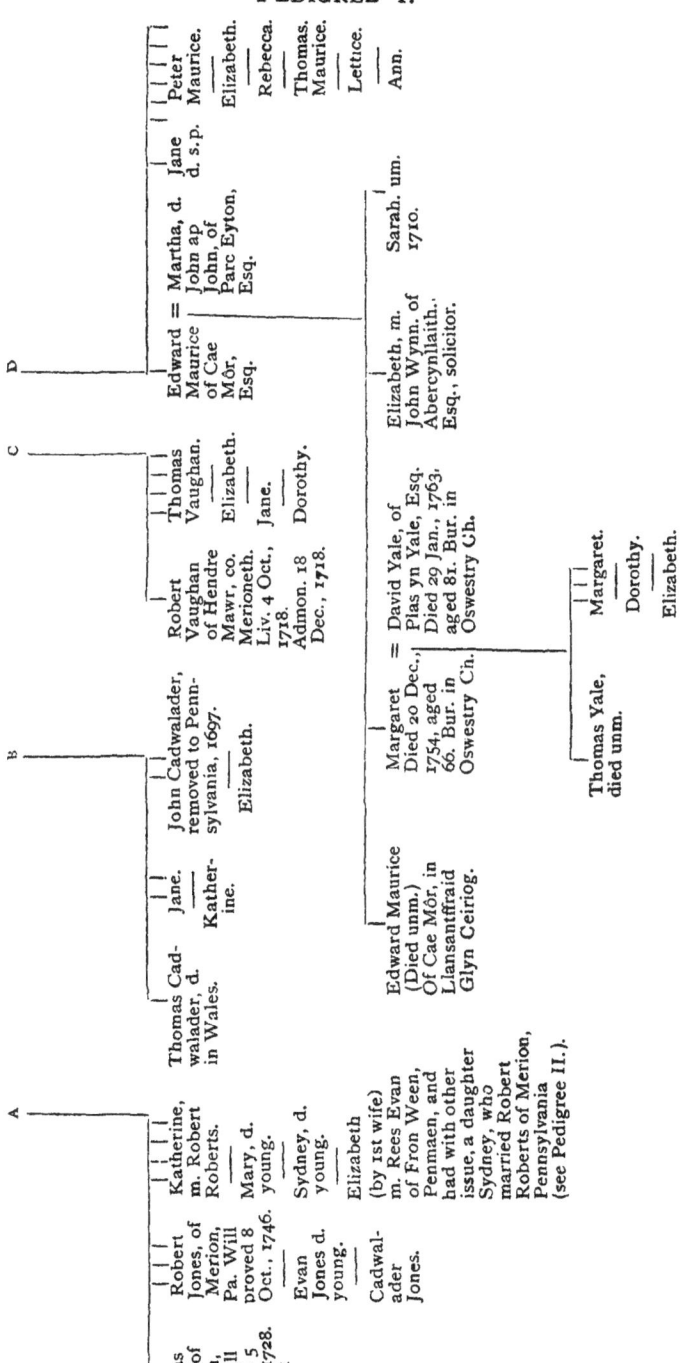

1 Owen ap Hugh had other issue, of whom Mably m. Edward Rees, Prees or Price, who removed to Pennsylvania 1682, Ellen and Gwen, and a son, name unknown.

ADDENDA TO PEDIGREE I.

MS. Pedigree of John Thomas.

The following is a copy of a pedigree, dated 1682, of John Thomas, of Llaithgwm, gentleman, brother of Cadwalader Thomas ap Hugh. The original is on vellum, and was brought to Pennsylvania by the family of John Thomas, on the Ship, " Morning Star," Thomas Hayes, Master, which arrived at Philadelphia in November, 1683.[1] Katherine Robert, the widow (she was the second wife), and the surviving children of John Thomas (two children having died at sea), with the exception of Elizabeth, who remained in Wales, settled in Merion upon a tract of land purchased by John Thomas in 1682. The original conveyance to " John Thomas of Llaithgwm," as he is called on the original draft and return of survey on file among the State Archives at Harrisburg, Pennsylvania,[2] or " John Thomas of Llaithgwm in the Parish of Llanvawr (Llanfor) in the County of Merioneth," as he is described in the Lease and Release, was executed 1 April, 1682.[3] The allotment to him had been 1250 acres, but, for reasons which it is unnecessary to explain here, only 612 acres of this land were surveyed in Merion, and the balance in Goshen. John Thomas, by his will executed in

---

[1] " John ap Thomas and his Friends," by J. J. Levick, M.D., " Pennsylvania Mag. of Hist. and Biog.," vol. iv. ; Glenn's " Merion," 298.

[2] " The lands of Edward Jones and Company in Merion," by Benjamin H. Smith, " Pa. Mag.," vol. xxvi., No. 101, 42.

[3] Deed Book, C I., Philadelphia.

Wales, 9 February, 1682-3, and proved at Philadelphia in 1688[1] (he died at Llaithgwm, Llanfor, 3 May, 1683[2]), devised the said 1250 acres to his sons, Thomas, Robert, Evan, and Cadwalader John, or as they called themselves, *Jones*, share and share alike. They at first named the plantation Gelli y Cochiad; but when Thomas Jones, the eldest son, married, and built a home for himself, he called it Llaethgwm (Llaithgwm) House.[3]

Katherine Thomas, or Robert, the widow of John Thomas, purchased, soon after her arrival, 650 acres of adjacent land in Merion, and her son Robert Jones secured an additional 165 acres in 1704. The re-survey of the Goshen property showed it to contain 635 acres, and by a re-survey the original Merion lands were found to contain 679 acres, so that the family at the beginning of the 18th century held, altogether, 2,129 acres of land. Much of the Merion property remained in the family until quite recently, and some is yet, or was in 1900, held by descendants.[4]

The family papers of John Thomas passed, as can be proved, to his eldest son, Thomas Jones. The latter died at Llaithgwm House in Merion, in 1727, and the family Bible, seal of John Thomas, pedigree, and other papers, passed into the possession of his brother, Robert Jones.[5] The latter, in his will proved at Philadelphia, 17 Oct. 1746,[6] bequeathed the family Bible to his daughter Elizabeth.

---

[1] Will Book A, folio 77, Philadelphia.

[2] Jones Family Bible, Levick MSS.

[3] Letter in Levick Collection, written in Wales, 1710, signed Edward Maurice (of Cae Môr) and directed to " Mr. Thomas Jones at Llaetcum (Llaethgwm) house in Merion Township, County of Philadelphia, Pensilvania."

[4] "The Lands of Edward Jones and Company in Merion," by Benjamin H. Smith, " Pa. Mag."

[5] Robert Jones was one of the trustees under the will of his brother Thomas, whose son was under age at the time of his father's death.

[6] Dated 21 Sept., 1746. Will Book H, folio 161, &c., Philadelphia.

The latter appears to have died unmarried; at any rate, the Bible, pedigree and other papers, seem to have passed to the family of her sister, Ann Paul, as indicated by Paul family papers, dating down to 1761, if not later, being included in the collection of Dr. Levick. It has not been explained precisely how these papers came into the Levick family. Elizabeth, the mother of Dr. Levick, was, however, the daughter of Isaac Jones, of Burlington, New Jersey (born 1743), whose father, James Jones (born in Wales, 1699), was a son of David Jones of Ciltalgarth, whose sister, Ellen Jones, married Robert Jones of Merion (died 1746), second son of John Thomas, of Llaithgwm, Merionethshire. Isaac Jones, therefore, was a third cousin of the children of Ann, daughter of Robert Jones, of Merion, and James Paul; and Elizabeth, the daughter of Isaac, who married in 1816, Ebenezer Levick, a third cousin once removed. The families are understood to have been intimate, which would satisfactorily account for the documents coming ultimately into the possession of J. J. Levick, M.D., the son of Ebenezer Levick and Elizabeth Jones. I am also informed that there was some other connection between the Paul and Levick families, through Ebenezer Levick.

After the death of Dr. Levick, the manuscripts passed into the hands of his sister, Miss Elizabeth R. Levick, of Philadelphia, and they were afterwards in the keeping of Richard Cadbury, Esq., Attorney at Law, Philadelphia. The MS. pedigree of John Thomas is at present (1910) deposited in the Library of the Historical Society of Pennsylvania.

This pedigree was examined by the writer, and compared with copy herewith, in 1889. The copy appended was made in 1874, from the original, and printed in the "Pennsylvania Magazine of History and Biography" (the official publication of the Historical Society of Pennsylvania,) vol. v. (1880), No. 4, pp. 477-481, under the title "An Old

Welsh Pedigree." An introduction was written by J. J. Levick, M.D., and the whole was under the careful editorship of John W. Jordan, L.L.D., the present Librarian of the Society. The article was reprinted by Dr. Levick, and privately distributed. A copy of the original MS. pedigree is in the hands of the writer, and the original has been photographed, and copies are in the possession of the Cadwalader family.

The same pedigree, from Thomas Hugh, of Wern Fawr, Llaithgwm (the father of John and Cadwalader Thomas) back to Marchweithian, is preserved in the Cae Cyriog MSS. under "Cae Môr." A copy of this version, which agrees in almost all essential details (except spelling), with the John Thomas pedigree, of 1682, will be found in the "History of Powys Fadog," by J. Y. W. Lloyd, of Clochfaen, Esq., M.A., K.S.G., London, 1884, vol. iv., 108, and is as follows :—

"Maurice ab Edward of Cae Môr, 1709 = Elizabeth, d. of Thomas ab Hyw [Hugh] of Wern Fawr, co. Meirionydd, ab Ieuan ab Rhys Goch ab Tudor ab Rhys ap Ieuan Goch of Cwm Pen Aner, in the parish of Caer y Drudion, ab Ieuan Ddu ab David ap Einion of Caer y Drudion, ab Cynwrig ab Llywarch ab Heilin ab Tyfyd of Carwedd Fynydd." [To Marchweithian.]

A few words may be added regarding the pedigree itself. From the foregoing pages it will be seen that it has been proved by existing official records, including Heraldic Visitations, back to Marchweithian, lord of Isaled. It is a fact, therefore, that each man named on the old pedigree, from John Thomas, of Llaithgwm, gentleman, back to Marchweithian, the Welsh chieftian of Isaled, actually lived and played his part in the history of Wales. Many of the descendants of these men rose to great distinction at various times, both in peace and in war. The effigies of some of them in country churches remind us of their military fame in their native land—as, for instance, that of Rhys ap Maredydd Fawr of Yspytty Evan, who upheld the Great Standard of England on Bosworth Field, after Sir William Brandon, the former standard bearer, had fallen, or that of Cynwrig Fychan, a distinguished soldier, in the lonely Church of Llannefydd, which was founded by one of his race five generations before his time. What little has been gathered, and here preserved, is as nothing to what, doubtless, exists, relative to each generation, in the mass of records remaining in the Public Record Office, the Library of the British Museum, and in private hands, so that what Dr. Levick considered to be merely a curious record of a line of obscure Welsh husbandmen, turns out to be the skeleton genealogy of a branch of one of the most famous families in Denbighshire.

It is worthy of note, also, that this branch of the family held the same lands for at least some eight centuries. Cerrig y Druidion had, it is said, been part of the possessions of Marchweithian, and much of the land contained in this parish descended to Einion ap Cynwrig, who came here to live in the time of Edward III. His lands became, in course of time, according to the Welsh law of gavel kind, divided amongst his posterity, so that when the Act of 34 Henry VIII. did away with the custom of equal partition of land among all of the sons, many of Einion's descendants in Cerrig y Druidion possessed but comparatively small estates, which however were, for the most part, portions of the broad acres of their ancestor Einion.

Regarding Marchweithian himself, the hitherto accepted statement that he flourished in the beginning of the 8th century[1] is most certainly wrong. Cynwrig Fychan, his descendant, was living 8 Edw. III. and was probably born not much earlier than 1270. Allowing an aver-

---

[1] See "Cambrian Register."

age of about 30 years to each generation, the approximate date of Marchweithian's birth is placed at 1000, but 30 years is very long to allow for generations at this period in Wales, and it is more probable that he was born much nearer to the year 1050. This computation agrees with the marriages of his descendants, and with the fact that there is evidence to show that he was contemporary with Prince Gruffydd ap Cynan, who reigned in North Wales from 1080 to 1137, and that he lived, therefore, during the reigns of William the Conqueror, William II., and the first years of Henry I., Kings of England.

The Pedigree goes on to give the descent of Marchweithian from Urien Reged (or Rhegid). Four generations only connect him with the latter chieftain, *viz.*, Llud, Llen, Llanimod Angel, and Pasgen. The Berain pedigree reads: "Marchwithion .... mab oedd ef y Tangwell ap Llydd ap Llewelyn ap Lluynod angel ap Pasgen." The "Hen Llyfr Madog ab Llewelyn ab Howel, Esq^e." calls Marchweithian the son of Tangno, which is intended for Tangwell. Four or five generations, however, are too few to cover the four centuries between Urien and the approximate date of Marchweithian's birth. It is therefore evident that a great many generations have been omitted, and that in this case, as in several others, in very old pedigrees, the "ab" stands for *descended from*, instead of "son of." There is no reason to doubt, however, that Marchweithian was actually descended from Urien Reged, who was a real person, a chieftain of Cumberland, whom many Welsh families claim as their ancestor. The balance of the pedigree, back to Beli Mawr agrees with a pedigree of the middle of the 10th century, which is a copy of a much older one, the probable accuracy of which, for many generations, is acknowledged by the highest authorities of the present day. Beli Mawr, however, was not a son of Monagan, and the earlier portion of the genealogy is fabulous. That is to say, it is certainly not the pedigree of Beli, or Belinus, Mawr, otherwise Cunobelinos, who was the son of Tasciovanus (as proved by coins and other irrefutable evidence) who was over-king of the Brythons in the first century B.C., and a descendant of Diviciacos, the great Gaul, who ruled also in Britain, and who was remembered by men of Cæsar's time, and whose coins are still found. This fabulous pedigree, of Cunobelinos, however, has also a very respectable antiquity, for it passed current before the twelfth century, and if we eliminate *Monagan*, which is not a name at all, but a mistake for *Minocynobelinum*, which should read *Adminio Cynobellini* . . . *filio*, and some other generations which most certainly belong to real persons who lived several centuries later, we have a string of names reaching from Cappoir back to Brute, that are certainly not Brythonic, and which may have actually belonged partly to rulers who lived just prior to the Brythonic invasion, which only commenced after the time of Pytheas, and partly to chieftians of the Aborigines, prior to the first Aryan invasion, which occurred not later than 600 B.C. There seems to be ground for this suggestion, insomuch as the list itself, and the very ancient legends which surround some of the names, as that of Lyr (Lear), point to succession through females only, which was the custom among the Aborigines. If this theory would hold water, it is perfectly conceivable that one of the early Brythonic over-kings, having married a descendant of these prehistoric chieftains, the list of his wife's predecessors and kinsmen, in process of time, through much transmissions by word of mouth, became confused with his own pedigree. Indeed, it is also possible, and probable, that this was purposely done to delude the remote and savage tribesmen into the belief that the Brythonic kings were descendants of their ancient chieftains. The subject of these ancient pedigrees, many generations of which are being verified in a wonderful way by recent research, and the early history of the Welsh people, is referred to at length elsewhere,

It is sufficient to say here that at the time of Cæsar's invasion the Brythons, as distinguished from the wild tribes, such as the Picts, mostly subject to them, were a civilized people, having commercial and diplomatic relations with Rome, and other countries, and their kings, whose predecessors had been emperors of Gaul, Britain having formed a part of the possessions of the older dynasty, which crumpled up before the Roman legions, minted coinage, had ships upon the seas, disciplined and well-equipped troops, and were rapidly subduing the wild tribes of the northern and western portions of the island when Rome pounced upon them. There is evidence, amounting almost to a certainty, that one of these early Brythonic kings, from whom most of the latter princes and nobles of Wales traced their descent, espoused the daughter of a house of Roman bankers, which at that time ruled the finances of the world, and which most certainly financeered the Brythonic government. To those who believe in hereditary, and that certain traits of character are capable of transmission through many generations, the fact that very many of the most successful financeers of England and America can be traced, in one way or another, to this marriage, may furnish food for comment. Here follows a copy of the original pedigree of John Thomas.

Pedigree of John ap Thomas ap Hugh, of Merionethshire, North Wales.

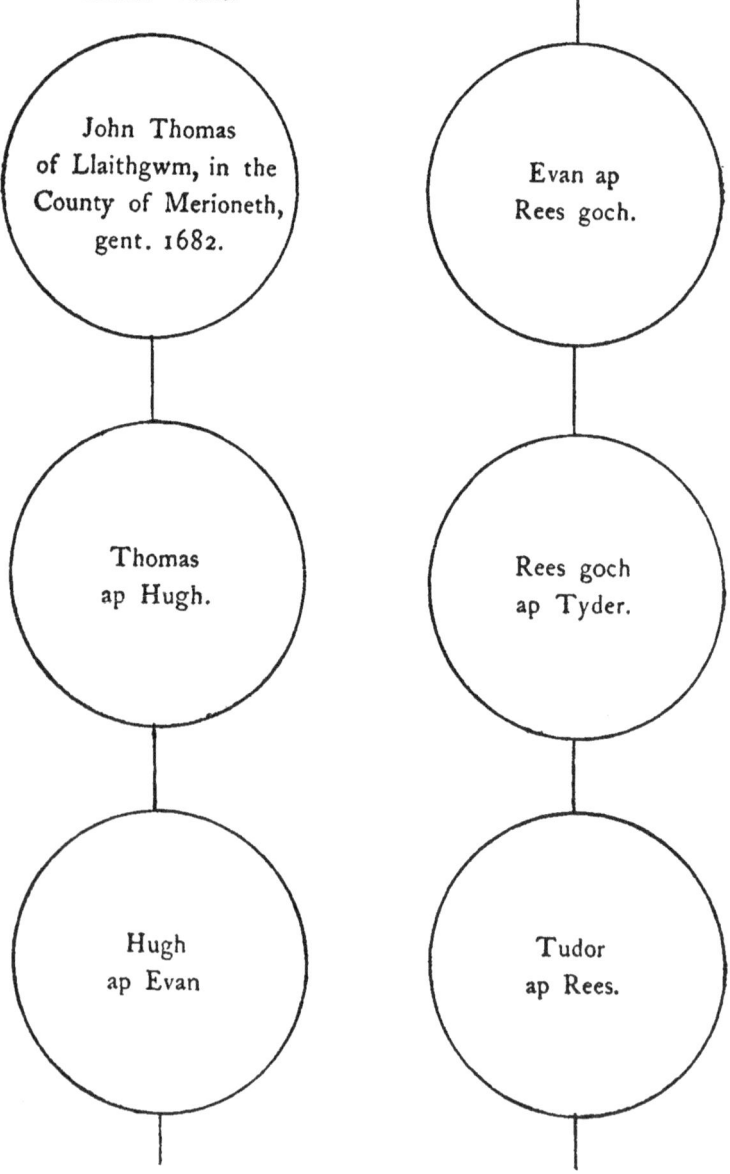

Pedigree I.—Addenda

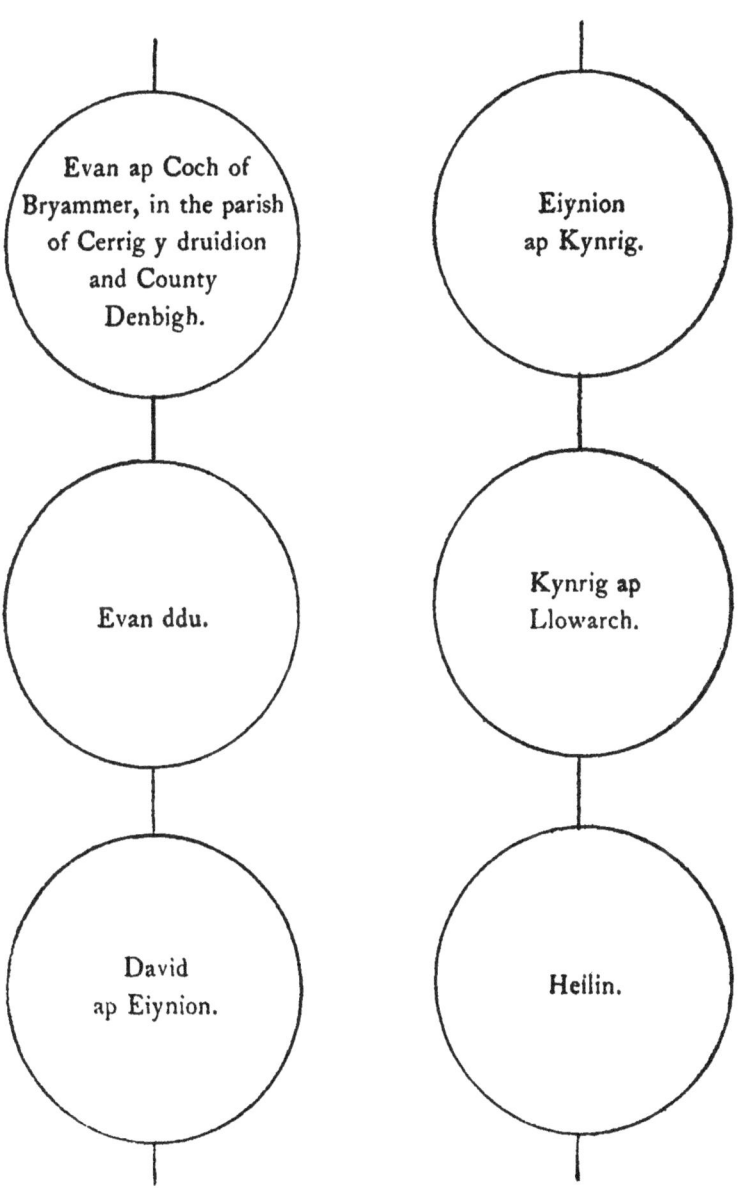

Evan ap Coch of Bryammer, in the parish of Cerrig y druidion and County Denbigh.

Evan ddu.

David ap Eiynion.

Eiynion ap Kynrig.

Kynrig ap Llowarch.

Heilin.

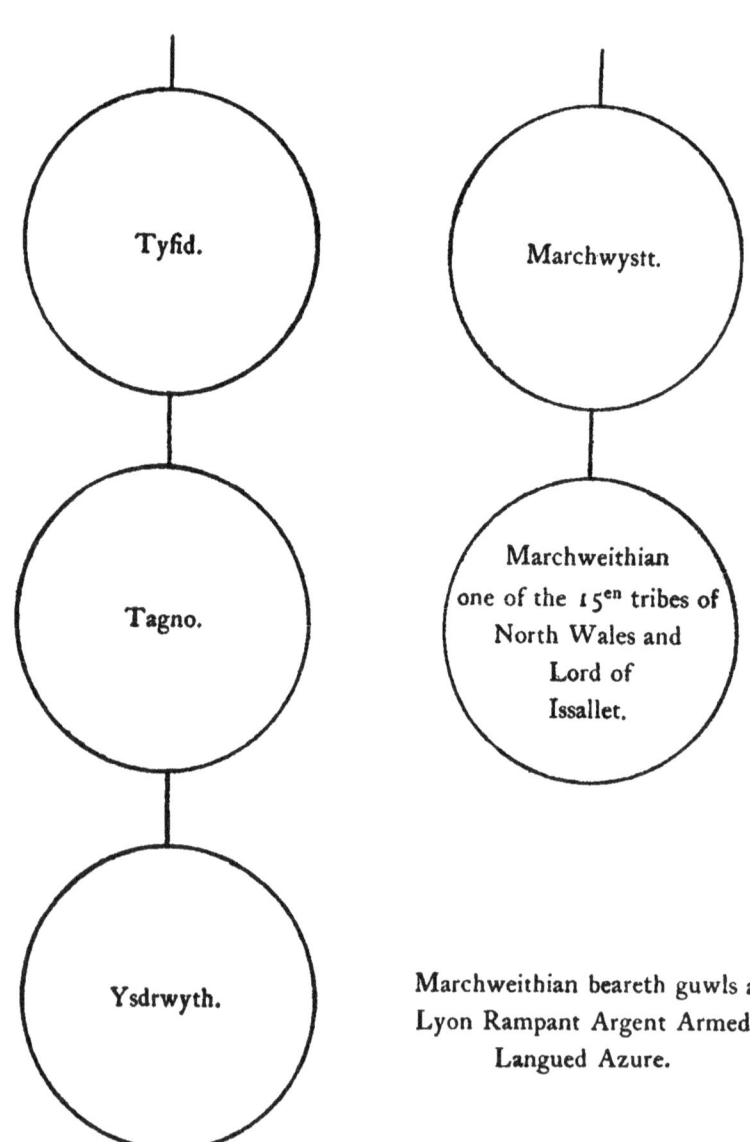

Pedigree I.—Addenda

Marchweithian . . . .

- ap Llud
- ap Llen
- ap Llanimod angel
- ap Pasgen
- ap Urien redeg
- ap Cynvarch
- ap Meirchion gul
- ap Grwst Ledlwm
- ap Cenan
- ap Coel godebog
- ap Tegvan
- ap Deheufraint
- ap Tudbuyll
- ap Urban
- ap Gradd
- ap Runedlwych
- ap Rydeyrn
- ap Endigaid
- ap Endeyrn
- ap Enid
- (ne Elvid o enw arall)
- ap Endog
- ap Endollen
- ap Avallach
- ap Affleth
- ap Beli mawr
- ap Monogen
- ap Cappoir
- (ne Pabo o enw arall)
- ap Pyrr
- ap Saml Penissel
- ap Rhytherich
- ap Eidiol
- ap Arthvael
- ap Seissyllt
- ap Owain
- ap Caph
- ap Bleuddut
- ap Meiriawn
- ap Gorwst
- ap Clydno
- ap Clydawr
- ap Ithel
- ap Urien
- ap Andrew
- ap Kerryn
- (ne Thoryn o enw arall)
- ap Porrex
- ap Coel
- ap Caddell
- ap Gerant
- ap Elidr mawr
- ap Morudd
- ap Dan
- ap Seissyll
- ap Cyhelyn
- ap Gwrgan sunsdrwth
- ap Beli
- ap Dyfnwal moel mud
- ap Dodion
- ap Cynvarch
- ap Aedd mawr
- ap Antonius
- ap Seissyllt
- ap Gorwst
- ap Riwallon
- ap Cunedda
- ap Regan
- Ferch Lŷr
- ap Bleuddut
- ap Rum baladr bras
- ap Lleon
- ap Brutus Darianlas
- ap E'vroc Cadarn
- ap Membyr
- ap Medoc
- ap Locrinus
- ap Brutus
- ap Silvius
- ap Ascanius
- ap Æneas
- ap Anchises
- ap Capius
- ap Assaracus
- ap Tros
- ap Ericthonius
- ap Dardon
- ap Jupiter
- ap Saturnus
- ap Coelus
- ap Ciprius
- ap Chetim
- ap Javan
- ap Japheth
- ap Noahen
- ap Lamech
- ap Methusalem
- ap Enos
- ap Seth
- ap Adda
- ap Duw

John Thomas of Llaithgwm.

John Thomas, otherwise John ap Thomas, and John Thomas ap Hugh, was twice married. His first wife being Ann Lloyd, who was buried at Llandderfel 31 August, 1665. This was before John Thomas joined the Society of Friends. The entry, in Latin, in the Llandderfel Parish Register calls her " Anna Lloyd uxor John Thomas ap Hugh." She was the daughter of John Lloyd and the sister of Dr. Edward Jones (i.e. Edward Johns), of Merion. This satisfactorily accounts for Dr. Edward Jones signing himself, in a letter to John Thomas, "thy Lo' friend and *Bro*," and explains why Thomas Jones of Merion, in his will of 1728, calls Jonathan Jones, son of Dr. Edward, " my cousin." It thus appears that Dr. Edward Jones discarded the surname of Lloyd, and assumed that of Jones, from his father's baptismal name, John, just as the Foulke family of Gwynedd dropped their surname of Lloyd, and called themselves Foulke. Such was the custom in Wales at that time. John Thomas married, secondly, Katherine Robert. She was certainly not a sister of Hugh Roberts, of Merion, as has been suggested. There is, however, a letter extant written after 1700, from one Hugh Roberts, living near Bala, to Thomas Jones, of Merion, signed "your uncle." The writer of this letter may possibly have been a brother of Katherine Robert, and thus uncle by marriage to Thomas Jones, but it is more probable that the relationship was that of first cousin to the latter's father. At any rate, the letter speaks of the writer's father, Robert, being in Pennsylvania, and of "uncle Robert ap Rhydderch."

By his first wife, John Thomas had two children: Elizabeth, who married Rees Evan, of Fron Ween, Penmaen, parish of Llanfor; and Thomas, who assumed the surname of Jones. By his second wife, John Thomas had Robert, Evan, Cadwalader, Katherine wife of Robert Roberts, son of Hugh, Mary, died at sea, Sidney died at sea (see Glenn's " Merion," 301; but for "*his*," in 3rd line from bottom of page, read "*their*"). An abstract of the will of John Thomas has been given on a preceding page, and more fully in "Merion," 300. It is dated (in Wales) 9 February, 1682, and was proved at Philadelphia, 1688. He appoints as overseers, John ap John, of the parish of Rhiwabon, Co. Denbigh, Thomas Ellis, of Cyfanedd, Co. Merioneth, Thomas Wynne, late of Bronvadog, near Caerwys, Co. Flint, Robert David, of Gwernevel, Co. Merioneth, Hugh Roberts of Kiltalgarth, said Co., Edward Jones late of Bala, Chirurgion [his brother-in-law], Robert Vaughan, of Gwernevel, aforesaid [his nephew], Edward Moris, of Havodgyfaner, in Co. Denbigh, [his nephew], Robert Owen, late of Fron Goch [a kinsman], and his son-in-law, Rees Evans, of Fronween. Thomas Jones, the eldest son, died 1728, and had children, Evan, Elizabeth, Katherine, Ann, Mary, and Sarah. On page 302 of " Merion," under children of Thomas Jones. omit *Robert*. The will of Thomas Jones was dated 6 month, 31st, *1727*, not *1728*, and proved 5 August, *1728*. On page 303 of "Merion," 14th line from top, for " Ann, b. 7-mo. 14th, 1702; m. *James Jones*," read "Ann, b. 7-mo. 14th, 1702; m., *1724, James Paul.*" This James Paul, born 4-mo. 14th, 1692, married, first, 1716, Jane Wilmerton, by whom he had no issue. He married, secondly, Ann Jones, as above, and, thirdly, a daughter of Morris Morris. He died in 1761, leaving issue, Robert, John, Jacob, Susanna, Hannah, Margaret, m.—Edge, and Ann Paul, who married—Knight. The descendants of John Thomas are now numerous. A branch intermarried with the Levering family, and some account of that branch will be found in the "Levering Genealogy." J. Levering Jones, of Chestnut Hill, Philadelphia, is the representative of that line. He married Miss Elizabeth Mercer Maclean. The late Howard Williams Lloyd, of Germantown, commenced a genealogy of the descendants of Gerrard Jones, of Merion, (son of Robert, son of John ap Thomas), who married, 1729, Sarah Lloyd. Mr. Lloyd's MS. may be consulted at the Historical Society of Pennsylvania. Mrs. David Aiken, jr., of Pittsburg, Pennsylvania, is a descendant of this line, being the daughter of Rees Jones, born 1772; died in

Ohio, 1849, son of Paul Jones, born 1737, son of Gerrard Jones, born 1705-6, son of Robert Jones, son of John Thomas, of Llaithgwm (see " Merion," 304). Mrs. Aiken's sisters were, Rebecca, married Francis Laesher ; Hannah, married Charles Sontag ; Ellen, married Rev. John McIlhenny ; Catherine, married William Thorne ; Lydia, married Ralph Means ; Mary, married George W. Morris. The sons of Rees Jones were, Benjamin, Rees Roberts, Paul, David, William Lloyd, Marcus Aurelius, and George.

PEDIGREE II.

David,[1] of Penmaen, who was father of :

Rees David, of the township of Penmaen, parish of Llanfor, Merioneth.

> 13 Car. I. (1637), 19 June. Rice (Rees) David and Elizabeth his wife, and Evan Price (otherwise Rees), son and heir apparent of the said Rice, deforciants (John David, fuller, being plaintiff), *in re* 3 messuages and lands, in Penmaen. [Rolls of the Feet of Fine, Merionethshire, Spring Bdle., 13 Car. I., Pub. Rec. Office, London.]
>
> Rees David had issue by Elizabeth, his wife :
> i. Evan, *of whom presently.*
> ii. Gwen Rees.

Evan Rees (otherwise ap Rees or Price), of Penmaen, eldest son and heir of Rees David.

> 13 Car. I. (1637), 19 June. A deforciant in Fine levied as cited *supra.*
>
> 26 Car. II. (1674), 7 Sept. Evan Rees, plaintiff, Rice (Rees) Jones and Elizabeth his wife, Edward Jones, and Evan William and Jane his wife, deforciants, *in re* 4 messuages and lands, in Penmaen. [Rolls of the Feet of Fine, Merionethshire, Sess. at Harlech, 7 Sept., 26 Car. II., Pub. Rec. Office, London.]
>
> 1682, 18 March. Deed, executed at Bala, Edward Jones, of Bala, and John Thomas, of Llaithgwm, to Evan Rees, of Penmaen, grocer, for 312½ acres of land to be surveyed to him in the Province of Pennsylvania. [Recorded at Philadelphia, Deed Book C, I.]
>
> 1683, 28 June. Deed, Evan Rees, of Penmaen, to Robert David and Griffith John, for the same 312½ acres. [Recorded at Philadelphia ; " Penna. Mag.," xxvi., 56.]
>
> Evan Rees did not remove to Pennsylvania. He married ——, daughter of David John, of Ciltalgarth, parish of Llanfor.
>
> ISSUE :
> i. Rees Evan, *of whom presently.*

---

[1] David is supposed to be identical with David ap Evan ap Howel, a free-holder of Llanfor, who was living 1636.

Pedigree II.

Rees Evan, of Fron Ween, Penmaen, parish of Llanfor.

1681-2, 18 March. Witness to deed to Robert David, for land in Pennsylvania. [Deed Book C, I., Philadelphia.] 1682, 1 April. Witness to deed to William ap Edward, for land in Pennsylvania. [Deed Book C, I., Philadelphia.]

1682, 9 Feb. Rees Evan, of Fronween, near Bala, "my son-in-law," named in will of John Thomas, of Llaithgwm. [Will Book A, fos. 77-88; Philadelphia.]

Draft of the will of Rees Evan, of Penmaen, in the parish of Llanfawr (Llanfor), in the county of Merioneth.

Dated after 1690 and before 1699-1700. The testator mentions a deed of trust, dated—Jac. II. (1685-1688), between Edward Cadwalader, of Ucheldre, gentleman, Rees Evan, of Penmaen, gentleman, (the testator), and Elizabeth, his wife,[1] of the one part, and Edward Morris,[2] of Cae Môr, in the county of Denbigh, and Lewis Owen, of Gwanas, gentleman, of the second part. The testator leaves bequests to his aunt Gwen vch. [daughter of] Rees, and to his aunt Jane vch. David.[3]

He names children: Evan, John, David, and Sydney.

Executors: Testator's "cousin," David Jones,[4] of Kiltalgarth (Ciltalgarth), in the county of Merioneth, gentleman, and "cousin" Thomas Cadwalader,[5] of Hendre Mawr. Overseers: Testator's father, [Evan Rees], "cousin" Robert Vaughan, Thomas ap Robert, David Vaughan, and testator's brother [in-law] Thomas Jones [of Merion, Pennsylvania.] [MS. found with papers of Thomas Jones, of Merion (died 1728), son of John Thomas of Llaithgwm. Original cannot be found at St. Asaph.]

Rees Evan married, before 9 Feb., 1682, Elizabeth, daughter of John Thomas, of Llaithgwm. [Will of J.T., 1682, cited in pedigree I.]

ISSUE:

i. Evan Rees, son and heir. He removed to Pennsylvania, and settled in Merion, where he died, 1752; called "yeoman." Will dated 4 June, 1752; proved at Philadelphia, 25 July, 1752; Will Book K, fo. 1, &c.] He appoints Lewis Jones[6] of Blockley, his cousin, one of his executors. Evan Rees had one child, Mary, living 4 June, 1752, and then of unsound mind.

ii. John Rees, supposed to have succeeded to the Penmaen lands.

iii. David Rees, said to have removed to Pennsylvania.

iv. Sydney Rees,[7] born 1690. Removed to Pennsylvania, and married, 1709, Robert Roberts, son of John of Merion.

---
[1] Daughter of John Thomas, of Llaithgwm; see pedigree I.
[2] First cousin of testator's wife; see pedigree I.
[3] She was daughter of David John, testator's maternal grandfather.
[4] Son of John David, of Ciltalgarth; see pedigree III.
[5] Probably his wife's first cousin; see pedigree I.
[6] Lewis Jones, of Blockley, was son of David Jones, of Ciltalgarth; see pedigree III.
[7] Sydney was an ancestress of the Roberts family, of Pencoyd, and Philadelphia. The late George B. Roberts, President of the Pennsylvania Railroad Company, was a descendant.

Phineas Roberts, son of Robert Roberts and Sydney, born 13 May, 1722; married, 1743, Ann, daughter of Thomas Wynne. For descendants, including the Cook family, of Philadelphia, see Wynne pedigree on another page.

PEDIGREE III.

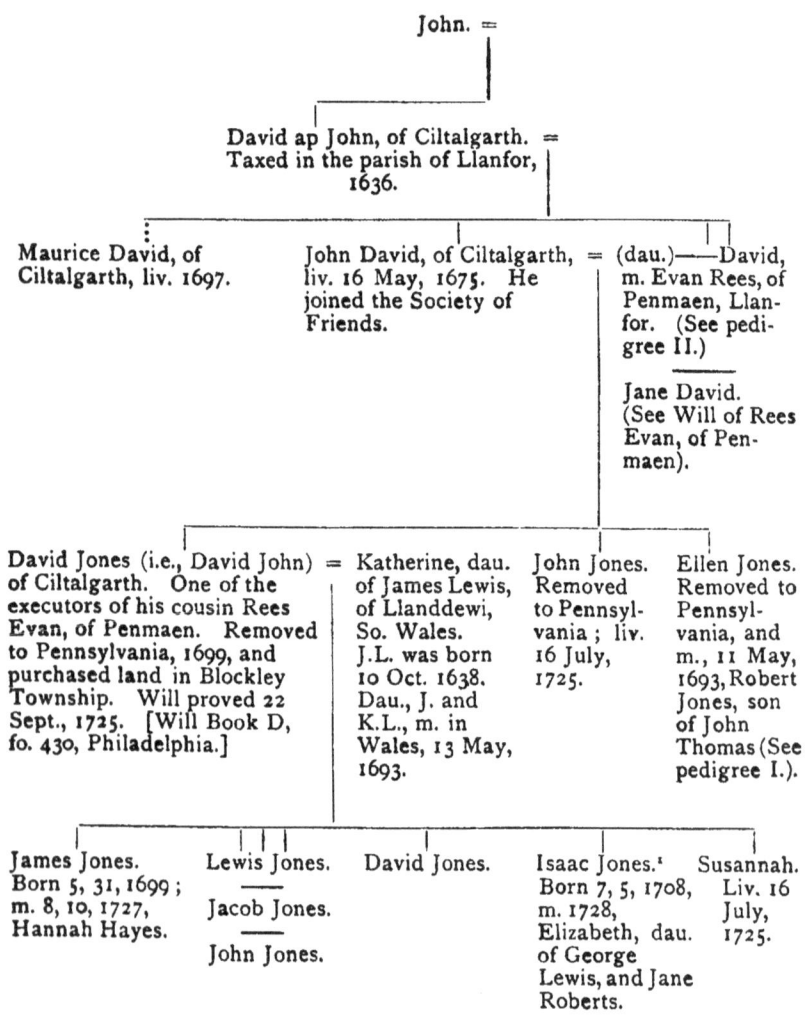

[1] The Levick family, of Philadelphia, descend from this line.

PEDIGREE IV.

David Vaughan, of the parish of Llanwddyn, Montgomeryshire, son of Bedo ap Jenkin ap Ieuan of Caer Einion; descended from Rhodri Mawr. David Vaughan married Catherine, daughter of Maurice ap Howel Vaughan, of Llwydiarth, Montgomeryshire. Howel Vaughan is named in a grant under the conventual seal of the Abbey of Strata Marcella, 12 Sept., 1522, and was ancestor to the family of Vaughan of Llwydiarth. [" Hist. Powys Fadog," iv., 367; Dwnn, i., 321; Harl. MS. 1969; " Montgomeryshire Collections," xiv., 373.]

ISSUE :
  i. John David Vaughan, of Llanwddyn; died before 39 Eliz. (1598). He had issue, *inter alia*, (a) Edward Wynne, of Eunant, gent. [Lay Subsidy Roll, 39 Eliz., and 3 Jac. I. (1605), Nos. $\frac{222}{381}$ and $\frac{222}{387}$, Pub. Rec. Office.] On Grand Jury 27 Eliz. [" Montgomeryshire Collections."] (b), Owen ap John David Vaughan. [Lay Subsidy Roll 3 Jac. I., No. $\frac{222}{387}$.] (c), Morris John, of Llanwddyn, living 1627. [Llanwddyn Parish Register.]
  ii. Howel ap David Vaughan, of Llanwddyn, *of whom presently.*
  iii. Morris ap David Vaughan.

Howel ap David Vaughan, of Llanwddyn. He died before 39 Elizabeth (1598). [" History of Powys Fadog," iv., 367; Dwnn, i., 321; Harl. MS., 1969.]

ISSUE :
  i. John ap Howel, *of whom presently.*
  ii. Thomas ap Howel, named under Llanwddyn, in Lay Subsidy Roll 39 Eliz. (1598), No. $\frac{222}{381}$, and in that of 3 Jac. I. (1605), No. $\frac{222}{387}$, Pub. Rec. Office.] Designated, as one of the Wardens of the parish, *Thomas ap Howell David Vaughan*, in the Parish Reg. of Llanwddyn, 1628. Buried at Llanwddyn, 27 March, 1640. He had: John Thomas ap Howell, of the township of Yspytty, Llanwddyn, who joined the Society of Friends. He was several times presented before the Grand Jury for non attendance at National Worship, and 1 April, 1678, under the designation of *John Thomas ap Howel*, with his wife Ann; again in 1682, then described as " John Thomas ap Howell of Prespytty (yspytty), in Llanwddyn, he is presented with "Thomas John his son." [Goal Files: " Montgomeryshire Collections," xxiv., 218; 55; xxvi., 63, &c.] Also 18 Augt., 1684, and 8 Mch., 1685-6. [" Montg. Colls," xxvii., 56; 67.] John Thomas ap Howel had issue : (a) John baptd. at Llanwddyn, 26 Oct., 1644; (b) Thomas John ap

Thomas (otherwise *Thomas Jones*) of whom presently; (c) Catherine, baptd. at Llanwddyn, 9 Oct., 1650; (d) Edward, baptd. 1652; (e) Margaret, baptd. 20 Feb., 1652 (twins); and perhaps others.[1]

Thomas John Thomas, the eldest son, was presented as a Quaker, and for absence from National Worship (being described as Thomas John, son of John Thomas ap Howell of Yspytty, in the parish of Llanwddyn) in 1682. Under the designation of "Thomas Jones of the parish of Llanwthin in the said County of Montgomery, Yom" (Yeoman), Thomas John Thomas is grantee in a deed, executed in Wales, dated 24 April, 1683, from Charles Lloyd of Dolobran, gentleman, and Margaret Davies of the same place, widow, for 156¼ acres of land in Pennsylvania. [Recorded at Philadelphia, 28th 3 month, 1684.]

This land was surveyed in Merion. The will of Thomas John Thomas (otherwise Thomas Jones), he being then of Merion, in the Province of Pennsylvania, is dated 25 May, 1701; proved at Philadelphia, 16 Sept., 1723. He leaves the above plantation in Merion to his "cousin Benjamin Humphreys." Mentions his nephews, Morris Thomas, John Thomas, and Thomas Edward, and speaks of Margaret, wife of James Mortimer. Thomas John Thomas died unmarried, and, during the latter part of his life lived with Benjamin Humphreys, who was his second cousin once removed.

Edward John, son of John Thomas ap Howel, had a son Thomas Edward, who removed to Pennsylvania about 1700. Catherine, daughter of John Thomas ap Howel, married Thomas Morris of Llanwddyn, and had Morris Thomas, John Thomas, Jane and Margaret Thomas, who all removed to Pennsylvania in or about 1708. The certificate of Morris Thomas was from Dolobran Mtg., 1708. ["Mongomeryshire Collections," xi., 117.] Margaret, the other daughter of John Thomas ap Howel of Llanwddyn, married James Mortimer,[2] who also removed to Pennsylvania, and had issue James and Margaret Mortimer and perhaps others.

---

[1] The Parish Register of Llanwddyn is defective and partly illegible for some years, particularly for 1641-2, 1645-48, 1652-60.

[2] James Mortimer had a sister, Margaret Mortimer, who married Francis Howell, of Llandissilio, Carmarthenshire (partly in Pembrokeshire), who removed to Pennsylvania, and settled in Merion, where he died 1696, s. p. His will is dated 1 month 15, 1695; proved 16 Sept., 1696. [Will Book A, folio 344.] He bequeathed a plantation of 300 acres, called Duffdryn Manor, and 100 acres in Merion, to his brother, Thomas Howell, and mentions his sisters, Elizabeth, Margaret, Mary and Susan, wife Margaret, and James Mortimer. The will of Margaret Howell, widow (of Francis), is dated 12 Sept., 1696; proved at Philadelphia, 25 Sept., 1696. [Will Book A, folio 341.] She mentions "my brother, James Mortimer," "my sister (in law) Margaret Thomas," "James Mortimer my nephew," "cousin James Mortimer," "brother-in-law David Janes [married ...... Mortimer] and others. Another sister of James Mortimer became the wife of David James, as above. This family of Mortimer was long seated in the county of Cardigan, and intermarried so much and for so long a time with Welsh families that they came to be considered as of that nationality. The first of the family named in any pedigree which has come under the notice of the writer is Roger Mortimer, who was Lord of Generau glyn and Coed Mawr, a descendant of the ancestors of the Earls of March, the Mortimers always holding vast estates in Wales. James became a family name in this branch.

PEDIGREE IV.

John ap Howel, son of Howel ap David Vaughan, of Gadfa in the township Rhiwargor in the parish of Llanwyddyn, called also John ap Howel Goch, and John Powell.[1]

30 Eliz., 20 Sept., "1588." Pedigree "Plwyv Llan Armon, Pennarth Sir Arvon, Evionydd"; "Plant Hugh Gwyn, Wm. Wyn Rolant, Owen, Robt. mort. Mredd *Sibl = John Powel o Lan Wddyn*, Elsbeth Mary, Lowri, Sian." [Dwnn, ii., 172.]

[A note by Meyrick to Dwnn's printed Visitations, states that the latter portions of this pedigree have been added subsequent to the date. This marriage, therefore, may have taken place several years after 1588. Their daughter Elizabeth could probably have well been born as late as 1610-11.]

Pedigree of Rowland Ellis, of Bryn Mawr, near Dolgelley (who removed to Pennsylvania), compiled *circa* 1697, gives:

Hugh John— = Sibill vch. Hugh Gwyn Penarth
| |
Hu'phry = Elizabeth

[Glenn's "Merion," plate facing p. 220.]

39 Eliz. (1596-7). John ap Howell, assessed in land in the parish of Llanwddyn at 40 shillings. [His brother Thomas ap Howell, the next above name on the roll, also 40 shillings.]

Lay Subsidy Roll for Montgomeryshire, parish of Llanwddyn, hundred of Llanvillinge, 39 Eliz., No. $\frac{222}{381}$, Pub. Rec. Office, London.]

3 Jac. I. (1605). Rated, under the designation of John Powell, as a freeholder, at 40 shillings. [Lay Subsidy Roll for Montgomeryshire, parish of Llanwddyn, 3 Jac. I., No. $\frac{222}{387}$, Pub. Rec. Office, London.]

1636, 24 July. John ap Howell Goch, of Gadfa, buried at Llanwddyn Church. [Llanwddyn Parish Register.]

ISSUE:

i. Thomas ap John ap Howel Goch, of Gadfa, living 1630. He had a daughter baptized 11 July of the above year, and he appears to be the same person as Thomas Jones (i.e. Johns, or ap John) who was rated at 1 hearth in Rhiwargor, 14 Car. II. [Lay Subsidy Roll, Montgomeryshire, No. $\frac{265}{7}$, Pub. Rec. Office, London.]

ii. Howel John ap Howel; buried at Llanwddyn, 2 June, 1635; there is nothing to indicate that he left issue.

iii. Elizabeth, married Humphrey ap Hugh, of Llwyn du, *of whom presently*.

iv. Mary.

[There were perhaps other daughters.]

---

[1] Powel was the common Welsh contraction for *ap Howel*.

Humphrey ap Hugh, of Llwyn du, township of Llwyngwril, parish of Llangelynin, gentleman. He was son of Hugh ap David ap Howel ap Gronwy ap Einion. [MS. ped. of Rowland Ellis; Dwnn, ii., 252.] His mother was Catherine, daughter of Rhydderch ap John, of Abergynolwyn. Humphrey ap Hugh married Elizabeth, daughter of John ap Howel (otherwise John Powell), of Gadfa, Llanwddyn, Montgomeryshire. The match may have been brought about from the fact that her uncle by marriage, Rev. Richard Nanney, was at the time Rector of Llangelynin.

> 1649, 1 Jan. Indenture between Rees Lewis ap John Gruffith, of Dyffrydan, co. Merioneth, gentleman, of the first part, Humffrey ap Hugh, of Llwyngwril, said co., gentleman, of the second part, and Richard Nanney, of Llwyngwril, and David Ellis of Gwanas, said co., gentlemen, of the third part. Touching a settlement concerning the intended marriage of Ellis Rees (otherwise Ellis Price), second son of the said Rees Lewis ap John Gruffith, with Anne Humffrey, one of the daughters of Humffrey ap Hugh. Witnesses: John ap William ap Humffrey, David John ap Hugh, Griffyth ap Rees Lewis, Tudor Vaughan, and John ap Hugh. [Original in possession of Edward Griffith, Esq., of Coedcymmer, Dolgelley.]

> ISSUE:
> i. Hugh, baptd. 7 April, 1628; bur. 22 May, 1628. [Llangelynin Reg.]
> ii. Owen, baptd. 13 April, 1629; *of whom presently.*
> iii. Catherine, baptd. 15 April, 1631; bur. 29 Nov., 1631.
> iv. John, baptd. 16 Nov., 1632; married Jane, sister of Richard Humphrey, of Llangelynin; removed to Pennsylvania 1683, settled in Merion, d. s. p.
> v. Anne, married Ellis ap Rees (alias Price), and was mother of Rowland Ellis, who removed to Pennsylvania.
> vi. Samuel, baptd. 22 Jan., 1635; *of whom presently.*
> vii. —— dau., living 1649.

Owen Humphrey, of Llwyn du, Esquire, second son and heir of Humphrey ap Hugh.

> 1629. "Owinus filius humffredi ap hugh dd bapt. fuit 13° Aprilis." [Llangelynin Reg.]
>
> He early joined the Society of Friends. It is stated that he was an officer under Cromwell, and that during the Protectorate he held a commission as Justice of the Peace for his County.

(*To face page 44.*)

Edmund Langley, Duke of York, s. Edward III.
|
Constance Plantagenet, m. Edmund Holland, Earl of Kent.
|
Eleanor Holland, m. Sir James, Lord Audeley.
|
Constance, m. Robert Whitney.
|
Eleanor Whitney, m. John Puleston, Constable of Carnarvon; Chamberlain of North Wales.
|
Jane Puleston, m. Sir William Griffith, of Penrhyn, Knt.; Constable of Carnarvon, Chamberlain of North Wales: des. fr. Edward I.
|
Sibil Griffith, m. Owen ap Hugh of Bodowen, High Sheriff of Anglesey, 1579-80.
|
Jane Owen, m. Hugh Gwyn, of Penarth; High Sheriff co. Carn., 1600.
|
Sibil, m. John Powel, of Gadfa, Llanwddyn.
|
Elizabeth, m. Humphrey ap Hugh, of Llwyn du, liv. 1649.
|

| | | | | |
Hugh, d. inft. | Owen Humphrey, of Llwyn du. | John Humphrey. | Samuel Humphrey. | Catherine —— Anne, m. Ellis ap Rees. —— . dau.)

Pedigree IV.

1662. Owen Humphrey, as well as his brother Samuel, having "refused to pay a demand for tithes," was prosecuted in the Sheriff's Court, and execution was awarded against him, by which his cattle were seized. [Besse.]

1678, 6 March. Bond. Owen Humphrey of Llwndu, gentleman, to Robert Owen, of Vron Goch in the commot of Penllyn, gentleman, given as surety for the performance of an agreement between Gainor John, of Vron Goch, widow, mother of the said Robert Owen, and the said Owen Humphrey, touching the intended marriage of Robert Owen and Rebecca, eldest daughter of the said Owen Humphrey. Witnesses: Rowland Ellis, Edward Vaughan, John ap Thomas, and Cadwalader Thomas. [Original in possession of Charles Morton Smith, Esq., of Philadelphia.]

1678-9, 11 March. As father of the bride, Owen Humphrey signs marriage certificate of Robert Owen, "Eldest son of Owen ap Evan (deceased) late of Vron goch in the comot of Penlin & in the County of Merioneth" and "Rebecca Owen, first daughter of Owen Humphrey of Llwyn du." [Original, in 1896, in possession of Mrs. Mary A. Haines, of Rosemont, Penna.]

Owen Humphrey married, first, Margaret Vaughan. His second wife was Elizabeth Thomas.

ISSUE:

i. Humphrey, baptd. Feb., 1653 (twin); died Feb., 1653.

ii. John, baptd. Feb., 1653 (twin); died Feb., 1653.[1]

iii. Humphrey Owen, of Llwyndu; he had a daughter and sole heiress, Anne, who married Owen Lewis Owen, of Tyddyn y Garreg, gentleman. ["Montg. Colls.," xv., 416.]

iv. John Owen; removed to Pennsylvania, 1687; settled in Merion. Certificate of Removal from Tyddyn y Garreg Mtg., 3 month 7, 1687, speaks of him as "ye 2d son of Owen Humphrey of Llwyndu." He appears to have died unmarried.

v. Joshua Owen. His certificate describes him as "of Llwyn du in the parish of Llangylynin in the County of Merioneth, Batchelor"; is signed by Owen Humphrey, his father, and dated 5 month 27, 1683. He settled in Merion, and married, 1 month 19, 1697, Martha, daughter of John Shinn, of West Jersey. He had several children born in Merion, and afterwards removed to Burlington, where he, or a son of the same name, was living in 1739.

vi. Owen Owen.

vii. Rebecca Owen, married Robert Owen, of Fron Goch. They removed to Pennsylvania, in 1690.

---

[1] The Llangelynin Register contains this entry: "Humffredus et Joannes didymi filii Owen Humffrey sepulti sunt ffeb. : 26, 1653. Sepulturâ asine sepulti [sine] ministro & debito mortuori ritu."

viii. Elizabeth Owen, born *circa* 1676 (prob. by 2d. wife); removed to Pennsylvania; married, 1692, John Roberts, of Merion, miller. He was an aged man (70) from Pen y Clwyd, Denbighshire.

Samuel Humphrey, fourth son of Humphrey ap Hugh of Llwyndu.

1635. "Samelus filius humffredi ap hugh dd bapt. fuit 22° Jan." [Llangelynin Reg.]

Samuel Humphrey joined the Society of Friends, and much concerning him may be found in Besse's "Sufferings." He died in Llangelynin 17 Sept., 1677, and was buried on the 19th of the same month in the burial ground called Bryn Tallwyn.

[Humphreys Family Bible, late in possession of Mr. Philip Sharpless of West Chester, Pennsylvania.]

Samuel Humphrey married Elizabeth Rees, daughter of Rees Hugh.

ISSUE:[1]

i. Lydia, born 1 month 26, 1659; married, in Pennsylvania, Ellis Ellis.

ii. Daniel, born 6 month, 1660; *of whom presently.*

iii. Joseph, born 5 month, 1662; removed to Pennsylvania, 1683; married Elizabeth Medford, and died in Philadelphia, 1693. He may have been father to Owen Humphrey, of Phila., inholder, 1726.

iv. Benjamin, born 5 month, 1662 (twin with Samuel); *of whom presently.*

v. Rebecca, born 7 month 26, 1664; married in Pennsylvania (as his 2d wife), Edward Rees, of Merion.

vi. Anne, born 3 month, 1666; married in Pennsylvania, Edward Roberts, son of Hugh, of Merion.

vii. Gobitha, born 8 month, 1668; removed to Pennsylvania.

viii. Elizabeth, married, in Pennsylvania, Thomas Abel.

Daniel Humphrey, eldest son of Samuel, born in the parish of Llangelynin, 6 month (Augt.), 1660. Removed to Pennsylvania, 1682, and settled in Haverford. He married, 8 month 25, 1695, Hannah, daughter of Dr. Thomas Wynne.

ISSUE:
i. Samuel, born 6 month 3, 1696.
ii. Thomas, born 4 month 20, 1697.

---

[1] The children of Samuel Humphrey at first called themselves *Samuel*, which they afterwards changed to Humphrey, many descendants adding a final s.

Pedigree IV.

iii. Jonathan, born 7 month 9, 1698; married Sarah ———.
iv. Hannah, born 11 month 7, 1669.
v. Benjamin, born 11 month 7, 1701-2; married Esther, daughter of Isaac Warner.
vi. Elizabeth, born 8 month 16, 1703.
vii. Mary, born 12 month 10, 1704-5.
viii. Solomon, born 10 month 16, 1706.
ix. Joshua, born 1 month 10, 1707-8; married Sarah, daughter of Edward Williams of Blockley, son of William ap Edward (see another pedigree) by Eleanor, daughter of David Lawrence, and had: Joshua Humphreys, born 1751, the shipbuilder, called "Father of the American Navy," Clement, Hannah, Daniel and Jane.
x. Edward, born 12 month 28, 1709; a physician; died unm., Jan., 1776.
xi. Martha, born 9 month 9, 1711.
xii. Charles, born 7 month 19, 1714; elected to Continental Congress, 1775, and voted for the Declaration of Independence.
xiii. Rebecca, born 10 month 2, 1716.

Benjamin Humphrey, third son of Samuel, was born in the parish of Llangelynin 5 month, 1662; removed to Pennsylvania, 1683; settled in Merion. Under the will of his "cousin," i.e. his father's second cousin, Thomas John Thomas, otherwise Thomas Jones, dated 25 May, 1701, and proved at Philadelphia, 16 Sept., 1728, he inherited the latter's plantation in Merion. [Will Book D, 366, Philadelphia.] He died in Merion 1738, and his will, dated 12 month 2, 1737-8, was proved at Philadelphia, 17 Jan., 1738, he being described as of Lower Merion. Benjamin Humphrey, or Humphreys as he later called himself, married Mary Llewelyn.

ISSUE:
i. John, born 7 month 8, 1695; *of whom presently.*
ii. Joseph, born 11 month 11, 1697.
iii. David, born 2 month 6, 1703.
iv. Ann, born 5 month 24, 1708; married Gerard Jones, son of Robert, of Merion.
v. Owen, born 11 month 27, 1713; married 7 month 29, 1738, Sarah, widow of John Hughes, of Haverford.
vi. Elizabeth, married 1741, John Scarlet, son of John, of Lancaster County.

John Humphrey, eldest son of Benjamin, was born in Merion, 7 month (Sept.) 8, 1695, and died in the same township, then called Lower Merion, 1761, intestate. He inherited from his father the plantation in Merion, situate along what is now called Grey's Lane, near Haverford Station, which Thomas John Thomas, by his will proved 1728 (above cited), had bequeathed to his "cousin Benjamin Humphrey."

ISSUE :
i. Benjamin, of Lower Merion, died Jan., 1830. Letters of Admon. granted 14 Jan., 1830. He left an only daughter, Jane Humphreys, who married —— Price; she died a widow, 16 Oct., 1834.
ii. Joseph, d. s. p.
iii. David, married Jane ——.
iv. Morris, died unmarried.
v. Ellis, d. s. p. prior to 1766.
vi. Robert, d. s. p. prior to 1766.
vii. Catherine, d. s. p.
viii. Elizabeth, married —— Davis, and had issue :
  (*a*) James Davis.
  (*b*) William Davis, died before 1834, leaving issue.
  (*c*) Elizabeth Davis, living 1834; married Jesse Rees.
ix. Jane, married —— Maris, and had issue :
  (*a*) John Maris.
  (*b*) Asa Maris.
  (*c*) Ellis Maris.
  (*d*) George Maris.
  (*e*) Ann Maris, married Samuel Lindsay.
x. Mary, d. s. p. before 1766.
xi. Patience, married Thomas Wildey (or Wilde), and had issue :
  (*a*) Elizabeth Wilde.
  (*b*) Lydia Wilde, married —— Smith.
xii. Margaret, married Thomas Cochran, but d. s. p.

PEDIGREE V.

Ivor ap Llewelyn, said by some to have been descended from Gwrgan, Prince of Glamorgan, but according to the MS. of Robert Vaughan of Hengwrt, and other authorities, he was of the line of Meuric, lord of Dyfed (or Dyfet), whose arms his posterity bore.

PEDIGREE V.

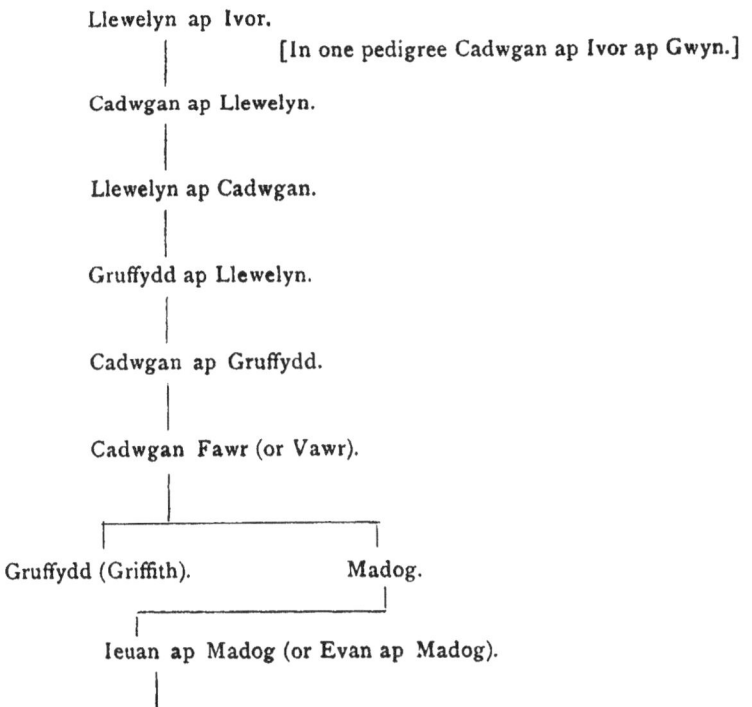

Cadwgan ap Ieuan ap Madog, of Kidwelli, near Carmarthen, South Wales. He "married a gentlewoman of North Wales, yᵉ daughter of dd ap Ieuan Vauⁿ," of Gwythelvynydd in yᵉ parish of Towyn, one of yᵉ greatest men in his countrey, & he sold his lands in Kidweli & came to live in North Wales to his wives' friends, where he bought lands in yᵉ hundred of Talybont & Estimanner, & left yᵉ same to Evan his son by his sayd wife." [MS. Vaughan of Hengwrt.] She was Gwenhwyfar, daughter of David ap Ieuan Vychan ap David Wyn Wydell ap Ednowain ap Bradwen, Lord of Talybont.

Ieuan ap Cadwgan, son of Cadwgan ap Ieuan ap Madog, married Lleuku, daughter of Rhys Vychan ap Rhys Goch ap David ap Rhydderch, and had:

Gruffydd Ddu, who married Gwenllian, daughter of Rhys ap Maredydd, and had:

Llewelyn ap Gruffydd Ddu, who "sould his lands & tenem^{ts} in Keven y rhos called Llawegros, Tyddyn Einion Gryc & divers other lands in Estimaner, to Tud^r ap Ieuan ap Tud^r ap Gruff. of Caethle, as by ye Records & evidences of y^t house is manifest, and came to dwell to Talybont. He lived in the dayes of King Hen. VI., & was of the grand jury for said county in a Sessions kept at Caernarvon before Thos. Stanley, Justice of North Wales, in the 32^d year of the said King. I find him also in divers other grand enquests An° 31, 32, 33, 34 of King H. VI., & always ranked and placed with the best of the gentry." He had:

Howel ap Llewelyn, of Talybont. [A note by Meyrick to Dwnn, assigns to him the service on juries &c., which is assigned in most transcripts of the Hengwrt MS., as above, to Llewelyn ap Gruffydd, his father.] Living, 34 Hen. VI. [MS. pedigree from Hengwrt MSS., in possession of the compiler.] Howel married Gwenhwyfar, daughter of Meuric ap Gruffydd ap Ieuan Lloyd, and had:

Owen ap Howel, who married Gwenhwyfar, daughter and heiress of Meuric ap Ieuan ap Einion, lineally descended from Ednowain ap Bradwen, of Talybont, and had:

Lewis Owen, Esquire, of Plâs yn dref in Dolgelley, Vice Chamberlain of North Wales, and Baron of the Exchequer of Carnarvon, M.P. for Merionethshire, 1547, 1552, 1553, 1554, High Sheriff 1543, 1552, 1554, in which last year he was murdered by outlaws. The following account of his murder was written by his great grandson, Robert Vaughan, of Hengwrt:

"Afterwards the sayd Lewys Owen, being high shiriffe of y^e County of Merioneth, & having occasion to goe to Montgomery shire assizes, to treat wth the Lord Mouthewy, about a marriage to be had betweene Jo^n Owen, his sonne and heire, & y^e daughter of y^e sayd Lord of

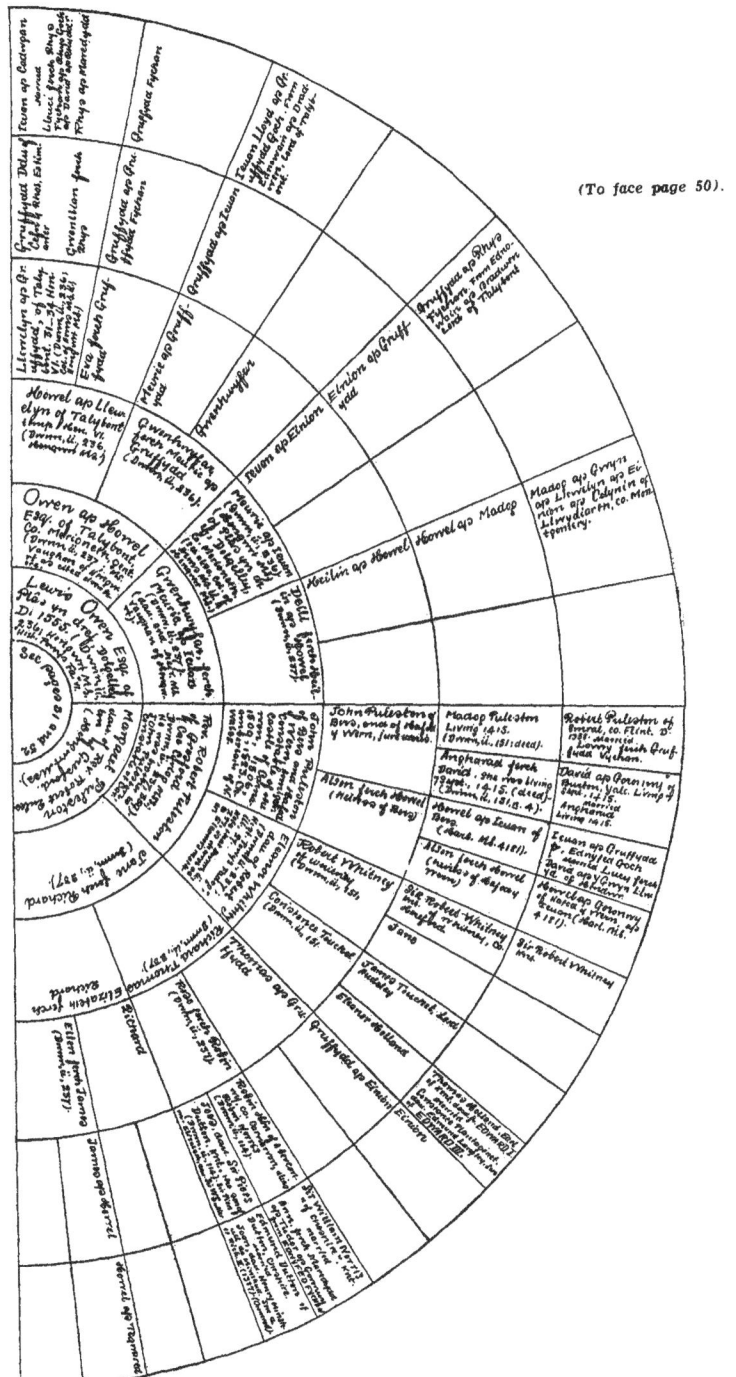

(To face page 50).

Mouthwy, was in his returne met by a damned crew of thieves & outlawes, who in thick woods of Mouthwy lay in wayt for his coming, & had cutt downe long trees to crosse y^e way & hinder his passage, & being come to the place, they lett flie att him a shower of arrowes, whereof one lighted in his face, the which he took out with his hand & brake it, then they fell upon him with theire bills & javelings & killed him—his men upon the first assault fledd & left him onely accompanied with his son in law John Lloyd, of Keiswyn, Esqre, who defended him till he fell down to the ground as dead, where he was found having above 30 bloody wounds in his body. This cruell murther was committed about alhallowtide in ye year of our Lord 1555. And the murtherers soone after were for ye most parte taken & executed, some few fled, the land, & never returned, And soe, wth the losse of his life, he purchased peace & quietnes to his countrey."

"Baron" Owen was killed 11 Oct., 1555, and the place where he was assassinated is yet known as Llidiait-y-Barwn, the Baron's gate, and the woodland adjoining as Ffridd-y-Groes, the enclosure of the cross, a cross having probably been erected on the spot where he fell.

The Sheriff had made himself very obnoxious to these outlaws, and a short time before they killed him, in conjunction with John Wynn, had captured 80 of them, most of whom were hanged.

Lewis Owen married Margaret, daughter of Sir (Rev.) Robert Puleston, Clerk, Parson of Gresford. He was brother of Sir John Puleston, knt., of Bers.

   ISSUE:

 i. John Lewis Owen; married Ursula, daughter of Richard Mytton, Lord of Mawddwy.

 ii. Hugh Lewis Owen, of Caer Berllan, Barrister-at-law; married Catharine, daughter of John Pugh, of Mathavarn, Esquire.

 iii. Edward Owen, of Hengwrt (see *infra*).

 iv. Gruffydd Owen, of the parish of Llanegryn; married Elizabeth, daughter and eventually heiress of David William Lloyd, of Peniarth, Esquire.

v. Robert Owen, *of whom presently.*
vi. Simon Owen, of Garth Angharad; married Margaret, daughter and sole heiress of Gruffydd ap Howel.
vii. Ellis Owen, or Wynn.
viii. Elin, married David Lloyd ap Tudor Vaughan.
ix. Elizabeth, married Richard Nannau (Nanney), of Cefn Deuddwr.
x. Catharine, married Ieuan ap David Lloyd Ceiswyn (called also John Lloyd).
xi. Mary, married John Wynn, of Llwyn yn and Caer Ddineu.

Robert Owen, of Dolserey "gent.," an attorney in the Court of the Marches of Wales. Born before 1555. He married Elizabeth, daughter of Robert ap Morgan, of Llanaber.

ISSUE:
i. Humphrey, *of whom presently.*
ii. Harry, of London.
iii. Simon.
iv. Rev. John Owen.

Humphrey Owen, of Dolserey, near Dolgelley, Merionethshire. He married ———.

ISSUE:
i. Humphrey.
ii. Robert, *of whom presently.*

Robert Owen, of Dolserey, near Dolgelley, second son of Humphrey Owen. He had been a captain under Cromwell, and was Governor of Beaumaris castle, under the Protectorate, and a Justice of the Peace. About 1660 he joined the Society of Friends, and was frequently fined and imprisoned, once for ten years, on account of his refusal to comply with the Acts of Parliament then in force. In 1684, being then quite aged, he removed, with his wife Jane and sons, Dr. Griffith Owen, who had been practising medicine in England, and Lewis Owen, to the Province of Pennsylvania. They sailed on the ship "Vine," Captain Preeson, master, which arrived at Philadelphia (or more probably Chester), 17 Sept., 1684, and proceeded to Duck Creek, New Castle County, then in Pennsylvania, but now in Delaware, where another son, Edward, had already settled.

(*To face page 52*).

Authorities :—To the marriage of Wm. Anwill with Margaret vch. Robert Symon Owen, *Peniarth MS. 288* (Griffith Vaughan's "Big Book of Pedigrees") fo. 1099 et. seq.
From that marriage onwards ; Wills, Parish Registers ; Inscriptions, Family Bibles, &c.

Lewis Owen, Esq., Baron of the Exchequer.=Margaret, da. of Robert Puleston, clerk of Gresford.

Symon Owen, of Hafod Tywyll,=Margaret, da. & h. of Griffith ap Howel
Dolgelley, 6th son. | ap Griffith, of Hafod Tywyll.

Lewis Owen, of Hafod Tywyll.   Robert Symon Owen, of Ty Gwyn, Dolgelley =Gwen llwyd, da. of John ap Ieun llwyd
                                Died 1637. Will at Bangor.   ap Lewis ap Ieun ap dd. [Lewis ap
                                                                            Ieuan of Festiniog's dau., Lowry, was
                                                                            mother of the 1st Anwyl (Lewis d.
                                                                            1605), of Parc, Llanfrothen.

John Owen,   Edward O.,   Ieuan O.,   Elizabeth, ux.   Margaret,=William Anwill, s. & h.   Ann, un. Wm.
of Ty Gwyn. jure, ux., of of Pant   John ap Robt.   not mar. | of Evan Lewis Anwill,   ap Lewis ap Wm.
             Garth   Phylip,   ap John Lewis,   in 1637, of Festiniog, 3rd s. of   of Bwllarthog.
             Angharad,   Llangel-   of Glyn   but soon Lewis Anwill, of Parc,
             Dolgelley.   ynin.   Maldan.   after.   Llanfrothen. Aged 26,
                                                                   12 Feb., 1635-6 : *Chanc.
                                                                   Proc: Dep. Eliz. to
                                                                   Chas. I.*, A 7/17.

                  Griffith Vaughan, of Dolmelynllyn,=Catherine,
                  s. of Robt. V., the Antiquary. | d. & h.

Rev. Evan Anwill, clerk, of Panteinion,=Catherine, da. of John Ellis [? of Llangelynin]   Anne A., bapt. Dolgelley,
Tremorfa, Llangelynin, co. Merioneth.   Marr. at Dolgelley, 24 March, 1658-9.   1647 ; d. unmd. 1707.
Baptd. Dolgelley, 5 May, 1643; of   Liv. a widow, 1703. Bur. Llangelynin, 14
Jesus Coll., Oxon. Liv. at Llangelynin, Dec. 1723.
1678; ?Curate there. Died before 1703

William Anwill, of Panteinion, s. & h.=Susan, da. of John   John Anwill, of Dolgleder, Dolgelley=Elizabeth Argas.
Marr. sett. 19 Feb. 1703-4 ; died 1718; | David, of Cyfanedd, and Llangelynin, gent ; baptd. Dol-
bur. Llangelynin.   Llanegryn. Died   gelley, 31 July, 1668, or Llangelynin.   [So, in Register,
                                         1715.   12 March, 1669 [?two sons named   Llangelynin.]
                                                              John, 1st ob. infs.];?bur. Llanegryn,
                                                              3 Mch., 1733-4.

Evan Anwyl, of Harlech, Llandanwg, co. Mer., gent,=Elizabeth, dau. of Watkin Solomon, of Barmouth,
eld. son; bapt. Dolgelley, 18 May, 1702; died 29   Llanaber, Merchant, by Jane, his wife; marrd. at
July ; bur. Llandanwg, 31 July, 1759 (aged 57 ; slab. Llanaber, 18 May, 1733; bur. Llandanwg, 31 May,
inscr.). Will, Bangor. [I have his Family Bible   1794. Will at Bangor.
with his children's births, &c., in it. It was printed
1678, and appears to have belonged to his father,
as it has J.A. in early type stamped on front page of
Old Test.—P. H. L.]

Watkin A.   Jane Anwyl, born 17 May, 1743 ; baptd. Llandanwg,=Solomon Griffiths, of Llandanwg, afterwards
             20 May, 1743 ; marr. there by lic. 9 June, 1764.   of Llanfechell, Anglesey. Died at Llandanwg
Anwyl of Dolgelley, &c.   Living 1794 at Llanfechell, Anglesey. (Harlech); bur. 21 June, 1788, aged 47.

John Griffiths, of Hafodonen,   Anne Griffiths, baptd. Llandanwg,=Robert Jones, of Amlwch, co. Anglesey, son
Amlwch, Anglesey.   17 April, 1768 ; died Aulwch, 13 of Robt. Jones, of Felin Adda, Amlwch,
                                   Jany., 1849, aged 80.   yeoman and miller. Bapt. 31 March, 1766 ;
                                                                     died 29 Aug., 1825.

       Mary Jones, baptd. 19 March, 1796,=Richard Owen, son & h. of Richd. Owen, of Ty'n Coed,
       marr. at Amlwch, 9 June, 1812. | Amlwch, desc. from Owen, of Llanfaethlu, Anglesey [Hwfa
                                            ap Cynddelw.] Bapt. 17 Aug., 1788 ; d. 14 Dec., 1842.

       Anne Owen, b. 1820,=Hugh Hughes, of Amlwch, son and h. of John Hughes ap Hugh ap John
       marr. 19 March, 1847; ap Howell, etc. (from Wm. ap Howel ap Dafydd ap Iorwerth, of Tregaian,
       died 6 Jany., 1883.   who died 1581, aged 105). Born 21 July, 1819 ; died 28 March, 1897.

       Elinor, b. 16 Jan., 1855;=William Lawson, 2nd son of Capt. John N. Lawson, of Whitby, Yorks.,
       married 20 Dec., 1885. | desc. from Lawson, of Brough, Catterick, co. York, earlier of
                                   co. Northumberland ; born 28 Nov., 1855 ; of Newton by Chester.

              Philip Hugh Lawson, of Newton by Chester ;
              b. 15 March, 1887. Liv., unm.

With his son Lewis, he appears as witness to a deed dated there, in 1685, and a commission of Justice of the Peace and County Courts had been prepared for him in anticipation of his coming.

Robert and Jane Owen were very old people at the time of their arrival, and died within a few days of each other, 1685-6, at Duck Creek. There are several sketches of their lives in various volumes of Friends' "Memorials"; but of these, one in print and another in MS., both written long after the decease of this couple, confuse them with Robert Owen and Rebecca his wife, who settled in Merion township, near Philadelphia, in 1690, and died 1697, and whose pedigree is given in "Merion," and in vol. ii. of this work.

Robert Owen, of Dolserey, married Jane, daughter of Robert Vaughan, of Hengwrt, Esquire, the celebrated Antiquary. See *infra*.

ISSUE:

i. Robert of Dolserey; inherited the Welsh estates, and disowned the Society of Friends. He married, and had the following children baptized in Dolgelley Church: (*a*) Humphrey, 1694, (*b*) Hugh, 1699, (*c*) Katherine, 1700, (*d*) Anna, 1703, (*e*) William, 1785 (by Jane ——, perhaps a second wife).
ii. Griffith, *of whom presently*.
iii. Rowland.
iv. Edward, *of whom presently*.
v. Lewis, *of whom presently*.
vi. Humphrey.

(There are said to have been three others who died in Wales).

Dr. Griffith Owen, son of Robert and Jane, born at Dolserey, practised medicine in England, and removed to Pennsylvania with his parents in the ship "Vine," 1684. He settled first in Merion, but afterwards removed to Philadelphia, where he died in January, 1717-18. Will dated 20 Sept., 1717; proved 14 January, 1717-18, at Philadelphia. He married Sarah, daughter of John Songhurst, and widow of —— Sanders; formerly widow of

Zachariah Whitpaine. Dr. Owen was a member of the Provincial Council of Pennsylvania, and held other important offices. He was also esteemed as a skilful surgeon.

ISSUE:
i. Robert.
ii. Sarah, married Jacob Minshall.
iii. Eleanor.
iv. Catherine.
v. Rebecca, married Isaac Minshall; *of whom presently.*
vi. Jane, married : 1st, Jonathan Coppock ; 2dly, —— Taylor.
vii. John, *of whom presently.*
viii. Edward, a physician in Philadelphia; d. s. p., 1729; married 15 Oct., 1724, Susanna, daughter of Philip Kearney.
ix. Griffith, living 2 Sept., 1729.
x. Ann, married John Whitpaine.

John Owen, son of Dr. Griffith Owen, married Jane, daughter of Samuel Harriott, of Philadelphia. She died after 18 Feb., 1741-2.

ISSUE:
i. Samuel, of Philadelphia; married Anne ——; died after 2 May, 1766.
ii. Sarah.
iii. Elizabeth.
iv. Griffith, of Philadelphia, d. s. p. will proved 18 Feb., 1741.
v. John, died after 16 July, 1733.

Rebecca Owen, daughter of Dr. Griffith Owen. She travelled very extensively in connection with the Society of Friends, of which she was a member. Married, first, 9-11-1707, Isaac Minshall, of Providence, Chester County, Pennsylvania, who died 1731 ; secondly, 8-5-1748, Job Harvey, of Darby, near Philadelphia.

ISSUE:
i. Aaron, born 8 month 10, 1708.
ii. Rebecca, born 4 month 1, 1710; married, 1 month 5, 1740; Richard Blackburn, d. s. p.
iii. Griffith, born 4 month 1, 1712 ; married Sarah Minshall.
iv. Isaac, born 8 month 29, 1718 ; married Lydia Ellis.
v. Samuel, born 8 month 26, 1724 ; married Jane ——.
vi. Edward, born 4 month 28, 1727 ; died young.
vii. Jacob, born 5 month 10, 1729 ; died young.

Pedigree V. 55

Edward Owen, son of Robert and Jane, born at Dolserey. He is grantee in a deed dated 1 April, 1682, for 312½ acres of land to be surveyed to him in Pennsylvania," he being described therein as "late of Doleysorre, gentleman." He also purchased land in Newcastle County (now in Delaware) and settled on Duck Creek. In 1685, he sold his land, which had been surveyed to him in Merion, to his brother, Dr. Griffith Owen, and his father Robert, and brother Lewis Owen witnessed the deed. He married, 15 Jan. 1684-5, Hannah Baxter, and afterwards removed to Kent County. Died in Maryland.

ISSUE:
 i. Thomas, died 1716, at Philadelphia, "aged 26 to 30 years."
 ii. Robert, *of whom presently.*
 iii. Edward, " of Maryland," living 1754.
  ["Other children" are named in Edward Owen's will, but their names have not been obtained. One MS. genealogy, however, states that there was a son Lawrence.] (Perhaps died at St. George's Hundred, 1774?)

Robert Owen, son of Edward and Hannah, born on Duck Creek, Newcastle County; removed to Maryland; but inheriting the Duck Creek plantation, returned to that place, where he died about March, 1754. He married Jannet——.

ISSUE:
 i. William, living in Little Creek Hundred, 1785.
 ii. Edward; had Edward and other issue.
 iii. Owen; had Owen and other issue.
 iv. Evan.
 v. Robert, living in Little Creek Hundred, 1785.
 vi. Ammon, living in Little Creek Hundred, 1785.
 vii. Sarah.

Lewis Owen, born at Dolserey; removed to Pennsylvania, with his parents, 1684; settled on Duck Creek, and died 1708-9. He married Lowry——. Will 22 Jan., 1708-9.

ISSUE:
 i. Lewis, born 1685.
 ii. John, born 1687.
 iii. Ann.
 iv. Ellen.
 v. Jane.

Edward Owen, third son of "Baron" Lewis Owen, of Dolgelley, was of Hengwrt, and so described in a deed dated 20 Nov., 1558-9 (1 Eliz.). He married Elin Llwyd, daughter of Robert ap Morgan, Vicar of Llanaber, and was living, 10 May, 1601.

ISSUE :

i. Robert, living 24 Nov., 1608, whose only child supposedly d. s. p.
ii. Elizabeth, married Morgan ap John ap Thomas, of Plassau Gwynion, party to a deed dated 11 Sept., 1598.
iii. Margaret, *of whom presently*.

Margaret Owen, second daughter of Edward Owen, of Hengwrt. She had Hengwrt as her share of her father's estate, and married Howel Vaughan ap Gruffydd ap Howel of Gwengraig, gentleman, (descended from the Nannau, or Nanney, family), who is named as party to a bond, dated 24 Nov., 1608. Their eldest son was:

Robert Vaughan, of Hengwrt, the celebrated Antiquary, who was born at Hengwrt 1592, and died 16 May, 1667. He married Catherine, daughter of Gruffydd Nannau, of Nannau, Esq., who was born 11 June, 1568, and was M.P. for Merionethshire, 1592. The latter was son of Hugh Nannau, High Sheriff of Merionethshire, 1587, and married Anne, daughter of Rhys Vaughan, of Cors y Gedol, High Sheriff of Merionethshire 1548, 1557.

ISSUE :

i. Howel Vaughan, of Hengwrt, High Sheriff of the co. of Merioneth, 1672, and M.P. for the same co. Ancestor of the Vaughans of Hengwrt, Baronets.
ii. Ynyr, d. s. p. 1668.
iii. Hugh, married Elizabeth Meyrick.
iv. Gruffydd, *of whom presently*.
v. Margaret, married Tudor Vaughan.
vi. Jane, married Robert Owen, of Dolserey, and died in Pennsylvania (see *supra*).
vii. Ellin.
viii. Ann.

Pedigree V.

Gruffydd Vaughan, fourth son of Robert Vaughan the Antiquary, was born 20 Oct., 1628, and was of Dolmelynllyn and Glynmalden, in the parish of Dolgelley. He married, 1652, Catherine, daughter and sole heiress of John ap Robert ap John ap Lewis ap Maredydd, of Glynmalden. Her mother was Elizabeth ——. The mother of John ap Robert was Gainor Rowland. [Peniarth MS. 288, fo. 404.] Here follows an abstract of the marriage settlement of Gruffydd Vaughan and Catherine, now in the possession of their descendant Edward Griffith, of Coedcymmer, Dolgelley, Esq.

This INDENTURE made the tenth Day of July in the yeare of our Lord one thousand sixe hundred Fiefty two BETWEENE John ap Robert John of Dolegleder in the Countie of Merionyth gent. and Elizabeth his wife, Robert Vaughan of Hengwrt in the Countie aforesaid esquier, and Hugh Gruffyth ap Evan of Tr (r) morva in the Countie aforesaid yeoman and Catherine his wiefe of the one partie, And Howell Vaughan of Gwengraige in the County aforesaid esquier and Edward Owen of Dolegleder aforesaid in the said Countie gent. of the other partie WITNESSETH that as well as for and in Consideration of a Lawfull marriage hereafter by God's permission .... to be had and solemnized betweene Gruffyth Vaughan gent. one of the sonnes of the said Robert Vaughan and Catherine Jones Daughter of the said John ap Robert John, and of the sume of fortie poundes lawfull moneys of England already paid and satisfied by the said Robert Vaughan unto the said John ap Robert John for the marriage portion of the said Gruffyth Vaughan and for his preferment in or to the said marriage......... and......... he the said John ap Robert John Doeth acknowledge himself fully Satisfied Contented and paid and thereof and of everie parte and parcell thereof Doeth exoneratte acquitte and Discharge the said Robert Vaughan his heires executors, and administrators and every of them by thei's p'sents.

And for the Selinge.................. and Conveyinge of all and singuler the messuage Lands Tenements wth the appurtencs hereinafter ment'oed for such uses and behoofes as are herein hereafter Declared, expressed......... for and concernnige the same and everie of them, as alsoe for Divers other good Causes and lawfull considerations (them the said John ap Robert John and Elizabeth his wiefe, Robert Vaughan, and Hugh Gruffyth ap Evan and Catherine his wiefe thereunto especially moveinge) IT is Coven'nted and agreed uppon by and between the said parties That they the said John ap Robert John and Elizabeth his wiefe, Robert Vaughan, and Hugh Gruffyth ap Evan and Catherine his wiefe shall and will at or before the next greate Sessions to be holden and......... for and w'thin the said Countie of Merinyth acknowledge and Leavy unto the said Howell. Vaughan and Edward Owen and their heires or to the heire's of one of them one Fine for the acknowledgement of there Right as that wch the said Howell Vaughan and Edward Owen have of there gift to be recorded and engrossed......... thereuppon to be had according to the Lawes and Statutes in that Case made and Provided of and uppon all and singuler that messuage tenement and Lands.........called tythyn Der*was?* and of.........all and singuler these severall messuages Lands and tenements and hereditants wth the appurtanc's Co'enly called and known by the severall names of Glynne Maylda.........and Llwynniarth all........... Lieinge in Dolegleder in the Countie of Merionyth aforesaid, and all other the messuages, Lands, tenements,.........hereditmts.........of the said John ap Robert John or whereof he the said John ap Robert John nowe is or by right ought to be seized of any estate Inheritance or freehold in possession, remainder..........Situate and lieinge in Dolegleder aforesaid in the said Countie or elsewhere in the said Countie, And alsoe of and uppon all and singular that messuage tenement and Lands wth the appurtennc's Called by the name of Doleymelynllyn situate and Lieinge in Llanysltyd in the Countie aforesaid.........beinge the Lands and Inheritance of the said Robert Vaughan, And likewise in and uppon all and singuler that messuage tenements and Lands &c..........Called by name of Pant Phillip situate lieing and being in Cregemran in the Countie aforesaid beinge sometime the Lands and Inheritance of the said Hugh Gruffyth ap Evan.........being 10 mess, 6 tofts, 15 gardens, 120 a land, 100 a meadow, 250 acres of pasture, 40 acres of wood, 120 acres of bruen and 44 ? acres of moore.........And it is further Covenanted declared and agreed uppon by and betweene the said parties.........that Howel Vaughan shall hold said premises in trust.........

Here follow provisions for Gaynor Rowland, mother of John ap Robert John, and Elizabeth, wife of John ap Robert John, who is in receipt of a separate mentenance, allowed her by court as alimony, and paid her by John ap Edward of Dolgelley, yeoman. The life tenancy of John ap Robert John is secured.

Signed :
Wm. ap Robert.
Elizabeth, [his wife.]
Hugh Gruffyth ap Evan.
Robert Vaughan.
Edward Owen.
   Witnessess :
Charles Morris.
Thomas Price.
Wm. ? Hughes.
Rob Lloyd.
Thomas Griffithes of Shrewsbury in ye Countie Salop.
John Lewis Gruffyth.
Owen Hughes.

Gruffydd Vaughan died 1700.

ISSUE :
 i. John, born 2 Sept., 1662.
 ii. Robert.
 iii. Hugh.
 iv. Elizabeth, born 15 Nov., 1656 ; married Hugh Jones ap John Pugh.
 v. Margaret, married David Williams ap William Lloyd of Brynllefrith.

PEDIGREE V. 59

vi. Ellen, married Owen Tudder, of Cefnrowen, *of whom presently*.
vii. Ann, married Robert Lloyd ap Hugh Lloyd, of Dduallt.
viii. Catherine, married Lewis Anwyl.
ix. Jane, married Lewis Owen ap John Owen, of Erwgoed.
x. Gemelli, born 8 Nov., 1676, [sic.]

Ellen Vaughan, third daughter of Gruffydd Vaughan, of Dolmelynllyn and Glynmalden, married Owen Tudder, of Cefnrowen, in the parish of Dolgelley, Merionethshire. This Owen Tudder was son and heir of Tudder Owen[1] (baptized 1650, died 1700), and Catherine his wife (born 1645, died 1686).

ISSUE:

i. John, died 1764, aged 61, unm.
ii. Edward, died 1791, aged 88, unm.
iii. Robert, died young.
iv. Lewis, died 1774, aged 66; married Margaret (bapt. 1726, died 1781), daughter of Lewis Griffith, of Bwlchcoch, by whom he had an only daughter, Ellen (bapt. 1763, died 1855), who married, 1792, John Edwards of Ty'nycoed, High Sheriff for co. Merioneth, 1818 (died 1834, aged 76 years without issue).
v. Catherine, married John Evans, owner of Gellilwyd, by whom she had an only daughter, Ellen, who died 1779, unm.
vi. Mary, married Robert Parry, *of whom presently*.
vii. Ann, born 1710, died unm.
viii. Ellen, married, Dec., 1758, Griffith Lewis, of Bwlchcoch; son of Lewis Griffith, of Bwlchcoch, who married Ann, daughter of Morris Owen, of Tygwyn, fourth in descent from Simon Owen, son of "Baron" Lewis Owen, of Dolgelley. They had, Lewis Griffith (bapt. 1760, died 1818), married Ann, daughter of John Jones, of Brynrhyg, and had an only daughter, Ellen Owen, married W. Jones, and died 1893, without issue.

---

[1] Owen Tudder's pedigree is as follows: Tudder Owen, (said to be descended from Gruffydd Derwas, esquire to the body of Henry VI., living 1416, son of Meuric Llwyd, of Nannau), was father of Ieuan ap Tudder Owen, who had Tudder ap Ieuan ap Tudder Owen, baptd. at Mallwyd, 21 May, 1584, and buried at Dolgelley, 1660. In 1632 he bought the farm of Hafodygoesfon, for his son Owen, and in 1638, he bought Pandyrgader from Watkin Lloyd of Peniarth. His name appears in the Lay Subsidy Roll for Merionethshire, for 1636, as a freeholder in the parishes of Mallwyd and Dolgelley. He was father of Owen Tudder, a gentleman of considerable property. The latter purchased the Cefnrowen estate from William Oxwick, and he also bought Caeiago Erwgwyddil (Tynewydd Islawrdref). He was one of those who signed the agreement as to dispasturage of Tir Extent Mawr, 1654. His family Bible is in the possession of his descendant, Edward Griffith, Esq., of Coedcymmer, to whom the compiler is indebted for information regarding this family. The will of Owen Tudder of Cefnrowen in the parish of Dolgelley, gentleman, is dated 24 May, 1683, and was proved at Bangor. He married Gwen———, and had issue; (1) Tudder Owen (Bapt. 1650, died 1700), married Catherine———, and had (a) Owen Tudder, above named, who married Ellen Vaughan (b) Gwen, born 1669 (c) Elizabeth, born 1671 (d) Mary, born 1675 (e) Lewis, born 1678 (f) Ann, born 1680. Owen Tudder had also (2) Ellen, married, ———, (3) Mary, born 1647, d.s.p. (4) Catherine, bapt., 1654, married Rowland Ellis, of Gwanas (5) Griffith, bapt. 1657, (6) Hugh, bapt. 1660.

Mary Tudder, sixth daughter of Owen Tudder, of Cefnrowen, married Robert Parry, of Wain, Islawrdref.

ISSUE :
i. Hari, *of whom presently.*
ii. Owen.
iii. Robert.
iv. John.
v. Lewis.
vi. Edward.
vii. Ellen.
viii. Ann.
ix. Betti.
x. Catherine.
xi. Margaret.

Hari Roberts, eldest son of Robert Parry, of Wain, Islawrdref, and Mary, daughter of Owen Tudder, of Cefnrowen, his wife, served with the 30th Regiment of Foot, and lost his arm in the defence of Gibraltar against the Spanish and French forces during the years 1770 to 1782, and subsequently returned to Dolgelley. He married at Gibraltar, 16 Nov., 1766, Mary Carss, widow.

ISSUE :
i. Catherine, married Tudder Owen, son of Owen, the second son of Mary and Robert Parry, but died without issue. Her husband Tudder Owen, died 1840, aged 69 years.
ii. Mary, married Griffith Dafydd, *of whom presently.*

Mary Roberts, second daughter of Hari Roberts, died 1844, aged 70 years. She was considered the beauty of the county, and is mentioned by Mr. Warner, the eminent tourist, who says, "we had scarcely ever seen a girl more lovely or interesting. She was tall and elegantly shaped, her complexion fair, her large blue eyes becoming kindness and ingenuity, her flaxen hair flowing in negligent ringlets over her shoulders. Her voice musically sweet, and her manners wonderfully soft." This was in 1797.

She married Griffith Dafydd, of Maesygarnedd, Llanelltyd, who died 1843, at the age of 69 years. Their children assumed the surname of Griffith.

ISSUE :
i. David, *of whom presently.*
ii. Harry, died 7 Dec., 1867, aged 63 years.
iii. Griffith, died 1866, aged 56 years.
iv. Catherine, died 1858, aged 53 years.
v. Mary.
vi. Ann.

(*To face page* 60).

TUDOR OF CEFNROWEN.
[Peniarth MS. 287, f. 439-440.]
(Compiled by Mr. Philip H. Lawson, Chester, from a transcript of the orig. MS. ;
and authorities cited).

Gruffydd Derwas of Cemmaes, 2nd son of Meurig, lord of Nannau, son of Meurig (or Meuric), son of Ynyr Vychan, lord of Nannau ; descended from Cadwgan, son of Bleddyn, Prince of Powys (Peniarth MS. as cited ; Dwnn, ii., 226; Harl. MSS. 1969, 1977). Cadwgan, after a distinguished career, was slain at Welshpool about 1109. Ynyr Vychan did homage and fealty for his lands to Prince Edward, at Conway, 28th April, 29 Edw. I. (1301). (Pat. Roll, 18 Edw. III.) Petitions for office of Raglor of Talybont, 33 Edw. I. ("Records of Caer," 220). Charged, with others, with attacking the Castle of John Grey of Ruthin at Michaelmas, 15 Edw. II. (Rot. Parl., i., 397). The effigy of Meurig ap Ynyr Vychan is in Dolgelley Church, with inscription : Hic Iacet Meuric ap Uner Vachan.

Gruffydd Derwas was liv. at Michaelmas, 5 Hen. V., and later ; according to Randal Holmes he was Esquire of the Body to Henry VI. (Dwnn, ii., 84, *n.* 6). He was father of *Maredydd*, who was father of *Howel*, who was father of *Owen,* who was father of *Thomas*, who was father of *Owen ap Thomas* (2nd son), who (by Mary, dau. of Elise ap Ynyr ap Llewelyn ap Ynyr) had : (a) Thomas ap Owen, (b) David ap Owen, (c) Tuder Owen, *of whom presently*, (d) Catrin, m. Humffrey ap Lewis ap Howel ap Ynyr, (e) Annes, m. Simon ap Lewis ap Tudor Goch of Bwlchcôch, (f) Margaret, m. Gruffydd ap Richard ap Gruffydd Vychan.

Tuder Owen, 3rd son of Owen ap Thomas, was liv. 1578, and married —— dau. of Lewis ap Tudor Goch of Bwlchcôch, by whom he had : (a) Ieuan ap Tuder Owen, *of whom presently*, (b) David ap Tudder Owen, Student of the Inner Temple, burd. at Mallwyd 13th Sept., 1577 ; will provd. at St. Asaph, 1578, (c) Robert, (d) Ellis, (e) —— (dau.), m. Lerois [? Lewis] ap John ap Gruffydd ap Richard.

Ieuan ap Tuder Owen, eldest son of Tuder Owen, was of the parish of Mallwyd, and is mentioned 1578, at which time he and his father were exors. of the will of his brother, David ap Tudder Owen. He was father of *Tudder ap Ieuan*. bapt. at Mallwyd, 21st May, 1584 ; burd. at Dolgelley, 1660 (see *n.* 1., p. 59). *Tudder ap Ieuan* was father of *Owen Tudder* of Cefnrowen, whose will of 24th May, 1683, was provd. at Bangor, and who married Gwen, daughter of Hugh ap Elisse ap David ap Owen, by whom he had (besides a daughter Catherine, wife of Rowland Ellis of Gwanas). *Tudder Owen*, bapt 1650, died 1700, who married Catherine, dau. of David Ellis of Gwanas, by whom he was father of *Owen Tudder* of Cefnrowen, who married Ellen, dau. of Gruffydd Vaughan of Dolmelyllyn, son of Robert Vaughan of Hengwrt. The Antiquary (see pp. 57-59 of this vol.). Gruffydd Vaughan was brother of Jane, wife of Robert Owen of Dolserey, who removed to Pennsylvania, 1684.

Pedigree V.

David Griffith, eldest son of Griffith Dafydd and Mary, daughter of Hari Roberts, his wife, died 1849, aged 49 years. He married Lowry Griffiths, who died March, 1882, aged 78, who lived at the Angel Hotel, Dolgelley, for 40 years; she purchased the property in 1854.

ISSUE:
i. Griffith, died 1850, aged 21 years.
ii. Edward, *of whom presently.*
iii. David, died 1890, aged 51 years; married Elizabeth, daughter of R. Roberts, of Dolgelley.
iv. Richard, married Anne, daughter of W. Parry, of Caerwegi, Capel Curig.
v. Margaret, married Evan Evans, of Dolobran, Mallwyd.
vi. Mary, married William Owen, Liverpool House, Dolgelley.
vii. Catherine, died 1879, aged 37, married William Williams, Dolgelley.
viii. Laura, married John Ellis, accountant, Dolgelley.

Edward Griffith, eldest son of David Griffith, of Coedcymmer, Dolgelley, Esq. As lineal descendant he is owner of all the land and property that belonged to the Tudders, viz., Cefnrowen, Caeiago, Erwwen, Pandyrgader, Maescoch. Edward Griffith married Gwen, the only surviving daughter of Robert Jones, of Dolgelley, and Jane his wife, daughter of Ellis Rees, of the same place. Jane, on her mother's side, was a granddaughter of Robert Oliver, of the Angel Hotel, Dolgelley. She married, secondly, William Williams, of Ivy House, Dolgelley, and died 1 June, 1881, aged 70. Robert Jones, father of the said Gwen, died in 1840, aged 30. He was the owner of Maesynghared and Llwyniarth, under the will of his uncle, Robert Jones, of Sylfaen, in the parish of Llanaber.

ISSUE:
i. David, born 1859; died 1863.
ii. Robert, born 1862, died 1906; married Phoebe Salisbury, and had, Elizabeth Gwendoline, born 28 July, 1894.
iii. Jane, married John Morris Owen, of the Anchorage, Carnarvon. They have Elsie Mair, born 1 Oct., 1891.
iv. Laura Catherine, born 1866; died 1887.
v. Winifred, born 1869, married John Trevor Owen, M.A., Head Master of the Swansea Grammar School. They have Gwendoline Anne, born 23 July, 1896, John Iorwerth Trevor Owen, born 25 Jan., 1898.

PEDIGREE VI.

Ellis ap Rhydderch, of the parish of Llanvawr (Llanfor). Will proved 5 May, 1638. [Probate Registry, St. Asaph.] = Mary vch. Hugh.

Children:
- Hugh ap Ellis.
- Rowland ap Ellis. — Margaret.
- David ap Ellis, of the parish of Llanfawr (Llanfor), Merionethshire. Will dated 4 March, 1678; proved 24 Feb., 1679 (1679-80). [Probate Registry, St. Asaph.] = Sibill ——. Living in the parish of Llanfor, 4 March, 1678.

Children of David ap Ellis and Sibill:

- Hugh David, eldest son and heir.[1]
- Robert David; he was of the township of Ciltalgarth, Llanfor, 1675. Removed to adjoining township of Gwernefel Isymydd, Llanycil, before 1682-3. Lived at "Tudygnant." Deed to him for 312½ acres of land in Pennsylvania (executed in Wales) 18 March, 1681. [Deed Book C.I. folio 175, Philadelphia.] Certif. of removal, Penllyn Mtg., 5 month, 18, 1683. Will of Robert David, of Merion, Pennsylvania, dated 26 April, 1732; proved 18 Oct., 1732. [Will Book E, folio 194, Philadelphia.] = Elizabeth ——.
- Ellis David, named in will of his father, 4 March, 1678; living, and named in will of his brother, Robert David, of Merion, 26 April, 1732.
- John David.
- William David.
- Rowland David.
- Margaret.
- Jane.

Children of Robert David and Elizabeth:

- Jane. Born 2 month, 28, 1678; m 10 month, 27, 1710, John Roberts.[2]
- Catherine. Born 1 month, 25, 1680; died 8 month, 12, 1683.
- Thomas David (or Davids) living in Merion, 1732.
- David David. Born 3 month, 4, 1685; died 5 month, 3, 1685.
- Katherine. Born 1 month, 4, 1687; died 6 month, 10, 1690.
- Elizabeth. Born 4 month, 19, 1689.
- David David. Born 10 month, 13, 1691; died s.p.
- Robert David. Born 8 month, 31, 1697; died 1700.

---

[1] This was probably the Hugh David, or Davies, who settled at Gwynedd, and was also in Merion, but there is no certainty.

[2] Son of Matthew Roberts, from Pen y Clwyd, Denbighshire, brother of John, of Merion, who married, as an old man, Elizabeth Owen.

PEDIGREES VII. & VIII.

PEDIGREE VII.

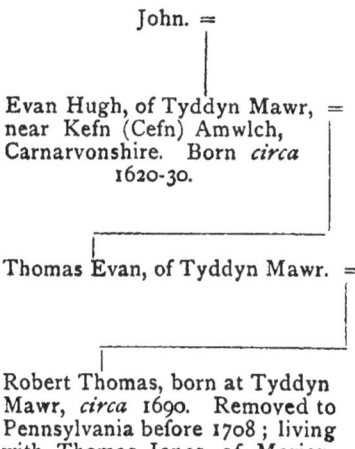

John. =

Evan Hugh, of Tyddyn Mawr, =
near Kefn (Cefn) Amwlch,
Carnarvonshire. Born *circa*
1620-30.

Thomas Evan, of Tyddyn Mawr. =

Robert Thomas, born at Tyddyn
Mawr, *circa* 1690. Removed to
Pennsylvania before 1708; living
with Thomas Jones, of Merion,
1708. [Letter to Robert Vaughan,
of Hendre Mawr, Levick MSS.]

PEDIGREE VIII.

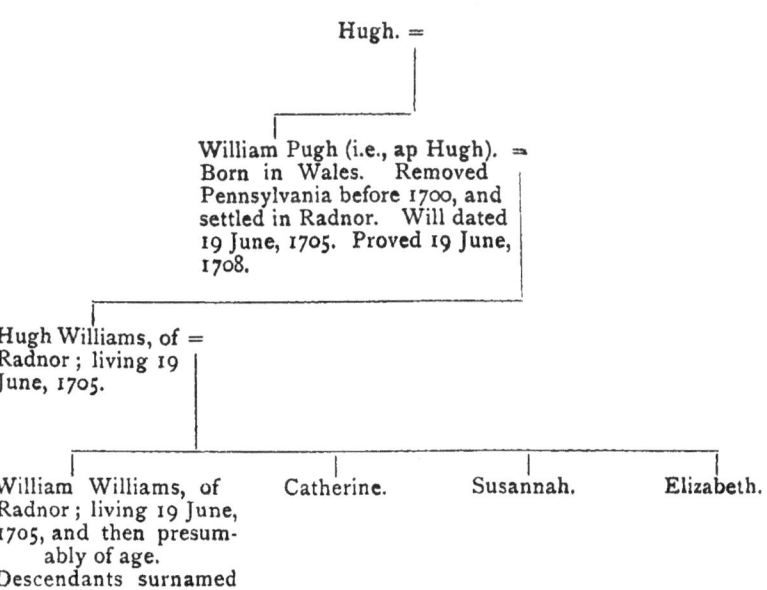

Hugh. =

William Pugh (i.e., ap Hugh). =
Born in Wales. Removed
Pennsylvania before 1700, and
settled in Radnor. Will dated
19 June, 1705. Proved 19 June,
1708.

Hugh Williams, of =
Radnor; living 19
June, 1705.

William Williams, of
Radnor; living 19 June,
1705, and then presum-
ably of age.
Descendants surnamed
Williams.

Catherine.   Susannah.   Elizabeth.

PEDIGREE IX.

Howel. = Descended from Meurig Vychan, lord of Nannau.

William Powel (i.e., ap Howel), = of the parish of Llanvachreth, Merionethshire.

Letters of Attorney. Dated 27 July, 1683, Evan ap William, of Llanvachraeth, co. Merioneth, and David Evans, of same place, to John Roberts, of Llangian, co. Carnarvon, to take possession of 312½ acres of land in Pa.

Evan William Powel, = Gwen———. of the parish of Llanvachreth, gentleman, (alias Evan William, and Evan ap William). Deed 30, 31 July, 1682, for land in Pennsylvania. [Deed Book C.I. 252. Phila.] Sailed for Pennsylvania 1684 ; died at sea.

John William. =

Gainor = David Evans, born in = Mary Jones.
———.   Llanvachreth. Removed   M. 1690,
         to Pennsylvania, 1684.   8 month 23.

Philip Evans. Removed to Pennsylvania, 1684; m. 1690, at Merion, Sarah Thomas, d.s.p. before 12 month 28, 1693.

Evan John William, d. s. p.

Caleb Evans, of co. of Chester, yeoman. Will signed 17 March, 1745: proved 29 March, 1746. [Will Book H, p. 109, Phila.] Issue : Mary, Jane, Caleb, David. (See Penna. Archives, 3 Ser.; vol. 1, 12).

Joshua Evans.

Evan Evans.

David Evans, of Merion, Issue.
———
John Evans.

Philip Evans.
———
Gwen.
———
Margaret.
———
Sarah.

---

[1] A branch of this Evans family removed to Virginia. The family of the late Colonel Dudley Evans, of New York, President of Wells, Fargo and Company, and Rear Admiral Evans, U.S.N., " Fighting Bob Evans," are descended from the Virginia line.

PEDIGREE X.

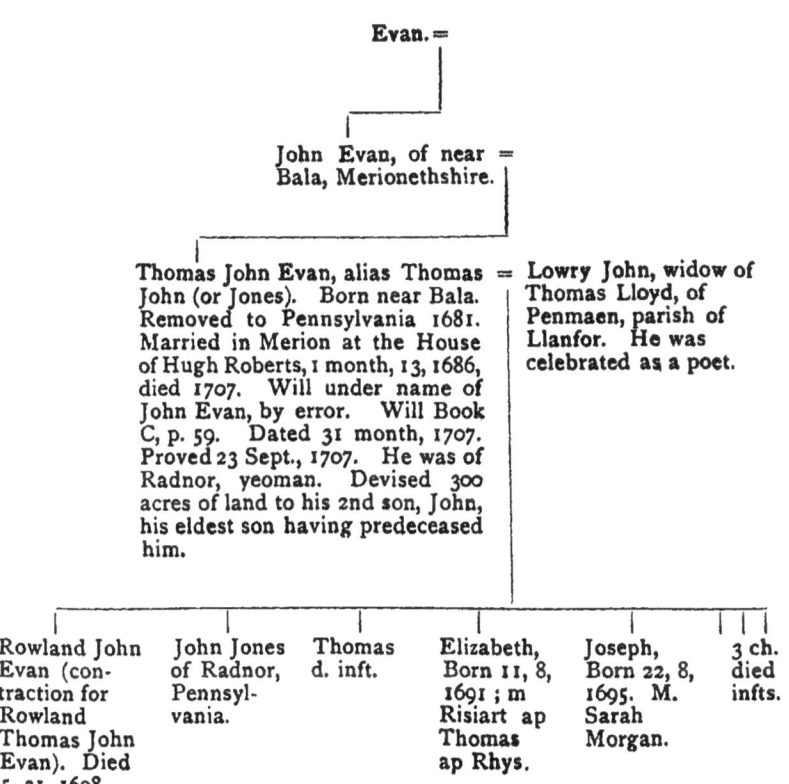

Note.—The Miles family, of Pittsburg, Pennsylvania, are descendants of this line.

PEDIGREE XI.

John Lloyd, of Llangower, = Merionethshire. Living about 1670.

Thomas Lloyd, of Llangower, yeoman. Grantee in a deed, executed in Wales, dated 1 April, 1682, for 156¼ acres of land in Pennsylvania. [Deed Book C. I., No. 3, p. 228, Phila.] He died in Wales without issue and bequeathed his lands in Pennsylvania to his nephew, John Roberts.

Robert Lloyd, of Llangower. Alias Robert John, and Robert Jones. [Deed Book X, p. 357, West Chester, Pennsylvania.]

John Roberts, of the parish of Llangower, cordwainer. He removed to Pennsylvania, and settled in Merion. He inherited the land, in Merion, of his uncle, Thomas Lloyd, and sold the same to Josiah Haines, by deed 16 Dec., 1710. [Deed Book X, p. 357. West Chester, Pa.] = (1st wife) ———. (2nd wife) = Mary.

PEDIGREE XII.

John. =
|
David John, of near Bala, Merion- =
ethshire. Living *circa* 1636. He
may have been, and probably was,
identical with David John, of
Ciltalgarth; see pedigree III.
|
William David John, of near Bala; =
living 1708.
|
Humphrey William. Removed to
Pennsylvania *circa* 1700. Living with
the family of Griffith John, deceased,
in Merion, Pennsylvania, in 1708.
[Levick MSS.]
|
Descendants are believed to
have assumed the surname
of Humphreys.

PEDIGREE XIII.

Griffith. =
|
James Griffith, of near =
Bala, Merionethshire.
Living 1708.
|
Thomas James, of near =
Bala.
|
Robert Thomas, born near
Bala. Removed to Pennsylvania *circa* 1700. Living
in Merion, 1708. [Levick
MSS.]

PEDIGREE XIV.

Evan, of Hirnant. =

Rhydderch ap Evan, = of the parish of Hirnant, Montgomeryshire, yeoman.

John Rhydderch, of the parish of Hirnant. Born 1651. He had a deed, executed in Wales, dated 1682-3, for land in Pennsylvania. Removed to Pennsylvania 1683. Certificate of removal dated 5 month, 31, 1683. Admon. on his estate, 11 month, 4, 1688. Letters to David Rhydderch. He m. Gwen, vch. John. ["Montg. Colls." xxvi., 63.]

David Rhydderch, of = Hirnant. Removed to Pennsylvania before 31 January, 1688.

Hannah. Born 5 month, 17, 1698. [Penna. Archives vol. I., 3 ser. p. 23.]

PEDIGREE XV.

Cadwalader, of the parish of Llanvawr (Llanfor), Merionethshire. =

Morgan Cadwalader, of the parish of Llanvawr (Llanfor), Merionethshire, yeoman. He held, among other lands, those called y Tir ar gyfor y garreg hir, y Tir nenredd, y Tir Mawr yn Llan, and which he bequeathed to his youngest son, David Morgan. Will dated 4 April, 1696. Proved 11 May, 1696. [Probate Registry, St. Asaph, vol. $\frac{1694}{1699}$, folio 96.] = Ellen, vch. William. Living May, 1696.

Cadwalader Morgan. Prior to his removal to Pennsylvania, he resided on a farm in Gwernefel, near Bala, and is called yeoman. He had a deed, executed in Wales, dated 1 April, 1682, for land in Pennsylvania. [Deed Book C I., p. 212, Phila.] Certificate of removal 5, 8, 1683. Died in Merion, Pennsylvania, 1711. Will dated 10 Sept., 1711. Proved at Phila., 10 Oct., 1711. [Will Book C, p. 259.] He mentions his brothers, John Morgan and Lewis Morgan. = Jane (Living 1698), daughter of Richard Price.

John Morgan, named in his father's will 4 April, 1696. Living, supposedly, 10, Sept., 1711.

Robert Morgan. Living 4 April, 1696.

Lewis Morgan, named 4 April, 1696. Living 10 Sept., 1711.

David Morgan. Living 5 April, 1696.

Margaret, Living 4 April, 1696.

Morgan Cadwalader. Born 6 month, 25, 1679; died 12 month, 1698. See "Piety Promoted," Dublin, 1721, p. 135.

Edward Cadwalader. Born 6 month, 22. Died s. p. before 1711.

Jane, m. Robert Evan, son of Thomas, of Gwynedd.

Catherine. Born 3 month, 3, 1685; died 6 month, 11, 1708, s. p. m. 8 month, 4, 1706, Hugh Evans.

———, dau. m. Abel Thomas.

PEDIGREE XVI.

[Cae Cyriog MS.; Harl. MS., 2299; Maryland Colonial Records.]

Madog Puleston, of Bers, second son of Robert Puleston of Emral, married Angharad, daughter of David ap Goronwy, of Burton and Llai.

ISSUE:
i. John, of Bers, and *jure uxoris* of Hafod y Wern.
ii. Edward; *of whom presently.*

Edward Puleston, of Cristionydd in Esclusham, Denbighshire, who, by Isabel Brereton, had:

Howel Puleston, of Plâs Uchaf, Cristionydd. [The family now discontinued the ancient surname of Puleston, and presently assumed that of Wynne or Wynn.] He had by Margaret, his wife, daughter and heiress of Ieuan ap Howel ap Ieuan Bach, of Rhiwabon:

Edward ap Howel, of Trefechan, who married Alice, daughter of John ap Ieuan, of Llanerch Rugog, and had:

John Wynn, of Trefechan alias Cristionydd Fechan (Vychan). The parish of Rhiwabon (Ruabon), Denbighshire, is called Cristionydd, and contains y Dref Fawr, or Cristionydd Cynwrig, y Dref (Tref) Fechan (Vychan), or Cristionydd Fechan, which is now called Dinhinlle Uchaf, and Coed Cristionydd.

John Wynn was living 1563, and had, with his wife, two portions of land in Cristionydd Cynwrig, called Plâs Ty Mawr. He married Elizabeth, daughter and co-heiress of David Lloyd ap John Puleston, of Plâs Uchaf.

ISSUE:
i. Richard, *of whom presently.*
ii. Anne Wen, married David ap Ieuan (Evan).
iii. Catherine Wen, d. s. p.

Pedigree XVI.

Richard Wynn, of Plas Ty Mawr and Trefechan, died after 1563; married Mary, daughter of William Edisbury, of Marchwiail.

> ISSUE:
> i. Robert, of Trefechan, living 1620.
> ii. Gruffydd; *oj whom presently.*
> iii. Richard, went to Kent, England.

Gruffydd Wynn, of Bryn yr Owen, married Elizabeth, daughter of John Sonlli, of Cord, in the parish of Wrexham, fourth son of John Sonlli, of Fron Deg. Her mother was Elizabeth, daughter of Edward ap Rhys, of Rhiwabon (Ruabon).

> ISSUE:
> i. John, d. s. p.
> ii. Robert Wynn, "went abroad"; supposedly to Pennsylvania, or the Carolinas.
> iii. Thomas Wynn,[1] "went to Maryland" before 1671. His descendants settled in Pennsylvania.
> iv. Elizabeth, married Richard Holland, of Wrexham; he died 1695. Admon. at St. Asaph Probate Registry.
> v. Jane, married Joseph Bromfield, of Wrexham.

---

[1] Thomas Wynn was in Maryland as early as 1671; he was Deputy Sheriff in 1678, and at one time Door-keeper of the Assembly.

THE LANDS OF EDWARD JONES AND COMPANY IN MERION.

An original draft and return of survey on file among the records at Harrisburg is of interest and value as showing the first subdivisions of the tract the outlines of which are represented on Holme's map of the Province of Pennsylvania and designated as the land of "Edward Jones and Company 17 Families," and on the original draft of the Welsh Tract "Edward Joans and Company Containg 2500 acres being 17 devisions." Attached to the draft is the certificate of David Powell, deputy surveyor, to the effect that the land was "laid out and subdivided" 1 mo. 25, 1684, in pursuance of a warrant from [Captain Thomas Holmes] the Surveyor-General dated the 24th day of the same month. We have some evidence, however, that the tract was subdivided nearly two years earlier by Charles Ashcom, then a deputy surveyor, for a note below the certificate reads "first p War^t per me dat^d 24th 6mo 82 directed to C Ashcom" and "After p War^t from ye Govr dat^d 22^d 1mo 83." In a letter from Edward Jones to John ap Thomas, dated "Skoolkill River ye 26th of ye 6 mo 1682," the first survey by Ashcom is evidently the one referred to in the following passage :

"Y^e name of town lots is called now Wicoco ; here is a Crowd of people striving for ye Country land, for ye town lot is not divided, & therefore we are forced to take up ye Country lots. We had much adoe to get a grant of it, but it Cost us 4 or 5 days attendance, besides some score of miles we traveled before we brought it to pass. I hope it will please thee and the rest yt are concerned, for it hath most rare timber, I have not seen the like in all these parts, there is water enough beside.

THE LANDS OF EDWARD JONES AND COMPANY 73

The end of each lot will be on a river as large or larger than the Dye at Bala, it is called Skool Kill River. I hope the Country land will within this four days [be] surveyed out. The rate for surveying 100 Acres [is] twenty shilling, but I hope better orders will be taken shortly about it."

At the date of this letter the summer was far advanced and the settlers were naturally anxious to have their allotments located as soon as possible. Owing to this urgency, it is likely that the original lines were hastily run and imperfectly marked on the ground, to correct which the subsequent warrants were obtained and the Powell survey of 1684 executed. Although several changes in title had been made prior to that date, they are not noted on the draft. It shows seventeen divisions, the several areas of which practically agree with the allotments called for in the original deeds to the seventeen grantees. Hence we may safely conclude that this draft shows the original subdivision that was being made on the ground, while Edward Jones was writing that "each lot will be on a river as large or larger than the Dye at Bala."

The seventeen persons concerned in this purchase had their homes in the neighbourhoods of Bala and Dolgelley, Merionethshire, Wales, and besides being neighbours and friends, were more or less connected by ties of blood and intermarriage. Prominent and respected citizens in their own country, those who came to Pennsylvania took a leading part in the development of the new colony, and many of their descendants have borne distinguished names in literature, science, and public affairs. Being all, by convincement, Quakers, and having suffered for many years much annoyance, loss of property, and even imprisonment by reason of the severe laws against non-conformists, they were among the first to appreciate and welcome the

---

NOTE.—This article, by Benjamin H. Smith, Esq., was printed in the "Pennsylvania Magazine," vol. xxvi., No. 101, April, 1902, and because it illustrates certain parts of the subject matter of this volume, is here inserted almost verbatim. A few corrections have been made in the text. The footnotes are mine.—T. A. GLENN.

"Concessions or Constitucons" published by William Penn July 11, 1681. In accordance therewith they subscribed one hundred pounds for the purchase of five thousand acres to be allotted and set out in the Province of Pennsylvania. The deeds of lease and release are dated September 16-17, 1681, the grantees named being John Thomas, of Llaithgwm, and Edward Jones, of Bala, who afterwards executed deeds, or declarations of trust, to the other contributors and to each other, covenanting to release and confirm the proportion of land to which each was entitled by reason of his contribution, as soon as the five thousand acres should be laid out.

The following is a list of the contributors in the order in which their names appear on the draft, with the dates of their deeds, amounts subscribed, and the number of acres to which each was entitled.

			£	s.	d.	Acres.
1.	John Thomas, of Llaithgwn[1]	Apr. 1, 1682	25	0	0	1250
2.	Hugh Roberts, of Kiltalgarth[2]	Feb. 28, 1681	12	10	0	625
3.	William ap Edward, of Ucheldre	Apr. 1, 1682	3	2	6	156¼
4.	Edward Rees, of Kiltalgarth	Apr. 1, 1682	3	2	6	156¼
5.	Edward Jones, of Bala	Apr. 1, 1682	6	5	0	312½
6.	Edward Owen, of Doleyserre[3]	Apr. 1, 1682	6	5	0	312½
7.	John ap Edward, of Nant Lleidiog[4]	Mch. 18, 1681	6	5	0	312½
8.	Robert David, of Gwernevel, Ismynydd[5]	Mch. 18, 1681	6	5	0	312½
9.	Rees John William, of Llanglynin[6]	Apr. 1, 1682	3	2	6	156¼
10.	Thomas Prichard, of Nant Lleidiog	Apr. 1, 1662	3	2	6	156¼
11.	Gainor Robert, of Kiltalgarth	Apr. 1, 1682	3	2	6	156¼

[1] Llaithgwm (not Llaithgwn), or Llaethgwm, a township in the parish of Llandderfel (formerly written Llanddervel), now, for civil purposes, in Llanfor, co. Merioneth (Hundred of Penllyn).

[2] Ciltalgarth, a township in the parish of Llanfor (formerly written Llanvawr, Llanfawr, &c.).

[3] Dolserey, a mansion and estate near Dolgelly, co. Merioneth.

[4] Nant-lleidiog, a township in Llanfor.

[5] Gwernefel (Ismynydd), a township in the parish of Llanycil.

[6] Llangelynin, a parish in the Hundred of Talybont, co. Merioneth.

THE LANDS OF EDWARD JONES AND COMPANY 75

			£	s.	d.	Acres.
12.	Cadwalader Morgan, of Gwernevel	Apr. 1, 1682	3	2	6	156¼
13.	Thomas Lloyd, of Llangower	Apr. 1, 1682	3	2	6	156¼
14.	William John, of Bettws	Apr. 1, 1682	3	2	6	156¼
15.	John Watkin, of Gwernevel	Apr. 1, 1682	3	2	6	156¼
16.	Hugh John, of Nant Lleidiog	Mch. 18, 1681	3	2	6	156¼
17.	Evan Rees, of Penmaen	Mch. 18, 1681	6	5	0	312½
			£100	0	0	5000

Having thus secured land rights in the new Province which would enable them to settle together in one place and at the same time afford means of support, these people made active preparations for the long voyage which was to separate them permanently from their old homes. The first to depart were Edward Jones, Edward Rees, Robert David, William ap Edward and probably his brother John ap Edward, and William John, with their families and servants, who arrived in the Schuylkill River 6 mo. 13, 1682, on the ship "Lyon," from Liverpool, John Compton, master, and, as we have seen, lost no time in selecting a suitable tract of land for their future homes. Remembering their native county in Wales, they called the new settlement Meirioneth or Merioneth (later Merion), which name, for some time, was confined to the tract under consideration. It extends along the city line from the Schuylkill River to a short distance beyond Overbrook, and northwestward to a point opposite Manayunk, having an average width of two miles. It includes Merion and Narberth on the main line, and Bala and Cynwyd Stations on the Schuylkill division of the Pennsylvania Railroad. The old Lancaster Road traverses the tract diagonally for two and a half miles.

The grant from William Penn carried with it the privilege of taking up "in the first great town or city" the proportion of ten acres for every five hundred acres purchased, which in this case amounted to one hundred acres. Edward Jones, in the letter above mentioned, says "ye town lot is not divided, & therefore we are forced to take up ye country lots." We accordingly find that the town lots were not surveyed at that time, and, on account of the urgent demand for "ye Country land," the remaining four thousand nine hundred acres could not be taken up in one place convenient to the city. It was determined, therefore, to locate half of the grant at once on the Schuylkill River, and have it subdivided so that each purchaser should have half of his allotment there. The draft shows how closely this plan was carried out, the areas of the several lots thereon aggregating two thousand four hundred and forty-four and three-quarters acres. According to modern surveys, the actual area is about three thousand two hundred acres. The other moiety of the grant was surveyed in Goshen by virtue of the general warrant for the survey of the Welsh Tract dated 1 mo. 13, 1684, and is shown on the draft of the Welsh Tract at the head of Chester Creek, bearing the name of "Griffith Owen and Comy 2400 acres." The one hundred acres of city lots appurtenant to the grant, denominated Liberty land, was surveyed in one tract in Blockley 2 mo. 23, 1692.

Upwards of twenty years elapsed before the titles to these Merion and Goshen lands were confirmed by patents, and in the meantime many changes both in ownership and boundries had been made, either through inheritance from the original owners or by sales or exchanges of lands, with or without formal conveyances. Taking up the subdivisions in the order shown on the draft, the following notes will illustrate some of the changes and furnish the names of subsequent owners, who should also have the credit of being among the first settlers of Merion.

1. Katherin Thomas ye Relict of John Thomas 612^a. John áp Thomas, of Llaithgwm, commot of Penllyn, trustee with Edward Jones, and owner of a one-fourth interest in the purchase, was not destined to come to

The Lands of Edward Jones and Company 77

Pennsylvania, but died at his home in Wales 3 mo. 3, 1683, having devised his rights in the twelve hundred and fifty acres to his four sons Thomas, Robert, Evan, and Cadwalader John (Jones) in equal shares. The widow Katherin,[1] with her children, accompanied by Hugh Robert and his wife Jane (verch Owen) and children, his sister Gainor Robert (ap Hugh), and probably Hugh John Thomas, Cadwalader Morgan, and John Roberts, of Caernarvon, arrived at Philadelphia about the middle of November, 1683, on the ship "Morning Star," from Liverpool, Thomas Hayes, master. Katherin Thomas settled upon the tract of six hundred and twelve acres, which had been laid out for her husband the preceding year, and which they called "Gelli yr Cochiad." The records show that she soon acquired other real estate. The following summer she purchased a dwelling-house, "lately erected," with one hundred and fifty acres on the west side of the Schuylkill in Philadelphia, between the lands of Barnabas Willcox and Joseph Harrison. Five years later she bought of Joseph Wood, of Woods Mount, Darby, five hundred acres of land on the Schuylkill, immediately north of the Merion land, the deed being dated December 10, 1689. This plantation was called "Glanrason," and doubtless was first settled and improved by Katherin Thomas or her sons. It is the tract bearing erroneously the name of William Sharlow on Holme's map. It was, however, first surveyed to William Wood 7 mo. 30, 1684, and confirmed by patent to his son Joseph in 1689. The next tract above, of five hundred acres, was the one surveyed at the same time to Sharlow, and was afterwards called "Mount

---

[1] She was also known as Katherin (or Catherine) Robert, the latter being her father's baptismal name. She was the second wife of John Thomas, of Llaithgwm, parish of Llandderfel, Penllyn; his first wife having been Ann Lloyd, sister to Dr. Edward Jones, of Bala. Ann was buried in the churchyard of Llandderfel, 31 Augt., 1665, before her husband became a Friend. Thomas Jones, the eldest son of John Thomas, and his sister, Elizabeth, who married Rees Evan (or Evans), of Penmaen, were by Ann.

Ararat Plantation." Robert Jones, son of Katherin, obtained a patent for one hundred and sixty-five acres of the Sharlow tract February 12, 1704. Katherin Thomas died 11 mo. 18, 1697, and her son Evan a month later.

The remainder of the John Thomas purchase was laid out in Goshen, on Chester Creek, between the lands of Hugh Robert and Edward Rees. Thomas,[1] Robert, and Cadwalader Jones obtained a patent for both the Merion and Goshen tracts 11 mo. 3, 1703, the former having been found, on resurvey, to contain six hundred and seventy-nine acres and the latter six hundred and thirty-five acres. Some of these lands still remain in possession of the family.

2. *Hugh Robart 306^a*. Hugh Roberts,[2] of Kiltalgarth, who arrived in Pennsylvania in November, 1683, settled with his family on the tract that had been allotted to him, containing three hundred and six acres. In addition, he bought the share of John Watkin 4 mo. 23, 1684, and the adjoining seventy-six and a half acres of William ap Edward 6 mo. 17, 1694. He soon became an extensive land-owner, the records showing conveyances from John ap John and Thomas Wynne for nine hundred acres, from Peter Young, of Bristol, for five hundred acres, from Francis Cook (in right of James Claypoole) for four hundred acres, and from Wood and Sharlow. These lands were surveyed in the upper part of the Welsh Tract and in Merion and Blockley. The Goshen tract, containing five hundred and forty-nine acres, was surveyed on Ridley Creek, between the lands of the Jones brothers first mentioned, John Roberts, and Griffith Owen. The upper

---

[1] Thomas Jones called his home Llaithgwm House, after his old home [Letter of Robert Vaughan.] Llaithgwm is a township, but there is a farm of the same name within it. Thomas ap Hugh, the father of John Thomas, lived on a farm called Wern Fawr, adjacent to Llaithgwm farm, but whether he held the latter also is doubtful. It is most probable that where John Thomas is described as of Llaithgwm, the township, not the farm, is intended to be understood.

[2] Ciltalgarth, a township, as well as a farm, in the parish of Llanfor.

THE LANDS OF EDWARD JONES AND COMPANY 79

portion, containing two hundred and ninety-five acres, was sold to Cadwalader Ellis, and the balance, containing on resurvey three hundred and thirty-eight acres, was confirmed by patent to the executors of Hugh Roberts, March 26, 1706. On March 23, 1701, Hugh Roberts obtained a patent for two hundred acres in Blockley, on the old Lancaster Road, which he called "Chestnut Hill," and where he resided until his death 6 mo. 18, 1702. This plantation, with adjoining lands purchased of Wood and Sharlow, was devised to his youngest son, Edward Roberts. A large part of these lands is now within the limits of Fairmount Park, that portion known as George's Hill having been presented to the city by Jesse and Rebecca George, whose ancestors derived their title from Edward Roberts.

Hugh Roberts devised his Merion lands to his sons Robert and Owen, who, on March 26, 1706, obtained patents for them in two tracts containing two hundred and twenty and two hundred and thirty-one acres respectively. By deed dated October 16, 1707, Robert Roberts, then residing in the Province of Maryland, conveyed the above two hundred and twenty acres to Edward Rees, together with ten acres at the head of Mill Creek, which had also been willed to him by his father under the name of "Clean John's Meadow." The tract conveyed to Edward Rees extended along the old Lancaster Road from the Merion Friends' Meeting-House to the junction of the Gulf Road. As to the two hundred and thirty-one acres comprising the easterly end of the original purchase, Ann Roberts, of Nantmell Township, Chester County, widow of Owen Roberts, conveyed the same to Jonathan Jones, of Merion, by lease and release October 13-14, 1726.

3. William Edward 76½ᵃ. William ap Edward[1]

---

[1] William ap Edward was, at the time of his removal to Pennsylvania, a resident of the township of Ucheldre, parish of Llanfor (anciently written Llanvawr, Llanfawr, &c.), in Penllyn, co. Merioneth. In March, 1672-3, he was tenant of a farm called Tythyn y Corne, alias Tythyn y Gessel, belonging to Evan Lloyd ap Rhydderch, of Garn, in the parish of Llanfor, and probably continued to live thereon until 1682.

or Bedward, son of Edward ap John, of Cynlas, near Bala, with his wife[1] Jane (verch John ap Edward) and daughters Elizabeth and Katherin, arrived in 1682 on the ship "Lyon," as before mentioned. The draft shows one hundred and fifty-three and a quarter acres in his name and that of his fellow-passenger Edward Rees, with the division line partly drawn. William ap Edward's half extended from that line to the Schuylkill, with the courses of the side lines changed to conform to a small stream flowing into the river, and on this tract he doubtless built his temporary cabin or dugout in the fall of 1682, in which the family continued to live until their removal to Blockley. The one hundred acres of Liberty land, surveyed in Blockley 2 mo. 23, 1692, as above related, were conveyed by the owners to William ap Edward 10 mo. 27, 1693, which may approximate the date of his removal. Having purchased other rights to Liberty land, he obtained a patent for the whole in one tract of two hundred and seven acres nine perches 3 mo. 4, 1702. The present suburban town of Overbrook is upon this land. William Edward conveyed his original purchase of seventy-six and a half acres in Merion to Hugh Roberts, 6 mo. 17, 1694, and his seventy-five acres in Goshen to Robert William, January 21, 1703. He continued to reside upon his Blockley plantation until his death in 1714, having devised the same to his only son Edward William, whose wife Ellin or Eleanor was the daughter of David Lawrence, of Haverford. William ap Edward's first wife, Katherin, was a daughter of Robert ap Hugh.

4. Edward Rees 76¾ª. Edward Rees, of Kiltalgarth,[2] settled in 1682 on the west half of the tract on which his name is associated with that of William Edward on the

---

[1] Jane was his second wife.

[2] Ciltalgarth Township. He was son of Richard Price, of Glanlloidiogin, parish of Llanfor, a brother-in-law of Rees John William, and a cousin to William, and John ap Edward.

THE LANDS OF EDWARD JONES AND COMPANY 81

draft. He purchased one hundred and twenty-five acres of the adjoining land of Thomas Lloyd, the Deputy-Governor, 5 mo. 5, 1691, and two acres of Edward Jones, which, with his original purchase, were confirmed to him by patent January 1, 1704, the three parcels containing together one hundred and ninety acres. The Merion Meeting-House lot occupies the northeast corner of this patent being divided from the main portion by the old Lancaster Road. Having purchased the adjoining plantation on the north, containing two hundred and twenty acres, of Robert Roberts in 1707, as before related, he granted one moiety of both tracts to the use of his son Rees Prees and his wife Sarah, only daughter of David Meredith, late of Plymouth, in a marriage settlement dated August 7th, 1705. Edward Rees sold his land in Goshen, together with seventy-eight acres bought of John William in 1697, to Ellis David January 9, 1707-8. This land was on Chester Creek, between the lands of Thomas Jones and brothers and Evan Jones and company, and, with other lands, was confirmed by patent to David Davis, son of Ellis, October 10, 1735. Edward Rees died at his home in Merion in 1728.

5. Edward Joans 153¼^a. Edward Jones, of Bala, Chirurgeon,[1] sometimes called Edward Jones, Senior, who arrived in 1682, was trustee with John ap Thomas, and took a leading part in the selection and subdivision of the land in Merion. The draft shows his own allotment as a narrow strip extending from the Schuylkill to the west boundary of the grant, but his patent for one hundred and fifty acres (4 mo. 22, 1703) comprises the west half only of that strip and the west half of the adjoining allotment of Edward Owen, implying an exchange in ownership before the date of the patent. At about the same time (4 mo. 21, 1703) he obtained a patent for the adjacent tract on the south containing one hundred and eighty-eight acres, which he

---

[1] Dr. Edward Jones (*viz.*, Edward Johns—meaning Edward, John's son), was son of John Lloyd, and brother-in-law of John Thomas, of Llaithgwm.

had purchased of Edward Jones, Junior. Dr. Edward Jones and Mary his wife were still living upon their Merion lands in 1731, when they gave them by deed to their son John Jones, who afterwards removed to Philadelphia, and sold the lands to Anthony Tunis in 1741. The road leading eastward from Merion Meeting-House forms part of the north boundary of this tract, which crosses the Pennsylvania Railroad near Narberth Station.

With the above patents to Edward Jones were included two tracts of one hundred and twenty-five acres and four hundred and two acres in Goshen, located to the eastward of Griffith Owen's land, the title to which was derived from his original purchase and rights bought of Edward Jones, Junior, and Richard ap Thomas. He sold three hundred acres of these lands to Robert Williams in 1707 and the balance to Ellis Williams in 1720. He also held a patent for one hundred and sixty-one acres in Blockley on the old Lancaster Road, adjoining the Merion line, and bounded by lands of William Edward, Jonathan Wynne, and Hugh Roberts. Dr. Edward Jones died in 1737, aged ninety-two years.

6. *Edward Owen 153¼ª*. The time of the arrival of Edward Owen is not known, but at the date of his deed (April 1, 1682) he is mentioned therein as *late* of Doley-serre[1] in the county of Merioneth, and may have been in Pennsylvania or on his way there at that early period. At that time the Merion lands had not been surveyed, which may account for his settlement at Duck Creek in New Castle County, at which place he resided when he executed (1 mo. 9, 1684-5) an assignment of his interest in his three hundred and twelve and a half acres to his brother Griffith Owen, "Practicioner in Physick," who in the mean time had settled upon the Merion allotment. By deed dated

---

[1] Dolserey, an estate near Dolgelley, co. Merioneth, belonging to his father, Robert Owen. His mother was Jane, daughter of Robert Vaughan, of Hengwrt, the Antiquary.

1 mo. 1, 1694, Dr. Griffith Owen conveyed the latter to Robert David, who owned the adjoining tract. It then comprised the east half of the lands of Edward Jones and Edward Owen, as shown upon the old draft. Griffith Owen, having purchased other land rights of Richard Davis, of Denbigh,[1] and of the Commissioners of Property, had the whole surveyed in one tract in Goshen containing seven hundred and seventy-five acres, which was confirmed to him by patent December 13, 1703. The Goshen Friends' Meeting-House and graveyard are located near the middle of this tract, the land having been granted by Griffith Owen to trustees for those uses. He afterwards conveyed thirty-three acres to Robert William, the deed being dated October 21, 1707. He also bought four hundred and forty-one acres in Goshen of John Fincher November 17, 1705, a tract which had been formerly surveyed to Hugh Roberts, but resurveyed and patented to Fincher by order of the Commissioners, May 27, 1705. Griffith Owen devised this land to his four daughters, Sarah Minshall, Rebecca Minshall, Jane Coppock, and Ann Whitpain, and the large tract to his three sons, John, Edward, and Griffith Owen, who in 1725 sold it to Stephen Beaks, of West Town. At that time the eldest son, John, was a "mariner," and Edward and Griffith "practicioners in physick" in Philadelphia. Dr. Griffith Owen's will is dated 1 mo. 15, 1716.

7. *Edward Joans Ju^r 153¼^a*. John ap Edward,[2] who probably arrived with his brother William on the ship "Lyon" in 1682, died the following year, and his eldest son, Evan, to whom his three hundred and twelve and a

---

[1] Is this not Richard Davies, of Welshpool?

[2] John ap Edward, of the township of Nant-lleidiog, parish of Llanfor, was the son of Edward ap John, of Cynlas (and Nant-lleidiog), and was baptized at Llandderfel, 19 June, 1635. Besides William ap Edward, already mentioned, there were two other brothers, Thomas ap Edward, of Cynlas, and Evan ap Edward. The latter's son, John Evans, or John Evan Edward, held a farm in Radnor, Pennsylvania, and married, 1686, Mary Hughes. See pedigree on another page.

half acres had been devised, having also died, the land descended to his surviving son and heir at law, Edward ap John, who was commonly called Edward Jones, Junior, to distinguish him from Edward Jones, Senior, the surgeon. The Merion allotment was traversed by the old Lancaster Road, and extended across the present line of the Pennsylvania Railroad between Merion and Narberth Station. Edward Jones, Junior, soon after attaining his majority, conveyed both his Merion and Goshen lands to Edward Jones, Senior, 2 mo. 13, 1703, as before mentioned.

8. *Robert David, 148½ᵃ.* Robert David,[1] of Gwernevel,[2] settled on the tract bearing his name on the draft in the fall of 1682 and lived there for fifty years. Having purchased the adjoining one hundred and fifty acres on the north (1 mo. 1, 1694) of Dr. Griffith Owen, he sold off twenty-five acres to Richard Walter in 1694 and obtained a patent for the remainder, containing two hundred and eighty acres, 5 mo. 20, 1703. In addition to his original purchase, Robert David bought one moiety, or one hundred and fifty-six and a quarter acres, of that of Evan Rees, of Penmaen, 5 mo. 28, 1683, seventy-five acres of which he sold to Richard Walter, December 1, 1694. The balance, together with his own rights and land purchased of Richard Thomas,[3] was surveyed in one tract of three hundred and forty-six acres in Goshen and included in the patent above mentioned. Robert David died in October, 1732, having devised his plantations in Merion and Goshen to his only son Thomas David.[4] The Goshen land was located on Chester Creek, between the tracts of Griffith Owen and John Roberts.

9. *Rees Joans, 76½ᵃ.* Rees John William, of Llangelynin, commonly appearing in the records as Rees John

---

[1] Robert David was the son of David ap Ellis, of Llanfor (d. 1679).
[2] Gwernefel Isymynydd, Llanycil.
[3] Of Whitford Garn, co. Flint.
[4] Or Davies ; see pedigree on another page.

The Lands of Edward Jones and Company 85

or Jones, arrived with his wife Hannah[1] and three children on the ship "Vine," of Liverpool, 7 mo. 17, 1684. Before leaving Wales he had purchased (July 16, 1684) the rights of Thomas Prichard to one hundred and fifty-six and a quarter acres, so that he was entitled, in all, to three hundred and twelve and a half acres. He settled upon the tract bearing the name of Thomas Richard[2] on the draft, and which includes the present site of Merion Station. By deed dated 4 mo. 18, 1694, he conveyed seventy-six and a half acres of his land on the Schuylkill to Cadwalader Morgan, who owned the adjacent land. Rees John William died in 1702, having devised his dwelling and plantation in Merion to his son Richard Jones, and his land in Goshen to his sons Evan and John Jones. The latter tract was on Chester Creek, between the lands of David Davis and Richard ap Thomas.

Richard Jones (November 8, 1720) bought thirty-nine and a half acres adjoining his Merion land, of John Roberts, a nephew of Thomas Lloyd, of Llangower, and having removed to Goshen, he and his wife Rebecca, by lease and release dated June 26-27, 1729, conveyed their Merion plantation, then containing one hundred and fifty-five acres, to Hugh Evans, in Merion. His tract of one hundred and fifty-seven acres in Goshen adjoined that of his brothers Evan and John, and was bounded by the lands of Griffith Owen and Thomas Lloyd. The title to a portion of this tract was derived from his uncle Evan John William, a purchaser under Richard Davies.

10. Thomas Richard, 76½ª. Thomas ap Richard,[3] or Prichard, did not come to Pennsylvania, but assigned his rights in the purchase to Rees John William, July 16, 1684, as above related.

---

[1] Sister to Edward Rees.
[2] Son of Richard Price, of Llanfor.
[3] Thomas ap Richard, of the township of Nant-lleidiog, parish of Llanfor, was the brother of Edward Rees, or Price, and of Hannah, wife of Rees John William, they being the children of Richard Price (Prees, or ap Rees), of Glanlloidiogin, Llanfor. See "Merion," Glenn, 77.

11. Gaynor Robart, 76½ᵃ. Gainor Robert, of Kiltalgarth,[1] spinster, was a passenger, with her brother, Hugh Robert, on the ship "Morning Star." She became the wife of John Roberts, of Carnarvonshire, 1 mo. 20, 1684. John Roberts arrived at Philadelphia 9 mo. 16, 1683, probably also on the "Morning Star," and settled at the place he called Pencoid, which is on the easterly end of the tract bearing the name of Evan Rees on the draft, which land he held in right of his wife's original purchase, and it has ever since continued in possession of the family. Under the notice of Robert David (No. 8) it was mentioned that Evan Rees, of Penmaen, by deed dated 5 mo. 28, 1683, had assigned one moiety of his purchase to Robert David, the Merion portion of which was the half of the tract, or seventy six and a half acres, next the Schuylkill. But as this half was soon after in possession of John Roberts and wife, and the original tract of Gainor Robert, of the same area, in the ownership of Robert David, we may, in the absence of records, infer that an exchange of the lands was made at about that time. By deed dated December 1, 1694, Robert David conveyed the last-mentioned tract (originally Gainor Robert's), with twenty-five acres adjacent, to Richard Walter, who obtained a patent for the same 4 mo. 8, 1703, the area on resurvey proving to be one hundred and seventeen acres. This land is on the old Lancaster Road about half a mile north of the city line.

John Roberts purchased (7 mo. 7, 1687) the Goshen allotments of Hugh John and Cadwalader Morgan, containing one hundred and fifty-six acres, which, with the land there in right of his wife, was resurveyed by warrant dated 10 mo. 22, 1701, and found to contain two hundred and sixty-

---

[1] Township of Ciltalgarth, parish of Llanfor.

THE LANDS OF EDWARD JONES AND COMPANY 87

two acres. This land was on Chester Creek, between the large tract of Hugh Roberts on the east and the land of Robert David on the west.

12. Cadwalader Morgan, 76½ª. Cadwalader Morgan,[1] of Gwernevel, also probably a passenger on the "Morning Star" in 1683, settled with his family on his Merion allotment on the Schuylkill, and increased his holding by purchase of the adjoining seventy-six and a half acres of Rees John William on the north and west, and the seventy-six and a half acres of John Williams (son of William John) on the southeast, the deeds being dated 4 mo. 18, 1694. This land was all resurveyed in one tract of two hundred and twenty-three and a half acres in 1701. Cadwalader Morgan bought the adjoining land of Hugh Jones (Hugh John Thomas), containing ninety-two acres, January 19, 1707-8, and on May 30, 1709, sold both tracts to Robert Evans. These lands afterwards passed into possession of the Roberts family. Cadwalader Morgan died in Merion in 1711.

13. Thomas Lloyd, 76½ª. Thomas Lloyd, of Llangower Parish, Penllyn,[2] devised his share in the purchase to his nephew John Roberts, who sold the east end of the Merion tract, containing thirty-seven and a half acres, to Griffith John prior to 1703, and the west end, containing thirty-nine and a half acres, to Richard Jones, November 8, 1720. At that time John Roberts and Mary his wife lived in Cheltenham Township, Philadelphia. John Roberts held about one hundred and fifty-three acres in Goshen, half in right of Thomas Lloyd and half through a grant or gift from Evan John William, who had purchased one

---

[1] Cadwalader (or Cadwaladr) Morgan, of Gwernefel Ismynydd, parish of Llanycil, where he was a tenant farmer, was the son of Morgan Cadwaladr, of the adjacent parish of Llanfor (d. 1696) and Ellen vch. William, his wife. See pedigree on another page. Ellen vch. William was probably the daughter of William Owen, of Llanfor, and sister to Elizabeth Williams, mother of Hugh Roberts.

[2] Son of John Lloyd.

hundred and fifty-six and a quarter acres of Richard Davies in 1682. Thomas Lloyd did not emigrate to Pennsylvania.

14. William Joans, 76½ª. It is not certainly known that William John, of Bettws,[1] ever settled upon his Merion allotment. His nuncupative will, proved 1 mo. 1, 1685, furnishes us with the names of his four children, John, Alice, Katherine, and Gwen William, who had chosen Hugh Roberts and John Roberts, of Merion, feoffees in trust. By deed poll dated 4 mo. 18, 1694, the son, John William, conveyed the Merion tract to Cadwalader Morgan, and the seventy-eight acres in Goshen to Edward Rees 6 mo. 13, 1697, who sold the same to Ellis David[2] January 7, 1707-8.

15. John Wattkin, 76½ª. John Watkin, of Gwernevel,[3] Bachelor, by deed dated 4 mo. 23, 1684, conveyed his Merion and Goshen lands to Hugh Roberts, who (5 mo. 26, 1688) conveyed the seventy-six and a half acres in Merion, shown upon the draft, to Abel Thomas, who was probably the first settler thereon.

16. Hugh John Thomas 76½ª. Hugh John Thomas,[4] of Nant-lleidiog, Parish of Llanvawr (Llanfor) commonly known as Hugh Jones, and probably a passenger on the ship "Morning Star," settled upon the tract allotted to him soon after his arrival. He obtained a patent for his land November 8, 1703, the resurvey making the area ninety-two acres. Hugh Jones removed to Plymouth, and by deed dated January 19, 1707-8, in which his son-in-law Rowland Richard joined, he conveyed his Merion plantation to Cadwalader Morgan. Hugh Jones sold his seventy-eight acres in Goshen to John Roberts, of Pencoyd, as before related.

---

[1] In the parish of Llanfor.
[2] He was of Gwynedd.
[3] Parish of Llanycil. He was probably a cousin of John and William ap Edward, and a descendant of Watkin ap Edward, of Garth Llwyd, Llandderfel.
[4] He was a first cousin to William and John ap Edward.

The Lands of Edward Jones and Company 89

*17. Evan Rees 153¼*ᵃ. Evan Rees, of Penmaen, by deed dated July 28, 1683, conveyed one moiety of his three hundred and twelve and a half acres to Robert David and one moiety to Griffith John, and his name is no further associated with the settlement of Merion.[1] The moiety conveyed to Robert David has already been noticed. Griffith John, having purchased, in addition, thirty-seven and a half acres of John Roberts, the nephew of Thomas Lloyd, obtained a patent for the whole in one tract of one hundred and ninety-two acres, November 8, 1703. This land was on the old Lancaster Road, next the city line, and included the easterly ends of the allotments of Thomas Lloyd and John Watkin and part of the west half of that of Evan Rees, as shown on the draft. Griffith John was a son of John ap Evan,[2] and therefore first cousin to Jane (verch Owen), the wife[3] of Hugh Roberts. He was the first settler on his Merion land, and resided there until his death in 1707. He devised his dwelling and plantation to his son John Griffith, who married Grace Foulke, and whose descendants continued to occupy the land for many years.

---

[1] This statement needs modification. Evan Rees was the father of Rees Evan, of Penmaen, Llanfor, who married Elizabeth, eldest daughter of John Thomas, of Llaithgwm. The children of Rees Evan and Elizabeth were: Evan, John, David, and Sydney, who assumed the surname of Rees. Evan, who may not have been the eldest, removed to Pennsylvania after 1700, and purchased land in Merion, where he died in 1752. David Rees also came to Merion, and their sister, Sydney, became the wife of Robert Roberts, son of John, of Pencoid. The family held a small estate in Penmaen township, Llanfor, Penllyn, called Fron Ween, which seems to have descended to John Rees, the other brother, who may have been the eldest son. See pedigree on another page.

[2] John ap Evan, otherwise John Evan, was of the township of Penmaen, parish of Llanfor, Penllyn, co. Merioneth, yeoman, and was son of Evan Robert Lewis. His will, in which he describes himself as John Evan, of Penmaen, in the parish of Llanvawr (Llanfor), county of Merioneth, yeoman, is dated 4 Augt., 1696, and was proved at St. Asaph, 24 April, 1697. See pedigree in vol. ii.

[3] First wife. Hugh Roberts married, secondly, whilst on a visit to Wales, Elizabeth John, widow.

PEDIGREE XVII.

Ednowain Bendew,[1] lord of Tegeingl, a district in Flintshire, North Wales. According to the book of Ednop, he was lord of Tegeingl in 1079, and by Peter Ellis is said to have been the head of the Fifteenth Noble Tribe of North Wales. We find amongst the pedigrees attested by Gutyn Owain and others, that the name which genealogists call Ednowain Bendew, or Eden Owain Bendew, or Owain Bendew, is really Edwal ab Owen (or Owain) Bendew.

The Welsh records tell us little about him except that "he was brave, for he killed a wild boar without help." Bendew signifies the thick or strong-skulled.

Ednowain Bendew lived at a place called Llys y Coed, in the parish of Bodfari, and he is said to have held all of the parish of Bodfari and the adjoining parishes of Ysceifiog[2] and Caerwys, his descendants holding these lands *per baroniam.*

Madog ap Ednowain Bendew,[2] of the parish of Bodfari, called lord of Tegeingl. He married Arddyn, daughter of Bradwen, and a sister of Ednowain ap Bradwen, of Merionethshire. Her brother was living 1194. The following account of Ednowain ap Bradwen is taken from a MS. of about the middle of the seventeenth century.[3]

---

[1] "Royal Tribes of Wales," Yorke, 203-4; "Arch. Camb.," 5 Ser., vol. 8, 252, &c.; Dwnn, ii., 83.

[2] "Arch. Camb." 4 Ser., vii., 201; Dwnn, ii., 304; Add MSS., 9865, B. M.; Pennant; Blakeway MSS.

Madog is supposed to have given his name to Bron Vadog, or Bron Fadog,—*viz.,* Madog's Hill, in Ysceifiog, the home of some of his descendants.

NOTE.—This pedigree is abstracted from "Ancestry of Dr. Thomas Wynne," by Richard Y. Cook, Esq., of Philadelphia, compiled from searches made by the writer some years ago. A few alterations in the spelling of names of persons and places have been made, for the sake of uniformity, as, in old records, Welsh names are spelled in every conceivable way.

[3] "Cambrian Register," 1796; Dwnn, ii., 238.

Pedigree XVII.

" Ednowen ap Bradwen is by many writers called Lord of Merionydd, but I apprehend erroneously, for the Princes and their issue were always Lords of Merionydd. How be it, it might be that he (as others) took the same to farm, and therefore might be called Lord thereof. Yet certain it is that he and his issue were possessed of all Talybont, save Nanney and Prince's, Demesnes, and for the most part of the hundred of Estimaner in like manner. He is said to have lived in Gruffydd ap Cynan's time. The ruins of his house, Llys Bradwen, are to be seen in the township of Cregenan, in the hundred of Talybont Iscregenan. Llewelyn ap Tudor ap Gwyn ap Peredur ap Ednowain ap Bradwen, lived in the time of Edward the First, and did him homage with the Lords and gentry of Wales, as by the said King's records is manifest."

At the time of so doing homage Llewelyn produced his pedigree, with other evidences of his title to Talybont, which was recorded by David, Scrivenor to Iorwerth son of this Llewelyn as follows :

William Lleyn, the bard, out of an old book written in the days of Edward the First, by one David, Scrivenor to one Iorwerth ap Llewelyn ap Tudor, a descendant of this chief (Bradwen) gives the Bradwen pedigree thus : Bradwen ap Mael ap Bleddyn ap Morudd ap Cynddelw ap Cyfnerth ap Cadifor ap Run ap Mergynawc ap Cynfawr ap Hefan ap Cadifor ap Maeldaf hynaf ap Unwch Unarchen ap Ysbwys ap Ysbwch, which Ysbwys and Ysbwch, father and son, came into this island out of Spain with Aurelius Ambrosius, and Uther, A.D. 466, and first inhabited Moelysbidion Viyo, the Stranger's Mount, and when Aurelius had recovered his crown from Vortigern, the Usurper, he rewarded those men, being his retinue, with the whole hundred of Talybont, and part of Estimaner in Merinethshire, where their posterity flourish to this day.[1] Madog, Lord of Tegeingl, had issue by his said wife (*inter al.*):

---
[1] " Royal Tribes of Wales," Yorke, 206, 207.

Iorwerth ap Madog, of Bodfari and Ysceifiog in Tegeingl, who married Arddyn,[1] the daughter of Llewelyn ap Owain ap Edwin. The unfortunate person named Owain (above) obtained the undesirable cognomen of "Vradwr" (or the traitor), have joined Hugh, Earl of Chester, against his son-in-law, Prince Gruffydd ap Cynan. He died at the commencement of the twelfth century, from a disease of the lungs. Edwin of Tegeingl was founder of one of the Noble tribes of North Wales; was slain 1075, and buried at Northrop. Iorwerth ap Madog was succeeded by his son.

Rhirid ap Iorwerth, of the parish of Bodfari and Ysceifiog, who married Tibot, daughter of Robert de Pulford. The family of Pulford was seated for several generations at Pulford in the county of Chester. This Robert de Pulford was enfeoffed in the castle and demesne lands of Pulford by Ralph, son of Simon de Ormsby, or de Pulford, in the year 1240, so that his daughter and her husband must have been living 1240 to 1300. These dates are from original deeds. It is supposed that Rhirid was married about 1240. Rhirid ap Iorwerth had issue (*inter al.*):

Iorwerth ap Rhirid,[2] of the parishes of Bodfari and Ysceifiog, who died prior to 1339. He married Nest, daughter and heiress of Iorwerth ap Grono ap Einion ap Seissyllt. This lady's grandfather, Grono, married Middyfis, daughter of Owain Cyfeiloc, of Powys. It appears by an inquisition taken at Bala, on the next Monday after the Feast of St. Michael,[3] 6 Henry VI. (6 Oct., 1427) "*Quod quidam Eignion ap Seyssyllt fuit seisitus in dominico suo ut de feodo de tota terra quod fuit et est*

---

[1] "Arch. Camb.," 4 Ser., viii., 51, etc. This does not, however, or do other pedigrees, accord with Dwnn, ii., 304. The above, however, appears to be correct.

[2] Dwnn, ii., 304; but marriage there given erroneous, according to "Arch Camb.," 4 Ser., viii., 52, 53; "Arch. Camb.," 5 Ser., viii., 258-9; Col. Jones MS, pedigree, College of Arms.

[3] "Arch. Camb.," 4 Ser., viii., 54; Dwnn, ii., 222; "History of Powys Fadog."

Pedigree XVII.

inter aquas de Dyvi et Dewlas, tempore Llewelyn ap Iorweth nuper principis, et quod terra illa tunc fuit pars et parcella Comoti de Estimaner in Comitatu Merioneth, et adhuc de jure," &c.

Iorwerth ap Rhirid had issue (*inter al.*):

Rotpert ap Iorwerth, of Bodfari and Ysceifiog. He married Adles, daughter of Ithel Vychan, of Mostyn, ap Ithel Lloyd ap Ithel Gam ap Maredydd ap Uchtred ap Edwin, of Tegeingl. Her mother being Adleis, sole heiress of Richard ap Cadwaladr, lord of Ceredigion. Rotpert ap Iorwerth was living 1339, and his brother, Gwyn, in 1313. Ithel Vychan was living temp. Edward I. Rotpert (or Robert) ap Iorwerth had issue:

    i. Ithel Vychan, Archdeacon of Tegeingl, living 1375, 1393; d.s.p.
    ii. Cynric (Kynveig); *of whom presently.*
    iii. Llewelyn ap Robert.

Cynric ap Rotpert,[1] of Bodfari and Ysceifiog, in both of which parishes he held lands, married several times. By his second wife, Angharad, daughter of Gruffydd Vychan, he had a daughter, Gwerfyl, who married 1st., Thomas ap Madoc, of Eyton, and 2dly., Iorwerth ap Simon. His first wife Angharad, daughter of Madog Lloyd of Bryncunallt, ap Iorwerth Voel, descended from Tudor Trevor.[2] We are told that Cynric, brother of the Archdeacon, " went to live at Caerwys, and having married a descendant of Prince David, so cruelly murdered by the English [?], was father of Ithel Vychan, a surname given him to distinguish him from his uncle, the Archdeacon."[3] He had issue by his first wife:

    i. Ithel Vychan; *of whom presently.*
    ii. David, m. Nest, dau. of Meuric Lloyd, of Nannau.
    iii. Rhys.

---

[1] Dwnn, ii., 304; "Arch. Camb." 4 Ser., viii., 56.
[2] Ibid., vi., 38.
[3] Ibid., 5 Ser., viii., 258-9; Hengwrt MS. 96.

NOTE.—The wife of Cynric ap Rotpert was descended from Emma Plantagenet, sister of Henry II., of England, and daughter of Geoffrey Plantagenet, Count of Anjou.

Ithel Vychan,[1] of Holt Denbigh and Northrop, in right of his wife, and of Bodfari and Ysceifiog, married the heiress of Robin, brother of Robert ancestor of the Gwydir family, and descended from Owain Gwynedd, Prince of North Wales. This Robert was alive 9 Henry IV., 1304. "The History of the Gwydir Family," by Sir John Wynn, states that: "John Tudor, one of our Welsh Heralds, sayeth that there was a third brother called Robin, whose daughter and heire Ithel Vaughan married, and therefor those descended from him doe quarter Owen Gwynedd's Egletts." John Tudor died 1602 and was a very noted and skilful herald.

After his marriage, Ithel Vychan went to live upon his wife's estate at Holt, in Denbighshire. His great-grandson, Richard, was living at Holt in 1488, but *his* son William succeeded his uncle, John, at Chilton in Shropshire, which had been granted by Henry VII. to his branch of the family for services on Bosworth Field, together with a new coat of arms of the tinctures borne by Henry himself in this battle, *viz.* : *Argent and vert.*

ISSUE :
i. Cynric, *of whom presently.*
ii. David.

Cynric ap Ithel Vychan,[2] of Bodfari and Ysceifiog, living after 1420, married Tanglwyst, daughter and heiress of Gruffydd Lloyd ap David ap Maredydd ap Gruffydd. Other authorities state that he also married a daughter of Gruffydd ap David ap Maredydd ap Rhys. He had by one or the other of these wives issue as follows :

i. John.
ii. Rhys.
iii. Harri, *of whom presently.*

---

[1] Dwnn, ii., 304 ; "Arch. Camb.," 5 Ser., viii., 260; "History of the Gwydir Family," Wynne.

[2] Dwnn, ii., 304; "Arch. Camb.," 5 Ser., viii., 58.

Pedigree XVII.

Harri ap Cynric,[1] of Ysceifiog,[2] was born probably about 1485, and was a man of very considerable standing in his county. Bron Vadog, in Ysceifiog, appears to have been a part of his possessions.

Harri ap Cynric married Alice, daughter of Simon Thelwall,[3] of Plas yn Ward, Esq., by Janet, daughter of Edward Langford, of Ruthin, in the county of Denbigh.

This Simon Thelwall was son unto David Thelwall of Plas yn Ward, by Tibot, or Tabitha, daughter of Jenkin de Weild, of Borasham.

The Langford family was of Allington and Ruthin, in Denbighshire. John Langford was constable of the Castle of Ruthin, and steward of Dyffryn Clwyd, and his son, Richard Langford, was likewise constable of the same castle, and died 12 July, 1466. He was succeeded by his son, Edward Langford, constable of Ruthin Castle, who died 16 Henry VII., and whose wife, Eleanor, daughter of John Dutton, of Dutton, died 5 Edward IV.

ISSUE:
i. John Wynne ap Harri, *of whom presently.*
ii. Thomas ap Harri, of Ysceifiog, who had issue, *inter al.*, Rees Wynne ap Thomas ap Harri, of Ysceifiog, who had Thomas Wynne, baptized 1581, and other issue.[4]

John Wynne ap Harri[5] was of the parish of Ysceifiog, where he was born and where he died, probably prior to

---

[1] Dwnn, ii., 304.

[2] I cannot find that he held any considerable lands, if any at all, in the parish of Bodfari, and the farms there seem to have gone to his brothers. Rhys ap Cynric, called Rees Wyn (Wynne), was of the township of Aberwhiler, or Aberweeler, in Bodfari. He was born 1487, and had several sons who were freeholders there. One of them, John ap Rees Wyn, was buried at Bodfari, 1607, aged 93 years. Harri ap Cynric, however, was possessed of part of Ysceifiog, including Bron Vadog, the home of Dr. Thomas Wynne, to whose immediate family it descended.

[3] Dwnn, ii., 304; "History Powys Fadog," iv., 306.

[4] Bodfari parish register.

[5] Dwnn, ii., 304; Lay Subsidy Rolls and other records.

1572. He married Katherine, daughter and heiress of Ithel ap Jenkin ap David ap Howel, and had issue by her:

    i. John Wynne, called also John ap John, Vicar of Caerwys, who left issue.
    ii. Ellis Wynne.
    iii. Griffith (or Gruffydd) Wynne.
    iv. Howel ap John Wynne, m. Jane, daughter of Thomas Gruffydd, and had by her John, father of Rees Wynne, of Galedlom, Hugh, Rees, and Lowry.
    v. Ithel ap John Wynne, of Ysceifiog, whose son, Rees, was assessed as a landholder there in 1592.
    vi. Rees ap John Wynne; *of whom presently.*
    vii. Margare m. Thomas Ellis.
    viii. Alice, m. John Benet.
    ix. Tabitha, m. Ieuan ap Richard.
    x. Gwen, m. 1st Howel ap David.
    xi. Jane, m. Robert ap Griffith (or Gruffydd) Lloyd.
    xii. Elizabeth, d. unm.
    xiii. Gwensi, d. unm.

Rees ap John Wynne was born in the parish of Ysceifiog, *circa* 1538, and is assessed as a freeholder there in the subsidy of 1592, being the 2d payment of the 2d subsidy, for the Hundred de Ruthllan. The date of his death is unknown.[1] His wife's name not ascertained. Rees ap John Wynne had issue:

    i. John ap Rees ap John Wynne; *of whom presently.*
    ii. Edward ap Rees ap John Wynne; baptd. 2 July, 1572.
    iii. Harri ap Rees ap John Wynne; baptd. 6 March, 1574.
    iv. Catherine; baptd. 1 March, 1577.
    v. Janett; baptd. 2 November, 1579.
    vi. Jane; baptd. 10 June, 1581.
    vii. Hugh ap Rees ap John Wynne; baptd. 19 February, 1583.

---

[1] It should be noted that he died in the parish of Ysceifiog (spelled also in old records, Yskeiviog, Sceiviog, Skivog, etc.), and was doubtless buried at the church belonging to that parish. A number of records concerning his immediate family are, however, in the parish register at Bodfari, for the reason that when Ysceifiog parish happened to be without a vicar, the parishioners, buried, baptized and married at Bodfari, or else the Rector of Bodfari conducted services at Ysceifiog, which happened very frequently. The earlier records of Ysceifiog (prior to 1662) have been lost. The Register of Bodfari contains an entry of the burial of a Rees John Wynne, a freeholder of Aberwheeler, 20 February, 1901, but this was a kinsman, as explained *ante.*

NOTE.—The name is here spelled, for the purpose of uniformity, *Wynne,* but upon the records it is written in many different ways, as *Winne, Wynn, Wyn,* &c.

Pedigree XVII.

John ap Rees Wynne, of the parish of Ysceifiog, was born *circa* 1570. The records of Bodfari begin in 1572, and the living of Ysceifiog appears to have been vacant for several years about this time.

He married at Bodfari Church, 29 October, 1588, Grace Morgan. The entry in the Parish Register reads as follows: "(1588) *John ap Rees ap John Wynn and Grace vc. Morgan were married the XXIXth October.*" The exact date of his death is unknown, but it was prior to 1640. He was prominent in the affairs of his county, and esteemed a wealthy and influential man. The children of John ap Rees Wynne were:

    i. Thomas ap John Wynne; baptd. 20 December, 1589; *of whom presently.*
    ii. Mary; baptd. 10 March, 1590.
    iii. Jane; baptd. 9 June, 1595.

Thomas ap John Wynne, of the parish of Ysceifiog, was born 1589, and baptised 20 December, 1589, at the parish church of Ysceifiog.[1] He lived at Bron Vadog in this parish, where he died in the year 1638-9.[2] During the years which preceded the civil war in England he suffered severely from taxes and fines imposed so unjustly during that period. The name of his wife is unknown. Thomas ap John Wynne had issue:

    i. Harri; baptd. 6 November, 1619.
    ii. Edward; baptd. 9 April, 1622.
    iii. John; baptd. 13 April, 1625; removed to Pennsylvania with his brother, Dr. Thomas Wynne, in 1682. Nothing else is known of him, except that he was bred to the law and practised as an attorney in Sussex County (now Delaware).
    iv. Thomas; baptd. 20 July, 1627; *of whom presently.*
    v. Peter; baptd. 30 January, 1630.

---

[1] Bodfari parish register.
[2] There is a record of a burial of a Thomas ap John Wynne, 7 October, 1633, in Bodfari records, but this was clearly a cousin. It must be remembered that the entries in the Bodfari register relating to Ysceifiog only occur when the latter parish was without a vicar, and that the records of Ysceifiog itself are missing.

Dr. Thomas Wynne, the son of Thomas ap John Wynne, of Bron Vadog,[1] in the parish of Ysceifiog, Flintshire (near Caerwys), was baptized 20 July, 1627. About the year 1655-7 he married, as his first wife, Martha Buttall, of the Buttalls of Wrexham. She was the sister of Jonathan Buttall, of Battersea, County of Surrey, whose will was proved at London, 19 September, 1695. Martha Wynne died 1670. Dr. Wynne married, secondly, Elizabeth Rowden, who died in 1676, and he then married, thirdly, 20th of 5th month, 1676, Elizabeth Maude, of Rainhill, Lancashire, who survived him.

Thomas Wynne took great interest in the religious society of which he was an early member. He became an able minister and appears to have visited various places giving forth his religious views. In 1677 he wrote a pamphlet on : *" The Antiquity of the Quakers, proved out of the Scriptures of Truth. Published in Love to the Papists, Protestants, Presbyterians, Independents and Anabaptists. With a Salutation of Pure Love to all the Tender-hearted Welshmen. But more especially to Flintshire, Denbighshire, Caernarvonshire and Anglesea. By their Countryman and Friend, Thomas Wynne." Printed in the year* 1677.

Besides the English part, this address contains two pages of Welsh. He signs himself your real friend, Thomas Wynne. These words are added : *" Y Llythyr i anner chfy an wy i wladwyr y Cymru."*[2]

Carwys y 4 *mis yr ail dydd* 1677.

A Welshman named William Jones wrote a reply to this pamphlet.

In the front of this reply there is a curious, finely etched portrait of Thomas Wynne tempted by the Devil.

---

[1] Bron Vadog, or as it is now usually written, Bron Fadog, is, in English, Madog's Hill, and was probably so called from having been the home of Madog ap Ednowain ap Bradwen, the remote ancestor of Dr. Thomas Wynne.

[2] This is very incorrect Welsh.

PEDIGREE XVII. 99

In 1679 Thomas Wynne printed: *An Anti-Christian Conspiracy Detected and Satan's Champion Defeated. Being also a vindication of my Book entitled The Antiquity of the Quakers, From the Base Insinuations, False Doctrine and False Charge therein contained against me, my Book and against God's People, called Quakers in general. By me Thomas Wynne.*[1]

Thomas Wynne was a successful Chirurgeon and "Practitioner in Physics," the latter being what he styles himself in his will. He is said to have practised in London. Thomas Wynne was also well versed in the law.

Richard Davies, in his autobiography, writing of one of his visits to North Wales in 1681, says: "I acquainted my friend William Penn and some Friends that I intended to give Bishop Lloyd a visit." [This was Dr. William Lloyd, who had been in charge of St. Martin's in London, afterwards Bishop of St. Asaph.] "I went to my friend Thomas Wynne's, who lived in [near] Caerwys, in Flintshire,[2]

---

[1] It's known to many now living, in this my Native Country wherein I live (and it being also near the place where I was Born), that my genious from a Child did lead me to Surgery, insomuch that before I was Ten Years old, I several times over-ran my School and Home when I heard of any one's being wounded or hurt, & used all my endeavours, then to see Fractures and Dislocations reduc'd, and Wounds dressed, and have been so long missing, that my Parents thought they had lost me, for which I underwent severe Correction, and the troublesome Times being then, my Parents sustained great Plunder, and my Father dyed before I was Eleven Years old, and my Mother not being then able to produce so great a Sum of Money as to set me to Chyrurgery, I betook my self to this honest & necessary Calling, with several other things that in those dayes pleased my mind; yet during all this time, I lost no opportunity to inform my self in the Practice of Chyrurgery, and continued thus until I became acquainted with an honest Friend, and good Artist in Chyrurgery, whose Name was *Richard Moore of Salop*, who seeing my forwardness to Chyrurgery, did further me in it, and brought me to Desections in Salop ; the Anatomists being men of known worth in that Practice, whose Names are *Dr. Needham* and *Dr. Hollins,* who at this day are doubtless of deserved Repute in their Professions (in *England*), and I being then expert in Drills, and Handy in Knife and Lancet, & other Instruments for that purpose, I set on making a Skellton of a mans Bones, which I only with the assistance of *Richard Moore* performed to their content, at which time they thought me fit to be Licensed the practice of Chyrurgery, and this is near 20 Years ago, and soon after I being taken a Prisoner to *Denbigh,* where I remained a Prisoner near six years for the Testimony of Jesus, I then betook my self wholly to the Practice of Chyrurgery.—[*Dr. Thomas Wynne's Reply, 1679.*]

[2] This was after his removal from Bronvadog, Ysceifiog, his native place.

not far from the bishop's palace, and he went with me. When we came there the bishop's secretary came to the gate. I asked him whether the bishop was within; he said he was. . . . . . . The Bishop sent for us, in there were several clergymen with him, among the rest the dean of Bangor. . . . . We went soon to dispute about water-baptism. I told them, there was one Lord, one faith and one baptism. . . . . . So this and such like discourse, held us till it was late at night, and then I went to my friend's house."

In the early part of the year 1682 there was a committee appointed to visit Whitehall to try to induce Lord Hyde, Sir Lionel Jenkins, Secretary of State, and others in authority, to influence the king to relieve the sufferings of the Friends of Bristol. The three friends on the committee from the country were Charles Lloyd, Thomas Wynne and Richard Davies. Before this Thomas Wynne was a resident of Bron Vadog, or Bronvadog, and was one of the overseers of the will of John ap Thomas, which was dated 9th February, 1682, being styled "Thomas Wynne, late of Bronvadog, near Caerwys, in the county of fflynt churyrgeon." Ysceiviog, the parish in which this place is located, is four miles southwest of Holywell, on the road from Nannerch to Whitford.

Thomas Wynne in connection with John ap John, for themselves, as well as trustees for others, purchased from Penn 5,000 acres to be laid out in the Welsh Tract. The Proprietor departed from England in the sixth month, 1682, on the ship "Welcome."

Dr. Wynne was a passenger aboard, and practised his profession, administering medicine and relieving the sufferings of those overtaken by the smallpox, which broke out soon after leaving port.

At the preliminary Legislative Assembly held at Chester the 4th day of the 10th month, 1682, Nicholas Moore presided. Thomas Holmes, Surveyor General; Thomas

Wynne, William Clark and Edward Southbrin, were appointed a committee to desire the Governor to transmit a "Constitute" [Constitution.] The session lasted three days.

Among the various accounts which have been written of Philadelphia, one states that among the first brick houses built was that of Thomas Wynne. It was located on Front Street, west side, above Chestnut Street, the latter being for a short time called Wynne Street. Having some business to attend to in the old country, he laid before his monthly meeting, 1st of 5th month, the prospect he had of a visit with his wife to England.

It is supposed that Thomas Wynne accompanied Penn to England in the ketch "Endeavour," which sailed from Philadelphia the 12th of 6th month, 1684. On the 23d of 9th month, in London, William Gibson was buried. It was he who had written the postscript to the Doctor's last publication. On this occasion a meeting was held in White Hart Court Meeting-House. It is stated that more than a thousand persons were at the burial-place, when it was publicly said of the body "That it had been often beaten and imprisioned for Christ's sake." At another time, while Thomas Wynne and twenty-three others were on their way to the meeting-house at White-Hart Court they were arrested in Angel Court and sent to prison.

The length of time that Thomas Wynne remained in England is unknown. On his return he settled on an estate he had purchased at Lewes. He again took part in public affairs.

During the year 1688, while holding the position of Associate Justice of Sussex County, he was also a representative from that county in the Assembly at Philadelphia, This body met on the 10th day of 3d month. In the same year on the 6th of 5th month Rachel Lloyd, a daughter of Thomas Lloyd, Deputy-Governor of the Province, was married to Samuel Preston, a meeting being held for that purpose at the house of Frances Cornwall, in Sussex. Among the signers to the marriage certificate were Thomas Wynne, his wife and children. In the year 1691 Dr. Wynne was in Philadelphia. He attended the Monthly Meetings held in the 11th month and 12th month. Soon after he was taken sick, and died. He was buried on the 17th of 1st month, 1692. He made his will on the "16th day of first month, 1691-1692." This was probated 2d month, 20th, 1692, at Philadelphia [Book A, p. 200.] In it he is called "Thomas Wynne, of Philadelphia, in the Province of Pennsylvania, practitioner in Physic." He gives his messuage and plantation, near the town of Lewes, to his wife, Elizabeth Wynne, during her natural life, after her death to his son Jonathan Wynne. He also gives to the latter the plantation of two hundred acres at Cedar Creek, in the County of Sussex. He gives one-half of his personal estate to his children in America, *viz.* : Jonathan, Mary, Rebecca, Sidney, and Hannah. His daughter Tabitha was living in England ; he gave her fifty shillings as a last mark of love. "She hath already sufficiently partaken of my fatherly care and tenderness of her." The other half of his personal estate he bequeathed to his beloved wife, Elizabeth, who was made executrix.

The Children of Thomas and Martha Wynne were :

i. Mary, born *circa* 1659 ; m. Dr. Edward Jones.
ii. Tabitha, remained in England and was probably married.
iii. Rebecca, born 1662 ; m. 1st, Solomon Thomas, in 3d mo., 1685, at Thirdhaven Meeting, Talbot County, Maryland, who d.s.p. 2dly, John Dickinson, of Talbot County, planter, at his house, 23d of 7 month, 1692. He was a son of Walter Dickinson, of Crosia-Doré, and an uncle of Samuel Dickinson, who married Mary Cadwalader, daughter of John Cadwalader and Martha Jones. The latter a daughter of Dr. Edward Jones and Mary Wynne.
iv. Sidney, m. 10th mo. 20th, 1690, William Chew, son of Samuel and Ann Chew, of that place.
v. Hannah, m. at Merion Meeting, 8 mo. 25th, 1695, Daniel Humphrey, son of Samuel and Elizabeth Humphrey.

Pedigree XVII.

vi. Jonathan, only son and heir. His will, dated January 29, 1719, was probated at Philadelphia, May 17, 1721. He married about the year 1694, Sarah [Graves or Greave?]. In the year 1705, on the 18th of 4th month, he applied to Edward Shippen, Griffith Owen and James Logan, Commissioners of Property, for a warrant for 400 acres in the Welsh Tract. He alleged that his father's joint purchase with John ap John of 5,000 acres was not fully taken up. His request was granted, and an order issued to David Powel, Surveyor. The latter part of his life he resided in Blockley township, Philadelphia County. He left to his eldest son, Thomas, all the home plantation after the death, or second marriage, of his widow. To his son, John, 250 acres near the Great Valley (Chester Valley). To son Jonathan, 250 acres in the same locality. To each of his two eldest daughters, Hannah and Mary, lot in High Street, Philadelphia, 60 x 300 ft., to be equally divided. To his three younger daughters, Sidney, Martha and Elizabeth, 400 acres near the Great Valley, "or in the great meadows," to be equally divided, with power to sell at 18 or marriage. His trustees were his brothers-in-law, Edward Jones and Daniel Humphrey; in case of their decease, John Cadwalader and Jonathan Jones. His wife, Sarah, executrix. JONATHAN WYNNE had THOMAS WYNNE 2d, of Merion and Blockley, who had ANNE WYNNE who married PHINEAS ROBERTS [1] of Merion, and had HANNAH ROBERTS, b. 1747, d. 1792; who married Lt. ABRAHAM STREEPER [2]—had MARY STREEPER, b. Oct. 28, 1770; d. Apr. 14, 1855, who married TITUS YERKES 2d,[3] and had MARY PAUL YERKES, b. June 12, 1814; d. Dec.

---

[1] John Roberts, the first of this family in Pennsylvania, was the son of Richard Roberts, of Cowyns, Parish of Llanengan, Carnarvonshire. John Roberts was born in 1648. He arrived in Pennsylvania 16th of ninth month, 1683. He bought land and settled at "Pencoid," in the Township of Merion, and married Gaynor, daughter of Robert Pugh, of Bala, Merionethshire. John Roberts became a very prominent man in the Colony. He held the office of Justice of the Peace and was elected to the Provincial Assembly.

ROBERT ROBERTS, only son of John and Gaynor Roberts, was b. December 15, 1685, died March 17, 1768. He married, April 17, 1709, Sidney Rees, and had Phineas, b. March 13, 1722. Phineas Roberts married, April 27, 1743, Anne Wynne, danghter of Thomas Wynne, 2d. Sydney Rees was daughter of Rees Evan, of Fron Ween, Penmaen, parish of Llanfor, Penllyn, and Elizabeth, his wife, daughter of John Thomas, of Llaithgwm, parish of Llandderfel. See pedigrees I. and II. in this volume.

[2] Lieutenant Abraham Streeper was born near Abington, September 4, 1747, and in 1770 married Hannah Roberts. He was the third generation from William Streeper, b. 1650, d. November, 1717, who was one of the early settlers of Germantown. Abraham Streeper was First Lieutenant in Warner's Battalion, Philadelphia County Troops, and was captured by the British after the battle of Brandywine, and confined in Walnut Street jail, Philadelphia. Leonhart Streeper, the grandfather of Abraham Streeper, was a large landholder, owning one tract of 5,000 acres in Bucks County. (See MS. Collection Historical Soc., of Pa.; also Mt. Book I, Board Prop., of Pa., Penna. Archives xix., 748).

[3] Titus Yerkes 2d, b. November 15, 1762, d. June 15, 1846, was the third generation from Anthony Yerkes, who came from Crefeld, Germany, in the year 1700, and was Burgess of Germantown in 1703.

4, 1890; who married JOEL COOK 2d[1] and had GUSTAVUS BENSON COOK, b. July 18, 1838, d. Jan. 6, 1867; JOEL COOK 3d, b. March 20, 1842, married MARY E. EDMUNDS; RICHARD YERKES COOK, b. Feb. 25, 1845; WILLIAM COOK, b. July 18, 1848; d. May 16, 1893, married MARY EARLE, daughter of GEORGE H. EARLE, and eighth generation from Captain RALPH EARLE, of Portsmouth, R. I. RICHARD YERKES COOK, who married LAVINIA BORDEN[2] (seventh generation from Richard Borden, of Rhode Island), had one son, GUSTAVUS WYNNE COOK, b. Dec. 12, 1868, who married NANCY MUMFORD BRIGHT, of Williamsburg, Va., had NANCY WYNNE COOK[3] and LAVINIA EMLEY COOK.

Other Descendants of Dr. Thomas Wynne. The Wister Branch.

DANIEL WISTER, the oldest son of John and Catharine Wister, was born in Philadelphia on 2d mo., 4th, 1738-9, and died 10th mo. 27th, 1805, æt. 68 years. On the 5th of the 5th month, 1760, he married LOWRY JONES, daughter of OWEN JONES and SUSANNAH, his wife. Owen Jones was son of JONATHAN JONES, eldest son of Dr. EDWARD JONES and MARY, daughter of Dr. THOMAS WYNNE. Daniel Wister was educated at Ephrata, Lancaster County, Pennsylvania. He was a prominent merchant of Philadelphia, and together with his father was a signer of the non-importation act, which was so important a measure, historically. His wife, Lowry Wister, was born 1743, and died 2d mo, 15th, 1804, æt. 61 years.

---

[1] Joel Cook 2d was the sixth generation from Captain Thomas Cooke, who was b. on the border of the parish of Earle's Colne, Essex, England. Captain Cooke came to America in 1635, landing at Boston, and being the first of the name in New England. In 1643, in company with Ralph Earle and Richard Borden (both being also the first of the name in America), he founded the town of Portsmouth, Rhode Island, where he died in 1677. Both the father of Joel Cook 2d (Joel Cook) and grandfather (William Cook 2d) were in the Continental Line (New Jersey troops) during the Revolutionary War. Joel was in the Infantry, and William was a commissioned officer in Captain Shreve's Troop, Burlington County Light Horse. (See *infra*).

[2] Lavinia Borden (of the Bordens of Bordentown) is the fifteenth generation in direct descent from Henry Borden, b. 1370, and Robergia, his wife. (See Canterbury Wills, vol. ii., folio 1). They are buried in the Church of St. Peter and St. Paul, Headcorn, County Kent, England. Henry Borden was descended from the Bordens of Borden, of whom Simon de Bourden gave the ground and built the parish church of Borden (still standing) in the seventh year of the reign of King John, A.D. 1206. (See pedigree of Richard Borden, by T. A. Glenn).

Richard Borden, b. 1601, died May 25, 1671, the first of the name in America, married Joan Fowle, daughter of Francis Fowle, of Cranbrooke, County Kent, England. He was prominent in the affairs of his Colony. He was one of the Committee to treat with the Dutch, May 18, 1653; "Assistant" of the Town of Portsmouth, 1653-1654; Commissioner, 1654-1656-1657; Treasurer, 1654-1655. In 1667 and 1670, he served as a Deputy from Portsmouth to the Assembly, and in the same year made extensive purchases of land in East Jersey.

[3] Nancy Mumford Bright, the daughter of Captain Robert A. Bright, of Williamsburg, Va., is the fifth generation from the Rev. Alexander Macaulay (great uncle of Lord Macaulay, the Historian) and Lady Helena Maxwell, sister of Sir William Maxwell, of Roslyn, Scotland.

Pedigree XVII.

Daniel and Lowry Wister had 9 children, *viz.*, Sarah (the authoress of " Sally Wister's Journal of the Revolution "), born 4th mo. 20th, 1761, and died s. p. 4th mo. 21st, 1804, æt. 43 years. Elizabeth, born 2d mo. 27th, 1764, o. s. p. 1812, æt. 48 years. Hannah, born 11th mo. 19th, 1767, o. s. p. (*circa*) 1827. Susannah, born 2d mo. 24th, 1773, obt. 11th mo. 27th, 1862, æt. 90 years. John, born 3d mo. 20th, 1776, obt. 12th mo. 12th, 1862, æt. 86 years. Charles Jones, born 4th mo. 12th, 1782, obt. 7th mo. 2d, 1865, æt. 84 years. William Wynne Wister, born 4th mo. 16th, 1784, obt. 11th mo. 16th, 1806, æt. 23 years, s. p.

JOHN WISTER, of Vernon, Germantown, son of Daniel and Lowry Wister, was married, 1798, to Elizabeth Harvey, of Bordentown, N. J., and had nine children who came to maturity. Of these, William, born 2d mo. 2d, 1803, obt. 11th mo. 19th, 1881, married, 9th mo. 26th, 1826, Sarah Logan Fisher, had six children who came to maturity: Of these, William Rotch, m. 3d mo. 4th, 1868, Mary Eustis of Milton, Mass., had children : (1) Mary Channing ; (2) Frances Anne ; (3) Ella Eustis ; (4) John Caspar.

Cadwalader Branch of the Wynne Family.

John Cadwalader, son of Cadwalader Thomas ap Hugh, of Ciltalgarth and Llandrillo, Merionethshire (see Pedigree I.), removed to Pennsylvania and m. 29 December, 1699, Martha, daughter of Dr. Edward Jones and Mary Wynne (daughter of Dr. Thomas Wynne) his wife. They had issue : Dr. Thomas Cadwalader, d. near Trenton, N.J., 14 November, 1779, who m. 18 June, 1738, Hannah, daughter of Thomas Lambert, of New Jersey. They had issue: 1. Anne, b. 1738, d. 30 July, 1739 ; 2. Martha, b. 1739, m. Capt. John Dagworthy ; 3. John, b. 1742, m. (1) Elizabeth Lloyd ; (2) Williamina Bond ; 4. Lambert, m. Mary McCall ; 5. Mary, b. 1745, m. Philemon Dickinson ; 6. Rebecca, b. 1746, d. s. p. (2d wife of Philemon Dickinson) ; 7. Margaret, b. 1748, m. Samuel Meredith ; 8. Elizabeth, b. 1760, d. 13 April, 1799.

John Cadwalader, b. 1742 (as above), had issue by his 1st wife : 1. Anne, b. 1771, m. Robert Kemble ; 2. Elizabeth, b. 1773, m. Archibald McCall ; 3. Maria, b. 21 February, 1776, m. Samuel Ringgold, of Maryland. General John Cadwalader had issue by his 2d wife : 1. Thomas, b. 28 October, 1779, m. Mary Biddle ; 2. John, b. 1 May, 1784, d. 10 July, 1785 ; 3. Frances, b. 1781, m. David, Lord Erskine.

Thomas Cadwalader, b. 1779, was Lieutenant-Colonel of Cavalry and Major-General of Pennsylvania Troops. He m. Mary, daughter of Colonel Clement Biddle, and had issue : 1. John, b. 1805, m. (1) Mary Binney ; (2) Henrietta Maria

Bancker. Issue by 1st wife: 1. Mary Binney, m. William Henry Rawle; 2. Elizabeth Binney, m. George Harrison Hare. Issue by 2d wife: 1. Sarah B.; 2. Frances; 3. Thomas, d. inf.; 4. Charles Evert, M.D., Lieutenant-Colonel of U. S. Vols.; 5. Anne, m. Rev. H. G. Rowland; 6. John; 7. George, d. inft.

The family of Francis H. Williams, Esq., of Philadelphia, is also descended from Dr. Thomas Wynne.

The Cook Family.

The Essex family to which Captain Thomas Cook belonged was descended from Adam Cook, lord of the manor of Beaumont, and was of "Cook's Hall," in West Burgholt, near Halstead. This Adam Cook is named as plaintiff in a Fine concerning premises in Wyston and Bures St. Mary, 50 Edw. III. [File 100 in case 222, No. 22, Pub. Rec. Office, Lond.] He is mentioned as "of Bergholt" in a Fine (Suffolk) 3 Rich. II., and 16 Rich. II. (1392), he, or his son Adam, and Robert Keterych granted a certain rent in Springfield to the Abbot and Convent of Coggeshall, the said Adam Cook retaining a messuage and lands in Horkesley. [Inq. ad quod damnum, File 421, No. 30, Pub. Rec. Office.] John Cook, son of John son of Adam (2), of Horkesley, died seized of Constantines (now Star Stile), near Halstead, Essex, and adjacent to Horkesley, which he held by ealty, homage and service, 16 Edw. IV. [Inq. P. M. 16 Edw. IV.] Henry Cook (or Cooke), aged 19 years and upwards, was his son and heir. Constantines consisted of a tenement and 40 acres of land. The said John held other lands in Pebmarsh and about Halstead. Henry Cook was father of John Cook, of Constantines, who d. before 17 Sept., 1561, and had (a) John Cook (or Cooke), of Halstead, who died seized of Constantines, 1570. Will 30 Oct., 12 Eliz. (1570). Proved 9 Nov. 1570. [Archdeaconry of Midd. Ct., 110 Reymond.] (b) William Cook (or Cooke), of Colne Engain, d. s. p. Will 15 Augt., 1580; proved 11 Oct., 1580. [Consist. Ct. of Lon.; filed will.] (c) George Cook (or Cooke), of Wakes Colne, d. 1589. Will 26 Feb., 1589. Proved 26 May, 1590. [Archdeaconry of Midd. Ct., 215 Mansfield.] (d) Rose, m. John Syston, of Wakes Colne. She is named in the will of her brother George Cook, of Wakes Colne, 1589, and in Inventory of estate of John Cook, of Constantines, 1570. George Cook, of Wakes Colne (d. 1590), had issue: (a) John Cook (or Cooke), of Earls Colne, named in will of his uncle William Cook, 1580; (b) John Cook (2d child of the name) mentioned in will of his uncle William Cook, 1580, died in Colchester, 1614; (c) Thomas Cook (or Cooke), *of whom presently* ; (d) George Cook ; (e) Robert Cook, of Earls Colne; (f) Anthony Cook, **of Earls**

Colne. Thomas Cook (or Cooke), son of George, is named in will of his uncle, William Cook of Wakes Colne, 1580. He lived at Chockley, a mill and farm on the borders of the parishes of Earls Colne and Great Tey. Will 3 Augt., 1597 ; no probate. [Archdeaconry of Colchester Ct.] He had issue : (a) Edmund Cook (or Cooke) ; (b) Captain Thomas Cook (or Cooke), who removed to New England, as above. It should be noted here that the date 1603, sometimes given as that of the birth of Captain Thomas Cook, is wrong, as is proven by New England and Essex records. He was probably 10 years, *or more* older. His will is dated 6 Feb., 1673. The name, in records and family documents in New England and Essex is frequently written *Cooke*, and in various other ways. Colonel Thomas Cooke, of Pebmarsh, near Halstead, a celebrated officer under Cromwell, was of this family, as was Sir Walter Cook, Knt., one of the ancestors of Dr. Thomas Wynne, whose pedigree is here traced. (See Chart, pedigree I.) There is evidence to indicate that Captain Thomas, when a lad, was indentured to his uncle, John Cook, of Colchester, whose will was proved 1614. [Archdeaconry of Colchester Ct.]

PEDIGREE XVIII.

Rhirid Flaidd,[1] son of Gwrgeneu, is called lord of Penllyn, Pennant Melangell, and the eleven towns in the cantref Trefryd, and of Gest in Eifionydd; but his authority in Penllyn must have been purely governmental, as it is not proved that he held any land there. He was, however, chief *uchelwr* (nobleman) in Pennant Melangell, and resided at Llys Celynin in that parish.[2] He was slain

---

[1] Flaidd, or Blaidd, *viz.*, Rhirid the Wolf. His father is called by the same surname, and the family bore a wolf rampant, the three wolves' heads having been assumed by their descendants at a much later period.

[2] Robert Vaughan of Hengwrt states that Rhirid Flaidd dwelt at a place called Neuaddau Gleision, in the township of Rhiwaedog, but a contemporary authority distinctly states that his home was at Llys Celynin. [Harl. MS. 14, 886, fo. 91.] The place called Castel Pren, in the township of Celynin, in Pennant Melangell, is probably the site of the *Llys* (court). Another MS., which is a copy of one of the fourteenth century, gives Rhirid's residence at a place called Dre'r Ffynon, which is very near Castel Pren, but the latter, as the name implies, is more likely to have been the home of this chieftain, as such a dwelling, at that period, in Wales, would be a fortress built of trees, roughly hewn from the adjacent forest. Pennant suggests that Rhirid lived in Castle Carn Dochan, but this, as we will presently see, was the stronghold of Rhirid's great grandson, to whom it was granted by Edward I.

Rhirid is stated in nearly all pedigrees to have married Gwenllian, daughter of Ednyfed, Lord of Broughton son of Cynwrig, who was slain 1074, but, of course, this is impossible. It seems probable, however, that his wife was Gwenllian, daughter of some other Ednyfed.

about the year 1207, his brother Arthen falling about the same time. Another brother, David, was living, and party to a deed for land about Montgomery, which had belonged to Robert, the brother of Gwrgeneu their father, dated 1230 to 1240. [Myddelton deeds at Chirk Castle.]

ISSUE:

i. Madog, *of whom presently.*
ii. Rhirid Fychan,[1] ancestor to the Myddeltons, of Chirk Castle and Gwaunynog.
iii. Einion, slain at the siege of Dyserth Castle, at a spot still called Bryn Einion, 1263. According to a MS. of Gruffydd Hiraddug, the cross which was erected over Einion's grave, and which was removed to Dyserth churchyard, bore this inscription: HOC SI PETATUR LAPSIS ISTE CAUSA NOTATUR | EINION OXI' RIRID VLAIDD FILIUS HOC MEMORATUR.

Einion's son, Einion, called by the Welsh genealogists *Einion Greulon*, lord of Crugaeth, Oswestry, under the designation of *Eynon de Greulon*, was one of the jury in an inquest held at Oswestry, 18 May, 30 Edw. I. (1302). [Chancery Inq. P. M., 30 Edw. I. No. 30.]

iv. Rhys. [Dwnn, ii., 107.]
v. Maredydd. [Dwnn, ii., 109.][2]
vi. Gwenllian, m. Gruffydd, of Henglawd, ap Ednyfed Fychan.
vii. Gwenllian, m. Gruffydd, ancestor to the Owens of Bodeon, Anglesey.

Madog ap Rhirid Flaidd. He succeeded to his father's lands in Pennant Melangell, and is stated in a number of pedigrees to have married Arddyn, daughter of Philip Uchtryd, lord of Cyfeiliog, but this, on account of the date, is improbable, and Harl. MS. 2288, is, doubtless, correct in giving his wife as Efa, daughter of Philip Ddu ap

---

[1] Rhirid Fychan was father of David y Bothan Flaidd, of Penllyn, who killed the steward of the English as he was sitting upon his bench in the court. David's grandson, Rhirid ap David (brother of Gruffydd ap David, summoner of the Court of Pennllyn, at Michaelmas, 16 Rich. II., 1392), married Cecelia, daughter and heiress of Philip Myddelton, and assumed his wife's surname. He was ancestor to Sir Hugh Myddelton, Baronet, of London Water Works fame, and to Sir Thomas Myddelton, of Chirk Castle, Knight, of the Parliamentary Army. Chirk Castle still belongs to a branch of this family.

[2] Maredydd ap Rhirid had a daughter, Lleuku, who married Owen Hên, ap Gruffydd ap Owain Brogyntyn. Bleddyn, the brother of Gruffydd, was living 2 Hen. III. (1218).

Pedigree XVIII.

Howel[1] ap Maredydd[2] ap Bleddyn ap Cynfyn, Prince of Powys. Dwnn (ii., 249) says that Efa was the daughter of Philip Dorddu.

ISSUE :
i. Iorwerth, *of whom presently.*
ii. Gwrgeneu. [Harl. MS. 2288.] He is described as of Rhiwaedog, Penllyn, and his descendant, Einion ap Ithel ap Gwrgeneu Fychan ap Gwrgeneu, of Rhiwaedog, was an esquire to John of Gaunt, Duke of Lancaster, with whom, in 18 Rich. II. (1395), he covenanted to attend for one year, with one man-at-arms, and one archer, on payment of a pension of 20 marks to issue out of the Manor of Halton. [MS. Robert Vaughan of Hengwrt.] Ithel was also High Sheriff of Merionethshire for life, and died 1401.

Iorwerth ap Madog, of the parish of Pennant Melangell, Montgomeryshire. He was senachall to Madog ap Gruffydd, Prince of Powys Fadog, and witnessed a deed of the latter to the Abbey of Valle Crucis, dated the day of the Nativity of the Blessed Virgin Mary, 1254. [MS. of W. W. E. Wynne, Esq.] Iorwerth was buried in the church of Pennant Melangell, where his effigy, in full armour, with a rampant wolf on the shield, and the inscription, HIC JACET ETWART (*i.e.* Iorwerth), remains.[3]

---

[1] Howel was a son of Maredydd ap Bleddyn by an alliance not entirely recognized by the Church in Wales, but which was sanctioned by the Welsh laws of the period, and the "Customs of Wales," and inherited, under the same a portion of his father's lands, called Main, in the parish of Meivod, in Montgomeryshire. [Harl. MS. 2299.] He was slain in 1140, according to one account, by some of his own household, but others state "that no one knew who killed him." Madog ap Maredydd, the half brother of Howel, was Prince of Powys from 1105 to 1130.

[2] Maredydd ap Bleddyn. The following notices of this prince are principally from "Brut y Tywysogion." In 1105, after having been imprisoned by Henry I. for four years, Maredydd escaped, and regained Powys. 1110. Maredydd ap Bleddyn took Madog ap Rhirid (his cousin) gave him to Owain ap Cadwgan, who pulled out his eyes and set him at liberty; but Owain and Maredydd shared Madog's lands between them. 1118. Maredydd defeats King Henry. 1122. Maredydd ap Bleddyn killed his nephew, Ithel ap Rhirid, and pulled out the eyes of his uncles, Goronwy, Rhirid, and Meilir, who had plotted to overthrow him. Then he emasculated them, and shortly afterwards he killed them. 1126. Llewelyn ap Sir Owain raised a revolt, but was captured, his eyes pulled out, and emasculated, by Maredydd, and at the same time Maredydd killed Ieuaf ap Owain.

"In 1130, Prince Maredydd ab Bleddyn ab Cynvyn died, the ornament, safety, and protection of Powysland, after having taken healthful penance for his body, and sincere repentance in his spirit, and having taken the Body of Christ and the oil *achagen.*"

[3] Until recently this effigy was mistakenly supposed to be that of Iorwerth ap Owain Gwynedd, who fell near by, but is now satisfactorily identified, by the arms, and other circumstances, to be that of the above Iorwerth. The effigy of Iorwerth's wife, Gwerfyl, likewise long figured as that of Saint Marcella, who died some centuries before, and is yet pointed out as such, despite positive proof to the contrary.

He married Gwerfyl, daughter of Cynwrig ap Pasgen ap Gwyn ap Gruffydd, lord of Cegidfa and Deuddwr. Gwerfyl's effigy is also in the church of Pennant Melangell.

ISSUE:
  i. Madog, *of whom presently.*
  ii. Gruffydd.
  iii. Iorwerth Fychan.
  iv. Gwenllian, m. Llewelyn ap Ithel, of Aelhairn, in Glyndyfrdwy.
  v. Maud, m. Goronwy ap Tudor ap Goronwy ap Ednyfed Fychan.

Madog ap Iorwerth. [Dwnn, ii., 232, &c.; "History of Powys Fadog," iv., 117, &c.] He was of Pennant Melangell, and Penllyn, Merionethshire, and was in the service of Edward I., and, about 1294, had a grant for life of the lands of Penanthlu, and castle of Carn Dochan, in the parish of Llanuwchllyn, Penllyn. [Extent of Penllyn, time Edw. I.]

33 Edw. I. (1305). Madog ap Iorwerth, of Penllyn, presents a petition to the Prince of Wales, at Kensington, praying that he might quietly enjoy certain lands, and the baliwick of one cantref in Penllyn and Ardudewey, which the King had given him for his services. [Records of Caernarvon.]

Madog ap Iorwerth married Efa, daughter of Gruffydd ap Einion. [Dwnn, ii., 232, note 4.]

ISSUE:
  i. Gruffydd, *of whom presently.*
  ii. Goronwy, m. Efa, daughter of Llewelyn ap Einion ap Celynin, of Llwydiarth, Montgomeryshire. Einion ap Celynin had a grant of land from Lord Powys, on the Thursday after the Decollation of St. John the Baptist, 14 Edw. III. (1340). ["Montgomeryshire Collections," v., 399.]
  iii. Gwerfyl, m. Iorwerth ap Hwfa, of Dudlyston.
  iv. Margaret.
  v. Gwenllian.

Gruffydd ap Madog, of Castle Carn Dochan, Penllyn (parish Llanuwchllyn).

17 Edward II. (1324), the Day of March next after the Feast of the Holy Trinity. Gruffydd ap Madog, under the designation of Griffith ap Madoc of the county of Merioneth, is 12th man on the jury on an inquisition held at Bala, before Thomas de Waynesburgh, Deputy to

Pedigree XVIII.

Lord Edmund, Earl of Arundell, Justiciary of Wales, regarding the rights of the Monastery of Strata Marcella to a diary called Pennantig3 and one plot of land called Kymman. [Inquisitions, 17 Edw. II., "Montgomeryshire Collections," v., 135-6.]

According to Harl. MS. 2288, Gruffydd married Alice, daughter of Bleddyn Fychan[1] ap Bleddyn, of Hafod Un Nos, who is there given as the mother of all his children; but, according to other accounts, all of his children, except Ieuan, were by Gwenllian, his second or third wife, daughter of Ieuan ap Howel ap Maredydd ap Howel ap Madog ap Cadwgan ap Elystan Glodrhudd, Prince of Fferlis (Herefordshire). ["History of Powys Fadog," iv., 118; Dwnn.]

Bleddyn Fychan above named was one of the witnesses to a charter of Henri de Laci, Earl of Lincoln to John de la Chambre, dated 3 Edw. I. (1274-5) for land about Denbigh, the said John being (probably afterwards), Bleddyn's son-in-law. [Chamber's MSS.] Alice, therefore, must have been born when Bleddyn Fychan was advanced in years, and the first wife of Gruffydd. I am inclined to suppose that she was the mother of Howel.

ISSUE:

i. Ieuan ap Gruffydd, of Llanuwchllyn. He "lived in great credit and esteeme in the days of King Edward III., who allowed him an annual stipend for guarding and conducting of ye justice of North Wales with a companie of archers, whilst he should soeiourne and stay in ye countie of Meirionydd." [MS. of Robert Vaughan of Hengwrt.] Meyrick, following Wynne, says of Ieuan ap Gruffydd: "His tomb is extant within the church of Llanuwchllyn, and if there is not a mistake in the inscription upon it, or a figure has been broken off, he died in 1370; but I find a person of the same name, and I am inclined to think him one of the jury in an inquisition held at Bala, upon the next Friday after the Festival of the Assumption, 48th Edward III. (1st September, 1374)." [Dwnn, ii., 229, note 15.]

"He was alive after this year [1370.] I think that a numeral, probably an 'x,' has been broken off at the end of the inscription." W. W. E. Wynne. ["History of Powys Fadog," vi., 69, note 1.] I have inspected this effigy, and there is no doubt that the final numeral has been chipped off. T. A. Glenn (1910).

He is represented recumbent in armour, with his shield charged with his arms, and this inscription: HIC JACET

---

[1] Meuric Llwyd, grandson of Bleddyn Fychan, and nephew of Alice, "finding himself and his tenants much oppressed by the English laws, did kill one of the judges, and hang divers other officers on oak trees in Uwch Dulas; on which account his lands and inheritance in Rhuvoniog escheated to the Crown, and so still remain, for the most part, to this day . . . whereupon he withdrew for his safety to the sanctuary of Halston." He afterwards was captain of a company of Free lances, recruited in the Marches of Wales, and gained distinction and wealth on the continent, returning to Wales, some years after, when he married the heiress of Llanvorda. [Robert Vaughan of Hengwrt.]

IOANNES AB GRIFFIT AB MADOG AB IERWERTH CVIVS ANIMÆ PROPITIETUR DEVS AMEN ANO DIVI MCCCLXX.—.
  ii. Howel y Gadair, *of whom presently*.
  iii. Rhys.
  iv. Goronwy ap Gruffydd, of Penllyn, who m. Isabel, daughter of Gruffydd ap Madog, of Rhuddallt, third baron of Glyndyfrdwy, who succeeded his father, the second baron, 11 Nov., 1306.¹ ["History of Powys Fadog," i., 196.] The mother of Isabel was Elizabeth, daughter of John L'Estrange, of Ness.
  v. Gruffydd, of Trefgoed.

Howel y Gadair, of Cadair Penllyn. He was living 1380, [Harl. MS. 2, 288], and married Mary, daughter of Goronwy Llwyd ap Iorwerth y Penwyn,² of Melai.

This Goronwy (or Grono) Llwyd, was of Bettws, Carnarvonshire, and was grantee of the "raglorie" of Nantconwy, and "avoterie" of Dolwyddelan and the mill of Penmachno, with their demesne lands, 1351, and was living 1356. ["Records of Caernarvon."] His wife was Lleuki (Dwnn says Gwenhwyfar), daughter and heiress of

---

¹ Madog ap Gruffydd, the second baron of Glyndyfrdwy, by English tenure, died 11 Nov., 1306. His wife was Gwenllian, daughter of Ithel Fychan of Helygen, lord of Mostyn, in Flintshire, son of Ithel ap Ithel Garn. ["Brut y Tywysogion"; "Llyfr Coch o Hergist."]

Llaneurgern, Sunday in the Vigil of St. Mark the Evangelist, 1317. Lease for 12 years of land at Nant Brynfron from Bledyn ap Iorwerth ap David of Helygen in Tegeingl to Ithel Vychan, son of Ithel Vychan, son of Ithel Garn, of Helygen in Tegeingl, at a yearly rent of 20 shillings. Witnesses: Madog ap Pled' ap Kynrick, Symon Kynrick Koch [and Griffith, his brother,] Bledyn ap Ithel, Iorwerth Wydel, David Wych, Bledyn ap Meuric and many others. [Original in possession of Lord Mostyn of Talacre, near Prestatyn, North Wales.]

Tudor, son of Ithel Vychan, and brother to Gwenllian (wife of Madog ap Gruffydd) is named as grantee in a deed from Kenwrick, son of Bledyn ap Iorwerth, of Helygen Wern, in Tegeingl, for 12 acres of land in Orwydvid (or Yrwidvit) in Helygen Wern, on Wednesday next after the Feast of St. Ambrose, 1333. [Original at Talacre.]

Gruffydd Fychan (or Vychan), first baron of Glyndyfrdwy, married Margaret, daughter of Gruffydd ap Cadwgan, lord of Eyton. This Gruffydd was third son of Gruffydd ap Madog, Prince of Powys Fadog, descended from Bleddyn ap Cynfyn, Prince of Powys. By a treaty dated on the Tuesday next before the Feast of St. Martin, 5 Edw. I. (1277), it is stipulated that Gruffydd Fychan shall do homage to the king for the lands he holds in Iâl, and to Llewelyn for the lands which he holds in Llewelyn's dominions. By charter dated at Rhuddlan, 12 Feb., 11 Edw. I. (1283), the King, at the request of John, Earl of Warren, granted the lands of Glyndyfrdwy to Gruffydd Fychan, and 22 July, 1284, the King granted him a new charter, correcting the first. [Rotuli Walliæ, 11 Edw. I., memb. 3, and 12 Edw. I., memb. 5.]

² Iorwerth, under the designation of "Yereward Penwyn," had a grant of a pension of 30 shilling yearly, for life, by the Crown, 1290. In 3 Edw. II., he was Rhaglor of Nantconwy, where he resided, and which office he had petitioned for, 33 Edw. I., and held the same until his death, *circa* 1320. Printed pedigree of Ffoulkes of Ereiviat.]

PEDIGREE XVIII. 113

Madog[1] ap Ellis, [Hengwrt MS. 198, fo. 36], son of Ellis[2] ap Iorwerth ap Owain Brogyntyn.[3]

ISSUE:
  i. Goronwy, *of whom presently.*
  ii. Tudor.
  iii. Ieuan, m. a daughter of Y Teg Vadog,[4] seneschall to Gruffydd, of Rhuddallt.

Goronwy ap Howel y Gadair, of Cadair Penllyn. [Harl. MS. 2, 288, Dwnn, ii. ; "History of Powys Fadog," vi., 108, 126.]

He died before Michaelmas, 1399, having married, first, Gwen, daughter of Gruffydd ap Llewelyn, of Cors y Gedol,[5] and, secondly, ——, daughter of Tudor ap Gruffydd Llwyd.

ISSUE by 1st wife :
  i. Tudor, *of whom presently.*

---

[1] Madog ap Ellis did homage to the Black Prince as Baron of Edernion, 17 Edw. III. (1344).

[2] A confirmation from the Crown to Ellisau, or Ellis, ap Iorwerth, of certain privileges in his manor of Llangar, in Edeirnion, is dated 22 July, 12 Edw. I. (1284). [Dwnn, ii., 109, note 7.]

[3] Owain Brogyntyn was the son of Madog ap Maredydd, Prince of Powys, by a daughter of the Maer Ddu, or Black Mayor of Rûg, and resided near Brogyntyn, near Oswestry. He was living 1215, and was then one of the witnesses to a deed of Owain de Brithdir to the Monks of Strata Florida. Owain Brogyntyn granted to the Abbey of Bassingwerk "Wenhewin," with all the men (nativi) of the same township, and with their appurtenances. [Charter given by Coleshill as MCCXL (1240).]

[4] Y Teg Vadog (or Madog), was steward or seneschall to Gruffydd of Rhuddallt, and did homage for his lands to the Black Prince, 1343. He was the son of Madog ap Gruffydd ap Owain Brogyntyn.

Lleuki and her sisters were co-heiresses of their brother, Leoline, Bishop of St. Asaph, who died 1375. The codicil to his will is dated on the next Friday after the Feast of St. Dionisius (12 Oct.), 1375. [Dwnn, ii., 112, note 1.]

[5] Gruffydd ap Llewelyn, of Cors y Gedol, was farmer of the office of High Sheriff of Merioneth, 46 Edw. III. (1373), Sheriff, 15 Rich. II. (1392), Woodwarden of the commot of Estimaner, between 7 July, 1382, and 12 Oct., 1385; died between 29 Sept., 20 Rich. II., and same day, 1 Hen. IV. (1399). His wife was Efa, daughter of Madog ap Ellis, and sister to Leoline, Bishop of St. Asaph. [Ped. of Peniarth, "History of Powys Fadog, vi., 153.]

Llewelyn was the son of Cynwrig (or Kenric), son of Osborn, surnamed "Wyddel" (the Irishman), who settled in Wales in the thirteenth century. Robert Vaughan of Hengwrt, in an MS. dated 1654, observes that Osborn "was a nobleman's son of Desmond in Ireland, of ye famous family of the Geraldines." It is stated by Gutyn Owain, one of the most eminent genealogists of the fifteenth century, that Osborn accompanied from Ireland to Wales, Gruffydd, one of the sons of Ednyfed Fychan, minister to Prince Llewelyn. This is probable, as Gruffydd was connected with the Geraldines. [See "The Geraldines"; Peniarth MS. 6.] Osborn is assessed in Llanabar towards the tax of a fifteenth, 1293-4.

Gwenllian's brother, Einion ap Gruffydd, of Cors y Gedol, was woodwarden of the commot of Estimaner, between 7 July, 1382, and 12 Oct., 1385; captain of forty archers for the king from Merioneth, 10 Rich. II.; living at Michaelmas, 20 Rich. II.

Tudor ap Goronwy, of Penllyn. [Harl. MS. 2, 288; Dwnn, ii.; "History of Powys Fadog," vi., 108.]

He was, supposedly, dead before 31 Hen. VI. (1451-2), and married Gwerfyl, daughter of Ieuan [1] ap Einion [2] ap Gruffydd [3] ap Howel,[4] of Bron y Voel, [Harl. MS. 2, 288; "History of Powys Fadog," vi., 108.]

ISSUE:

i. Goronwy, of Penllyn; married Margaret, daughter of Belyn ap Iockws Bach, of Dinmael.
ii. Einion; on Grand Jury, at Bala, Penllyn, 31 Hen. VI. (1453).
iii. Howel, m. his cousin, Tibot, daughter of Einion ap Gruffydd, of Cors y Gedol.
iv. Ieuan.
v. Maredydd, *of whom presently.*

Maredydd ap Tudor, of Penllyn. [Garth Llwyd ped., from MS. of J. Y. W. Lloyd, of Clochfaen, Esq., M.A., K.S.G.; "History of Powys Fadog," vi., 108; Harl. MS. 2, 228.]

---

[1] Ieuan ap Einion ap Gruffydd, of Bron y Voel, was living 23 April, 1389, and later. In his youth he had been a soldier of fortune, on the Continent, and is mentioned in Symond's "Switzerland," as Ieuan ab Einion ab Gruffydd, a valiant Welshman, who had defended Henry de Transtamare and the throne of Castile against the Black Prince, in the 39th and 40th of Edward III. (1366), and who afterwards accompanied Enguerrard de Courcy (son-in-law of the English King) in his expedition against the Duke of Austria, under pretence of demanding the dower due to him (Enguerrard) in right of his mother. Ieuan evidently married on his return to Wales, when he was beyond middle age. His wife is given in several pedigrees as daughter of Ynyr Vychan, of Nannau, but, as is evident from the dates, and other circumstances, she was the daughter of Meuric Llwyd (or Lloyd) ap Meuric ap Ynyr Vychan.

[2] Einion ap Gruffydd, of Bron y Voel, was living 27 July, 1352; Sheriff for life of the counties of Carnarvon and Merioneth; 29 Edw. III., for the former. His wife was Nest, daughter and co-heiress of Gruffydd ap Adda, of Dol Goch, in the parish of Towyn, a taxer of the fifteenth in 1293-4; Raglor of the commot of Estimaner, 3 and 7 Edw. III. His effigy in armour remains in Towyn Church.

[3] Gruffydd ap Howel, of Bron y Voel, married Angharad, daughter of Tegwared, illegitimate son of Llewelyn ap Iorwerth, Prince of Wales.

[4] Howel was the son of Maredydd ap Einion ap Gwgan ap Maredydd ap Collwyn ap Tangno, Lord of Llêyn, and his wife was Gwenllian, daughter of Gruffydd, son of Ednyfed Fychan.

Einion ap Gruffydd, above named, was brother to Sir Howel y Fwyall, who distinguished himself at the battle of Poitiers, and is said to have been the person who took the King of France prisoner. On this occasion he was knighted, and still more to commemorate his services, the King of England conferred upon him "a mess of meat, to be served before his pole-axe for ever. This mess, upon his death, was carried down to be distributed among the poor, for his soul's sake, till the reign of Elizabeth, when the custom was abolished." ["History of the Gwydir family."]

Pedigree XVIII.

31 Hen. VI. (1453). Maredydd ap Tudor ap Goronwy, of Penllyn, is named as 4th man on the jury in an inquisition "apud Penllyn," held before Thomas Burnaby, High Sheriff, at Bala. [Inquisitions for the co. of Mer. ; see also "History of Powys Fadog," vi., 148.]

Maredydd ap Tudor married Annesta, daughter of Maredydd[1] ap Tudor[2] ap Howel[3] ap Cynwrig[4] Fychan, ap Cynwrig[5] ap Llywarch; from Marchweithian, lord of Isaled.

ISSUE :

i. John Wynn, *of whom presently.*

John Wynn. He was of Garth Llwyd, in the township of Doldrewyn, parish of Llandderfel, Penllyn. In addition to the estate of Garth Llwyd, he held adjacent lands and tenements in the townships of Cynlas and Nant-lleidiog, about Sarn. [Pedigree by J. Y. W. Lloyd,[6] of Clochfaen, Esq., M.A., K.S.G., compiled principally from Harl. MS. 2, 228; "History of Powys Fadog," vi., 108; "Visitations of the three Counties of North Wales," by

---

[1] Maredydd (Meredith) ap Tudor was of Plâs Iolyn, in the parish of Yspytty Evan, Denbighshire, and was steward of the lands of the Monastery of Aberconwy, in Hiraethog, 1450. He married Efa, daughter of ap Rhys Gwyn, descended from Iorwerth y Penwyn, of Melai.

Rhys ap Maredydd, of Plâs Iolyn, brother to Annesta, was one of the Lancastrian captains at Bosworth Field (1485), and was entrusted by Henry VII. with the Standard of England, after the former Standard bearer, Sir Wiliam Brandon, had been slain. An MS. at Rhiwlas states, from his own account, that he slew Richard III. with his own hand, and this seems borne out by the favours received from the Tudors by his descendants. His effigy remains in Yspytty Church. [Harl. MS. 1977, fo. 64, 65; Harl. MS. 1969; Rhiwlas MS.; Dwnn, ii.]

[2] Tudor ap Howel died about 1450; his wife was Susanna, daughter and heiress of Maredydd ap Madog, from Ithel Felyn, lord of Iâl (Yale).

[3] Howel married Margaret, daughter of Howel ap Ithel ; from Bleddyn, Prince of Powys.

[4] Cynwrig Fychan, was of Llannefydd. At a court held at Llannerch, near Denbigh, on Thursday in Whitsun-week, 22 Edw. I. (10 June, 1294), Cynwrig Fychan, then a young man, was attached because he depastured the lord's land without leave. The damages amounted to 6d., and he was quit. [Ruthin Court Rolls, 82 Edw. I., Pub. Rec. Office.] He was living 8 Edw. III. (1334). Buried in Llannefydd Church, where his effigy in full armour, remains.

[5] Cynwrig ap Llywarch, under the designation of Kenewvek Ab llawar, is the fifth witness to the charter of Henri de Laci to Johan de la Chambre for two carucates of land in Llyweni (near Denbigh), 3 Edw, I. (1274-5). [Chambers MSS.]

[6] The pedigree of "Garth Llwyd," from MS. of J. Y. W. Lloyd, Esq., makes John Wynn the son of *Ieuan* and a *grandson* of Maredydd (Meredith) ap Tudor, of Penllyn. No further information is given concerning this *Ieuan*. A pedigree from the "Visitations," compiled 18 Jan., 1894, by an authorised Herald, and at a date when the grandchildren of John Wynn were alive, states that he was the *son* not the *grandson* of Maredydd ap Tudor. This also accords with known records, and as the statement is by an authority recognized by the College of Arms, it is, after the failure of a careful search to throw any further light on the the subject, accepted.

Lewys Dwnn, Deputy Herald, orig. folio lxxx.; dated 18 Jan., 1594; Will of Edward ap John Wynn, of Llandderfel, cited *infra.*]

John Wynn married Catherine, daughter of Howel[1] ap Jenkin. [Refer to "Visitations of the three Counties of North Wales," by Lewys Dwnn, MS., folio clxvi.; dated 22 July, 1588.] He seems to have died subsequent to 37 Hen. VIII. (1545).

ISSUE:

i. Edward[2] ap John Wynn, *of whom presently.*
ii. Roger[3] ap John Wynn, of the parish of Llandderfel, Penllyn; living 20 April, 1575, and then holding his brother Edward's estates, under a deed of trust. His daughter, Sioned, married Robert ap Owen, of the parish of Llandderfel, and had issue: Cadwaladr ap Robert, Ellis ap Robert, and David ap Robert [Dwnn, ii., 113; pedigree dated 15 July, 1596.]
iii. David[4] ap John Wynn, of the parish of Llandderfel; married Lowry, daughter of Howel. The will of David ap John Wynn, of Llandderfel, was proved at St. Asaph, 16 Jan., 1587, and letters testamentary were granted to Lowry vch. Howel, the relict and executrix of the deceased. [Act Book $\frac{1584}{1593}$, Probate Registry, St. Asaph.]
iv. Catherine,[5] m. Watkin ap John, of Branas Uchaf, parish of Llandrillo, and had issue: Hugh ap Watkin, and Morris (or Maurice) ap Watkin. [Dwnn, ii., 126.]
v. Lowry, living 20 April, 1675. [Will of her brother, Edward ap John, see *infra.*]

---

[1] Howel ap Jenkin, of Ynys y Maen Gwyn, died of the plague, 1494. His wife was Mary, daughter of Sir Roger Kynaston, Knt., High Sheriff of Shropshire, 1462, Constable of the Castle of Harlech, Merionethshire, 1472-73. Died 1517. The wife of Sir Roger Kynaston was Elizabeth, daughter of Henry Grey, Earl of Tankervill, whose wife was Antigone, daughter of Humphrey, Duke of Gloucester, son of Henry IV., King of England. (See chart and authorities hereafter given).

Jenkin ap Iorwerth, of Ynys y Maen Gwyn, married Ellen, daughter of Gruffydd Derwas (the latter an esquire to John of Gaunt).

Iorwerth ap Einion, the father of Jenkin, was farmer of the vill of Towyn (*viz.*, lessee of Crown Revenues there), and of the office of Raglor of the comot of Estimaner, at Michaelmas, 1415, and held in farm the office of Woodwarden of Estimaner, at Michaelmas, 1425, for a term of two years, that being the first. [Dwnn, ii., 230; "History of Powys Fadog," vi., 155.]

[2] Edward may have been so called after Edward ap Howel, or Edward Kynaston, who, in 1554, set up a claim to the Lordship of Powys.

[3] Roger may have been so named after Sir Roger Kynaston, who lived for several years after the approximate date of Roger ap John Wynn's birth, dying 1517, according to the best authorities.

[4] I am inclined to suppose that David was by a second wife of John Wynn.

[5] Catherine bore her mother's name.

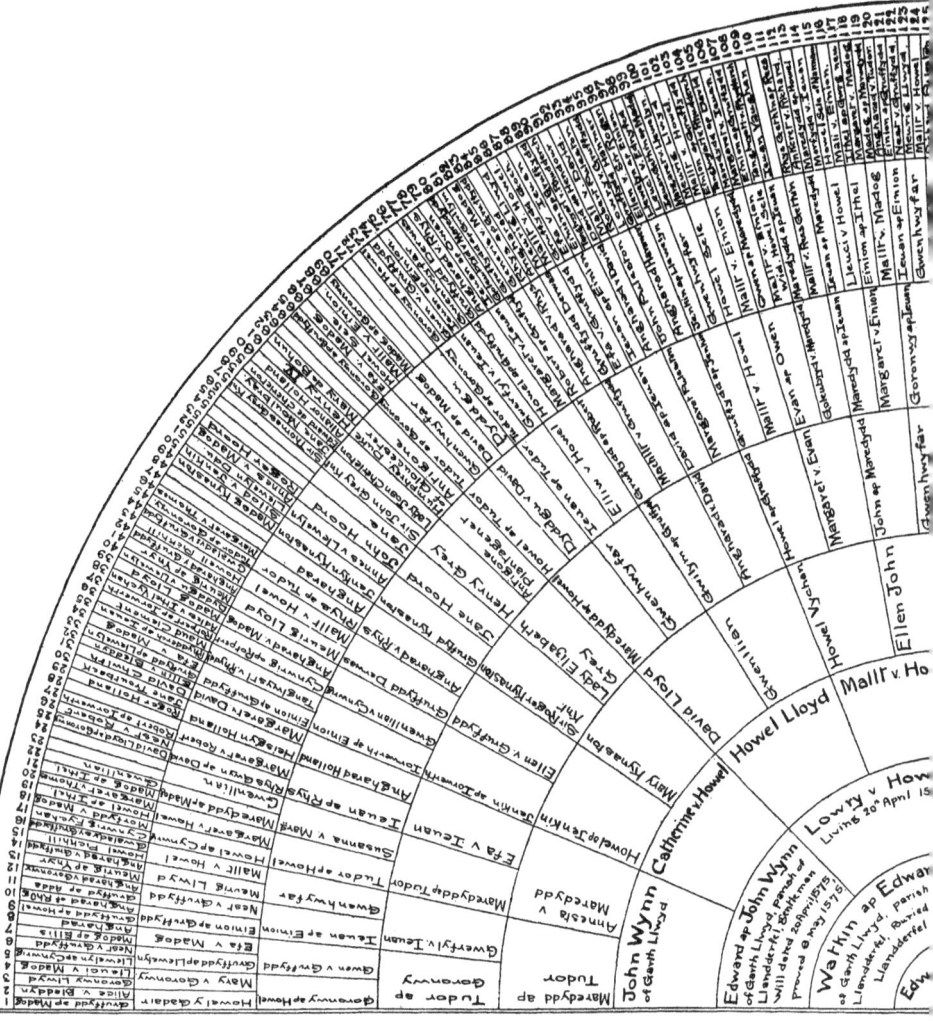

Authorities: Llandd. Reg.; L. Sub. Rolls; Chanc. Inqs.; Rolls of F. of Fine (as cited); Wills and Admons.; Mostyn deeds; Chambers MSS.; Recds. Dioc. Reg., St. Asaph; Visits, N.W., i., 326, ii., 70, 72, 81, 84, 86, 93, 94, 95, 150, 228-9, 230-2, 249, 309-10, &c.; Harl. MS. 1269, 1977, fo. 64-5, 14, 886, fo. 91, 2, 228, &c.; *Recds. of Caer.*; *Brut y Tywysogion*; *Rot. Wall.*; Pat. Rolls; *Montg. colls.*, v., 135-6, 399, 402 (and gen.); *Ruthin Ct. Rolls*; *Hist. of the Gwydir Family*; *Homage and Fealty to first English Prince of Wales*, Ed. Owen; Peniarth MSS. (Nat. Lib. of W.) (gen.), but espec. Hengwrt MSS.); *Myddelton of Gwaynog*; Cardiff MS. 50; 6, v. *H. Powys Fadog*, (gen.); Bridgeman; *Feudal Barons of Powys*; *Arch. Camb.* (gen.); Add. MS. 9864. When conflicting statements, principally due to careless transcription, have been found, an exhaustive search has been made, and most trustworthy MS. followed.

ROYAL DESCENTS. Fr. HENRY IV., as given; fr. EDWARD I., 46, 128, 240, 246 (accord. to Cardiff MS. 50, Ret. of Royal Commission, 1485-6; Burke's *Royal Descents*, Eleanor, dau. Edward I. m. Henri de Barr, and had Eleanor, m. Llewelyn ap Owen, rep. of Princes of S. Wales, and had Thomas ap Llewelyn, who m. Catherine, dau. Philip ap Ivor (by Catherine, ill. dau. of Prince Llewelyn, d. 1282), and had (a) Eleanor, m. Gruffydd Fychan of Glyndwr, and (b) Margaret, m. Tudor ap Goronwy. Gruffydd Vychan and Eleanor had Lowry, wife of Robert Puleston, and Tudor and Margaret had Rhys, whose dau. was one of the wives of Gruffydd Derwas.

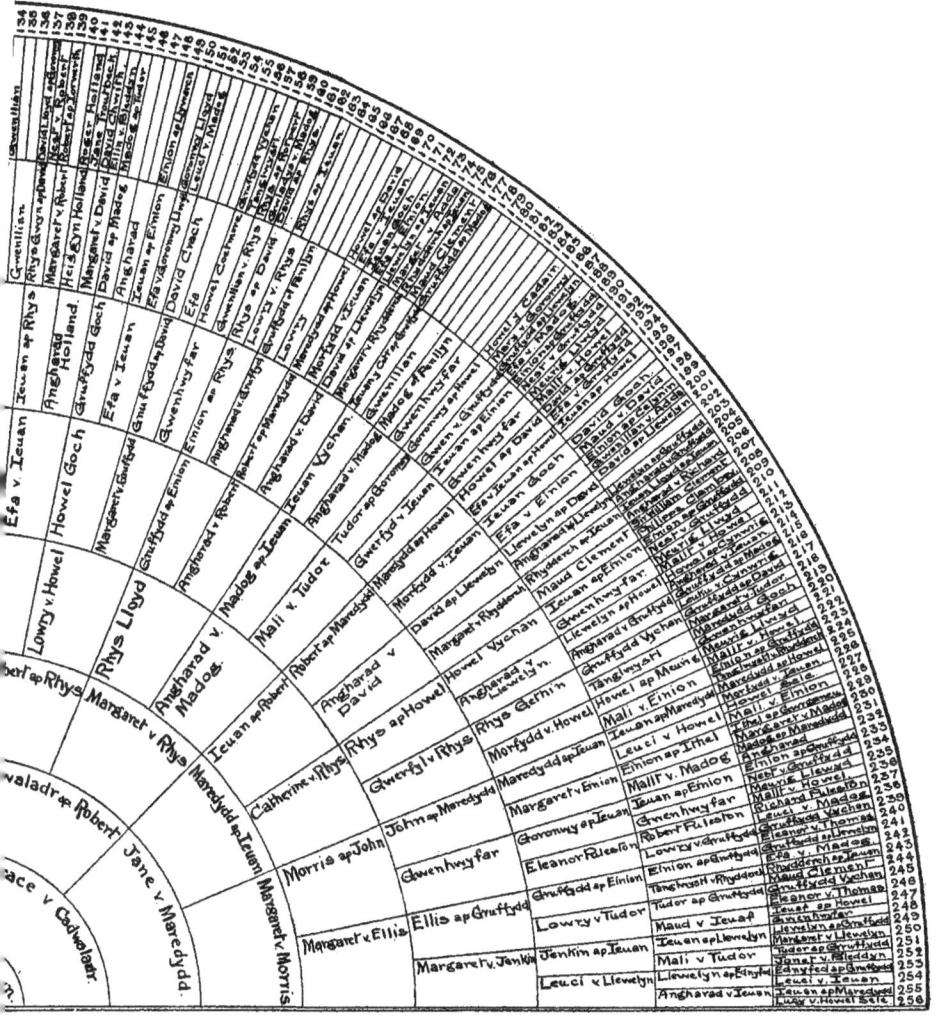

From GEOFFREY PLANTAGENET, about 40 dcts., of wh. are 15, 38, 43, 61, 62, 67, 77, 86, 102, 115, 124, 192, 212, 222, 227, 256, David, Prince of Wales, m, before 20 Hen. II. (1173); prob. 1170, Emma Plantagenet, dau. Geoffrey (Roll of the Gt. Pipe, 20 Hen. II., Rot. 2, Lans. MS., 249). Their dau. Angharad, m. Gruffydd ap Cadwgan (but not of Nannau), and had Anghard, who m. Sanddef Hardd of Morton, father of Moreiddig, f. of Howel, f. of Iorwerth, f. of Goronwy, f. of David, f. of Howel de Pickhill, f. of Malit, wf. of Mewrig Lloyd of Nannau. Other descts. th. Ithel Fychan of Mostyn, &c., appear in *H. Powys Fadog*, visit. N.W., and Harl. MSS. Fr. Bleddyn, Prince of Powys, th. 7, 13, 34, 41, 49, 67, 77, 85, 91, 94, 101, 115, 123, 127, 177, 191, 211, 221, 227, 235, 239, 245, 256, &c. Fr. "The Lord Rhys," Prince of So. Wales. Fr. Llewelyn, ap Iorwerth, 10, 46, 128, 240, 246, &c. The other important lines are fr. Rhirid Flaidd, "lord of Penllyn," 1, &c., Cors y Gedol (Fitz Gerald), Holland, Earls of Kent, de Bohun, de Mowbray and l'Estrange. Reference to details of these lines may be had on other pages of this vol.; Vist. N.W. (general); 6 vols. *H. Powys Fadog*; Harl. MS. peds., Peniarth MS., N. Lib. W.

EDWARD AP WATKIN (see p. 121) was father of John ap Edward, f. of Edward ap John of Cynlas, f. of Evan ap Edward, f. of Sarah (b, 1695), wf. of John Morgan (2d), f. of Hannah, wf. of Capt. James Hunter, f. Capt. John Hunter, f. Sarah, wf. of Wm. R. von. Löhr (Van Leer), f. Isaac Van Leer, father of Ellen Frances, wf. Geo. H. Earle, f. of George H. Earle, Jr., of Philadelphia (see other chart, this ped., ped. XIX., and chart ped. XX.).

Pedigree XVIII.

Edward ap John Wynn. [Authorities cited *supra*.] He inherited Garth Llwyd, in Doldrewyn, parish of Llandderfel, Penllyn, and adjacent lands and tenements in the township of Cynlas (then in Llandderfel) and Nantlleidiog (in Llanfor). The approximate date of his birth was 1490-1500. Died between 20 April and 6 May, 1575. [See his will cited *infra*.]

Edward ap John Wynn married Llowry,[1] daughter of Howel Lloyd,[2] of Bala, ap David ap Maredydd[3] ap Howel[4] ap Tudor ap Goronwy ap Gruffydd, of Llanuwchllyn; from Rhirid Flaidd. [Dwnn, ii., 249;[5] "History of Powys Fadog," vi., 71.]

1575. Will of Edward ap John Wynn, of the p'ish of Llanddervell. Dated 20 April, 1575. Proved at St. Asaph, 6 May, 1575. [Reg. $\frac{1569}{1575}$, folio 231, &c., Probate Registry, St. Asaph.]

The testator desires to be buried within the Parish Church of Llanddervell.

He bequeaths to his daughter, Katherine vch. Edward the sum of five pounds, to be paid her by his (the testator's) son [and heir] Watkyn ap Edward.

The testator gives and bequeaths unto his son Ieūn [*i.e.*, Evan] ap Edward, a tenement which Thomas ap dd ap Jon now dwelleth in and his part of the meadow which he bought of Ieūn ap gr goz.

He gives and bequeaths unto his son Robert a tenement called Cwm tale Sarne.

He gives and bequeaths unto his son Nicholas the tenement cal led Keven bordig.

The testator protests before God that he never assigned nor settled his lands to his brother Roger ap John Wynn but for the term of his natural life.[6]

---

[1] Llowry was living 20 April, 1575. Her father's younger half-brother, Sir John, was collated to the Rectory of Llanycil (Bala), 1537.

[2] Howel Lloyd, of Bala, married Mallt, daughter of Howel Vychan, of Llwydiarth, Montgomeryshire. This Howel Vychan, had a lease of a tenement called Tyddyn y Voel, in the parish of Llanbrynmair, from John, abbot of Ystrad Marchell (Strata Marcella), dated 30 August, 1530 ["Cambrian Quarterly," i., 328], and is named in Ministers' Accounts 32 Hen. VIII., and later. [Pub. Rec. Office.]

[3] Maredydd ap Howel, of Penllyn, was on a Jury, at Bala, 31 Hen. VI. (1453). His wife was Gwenhwyfar, daughter of Ieuan ap Tudor, who was one of the sureties for the farmer of the Raglorship of Penllyn at Michaelmas, 4 Hen. VI. (1425).

[4] Howel ap Tudor was farmer, under the Prince of Wales, of the Mill of Penaran, in the hundred of Penllyn, at Michaelmas, 1 Hen. IV. (1400). [Dwnn, ii., 249.]

[5] Dwnn has the marriages confused, and gives wrong mother for Lowry.

[6] It is evident that Edward ap John had suffered a recovery and executed a deed of trust to his brother Roger, entailing the greater part of his estate. This was a very common practice at this time.

The testator gives and bequeaths unto Cadwaladr ap Watkyn [his grandson], his heirs and assigns, a tenement of lands where Thomas ap dd ap Jon now dwelleth, paying yearly for the space of six years the rent thereof to testator's sons Ieūn and Robert.

To his daughter Gwen vch. Edward xx^s. rent per year due upon John ap Morice.

The testator mentions his wife Lowrie and his sister Lowrie, and appoints his sons Watkyn ap Edward and Nicholas ap Edward, executors, and Thomas ap Robert ap gr and John Wynn ap ₁Cadwaladr to be overseers.

Witnesses: John Gr. Lloid, Cadwaladr[1] ap Ieūn, Robert ap David,[2] John ap Morice,[3] Mr. Morgan Jones, clīco, Ellice ap holl ap Ilni ap holl, Ieūn ap Edward.

ISSUE:

i. Watkyn ap Edward, *of whom presently*.
ii. Ieuan (Evan) ap Edward named in his father's will, 20 April, 1575 ; he had under said will a tenement in Llandderfel, of which Thomas ap David ap John was then tenant ; his father's share of a certain meadow purchased of Ieuan ap Gruffydd Goch, and one half of the whole rent of a tenement of lands where the said Thomas ap David ap John dwelt, for the term of six years. [Reg. $\frac{1569}{1575}$, folio 231, &c., Probate Registry, St. Asaph.]
iii. Robert ap Edward, of Llandderfel, named in his father's will, 20 April, 1575 ; he had under said will a tenement called Cwm tale Sarne, and one half of the whole rent of a tenement of lands where Thomas ap David ap John dwelt, for the term of six years.
iv. Nicholas ap Edward, of Llandderfel, named in his father's will, 20 April, 1575 ; he had under said will a tenement called Keven bordig, and is named as one of his father's executors.
v. John ap Edward ap John Wynn, of Llandderfel ; m. Elizabeth, daughter of Morgan ap Robert, of Crogen, by whom he had no issue, and died before 20 April, 1575.
vi. Catherine, living 20 April, 1575.
vii. Gwen, living 20 April, 1575.

Watkyn ap Edward, eldest son and heir of Edward ap John Wynn, of Garth Llwyd, in the township of Doldrewyn, parish of Llandderfel, Penllyn. [Authorities cited *supra ;* Dwnn, ii., 229.] He held, adjacent to Garth Llwyd, lands and tenements in the townships of Cynlas and Nant-lleidiog, and elsewhere.

---

[1] Cadwaladr ap Ieuan (or Evan) was the grandson of the testator.
[2] Robert was son of David ap John Wynn.
[3] Probably son of Morris ap Watkin, of Llandrillo.

1575, 20 April. Named in his father's will, and probate granted to him and to his brother Nicholas ap Edward, 6 June following. [Reg. $\frac{1569}{1575}$, folio 231, &c., Probate Registry, St. Asaph.]

Watkyn ap Edward married Grace, daughter of Cadwaladr[1] ap Sir Robert[2] ap Rhys, of Plâs yn Rhiwlas, near Bala. [Dwnn, ii., 229; "History of Powys Fadog," vi., 109.] The mother of Grace was Jane, daughter of Maredydd[3] ap Ieuan ap Robert, of Dolwyddelan and Gwydir, and her mother was Margaret, daughter of Morris ap John ap Maredydd. The first wife of Maredydd ap Ieuan, was Alice, daughter of William[4] ap Gruffydd ap Robert, of Coch Wylyn.

1610-11, 22 Feb. Watkyn ap Edward, buried at Llandderfel. [Llandderfel Parish Register, anno 1610.]

ISSUE :

i. Edward ap Watkyn, *of whom presently.*

ii. Cadwaladr ap Watkyn ; married, 2dly,[5] daughter of Ellis

---

[1] Cadwaladr ap Robert, son of Sir Robert ap Rhys, of Plâs Iolyn, had a lease under the conventual seal of Strata Marcella, presumably dated 22 Hen. VIII., for the Grange of Penllyn (including Plâs yn Rhiwlas, which he held in 1540, and is mentioned as tenant of the same lands as late as 5-6 Philip and Mary. [Ministers' Accounts of the Abbey of Strata Marcella, 27-32 Hen. VIII., No. 209, Pub. Rec. Office ; *et seq.*] His grandson, Cadwaladr Wyn-Price, represented Merionethshire in Parliament, 1584.

[2] Robert ap Rhys had a lease under the conventual Seal of Strata Marcella dated 20 Feb., 1527, for 59 years, for a tenement afterwards in the possession of Ieuan ap Howel Vaughan. ["Montgomeryshire Collections," v. 402.] He had been chaplain to Cardinal Wolsey, and his effigy remains in Yspytty Evan Church (see vol. ii.) *In re* his father, see note, *supra*.

[3] Maredydd (Meredith) ap Ieuan (alias Wynn) was a very distinguished man, and ancestor to the Wynnes of Gwydir ; see [" History of the Gwydir family," Wynn.]

[4] William ap Gruffydd ap Robert (or Robin) was captain of lances at Bosworth Field, and was afterwards Sheriff of Carnarvonshire for life, 1496.

[5] She was his second wife. His first wife, by whom he probably had no issue, is stated in MS. pedigree to have been Susannah, daughter of Robert Lloyd, of Gwern y Brechtwn. Cadwaladr ap Watkyn in late pedigrees is called of Garth Llwyd, and his daughter Grace, is supposed to have carried that property to the Meyrick family, and this assumes that he was the eldest son, which is very improbable. In the first place, his grandfather, Edward ap John Wynn, by his will of 20 April, 1575, bequeaths him a farm (for which he is to pay rent for six years to his uncles) in fee simple. If Cadwaladr ap Watkyn had been the eldest son of Watkyn he would, of course, have been heir to the entire estate not alienated by the said will, or any deed of trust, and therefore his grandfather would be very unlikely to further provide for him. Secondly, he was, with his brother Nicholas, deforciant in a Fine, levied in 1614, by William Edward evidently to bar the remainder of Garth Llwyd, which, upon the death of the said William Edward, s. p., descended to Evan ap Edward, nephew of the said William, who died seized thereof in 1647. Thirdly, no contemporaneous records call him of Garth Llwyd, but only of Doldrewyn Township.

Now, the facts seem to be these. Watkyn ap Edward appears, as was then the custom, to have suffered a recovery and executed a feoffment, whereby he entailed Garth Llwyd, or a moiety thereof, and other lands to his son Edward, and after his decease, to the latter's son and heir, and to his issue in tail male, and in default of such issue, then to Cadwaladr, the second son of the said Watkyn, and to his issue male, and in default of such issue, then to Nicholas, another son of the said Watkyn, and to his heirs or assigns. Watkyn ap Edward

[*Note continued on page 120.*]

Vaughan, of Brinllech, by whom he had issue: (a) Grace, m. at Llandderfel Church, 5 Feb., 1618-19;[1] Edmund, son of Peter Meyrick; she was buried at Llandderfel, 25 Augt., 1629; (b) Elizabeth, unm. 1619; (c) Gwen, wife of Robert Evans. Cadwaladr ap Watkyn was of the township of Doldrewyn, parish of Llandderfel, and was buried at Llandderfel, 27 May, 1622. [Llandderfel Parish Register.]

iii. Nicholas ap Watkyn, deforciant (with his brother Cadwaladr) in Fine 8 Augt., 12 Jac. I. (1614). [Rolls of the Feet of Fine, Merionethshire, Spring Bdle., 12 Jac. I.] His daughter Jane is mentioned in the will of Oliver Thomas ap Robert, proved 1623, at St. Asaph.

iv. Ellis ap Watkyn. Thomas ap David ap Ellis ap Watkyn, of Llandderfel, was living 7 July, 1740. [Act Book $\frac{1637}{1670}$, St. Asaph.]

[*Note continued from page 119.*]

also, doubtless, provided for his sons Cadwaladr and Nicholas and Ellis. He probably left a will, but there are no wills at St. Asaph for 1610-11, and no Act Book. Nor can his will be found at Somerset House.

Edward ap Watkyn died in or before 1614 (I am inclined to suppose that 1614 was the year of his death), leaving at least four sons, *viz.*: William ap Edward, his heir, John ap Edward, who, either by enfeoffment in the lifetime of his father, or by will, or settlement or will of Watkin, his grandfather, was seized of certain lands in Llandderfel, which had belonged to Edward ap John Wynn and descended to Watkyn.

At the time of the death of Edward ap Watkyn (supposing this to have occurred 1614), William Edward, or William ap Edward, was aged about 46 years and unmarried. We may presume that he desired the Garth Llwyd property, or his share of it, to descend to the children of his brother John, instead of reverting to his uncles, or the latter's issue, and that he purchased the remainders. At any rate, he brought an action against both Cadwaladr ap Watkyn and Nicholas ap Watkyn to extinguish whatever interest they may have possessed in Garth Llwyd, and adjoining lands, as appears by the following:—

12 Jac. I. (1614), 8 Augt. William Edward and Reginaldus ap John ap David; plts., and Cadwalader Watkyn, Nicholas Watkyn, and Morice Kenricke, defts.—Two messuages with lands in Doledrewyn, Gwythelwerne, Nantfrier and Llandderfel. [Rolls of the Feet of Fine, Merionethshire, Spring Bdle, 12 Jac. I., Pub. Rec. Office.]

The above two messuages were part or all of Garth Llwyd, and probably Tyddyn y Marchell. Reignald ap John ap David was merely introduced into the case for customary legal purposes, the final concord showing that the fee remained to William Edward. Morice Kenricke, one of the defendants, was probably the trustee of Watkyn ap Edward. Neither Cadwalader ap Watkin or Nicholas ap Watkyn had issue male living in 1614.

William ap Edward of Doldrewyn died, s.p., 1645. He evidently enfeoffed Evan John, the eldest son of his brother John, for the latter died seized of Garth Llwyd, or part thereof, in 1647. The latter evidently also executed a deed of trust, reserving the right to charge the estate. What disposal was made of Garth Llwyd is uncertain. It may have gone to the eldest son of Edward ap John, Evans brother. Eventually, it became the property of the Meyrick family, by reason, as some say, of foreclosure of a mortgage.

[1] A settlement was made in favour of Edmund Meyrick and Grace his wife, and their heirs, 1619, as appears by the following: 5 July, 17, Jac. I. (1619). Edward Vaughan, gentleman and Morgan Lloyd (of Crogen), gentleman (Trustees) plts., Peter Meiricke, esq., Edmund Meiricke, gentleman, son and heir apparent of the said Peter, Grace, his wife. Cadder Watkyn, Elizabeth vch. Caddr, Robert Evans, gentleman, and Gwenne, his wife, defts, 38 messuages, 10 cottages, 30 gardens, 1 water corn mill, 1,000 acres of [arable] land, 500 acres of meadow, 1,000 acres of pasture, 60 acres of wood, 500 acres of furze and heath, and 40 acres of moor, in Ucheldre, Llygallog, Gwyddelwerne, Maesgwyn, Aberalwen, Corwen, Trewyn, Carrog, Mustwr, Crogen, Cwindadu, Llanywelyn, Penmaen, Llanfor, Llandderfel, Doldrewyn Kystle, and Nantffrier.

The greater part of this property belonged to the Meyricks.

Pedigree XVIII.

Edward ap Watkyn, of Garth Llwyd, township of Doldrewyn, parish of Llandderfel. ["History of Powys Fadog," vi., 84, citing Add. MS. 9864.] He died before 8 Augt., 1614, when his son, William ap Edward, levied a fine against Cadwaladr ap Watkyn and Nicholas ap Watkyn to recover the fee of two messuages and lands in Doldrewyn, Gwythelwerne and Nantfrier which had belonged to Watkyn ap Edward. [Rolls of the Feet of Fine, Merionethshire, Spring Bdle. 12 Jac. I., Pub. Rec. Office.]

Edward ap Watkyn married the daughter of Thomas ap Robert ap Gruffydd (Griffith), of Llandderfel.[1]

ISSUE:

   i. William ap Edward, born about 1571; he levied a fine against his uncles, Cadwaladr and Nicholas, 8 Augt., 1614, to recover the fee of two tenements with lands in Doldrewyn and elsewhere; d. s. p. "Willm ap. Edw. of Doldrewyn sepult. aged 75 years or thereabouts." Died 3 Feb., 1645. Buried 5 Feb. He is named as a freeholder in Penllyn on Lay Subsidy Roll, 3 Car. I. (1627-8). [No. $\frac{220}{330}$, Merionethshire. Pub. Rec. Office.]

   ii. John ap Edward, *of whom presently*.

   iii. Ellis ap Edward; living 17 Jan., 1621.

   iv. Watkyn ap Edward, who had Nicholas ap Watkin (or Watkyn), witness to will of Robert Lewis, of Llandderfel, 11 Feb., 1646. [St. Asaph.] Nicholas had Edward ap Nicholas bapt. at Llandderfel, 28 Sept., 1647.[2]

---

[1] This marriage is confirmed by the will of John Thomas ap Robert, of Llandderfel, proved at St. Asaph, 17 Jan., 1621. [Reg. $\frac{1620}{1623}$, folio 147, &c.], whereof the testator appoints his nephew, Ellis ap Edward, executor; Nicholas Watkyns, the uncle of Ellis; being one of the witnesses. Also by will of Evan John, 1647 (cited hereafter), wherein certain relations of the testator are mentioned. Also by the will of Oliver Thomas ap Robert of Llandderfel, proved at St. Asaph, 1623.

Thomas ap Robert ap Griffith was one of the overseers of the will of Edward ap John Wynn (cited *supra*), 1575, and Edward ap Watkyn seems to have been a double first cousin of his wife.

[2] Edward ap Nicholas is described as of Cynlas, parish of Llanfor, yeoman. One Richard Price, of Glanlloidiogin, in the parish of Llanfor, who had married one of the daughters of Edward ap John of Cynlas (d. 1667), died 1685, leaving a will and constituting his son, Richard ap Thomas sole executor, who renounced, and letters C. T. A. were granted to this Edward Nicholas, of Cynlas, one of the deceased's relations, and Thomas Edward of Nant-lleidiog, brother-in-law of the deceased, and second cousin to Edward Nicholas, is named with Thomas Richard (who renounced) as a bondsman.

v. Nicholas ap Edward. ["History of Powys Fadog," vi., 84, citing Add. MS. 9864.] His daughter, Jane, married 1st, John Pryse ; 2dly, Robert Maesmor.

vi. Agnes, m. William Owen, of Llanfor.[1]

John ap Edward, of the parish of Llandderfel. He held certain lands and tenements, partly in the township of Cynlas, then in Llandderfel, and partly in the adjoining township of Nant-lleidiog, parish of Llanfor, which had belonged to Watkyn ap Edward, and adjoining the lands called Cwm tale y Sarn, which Edward ap John Wynn, by his will of 20 April, 1575, bequeathed to his son Robert ap John Wynn. Under the designation of *Johanes Edwards* he is assessed for the same lands, 3 Car. I. (1627-8). [Lay Subsidy Roll for Merionethshire, under "Penllyn Commot," 3 Car. I., No. $\frac{220}{333}$, Pub. Rec. Office.] John ap Edward died before 24 March, 1646.

There is some evidence, not amounting to a certainty, that he married, about 1588, Jane, daughter of an owner of Y Vaner.[2]

ISSUE :[3]

i. Evan ap John, of Garth Llwydd ;[4] d.s.p.

---

[1] William Owen died 1640, and letters of admon. on his estate were granted Sept. of the same year to Agnes vch. Edward, relict of deceased. Their daughter, Elizabeth Williams, is named in will of Evan John, proved 1647; she married Robert Pugh, or ap Hugh, and was mother of Hugh Roberts, who removed to Pennsylvania. Elizabeth Williams died in Pennsylvania.

[2] He could not have been over 16 years of age at the time unless this marriage was subsequent to the date of the Visitation pedigree, which was frequently the case. This however, was not an unusually early age for marriage at that time in this neighbourhood. The Vaner ped. is confusedly drawn, and supposedly incorrect.

[3] Robert may not have been the second son, but Edward does not seem to have been so either, otherwise there would have been no necessity for the bequest in will of Evan John, as Edward would have been the next heir.

[4] The will of Evan ap John, of the parish of Llandderfel, in the county of Merioneth, is dated xxiiij. March, 1646, and was proved at St. Asaph, 15 May, 1647. [Reg. $\frac{1642}{1649}$, folio 125, &c.]

The testator, after charging the rents of his tenements and lands, called Tythyn y Marchel and Garth Llwyd with an annual payment to the poor of the parish, and after bequeathing to his brother, Edward ap John, certain tenements and lands, as will here-

ii. Robert ap John, of the parish of Llandderfel, who had issue : (a) John ap Robert ; (b) Edward ap Robert ; (c) William ap Robert ; (d) Cadwaladr ap Robert ; (e) Lowry ; (f) Jane.

iii. Edward ap John, *of whom presently.*

iv. —— (dau.), married Thomas ——, and had Hugh John Thomas, of Nant-lleidiog.[1]

v. —— (dau.), married Hugh ——[2], and had Thomas ap Hugh, living 24 March, 1646.

Edward ap John, of Cynlas, parish of Llandderfel, Penllyn.

1646. Will of Evan John " of the p'ish of llandervell." Dated xxiiijth day of March, 1646 (*viz.*, 1646-7). Proved at St. Asaph, 15 May (Decimo quinto menses Maij), 1647. [Reg. $\frac{1642}{1649}$, folio 125, &c., Probate Registry, St. Asaph.] (The original cannot be found).

The testator bequeaths as follows :

" Item, I give & bequeath to the poore of the p'ish of llanddervell the sume of xxs. to be yearlie payd unto them out of the rents issues and profitts of my mesuages lands and Tenemts called tythyn y marcheli and Garth lwyd for ever to be distributed between the poore of the said p'ish by the discrecon of my brother Edward John and his heires and the Churchwardens of the said parish for the time being within the space of two dayes before the feast day of the Nativity of our Lord god yearlie for ever And the said mesuages lands and tenemts to be charged therewith and that the Churchwardens of the said p'ish for the time being may distraine thereupon for the same in default of payment."

" Item, I give devise and bequeath to my brother Edward John all my mesuage lands and Tenemts with the app'tences situate lying and being in the sev'all townships of Nantleidiog & Kynlas Com'tt of Penllyn County of Merioneth To have and to hould to him his heires and assignes forever."

---

after more at large appear, makes bequests to the following persons: To his nephews, John Robert, Edward Robert, William Robert, and Cadwaladr Robert.

To nieces Lowry and Jane vch Robert.

To nephew, Thomas ap Hugh, niece Marion vch. Hugh, nephew Hugh John, cousin Cadwaladr ap Robert ap Moris. Marred vch. Cadwaladr, Gwen vch. Cadwaladr, Lowry vch. Thomas, cousin Gainor Evan, uncle John Jones, niece Jane vch. John, niece Lowry Griffith, Elizabeth vch. William, Margaret John Owen, William ap Griffith ap William, William ap Hugh ap William, the youngest son of Catherin vch. Robt. ap Ellise, John Thomas Ellise, Modlen Thomas, Elizabeth vch. John William, testator's godson, Evan Robert, nephew Evan ap Edward (a minor), nephew William ap Edward (a minor). The testator appoints his brother, Edward ap John, executor.

Witnesses : Gruffyth Lloyd, William David, Morgan John, Thomas Cadwalader, Rytherach ap Robert, Cadwalader ap Edwardes.

[1] Hugh John Thomas removed to Pennsylvania, 1682.

[2] Probably Hugh ap Evan, of Yspytty Evan.

The testator also, among other things, bequeaths certain monies to his nephews, Evan ap Edward and William ap Edward; and he constitutes and appoints his brother Edward ap John to be sole executor of the said will.

1663-4. Edward ap John,[1] under the designation of "Edwd John," is taxed as a freeholder of lands in Llandderfel, Penllyn Isavon, in Lay Subsidy Roll, 15 Car. II. [Lay Subsidy Roll for Merionethshire, 15 Car. II. No. $\frac{2 2 2}{3 3 1}$, Pub. Rec. Office.]

1667, 1 March. "Edwardus ap John de Kynlas sepultus est primo die Martii" (de anno 1667). [Llandderfel Parish Register.]

ISSUE:

i. Thomas ap Edward,[2] of Nant-lleidiog, living 1686.
ii. John ap Edward,[3] bapt. at Llandderfel Church, 19 June, 1635. Died in Merion, Pennsylvania, 1683.[3]
iii. William ap Edward,[4] died in Pennsylvania, 1714-15.
iv. Evan ap Edward, *of whom presently*.
v. —— (dau.), married Richard Price.

---

[1] "Edward ap John of Cynlas .... a freeholder of about £24 per annum .... a man of good repute and careful to bring up his children in the fear of the Lord, according to the Church of England." [Bible late in possession of Mrs. M. Creswell, Merion, Pennsylvania; "Penna. Mag. of Hist. and Biog.," x., 107 (1886).]

[2] See note *supra*.

[3] John ap Edward. The entry in the Llandderfel Parish Register reads: "Johannes ap Edward filius Edwardi ap John baptizatus fuit decimo nono die Junij dieqʒ Veneris," 1635.

He joined the Society of Friends, and removed to Merion, Pennsylvania, 1682. Under the designation of John ap Edward of Nantlleidiog, yeoman, he is grantee in a deed, executed in Wales, dated 18 March, 1681-2, for 312½ acres of land in Pennsylvania, of which part was surveyed to him in Merion, and part in Goshen. He arrived in Pennsylvania in August, 1682, and died the following year. Will dated 8 month, 16, 1683; proved at Philadelphia, 2 month, 8, 1683-4. He names children, Evan, Edward, and Elizabeth; brothers Evan ap Edward and William ap Edward, and nephew John Evan, son of his brother, Evan ap Edward. The children of John ap Edward were: 1, Evan, b. 2 month, 2, 1677; d. before 1699; 2, Sarah, b. 11 month, 8, 1673; d. young; 3, Edward, b. 8 month 5, 1681; 4, Elizabeth (surname Jones), b. 12 month, 18, 1671; m. 10 month, 25, 1699; Robert Fletcher, of Philadelphia. Edward, b. 1681; who assumed the surname of Jones, and was known as Edward Jones, jr., to distinguish him from Dr. Edward Jones, sold his Merion and Goshen lands, and it is not known what became of him, but he probably removed to Virginia. [Deed Book C. I., Phila.; Will Book A, folio 37, Phila.]

[4] William ap Edward. He is named in the will of his uncle, Evan John, of Garth Llwyd, Llandderfel, 20 April, 1646. With his brother John, he, about 1674, joined the Society of Friends. In March, 1672-3, he was tenant of a farm called Tythyn y Corne, alias Tythyn y Gessel, belonging to Evan Lloyd ap Rhydderch, of Garn, in the parish of Llanfor, and probably continued to reside in Ucheldre Township, Llanfor, until his removal to Pennsylvania, in 1682. Under the designation of William ap Edward, of Ucheldre, he had a deed, executed in Wales, dated 1 April, 1682, for 156¼ acres of land in Pennsylvania, part of which was surveyed to him in Merion. He removed from Merion to Blockley, where he died 1714-15. Will dated 29 Dec., 1714; proved at Philadelphia, 29 Jan., 1714-15. He married, 1st, Katherine, daughter of Robert ap Hugh, and, 2dly, Jane, daughter of John ap Edward, of near Bala. For issue see Glenn's "Merion." [Deed Book C. I., folio 217, Phila.; Will Book D, folio 25, Phila., and "Pennsylvania Magazine of History and Biography," x., 107.]

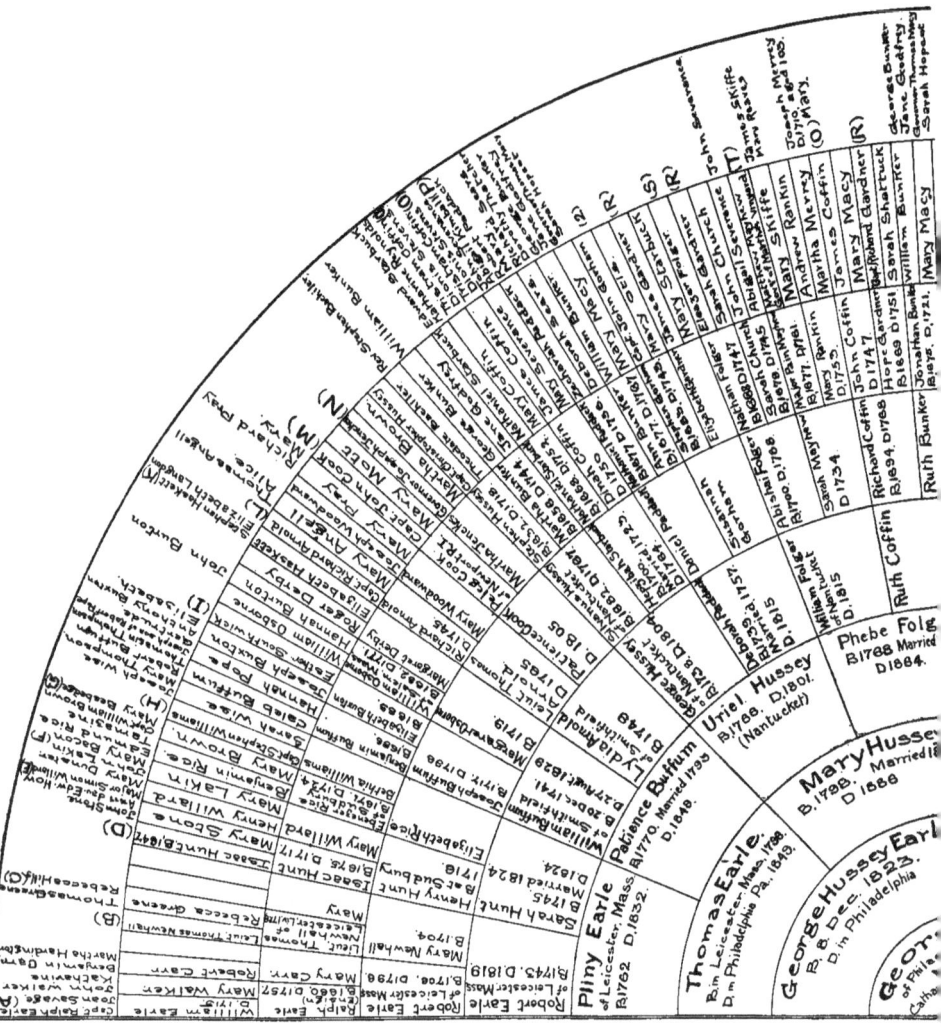

A.—Descendants of Ralph Earle, Earle. **B.**—Son of Ensign Thomas Newhall and Elizabeth, dau. Nicholas Potter, s. Thomas Newhall of Lynn, and Mary. **C.**—Thomas Greene of Malden, b. 1630, m. Rebecca, dau. Joseph Hills, s. Thomas Greene, b. 1606, and Elizabeth. Joseph Hills of Billericay, Essex (s. George Hills and Mary) settled in Charlestown, Mass., and m. Rose Clarke. **D.**—Isaac Hunt, s. Isaac (by Mary Stone), s. William, b. 1605 (by Elizabeth Best). Mary Stone, dau. John (by Ann, dau. Edward How), s. Gregory, b. Nayland, Suffolk, 1592 (by Margaret Garrad), s. David (by Elizabeth Hewit), s. Symond (by Agnes ——), s. David of Nayland (liv. 1510), s. Symond (and Elizabeth), d. 1510. **E.**—S. Richard Willard (and Margery Humphrie), s. Symon Willard of Goudhurst, Kent (d. 1584) (and Elizabeth his wife), s. Richard Willard, d. 1558. Ensign John Lakin, b. Reading, England, s. William Lakin (by Mary ——), s. William Lakin of Reading, d. in N.E. 1672. **F.**—Mary Bacon, dau. Michael of Charlestown, Mass. (and Mary ——), s. Michael of Dedham, Mass., d. 1648, s. Michael Bacon of Ireland. **G.**—Dau. Thomas Besbedge of Hedcorn, Kent, remd. to N.E. 1635. **H.**—Capt. Stephen Williams, b. Roxbury, 1640, s. Robert (and Elizabeth Stalham), b. Gt. Yarmouth, 1593, s. Stephen Williams and Margaret Cooke. **I.**—Dau. Daniel Southwick and Esther, dau. Joseph Boyce of Salem; s. Lawrence Southwick fr. Lancashire; remd. to N.E. 1627, and Cassandra his wf. **K.**—Son Stephen (and Elizabeth) of Marnshull, Dorset, d. 1648. **L.**—According to ped. in Austin's 160 Allied Families, the Arnolds were of Llanthony, Monmouthshire, and desct. there given back to Meiric ap Ynyr, Prince of Gwent. **M.**—Capt. John Cook was son of Capt. Thomas Cook (and Mary, dau. William Havens); s. Capt. Thomas Cook (see p. 106). Mary Mott was dau. of Jacob (and Joanna, dau. Giles [and Joan,] s. Anthony Slocum of Taunton), s. Adam Mott, of Cambridge, England, d. 1661. **N.**—Son of

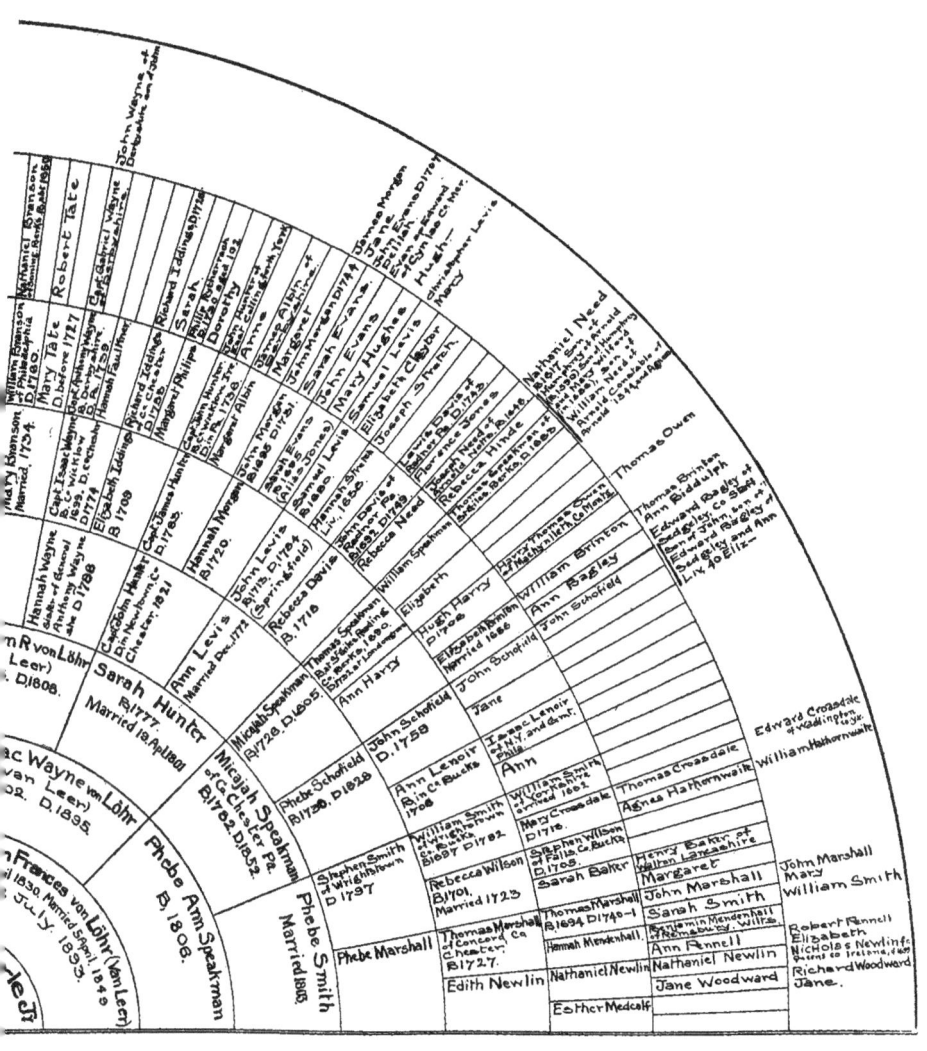

Joseph, b. Colebrook, Buckinghamshire, 1632 (and Hester, dau. Wm. Ballard), s. Joseph Jenckes, d. in Lynn, 1645, and Elizabeth. Gov. Joseph Jenckes m. Martha, dau. John Brown (by Mary, dau. of Obadiah (and Catherine) Holmes, or Hulme, of Reddish, Lanc.), s. Chad Brown, who arriv. N.E. 1638 (Boston), and Elizabeth his wife. Capt. Chris. Hussey, s. John of Dorking, Surrey, and Mary Wood. **O.**—Nicholas Coffin of Brixton, co Devon, s. Peter, and Mary dau. Hugh Boscawen (by Philippa Carminow), m. Joan ——, and had Peter, d. 1628; m. Joan, dau. Robert Keymber, and had Tristram, b. 1609-10; d. N.E. 1681. Dionis Stevens, dau. Robert (and Dionis), s. John Stevens of Brixton, co. Devon. **P.**—Dau., Richard (by Ursula Scott), s. Richard of Lawford, Essex, d 1619, and Elizabeth. Edmund Scott of Rattlesden, Suffolk, d. 1621, father of Henry, d. Sudbury, Mass., 1624-5; m. Martha, dau. Thomas Whatlocke of Rattlesden, d. 1608, f. Ursula, wife of Richard Kimball. **Q.**—Son Capt. John (and Desire Howland), Benefield, Northants, 1621; s. Ralph, b. 1575, s. James (by Agnes Bernington), b. 1550, b. John Gorham of Benefield. Desire Howland was dau. John Howland (*Mayflower*), by Elizabeth, dau. John Tilley (*Mayflower*). Mary Otis, dau. of John, b. Glastonbury, 1621 (by Mary, dau. Nicholas Jacob of Wales), s. John (and Margaret), s. Richard of Glastonbury, b. 1611. **R.**—James Gardner, s. Capt. Richard (by Sarah Shattuck). s. Thomas Gardner and Margaret Frier. James Gardner m. Mary, dau. Nathaniel Starbuck, s. Edward. **S.**—Son Peter Folger (by Mary Morrell), s. John Folger of Norwich, and Meribell Gibbs. **T.**—Simon Mayhew of Dinton, Wilts, father of Robert of Dinton, m. Jone, dau. John Bridmore, f. Thomas of Tisbury, d. 1590, f. Matthew of Tisbury, d. 1614 (m. Alice, dau. Edward and Edith Barter), f. Gov. Thomas Mayhew, who m. Martha Parkhurst, f. Rev. Thomas Mayhew, who m. Jane, dau. Thomas Paine, f. Gov. Matthew Mayhew.

PEDIGREE XVIII.

Evan ap Edward, born in Cynlas, parish of Llandderfel.

1646, 20 April. Named as "my nephew Evan ap Edward," in will of his uncle, Evan John, of Garth Llwyd (cited *supra*), and then a minor.

1683, 16 Oct. Named in the will of his brother, John ap Edward, then of the township of Merion, Pennsylvania (cited *supra*).

ISSUE:

i. John Evans, *of whom presently*.

John Evans, son of Evan ap Edward, of Cynlas, alias John Evan Edward, and John Evan. He was born in Cynlas, and removed with his kinsmen to Merion, Pennsylvania.

1683, 16 Oct. Named in the will of his uncle, John ap Edward, of Merion, Pennsylvania (cited *supra*).

1686, 16 July. John Evans married Mary Hughes. [Records of Merion, Radnor, and Haverford Mtg., Philadelphia.] William ap Edward and family sign marriage certificate as nearest relatives of the groom.

John Evans takes up land on rent, in Radnor Township.

1696, John Evans, being then of Radnor, subscribes to the Susquehanna Land Company over the signature Jno. Evan Ed^w., to distinguish him from John Evans, or Evan, late of Nantmell, also of Radnor.

ISSUE (*inter alia*):

i. Sarah, born 11 of 11 month, 1695; married, 7 month, 10, 1717, John Morgan, son of John and Sarah of Radnor.

126   WELSH FOUNDERS OF PENNSYLVANIA

John Morgan, of Radnor, Penna. = Sarah dau. John Evans,
Will proved 4 March, 1731; s.   s. Evan ap Edward, of Cynlas.
John Morgan and Sarah, dau.   M. 17, 10, 1717. From Watkyn
John Evans, late of Nantmell.   ap Edward, of Garth Llwyd.
(See Morgan).

James Morgan, d. young.

Hannah Morgan, b. 1720. Will proved 3 Dec., 1803. = Capt. James Hunter. Will proved 24 March, 1783.

James Hunter.

Capt. John Hunter, of Newtown, county of Chester; d. Dec., 1821. Will proved 17 Dec., 1821. = Ann Levis, m. 8 Dec.. 1772, at St. David's Ch., Radnor, Penna.

George Hunter, m. Grace Brick.
Sarah, m. Evan Lewis.
Mary, m. Hugh Jones.

Ann.
Peter Hunter.
Samuel Hunter.

James Hunter. d. s. p.

Rebecca, M. b. 3 Sept., 1775.

Sarah Hunter. =

William R. von Löhr (Van Leer), b. 30 May, 1775; d. 25 May, 1808. M. in Christ Church, Phila., 19 April, 1801. (See another page).

Elizabeth, b. Augt., 1780.

John Hunter, b. 13 Dec., 1782.
Hannah, b. 26 May, 1785.
Thomas Hunter, d. young.

Isaac Wayne von Löhr (Van Leer), b. 26 March, 1802; d. 1895. = Phebe Ann Speakman (1st wife); m. 7 June, 1827.

Hannah, d. inft.

Ann Louisa, b. 12 Nov., 1804; d. 22 Dec., 1874; m., 1 Dec., 1829, J. B. Willaner, M.D. (See another page).

Anne, m. William Huddleston.
Isaac Wayne Van Leer. Mortally wounded in action at Seven Pines, 15 June, 1864.

Ellen Frances von Löhr (Van Leer). B. 5 April, 1830; m. 5 April, 1849; d. July, 1893. =

George Hussey Earle, b. 8 Dec., 1823. (See folding Chart II., ped. xviii.).

Hunter Evans Van Leer, m. Clara Wills.
Archer W. Van Leer, m. Josephine Colladay.

Frances Van Leer, m. Edward Hine Johnson, of Brooklyn, N.Y.

Florence, m. (1) William Nicholson; (2) Edward H. Coates, 7 Jan., 1879.
Alice, m. Reginald Herbert Jones.

Mary, m. William Cook. (See another page).

George H. Earle, Jr., of Philadelphia. = Catherine Hansell, daughter of Clayton French.

Catharine Ann Earle, m. Victor Charles Mather, and has Catherine Earle Mather, and Charles E. Mather, Jr.

Caroline French. Died.

Mary. Died.

Frances von Löhr Earle, m. Lawrence Dilworth Beggs, of Pittsburg, and has Lawrence Dilworth Beggs.

George Howard Earle.

Ralph Earle.

Clayton French Earle.
Hansell French Earle.
Edith Earle.
Gladys Howland Earle.

PEDIGREE XIX.

Maredydd Goch, son of **Rhys Gloff** (alias Rhys Wendot, and Rhys, or Res, Vychan, or Fychan), of Dynevor (from Princes of South Wales). He seems to have become possessed, in the lifetime of his father, of certain lands in Radnorshire, and does not appear to have been forfeited with his father after the rebellion of 1282-3. He had:

Iorwerth ap Maredydd, who had:

Ieuan ap Iorwerth, who had:

David Lloyd, who inherited large estates in the neighbourhood of Preisteign, including Boultibrook in the parish of Norton. He lived in the reign of Edw. III., and had issue:

    i. Robert Lloyd, *of whom presently.*
    ii. Gruffydd Lloyd, of Boultibrook.

Robert Lloyd, son of David, of Pen y Bourth, married Janet, daughter of Gruffydd Vychan ap Gruffydd Goch, and had:

Llewelyn ap Robert Lloyd, of Pen y Bourth. He married Efa, daughter of Rhys Ddu, of the parishes of Llanddeiniol and Llanrhystyd, Cardiganshire, by Gwenllian, daughter of Ieuan ap Einion, of Efionydd, Carnarvonshire. [Dwnn, i., 267.] Rhys Ddu was the son of Llewelyn ap Kydwgan (or Cadwgan), of Carog, Llanddeiniol (by Gladys, daughter of Maredydd Vychan, of Blaen Trean, in the parish of Llan y Beddair, Carmarthenshire), ap Kydwgan ap Kydwgan Vawr ap Richard ap Rhys, of Pont y Chan, ap Rhys (Rys) ap Rhydderch, of Castle

Howel, descended from Kydivor (Kydifor) ap Dyfnwal, of Castle Howel, Cardiganshire, an officer under the "Lord Rhys," and who took by escalade the castle of Cardigan for that prince, subsequently marrying his daughter, Katherine. The wife of Kydwgan Vawr was Efa, daughter of Einion Sais, by Peredar his wife, descended from Rhys Gryg, son of the Lord Rhys.

Ieuan ap Einion, of Efionydd, father of Gwenllian, wife of Rhys Ddu, was party to a deed dated, at Wheeloc, on the next Friday after Easter, 12 Rich. II. [23 April, 1389], and her brother, Madog, was party to a deed dated 10 Hen. V. (1415).

This Ieuan ap Einion was of Bron y Foel, in the parish of St. Catherine, in Efionydd, and is mentioned in Symond's Switzerland as a valiant Welshman who had defended Henry of Transtamare and the throne of Castile against the Black Prince, in the 39th and 40th years of Edw. III. (1366), and who afterwards accompanied Enguerrad de Coucy (son-in-law of the English king) in his expedition against the Duke of Austria, under pretence of demanding the dower due to him (Enguerrad) in right of his mother. [MS. Pedigree of Nannau; note by Meyrick to Dwnn, ii., 93-4, *n.* 8.]

Ieuan had a brother, Howel, called Sir Howel y fwyall, or of the battle axe, who was distinguished for his prowess in the wars in France, in the time of Edward III. His countrymen have ever competed for him, with Denis de Morbeque, the honour of taking the French king prisoner. "This Howel," observes Sir John Wynn in his "History of the Gwydir Family," "was knighted at the field of Poyctiers, and by our countrymen is reported to have taken the French King; but, however it was, he did such service there that the Prince bestowed a messe of meate, to be served up dayly during his life, before his battle axe, which after was bestowed on the poor, whereof he was called Sir Howel y fwyall."

Pedigree XIX.

Einion ap Gruffydd, of Bron y Foel, the father of these brothers, is named as one of the heirs of "Wele Gogan in the villes of Whyloc" (Chwilog), Glasvryn, in the extent of the commot of Eivionydd, taken at Cricciaeth, and was High Sheriff of the Counties of Carnarvon and Merioneth. For the former he appears to have held the office in the 29th year of Edw. III., and for life. [Note of Meyrick to Dwnn, ii., 93, *n.* 6.] Einion ap Gruffydd was son of Gruffydd ap Howel ap Maredydd ap Einion ap Gwgan ap Maredydd ap Collwyn ap Tangno, lord of Llêyn.

The wife of Einion ap Gruffydd was Nest, daughter and heiress of Gruffydd ap Adda, of Dolgoch, Merionethshire, Raglor (governor) of the commot of Estimaner, 3 and 7 Edw., III., whose tomb, on which is his effigy in armour, remains in the church of Towyn.[1] He was the owner of Ynys y Maengwyn and other great estates in Estimaner and Ardudwy.

The wife of Ieuan ap Einion was Gwenhwyfar, daughter of Meuric Llwyd (or Lloyd) ap Meuric ap Ynyr ap Ynyr, of Nannau, Merionethshire, descended from Bleddyn ap Cynfyn, Prince of Powys. [Dwnn, ii., 93.] This Ynyr ap Ynyr (or Ynyr Vychan), lord of Nannau, presented a petition to Edward, Prince of Wales, at Kensington, 33 Edw. I. (1304-5), for the office of Raglor of the commot of Talybont, Merionethshire, stating that the king had given it to him for taking Madog ap Llewelyn, who, in the last war, had made himself Prince of Wales. The petition, however, was not granted, as no charter could be shown, and in the Parliament of 15 and 16 Edw. II. (1322-3), he and others were charged with attacking, on the next Wednesday after the Feast of St. Gregory, in the 15th of Edward II., the castle of John Grey, at Ruthin, setting fire to the town, and killing two men. ["Records of Caernarvon," 220; Rolls of Parlt., vol. i., p. 397.]

---

[1] She was also wife to Llewelyn ap Cynric, of Cors y Gedol.

Llewelyn ap Robert Lloyd, who was living *circa* 1460, left issue, *inter alia:*

Walter Llewelyn, of Pen y Borth (*circa* 1500), who married Mallt (Mary) daughter of David Lloyd ap Philip, and had:

Howel ap Walter, of the parish of Nantmell, Radnorshire. He held the Hall of Nantmell and various lands in Vaynor, or Vainor, a township in the same parish. Died before 1597. He married Gwenllian, daughter of Llewelyn ap Howel ap Rhys Gethin. [Dwnn, i., 267.]

ISSUE:
i. Rev. Owen Howel, Vicar of Llanbister, Radnorshire; died before 1567; married Maud, daughter of Howel ap Owen. [Dwnn, i., 268, 261.]
ii. Philip Walter. [Dwnn, i., 268.]
iii. Edward Gwyn, *of whom presently.*
iv. Evan Gwyn, of Nantmell, living 1597; married Elizabeth, daughter of Thomas ap Evan Lloyd, and had issue: (a) David ap Evan of Nantmell (died before 1 Car. I. (1625-6), who had Evan ap David, taxed in Nantmell 1 Car. I. (1625-6). [Dwnn, i., 268; Subsidy Roll, No. $\frac{224}{583}$a, Radnorshire]; (b) John ap Ieuan (Evan), called John ap *Jenkin.*
v. Mallt, married Howel ap David ap Maredydd (Meredith).
vi. Annest, married David ap Ieuan ap Rhydderch.

Edward Gwyn, (or Wyn) ap Howel, of Nantmell, living 1597. He held the Hall of Nantmell, and various lands in Vaynor or Vainor in the same parish. Died before 1 Car. I. [Dwnn, i., 268; Subsidy Roll No. $\frac{224}{583}$a, Radnorshire.] He married Eleanor Philips,[1] daughter of Owen Philips, Esquire, of Llanddewi Ystradyny, Radnorshire. Owen Philips was the son of Howel ap Philip ap Cadwgan Vychan ap Cadwgan ap Philip Dorddû, descended from Elystan Glodrydd, Prince of Fferlis, and he married Marged, daughter of James ap Rhys, of Y Mynchdy. [Dwnn, i., 260.]

Pedigree XIX.

James ap Rhys (No. 1) was son of Ieuan ap James ap Rhys, son of James ap Rhys ap David ap Howel Vain; descended from Elystan Glodrydd.

ISSUE:

i. John ap Edward Wyn (Gwyn) alias John Wyn, married Juliana, daughter of John ap Rhys. [Dwnn, i., 268.] He was living 1597; died before 1 Car. I., when his son Rees ap John Wyn was possessed of his estates. [Subsidy Roll, No. $\frac{224}{583}$a, Radnorshire.]

ii. Richard ap Edward Wyn. [Dwnn, i., 268.]

iii. Rhys (Rees) ap Edward, married Jane, daughter of Rhys ap David. [Dwnn, i., 268.]

iv. Morgan, *of whom presently.*

v. Hugh Gwyn, living 1 Car. I. (1625). [Subsidy Roll, No. $\frac{224}{583}$a. Radnorshire.]

vi. Thomas ap Edward. [Dwnn, i., 268.]

vii. Joyce, married David ap Evan. [Dwnn, i., 268.]

viii. Goleubryd. [Dwnn, i., 268.]

ix. Ellen. [Dwnn, i., 268.]

Morgan ap Edward, of Nantmell and Vainor in Nantmell, gentleman, son of Edward Gwyn. He is mentioned as living 1597. [Dwnn, i., 268.] Died before 1 Car. I. (1625). [Subsidy Roll No. $\frac{224}{583}$a, Radnorshire, Pub. Rec. Office, London], and had:

i. Lewis Morgan, *of whom presently.*

ii. Hugh Morgan, taxed in Nantmell 1 Car. I. (1625), and 4 Car. I. (1628).

iii. Edward Morgan, of Vainor, living 1666.

iv. John Morgan, will proved 25 May, 1663. [Hereford Probate Registry.]

Lewis Morgan, of Nantmell, gentleman, son of Morgan Edward, was taxed as one of the largest freeholders of Nantmell, 1 Car. I. (1625). [Subsidy Roll, No. $\frac{224}{583}$a, Radnorshire], and 4 Car. I. (1628). [Subsidy Roll No. $\frac{224}{584}$.] Will proved 28 August, 1671. [Hereford Probate Registry.] He was then probably 80 to 90 years old.

ISSUE:
i. Morgan Lewis, *of whom presently.*
ii. David Lewis, of Vainor.
iii. Evan Lewis, of Vainor; (see John Evans, of Nantmell), acquired lands in Vainor in his father's lifetime.

Morgan Lewis, of Nantmell, who acquired lands in Vainor in his father's lifetime, and was taxed there (in Vainor, Nantmell), 18 Car. II. (1667-7) and later. [Subsidy Roll, No. ###, Radnorshire.] He had:

James Morgan, born in Vainor, parish of Nantmell, Radnorshire, *circa* 1645. He married Jane ——. They removed with their children to the Province of Pennsylvania, in 1691. She died on shipboard 9 Sept., 1691. He died on their arrival, 14 Nov., 1691, and was buried at the head of Bohemia Bay, Bohemia Manor, on the Chesapeak, Maryland. [Morgan Family Bible, copy by the late Mr. Bruner, 1897.]

ISSUE:
i. Margaret, born 1 March, 1666.
ii. John, born 22 Nov., 1669; *of whom presently.*
iii. Evan, born 29 Nov., 1672.
iv. James, born 1 May, 1675; of Bristol; d.s.p.

John Morgan, eldest son and heir of James, born in Vainor, parish of Nantmell, Radnorshire, 22 Nov., 1669; removed to the Province of Pennsylvania 1691. [Family Bible Record.] He settled in the township of Radnor, County of Chester, near Philadelphia, and his wife was Sarah, daughter of John Evans, of Nantmell, Radnorshire, "gentleman," his kinsman.

John Morgan acquired three plantations in Radnor, near "Morgan's corner," which he called "Nantmeal [Nantmell] Hall," "Vainor," and "Brui Lion." He died about Dec. 1744. Will proved 9 Dec., 1744. [Recorded at Philadelphia. Will Book G, p. 153, &c.]

ISSUE:
i. John, born 1695; *of whom presently.*
ii. Hannah, born 1697.

Pedigree XIX.

iii. Sarah, born 1698; married Joseph Evans.
iv. James, born 1700; died 1 May, 1701.
v. James, born 1702, d. s. p.
vi. Evan, born 1704.
vii. Thomas, born 1706.
viii. Mary, born 1708.
ix. Samuel, born 1709.
x. Mordecai, born 1713; *of whom presently.*

John Morgan, eldest son of John, born 1695. He married, first, 17 Dec., 1717, Sarah, daughter of John Evans and Mary Hughes, his wife. She was born in Merion township, near Philadelphia, 11 Jan., 1695. John Evans was son of Evan ap Edward, of Nant-lleidiog, Penllyn, Merionethshire, Wales. (See pedigree xviii.). John Morgan married, secondly, Patience ——. He died prior to his father. Will dated 1 Feb., 1731; proved 4 March, 1731. [Will Book E, p. 180, Philadelphia.]

ISSUE BY FIRST WIFE:
i. James, d. s. p.
ii. Hannah, born 1720; married James Hunter; *of whom presently.*

ISSUE BY SECOND WIFE:
iii. Mary, unmarried, 17 Jan., 1753.

Hannah Morgan, daughter of John, married 1742, Captain James Hunter. He was born at Rathdrum, County Wicklow, Ireland (son of John and Margaret); died in Newtown Township, Delaware (then Chester) County, in March, 1783; buried at St. David's, Radnor. Will dated 12 May, 1773; proved 24 March, 1783. [Will Book 7, 39, West Chester.] James Hunter was commissioned captain in Colonel William Moore's Regiment, Chester County Troops, during the French and Indian Wars, 8 Feb., 1747-8. ["Penna. Arch." II., 506-7.] Hannah, wife of James Hunter, died *circa* 1 Dec., 1803. Will dated 12 May, 1802; proved 3 Dec., 1803. (Will Book A. 1, 417, Media, Pa.]

ISSUE:
i. James.
ii. John ; *of whom presently.*
iii. George, married Grace Brick.
iv. Sarah, married Evan Lewis.
v. Mary, married Hugh Jones.
vi. Ann.
vii. Peter.
viii. Samuel.

Captain John Hunter, son of James and Hannah, born in Newtown, Chester County; died there in Dec., 1821. He married, 8 Dec., 1772, Ann, daughter of John Levis, of Springfield, Delaware (then Chester) County. He was a captain 4th Company, 6th Battalion, Chester County Troops, during the Revolution. [Penna. in Rev. (4) Assoc. and Militia, 11, 92, " Pa. Archives."] Will of John Hunter dated 6 Sept., 1813; proved 17 Dec., 1821.

ISSUE:
i. James, d. s. p.
ii. Rebecca Matlack, born 3 Sept., 1775.
iii. Sarah, married William R. von Löhr (Van Leer); *of whom presently.*
iv. Elizabeth, born August, 1780.
v. John, born 13 Dec., 1782.
vi. Hannah, born 26 May, 1785.
vii. Thomas, d. young.

Sarah Hunter, daughter of John and Ann, married 19 April, 1801, William R. von Löhr (Van Leer), son of Captain Samuel von Löhr (Van Leer) and Hannah, his wife, daughter of Captain Isaac Wayne.

William R. von Löhr (Van Leer)[1] was born in the County of Chester, Penna; 30 May, 1775; died there 25 May, 1808.

---

[1] William R. von Löhr was the son of Captain Samuel von Löhr (or Van Leer) of the county of Chester, Pennsylvania, and Hannah, his wife, daughter of Captain Isaac Wayne, and sister to Major-General Anthony Wayne.

Captain Isaac Wayne was born in County Wicklow, Ireland, and was son of Captain Anthony Wayne of Wicklow, an officer of dragoons at the battle of the Boyne, son of Captain Gabriel Wayne, of Derbyshire, an officer of the Parliamentary Army. Captain Isaac Wayne married Elizabeth, daughter of Richard Iddings, of the county of Chester, son of Richard Iddings, who removed to Pennsylvania from the Marches of Wales about 1700, and was of Welsh descent.

The wife of the second Richard Idding, and grandmother of Major-General Anthony Wayne, was Margaret Philips, daughter of Philip Rhytherrach (or Rhydderch), who was born in Carmarthenshire, 1627-8, and lived to the age of 102 years. He removed to Pennsylvania 1690, and died 1730. See notice of him on another page. He was descended from the Princes of South Wales.

Pedigree XIX.

ISSUE:
i. Isaac Wayne, born 26 March, 1802. (See preceding pedigree of George H. Earle, Jr.).
ii. Hannah, died young.
iii. Ann Louisa, born 12 Nov., 1804; died 22 Dec., 1874; married 1 Dec., 1829, J. B. Willaner; had: William, died infant; Isaac Wayne, died infant; Eleanor, married 15 Sept., 1869, Andrew W. Wills; has: Wayne and Eleanor

Mordecai Morgan, son of John, born 12 July, 1713; married, June 1749, Mary, daughter of David and Catherine Pugh, of Great Valley and Tredyffrin Township, He died 29 Dec., 1782.

ISSUE:
i. Mordecai, born 19 June, 1750, *of whom presently.*
ii. Joseph, born 10 June, 1752; died 1752.
iii. Hannah, born 13 Jan., 1755.

Captain Mordecai Morgan, jr., born 19 June, 1750; died 9 August, 1794; married, 12 Sept., 1772, Mary, daughter of James and Mary Davis. She died 30 July, 1832. Of Tredyffrin Township, Chester County.

ISSUE:
i. James, born 1 Jan., 1775; died in Philadelphia, 4 Oct., 1846.
ii. Hannah, born 3 Nov., 1776; died 24 April, 1778.
iii. Joseph, born 28 Dec., 1778; died at Radnor, 5 Nov., 1807.
iv. Samuel, born 8 March, 1781; died, 4 May, 1857.
v. John, born 26 March, 1784; *of whom presently.*
vi. Maria, born 26 Dec., 1787; died in Philadelphia, 12 Jan., 1856.
vii. Mordecai, born 5 July, 1790; died at Pensacola, Florida.

John Morgan, son of Captain Mordecai, born 26 March, 1784; died 5 Sept., 1871, married, 9 May, 1811, Mary, daughter of Jacob and Mary W. Buckwalter, of Charleston, Chester County.

ISSUE:
i. Joseph, born 24 Feb., 1813; *of whom presently.*
ii. Jacob, born 18 Dec., 1814; died at Phœnixville, 1896.
iii. John, born 26 Nov., 1816; died at Jeansville, Wis., 1853.
iv. Mordecai, born 20 Nov., 1819; died at Phœnixville, 24 Nov., 1867.
v. Mary, born 22 April, 1821.

vi. Emily, born 4 July, 1823; died at Phœnixville, 26 July, 1826.
vii. Cornelia, born 7 Dec., 1825.
viii. George, born 29 Dec., 1827; died at Reading, Pa., 30 Dec., 1832.
ix. Harriet, born 7 Feb., 1829.
x. Sarah, born 20 Nov., 1831.
xi. Anna F., born 24 Sept., 1833; died 11 Dec., 1886, at Phœnixville.

Joseph Morgan, son of John, born 24 Feb., 1813; died in Philadelphia, 19 March, 1895; married in Philadelphia, 13 Oct., 1841, Sarah, daughter of Thomas and Rebecca Phipps.

ISSUE:
i. Joseph, born 27 July, 1842; *of whom presently*.
ii. Thomas P., born 29 Dec., 1845.
iii. Deborah, born 21 Jan., 1848.

Joseph Morgan, son of Joseph, born 27 July, 1842; married 14 June, 1871, Frances Augustine Eyre, at Wilmington, Delaware.

ISSUE:
i. John Eyre, born 11 August, 1872, Edgemore.
ii. Robert Churchman, born 10 Oct., 1873, Edgemore.
iii. Charles Cox, born 25 Feb., 1876; died 2 Feb., 1877.
iv. Ellen Eyre, born 25 Nov., 1877, Wilmington.
v. Frances Augustine, born 24 Feb., 1881, Johnstown, Pa.
vi. Webster Lowerman, born 30 Nov., 1882; died 4 Jan., 1883.

PEDIGREE XX.

Harry Thomas Owen, of the parish of Machynlleth. (For pedigree of Thomas Owen, of Machynlleth, see folding chart). He joined the Society of Friends. Presented to the Grand Jury, as a Quaker, April Sessions, 1681. ["Montgomeryshire Collections," xxvi., 51.]

ISSUE:
i. Hugh Harry, *of whom presently*.
ii. Daniel Harry, removed to Pennsylvania, 1684; settled in Merion.
iii. Evan Harry, removed to Pennsylvania before 1797; m. 3 month, 11, 1697, Katherine David, widow. He was of Merion.

Pedigree XX.

Hugh Harry, son of Harry Thomas Owen, of Machynlleth, Montgomeryshire. He removed to Pennsylvania, 1684, coming on the ship "Vine," which arrived at Philadelphia 7 month, 17, 1684, and purchased a plantation in the township of Birmingham, county of Chester, and he had a deed, 1707, for 430 acres of land in Marlborough Township. He died about the end of September, 1708. His will, in which he calls himself Hugh "Harris,"[1] is dated 1 month 27, 1708, and was proved at Philadelphia, 28 Sept., 1708. He married, 2 month, 12, 1686, Elizabeth, daughter of William Brinton, late of the parish of Sedgeley, Staffordshire.[2]

ISSUE :
   i. Evan, m. Elizabeth ——.
   ii. William.
   iii. Hugh.
   iv. John.
   v. Elizabeth, m. 1728, Robert Eachus.
   vi. Ann, m. Thomas Speakman ; *of whom presently.*
   vii. Jane.
   viii. Lois.
   ix. Olive, m. 1 month, 16, 1720, Daniel Bailey.

Ann Harry (or Harris), daughter of Hugh, married, 1714, Thomas Speakman, son of William and Elizabeth, of the parish of St. Giles, Reading, county of Berks. Thomas Speakman was of Londongrove, county of Chester. Died 1732. He removed to Pennsylvania, 1712.

ISSUE (surname Speakman) :
   i. William, b. 8, 8, 1715.
   ii. Hugh, b. 9, 2, 1717.
   iii. Ann, b. 10, 18, 1719 ; m. Nicholas Newlin.
   iv. Thomas, b. 11, 11, 1721 ; m. Abigail ——.
   v. Ebenezer, b. 5, 14, 1724 ; m. Mary Hayes.
   vi. Micajah, b. 9, 26, 1726 ; *of whom presently.*
   vii. Joshua, b. 5, 20, 1731 ; m. Ann Miller.
   viii. Margaret, m. —— Newlin.

---

[1] The name Harry is usually written, in Welsh, Hari or Harri, hence Hugh, the son of Harri, would be written Hugh Harris.

[2] William Brinton was baptized in Sedgeley Church, 1 Dec., 1636, and was son of Thomas Brinton and Ann, daughter of William Biddle (Biddulph), and was a descendant of the Mason and Grazebrook families, of Staffordshire. William Brinton's wife was the daughter of Edward Bageley, of Sedgeley.

Micajah Speakman, born 1726; married, first, 4, 22, 1752, Mary Griffiths, who died 1774. He married, secondly, 5, 23, 1781, Phebe, widow of Nathaniel Yarnall (born 7, 16, 1739; died 11, 16, 1828), and daughter of John Schofield, of the county of Bucks, Pennsylvania, and had by her:

Micajah Speakman, jr., born 1782; died 5, 22, 1852. He was of the county of Chester, and married, first, 10, 4, 1803, Phebe, daughter of Stephen Smith, and secondly, 10, 17, 1833, Sarah (Taylor) Briggs, widow.

ISSUE:

i. Stephen, b. 10, 28, 1804; m. 1827, Mary Smith, wid; d. 10, 19, 1848.
ii. Phebe Ann, b. 10, 18, 1806; m. Isaac W. von Löhr (Van Leer) (see preceding pedigree).
iii. William Allibone, b. 12, 3, 1808; m. 4, 8, 1852, Elizabeth Dingee.
iv. Rebecca, S., b. 4, 30, 1811; m. 2, 12, 1829, David Potts.
v. Sarah, A., b. 3, 1, 1813; m. 10, 1, 1840, J. Miller McKim.[1]

---

[1] Charles F. McKim, of New York, is a descendant.

Authorities: Cedwyn MSS.; M.Col. x., 25, et seq.; Visit. Salop; Visit. N.W. (Montg.); *Morgan et Glam.* (Herbert); Montg. Colls. (Record Series); Wills at St. Asaph; Visit. N.W. (general). **A.**—Myddleton deeds; *Myddleton of Gwaynog;* Vist. N.W. (Myddelton); Ormerod; *Montg. Colls.* **B.**—See p. 107. **C.**—Bleddyn ap Cynfyn, Prince of Powys, 1062-1072; see H. Powys Fadog, i., 109, &c., and other vols. for these lines. **D.**—Osborn Fitz Gerald was ancestor to the Corsygedol and other families; see Visit. N.W. (Dwnn, ii.) under Corsygedol, and numerous peds. in the 6 vols. H.P.F. **E.**—*Morgan et Glamorgan,* Clark. **F.**—H. Powys Fadog, i. 307, &c. **G.**—H.P.F. (general). **H.**—H.P.F., i., 10, &c. (Brochwel *alias* Brochmael was Prince of Powys). **K.**—Sir Thomas Stanley m. Joan, dau. Sir Robert Goushill, by Elizabeth, dau. Richard Fitz Alan, by Elizabeth, dau. William de Bohun, s. Humphrey de Bohun, by Elizabeth, dau. Edward I. For Holland and Touchet descent fr. Edward III., see chart facing

page 44. Edmund Langley, s. Edward III., had Constance, who m. (marriage disallowed) Edmund Holland, E. of Kent, and had Eleanor, wf. James Touchet, Lord Audeley. Auths. for these lines: Dougdale, 1, 180,&c.; *Test. Vet.*, Nichol, 60, 129; Weever's F. Mts., 77, Ormerod; Inqs. P.M. (Chanc.); Harl. MS. 2151, fo. 16b; Collins, iii., 40; ed. 1779; Harl. MS. 1424, fo. 1287, 1424, fo. 136b; Visit. N.W.; Peniarth MS. (MS. Vaughan of Hengwrt as to Clifford); ped. by Thomas Jones of Fountain Gate, Tregaron, Dwnn, ii., apx.

Hugh Harry, s. Harry Thomas Owen of Machynlleth (see p. 136), was father of Ann, wf. of Thomas Speakman, f. of Micajah Speakman, f. of Micajah Speakman, f. of Phebe Ann, wf. of Isaac W. von Löhr (Van Leer), f. of Ellen Frances, wf. of George H. Earle, f. of George H. Earle, Jr., of Philadelphia.

PEDIGREE XXI.

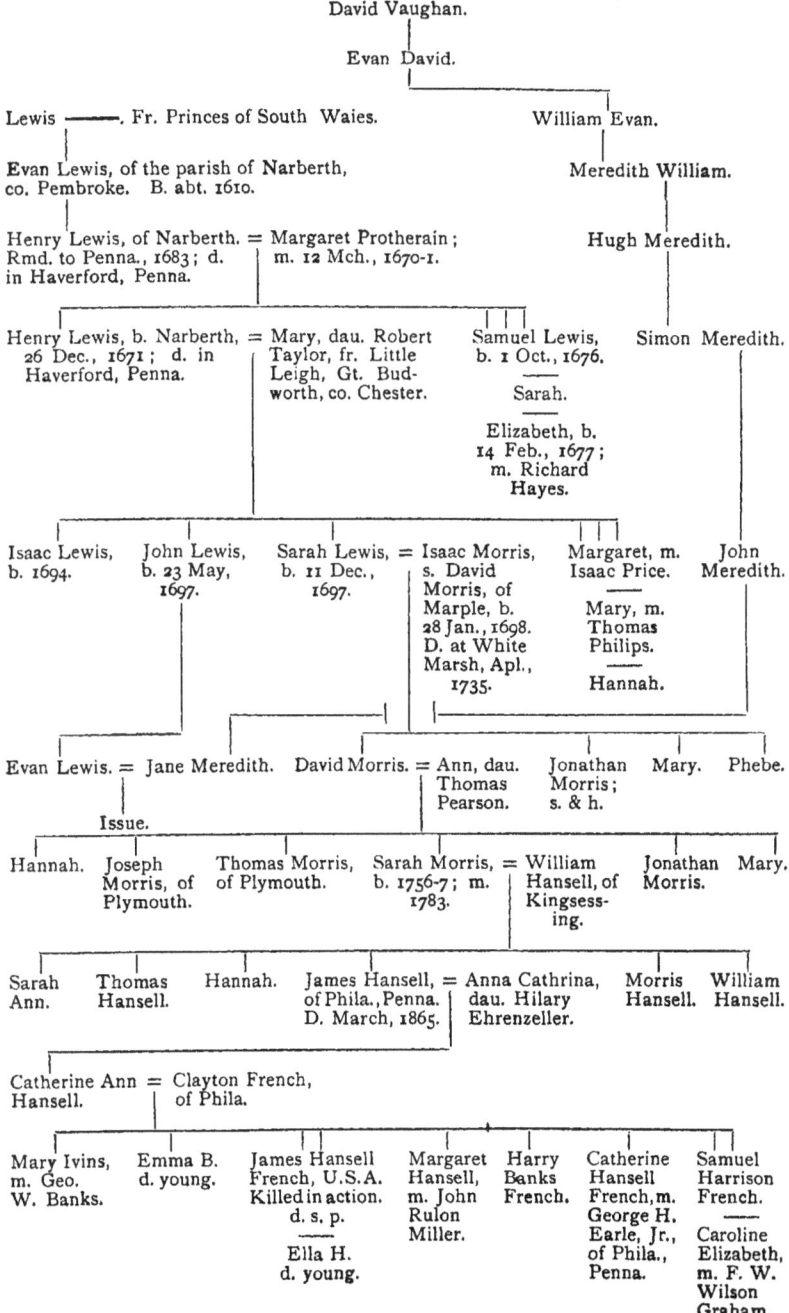

PEDIGREE XXII.

Cadwgan, lord of Nannau, near Dolgelley, Merionethshire, son of Bleddyn ap Cynfyn, Prince of Powys.

Madog, lord of Nannau.

Einion ap Madog, lord of Ciltalgarth (or Kiltalgarth), near Bala. This lordship extended to Yspytty Evan, Denbighshire.

Madog Hyddgam, of Ciltalgarth. He sold a certain portion of his lands in Ciltalgarth to the monks of the Cistercian Monastery of Ystrad Marchell, and the boundaries of these lands are given in the *Inspeximus* Charter of Edw. I., dated 12 March, 1287. [Harl. MS. 1969; " Montg. Colls." v., 109.]

Cadwgan, of Ciltalgarth.

Maredydd [MS. pedigree by Edward Foulke of Gwynedd]; see "Historical Collections of Gwynedd," by Howard M. Jenkins, Philadelphia, 1897 (2d Ed.).

Einion [MS. ped., by Edward Foulke.]

Madog of Ciltalgarth. [MS. ped. by Edward Foulke; Harl. MS. 1969.]

Gruffydd of Ciltalgarth. [Authorities cited *supra*.][1]

Ieuan (Evan), of Ciltalgarth, surnamed *y Cott*, from which circumstance his descendants were called *y Cottiad*. [Harl. MS. 1969.] The MS. of Edward Foulke, however, applies this epithet to this Ieuan's son, named Ieuan (Evan) Fychan (or Vychan, *viz.*, the little, or junior).

Ieuan (Evan) Fychan (or Vychan), of Ciltalgarth. [Authorities cited *supra*.]

Madog, of Ciltalgarth, married.
Mali, daughter of Tudor ap Goronwy ap.
Howel y Cadair, of Cadair Penllyn.
[Authorities cited *supra*.]

David, of Ciltalgarth, married. Mallt, daughter of Ieuan . . . . [Authorities cited *supra*.]	Angharad married Rhys Lloyd of Gydros, Llanfor.

A

---

[1] From Gruffydd ap Madog to William ap Hugh of Cae Fadog, Harl. MS. 1969 and MS. ped. by Edward Foulke, agree. The latter genealogy was in Edward Foulke's possession before 1698, although his MS. account of his family was written a few years later.

Pedigree XXII. 141

Thomas, of Ciltalgarth. [Authorities cited *supra*.]

Hugh ap Thomas, of Cae Fadog, in Ciltalgarth [Authorities cited *supra*], married Margaret, daughter of Thomas Lloyd Gethin, of Y Ddwyfaen in Dinmael, eldest son of Howel Lloyd ap David ap Maredydd, of Bala.

William ap Hugh, of Cae Fadog. [Authorities cited *supra*.] He is named in Lay Subsidy Roll for Merionethshire (under Penllyn), 3 Car. I., as father of Ellis ap William ap Hugh (Ellis Williams), and was then dead. [Lay Subsidy Roll, Merionethshire, No. $\frac{220}{330}$, Pub. Rec. Office, London.]

Ellis Williams (*alias* Ellis William ap Hugh, &c.), of Cae Fadog. [MS. ped. by Edward Foulke of Gwynedd, " Historical Collections of Gwynedd," Jenkins ; MS. Gen. of Owen and Evans' families, original bound with " Some Records relating to Radnor and Merion Mtg.," in MS. Collections of Gen. Society of Penna.]

    3 Car. I. Named in Lay Subsidy Roll, Merionethshire, under Penllyn Hundred. [Lay Subsidy Roll, Merionethshire, 3 Car. I., No. $\frac{220}{330}$, Pub. Rec. Office, London.]

    1636. Named in Lay Subsidy Roll, Merionethshire, under parish of Llanvawr (Llanfor). [Lay Subsidy Roll, Merionethshire, 1636. "The Cambrian Quarterly Magazine and Celtic Repertory," iii., 449, 1831.]

    16 Car. I., 14 Sept. (Autumn Sess., 1640). Feet of Fine, Merionethshire. Eliceus Wil'ms (Elice, or Ellis, Williams), gentleman, plaintiff, and William Kyffyn, gentleman, and Gwennia his wife, deforciants. 3 messuages and lands in the township of Penmaen, parish of Llanfor (adjoining Ciltalgarth). [Rolls of the Feet of Fine, Merionethshire, 16 Car. I., Pub. Rec. Office, London.]

    1645, 26 Feb. Administration of the personal estate of Ellis William ap Hugh, of the parish of Llanvawr (Llanfor), granted to Marrett vch. John, relict of the deceased. [Act Book, $\frac{1637}{1646}$, anno 1645, Probate Registry, St. Asaph.]

    Ellis Williams, of Cae Fadog, married Marrett, daughter of John ———; living 26 Feb., 1645.

        ISSUE :

        i. Margaret. [Owen and Evans MS. Gen.]
        ii. Douse. [Owen and Evans MS. Gen.]
        iii. Gwen, married Hugh ap Cadwaladr ap Rhys, of the parish of Yspytty Evan (Spytu or Sputty), Denbighshire, and had issue : (a) John Pugh (*viz.*, ap Hugh), *who removed to*

Gwynedd, Pennsylvania, about 1698. [Owen and Evans MS. Gen. cited *supra*.] For some reference to him see Jenkin's "Gwynedd," (b) Eleanor, or Ellin, married *Edward Foulke*[1] (son of Foulke ap Thomas), *who removed with his family to Gwynedd, Pennsylvania*, 1698. [MS. cited, Foulke MS.; see Jenkin's "Gwynedd."] (c) Jane, married *William John*,[2] son of John ap Evan (or John Evan) of Penmaen, and removed to Gwynedd, Pennsylvania, 1698. [See will of Cadwalader ap Evan of Coed y Foel, dated 25 Dec., 1688 :[3] "To nephew W^m. Jo^n. Evan . . . . &c., upon condition y^t *his father-in-law*, Hugh Cad'der shall likewise give him the said" sum.]

There may have been other children.

iv. Eleanor, married John Morris, of Bryn Gwyn, Denbighshire, and had Eleanor, or Ellin, who married *Cadwalader Evans*[4] (son of Evan Lloyd Evan, or Evan ap Evan), *who removed to Gwynedd, Pennsylvania*, 1698. [MS. cited, *supra*.]

---

[1] For pedigree of Edward Foulke see account of his ancestry from a MS. in his own handwriting, printed in full in "Historical Collections of Gwynedd," by Howard M. Jenkins; also genealogy of his descendants; see also "Pedigree of Edward Foulke," Folio, Lithographed, Hist. Soc. of Penna., and Glenn's "Merion," and on another page of this volume.

[2] Called also William Jones; his children assumed the surname of Williams; see Pedigree i.

[3] Register "Copies of Wills " $\frac{1684}{1690}$, folio 228-30, Probate Registry St. Asaph.

[4] For ancestry of Cadwalader Evans, see Pedigree i.; for descendants, see "Gwynedd," Jenkins.

MANUSCRIPT PEDIGREES
Brought from Wales to Pennsylvania by the First Colonists.

The following pedigrees of some of the Welsh Founders of Pennsylvania are copies of original MSS. brought to the Province, or compiled by the Colonists from family documents, or information furnished by kinsmen in Wales, soon after their arrival. The majority of these genealogies, I believe, have, at one time or another, appeared in print. All known to be extant, with the exception of that of John Thomas, of Llaithgwm, which will be found elsewhere in this volume, are here included, with notes and corrections, after careful comparison with the original MSS., or with dependable transcripts thereof.

Evan ap Evan, Father of the Evans Brothers, of Gwynedd, 1698.

The original MS. of the following pedigree was brought to Gwynedd by one of the sons of Evan ap Evan, son of Evan Robert Lewis "of Fron Goch," in 1698, and, with other family "information," was given to Cadwalader Evans of Philadelphia, in October, 1797, by John Evans, Sr., of Gwynedd, and his sister Elizabeth. John was at this time 67 years old, and his sister 71.

Evan[1] ap Evan[2] ap Robert[3] ap Lewis ap Griffith ap Howel Goch[4] ap Einion ap Deikws ddu ap Madoc ap Ieuan Goch ap David Goch ap Trahnarn Goch of Madoc ap Rhys Gloff ap Rhys Vaughan ap Rhys Mechyllt ap Rhys Grug ap Rhys ap Griffith ap Rhys ap Tewddur Mawr ap Einion ap Owen ap Howel dda ap Cadelh ap Rodri Mawr ap Mervyn Vrych.

The above is from a copy, made by Mrs. William Parker Foulke, of the original, then in possession of the late Rowland E. Evans, Esq., and compared by the writer with an amplified copy of the same (in handwriting of Rowland E. Evans), in the possession of Rowland Evans, of Haverford, Pennsylvania, Esq., in 1889. At that time the original was stated to be among the Rowland E. Evans MSS., but inaccessible.

---

[1] He was called, also, Evan Lloyd Evan, and was of the township of Ucheldre (Fron Goch farm being partly in that township), in the parish of Llanfor, and was buried at Llanfor, 25 April, 1690.

[2] Usually called Evan Robert Lewis; for genealogy of his descendants see vol. ii.

[3] For all of these generations see vol. ii.

[4] The Visitation pedigree omits the epithet *Goch*.

John Hugh of Gwynedd.

The following is a copy of a copy (made about 1790) of an original MS. compiled shortly after 1700. Some later information was added by the 1790 (*circa*) transcriber, who also made one or two palpable clerical errors, which are here corrected. Another copy of this MS. which I have seen is more accurate. The original from which this is taken is in the possession of the Historical Society of Pennsylvania; see also vol. ii.

Ellis Williams of Cai [Cae] fadog[1] had four Daughters, vizt Margaret, Douse, Gwenn & Ellin.

The said Ellin married John Morris of Brin Gwin in Denbighshire, by her had one daughter named Ellin who married Cadwalader Ab Evan[2] late of Gwynedd deceased.

Gwenn, another daughter of the said Ellis Williams had three children[3] who came to Pennsylvania viz$^{t.}$

1 Ellis [should be John, father of Ellis] Pugh late of Gwynedd deceased.

2 Ellin married to Edward Foulke late of Gwynedd dec$^{d.}$

3 Jane, married to W$^{m.}$ John[4] of Gwynedd, also deceased.

Hugh Meredith of Radnor, about 1683.

This Hugh Meredith was father of Simon Meredith, father of John Meredith, father of Jane Meredith, who married Evan Lewis, son of John Lewis of Haverford (born 1697).

Hugh Meredith ap William ap Evan ap David Vaughan.

---

[1] Cae Fadog is in Ciltalgarth, near Bala. Ellis Williams was a freeholder in Llanfor, and letters of admon. on his personal estate were granted 1645.

[2] Son of Evan ap Evan, alias Evan Lloyd Evan, of Uwcheldre, Llanfor.

[3] Gwen, daughter of Ellis Williams, of Cae Fadog, married Hugh ap Cadwaladr ap Rhys, of the parish of Yspytty Evan, Denbighshire.

[4] Son of John ap Evan, of Penmaen, son of Evan Robert Lewis, of Fron Goch. The will of Cadwalader ap Evan, of Coed y Foel, 1688, contains a bequest to his "nephew Wm Jon Evan" upon condition that "his father-in-law, Hugh Cadwaladr, shall give him a like sum."

MANUSCRIPT PEDIGREES OF FIRST COLONISTS 145

HUMPHREY WILLIAM OF GWYNEDD, 1708.

From draft of a letter of Thomas Jones, of Merion, to Robert Vaughan, in Levick MSS. Humphrey William was from near Bala.

Humphrey ap William ap David ap John.

ROBERT THOMAS OF MERION, 1708.

He was born at Tyddyn Mawr, near Kefn Amwlch, Carnarvonshire, about 1690.

Robert ap Thomas ap Evan ap Hugh.

DAVID THOMAS OF RADNOR, BORN 1671.

He was from Carmarthenshire.

David Thomas ap Lewis ap Philip ap Rhydderch.

EDWARD PREES (OR REES AND PRICE) OF MERION, 1690.

Edward Prees (or Rees and Price) removed to Merion, Pennsylvania, from near Bala, 1682, and the following is an answer from Wales to his request for information regarding his family, and is addressed to John Harry, of in or near Merion. The date of the MS. is supposed to be about 1685, or not later than 1700, and this transcript was made from a copy in the possession of Gilbert Cope, of West Chester. See also Glenn's "Merion," 77.

My old friend Edward Prees [alias Price] hath w[ritten] in his letter to Thomas Lloyd, Requesting to send him some intelligence of his Pedigree. I know but a little thereof at this time but give him this much while he stays for more.

Edward Price son of Richard,[1] son of Griffith son of Re[es.] .... [I Know] no more than this of his Father's side these were own[ers] of that Land where you have seen William ap Robert .... [live] .... and the name of that land is Tyddin Tyfod .... And the mother of Rees Prichard, was Mary the D[aughter of] Thomas[2] son of Robert, David Lloyd the son of D[avid] [the son of Evan] Vaughan[3] son of Griffith son of Evan

---

[1] Richard ap Griffith, otherwise Richard Price, was of Glanlloidiogin, in the parish of Llanfor, and died 1686.

[2] Thomas Lloyd was buried at Llandderfel, 21 May, 1612.

[3] The pedigree should run: David ap Evan (or Ieuan) Vaughan ap Ieuan ap Gruffydd ap Madog ap Iorwerth ap Madog ap Rhirid Flaidd. (Same descent as Edward Foulke, of Gwynedd).

Son of .... Madock, the son of Ierwith the son of Madock [the son of Rhirid] Flidd of Glan y LLyn [alias] Lake's Bank .... these followed further by Ann, ... John Vaughan of .... Mein y [alias] Stone Pen that comes over. The mother of Mary the daughter of Thomas Lloyd of Gwern y Brychdwyn [alias Owlars Brindle Bush] was Catharine the daughter of Robert,[1] the son of Griffith the son of Côch, or Red the son of Ddu the son of David, the son of Einion, the son of Canwrig Vaughan, the son of Canwrig, the son of Heilin, the son of Tyvid, the son of Tago, the son of Ystwyth, the son of Marchwyth, the son of Marcheithian of the fifteen tribes of Gwynedd North Wals, from the Lord Is Aled. The mother of Catherine vch Robert or daughter of Robert, was Margaret the daughter of Cadwalader, son of Rees Lloyd of Cydros Linealy descending from Enion Ardudwy, the mother of Robert, the son of Griffith, was Marred the daughter of Tudor the son of Ewan [Evan] Lloyd of the Upper Plas in Llanfair [alias] Mary's Church Dyffryn (or Valley Clywd). The mother of Griffith, the son of Evan, the son of Côch .... was Gwenhwyfir the daughter of Thomas David. ... (or having one eye) of the Court in Fenel Hill. Lineally .... [descend]ing from the L[or]d y[s] Dulas [alias] Gray. The mother [of] [Thom]as the son of Robert Lloyd of Gwern Brychdwyn [was] .... the daughter of Raynold the son of Griffith the [son of] .... of Upper Branas, the mother of Richard Griffith .... [Gwen]llian the daughter of Rees of the House where ... [O]wen Lived. *For John Harry.*

ROWLAND ELLIS, OF MERION, AND WIVES, 1697.

The following is from the original in the handwriting of Rowland Ellis, in the possession of Rowland Evans, of Haverford, Pennsylvania, Esq. This pedigree was compiled before 1697, because the name of his daughter Catherine, born in that year, is not in his handwriting, but has been added by someone else. The original is in chart form. A portion of this pedigree was printed by the writer in "Merion" (pp. 210-11), and a few corrections are here made, after a careful reading of a photograph of the original document.

---

[1] Robert ap Gruffydd (or Griffith), of Cerrig y Druidion. (See pedigree i. in this vol.).

Manuscript Pedigrees of First Colonists 147

Rowland Ellis[1] [ap] Ellis[2] [ap] Rees [ap] Lewis [ap] Sion : Gruffydd ap Howell

[The mother of Rowland Ellis was] Ann [vch.] H'mph'y[3] [ap] Hugh [ap] David ap Howell ap Gronw

[The mother of Ann vch. Humphrey was] Elizabeth [vch.] John[4]

[The mother of Elizabeth vch. John was] Sibill vch Hugh Gwyn[5] Penarth

[The mother of Sibill vch. Hugh Gwyn was] Jane v^{ch} S^r. Hugh Owen.[6]

[The mother of Humphrey ap Hugh was] Catherin v^{ch} Sion ap Rydderch Abergynolwyn

[The mother of Hugh ap David ap Howell was] Mary v^{ch} Hugh Sion Bedo

[The mother of Ellis ap Rees ap Lewis was] Catherin [vch.] Elissa [ap] Davidd ap Owen ap Tho : ap How^{ll} ap Mrhedydd ap Gruffydd Derwas

[The mother of Catherin vch. Elissa was] Mary v^{ch} Sion ap dd ap Gruffydd

[The mother of Rees ap Lewis was] Ellin v^{ch} Howell Gruffydd

[The mother of Lewis ap Sion Gruffydd was] Elsbeth v^{ch} Dd Llwydd

[The first wife of Rowland Ellis was] Margaret [vch.] Ellis [ap] Moris [ap] . . . .

---

[1] Rowland Ellis was born 1650.

[2] Settlement, *in re* marriage of Ellis ap Rees, Son of Rees Lewis ap John Gruffith, of Dyffrydan, co. Merioneth, gentleman, to Anne Humffrey, daughter of Humffrey ap Hugh, of Llwyngwril, said co., gentleman, is dated 1 Jan., 1649. [Original in the possession of Edward Griffith, of Dolgelley, Esq.]

[3] Living 1 Jan., 1649. His second son and heir, Owen Humphrey, was baptd. at Llangelynin, 13 April, 1629.

[4] John ap Howel, alias John Powel, of Llanwddyn, Montgomeryshire; see his pedigree on another page of this vol.

[5] Of Penarth, or Peniarth, Carnarvonshire. He was High Sheriff of his county, 1600.

[6] She was sister, not daughter, to Sir Hugh Owen, of Bodowen, Anglesey. Her father was Owen ap Hugh, of Bodeon, High Sheriff of Anglesey, 1579-80; d. 1613.

Ellissa ap Howell ap Tyddur ap . . . . ap How : Mhrd : Gruffydd

[The mother of Margaret was] Jane [vch.] Ellis ap Sion . . . .

[The mother of Jane was] Margaret [vch.] Ellissa ap Gruffydd ap Rich ap How : a. Mredydd ap Gruff: derwas.

[The mother of Ellis ap Moris was] Ellin vch Owen ap Lewis ap Sion ap Gru : ap Howell

[The mother of Moris ap Ellissa was] —— v^{ch} Moris ap Howell bedo

[The mother of Ellin vch. Owen was] Mary v^{ch}. Tyddur.

[The mother of Owen Lewis was] Ellin v^{ch}. Howell Gruff :

[The second wife of Rowland Ellis was] Margaret [vch.] Robert [ap] Owen [ap] Lewis [ap] `Sion : Gruffrydd ap Howell

[The mother of Margaret vch. Robert was] Margaret [vch.] Sion [ap] Lewis [ap] Tyddur ap Ednyved ap Howell ap Mrhedydd ap Gruffydd Derwas

[The mother of Margaret vch. Sion ap Lewis was] Agnes [vch.] Owen [ap] Tho : ap Owen ap Tho : ap Howell ap Mrhedydd ap Gruff. . . . . .

[The mother of Agnes vch. Owen ap Thomas was] Mary v^{ch} Ellisa [Bynn ?]

[The mother of Robert ap Owen ap Lewis was] Mary [vch.] Tudur V[aughan] ap dd Llwyd ap Tydur Vaughan ap Howell

[The mother of Mary vch. Tudur Vaughan was] Agnes v^{ch} Lewis . . . .

[The mother of Owen ap Lewis was] Ellin v^{ch} Howel Gruffydd

[The mother of Lewis ap Sion Gruffrydd was] Elsbeth v^{ch} dd Llwyd

[The mother of Lewis ap Tyddur ap Ednyved was] [Elizabeth ?] v^{ch} Howell dd Meirig

[The children of Rowland Ellis by his first wife] Ann[1] [and] Jane

[Children by second wife] Elizabeth [,] Rowland [,] Robert [,] Ellin [,] Catherin. [The latter added in a different handwriting.]

JOHN ROBERTS OF MERION, 1685.

Original MS. in possession of his descendants, see Glenn's " Merion," 100, and is entitled "An Account of John Roberts left to my Posterity." He removed to Merion, Pennsylvania, 1683.

A short account of John Roberts formerly of Llyn, being son of Richard Roberts, and Grand-son of Robert Thomas Morris, who lived at Cowyns, in the Parish of Llanergan, and County of Carnarvon; My Môther being Margaret Evans, daughter of Richard Evans of the Parish of Llangian and county aforesaid. . . . . I took to wife Gaynor[2] Roberts, daughter to Robert Pugh from Llyndedwydd near Bala in Merionethshire, her mother being Elizabeth[3] William Owen.[4] . . . .

EDWARD FOULKE OF GWYNEDD, 1702.

There are a great many copies of Edward Foulke's original MS., or rather, of the translation made by his son Samuel. The original MS. bore date 14 January, 1702. The following is from a copy made by the late Howard M. Jenkins, with a few corrections upon comparison with another MS.

I, Edward Foulke, was the son of Foulke[5] ap Thomas[6] ap Evan[7] ap Thomas[8] ap Robert ap David Llwyd

---

[1] The Parish Register of Dolgelley contains this entry of her baptism: "Anna filia Rowlandi Ellis Margretæ uxoris ejus baptizat fuit decimo nono die February, Anno Domini, 1672." She married Rev. Richard Johnston, Curate of Dolgelley. Their descendant, Edward Griffith, of Coedcymmer, Dolgelley, to whom the writer is much indebted for valuable information, has several deeds in his possession illustrating the above pedigree.

[2] She was sister to Hugh Roberts, of Merion.

[3] Elizabeth Williams is named in the will of Evan John, of Garth Llwyd, Llandderfel, dated 24 March, 1646. Her mother was Agnes, or Ann, daughter of Edward ap Watkyn.

[4] William Owen was a freeholder in Llanfor, and letters of admon. on his estate were granted 8 Sept., 1640, to Agnes vch. Edward, his wife.

[5] Foulke ap Thomas (whose father's surname was Lloyd) was baptized at Llandderfel, 14 April, 1623.

[6] Thomas ap Evan Lloyd was Sheriff, 1623; died Nov., 1649, married Catherine, daughter of William David, of Llandderfel.

[7] Evan ap Thomas Lloyd, of Nant y Friar, Llandderfel; buried at Llandderfel, 16 May, 1640. His will was proved at St. Asaph, 29 May, 1640, and letters testamentary were granted to his son Thomas ap Evan Lloyd. Act Book $\frac{1637}{1670}$.

[8] Thomas Lloyd, gentleman, was buried at Llandderfel, 21 May, 1612.

ap David ap Evan Vaughan [ap Evan, or Ieuan] ap Griffith ap Madoc ap Jerwert ap Madoc ap Ririd Flaidd Lord of Penllyn, who dwelt at Rhiwaedog.

My mother's name was Lowry,[1] the daughter of Edward ap David ap Ellis ap Robert of the Parish of Llanvor in Merionethshire.

I was born on the 13th of the 5th month [July], 1651, and when arrived at mature age, I married Eleanor the daughter of Hugh ap Cadwalader ap Rhys, of the Parish of Spytu in Denbighshire; her mother's name was Gwen, the daughter of Ellis ap William [2] ap Hugh ap Thomas ap David ap Madoc ap Evan ap Cott ap Evan ap Griffith ap Madoc ap Einion ap Meredith of Cai Fadog; and [she] was born in the same parish and shire with her husband.[3]

I had, by my said wife, nine children, whose names are as follows:[4] Thomas, Hugh, Cadwalader, and Evan; Grace, Gwen, Jane, Catherine, and Margaret. We lived at [on] a place called Coed y foel, a beautiful farm, belonging to Roger Price, Esq., of Rhiwlas, Merionethshire, aforesaid.

---

[1] "Lowrea vch. Edward vidua et relicta fulconis Thomas nup defuncti sepulta fuit 5to diè July, A.D. 1677" [Llandderfel P. R.].

[2] Ellis Williams was of Cae Fadog, Ciltalgarth, parish of Llanfor, and Admon. of his personal estate was granted to his widow, Marrett vch. John, 26 Feb., 1645.

[3] This is a mistake, as Gwen's father, Ellis Williams, lived at Cae Fadog, in Llanfor, where, under the designation of *Elliseus ap Wm ap Hughe and Ellisey ap William ap Hugh*, he is assessed in land 3 Car. I., and 1636.

[4] Coed y Foel, in Penmaen, subsequently divided into Coed y Foel uchaf, Coed y Foel issaf, originally belonged to one Cadwaladr ap Maredydd (Meredith), one of whose daughters and co-heiresses, married Thomas Wynne, of Garth Meilio, and her descendant, John Wynne, of Coed y Foel, held one half of the original property, in 1697, which, by his will dated 20 March, 1697-8, he bequeathed to his son, John Wynne. Another daughter of Cadwaladr ap Maredydd, appears to have been the first wife of Evan Robert Lewis, at any rate, Cadwalader ap Evan, eldest surviving son of Evan Robert Lewis, died seized of the other half of Coed y Foel, in 1688. The will of this Cadwalder ap Evan, of Coed y Voel . . . . . gen. (gentleman), is dated 25 Dec., 1688, and was proved at St. Asaph, 31 Jan., 1688 (1688-89). Edward Foulke is one of the witnesses, and his signature is the same as that of Edward Foulke of Gwynedd.

This Cadwalader ap Evan, who was the uncle of the Evans' brothers, of Gwynedd, and of Robert Owen, of Merion, executed "a deed of ffeoffment" the 28 May prior to his decease, creating Andrew Jones, of Llanycil, his trustee. Coed y Foel was, by this deed, to be held by the grantee for certain uses. Grace, widow of Cadwalader, probably died soon after, and this portion of Coed y Foel, of which Edward Foulke was the tenant, passed by sale to Roger Price, of Rhiwlas, Esq., before 1698.

PEDIGREE XXIII.

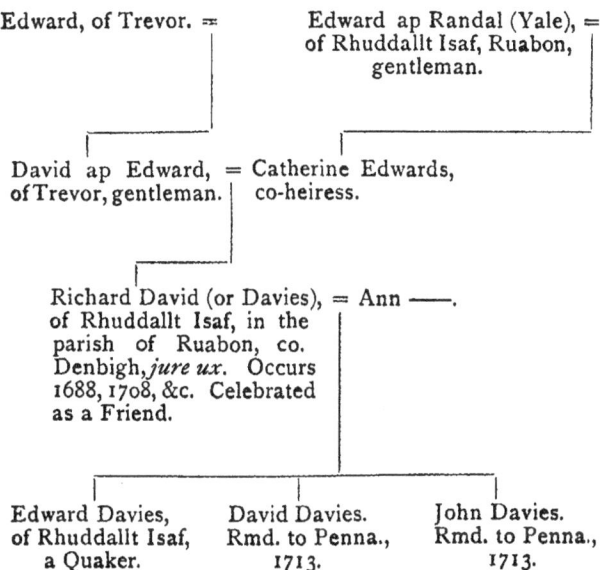

Welsh Founders of Pennsylvania.

The following list of some of the Welsh Founders of Pennsylvania is not intended to be exhaustive; but it will probably be of value because of the positive identification of numbers of persons among the Welsh bearing the same name, but not related to each other. The localities in Wales from whence a large proportion of these colonists came are given, as well as, in most cases, their occupation, and when obtainable, the name of the religious body to which they belonged at the time of their removal to the Province. It should, however, be borne in mind in this connection, that many who were members of the Church of England, when they arrived, soon afterwards joined the Society of Friends, and that numbers of the latter, especially children of the original colonists, returned to the Church, or joined the Baptists and Presbyterians. The particulars concerning individuals are purposely as brief as possible. The principal abbreviations are: s. = son of; dau. = daughter of; b. = born; d. = died; m. = married; Ch. E. = Church of England; Fd. = Friend (i.e., Society of Friends); Bpt. = Baptist; rmd. = removed; certif. = certificate; ld. = land; wid. = widow; fr. = from; liv. = living; prob. = probably. The children of persons mentioned, are not, perhaps, in some cases, all given, and sometimes not in the order in which they were born. It should be noted that the descriptions in various documents of the same individuals do not always agree. For instance, some of those described as "gentleman" in one deed are not unlikely to be called "yeoman," in another, especially if an Englishman drew up the instrument. Likewise "weavers" are sometimes called "tailors"; but it may be presumed that these persons followed both trades.

THOMAS ANDREWS, prob. of near Bala, co. Mer. Rmd. to Philadelphia, Penna., abt. 1685; perhaps earlier. Ch. E.; d. 1698.

(To face page 152.)

John de Beaufort, Earl of Somerset, d. 1440 ; s. John of Gaunt, and gds. Edward III. ; m. Margaret, dau. Thomas Holland, Earl of Kent.
|
Edmund Beaufort, fell at St. Albans, 1455; m. Eleanor, dau. and co. h. Richard Beauchamp, Earl of Warwick.
|
Henry Beaufort, beheaded 1463.
|
Charles Somerset, created Earl of Worcester, 1514 ; d. 1526.
|
Henry Somerset, 2d Earl of Worcester.
|
Eleanor Somerset, m. Sir Roger Vaughan, of Porthaml, Knt.
|
Watkin Vaughan, of Talgarth ; m. Joan, dau. Evan ap Gwilym, of Peyton Gwyn.
|
Sir William Vaughan, of Porthml ; d. 1564 ; m. Catherine, dau. Jenkin Harvard, of Tredomen.
|
Catherine Vaughan, m. David Evans, of Neath, High Sheriff of co. Glamorgan, 1563.
|
Mary, m. Thomas Basset, of Miscin.
|
Catherine, m. Richard ap Evan, of Collenna.
|
Jane, m. Evan ap John, of Treferig, and had John Bevan, of Treverig.

Wives: (1.) —— ; (2.) Elizabeth Owen, dau. Owen ap Hugh (bro. Thomas ap Hugh, of Wern Fawr, Llaithgwm, par. of Llandderfel, co. Mer.); m. 1689. She d. 1718.

Children (surname Andrews): 1. Simon; 2. Ellen (both by 1st wife.)

ROBERT ARTHUR, of near Bala, co. Mer. Rmd. to Merion, Penna., supposedly, 1698.

MARTHA AUBREY (or Awbrey), dau. William Aubrey, of Llanelyw, co. Mon., gentleman, by Elizabeth, illegitimate dau. William Aubrey, of Llanelyw. Rmd. to Penna., 1683. She m., 1692, Rees Thomas, of Merion, to whom she had been engaged since 1682 (see his certif. of rml., 1683, which states that he was not then clear of Martha Aubrey. Such a long engagement at that time, when wives were scarce, is remarkable).

CHARLES BEVAN (alias ap Evan), of Treverigg, par. of Llantrisant, co. Glam., gentleman; 2nd. s. Evan ap John, of same place, gentleman. Rmd. to Penna., 1683. Ch. E. Freeholder in Haverford. He returned to Wales, and resided in par. of Llantwit Vardre.

Wife: Florence, dau. Morgan ap Evan, of Gelligaled.

Child: Evan, grad. Oxford. Matric. 11 Feb., 1695-6, aged 18.

EVAN BEVAN, of Treverigg, par. of Llantrisant, co. Glam.; b. 1666-68; s. John Bevan (alias John ap Evan), of the same place, gentleman, and Barbara, his wife. Rmd. to Penna., 1683. Fd. D. in Merion, Penna., 1720.

Wife: Eleanor, dau. John Wood, of Darby, Penna. (M. 1693).

Children (surname Bevan): 1. John, b. 1694; heir to Treverigg, where he died; 2. Barbara, b. 1696; 3. Evan, b. 1698; 4. Aubrey; 5. Charles; 6. Ann; 7. Catherine; 8. Jane, b. 1707-8.

For descts. see "Merion in the Welsh Tract," Glenn, 165, &c.

JOHN BEVAN (alias John ap Evan) of Treverigg, par. of Llantrisant, co. Glam., gentleman; s. Evan ap John, of same place, gentleman. Rmd. to Penna., 1683, Fd. A first purchaser of 2000 a. ld. surveyed to him in Merion and Haverford. He made several visits to his native country, and finally returned to Treverigg to live. D. there 1726. Memb. Prov. Assembly, and J.P. for co. Phila.

Wife, Barbara, said to have been sister of William Aubrey, of Pencoed. (See "Merion.") She d. 1710.

Children (surname Bevan): 1. Evan, m., 1693, Eleanor Wood; 2. Jane, m. John Wood; 3. Ann, m. Owen Roberts; 4. Elizabeth, m. Joseph Richardson; 5. Barbara, d. unm., 1705. For ped. and descts. see "Merion in the Welsh Tract," Glenn, 154, &c., and "A Royal Pedigree," by Hon. Samuel W. Pennypacker, Ex-Governor of Pennsylvania, a descendant.

JANE CADWALADER, "a widow for these many years," of near Bala, co. Mer., with her s. Humphrey Ellis, rmd. to Penna., 1697. She was sister to John Cadwalader Rowland, and mother of Gwen Ellis, who came at the same time, and are included in same certif., from Hendre Mawr Mtg., 12, 16, 1696. Fd.

JOHN CADWALADER ROWLAND, of near Bala, co. Mer., yeoman; s. Cadwalader Rowland, of same place. Rmd. to Penna., 1696. Fd.

JOHN CADWALADER, of near Bala, co. Mer.; s. Cadwalader Thomas ap Hugh, formerly of Ciltalgarth, par. of Llanfor; who d. in par. of Llandrillo, 1680. Rmd. to Merion, Penna., 1697, from co. Pembroke, where he had been educated, and where he was then a teacher. Rmd. from Merion to Philadelphia. Fd. For ped. see another page.

Wife, Martha, dau. Dr. Edward Jones, of Merion. (M. 1699).

For dests. see Keith's "Provincial Councillors of Pennsylvania."

ROBERT CADWALADR, of par. of Llanuwchllyn, co. Mer., yeoman (late of Llangower, and Penbryn, Llanycil); s. Cadwaladr ap Robert. Rmd. to Gwynedd, Penna., about 1700. Ch. E. D. prior 1710.

Wife, Jane, dau. John Evans (or John ap Evan), of Penmaen, par. of Llanfor, who d. 1697. For ped. of both see "Welsh Founders of Penna.," vol. ii.

Children (surname Roberts): 1. Cadwalader (or Cadwaladr), bapt. 1 June, 1673; m., 1714, Eleanor Humphrey; 2. Margaret, bapt. 27 June, 1675; 3. Morris, bapt. 9 May, 1677; m., 1718, Elizabeth Robeson; 4. John, bapt. 7 Jan., 1678-9; 5. John, bapt. 11 Sept., 1681; m., 1706, Elizabeth Edward; 6. Nicholas, m. Margaret Foulke; 7. Rowland, bapt. 29 March, 1685; m. (1), 1713, Mary Pugh; (2), Ann Bennet; 8. Elizabeth, bapt. 9 Dec., 1688; m. Daniel Morgan.

RICHARD COOK, of par. of Llangunllo, co. Rad., glover. Rmd. to Radnor, Penna., 1683. Ch. E. Freeholder of 100 a. ld. in Radnor. Deed 19-20 June, 1682.

Wife, ——.

Child: Elizabeth Cook, sole heiress. She sold the Radnor lands to Samuel Powel.

ELIZABETH COOPER, of Pontymoel, co. Mon., spinster; dau. Anthony Cooper, of same place. Rmd. to Penna., 1699. Fd.

JOYCE COOPER, of co. Carn.; bound for 4 years' servitude. Sailed "for Virginia," 1698, 19 Oct.

RICHARD CORNE, of par. of Llangunllo, co. Rad., glover. Rmd. to Penna. about 1683, but prob. returned to Wales. Fd. Freeholder of 50 a. ld. in Radnor.

Wife, ——.

Children: 1. William, who sold his father's right in the above land to John Evans; prob. others.

DAVID DAVID (alias Davis), of par. of Machynlleth, co. Montg., yeoman; s. David ——. Rmd. to Radnor, Penna., 1684. Fd. Freeholder of 200 a. ld. in Radnor. (Pat. 1685). His sister, Katherine David, m. in Wales, Tudor ——, and had Mary Tudor, m., 1686, Richard Orme. David David was also bro. in law to William Thomas, of Radnor, who m. Ann David.

Wife ——.

ELLIS DAVID, prob. of par. of Llanfor, co. Mer., yeoman. Rmd. to Gwynedd, Penna., 1698. Perhaps he had been in Merion before this. Fd. Freeholder of 231 a. ld. in Gwynedd (by deed 1698). He purchased land in Goshen, 1707.

Wife, ——.

Children (surname Davies): 1. John, m., 1705, Mary James. Prob. others.

It is possible that he returned to Wales, and may have died there, or else another colonist of the same name.

HUGH DAVID, of near Bala, co. Mer., gentleman. Rmd. to Penna., with Penn, on his 2d. voyage, 1700. Lived near Gwynedd. Left descendants, surname David. One of these, Tacey David, m., as his 2d. wife, William Ogden, of Phila.

Hugh David was prob. s. David ap Ellis, of Llanfor; see ped. on another page.

JENKIN DAVID, prob. of near Bala, husbandman. Rmd. to Merion, Penna., about 1700. Living 1714. He was a neighbour of William ap Edward, of Merion and Blockley, and had been in his service in Wales.

JOHN DAVID (otherwise Davis), s. Lewis David and Florence; b. Haverford, Penna., 1692. D. 1749. He was of Darby, co. Chester. Memb. Provincial Assembly, fr. co. Chester, 1732, 1733, 1748.

Wife, Rebecca, dau. Joseph Need, of Arnold, Notts. (Descd. from William Need, constable of Arnold, 1544).

Children: 1. Joseph, b. 1715; 2. Lewis, b. 1716; m. Hannah, wid. Richard Lloyd, and dau. Samuel Sellers; 3. Rebecca, b. 1718-19; m. John Lewis, of Springfield; 4. Ann, b. 1721; m. William Parker; 5. Hannah, b. 1724; m. —— Smith; 6. John, b. 1727; d.s.p.; 7. Mary, b. 1731; 8. Sarah, b. 1734; 9. Nathaniel, b. 1737; d. 1746.

Ann, dau. John Lewis and Rebecca Davis; m. Capt. John Hunter. (See Morgan ped. on another page).

KATHERINE DAVID (or Davis), of par. of Machynlleth, co. Montg., wid. Tudor ——, and sister to David David (of same place). Rmd. to Penna., 1684.

Children (surname Tudor, or Tyder): 1. Mary, m., 1686, Richard Orme; others unknown.

LEWIS DAVID, of par. of Llandewi Velfrey, co. Pemb., gentleman. He had been severely persecuted as a Friend. Besse says, "they took from him all he had in Llandewy; but he had houses and lands in Carmarthenshire."

He purchased 3000 a. ld. in Penna, 1682, and soon after rmd. there (about 1690). D. 1708. Fd.

Wife, ——.

Children: 1. James (surname Lewis); 2. prob. Lewis. Others living in Wales, in 1708.

LEWIS DAVID. Rmd. to Penna., before 1690. Fd. Lived in Haverford. D. 1743 (July).

Wife, Florence Jones; m., 1690, at Haverford.

Children: 1. John, b. 1692; d. 1749 (surname Davis); m., 1714, Rebecca, dau. Joseph Need, of Arnold, Notts.; 2. Ann, b. 1694; 3. William, b. 1696; 4. Mary, b. 1698; 5. Hannah; 6. Benjamin, b. 1704; 7. Lewis.

MERICK DAVID (or Davies), s. William Davies; lived for a time in Haverford, near Darby Creek. Fd. Freeholder.

Wife, Mary ——.

Children: 1. James, b. 1720; and perhaps others.

MORGAN DAVID, of Lithrens Castle, co. Pemb., yeoman. Rmd. to Merion, Penna, before 1694. Fd. Freeholder of 354 a. ld. in Merion. D. 1695.

Wife, Catharine ——. She m. 2d., 1697, Evan Harry, and 3d. (?) James Thomas.

Children (surname uncertain): 1. John; 2. Evan; 3. David; 4. Katharine; 5. Elizabeth.

ROBERT DAVID, of Tyn y Nant, Gwernefel Isymydd, par. of Llanycil, yeoman; s. David ap Ellis, of par. of Llanfor. Rmd. to Merion, Penna., 1683. Fd. Freeholder of 312 a. ld. in Merion, and elsewhere (orig. purchase), to which he added several plantations. D. 1732. (See pedigree on another page).

Wife, Elizabeth ——.

Children (surname David, Davids, or Davies): 1. Jane, b. 1678; m., 1710, John Roberts; 2. Catharine, b. 1680; d. 1683; 3. Thomas, liv. 1732; 4. David, b. 1685; d. 1685; 5. Katherine, b. 1687; d. 1690; 6. Elizabeth, b. 1689; 7. David, b. 1691; d. s. p.; 8. Robert, b. 1697; d. 1700.

THOMAS DAVID, prob. of near Bala, co. Mer. Rmd. to Merion, Penna., before 1692. Fd.

TREHARN DAVID, of Treverigg, par. of Llantrisant, co. Glam., husbandman. Rmd. to Penna., 1683. Fd.

Wife, Janne ——.

WILLIAM DAVID, of So. Wales, yeoman. Rmd. to Radnor, Penna., before 1685. Fd. Freeholder in Radnor.

Wife, Gwenllian Philips, of Radnor, Penna.

Children (surname Williams): 1. William, m., Ann, dau. James Morgan; 2. Meyrick, m. Mary ——; prob. others.

WILLIAM DAVID (or Davis or Davies), of So Wales; s. William. Rmd. to Radnor, Penna., 1685. Ch. E. Rmd. to Carnarvon, Penna. (Lanc. Co.). D. 1739.

Wife, Ann, dau. James Morgan, late of Llanfihangel Helygen, co. Rad.; m. after 1685, in Penna. She d. 1734.

Children : 1. Meyrick; 2. Gabriel; 3. John; 4. John; 5. William, m. Margaret Hughes; 6. Mary, m. Hugh Hughes; 7. Susannah, m., 1709, Nathan Evans; 8. Ann, m. Evan Hughes; 9. Elizabeth, m., 1735, David Jones.

DAVID DAVIES, of Welshpool, co. Montg.; s. Richard Davies, of Cloddau Cochian, co. Montg., the celebrated Quaker. Rmd. to Penna, 1683. He prob. married and left issue.

DAVID DAVIES, of Rhuddallt Isaf, par. of Ruabon, co. Denbigh; s. Richard and Ann Davies, of same place. Rmd. to Penna., 1713. Fd. See ped. on another page. He prob. married and left issue.

JOHN DAVIES, of Nantwich, co. Chester, yeoman; s. Richard and Ann Davies, of Rhuddallt Isaf. par. of Ruabon, co. Denbigh. Rmd. to Penna., 1713. Fd. See ped. on another page.

JOHN DAVIES, of co. Denb., grocer, bound for 4 years' servitude. Sailed "for Virginia," 1698, 19 Oct.

Those who are stated to have gone to Virginia are included in this list because many of the ships clearing "for Virginia," were really bound for Pennsylvania, and also because many of those Welshmen who were shipped to Virginia subsequently went north to Pennsylvania.]

MARGARET DAVIES, of Dolobran, co. Montg., wid. Fd. She was a near relation to Charles and Thomas Lloyd, of Dolobran, and, in 1681-2, was a joint purchaser with the former, of 5000 a. ld. in Penna. which was resold to various persons, and it is supposed that she did not remove to the Province.

RICHARD DAVIES, of Rhuddallt Isaf, par. of Ruabon, co. Denbigh, gentleman; s. David ap Edward, of Trevor. (See ped. on another page). He was noted as a minister among Friends, and although he did not go to Pennsylvania, he had much to do with the emigration movement in Wales, and was the

SOME OF THE FOUNDERS 159

personal friend of Penn, Dr. Wynne, Dr. Jones, of Bala, and others. His sons, however, removed to the Province.

Wife, Ann ——.

Children (surname Davies): 1. Edward, of Rhuddallt Isaf; 2. John, rmd. to Penna., 1713; 3. David, rmd. to Penna., 1713. Prob. others.

RICHARD DAVIES, of Cloddiau Cochion, Welshpool, co. Montgomery, gentleman; the celebrated minister among Friends. He was a first purchaser of 5000 acres of land in Penna., a great part of which was surveyed in Radnor; but disposed of the same to various persons, immediately after 1 June and July, 1682. He did not remove to the Province.

EVAN AP EDWARD, of near Bala, co. Mer.; s. Edward ap John, of Cynlas, par. of Llandderfel (now Llanfor), gentleman. Stated to have rmd. to Merion, Penna., with his bros., John and William, 1682. Named in will of his bro. John ap Edward, 1683. (See ped. on another page).

Wife, ——. (M. abt. 1663-4).

Children (surname Evans) : 1. John (otherwise John Evan Edward), m., 1686, Mary Hughes, and was in Radnor, 1692. Prob. daughters.

HUGH AP EDWARD, of near Bala. co. Mer. Rmd. to Gwynedd, Penna., abt. 1700. He was a nephew of David Cadwalader ap Hugh, of Gwynedd. (D. 1701).

JOHN AP EDWARD, of Nant-lleidiog, par. of Llanfor, co. Mer., yeoman; s. Edward ap John, of Cynlas, gentleman. Rmd. to Merion, Penna., 1682. Fd. Freeholder of 312½ a. ld. in Merion, and elsewhere. D. 1683. (See ped. on another page).

Wife, ——.

Children (surname Jones): 1. Elizabeth, b. 1671; 2. Sarah, b. 1673; 3. Evan, b. 1677; 4. Edward, b. 1681. The latter was known as Edward Jones, Jr., to distinguish him from Dr. Edward Jones, of Merion, to whom he sold his lands.

WILLIAM AP EDWARD, of Ucheldre, par. of Llanfor, co. Mer., yeoman; s. Edward ap John, of Cynlas, gentleman. Rmd. to Merion, Penna., 1682. Fd. Freeholder of 156¼ a. ld. in Merion and elsewhere. Rmd. fr. Merion to Blockley. D. 1749. (See ped. on another page).

Wives: (1) Katherine, dau. Robert ap Hugh; (2) Jane, dau. John ap Edward (ap Hugh), of par. of Llandderfel, co. Mer., yeoman.

Children (surname Williams): 1. Elizabeth, b. 1672; m. Thomas Lloyd; 2. Katherine, b. 1676; d. s. p. (by 1st. wife); 3. Sarah, b. 1685; m. Thomas Lawrence; 4. Edward, b. 1689; 5. Ellen, b. 1691; m. Henry Lawrence; 6. Mary, b. 1697; m. Richard Preston.

GRIFFITH EDWARD, of par. of Llanycil, co. Mer.; s. Edward Griffith, and gd.-s. Griffith ap Evan, of Ucheldre, par. of Llanfor. Rmd. to Penna., 1698, or soon after. He was then a young man, and unm. (See ped. in vol. ii.).

JANE EDWARD, of par. of Llanycil, co. Mer., spinster, dau. Edward Griffith, and sister of Griffith Edward. Rmd. to Penna., 1698, or shortly after 1700. She m., 1713, John Jones, of Montgomery, Penna. (See ped. in vol. ii.).

THOMAS EDWARD, of par. of Llanwddyn, co. Montg.; s. Edward Thomas ap Howel, of same place. Rmd. to Penna., prob. 1684. Liv. 1723. Fd. (See pedigree on another page).

THOMAS EDWARD, of near Bryn y maen, par. of Llandeilo Fawr, co. Carm., yeoman; s. Edward ———. Rmd. to Penna., 1713. Fd.

Wife, Elinor ———.

ALEXANDER EDWARDS, of par. of Machynlleth, co. Montg., yeoman. Rmd. to Radnor, Penna., 1684; rmd. from Radnor to Montgomery, before 1700. Freeholder of 1100 a. ld. in Montgomery. D. 1712.

Wives: (1) Margaret ———; (2) Catherine ———.

Children (surname Edwards): 1. Alexander, m., 1703, Grace Foulke; 2. Thomas, m., 1715, Margaret Price, of Gwynedd; 3. Margaret; 4. Martha; 5. Bridget, m. Griffith Miles; perhaps others.

EDWARD EDWARDS, of near Dolgelley, co. Mer., labourer, servant to Robert Owen, of Dolserey, gentleman. Rmd. to Duck Creek, Penn., 1684.

LOWRY EDWARDS, of near Dolgelley, co. Mer., spinster; maid to Robert Owen, of Dolserey, gentleman. Rmd. to Duck Creek, Penna., 1684. Prob. sister to Edward Edwards.

Some of the Founders

MARGARET EDWARDS, of near Dolgelley, co. Mer., spinster; maid to Robert Owen, of Dolserey, gentleman. Rmd. to Duck Creek, Penna., 1684. Prob. sister to Edward Edwards.

PETER EDWARDS; had a deed, 1682, for 100 a. ld. in Penna., and prob. rmd. there, 1683.

WILLIAM EDWARDS, of co. Glam., yeoman. Rmd. to Middleton, Penna., before 1688. Fd. Freeholder in Middleton. Died, 1716.

Wives: (1) ——; (2) Jane Atkinson, from co. York.

Children (surname Edwards): 1. John; 2. Sarah (by 2d wf.), m. Joseph Pratt; and prob. others. John Edwards, s. William, d. 1749. Children: John, Nathan, Moses, Joseph, Amos, Mary, Elizabeth, Hannah, and Phebe.

CADWALADER ELLIS. Rmd. to Penna. about, or before, 1700. He purchased 295 a. ld. on Ridley Creek, Goshen, from Hugh Roberts or his executors, before 26 March, 1706.

ELLIS ELLIS, of Iscregenan, co. Mer.; s. Thomas Ellis, of same place, gentleman. Rmd. to Haverford, Penna., 1683 (with his father). Fd. D. 1706.

Wife, Lydia, dau. Samuel Humphrey, decd.; m. 1685.

Children (surname Ellis): 1. Rachael; 2. Thomas; 3. Elizabeth; 4. Bridget; 5. John; 6. Joseph; 7. Evan; 8. William; 9. Benjamin; 10. Rebecca.

GWEN ELLIS, of near Bala, co. Mer., spinster. Rmd. to Penna., 1697. Fd.

HUMPHREY ELLIS, of Iscregenan, co. Mer.; s. Thomas Ellis, of same place. Rmd. to Haverford, Penna., 1683 (with his father). Fd.

Wives: (1) Gwen Rees, m. 1684; (2) Jane David, of Haverford; m. 1687.

Children: 1. Thomas; 2. Lydia (by 1st. wife); 3. Humphrey; 4. Sublimus; 5. Jeremiah; 6. Margaret; 7. Jane; 8. Rachael; 9. Ellen.

HUMPHREY ELLIS, of near Bala, co. Mer.; s. Ellis ——., and Jane, dau. Cadwalader Rowland, his wife. Rmd. to Penna., with his mother, Jane Cadwalader, then a wid., and his uncle, John Cadwalader Rowland, 1696. Fd.

MARY ELLIS, of near Dolgelley, co. Mer., wid. of ——. Rmd. to Penna., prob. 1683. Certif. undated. Fd.

Children: 1. ——, m. Evan Jones; 2. Gemima.

ROBERT ELLIS, of near Tyddyn y Garreg, co. Mer., gentleman; s. Ellis ——. Rmd. to Merion, Penna., 1690. (Certif. from Tyddyn y Garreg Mtg.). Fd. Freeholder in Merion.

Wife, Ellin ——.

Children (surname Roberts): 1. Abel; 2. Moses; 3. Ellis; 4. Aaron, of Norriton (now Norristown); m., 1727, Sarah Longworthy; 5. Evan; 6. Rachel; 7. Jane.

ROBERT ELLIS, s. Rowland Ellis, of Bryn Mawr; b. Bryn Mawr, near Dolgelley, co. Mer. Rmd. to Penna. (with his father), 1696. Fd.

Wife, Margaret, dau. William John (or Jones), of Gwynedd. (See ped in vol. ii.)

Children (surname Ellis): 1. Jane.

ROWLAND ELLIS, of Bryn Mawr, near Dolgelley, co. Mer., gentleman; b. 1650; s. Ellis ap Rees (alias Ellis Price), of Bryn Mawr (see ped. "Merion," 219). Rmd. to Merion, Penna., 1686. Returned to Wales, and re-embarked with his family, 1696. Fd. Freeholder.

Wives: (1) Margaret, dau. and h. of Ellis Morris (or Maurice), of Dolgun-issa; (2) Margaret, dau. of Robert ap Owen, of Dyffrydan (his cousin).

Children (surname Ellis): 1. Anne (by 1st wife), m., before 9 Jan., 1696, Rev. Richard Johnson, Curate of Dolgelley; 2. Jane (by 1st. wife); 3. Elizabeth; 4. Rowland; 5. Robert, m. Margaret, dau. William Jones (or John), of Gwynedd, and had dau. Jane Ellis; 6. Ellin (or Eleanor), m. John Evans, of Gwynedd, s. of Cadwalader; 7. Catherine.

The Rev. Richard Johnson, died without issue. The marriage settlement of R. J. and Anne, daughter of Rowland Ellis, remains in the possession of Edward Griffith, Esq., of Coedcymmer, Dolgelley, and the following is an abstract thereof.

Indenture Quadrapartit, made 9 Jan., 8 William III., 1696. Between Rowland Ellis of Brynmawr in the co. of Merioneth gent. and Jane Ellis one of the daughters of the sayd Rowland Ellis spinster of the first part, Richard Johnson of Doleythowgrid in

(To face page 162.)

Henry IV.
|
Humphrey, Duke of Gloucester.
|
Antigone, m. Henry Grey, Earl of Tankerville.
|
Elizabeth Grey, m. Sir Roger Kynaston, Knt.
|
Mary Kynaston, m. Howel ap Jenkin, of Ynysymaengwyn.
|
Humphrey ap Howel, m. Anne, dau. Sir Richard Herbert, Knt.
|
Jane, m. Griffith Nannau, of Nannau, Dolgelley.
|
John Griffith Nannau, m. Elizabeth, dau. David Lloyd.
|
Lewis ap John Griffith, of Dyffrydan, Dolgelley, liv. 1654.
|
Rees Lewis ap John Griffith, of Dyffrydan, liv. 1649.
|
Ellis ap Rees (alias Ellis Price), of Bryn Mawr, liv. 1678; m. Anne, dau. Humphrey ap Hugh, of Llwyn du (see ped iv.), des. fr. Edward III.
|
Rowland Ellis, of Bryn Mawr.

the said co. and Anne his wife another of the daughters of the said Rowland Ellis, of the second part, Lewis Owen of Tyddyn y garegg in the said co., gent., and John Vaughan of Penarth in the said co. gent. of the third part, Howell Vaughan of Hengwrt in the said co. esq. and Gryffith Vaughan of Dollymelonllyn in said co. gent. of the fourth part, citing a marriage heretofore solemnized between the said Richard Johnson and Anne his said wife and payment of £250 by the said Richard and Anne to said Rowland and Jane as consideration. Also an agreement formerly made between the said Rowland Ellis and the said Richard Johnson. Provides for a Fine to be levied upon those messuages and tenements called and known by the several names of Tyddyn y Brynmawr alias Tyddyn y Groes and Llyncae dy, situate in the township of Dyffrydan in the parish of Dolgelley in co. Merioneth, in favour of the said Lewis Owen and John Vaughan and the heirs of the said Lewis Owen to the use and behooff of the purposes thereafter mentioned, viz. to the use of the said Richard Johnson and his assigns for the term of his natural life and after his death to the use and behoof of the said Howell Vaughan and Gryffith Vaughan their executors and assigns for and during the term of One hundred years under limitations and conditions set forth. That is to say, to use of Anne wife of the said Richard during her natural life, and then to the issue of said Richard and Anne in tail male, and in default of issue male, then to the issue female of the said Richard and Anne, and in default of such issue to Jane the other daughter of the said Rowland Ellis and her heirs, and in default of such issue to the right heirs of the said Rowland Ellis forever.

Signed and sealed by: Rowland Ellis, Jane Ellis [Mark.], Richard Johnson, Anne Johnson.

Witnesses: J. Humphrey, Edw. (?) Owen, Gryffith Jones. [The signature of Rowland Ellis to this deed is identical with his signature attached to documents relating to Penna.]

ROWLAND ELLIS, s. Rowland Ellis, of Bryn Mawr, co. Mer., b. Bryn Mawr, near Dolgelley. Rmd. to Penna. (with his father), 1686. Fd. D. 1737, s.p.

ROWLAND ELLIS. Rmd. to Philadelphia, Penna. abt. or shortly after 1700. D. in Philadelphia, 1726, s.p.

THOMAS ELLIS, of Iscregenan, co. Mer., yeoman. Rmd. to Penna., 1683. Certif. fr. Mtg. at Dolserey,

5 mo. 27, 1683. Fd. Freeholder of large tracts of land in Haverford and elsewhere. D. 1688. Reg. Gen. of Penna.

Wives: (1.) ——; (2.) Elliew, or Ellin, dau. Rees Hugh, of co. Mer., and sister to Elizabeth Rees, wife of Samuel Humphrey, of Llangelynin.

Children (by 1st wife): 1. Ellis, m. Lydia Humphrey; 2. Humphrey, m. (1) Gwen Rees; (2) Jane David; 3. Eleanor, m. David Lawrence; 4. Bridget, m. —— Jones.

Fds. records show a certif. to a Thomas Ellis, fr. Redstone Mtg., Pembrokeshire, 7 mo., 2, 1683. Thomas Ellis traced to the ancient nobility of Wales. He was *not* a near relative of Rowland Ellis, as some have supposed.

THOMAS ELLIS. Rmd. to Penna., 1683. Certif. fr. Redstone Mtg., co. Pemb., 7 mo., 2, 1683. According to some accounts he was father of the children usually assigned to Thomas Ellis, the Reg. Gen. One of these persons was father to Rachel Ellis, who m. Robert Wharton.

OWEN AP EVAN (alias Evans), of South Wales, yeoman; s. Evan ap Evan. Rmd. to Chester Co. Penna., about 1700.

Wife, Elizabeth ——.

Children (surname Evans): 1. John, d. unm.; 2. Thomas, m. 1720, Elizabeth Griffith; 3. Robert, m., 1717, Ellen ——, and had Peter Evans; 4. Griffith. Thomas Evans, 2d. s. Owen ap Evans, had, by Elizabeth, his wife, 1. Owen; 2. Edward, b. 1730; 3 Thomas, b. 1733; 4. Griffith, b. 1735; 5. John, b. 1737.

REES EVAN, of Fronween, Penmaen, par. of Llanfor, co. Mer., gentleman; s. Evan Rees, of same place, grocer. D. in Wales. Fd. (For ped. see another page). Freeholder in Merion.

Wife, Elizabeth, dau. John Thomas, of Llaithgwm, gentleman. (For ped. see another page).

Children (surname Rees): 1. Evan; 2. John; 3. David; 4. Sydney, m., 1709, Robert Roberts, s. John, of Pencoyd, Pennsylvania. Two of the sons rmd. to Penna.

THOMAS SION EVAN (alias Thomas Jones), of near Bala, co. Mer., yeoman; s. Thomas Sion (John). Rmd. to Penna., 1682. He arrived near the spot upon which Philadelphia was afterwards built, 16 April, 1682, being the first Welshman in the province. Ch. E. Freeholder of 300 a. ld. in Radnor. D. 1707.

Wife, Lowry, wid. Thomas Lloyd, of Penmaen, par. of Llanfor. The latter had been a poet of note before he joined Friends. (M. in Penna, 1686).

Children (surname Jones): 1. John; 2. Joseph, b. 1695; m. Sarah Morgan; 3. Rowland, d. 1698; 4. Elizabeth, m. Risiart (Richard) ap Thomas ap Rhys. Four others d. young. All b. in Penna.

CADWALADER EVANS, of Ucheldre, par. of Llanfor, co. Mer., yeoman, b. 1664; s. Evan Lloyd Evan of Ucheldre, yeoman (d. 1690). Rmd. to Gwynedd, Penna., 1698. Ch. E. Freeholder of 609 a. ld. in Gwynedd. D. 1745. (For ped. see "Welsh Founders of Penna.", ii.)

Wife, Ellen, dau. John Morris, of Bryn Gwyn, co. Denb. (For ped. see another page).

Children (surname Evans): 1. John, m. Ellen Ellis; 2. Sarah, m. John Hanke. Two ch. d. at sea, 1698. (For dests. see "Historical Collections of Gwynedd," Jenkins).

DAVID EVANS, of par. of Llanvachreth, co. Mer., gentleman; s. Evan William Powel, of same place. Rmd. to Penna., 1684. Fd. Freeholder.

Wives: (1) Gainor; (2) Mary Jones. (M. 1690).

Children (surname Evans): 1. Caleb; 2. Joshua; 3. Evan; 4. David; 5. John; 6. Philip; 7. Gwen; 8. Margaret; 9. Sarah. (See pedigree on another page).

DAVID EVANS, prob. from North Wales, was in Philadelphia before 1700. Fd. Freeholder. Depty. Sheriff of Philadelphia, 1714-1721. D. 1745.

Wives: (1) ——; (2) Elizabeth, dau. Robert Owen, of Merion (s. Owen ap Evan, of Fron Goch, near Bala).

Children: 1. Evan, who had, Sidney, David and Rebecca Evans; 2. Rebecca, d. unm.; 3. Sidney, m., 1759, Joseph Howell; 4. Sarah, d. unm. 1762; 5. David, d. 1725; 6. Margaret, d. unm., 1734. Some of the above said to have been by 1st wife.

EDWARD EVANS, of par. of Nantmell, co. Rad., gentleman; bro. John Evans, of Nantmell, who rmd. to Penna., 1683, supposed to have rmd. to Penna. abt. same time. Prob. lived with his bro. (See ped. on another page).

Wife, ——.

Children: 1. Elizabeth, liv. 17 Augt., 1703.

JANE EVANS, of co. Rad., wid. 'Rmd. to Penna. 1684. She was prob. kinswoman to Rees Rees.

Children : 1. Sarah ; 2. Mary ; 3. Alice ; 4. Eliza ; 5. Joseph.

The surname of these children uncertain ; but prob. Evans, as her husband is supposed to have been named John Evans, although there is no certainty.

JENKIN EVANS, of South Wales, yeoman. Rmd. to Montgomery, Penna., before 1717. Ch. E. Freeholder of 108 a. ld. in Montgommery. D. 1770.

Wives : (1) Alice, dau. Edward Morgan, of Gwynedd (m. 1718) ; (2) Jane ———.

Children (surname Evans) : 1. Elizabeth; 2. Rachel; 3. Sarah ; 4. Mary ; 5. Eleanor ; 6. Jenkin, of New Britain, miller ; 7. Walter (by 2d wife). All b. Penna.

JOHN EVANS, of par. of Nantmell, co. Rad., gentleman ; s. Evan Lewis, of same place. Rmd. to Radnor, Penna., 1682-3. Ch. E. Freeholder of 350 a. land. D. 1707.

Wife, Delilah ———.

Children (surname Evans and Jones) : 1. Sarah, m. John Morgan, Sr., s. James, of Radnor ; 2. May, m. David Evan ; 3. Jane ; 4. Margaret, m. Hugh Samuel ; 5. Phebe, m. Edward David ; 6. Rees (surname Jones) ; 7. Thomas (surname Jones) ; 8. ———, d. inft.

JOHN EVANS (otherwise John Evan Edward, and John Evan ap Edward), b. near Bala, co. Mer.; s. Evan ap Edward, of Cynlas, par. of Llandderfel, co. Mer. Rmd. to Penna. with his father's family (which included his uncles, John ap Edward, and William ap Edward, of Merion, who arrived in the Province, 1682). He is mentioned as "my nephew" John Evans, in will of his uncle John ap Edward, 1683-4, and in his marriage certif., 1686 ; but, in 1692, signs himself *Jno. Evan. Edwd.* to distinguish himself from John Evans, late of Nantmell. He acquired land in Radnor. (See ped. on another page).

Wife, Mary Hughes ; m. 1686.

Children : 1. Sarah, m., 1717, John Morgan, Jr., (see Morgan). (Two John Morgans, father, and son, married women named Sarah, both of whom were daus. of a John Evans). There was other issue, names not satisfactorily ascertained.

OWEN EVANS, of Ucheldre, par. of Llanfor, co. Mer., yeoman ; s. Evan Lloyd Evan of Ucheldre,

SOME OF THE FOUNDERS 167

yeoman (d. 1690). Rmd. to Gwynedd, Penna., 1698. Ch. E. Freeholder of 538 a. ld. in Gwynedd. D. 1723, "in his 64th year." (For ped. see "Welsh Founders of Penna.", ii.).

Wife, Elizabeth ———.

Children (surname Evans) : 1. Thomas, m. Elizabeth Griffith; 2. John, died unm.; 3. Robert, m. (1) Ellen Griffith; (2) Ruth Richards; 4. Cadwalader, d. unm.; 5. Evan, m. Phœbe Miles; 6. Mary, m. (1) Ellis Pugh, jr., of Plymouth; (2) William Roberts; 7. Elizabeth, b. Penna., m. Samuel Richards, s. Rowland, of Tredyffrin; 8. Samuel, m. Hannah Walker; 9. Jane, b. presumably in Penna.; d. unm. (For dests. see "Historical Collections of Gwynedd," Jenkins).

PHILIP EVANS, of par. of Llanvachreth, co. Mer., gentleman; s. Evan William Powel, of same place. Rmd. to Penna., 1684. Fd. Freeholder.

Wife, Sarah Thomas; m. 1690. D.s.p. before 1693. (See pedigree on another page).

ROBERT EVANS, of Ucheldre, par. of Llanfor, co. Mer., yeoman; s. Evan Lloyd Evan of Ucheldre, yeoman (d. 1690). Rmd. to Gwynedd, Penna., 1698. Ch. E. Freeholder of 1034 a. ld. in Gwynedd. D. 1738, aged "about" 80. (For ped. see "Welsh Founders of Penna.", ii.).

Wife, Ellen ———.

Children (surname Evans): 1. Hugh, m. Margaret Roberts; 2. Evan; 3. Lowry, m. Thomas Siddon; 4. Mary, m. (1) Cadwalader Foulke; (2) Thomas Marriott; 5. Ann, m. William Roberts, of Merion; 6. Sarah, m. Richard Kinderdine; 7. Jane, m. Edward Parry. (For dests. see "Historical Collections of Gwynedd," Jenkins).

STEPHEN EVANS, of par. of Llanbister, co. Rad. Rmd. to Radnor, Penna., 1683. Ch. E. 100 a. ld. on rent in Radnor.

Wife, Elizabeth ———.

Children (surname Stephens, or Stevens): 1. John; 2. Phœbe.

THOMAS EVANS, of Ucheldre, par. of Llanfor, co. Mer., yeoman; s. Evan Lloyd Evan of Ucheldre, yeoman (d. 1690). Rmd. to Gwynedd, Penna., 1698. Ch. E. Freeholder of 1049 a. ld. in Gwynedd. D. 1738, aged 87. (For ped. see "Welsh Founders of Penna.", ii.).

Wives: (1) Ann ———; (2) Hannah Davies, wid., of Goshen. (M. 1722).

Children (surname Evans): 1. Hugh, m. (1) Catharine Morgan; (2) Alice Lewis; (3) Lowry Lloyd; 2. Owen. m. (1) Ruth Miles; (2) Mary Nicholas; 3. Evan, m. Elizabeth Musgrave; 4. Ann; 5. Lowry, m. Evan Jones; 6. Ellin, m. Rowland Hugh, widower; 7. Sarah, m. Edward Jones. (For dests. see "Historical Collections of Gwynedd," Jenkins).

EDWARD FOULKE, of Coed y Foel, par. of Llanfor, co. Mer., b. 1651; s. Foulke Thomas Lloyd of par. of Llandderfel (d. before 1677), and Lowry, dau. Edward David of Llanfor. (She was bur. at Llandderfel, 5 July, 1677). Rmd. to Gwynedd, Penna., 1698. Ch. E. Freeholder of 712 a. ld. in Gwynedd. D. 1741. (For ped. see "Historical Collections of Gwynedd," Jenkins. Foulke Ped., chart, and "Pedigree of Edward Foulke" MS., Hist. Soc. of Penna.).

Wife, Eleanor, dau. Hugh Cadwaladr, of par. of Yspytty Evan, co. Denb.

Children (surname Foulke): 1. Thomas, m. Gwen Evans; 2. Hugh, m. Ann Williams; 3. Cadwalader, m. Mary Evans; 4. Evan, m. (1) Ellen Roberts; (2) Anne Coulston; 5. Gwen, m. Alexander Edwards; 6. Grace, m. John Griffith; 7. Jane, m. Ellis Hugh (Hughes); 8. Catharine, m. Theophilus Williams; 9. Margaret, m. Nicholas Roberts. (For dests. see Historical "Collections of Gwynedd," Jenkins).

MARY FOULKE, prob. of near Wrexham, co. Denb. A purchaser of 200 a. ld. in Penna. from John ap John, 1682. It is not known whether she removed to the Province or not.

OWEN FOULKE, of par. of Bettws y Coed, co. Carn., tanner. He had a deed, 25 July, 1862, for land in Penna. Fd. He prob. remained in Wales; but uncertain.

THOMAS FOULKE, prob. fr. North Wales. Rmd. to Burlington, West Jersey, 1677. He was a commissioner of lands, 1677, and had interests in what was afterwards the Province of Penna.

Wife, ———.

Children: 1. Thomas, m., 1688, Elizabeth Curtis, and had Sarah Foulke, who m. Joseph Thorne.

Ancestor to the French family, of N. J. and Philadelphia.

HENRY GIBBONS, of Paverage, co. Derby. Rmd. to Darby, Penna., 1684. He was descended from the Gibbons, or Gibons family, of Salop, whose ancestor was Gibbon, or Gibon, son of Ithel ap Ieuan Fychan, 2d son of Ieuan Fychan, lord of Llys Pengwern, Tref Castell, and Tref Gwehelaith, and *jure uxoris*, of Mostyn. This Ieuan Fychan did homage for his lands, 1300, at Chester. Ithel Fychan, father of Gibbon (whose descendants assumed the surname of Gibbons), was slain at Whittington Castle, on the last Thursday in July, 1457.[1]

ABEL GRIFFITH, b. 1723; s. Griffith Griffiths, of East Nantmeal (Nantmell), co. Chester, Penna., planter. D. after 1799.

Wives: (1) Marget Bramer; m. 1763; (2) Mary ——.

Children: 1. Griffith, b. 1763; m. Mary Butler; 2. Gwen, b. 1765; d. unm., 1833; 3. Anna, b. 1767; d. unm.; 4. Benjamin, b. 1768; d. unm.; 5. Elijah, M.D., b. 1769. Surgeon of 1st. Penna. Cavalry, and a distinguished physician. D. 1847. M., 1815, Isabella, wid. James McCurach, and dau. Thomas Sharp, of Salem, N.J.[2]; 6. Amos, of New Britain, co. Bucks, M.D., b. 1771; 7. Salome, b. 1772; d. unm.; 8. Margaret, d. inft.

EDWARD GRIFFITH, of co. Mer., yeoman. Rmd. to Merion, Penna., before 1689. Fd. D. 1719.

Wife, Catherine Williams, of Merion; m. 1689.

Children (surname Griffith): 1. Ellin, b. 1690; d. inft.; 2. Ellin, b. 1691; m. Robert Evans, 1717, of Gwynedd; 3. Jane, b. 1693; 4. Elizabeth, b. 1696; m. Thomas Evans, 1720, of Gwynedd; 5. Thomas, b. 1699; 6. Jane, b. 1701; 7. Margaret, b. 1702.

GRIFFITH GRIFFITHS, of par. of Llanddewi Brefi, co. Card.; s. Griffith John Griffith, of same place, gentleman. Rmd. to co. Chester, Penna., abt. 1717. D. in East Nantmeal, 1760. Bpt.

Wife, Gwen, dau. Evan Thomas, of co. Chester; m. 1722.

Children: 1. Abel, b. 1723, m. (1), 1763, Marget Bramer; (2) Mary ——; 2. William rmd. to So. Carolina; 3. Evan, b. 1729; 4. Dan, a Magistrate for co. Chester; m. Rebecca ——; 5. Levi, Capt. in service U.S.A.; 6. Amos, of New Britain, co. Bucks; 7. Rebecca, m. John Howell, of co. Bucks.

---

[1] A daughter of Henry Gibbons married Samuel Sellers, ancestor to Horace Wells Sellers, of Philadelphia.
[2] Joseph Murray Griffiths, s. Dr. Elijah Griffiths, was Lt.-Colonel 39th Iowa Infantry, war of Rebellion, and his bro., Henry Holcombe Griffiths, was Captain Iowa Light Artillery, and served with conspicuous gallantry. Another son of Dr. Griffiths, Rev. Thomas Sharp Griffiths, was father of Foster C. Griffith, Esq., of Trenton, N.J. Henry Griffith Keasbey, of Eastbourne, England, is a grandson of Dr. Griffiths.

HUGH GRIFFITH, of near Bala, co. Mer., yeoman ; s. Griffith ap Evan, of Ucheldre, par. of Llanfor. Rmd. to Penna., 1696, and afterwards settled at Gwynedd. Fd.

Wife, ——; d. several years before his removal to Penna. (See his ped., vol. ii.).

Children (b. in Wales): 1. Griffith, m. 1718, Jane Roberts; 2. Evan, m. 1705, Bridget Jones; 3. Robert; 4. Edward; 5. David; 6. Ellin.

Some of these children appear to have assumed the surname of Hugh, or Hughes; others that of Griffith, or Griffiths. Griffith, the eldest son, who married Jane Roberts, dau. Robert Ellis, late of Radnor, 1718, was then called Griffith Hugh. Descendants lived about Gwynedd.

JAMES GRIFFITH, of near Bala. co. Mer. Rmd. to Penna., supposedly, 1698.

JANE GRIFFITH, of near Llangelynin, co. Mer., spinster, "a hopeful young woman." Rmd. to Penna., 1690. Fd.

JOHN GRIFFITH, of par. of Llanddewi Brefi, co. Card.; s. Griffith John Griffith, of same place, gentleman. Rmd. to Penna. abt. 1717. Fd. D. in Newtown, co. Chester, 1774.

Wife, Mary, dau. Samuel John.

Children: 1. William, b. 1736; m. Hetty Wynne; 2. John, b. 1737, d. Frederick Co.,Va., 1833, m. (1) 1768, Mary, dau. Jesse Faulkner; (2) Mary Ellis; 3. Samuel, m. (1) Amy George; (2) Mary Leiter; 4. Ruth, m., 1767, Samuel Fisher; 5. Anna, m., 1771, Jesse Wickersham, of East Nantmeal (Nantmell).[1]

ROBERT GRIFFITH, of par. of Llanfor, co. Mer.; s. Griffith ap Evan, of Ucheldre, Llanfor. D. at sea, on voyage to Penna., 1698. See ped. in vol. ii.

Wife ——.

Children: 1. Catherine, and three or more others, who were brought up at Gwynedd, Penna.

SUSAN GRIFFITH, of par. of Machynlleth, co. Montg., maid to John Richards, bound to serve 8 years from 1684. Rmd. to Penna., 1684.

---

[1] The descendants of John Griffith are, for the most part, living in Virginia, and Chicago, Ohio. The family is represented in Winchester, Va., by Richard Edward Griffith, Esq. and John Griffith, Esq., Joseph Clarkson Griffith, Esq., another brother, removed to Chicago.

Some of the Founders

WILLIAM GRIFFITH, of par. of Llanddewi Brefi, co. Card. ; s. Griffith John Griffith, of same place, gentleman. Rmd. to Easttown, Penna., abt. 1717. Bpt. Freeholder in Easttown. D. 1790.
Wife ——.
Children : 1. William ; 2. John ; 3. David ; 4. Sarah, m. Daniel McKachen ; 5. Ann, m. John Edwards.

HANNAH HARDYMAN, of near Haverford West, co. Pemb., spinster. Rmd. to Penna., 1683. She m. Samuel Carpenter, of Philadelphia, merchant. (For descendants see "Lloyd and Carpenter Families," by S. P. Smith ; "Notes on Lloyd, Pemberton and Hutchinson Families," by T. A. Glenn ; Carpenter Genealogy, by General Louis A. Carpenter, U.S.A., retired ; in preparation).

DANIEL HARRY, of par. of Machynlleth, co. Montg. ; s. Harry Thomas, of same place. Rmd. to Penna., 1684. Fd. Freeholder in Merion. (See pedigree on another page).

DAVID HARRY, Rmd. to Radnor, Penna., before 1696. Fd.
Wife, Lydia, dau. David Powell, of Penna. ; m. 11 mo., 19, 1699. (See pedigree on another page ; but it is uncertain if he was bro. to Hugh, Evan, and Daniel).

EVAN HARRY, of par. of Machynlleth, co. Montg. ; s. Harry Thomas Owen, of same place. Rmd. to Merion, Penna., before 1697. Fd. Freeholder in Merion.
Wife, Catherine David, wid. ; m. 1697. (See pedigree on another page).

HARRY REES HARRY, of near Cwmcawlid, co. Carm. ; s. Rees Harry. Rmd. to Penna., 1693. Fd.
(The above is intended for Harry, son of Rees, son of Harry).

HUGH HARRY (alias Harris), of par. of Machynlleth, co. Montg. ; s. Harry Thomas Owen, of same place. Rmd. to Chester, co. Penna., 1684 (ship Vine). Fd. Freeholder in Birmingham Twp. D. 1708. (See ped.).
Wife, Elizabeth, daughter of William Brinton, late of par. of Sedgeley, co. Staff., by Ann, dau. of Edward Bagley, gentleman, of same place. H. H. and E. B. mar. 1686.

Children (surname Harry or Harris): 1. Evan, m. Elizabeth; 2. William; 3. Hugh; 4. John; 5. Elizabeth, m., 1728, Robert Eachus; 6. Ann, m. Thomas Speakman; 7. Jane; 8. Lois; 9. Olive, m., 1720, Daniel Bailey.

JOHN HARRY, living in or near Merion, Penna., about 1690 to 1700, and prob. earlier. He was from near Bala. Nothing further has been found concerning him except that he was a man of considerable education, and perhaps a schoolmaster.

DAVID HAVERD, of South Wales. He had a deed, 1696, for land in Penna., and d. before 3 Dec., 1701.
Wife, Mary ———.
Children: 1. John, s. and h.; prob. others.

JOHN HAYES, of par. of Ilmiston, co. Pemb., husbandman; s. Richard, of same place. Rmd. to Haverford, Penna., 1687. Fd.

RICHARD HAYES, of par. of Ilmiston, co. Pemb., yeoman. Rmd. to Haverford, Penna., 1687. Fd. Freeholder. D. at an advanced age, 1697.
Wife, Issallt ———.
Children: 1. Richard; 2. John; prob. others d. y.

RICHARD HAYES, of par. of Ilmiston, co. Pemb., yeoman; s. Richard, of same place. Rmd. to Haverford, Penna., 1687. Fd. Freeholder in Haverford and elsewhere. Held many public offices. D. 1738.
Wife, Elizabeth, dau. Henry Lewis; m. 1697-8.
Children: 1. Joseph; 2. Richard; 3. Benjamin; 4. Mary, m. John Jacobs, of Perkiomen; 5. Hannah, m. James Jones, of Blockley.

REES HENT, of par. of Llanddewy, co. Pemb., yeoman. Rmd. to Newtown, Penna., 1688. Returned to Wales and brought his family to the Province in 1694.
Wife ———.
Children: 1. Jane, m. John Smith; prob. others.

FRANCIS HOWELL, of par. of Llanddissilio, co. Carm. (partly in co. Pemb.), carpenter. Rmd. to Merion, Penna., 1684. Fd. Freeholder. D. 1696.
Wife, Margaret Mortimer. She d. 1696.
No issue survived.

HUMPHREY HOWELL, of co. Denb., bound for 4 years' servitude. Sailed "for Virginia," 1698, 19 Oct. Penna. prob. intended to be meant.

Some of the Founders

JAMES HOWELL, of Pontymoel, co. Mon., yeoman. Rmd. to Radnor, Penna., 1684. Fd. Freeholder of ld. in Radnor.

Wives : (1) Gwenllian ; (2) Maudin, wid. John Kinsey. (M. 1690).

JOHN HOWELL, of Aberystwyth, co. Card., yeoman. Rmd. to Penna., 1697.

Wife, ——.

Children (surname Howell) : 1. Jacob, b. 1687 ; m. Sarah Vernon, dau. Randal, of Lower Providence ; 2. Evan, m. Sarah Ogden, of Edgemont ; 3. Sarah, d. unm.

REES HOWELL, of par. of Kilycwm, co. Carm., husbandman. Rmd. to Penna., 1699. Fd.

WILLIAM HOWELL, par. of Castel Bight, co. Pemb. Rmd. to Merion, Penna., abt. 1683. Fd. Freeholder of 500 a. ld. (deed 1682), in Penna., part of which was surveyed in Merion.

Wife, Mary Thomas ; m. 1687.

CADWALADER THOMAS AP HUGH (usually called Cadwalader Thomas), of Ciltalgarth, par. of Llanfor, co. Mer. ; s. Thomas ap Hugh of Wern Fawr, par. of Llandderfel. Fd. Although he did not remove to Penna., yet he is so identified with the events which led up to the settlement of Merion as to warrant his inclusion in this roll. He d. in the par. of Llandrillo, near Bala, of illness contracted during imprisonment for nonconformity, 1680.

Wife, Ellen Owen, dau. Owen ap Evan, of Fron Goch, sis. of Robert Owen (who d. in Merion, 1697).

Children (surname Cadwalader) : 1. Thomas ; 2. John, rmd. to Penna. ; 3. Jane ; 4. Catherine ; 5. Elizabeth. Cadwalader Thomas was bro. of John Thomas, of Llaithgwm. (See ped. i.).

DAVID CADWALADER AP HUGH, of near Bala, co. Mer. Rmd. to Gwynedd, Penna., 1698. D. s. p. 1701. He was bro.-in-law to Evan ap Hugh or Pugh, of Gwynedd.

EVAN AP HUGH (alias Pugh), of near Bala, co. Mer., yeoman ; prob. s. of Hugh Cadwaladr ap Rhys, of par. of Yspytty Evan, and bro. of John ap Hugh, (or John Hugh, or Pugh, of Gwynedd). Rmd. to Gwynedd, Penna., 1698. Ch. E. Freeholder of 800 a. ld. in Gwynedd.

Wife, Ann, dau. Cadwalader ap Hugh (sister to David Cadwalader ap Hugh, of Gwynedd, d. 1701).

Children (surname Evans): 1. Hugh, m., 1716, Mary, dau. Robert Jones, of Merion, decd.; 2. David; 3. Cadwalader, m., 1722, Sarah, dau. Rowland Richard, of Tredyffrin; 4. Catherine, m., 1717, Robert Hugh, s. Hugh Griffith, of Gwynedd; 5. Jane, m. Evan Roberts, of Gwynedd.

Evan ap Hugh, alias Pugh, appears to have also m. Grace ——.

JOHN AP HUGH, see John Hugh.

ROBERT AP HUGH (alias Pugh), of near Bala, co. Mer., yeoman. Rmd. to Gwynedd, Penna., 1698. Ch. E. Freeholder of 200 a. ld. in Gwynedd.

Wife, Sarah, dau. Evan Lloyd Evan, of Ucheldre (alias Evan ap Evan). (See ped. vol. ii.).

Children: 1. Sarah, m. Samuel Bell; 2. Evan, who rmd. to Virginia; 3. Ellen, m. (1) John Rogers, s. Roger Roberts, of Merion; (2) ——; 4. Sarah, m. Rowland Roberts, of Gwynedd. (See vol. ii.).

DAVID HUGH, prob. of near Bala, co. Mer., yeoman. Rmd. to Merion, Penna., before 1695. Rmd. from Merion to Haverford. Fd. D. 1709.

Wife, Martha, dau. Ralph Lewis, of Haverford. (M. 1696).

Children (surname Hughes): 1. David; 2. Ruth; 3. John; 4. Mary; 5. Samuel; 6. Caleb.

DAVID HUGH, prob. of co. Mer. Rmd. to Merion, Penna., before 1692.

DAVID HUGH. Rmd. to Merion, Penna., before 1696. Fd.

Wife, Martha Lewis. (M. 1696).

JOHN HUGH (alias ap Hugh and Pugh), of par. of Yspytty Evan, co. Denb., yeoman; s. Hugh ap Cadwaladr ap Rhys (alias Hugh Cadwaladr), of same place, yeoman. Rmd. to Gwynedd, Penna., 1698. Ch. E. Freeholder of 648 a. ld. in Gwynedd. (See ped. on another page).

Wives: (1) ——; (2) Ellin Williams, of Upper Merion. (M. 1716-17).

Children (surname Hugh and Pugh): 1. Ellis, m., 1713, Jane Foulke; 2. Rowland, m., 1708, Catharine Humphreys; 3. Jane, m., 1712, Thomas Ellis, of Gwynedd. Perhaps others.

MARGARET Hugh, of near Bala, co. Mer., spinster. Rmd. to Penna., 1696. Fd.

Some of the Founders

ROWLAND HUGH, of par. of Yspytty Evan, co. Denbigh, yeoman ; s. Hugh Cadwalader ap Rhys, of same place. (See ped. on another page). Rmd. to Gwynedd abt. 1700.
Wife, ——.

STEPHEN HUGH (alias Stephen ap Hugh). Rmd. to Springfield, Penna., 1683. D. 1683.
Wife, Frances ——. (M., 2d, Thomas Norbury).
Children : 1. Martha, m. Jonathan Taylor. She is called Martha Stevens in one record.

ROGER HUGHES, of par. of Llanfihangel Rhydrython, co. Rad., gentleman. He had a deed dated 1682, for 250 a. ld. in Penna., which he sold to Thomas Parry and David Meredith, and probably did not rm. to the Province, or if so returned to Wales. Ch. E.

HUMPHREY, see Humphrey William.

ANNE HUMPHREY (alias Anne Samuel), of par. of Llangelynin. co. Mer., spinster, b. 1666 ; dau. Samuel Humphrey, of same place, gentleman. Rmd. to Haverford, Penna., 1683. Fd. She m. Edward Roberts.

BENJAMIN HUMPHREY (alias Benjamin Samuel), of par. of Llangelynin, co. Mer., yeoman, b. 1662 ; s. Samuel Humphrey, of same place, gentleman. Rmd. to Merion, Penna., 1683. Fd. Freeholder of 100 a. ld. in Merion.
Wife, Mary, dau. Morris Llewelyn. (M. 1694).
Children (surname Humphrey or Humphreys): 1. John, b. 1695 ; 2. Joseph, b. 1697 ; 3. David, b. 1703 ; 4. Ann, b. 1708 ; m. Gerrad Jones s. Robert Jones, of Merion ; 5. Owen, b. 1713 ; m. 1738, Sarah, wid. of John Hughes, of Haverford ; 6. Elizabeth, m., 1741, John Scarlet.

John Humphrey, s. Benjamin, b. 1695, of Merion ; m. ——; d. 1761. Children : 1. Benjamin ; 2. Joseph ; 3. David ; 4. Morris ; 5. Ellis ; 6. Robert ; 7. Catherine ; 8. Elizabeth ; 9. Jane ; 10. Mary ; 11. Parthemia ; 12. Margaret.

DANIEL HUMPHREY (alias Daniel Samuel), of the par. of Llangelynin, co. Mer., yeoman, b. 1660 ; s. Samuel Humphrey, of same place, gentleman. Rmd. to Haverford, Penna., 1682. Fd. Freeholder in Haverford.
Wife, Hannah, dau. Dr. Thomas Wynne.

Children (surname Humphrey or Humphreys):
1. Samuel, b. 1696 ; 2. Thomas, b. 1697 ; 3. Jonathan, b. 1698 ; 4. Hannah, b. 1699 ; 5. Benjamin, b. 1701-2, m. Esther, dau. Isaac Warner ; 6. Elizabeth, b. 1703 ; 7. Mary, b. 1704-5 ; 8. Solomon, b. 1706 ; 9. Joshua, b. 1707-8 ; 10. Edward, b. 1709 ; 11. Martha, b. 1711 ; 12. Charles, b. 1714 ; 13. Rebecca, b. 1716.

ELIZABETH HUMPHREY (alias Elizabeth Rees), wid. of Samuel Humphrey (b. 1635 ; d. 1677) ; s. Humphrey ap Hugh, of Llwyndu, Llwyngwril, par. of Llangelynin, co. Mer , gentleman. She was dau. Rees ap Hugh. Rmd. to Haverford, Penna., 1683, with children : Benjamin, Lydia, Anne and Gobitha. Surname Samuel, which they changed to Humphrey, or Humphreys. Daniel and Joseph, elder ch. had rmd. to Penna. 1682. (See ped on another page).

ELIZABETH HUMPHREY (alias Elizabeth Samuel), of par. of Llangelynin, co. Mer., spinster ; dau. Samuel Humphrey, of same place, gentleman. Rmd. to Haverford, Penna., 1683. Fd. She m., 1693, Thomas Abel.

GOBITHA HUMPHREY (alias Gobitha Samuel), of par. of Llangelynin, co. Mer., spinster, b. 1668 ; dau. Samuel Humphrey, of same place, gentleman. Rmd. to Penna., 1683. Fd.

JOHN HUMPHREY, of par. of Llanwddyn, co. Montg., yeoman, bapt. at Llangelynin, co. Mer., 16 Nov., 1632 ; s. Humphrey ap Hugh, of Llwyndu, twp. of Llwyngwril, par. of Llangelynin, gentleman, (called also esquire). Rmd. to Merion, Penna., 1683. Fd. Freeholder in Merion. D. 1699, s. p. (For ped. see another page).

Wife, Jane Humphrey, sister to Richard Humphrey, of par. of Llangelynin. She predeceased her husband.

JOHN HUMPHREY, of par. of Llangower, co. Mer. ; s. Humphrey John (alias Jones), of same place, yeoman (burd. at Llangower, 1 Feb., 1678), and Gainor. Rmd. to Gwynedd, Penna., 1698. Ch. E. Freeholder of 574 a. ld. in Gwynedd.

Wives : (1) —— ; (2) Gwen, wid. John ——, of Llanfor, and dau. John Evans (or John ap Evan), of Penmaen. (See ped. vol. ii.).

Children (surname Jones) : 1. Humphrey, m., 1719, Catharine, dau. William John, and others.

Some of the Founders

JOHN HUMPHREY, of co. Denb., aged 12 years. Bound for 9 years' servitude to Mr. George Tyrer (assigned to Mr. Tildesley). Sailed "for America," 1702, 29 Jan. (Virginia or Penna.).

LYDIA HUMPHREY (alias Lydia Samuel), of par. of Llangelynin, co. Mer., spinster, b. 1659; dau. Samuel Humphrey of same place, gentleman. Rmd. to Haverford, Penna., 1683. Fd. She m. Ellis Ellis, of Haverford, s. Thomas Ellis.

JOSEPH HUMPHREY (alias Joseph Samuel), of par. of Llangelynin, co. Mer., b. 1662; s. Samuel Humphrey, of same place, gentleman. Rmd. to Haverford, Penna., 1682. Fd. D. in Philadelphia, 1693.

Wife, Elizabeth Medford.

MAURICE (or Morris) HUMPHREY, of co. Mer. (formerly of near Bala); s. Humphrey ap Morgan, and cousin to Cadwalader ap Evan, of Penmaen, decd. Rmd. to Penna., 1699. Fd.

Wife, ———.

Children (surname Humphrey): 1. Morgan; 2. Owen.

OWEN HUMPHREY, sup. s. Joseph (d. Phila., 1693), s. Samuel Humphrey (b. 1635), of par. of Llangelynin. He was of Philadelphia, Penna., innholder, 1726, and was then adminr. of est. of Rowland Ellis, decd. (prob. s. of Rowland Ellis, of Bryn Mawr).

REBECCA HUMPHREY (alias Rebecca Samuel), of par. of Llangelynin, co. Mer., spinster; b. 1664; dau. Samuel Humphrey, of same place, gentleman. Rmd. to Haverford, Penna., 1683. Fd. She m., 1713, as his 2d wife, Edward Rees (alias Price), of Merion.

RICHARD HUMPHREY, of par. of Llangelynin, co. Mer., gentleman; s. Humphrey ———. Rmd. to Radnor, Penna., 1683. Fd. Freeholder of 156 a. ld. in Radnor. D. 1692-3 s. p.

ROBERT HUMPHREY, of par. of Llangower, co. Mer.; s. Humphrey John (alias Jones), of same place (bur. 1 Feb., 1678), and Gainor. Rmd. to Gwynedd, Penna., 1698.

SAMUEL HUMPHREY, of par. of Llangelynin, co. Mer., gentleman; bapt. 22 Jan., 1635; s. Humphrey ap Hugh, of Llwyndu, Llwyngwril, par. of Llangelynin, co. Mer., gentleman. D. in Wales 1677. Fd.

Wife, Elizabeth, dau. Rees Hugh; m. 1658.

Children (surname Samuel, which, just prior to their rml. to Penna., they changed to Humphrey): 1. Lydia, b. 1559; 2. Daniel, b. 1660; 3. Joseph, b. 1662; 4. Benjamin, b. 1662; 5. Rebecca, b. 1664; 6. Anne, b. 1666; 7. Gobitha, b. 1668; 8. Elizabeth. All of whom removed to Penna., 1682-3.

JANET HUMPHRIES, of Haverfordwest, co. Pemb. (maid to George Painter). Rmd. to Penna., 1683. Fd.

RICHARD IDDINGS, "of the Marches of Wales." Rmd. to co. Chester, Penna., abt. 1700. Ch. E. Freeholder co. Chester. D. in Nantmell, Penna., 1726.

Wife, Sarah ——.

Children: 1. John; 2. Richard; 3. Elizabeth; 4. Ann; 5. William; 6. Mary.

RICHARD IDDINGS, b. 1650; s. Richard and Sarah. Rmd. from borders of Wales to Penna. (with his parents), abt. 1700. D. Newtown, co. Chester, 1753. Ch. E. Freeholder of 160 a. ld. in Newtown.

Wife, Margaret, dau. Philip Rhytharrach; m. 1705.

Children: 1. Priscilla, b. 1707; m. Humphrey Wayne; 2. Elizabeth, b. 1709; m. Isaac Wayne. She was the mother of General Anthony Wayne, and ancestress of George H. Earle, jr. (See chart elsewhere in this vol.).

ALICE JAMES (alias Lewis), of par. of Llandewi Velfrey, co. Pemb., spinster, dau. James Lewis, of Llandewi, (b. 10 Oct., 1638). Rmd. to Montgomery, Penna., before 1710. Lived at Gwynedd. She m., 1710, as his 2d wife, Hugh Evans, of Gwynedd.

DAVID JAMES, of par. of Glascomb, co. Rad., gentleman. Rmd. to Radnor, Penna., 1682. Fd. Freeholder of 100 a. ld. in Radnor. His wife and one child arrived 1683.

Wife, Margaret Mortimer.

Children: 1. Evan; 2. Mary, b. in Wales; she was ex. of her father's will; 3. Rebecca, m. John Miles.

David James was not b. in Glascomb, but had lived there several years, and had also resided in the par. of Llandegley. He was prob. b. in Llandilo Fawr (Vawr), co. Carm.

GEORGE JAMES, of South Wales, yeoman; s. James ——. Rmd. to co. Chester, Penna., before 1692.

Wife, ——.

HOWEL JAMES, prob. of par. of Malpas, co. Mon. Rmd. to Penna., 1699. Fd.

Some of the Founders

JAMES JAMES, prob. of co. Rad., yeoman. Rmd. to Radnor, Penna., before 1690. Rmd. from Radnor to Haverford. Fd. D. 1708.

Wife, ——.

Children (surname James) : 1. George ; 2. David ; 3. Sarah, m. David Lewis.

JOHN JAMES, of par. of Llandewi Velfrey, co. Pemb., yeoman ; s. James Lewis (b. 10 Oct., 1638). Rmd. to Montgomery, Penna., in or before 1710. Fd. Freeholder in Montgomery, and of 1000 a. ld. in New Britain, to which place he rmd., 1720.

Wife, Sarah ——.

Children (surname James) : 1. William ; 2. Thomas; 3. Josiah ; 4. Isaac.

MARGARET JAMES, of the par. of Newchurch, co. Radnor, spinster. Freeholder of 200 a. ld. in Radnor, Penna., 1682. She m. at Newchurch, 25 June, 1682, Samuel Miles, and rmd. to Penna., 1683.

She was prob. sister to David James, of Glascomb.

MORGAN JAMES, prob. of co. Carm., yeoman. Rmd. to Radnor, Penna., perhaps before 1690.

Wife, Elizabeth Prytherch ; m. 1694.

EDWARD JARMAN, of par. of Llangurig, co. Montg., yeoman ; kinsman to John. Rmd. to neighbourhood of Philadelphia, Penna., abt. 1700, or earlier. Fd.

Wife, ——.

JOHN JARMAN, of par. of Llangurig, co. Montg. Rmd. to Radnor, Penna., 1683. Fd. Freeholder in Radnor. D. 1697.

Wife, Margaret —— ; d. 1731.

Children : 1. John, 1684 ; d. 1769. He was celebrated as a mathematician, and published "The American Almanac"; 2. Margaret, b. 1687, m. David Evan ; 3. Elizabeth, b. 1691, m. Peter Taylor, jr. ; 4. Sarah, b. 1695, m. Thomas Thomas ; 5. Priscilla, m. Joseph Thomas of Newcastle. J. J. did not have a son named *Lewis* as stated in "Walker Genealogy."

LEWIS JARMAN, of par. of Llangurig, co. Montg., yeoman, a kinsman to John. Rmd. to co. Chester, Penna. before 1715. Fd.

Wife, ——.

EVAN JENKINS, of near Dolobran, co. Montg. Rmd. to Penna. 1715. Fd.

WILLIAM JENKINS, of Tenby, co. Pemb., "emasculator," b. 1648. Rmd. to Haverford, Penna., before 1685. Fd. Freeholder of upwards of 1000 a. ld. in Haverford and elsewhere. J. P. for co. Chester, Penna., Member of Assembly, and Provincial Council. D. 1712, in Abington.

Wife, Elizabeth, dau. Lewis Griffith, of Tenby. (M. 1673; died 1725).

Children (surname Jenkins): 1. Margaret, b. 1674; m., 1692, Thomas Paschall; 2. Sarah, b. 1675; 3. Elizabeth, b. 1678; 4. Stephen, b. 1680, m., 1704, Abigail Pemberton.

JOHN, see Jones.

JOHN AP JOHN, of Plâs Evan, in the hamlet of Trevor, par. of Llangollen, co Denb., yeoman; s. John —— (Trevor, near Ruabon); b. about 1625-30. A celebrated minister among Fds., and had been chaplain in the Parliamentary Army. He and Dr. Thomas Wynne had a patent dated 15 Sept., 1681, for 5000 a. ld. in Penna., the consideration being £100, and quit-rent. John ap John, who is described in the patent as of "the parish of Ruabon," sold his share of this land to various persons, but did not remove there as he originally intended, as he himself informs us. He d. at Whitehough, 1697. Phebe, dau. John ap John, m. John Mellor. Their dau. Phebe, wf. of William Hollins, was ancestress of Penelope Boothby, whose exquisite monument is in Ashbourne Ch., and whose portrait, by Reynolds, is well known.

GWEN VCH. JOHN (or Jones), of near Bala, co. Mer., wid. John ——, and dau. John Evans (otherwise John ap Evan), of Penmaen, par. of Llanfor, co. Mer. Rmd. to Gwynedd, Penna., abt. 1698. She m. 2dly, John Humphrey, of Gwynedd.

GRIFFITH JOHN, of near Bala, co. Mer., yeoman; s. John Evan (otherwise John ap Evan), of Penmaen, par. of Llanfor (d. 1697). Rmd. to Merion, Penna., 1690. Fd. Freeholder in Merion. D., 1707, in Gwynedd, Penna. (See ped. vol. ii.). He is sometimes called Griffith *Jones*.

Children (surname Griffith): 1. John, of Merion, m. Grace Foulke; 2. Evan, of Gwynedd, m. Jane Jones, his 1st cousin; 3. Ann, m. Thomas Jones, of Merion, s. John ap Thomas, of Llaithgwm, co. Mer.

I am inclined to suppose that the descendants of John Griffith assumed the surname Jones.

Some of the Founders

GRIFFITH JOHN, of co. Pemb., b. 1683; s. John Phillips and Ellen. Rmd. to co. Chester, Penna., 1709. Fd. Freeholder of upwards of 100 a. ld. in co. Chester. D. 1778.

Wife, Ann, dau Robert Williams and Gwen, his wife.

MARGARET JOHN, of par. of Llanfor, co. Mer., wid. of John Evan (alias John ap Evan), of Penmaen, Llanfor (d. 1697). Rmd. to Gwynedd, Penna., abt. 1698-1700, with others of her family.

MARGARET JOHN, of near Bala, co. Mer., wife of David Evan, and dau. John Evan (otherwise John ap Evan), of Penmaen, par. of Llanfor. She d. at sea on the voyage to Penna., abt. 1700.

Children: 1. Gwen, m. Thomas Foulke, of Gwynedd; 2. Gainor, m. Robert Humphrey, of Gwynedd. Perhaps others.

MARGARET JOHN, of par. of Llangelynin, co. Mer., wid. Rmd. to Penna., 1683. Fd.

MARGARET JOHN, sister to one William John (not of Gwynedd), who dying s.p. bequeathed her his land. She prob. rmd. to Penna. after 1700. Her will was proved at Philadelphia.

WILLIAM JOHN, of par. of Llanfor, co. Mer.; s. John Evans (otherwise John ap Evan), of Penmaen, Llanfor. Rmd. to Gwynedd, Penna., 1698. Fd. Freeholder of abt. 2000 a. ld. in Gwynedd and elsewhere. D. ——. (See ped. vol. ii.).

Wife, Jane, dau. Hugh Cadwaladr ap Rhys, of par. of Yspytty Evan, co. Denb. (See ped. vol. ii.).

Children: 1. Gwen; 2. Margaret; 3. Gainor; 4. Catherine; 5. Ellin; 6. John.

WILLIAM JOHN, of North Wales. Rmd. to Penna. prob. after 1700, and acquired land, which, dying s.p., he devised to his sister Margaret John, who d. in Penna., as appears by her will.

JONES, see John Lloyd.

ANN JONES, of co. Carmarthen, wid. Rmd. to Penna., 1684.

Children: 1. Ann Jones.

CADWALADER JONES, of par. of Llanfor, co. Mer. ; s. John —— (d. before 1698), and Ellin, dau. Evan Lloyd Evan (otherwise Evan ap Evan), of Ucheldre. Rmd. to Penna., 1698. Died at sea on the voyage.

Wife, —— Jones (b. in Wales).

Children (surname Jones): 1. Robert; 2. ——; 3. ——. They were brought up in Gwynedd. (See ped. vol. ii.).

CADWALADER JONES (or JOHN), of near Bala, co. Mer. Rmd. to Penna., supposedly in 1698.

CADWALADER JONES, b. near Bala, co. Mer. ; s. John ——, and Gwen, dau. John Evan (otherwise John ap Evan), of Penmaen, par. of Llanfor (d. 1697). Rmd. to Gwynedd, Penna., with his mother (then a wid., and who afterwards m. John Humphrey, of Gwynedd), abt. 1698.

CADWALADER JONES, of par. of Llanfor, co. Mer., yeoman ; s. John Jones, of same place, decd. Rmd. to Gwynedd, Penna., before 1719.

Wife, Martha, dau. David Thomas, of Radnor, Penna.; m. 1719. (See ped. vol. ii.).

CADWALADER JONES ; s. John ——. Rmd. to Penna., abt. 1700. D. in Uwchllan, co. Chester, Penna., 1758.

Wife, ——.

Children : 1. Evan (Jones) ; 2. Rebecca, m. John Thomas ; 3. Cadwalader ; 4. ——, m. —— Pugh. Cadwalader Jones, sr., had a sister Gwen John, liv. 1758.

DAVID JONES, of Ciltalgarth, par. of Llanfor, co. Mer. ; s. John David, of same place. Rmd. to Blockley, Penna., 1699. Fd. D. 1725. (See pedigree).

Wife, Katherine, dau. James Lewis, of Llandewi Velfrey, S. W. ; m. 1693.

Children : 1. James, m. Hannah Hayes ; 2. Lewis ; 3. Jacob ; 4. John ; 5. David ; 6. Isaac, m. Elizabeth Lewis ; 7. Susannah.

DAVID JONES, of near Haverfordwest, co. Pemb., husbandman. Rmd. to Penna., 1699-1700. Fd.

DAVID JONES, of the town of Carmarthen. He had a deed from John ap Evan (alias John Bevan), of the par. of Llantrisant, co. Glam., gentleman, dated 1682, for 125 a. ld. in Penna., and prob. rmd. there about that time.

SOME OF THE FOUNDERS 183

DAVID JONES, b. near Bala, co. Mer. ; s. John ——, and Gwen, dau. John Evan (otherwise John ap Evan), of Penmaen, par. of Llanfor (d. 1697). Rmd. to Gwynedd, Penna., with his mother (then a wid.), (and who afterwards m. John Humphrey, of Gwynedd), abt. 1698.

Wife, Lowry Roberts ; m. 1707.

EDWARD JONES (*viz.* Edward Johns), of Bala, co. Mer., surgeon, b. about 1645 ; s. John Lloyd (bro. Anne Lloyd, 1st wife of John Thomas of Llaithgwm). Rmd. to Merion, Penna., 1682. Fd. Freeholder of 306 a. ld. in Merion. D. 1737.

Wife, Mary, dau. Dr. Thomas Wynne (m. in Wales).

Children (surname Jones): 1. Martha, m. John Cadwalader ; 2. Jonathan, m. Gainor Owen ; 3. Edward ; 4. Thomas ; 5. Evan, m. (1) Mary Stephenson ; (2) —— dau. Col. Mathews ; 6. John, m. Mary Doughty, of New Jersey ;[1] 7. Elizabeth, m. Rees Thomas, jr. ; 8. Mary.

EDWARD JONES, of par. of St. Harmon, co. Rad., gentleman. He had a deed, dated 1682, for 250 a. ld., surveyed to him in Radnor. He sold his rights, by deed executed in Wales, to James Morgan, and prob. did not rm. to Penna.

ELIZABETH JONES, of Blackpool, co. Montg., spinster, dau. David Jones, of same place. Rmd. to Penna., " with the consent of her parents," 1699. Fd.

ELLIN JONES, of Ciltalgarth, par. of Llanfor, co. Mer. spinster, dau. John ap David, of same place, gentleman. Rmd. to Blockley, Penna., 1699. Her name is sometimes written Eleanor. She m. Robert Jones (s. John ap Thomas of Llaithgwm), of Merion. She was sis. to David Jones, of Blockley. (See ped. on another page).

ELLIS JONES, of par. of Nantmell, co. Rad., weaver. Rmd. to Radnor, Penna., about 1685. Ch. E. Freeholder of 100 a. ld. in Radnor, which he sold to William David, who resold it to John Morgan. He was liv. in Merion, 1696.

EVAN JONES ; see Evan John William.

---

[1] I am indebted for information *in re* the Doughty marriage to the late L. Taylor Dickson, Esq., of Philadelphia, a keen genealogist, and the best of friends. John Jones d. 1743, leaving issue : 1. Deborah, m., 1743, John Price ; 2. Thomas ; 3. Israel ; 4. Doughty, m., 1747, Hannah Gardiner ; 5. Edward ; 6. John ; 7. Whitehead, m., 1762, Ann Johns ; 8. Samuel ; 9. Amy ; 10 Mary ; 11. Martha, m., 1761, John Brook.

EVAN JONES, of par. of Llanfihangel, co. Mer., yeoman; s. John Pugh, of same place. Rmd. to Penna., before 1712. Fd.

Wife, Hannah, dau. Hugh David, of Gwynedd. (M. 1712).

EVAN JONES, of Llaithgwm, par. of Llandderfel (now in Llanfor), co. Mer.; s. John Thomas (or John ap Thomas), of Llaithgwm, gentleman. Rmd. to Merion, Penna., 1683. Fd. D. young, 1697, unm.

EVAN JONES, of near Dolgelley, co. Mer., yeoman; but not a native of that country. Rmd. to Penna. abt. 1683. (Certif. undated). Fd.

Wife, Hannah ——. (Her mother Mary Ellis, of Dolgelley).

FLORENCE JONES, of co. Glam., a kinswoman of John Bevan. Rmd. to Pennsylvania, prob. 1683. Married Lewis David, of Radnor, Penna.

FRANCIS JONES, of near Redstone, co. Pemb., husbandman. Rmd. to Penna., 1711.

HENRY JONES, prob. of So. Wales. Rmd. to Penna. before 1700. He had a warrant for 500 a. ld. to be surveyed in the Welsh Tract.

HUGH JONES, prob. of Bala, co. Mer., husbandman. Rmd. to Merion, Penna., about 1700. Freeholder near Bryn Mawr, Merion.

Wife, ——.

Children (surname Jones): 1. Hugh, b. 1705, owner of farm now called "Brookfield," north of Bryn Mawr; and prob. others.

The late Francis M. Brooke, of Philadelphia, was a descendant. He d. Jan., 1899. Also John Brooke, M.D., U.S.A., of Radnor.

JANE JONES, b. near Bala, co. Mer.; dau. John ——, and Gwen, dau. John Evan (otherwise John ap Evan), of Penmaen, par. of Llanfor (d. 1697). Rmd. to Gwynedd, with his mother (then a wid.), who afterwards m. John Humphrey, of Gwynedd, abt. 1698. She m., 1707, Evan Griffith, her first cousin.

JOHN JONES, prob. of co. Card., yeoman. Rmd. to Barbadoes, thence to Penna., 1683.

Wife, ——.

JOHN JONES; s. Thomas John (Sion) Evan, of near Bala, co. Mer.; b. in Radnor, Penna., abt. 1689. Lived in Radnor.

Wife, ——.

Some of the Founders

JOHN JONES, of Ciltalgarth, par. of Llanfor, co. Mer. ; s. John David, of same place. Rmd. to Penna., abt. 1700. (See ped. iii.).

JOSEPH JONES ; s. Thomas John (Sion) Evan, of near Bala, co. Mer. ; b. in Radnor, Penna., 1695.

Wife, Sarah Morgan ; m. 1727. (She was b. 1698, d. ——. John Morgan, of Nantmell, co. Rad., gentleman. See ped. on another page).

Children : 1. Hannah, m. Nathaniel Miles.

MATHEW JONES, of the town of Carmarthen, mercer. He had a deed from John ap Evan (alias John Bevan), of the par. of Llantrisant, co. Glam., gentleman, dated Augt., 1682, for 125 a. ld. in Penna., and prob. rmd. there about that time.

MARGARET JONES : see Margaret John William.

MARGARET JONES, of Holywell, co. Flint., aged 16 yrs. Transported to America to serve 7 years, 1706. No crime charged, but without support. (Cleared for Bohemia River). She appears to have had relatives in Pennsylvania, and was probably a kinswoman to Dr. Thomas Wynne, or to Richard Thomas, of Whitford, these places being adjacent to Holywell.

PETER JONES. He was a resident in Merion, 1696, and a man of considerable means.

REES JONES (otherwise Rees John William), of Iscreganen, par. of Llangelynin, co. Mer., husbandman ; s. John William, of same place, husbandman. Rmd. to Merion, Penna., 1684. Fd. Freeholder in Merion. D. 1702-3.

Wife, Hannah, dau. Richard Price, of Glanlloidiogin, par. of Llanfor, co. Mer., husbandman.

Children : See Glenn's " Merion," 81.

REES JONES, b. par. of Nantmell, co. Rad. ; s. John Evans, of same place. Rmd. to Radnor, Penna., 1682-3 (with his parents). Ch. E.

ROBERT JONES, sup. bro. of Hugh Jones, and uncle of Hugh Jones of " Brookfield." Rmd. to Merion, Penna., about 1700. Lived with Hugh Jones, near Rowland Ellis's home.

ROBERT JONES (or John), of par. of Llanfor, co. Mer. ; s. John —— (d. before 1698), and Ellin, dau. Evan Lloyd Evan (otherwise Evan ap Evan), of Ucheldre. Rmd. to Gwynedd, Penna., 1698. (See ped. vol. ii.). He was a Magistrate at Gwynedd for many years. (See ped. vol. ii.).

Wife, Gaynor Lloyd, of Merion, wid.; m. 1706.

H. M. Jenkins, in "Gwynedd," is in error regarding the identity of this Robert Jones, and H. W. Lloyd's information regarding him in article on Rees John William, in "Merion," is also incorrect.

ROBERT JONES (or John), of near Bala, co. Mer., yeoman; s. John Evan (or John ap Evan) Robert Lewis, of Penmaen, par. of Llanfor, co. Mer. Rmd. to Abington, Penna., 1696. Fd. (See ped. vol. ii.).

Wife, ——.

ROBERT JONES, of Llaithgwm, par. of Llandderfel (now in Llanfor), co. Mer., yeoman; s. John Thomas (or John ap Thomas), of Llaithgwm, gentleman. Rmd. to Merion, Penna., 1683. Fd. Freeholder of 1000 a. ld. in Merion. D. 1746.

Wife, Ellin, dau. John ap David, of Ciltalgarth, par. of Llanfor.

Children (surname Jones): 1. Elizabeth; 2. John, d. inft.; 3. John, d. inft.; 4. Katherine, m. Thomas Evans; 5. Ann, m. James Paul; 6. Gerrard, m. Sarah Lloyd; 7. Robert.

ROBERT JONES. He was in Merion and Gwynedd, abt. 1690 to 1700, and his signature indicates that he was not identical with any of the others of the name mentioned.

ROBERT JONES, b. 1690, of co. Denb., yeoman. Rmd. to Gwynedd, Penna., about 1710. D. 1773.

Wife, Ann Coulston; m. 1717; d. 1772.

Children: 1. William; 2. Margaret; 3. Ann, m. Jacob Bell; 4. Elizabeth; 5. Robert; 6. Josiah; 7. Grace, m. (1) —— Jones; (2) Owen Thomas; 8. Hannah, m. —— Prichard; 9. Enos.

SAMUEL JONES, of Haverford West, co. Pemb., husbandman. Rmd. to Penna., 1711.

SARAH JONES (or John), of near Bala, co. Mer., spinster; dau. John Edward, of same place. Rmd. to Merion, Penna., before 1708. Fd. She was maid in family of Edward Roberts, and afterwards in that of Thomas Jones, of Merion, 1708, and was related to both families, it being then the custom to take poor relations as servants.

Some of the Founders

THOMAS JONES, of Llaithgwm, par. of Llandderfel (now in Llanfor), co. Mer., gentleman ; s. John Thomas (or John ap Thomas), of Llaithgwm, gentleman. Rmd. to Merion, Penna., 1683. Fd. Freeholder of —— a. ld. in Merion. D. 1727. For ped. see another page.

Wife, Anne ——, dau. Griffith John, of Merion.

Children (surname Jones) : 1. Elizabeth ; 2. Katherine ; 3. Anne ; 4. Mary ; 5. Sarah ; 6. Evan.

THOMAS JONES (otherwise Thomas John Thomas), of par. of Llanwddyn, co. Montg., yeoman ; s. John Thomas, of same place. Rmd. to Merion, Penna, 1683-4. Fd. Freeholder of $156\frac{1}{4}$ acres in Merion. See pedigree. D. unm., 1723.

THOMAS JONES. Rmd. to Radnor, Penna., before 1700. Freeholder of 50 acres of land, prob. surveyed in Radnor. Had come over as a servant.

Wife, ——.

THOMAS JONES, b. par. of Nantmell, co. Rad. ; s. John Evans, of same place. Rmd. to Radnor, Penna., 1682-3 (with his parents).

Wife, ——.

THOMAS JONES, of par. of Glascombe, co. Rad., gentleman. He had a deed, 1682, for 100 a. ld. in Penna., which was surveyed to him in Radnor. Rmd. to Penna., 1683. His heirs sold the above land to William Davies.

THOMAS JONES, sr., was living in Merion, 1696. He is not the same person as Thomas Jones, s. John Thomas, and was evidently a man of property.

THOMAS JONES, living in Merion, about 1700 ; perhaps son of Thomas Jones, sr., of Merion (1696). Rmd. fr. Merion to Cheltenham ; prob. same person who m. Catherine Arrets.

WILLIAM JONES (or John), of Bettws, near Bala, co. Mer., yeoman ; s. John ——. Rmd. to Merion, Penna., 1684-5. Fd. Freeholder of 156 a. ld. in Merion and Goshen. D. 1685, perhaps on shipboard.

Wife, Ann Reynolds ; predeceased her husband.

Children (surname Williams) : 1. John ; 2. Alice ; 3. Katherine ; 4. Gwen. John Williams (or William), was of age in 1694. William Jones, or John, of Bettws, is the same person who witnessed deeds, in Wales, of the John Thomas and Edward Jones Company.

DAVID KINSEY, of par. of Nantmell, co. Rad., carpenter. Rmd. to Penna., 1683. Fd. Freeholder of 100 a. ld. in Penna. (deed 1682).

DAVID LAWRENCE, said to be from Pembrokeshire. Rmd. to Haverford, Penna., with Thomas Ellis, 1683. (See Ellis). Fd. Freeholder in Haverford. D. 1699. Wife, Ellen (or Eleanor), dau. Thomas Ellis. Children (surname Lawrence): 1. Daniel; 2. Henry; 3. Thomas, m. Ellen Williams; 4. Margaret, m. David Llewelyn; 5. Eleanor; 6. Rachel.

LEWIS, see James.

ANN LEWIS, of near Rayader, co. Radnor, spinster. Rmd. to Penna., 1698. Fd.

CADWALADER LEWIS, of near Bala, co. Mer., husbandman. Rmd. to Merion, Penna., about 1690. D.s.p. before 1697, and Robert Owen, of Merion, a kinsman, was appointed Adminr. Freeholder.

DANIEL LEWIS, of near Redstone, co. Pemb. Rmd. to Penna., 1701-2. Fd.

DAVID LEWIS, of par. of Eglwyslan, co. Glam.; s. David Lewis, of same place. Rmd. to Penna. after 1684.

ELLIS LEWIS, of co. Mer., b. 1680; s. Lewis ap Robert, of near Dolgelley.[1] A descendant of Cadwgan, lord of Nannau. Rmd. to Haverford, Penna., viâ Ireland, 1708. D. in Wilmington, Del., 1750.
Wife, Elizabeth Newlin.

---

[1] The definite statement that Ellis Lewis was s. of Lewis ap Robert, is from a carefully prepared pedigree of the family by Philip S. P. Conner, Esq., of Philadelphia. Hester Lewis, dau. Ellis Lewis, s. Robert, s. of the above Ellis Lewis, m., abt. 1790, George Eddy, and had: 1. George; 2. Charles; 3. James; 4. Lewis; 5. Mary Ann, m. Dr. Pickering; 6. Hester, m. Nathaniel Lewis; 7. Phœbe Waln; 8. Catharine, m. Samuel L. Chapman; 9. Lucy Lewis; 10. Frances. Lucy Lewis Eddy, dau. George, m., 1826, Samuel Harrold Gillingham, and had: 1. Francis Eddy, b. 1827; 2. Harrold, b. 1828; d. inft.; 3. Rebecca Harrold, b. 1829; d. inft. 4. Joseph Eddy, b. 1830; m. Clara Donaldson; 5. Lucy Eddy, b. 1831; d. inft.; 6. George E., b. 1835; d. inft.; 7. Louis Harrold, b. 1836; m. Louisa M. Bartle, and had: (a) William Gillingham, b. 1860; (b) Hattie Wells Gillingham. Frances Eddy Gillingham, m. Dr. Jared Kibbee, 1852, and had: (a) Ada F., m. Theodore Wright, and had Clara Gillingham Wright, and Ada Kibbee Wright; (b.) Harrold Gillingham; (c.) Lucy Gllingham; (d) Henry Clinton, m. 1888, Louise Halbig, and had: Henry C. and Clara L. Kibbee; (e) Frances Lewis, m. Cyrus Hovey, and had: Harrold Kibbee, and Eleanor Frances Hovey; (f) Nellie, William Gillingham, s. Louis, m. 1885, Anna Robinson, and had: Joseph E. Gillingham, born 1887. Hattie Wells Gillingham, dau. Louis, m., 1882, Edmund De Rueyter Conger, and had Edward Chamberlain and Mary Louise Conger.

Some of the Founders

Children: 1. Robert, b. 1714; 2. Nathaniel, b. 1717; 3. Ellis, b. 1719 (and father of Ellis Lewis, Chief Justice of Pennsylvania); 4. Mary, b. 1716, married Joshua Pusey. Philip S. P. Conner, of Philadelphia, is a descendant. See Glenn's "Merion."

ELLIS LEWIS. Rmd. to Merion abt. 1700. He was later of Upper Dublin, or perhaps he went there almost immediately after his arrival. Freeholder in Upper Dublin. Signs petition as to roads, 1711. D. 1753.

Wife, Anne ——, d. 1756.

Children (surname Lewis): 1. Ellis, m., 1729, Mary Tyson (she d. 1763); 2. Ellen, d. John Evans, of Gwynedd (see Jenkin's "Gwynedd," 369); 3. Lewis, m. Anne Lord; 4. Jane, m. Enos Lewis, of Gwynedd; 5. Elizabeth, m. William Spencer.

(For descts. see "Reifschneider—Gillam Genealogy," Glenn).

HENRY LEWIS, of par. of Narberth, co. Pemb.; s. Evan Lewis. Rmd. to Haverford, Penna., 1682-3. Fd. Freeholder of 1000 a. ld. in Haverford.

Wife, Margaret Protheroe (*viz.*, Margaret, dau. Rhydderch), (m. 1670).

Children (surname Lewis): 1. Henry, b. 1671; m., 1692, Mary, dau. Robert Taylor, of Little Leigh, par. Great Budworth, co. Chester, and had (a) Isaac, b. 1694; (b) Mary, b. 1696; (c) John, b. 1697; (d) Sarah, b. 1698; m. Isaac Morris; (e) Margaret, b. 1700; m. Isaac Price; (f) Mary, b. 1702; m. Thomas Philips; (g) Hannah, b. 1704; 2. Sarah, b. 1673, d. inf.; 3. Samuel, b. 1676; 4. Elizabeth, b. 1677; m. Richard Hayes; 5. ——, m. Richard Walter; 6. ——, m. William Roberts.

(The Hansell family, of Philadelphia, is descended from H. L. See ped. on another page).

JOHN LEWIS, of co. Pemb., yeoman. Rmd. to Haverford, Penna., 1683. Fd. Freeholder in Haverford. D. 1704.

Wife, Elizabeth ——.

Children (surname Lewis): 1. John, m. Sarah Price, of Merion, and had: Philip, Stephen, Josiah, and Elizabeth Lewis; 2. Elizabeth, m. John Reece; 3. Margaret.

RALPH LEWIS, of par. of Eglwysilan, co. Glam.; s. David Lewis, of same place. Rmd. to Penna., 1683. Fd. Freeholder in Haverford.

(For children and descendants of Ralph Lewis, see MS. of Howard Williams Lloyd, under "Ralph Lewis," in Lib. Hist. Society of Penna.).

RICHARD LEWIS, of Montgomeryshire, yeoman. Rmd. with his family to Penna., 1713.

THOMAS LEWIS, yeoman. Rmd. to Montgomery, Penna., about 1700. Ch. E. Freeholder of 484 a. 1d. in Montgomery, 1701. D. 1723.

Wife. ——.

Children (surname Lewis): 1. George, b. 1680 ; m. 1708, Jane Roberts ; 2. Richard (issue).

WILLIAM LEWIS,[1] of Eglwysilan, par. of Llantrisant, co. Glam. Rmd. to Haverford, Penna., 1686. Fd. Freeholder of a large plantation in Haverford.

Wife, Ann ——.

Children, 1. William, m., 1704, Gwen, dau. William John, of Gwynedd ; 2. Lewis, m. Mary Howell, of Bristol ; 3. Evan, m. Mary Hayes ; 4. David, m. 1695, Ann Jones, of Merion.

MORRIS LLEWELYN, of par. of Castle Bight, co. Pemb., gentleman, b. 1645 ; s. Llewelyn ——. Rmd. to Haverford, Penna., about 1686. Fd. Freeholder in Haverford.

Wife, Ann Young, b. 1647.

Children (surname Llewelyn): 1. David, m. (1) 1706, Margaret Thomas ; (2), 1709, Margaret Ellis, wid. ; 2. Morris, m. Elizabeth Thomas ; 3. Griffith ; 4. Mary, m. Benjamin Humphrey, of Merion.

CHARLES LLOYD, of Dolobran, co. Montg., gentleman ; b. 1637 ; s. Charles Lloyd, of Dolobran, Esq.

---

[1] William Lewis was descended in the direct male line from Einion Sais, of Llywell, co. Brecon, and his arms were *argent three cocks gules*, as is proven by his seal attached to a deed relative to Pennsylvania lands, being also the arms of Einion Sais. On his maternal side William Lewis was descended from the Collenna family, and from Henry Somerset, 2d Earl of Worcester, s. Charles (d. 1526), s. Henry (Plantagenet) Beaufort, gt.-gd.-s. Edward III., King of England.

John Thompson Lewis, of Philadelphia, a descendant of William Lewis, married, 1850, Maria Litchfield, dau. John Morin Scott, Esq., Mayor of Philadelphia, (descended from Thomas Lloyd of Dolobran), and had: 1. Mary Emlen Lewis; 2. Sophia D. Lewis ; 3. Rebecca C. Lewis, m. Allen Evans, of Haverford, Penna. ; 4. Maria L. Lewis, m. E. F. Beale ; 5. Helen S. Lewis, m. J. Ogden Hoffman ; 6. Frances Lewis, m. T. Dewit Cuyler ; 7. Amy Lewis, m. Pemberton S. Hutchinson.

Some of the Founders

Fd. He was jointly with Margaret Davies, of Dolobran, wid., a first purchaser of 5000 a. ld. in Penna., which was resold to various persons, and did not remove to the Province.

DAVID LLOYD, b. about 1756, supposedly in par. of Meifod, co. Montg.; stated to have been a kinsman of Thomas Lloyd, of Dolobran, Depty. Gov. of Penna., lawyer. Rmd. to Penna. 1686. Atty. Gen. of Prov.; Chief Justice, 1717; held many other offices. D. at Chester, 1731; d.s.p. Fd.

Wife, Grace Growden, who survived him 29 years.

EVAN LLOYD, of co. Rad., yeoman. Rmd. to Radnor, Penna., 1711. Fd. Freeholder in Radnor.

FRANCIS LLOYD, of town of Haverfordwest, co. Pemb., shoemaker. Rmd. to Merion, Penna., prob. 1686. Fd. Freeholder in Merion.

Wife, ——.

GAYNOR LLOYD, of par. of Llanfor, co. Mer., wid. of Rowland ——. Rmd. to Penna., abt. 1690. Fd. (She was sister to Robert and Thomas Lloyd, of Merion). She m., 2dly, Robert Jones, of Gwynedd.

HUGH LLOYD, of near Llandeilo Graban, co. Rad., widower, and labourer. Rmd. to Penna., 1699. Fd.

JOHN LLOYD, of par. of Disserth, co. Rad., glover. He had a deed, dated 1682, for 100 a. ld. in Penna. (surveyed in Radnor), upon which he settled. Ch. E.

Wife, ——.

Many descendants surnamed Lloyd.

JOHN LLOYD, of Treverigg, par. of Llantrisant, co. Glam., labourer, servant to John Bevan. Rmd. to Penna., 1683. Fd.

LOWRY LLOYD, wid. Thomas Lloyd, of Penmaen, par. of Llanfor, co. Mer. The latter a poet of note before he joined Friends. She rmd. to Penna. about 1685, and m., 2dly, 1686, Thomas Sion (John) Evan (alias Thomas Jones), of Radnor.

ROBERT LLOYD (otherwise Robert John or Jones), of par. of Llangower, co. Mer., yeoman; s. John Lloyd, of same place, yeoman. Freeholder of 76½ a. land in Merion and elsewhere. D.s.p. in Wales. One of the Edward Jones Company. (See pedigree on another page).

ROBERT LLOYD, of par. of Llanfor, co. Mer. ; b. 1667-8 ; s. Thomas Lloyd, of same place. Rmd. to Merion, Penna., abt. 1684. Fd. Freeholder of considerable land in Merion. D. 1714. (See ped. vol. ii.).

Wife, Lowry, dau. Rees John William ; m., 1698.

Children: 1. Hannah, b. 1699; m. (1) John Roberts; (2) William Paschall ; (3) Peter Osborne ; 2. Gwen, b. 1701 ; d. unm. ; 3. Sarah, b. 1703 ; m. Gerrard Jones ; 4. Gaynor, b. 1705 ; m. Mordecai James ; 5. David, b. 1707 ; m. Anna ——— ; rmd. to North Carolina ; 6. Rees, b. 1709; m. Sarah Cox ; 7. Robert, b. 1711 ; m. Catherine Humphrey ; 8. Richard, b. 1713-14 ; m. Hannah Sellers. (See ped. vol. ii.).

THOMAS LLOYD, of par. of Llanfor, co. Mer., yeoman ; s. Thomas, of same place (and bro. to Robert). Rmd. to Merion, Penna., abt. 1684. Fd. Freeholder in Merion. D. 1748.

Wife, Elizabeth, dau. William ap Edward.

Children : 1. Thomas, b. 1699 ; 2. Sarah, b. 1701 ; m. John Morgan, of Gwynedd ; 3. Jane, b. 1703 ; m. (1) Lewis Williams, of Gwynedd ; (2) ——— Darkins ; 4. John, b. 1704 ; m. Eleanor Pugh, of Merion ; 5. Elizabeth, b. 1706 ; m. Joseph Morgan, of Gwynedd ; 6. William Lloyd, b. 1708 ; 7. Evan Lloyd, b. 1713. (See ped. vol. ii.).

THOMAS LLOYD, of Dolobran, co. Montg., physician, b. 1640 ; s. Charles Lloyd, of Dolobran, Esq. Rmd. to Penna., 1682-3. Fd. Freeholder of 2000 a. ld. in Merion and Haverford. Dep. Gov. of the Prov. D. 1694.

Wives : (1) Mary, dau. Roger Jones (m. 1665) ; (2) Patience, wid. Robert Story (m. after 1682).

Children (surname Lloyd): 1. Hannah, b. 1666 ; m. (1) John Duval ; (2) Richard Hill ; 2. Rachel, b. 1667-8 ; m. Samuel Preston ; 3. Mordecai, b. 1669 ; lost at sea, 1694 ; 4. John, b. 1671 ; d.s.p. 1692 ; 5. Mary, b. 1674 ; m. Isaac Norris ; 6. Thomas, b. 1675 ; m. Sarah Young ; 7. Elizabeth, b. 1677 ; m. Daniel Zachary ; 8. Deborah, b. 1682 ; m. Dr. Mordecai Moore ; 9. Samuel, b. 1684 ; d. inft. ; 10. Margaret, b. 1685 ; d. 1693.

LLEWELYN MARTIN, s. Mathias Martin, of Charleston, co. Chester, Penna. ; d. in Charlestown, 1764.

Wife, Elizabeth ———.

Children: 1. Mathias, under age of 21 years, 1740-1; 2. Ann; 3. Hannah; 4. Esther; 5. Mary; 6. Martha.

MATHIAS MARTIN, of So. Wales. Rmd. to Charlestown, co. Chester, Penna., abt. 1682.

Wife, Ellien Bowen.

Children: 1. Llewelyn; 2. —— dau., m. Benjamin Harvey; 3. Lewis, living 1764, and then aged over 60 years.

[The family of Martin of So. Wales had long used that surname, being of Norman origin, and descendants of the Martins, lords of Caemes, whose ancestor was Martin de Tours.]

MARY MATTHEWS, of near Dolobran, co. Montg., spinster. Rmd. to Penna., 1707. Fd.

DAVID MEREDITH, of the par. of Llanbister, co. Rad. Rmd. to Radnor, Penna., 1683. Fd. Freeholder of 250 a. ld. in Radnor, and elsewhere.

Wife, Katherine ——

Children (surname Meredith): 1. Richard; 2. Mary; 3. John; 4. Meredith; 5. Sarah (b. in Wales).

HUGH MEREDITH, who was prob. a bro. of David Meredith, appears to have rmd. to Radnor, Penna., before 1700. His son, Simon Meredith, had John Meredith, whose dau. Jane, m. Evan Lewis, s. John Lewis (b. 1697). (See ped. on another page). Most of the name in Pennsylvania are descended from one or the other of these brothers.

ANN MILES, of par. of Llanfihangel Helygen, co. Rad., spinster, dau. of James, of same place. Rmd. to Radnor, Penna., prob. 1683. Ch. E. She m. William Davies (or Davis).

DAVID MILES, of par. of Llanfihangel Helygen, co. Rad.; s. James, of same place. Rmd. to Radnor, Penna., before 1688. Ch. E.

Wife, Alice ——.

Children: 1. Sarah; prob. others.

GRIFFITH MILES, of par. of Llanfihangel Helygen, co. Rad., s. James, of same place, b. 1670. Rmd. to Radnor, Penna., before 1688. D. 1719. Ch. E.

Wife, Bridget, dau. Alexander Edwards; m. 1692.

Children: 1. Hester, b. 1693; 2. Martha, b. 1695; m. John Carl; 3. Margaret, b. 1698; 4. Griffith, b. 1700; 5. Samuel, b. 1703; 6. John, b. 1709; m. Ann, dau. Meyrick Davis (or Davies). (For descts. see "Annals of Miles' Ancestry," Banes).

JAMES MILES, of par. of Llanfihangel Helygen, co. Rad., b. 1622, weaver. Rmd. to Radnor, Penna., 1683. Fd. Freeholder of 100 a. ld. in Penna., (deed 1682).

Wife, ——.

Children: 1. Samuel, m., 1682, Margaret James; 2. Richard, m., 1688, Sarah Evans; 3. Griffith, b. 1670; m., 1692, Bridget Edwards, dau. Alexander Edwards; 4. David, m. Alice ——; 5. Ann, m. William Davies, of Radnor, Penna. The above all removed to Penna.

[For details concerning Miles family, and descts. of Griffith Miles, see "Annals of Miles' Ancestry," by O. H. Banes, (Lippincott, co. Phila., 1895). Mr. George K. Miles, of Allegheny, Penna., has also compiled a genealogy of the descts. of Richard Miles, and has kindly furnished me with data regarding this branch of the family.]

RICHARD MILES, of par. of Llanfihangel Helygen, co. Rad., weaver; s. James, of same place. Rmd. to Radnor, Penna., before 1688. Bro. to Samuel Miles, of same place. Fd. D. 1713. Mar. Certif. calls him "tailor."

Wife, Sarah Evans; m. 1688.

Children: 1. Richard, m. Phebe Davis; 2. James, m. Hannah Pugh, dau. David Pugh, of Radnor; 3. Evan, m. Mary ——; 4. John, m. Rebecca James, dau. David James, of Radnor; 5. Jane, m. John Davis, of Plymouth; 6. Sarah, m. Benjamin Griffith, late of Llanllwny; 7. Hannah, m. Jonathan Pugh; 8. Abigail, m. John Davis; 9. Joanna, m. Joseph Powell.

[Sarah, wife of Richard Miles, is said to have been the daughter of John Evans, of Radnor. The latter, however, could not be identical with John Evans from Nantmell, as the latter's daughter Sarah married John Morgan.]

SAMUEL MILES, of par. of Llanfihangel Helygen, co. Rad.; s. James, of same place. Rmd. to Radnor, Penna., 1683. Fd. Freeholder of land deeded to him by conveyance executed in Wales.

Wife, Margaret James, of Newchurch, co. Rad. (m. 1682). She was prob. sister to David James, of Newchurch.

SOME OF THE FOUNDERS

Children: 1. Tamar James, b. 1687; m. 1708, Thomas Thomas, s. William Thomas, of Radnor; 2. Phebe, b. 1690; m., 1715, Evan Evans (Haverford); 3. Ruth, b. 1693; m., 1715-16, Owen Evans (not of the Gwynedd family).

EDWARD MOORE, of par. of Llanbardan Fawr, co. Rad., gentleman. Rmd. to Penna., 1698. Fd. Freeholder in co. Chester.

CADWALADR MORGAN, of Gwernefel, parish of Llanycil, co. Mer., yeoman; s. Morgan Cadwaladr, of adjacent parish of Llanfor, yeoman, and Ellen vch. William, his wife. Rmd. to Merion, Penna., 1683. Fd. Freeholder of 156 a. ld. in Merion. D. 1711. (See ped. xv.).

Wife, Jane, dau. Richard Price, of Glanlloidiogin, par. of Llanfor.

Children (surname Cadwaladr or Cadwalader): 1. Morgan, b. 1679, d. unm.; 2. Catherine, m., 1706, Hugh Evans, of Gwynedd; 3. ——, m., Robert Evan; 4. ——, m., Abel Thomas, of Merion; 5. Edward, d. young.

EDWARD MORGAN, of near Bala, co. Mer., tailor; s. Morgan ——. Rmd. to Gwynedd, Penna., about 1700. Ch. E. Freeholder of 800 a. ld. in Gwynedd. D. in Towamencin, 1727.

Wife, Dorothy ——; liv. 1727.

Children (surname Morgan): 1. Margaret, m., 1713, Samuel Thomas, of Montgomery; 2. William, m., (1) 1713, Elizabeth Roberts; (2) ·1731, Catherine Robeson; 3. John, m., 1721, Sarah Lloyd; 4. Daniel, m., 1718, Elizabeth Roberts; 5. Sarah, m., 1720, Squire Boone; 6. Joseph, b. Penna.; m. 1728, Elizabeth Lloyd; 7. Alice, b. Penna.; m., 1718, Jenkin Evans, of Montgomery; 8. Edward, b. Penna, 9. Jesse, b. Penna.

EVAN MORGAN, of Vainor, par. of Nantmell, co. Rad., gentleman; b. 1672.; s. James (d. in Bohemia Bay). Rmd. to Penna., 1691. Lived for a time in Radnor. Ch. E. (See ped. xix.).

JAMES MORGAN, of Vainor, par. of Nantmell, co. Rad., gentleman; s. Morgan Lewis, of same place. Rmd. to Penna. 1691. D. on arrival; burd. at head of Bohemia Bay. Ch. E. Had purchased ld. in Radnor, Penna., before sailing.

Wife, Jane ——; d. at sea, on the voyage.

Children (surname Morgan) : 1. John, b. 1669 ; m., Sarah Evans ; 2. Evan, b. 1675 ; 3. James, d.s.p. ; 4. Margaret, b. 1666. (See ped. xix.).

JOHN MORGAN, of Vainor, par. of Nantmell, co. Rad., gentleman ; b. 1669 ; s. James (d. in Bohemia Bay). Rmd. to Penna., 1691. Ch. E. Freeholder in Radnor. D. 1744. (See ped. xix.).

Wife, Sarah, dau. John Evans. late of Nantmell.

Children : 1. John, b. 1695 ; 2. Hannah, b. 1697 ; 3. Sarah, b. 1698 ; 4. James, b. 1700 ; d. 1701 ; 5. James, b. 1702 ; d. s.p. ; 6. Evan, b. 1704 ; 7. Thomas, b. 1706 ; 8. Mary, b. 1708 ; 9. Samuel, b. 1709 ; 10. Mordecai, b. 1713.

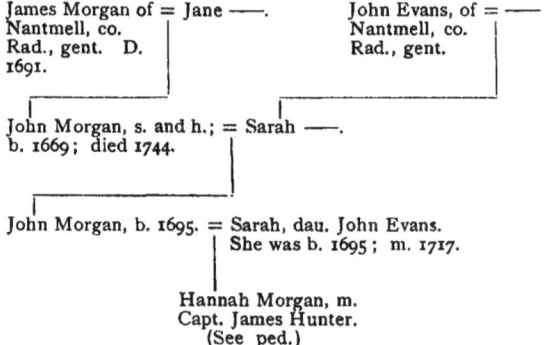

JOHN MORGAN, of near Bala, co. Mer., husbandman ; s. Morgan —— (bro. of Edward of Gwynedd). Rmd. to Gwynedd, Penna., about 1700. Ch. E. Liv. 1727.

Wife, ——.

Children (surname Morgan): 1. Elizabeth, m., 1710, Cadwalader Morris ; and perhaps others.

JOHN MORGAN, of Milnhouse, co. Durham, Eng. ; 6th s. of John Morgan, of Milnhouse, gentleman. Rmd. to Penna. about 1706. In 1730, his brothers being all dead without issue, he was advertised for as heir to the estate. The family was of Welsh descent.

JOSEPH MORGAN, of near Bala, co, Mer., husbandman ; s. Morgan —— ; (bro. Edward, of Gwynedd). Rmd. to Gwynedd, Penna., about 1700. Ch. E.

OWEN MORGAN, of par. of Machynlleth, co Montg., labourer. Rmd. to Penna., 1684.

Wife, Janne ——.

DAVID MORRIS, of ——. Rmd. to Philadelphia, Penna., and thence to Haverford, and Marple, before 1686. Ch. E.

Wife, Mary Philippin (m. in Penna., 1686).

Children (surname Morris): 1. David, b. 1686-7; 2. Isaac, b. 1689; 3. Jonathan, b. 1692; 4. Elizabeth; 5. Mordecai.

Isaac Morris, b. 1689; d. 1735; of Whitemarsh. He m. Sarah, dau. Henry Lewis of Haverford. Children: 1. Mary; 2. Jonathan; 3. David; 4. Phebe.

David Morris, s. Isaac, of Plymouth, m., 1755, Ann Peason. Children: 1. Hannah; 2. Joseph; 3. Thomas; 4. Sarah, b. 1756-7; m. William Hansell, s. Peter David, 1783, and had James Hansell, who m. Anna Catharina, dau. Hilary Ehrenzeller, and had Catharine Ann, who m. Clayton French, and had Catharine Hansell French, who m. George H. Earle, jr.

EVAN MORRIS. Rmd. to Penna., 1692. Fd.

Wife, Gainor ——.

Two children.

ELLIS MORRIS (or Maurice), of Dolgynuchaf, near Dolgelley, co. Mer., gentleman. He was a purchaser of 180 a. ld. in Penna., 1682, which he sold to Thomas Ellis, and did not remove to the Province.

EVAN MORRIS, of near Tyddyn y Garreg, co. Mer. Rmd. to Penna., 1690.

JANE MORRIS, of co. Mer., spinster (sister to William Morris, of Montgomery); dau. Morris Richard, of Dolgelley, co. Mer., tailor, who d. at sea on the voyage to Penna. Rmd. to Montgomery, Penna., before abt. 1710. Married, 1720, Thomas Williams, of Montgomery.

MADLIN MORRIS, of Denbigh Town, or neighbourhood; kinswoman to John and Benjamin Prichard, of Penna., and to John Roberts, a resident in Denbigh, 1710. Rmd. to Penna. about 1700 to 1710. Lived near Philadelphia. Ch. E.

JOHN (or Shôn) THOMAS MORRIS (i.e. John ap Thomas ap Morris), of par. of Llanwddyn, co. Montg., gentleman. He inherited a good estate, but falling into bad habits, mortgaged his lands. Joining to Society of Friends, he rmd. to Penna., 1683, and remained 30 years, when, having accumulated a considerable fortune, he returned to Wales, paid off the mortgage, and d. in Llanwddyn, unm. He wrote and published a history of the Society of Friends in Montgomeryshire.

THOMAS MORRIS, of Mochnant Issa., co. Montg., yeoman. He had a deed, dated 1683, for $156\frac{1}{4}$ a. ld. in Penna. Fd.

WILLIAM MORRIS, of co. Mer., tailor ; s. Morris Richard, of Dolgelley, co. Mer., tailor, who d. at sea on the voyage to Penna. Rmd. to Montgomery, Penna., before abt. 1710.

Wife, Catherine, dau. Richard Pugh. of Montgomery (m. 1719).

JAMES MORTIMER, of co. Card., South Wales. Rmd. to Penna., prob. before 1696. Fd.

Wife, Margaret, dau. John Thomas ap Howel, of Llanwddyn, co. Montg.

Children : 1. James ; 2. Margaret; perhaps others.

[The Mortimer family was seated in Cardiganshire, and formerly held Coed Mawr, and the lordship of Geneurglyn, and was an offshoot of the same family as the Mortimers, Earls of March.]

EVAN OLIVER, of par. of Glascomb, co. Rad., gentleman; s. Evan Oliver, of same place, gentleman. Rmd. to Radnor, Penna., 1692. Fd. Freeholder of 200 a. ld. in Radnor and elsewhere (deed 1682). Was Woodwarden or Forester for the proprietor.

Wife, ———.

RICHARD ORME, of co. Merioneth, yeoman. Rmd. to Radnor, Penna., before 1686. Fd. Freeholder of ld. in Radnor.

Wife, Mary Tyder (Tudor), dau. Tudor ———, and Katherine David, his wife, of Machynlleth, co. Montg.

Children : 1. Katherine ; 2. Elizabeth ; 3. Mary, m., 1715, John Thomas, s. William, of Radnor.

ANN OWEN, of near Dolgelley, co. Mer. Maid to Robert Owen, of Dolserey, to whom she was related. Rmd. to Penna., 1684.

EDWARD OWEN, of Dolserey, near Dolgelley, co. Mer., gentleman ; s. Robert Owen, of same place. Rmd. to Merion, Penna., 1683-4. Fd. Rmd. from Merion to Duck Creek and Kent co. D. in Md.

Wife, Hannah Baxter ; m. 1684-5.

Children (surname Owen) : 1. Thomas; 2. Robert; 3. Edward ; and others unnamed. (See ped. v.).

Some of the Founders

EVAN OWEN, b. Fron Goch, near Bala, co. Mer., 1682-3; s. Robert Owen, of Fron Goch. Rmd. to Merion, with his parents, 1690. (See "Merion," 131). D. in Philadelphia, 1727.

Wife, Mary, dau. Dr. Richard Hoskins.

Children : 1. Robert, d. 1712 ; 2. Robert, b. 1712, d.s.p.; 3. Martha, b. 1714; 4. Esther, b. 1716; m. 1743, William Davis; 5. Aurelius, b. 1718; d. 1721.

(For pedigree see "Merion," and "Welsh Founders of Pennsylvania," vol. ii.).

ELIZABETH OWEN, of par. of Llangelynin, co. Mer., spinster, b. 1675; dau. Owen Humphrey, of Llwyndu, Llwyngwril, par. of Llangelynin, Esq. (by his 2nd wife, Elizabeth Thomas). Rmd. to Merion, Penna., 1690. Fd. She married, 1691, John Roberts of Merion, millwright, an aged man.

ELIZABETH OWEN, of near Bala, co. Mer., spinster; dau. Owen ap Hugh ap Ieuan, of par. of Cerrig y Druidion, co. Denb. Rmd. to Penna., before 1689. Fd. She m., 1689, as his 2d wife, Thomas Andrews, of Philadelphia, and d. 1718. (See ped. i.).

GRIFFITH OWEN, of Lancashire, physician ; s. of Robert Owen, of Dolserey. Rmd. to Penna. 1684. Fd. Freeholder in Merion and elsewhere. D. 1717-18. (See ped. v.).

Wife, Sarah, dau. John Songhurst (or Longhurst) ; wid. of —— Sanders.

Children (surname Owen): 1. Robert; 2. Sarah, m. Jacob Minshall; 3. Eleanor; 4. Catherine; 5. Rebecca, m. Isaac Minshall; 6. Jane, m. (1) Jonathan Coppock; (2) —— Taylor; 7. John, m., Jane Harriott; 8. Edward, d.s.p., 1724; m. Susanna Kearney; 9. Griffith; 10. Ann, m. John Whitpaine. (See ped. v.).

JOHN OWEN, of par. of Llangelynin, co. Mer.; 2d. s. Owen Humphrey, of Llwyn du Llwyngwril, par. of Llangelynin, Esq. Rmd. to Merion, Penna., 1683. Liv. prob. unm., 1714.

JOHN OWEN, b. in Merion, 1692 ; s. Robert Owen, of Fron Goch and Merion. D. in co. Chester, 1752. Freeholder. Fd.

Wife, Hannah, dau. George Maris ; m. 1719.

Children : 1. Jane, m. Joseph West; 2. George, m. 1751, Rebecca Hains; 3. Elizabeth, m. James Rhoads ; 4. Rebecca, m., 1754, Jesse Maris ; 5.

Susannah, m. Josiah Hibbard. (For ped. see "Merion," and "Welsh Founders of Pennsylvania," vol. ii. For descendants see "Maris Genealogy").

JOSHUA OWEN, of par. of Llangelynin, co. Mer., schoolmaster; 3d s. Owen Humphrey, of Llwyndu, Llwyngwril, par. of Llangelynin, Esq. Rmd. to Merion, Penna., 1683. Rmd. from Merion to New Jersey. Liv. 1714. Fd.

Wife, Martha, dau. John Shinn, of W. Jersey.

Children (surname Owen): 1. Joshua, b. 1697; 2. Rebecca, b. 1699; 3. Margaret, b. 1701; 4. Martha, b. 1706; prob. others.

LEWIS OWEN, of Dolserey, near Dolgelley, co. Mer., gentleman; s. Robert Owen, of same place. Rmd. to Duck Creek, Penna., 1684. D. 1708-9. Freeholder. Fd.

Wife, Lowry ———.

Children (surname Owen): 1. Lewis; 2. John: 3. Ann; 4. Ellen; 5. Jane. (See ped. v.).

LEWIS OWEN, of Gwanas, co. Mer., gentleman. He had a deed, 1682, for 78 a. ld. in Penna., which he subsequently sold, and did not rm. to the Province. Fd.

MABLY OWEN, of near Bala, co. Mer., spinster; dau. Owen ap Hugh ap Ieuan, of par. of Cerrig y Druidion, co. Denb. (See ped. i.). She married Edward Rees, alias Price, who rmd. to Merion, Penna., 1683. (See Glenn's "Merion," under Edward Rees).

OWEN OWEN, b. in Merion, 1690; s. Robert Owen, of Fron Goch and Merion. D. in Philadelphia, 1741.

Wife, Anne Wood, m. 1714; d. 1743.

Children: 1. Robert; 2. Jane, m. Dr. Cadwalader Evans; 3. Sarah, m. John Biddle; 4. Tacey, m. Daniel Morris; 5. Rebecca, d. unm.

(For ped. see "Merion," and "Welsh Founders of Pennsylvania," vol. ii.).

ROBERT OWEN, of Dolserey, near Dolgelley, gentleman; s. Humphrey Owen, of same place. Rmd. to Duck Creek, Newcastle co., Penna., 1684. Fd. D. 1685-6.

Wife, Jane, dau. Robert Vaughan, of Hengwrt, the antiquary. She d. 1685-6.

Some of the Founders

Children (surname Owen) : 1. Robert, remained in Wales ; 2. Griffith ; 3. Rowland ; 4. Edward ; 5. Lewis ; 6. Humphrey. Three others, names unknown. (See ped. v.).

ROBERT OWEN, of Fron Goch, par. of Llanfor, co. Mer., gentleman ; s. of Owen ap Evan, of same place, gentleman. Rmd. to Merion, Penna., 1690. Fd. Freeholder of 450 a. ld. in Merion. J.P., Memb, Prov. Assembly. D. 1697.

Wife, Rebecca, dau. Owen Humphrey, of Llwyndu, par. Llangelynin, co. Mer., Esq., (m. in Wales, 1678-9).

Children (surname Owen) : 1. Gainor, b. 1681; m. Jonathan Jones ; 2. Evan, b. 1683 ; m. Mary Hoskins; 3. Jane, b. 1685 ; 4. Elizabeth, b. 1687; m. David Evans; 5. Owen, b. Penna., 1690; m. Anne Wood; 6. John, b. Penna, 1692; m. Hannah Maris ; 7. Robert, b. 1695, m. Susanna Hudson ; 8. Rebecca, b. 1697; d. inft.

ROBERT OWEN, b. in Merion, 1695 ; s. Robert Owen, of Fron Goch, and Merion. D. about 1730.

Wife, Susanna, dau. William Hudson, Mayor of Philadelphia. She m. (2) John Burr, widower.

Children : 1. Mary, b. 1719; m. Henry Burr, s. John ; 2. Hannah, b. 1720; m. (1) John Ogden; (2) Joseph Wharton, of Walnut Grove ; 3. Rachel, b. 1724; unm. 1740.

(For ped. see "Merion," and "Welsh Founders of Pennsylvania," vol. ii. For descendants see "Wharton Family," by Miss Annie Wharton, and Glenn's "Merion," 138., *et seq.*).

ROWLAND OWEN, of Gwanas, co. Mer., gentleman. He had a deed, 1682, for 183 a. ld. in Penna., which he subsequently sold, and did not remove to the Province. Fd.

THOMAS OWEN, prob. of co. Pemb., yeoman. Rmd. to Radnor, Penna., before 1692. Descendants, surnamed Owen, are numerous.

GEORGE PAINTER (or Paynter) of Haverfordwest, co. Pemb. Rmd. to Penna., 1683.

Wife, Eleanor ——.

Children : 1. George ; 2. Susan.

MARMADUKE PARDO, of par. of St. David's, Haverfordwest, " who for these several years past took upon him ye keeping of a private school in this Citty" (St. Davids). Rmd. to Penna., 1727. Ch. E.

Certif. from Curate and others of the inhabitants of the par. of St. Davids, 18 April, 1727, and from Mtg. of Haverfordwest, 6 mo. 18, 1727. He established a school in Haverford, but moved to Gwynedd before or in 1729.

Wife, Gainor Jones, of Merion ; m. 1729.

OWEN PARRY, of Dynunllo Issa, co. Denb., yeoman. A purchaser, 1862, from John ap John, of 150 a. ld. in Penna. Fd.

THOMAS PARRY, of par. of Llanelwi, co. Rad., weaver ; s. Henry (or Harry) Rees, of par. of Henllan, co. Card. Rmd. to Radnor, Penna., 1699. Fd. Freeholder of 125 a. ld. in Radnor.

Wife, Elinor, dau. John ap Edward, of par. of Llanelwi, (m. in Wales).

Children (surname Parry) : 1. Edward, m. 1710, Jane, dau. Robert Evans ; 2. Thomas, m. 1715, Jane, dau. Philip Philips, of Radnor.

REES PETER (or Petter) of par. of Machynlleth, co. Montg. Rmd. to Penna., 1683. Fd.

PHILIP PHILIPS, prob. of So. Wales. Rmd. to Radnor, Penna., before 1693. Ch. E.

Wife, Phebe Evans ; m. 1693.

EVAN WILLIAM POWEL (otherwise Evan Williams), of par. of Llanvachreth, co. Mer., gentleman ; s. William Powel (otherwise William ap Howel), of same place, gentleman. Died at sea on the voyage to Penna., 1684. Fd. (See ped. ix.).

Wife, Gwen ———.

Children (surname Evans) : 1. David ; 2. Philip (see Evans).

DAVID POWEL, of par. of Nantmell, co. Rad. Rmd. to Penna., 1698. Fd.

Wife, Gwen ———.

"Several children."

DAVID POWEL, prob. of North Wales. Rmd. to Penna., abt. 1683. He was Deputy Surveyor of the Province of Penna.

EVAN POWEL (Evan ap Howel), of par. of Nantmell, co. Rad., weaver ; prob. s. Howel ap Edward (liv. Nantmell 4 Car. I.), and was of Maesgwyn, Nantmell, 13 Car. II. Rmd. to Penna., 1698.

Wife, Gwen ——— ; d. in Penna.

Some of the Founders

HOWEL POWEL, of par. of Llansadwrnen, co. Carm., yeoman. Rmd. to Penna., 1713. Fd.

THOMAS POWELL, of par. of Llanbadarn fawr, co. Rad. Rmd. to Penna., 1698. Fd. Freeholder.

PRICE. "The children of David Price and Joan, his wife," of co. Brec. Rmd. to Penna., 1690.

DAVID PRICE, of co. Brec. Rmd. to Penna., 1690. Fd.

Wife, Joan ——; liv. 1690.

DAVID PRICE, of par. of Mothvey, co. Carm., gentleman; bro. James. He purchased 300 a. ld. in Radnor, Penna., after 1682-3, from James Price, but soon after sold the same to Henry Rees (before 1700). It is uncertain whether this David Price rmd. to Penna., or not.

PHILIP PRICE, of So. Wales, husbandman. Rmd. to Penna., prob. before 1692. Fd. Freeholder in Upper Merion, 1703; and in Whitpain, same date.

THOMAS AP PRICHARD, cordwainer; s. Richard ——. Rmd. to Philadelphia, Penna., before 1698. D. 1698.

Wife, ——.

Children (surname Prichard): 1. John; 2. Mathew, of Phila., cordwainer; m. 1699, Sarah Henley, of Phila.; 3. Benjamin; 4. Ann; 5. Jane.

ANN PRICHARD, of Denbigh Town, or neighbourhood. Kinswoman to John Roberts, who was living in Denbigh, 1710. Rmd. to Penna., abt. 1700. (She was sister to John and Benjamin Prichard).

BENJAMIN PRICHARD, of Denbigh Town, or neighbourhood, bro. to John, Ann, and Jane Prichard. Rmd. to Penna., abt. 1700.

JANE PRICHARD, sister to John Benjamin, and Ann Prichard. Rmd. to Penna., abt. 1700.

JOHN PRICHARD, of Denbigh Town, or neighbourhood; kinsman to John Roberts, who was living in Denbigh, 1710. Rmd. to Penna., abt. 1700.

KATHERINE PRICHARD, of Telcha, co. Glam., spinster (cousin to John Bevan, of Treverigg), a purchaser under the latter of land in Penna., and may have rmd. there. She d. unm., and her land vested in her only sister, Elizabeth Prichard, who sold the same, 1697.

DAVID PUGH, was of twp. of Radnor, Penna., before 1701, and Constable of same place, 1701 ; Supervisor, 1702. Freeholder of 174 a. ld. in Radnor, 1703.

Wife, Catherine ——.

Children (surname Pugh) : 1. Jonathan ; 2. Hannah, m. James Miles ; and others.

ELLIS PUGH (i.e., ap Hugh), of Brithdu, near Dolgelley, co. Mer., yeoman. Rmd. to Penna., 1686. Fd.

Wife, Sina ——.

As 9 "poor small children" of Sina are mentioned in their certif. it is presumed that they were by a former husband.

EVAN PUGH, of near Bala, co. Mer., yeoman. Rmd. to Gwynedd, Penna., 1698. Ch. E. Freeholder of ld. in Gwynedd.

Wife, Sarah, dau. Evan Lloyd Evan (otherwise Evan ap Evan), of Ucheldre, par. of Llanfor, according to earliest MS. ; but later MSS. differ. (See ped. in vol. ii.).

WILLIAM PUGH, of near Bala, co. Mer., yeoman. Rmd. to Radnor. Penna., before 1700. Freeholder in Radnor. D. 1708. Ch. E.

Wife, ——.

Children (surname Williams) : 1. Hugh ; 2. —— (dau.) m. near Bala, co. Mer., before 1682, Hugh John Thomas, of Nant-lleidiog, par. of Llanfor, who rmd. to Merion, Penna., 1682, and d. in Plymouth, 1727. Hugh Williams had : 1. William Williams ; 2. Catherine Williams, and prob. others.

WILLIAM PUGH (or ap Hugh), of near Dolgelley, co. Mer. yeoman. Rmd. to Penna., 1688. Fd.

Wife, Katherine ——.

Children : 1. Ann, b. in Wales.

DAVID REES, of Fron Ween, Penmaen, par. of Llanfor, co. Mer., yeoman ; s. Rees Evan, of same place, gentleman. (See ped. ii.). Rmd. to Penna., after 1700, and supposedly settled in Merion. Fd.

EDWARD REES (otherwise Prees and Price), of Ciltalgarth, par. of Llanfor, co. Mer., yeoman ; s. Richard Price, of Glanlloidiogin, same par., husbandman. (For ped. see "Merion," 92). Rmd. to Merion, Penna., 1682. Fd. Freeholder of 156¼ a. ld. in Merion, and elsewhere.

Some of the Founders 205

Wives: (1) Mably, dau. Owen ap Hugh (bro. Thomas ap Hugh, of Wern Fawr ; see ped. i.); (2) Rebecca, dau. Samuel Humphrey, of par. of Llangelynin, decd. (See ped. iv.)

Children (surname Price) : 1. Rees, b. 1678; m. (1) Sarah Meredith; (2) Elizabeth Ellis, (3) Ann Scothorn, wid. ; 2. Catherine, d. 1682 ; 3. Jane, m. (1) Jonathan Hayes ; (2) —— Maries.

EVAN REES, of Penmaen, par. of Llanfor, co. Mer., grocer (called gentleman in later record); s. Rees David, of same place. He was one of the Edward Jones Company, and a purchaser, in 1682, of 312 a. 1d. in Penna., a part of which was surveyed in Merion. He did not remove to the Province, but died in Wales. The children of his son, Rees, however, (except one) settled in Merion in after years. (See ped. ii.).

Wife, —— dau. David John, of Ciltalgarth.

Children : 1. Rees Evan, m. Elizabeth, dau. John Thomas, of Llaithgwm, gentleman.

EVAN REES, of Fron Ween, Penmaen, par. of Llanfor, co. Mer., yeoman ; s. Rees Evan, of same place ; gentleman. . (See ped. ii.). Rmd. to Penna., after 1700. Fd. Freeholder in Merion. D. 1752.

Wife, Mary ——.

Children : 1. Mary, liv., unm., and then of unsound mind, 1752.

REES REES, of co. Rad., husbandman. Rmd. to Penna., 1684. Ch. E.

Wife, Ann ——.

Children : 1. Richard ; 2. John ; 3. Mary ; 4. Sarah; 5. Phebe. (B. in Wales).

SYDNEY REES, b. 1690; dau. of Rees Evan, of Fron Ween, Penmaen, par. of Llanfor, co. Mer., gentleman. Rmd to Merion, Penna., after 1700. Fd. M., 1709, Robert Roberts, of Merion, s. John, of Pencoid.

JOHN RHYDDERCH, of par. of Hirnant, co. Montg., yeoman ; s. Rhydderch ap Evan, of same place, yeoman. Rmd. to Penna., 1683. Fd. Freeholder. D.s.p. 1688. (See ped. xiv.).

Wife, Grace (or Gwen) John, of Hirnant.

DAVID RHYDDERCH, of par. of Hirnant, co. Montg., yeoman ; s. Rhydderch ap Evan, of same place, yeoman. Rmd. to Penna. before Jan., 1688. Fd. Freeholder. (See ped. xiv.).
Wife, ——.
Children : 1. Mary, b. 1698.

RISIART (RICHARD) AP THOMAS AP RHYS, of ——. Rmd. to Radnor, Penna., about 1700. Prob. Ch. E.
Wife, Elizabeth, dau. Thomas Sion (John) Evan, (alias Thomas Jones) ; m. in Penna.

PHILIP RHYTHERRACH (Rhydderch), or Prothroe, b. co. Carm., 1627-8. Rmd. to Penna., 1690. D. in Newtown, co. Chester, Sept., 1730, aged 102 yrs. Benjamin Franklin, in the "Pennsylvania Gazette," of Sept., 1730, gives the following account of him :

"Sunday last, died of a Flux, at Newtown in Chester County, Philip Rhyddarch in the 102 Year of his Age. He was born in Caermarthenshire in South Wales, and came into Pennsylvania about 40 years ago. He was a Man of a peaceable Disposition, very religious, and remarkable for his Temperance, having never been overcome with Drink during his whole Life."

Wife, Dorothy ——.
Children (surname Philips) : 1. Margaret, m. Richard Iddings ; 2. Elizabeth ; 3. Mary.

Philip Rhytherrach was ancestor to General Anthony Wayne, the Hunter, and Van Leer (von Löhr), families, and George H. Earle, jr.

JOHN RICE, of near Redstone, co. Pemb., a minor ; s. David Rice, of same place. Rmd. to Penna., "with the consent of his parents," 1696. Fd.

THOMAS AP RICHARD (alias Thomas Prichard), of Nant-lleidiog, par. of Llanfor, co. Mer., yeoman ; s. Richard Price of Glanlloidiogin in the par. of Llanfor, husbandman. He had a deed, executed in Wales, 1682, for 156¼ a. ld. in Penna., of which 76½ acres were surveyed to him in Merion. If Thomas Richard rmd. to Penna., he did not remain long, and d. in Wales. He is named as executor in his father's will, provd. at St. Asaph, 1686, but renounced in favour of Edward Nicholas, of Cynlas, a kinsman. In 1684 he sold his Merion lands to Rees John William, who had m. his sister Hannah. Edward Price (alias Rees), of Merion, was a bro. of Thomas ap Richard.

Some of the Founders

EDWARD RICHARD, of Treverig, par. of Llantrisant, co. Glam., tailor. Rmd. to Haverford, Penna., about 1683. D. unm. and his land in Haverford went to his bro., Lewis Richard, who never came to Pennsylvania, but sold the land to John Bevan, from whom it was originally purchased.

JOHN RICHARD, par. of Llantrisant, co. Glam., labourer. Rmd. to Penna., 1683. Fd.

JOHN RICHARDS, of par. of Machynlleth, co. Montg. Rmd. to Penna., 1684. Fd.
Wife, Susan ———.
Children: 1. Hannah; 2. Bridget (b. in Wales). Prob. others.

MAUD RICHARD, of "Llanllough" (Llanllwch), par. of St. Peter's, Borough of Carmarthen, co. Carm., spinster. Rmd. to Penna., 1693. Certif. from inhabitants of Carmarthen, 4 July, 1694. Ch. E.

MORRIS RICHARD, of Dolgelley, co. Mer., tailor. D. at sea on the voyage to Penna., abt. 1710.
Wife, ———.
Children (surname Morris): 1. William, m., 1719, Catharine Pugh; 2. Jane, m., 1720, Thomas Williams, of Montgomery, Penna. Prob. others.

TRYALL RIDER, of Wrexham, co. Denbigh, flaxdresser. Fd. He was a purchaser under John ap John, of 400 a. ld. in Penna., which John ap John subsequently repurchased, and was liv. near Wrexham in 1697, where he d. some years after.

DAVID ROBERT, of near Tyddyn y Garreg, co. Mer., minor; s. Robert Tudor and Lowry his wife, (both decd.). Rmd. to Penna., 1686.

ELLEN ROBERT, of near Tyddyn y Garreg, co. Mer., minor; dau. Robert Tudor and Lowry his wife, (both decd.). Rmd. to Penna., 1686. Fd.

EVAN ROBERT, of near Bala, co. Mer.; yeoman; s. Robert ———. Rmd. to Gwynedd, Penna., 1698. Ch. E. Freeholder of 100 a. ld. in Gwynedd.

KATHERINE ROBERT (alias Thomas); dau. Robert ———, and wid. John Thomas (alias John ap Thomas), of Llaithgwm, near Bala, co. Mer. Rmd. to Penna., with her family, 1683. She was the 2d. wife of John Thomas. Fd.

MARGARET ROBERT, of par. of Llanfor, co. Mer., spinster; dau. Robert ———. Rmd. to Penna., 1698. Fd.

ANN ROBERTS, of par. of Llangian, co. Carn., spinster; dau. Richard Roberts, of Cowyns, in the par. of Llanengan. Rmd. to Merion, Penna., supposedly, 1683. Fd. She was sister to John Roberts.

CADWALADER ROBERTS, of par. Llanuwchllyn, co. Mer., yeoman; s. Robert Cadwalader, of same place; b. par. of Llanuwchllyn, 1673. Rmd. to Gwynedd, Penna., 1698; then unm. Ch. E. Freeholder of 140 a. land in Gwynedd, in 1710.

For ped. see "Welsh Founders of Pennsylvania," vol. ii.

Wife, Eleanor Humphrey, dau. Humphrey Ellis.

Children (surname Roberts): 1. Rebecca, m. William Erwin; 2. Robert, m. Sarah Ambler.

For dects. see "Welsh Founders of Pennsylvania," vol. ii.

EDWARD ROBERTS, supposedly from North Wales. Rmd. to Gwynedd, Penna., shortly after 1700. D. 1748-9, being "far advanced in years."

Wife, Anne ——. Liv. 1748.

Children: 1. Robert, m. Jane, dau. Robert Evans, of Merion; 2. Margaret, m. (1) Hugh Evans; (2) Robert Jones, of Merion; 3. Gainor, m. Edward Foulke.

ELIZABETH ROBERTS, of par. of Llanuwchllyn, co. Mer., spinster; dau. Robert Cadwalader, of same place; b. par. of Llanycil, 1688. Rmd. to Gwynedd, Penna., about 1700. Ch. E. She m., 1718, Daniel Morgan, s. Edward.

ELLIS ROBERTS, of near Bala, co. Mer., tailor; s. Robert ——. Rmd. to Gwynedd, Penna., abt. 1700. He became a Freeholder, 1714. Fd.

Wife, Elizabeth, dau. David Thomas, of Radnor; m. 1715.

Children: 1. Lydia; m. Benjamin Mendenhall; 2. —— (son); prob. others.

EVAN ROBERTS, of near Bala, co. Mer., yeoman. Rmd. to Gwynedd, Penna., 1698. Ch. E. Freeholder of 110 a. ld. in Gwynedd. Prob. single at time of arrival, and perhaps identical with Evan Roberts of Gwynedd, who m., 1709, Jane Evan, dau. Evan Pugh of the same place.

GAINOR ROBERTS, of Ciltalgarth, par. of Llanfor, co. Mer., spinster, b. 1652; dau. Robert ap Hugh (alias Pugh). She was sister to Hugh Roberts, of Merion. Rmd. to Penna., 1683, and m. in Merion, 1684, John Roberts, late of Llangian, co. Carn. Fd.

GRACE ROBERT, of near Tyddyn y Garreg, co. Mer., minor ; dau. Robert Tudor and Lowry his wife, (both decd.). Rmd. to Penna., 1686. Fd.

GRIFFITH ROBERT, of near Dolgelley, co. Mer. Rmd. to Penna., 1707. Fd. Descended from Cadwgan, lord of Nannau.

Wife, —— ; decd. in Wales.

Children (surname Griffith) : 1. Derwas ; 2. Margaret.

HUGH ROBERTS, b. abt. 1644 ; of Ciltalgarth, par. of Llanfor, co. Mer., gentleman ; s. Robert ap Hugh (or Pugh), of Llwyndedwydd. Rmd. to Merion, Penna., 1683. He made two or more voyages to Wales. D. 1702. (See ped. xxiv.).

Wives : (1) Jane, dau. Owen ap Evan, of Fron Goch ; m. 1672 ; (2) Elizabeth John, m. 1689. She was a wid., and had several " poor small children," by her first husband.

Children (surname Roberts) : 1. Robert, b. 1673 ; 2. Ellin, b. 1675 ; 3. Owen, b. 1677 ; 4. Edward, b. 1680 ; 5. William, b. 1683 (all by 1st wife).

HUGH ROBERTS, of near Bala, co. Mer., husbandman. Rmd. to Gwynedd, Penna., about 1700. Ch. E.

Wife, Ann Thomas, of Upper Merion (m. 1703).

JOHN ROBERTS, of near Bala, co. Mer., cordwainer ; s. Robert Lloyd, and gds. of John Lloyd. His uncle, Thomas Lloyd, of Llangower, yeoman, devised him 156½ a. ld. in Penna., of which 76½ a. were surveyed in Merion, and the balance in Goshen. John Roberts, who dropped the surname of Lloyd, rmd. to Penna., prob. about 1700. Ch. E. He had also land in Goshen by gift or grant of Evan John William. He sold his Merion lands before 1703, and by deed 1720. Freeholder in Cheltenham, 1720. (See ped. xi.).

Wife, Mary ——.

JOHN ROBERTS, of near Bala., co. Mer. (bro. to Ellis Roberts, of Gwynedd, tailor). Rmd. to Gwynedd abt. 1700. D. 1725, s.p.

Wife, Ellinor —— ; d. 1725.

JOHN ROBERTS, of par. of Nantmell, co. Rad., blacksmith. He "livid in Llanidloes (co. Montg.) many years . . . . since he buried his wife." Rmd. to Penna., 1698. Fd.

JOHN ROBERTS, of par. of Llanuwchllyn, co. Mer.; s. Robert Cadwalader, of same place ; b. par. of

Llanycil, 1681. Rmd. to Gwynedd, Penna., abt. 1700; rmd. from Gwynedd to Oxford, and thence to Montgomery. Ch. E. Freeholder of 100 a. ld. in Montgomery. D. 1773.

Wife, Elizabeth Edward, of Merion (m. 1706).

Children (surname Roberts): 1. Elizabeth, m. (1), John Jones; (2) John Blair. Prob. others.

JOHN ROBERTS, of par. of Llangian, co. Carn., gentleman, b. 1648; s. Richard Roberts, of Cowyns, in the par. of Llanengan. Rmd. to Merion, Penna., 1683. Fd. Freeholder of upwards of 1,000 a. ld. in Merion and elsewhere. D. 1724. For ped. and descts. see " Merion in the Welsh Tract," Glenn, 98.

Wife, Gainor Roberts, dau. Robert ap Hugh (or Pugh) (m. 1684).

Children (surname Roberts): 1. Robert, b. 1685; m. Sidney Rees (or Reese), dau. Rees Evan, of Penmaen, Llanfor, co. Mer. (See ped. ii.); 2. Elizabeth, b. 1692.

MATTHEW ROBERTS, of Pen y Clwyd, co. Denbigh, millwright (bro. John Roberts of same place). Rmd. to Merion, Penna., 1683; he was then advanced in years. Fd.

Wife, ——.

Children (surname Roberts): 1. John (only son); m., 1710, Jane, dau. Robert David. Perhaps daus.

MILES ROBERTS, sup. an early settler from S. Wales; of co. Chester, Penna., before 1720. His wife eloped with a neighbour, before 12 Augt., 1730.

MORRIS ROBERTS, of par. of Llanuwchllyn, co. Mer., yeoman; s. Robert Cadwalader, of same place; b. par. of Llangower, 1677. Rmd. to Gwynedd, Penna., 1698; then unm. Ch. E.

Wife, Elizabeth Robeson (m. 1718). Rmd. from Gwynedd to North Carolina, 1738.

Children (surname Roberts): 1. Susanna, m. Jacob Zimmerman; 2. Hannah, m. William Howe; 3. Sophia, m. John Cadwalader, of Gwynedd; 4. Lydia, m. Joseph Jones; 5. Morris, d. young; 6. Nehemiah, d. at Gwynedd.

NICHOLAS ROBERTS, of par. of Llanuwchllyn, co. Mer.; s. Robert Cadwalader, of same place. Rmd. to Gwynedd, Penna., about 1700. Ch. E. D. 1733.

Wife, Margaret, dau. Edward Foulke, of Gwynedd.

Children (surname Roberts): 1. Jane, m., 1741, David, s. Cadwalader Morris, of Philada. ; 2. Ellen, m. John Siddons ; 3. Elizabeth, m. David Humphrey, of Gwynedd, s. Robert.

RICHARD ROBERTS, of par. of Llangian, co. Carn., husbandman ; s. Richard Roberts, of Cowyns, in the par. of Llanengan. Rmd. to Merion, Penna., supposedly, 1683. Ch. E. Liv. 1722.

Wife, ——.

Children (surname Roberts): 1. Margaret, liv. 1722 ; and perhaps others.

ROGER ROBERTS, of Ciltalgarth, parish of Llanfor, co. Mer., husbandman (farmer for David Jones, of Ciltalgarth, gentleman, who rmd. to Penna., 1699). Rmd. to near Philadelphia, Penna., about 1700. Fd. D. July, 1720.

Wife, ——.

Children (surname Rogers): 1. John, m., 1717, Ellin, dau. Robert Pugh, of Gwynedd. Prob. others.

ROWLAND ROBERTS, of par. of Llanuwchllyn, co. Mer. ; s. Robert Cadwalader, of same place, b. par. of Llanycil, 1685. Rmd. to Gwynedd, Penna., about 1700. Ch. E. Rmd. from Gwynedd to Montgomery. Innkeeper. D. 1749.

Wives : (1) Mary Pugh (m. 1713) ; (2) Ann Bennet.

Children (surname Roberts) : 1. Eldad, b. 1713 ; m. (1) Elizabeth Mitchell ; (2) Jane Jones ; 2. Sarah, b. 1715.

TUDOR ROBERTS, of near Tyddyn Garreg, co. Mer., minor ; s. Robert Tudor and Lowry, his wife (both decd.). Rmd. to Penna., 1686.

WILLIAM ROBERTS (alias William Robert Ellis), of Tyddyn Tyfod, par. of Llandderfel, co. Mer., husbandman ; s. Robert ap Ellis, of same place. Rmd. to Merion, Penna., before 1697. Ch. E. Freeholder of 100 a. ld. in Blockley (to which place he rmd. from Merion), which he acquired by deed, 1697. D. 1719. Bur. Merion 7 mo., 18.

Wife, Affy, dau. Henry Lewis, of Haverford.

Children (surname Roberts): 1. John, d. 1720; 2. William, b. 1700 (about); d. 1796, "aged 96 years"; m. Elizabeth ——. Her maiden name is supposed to have been Warner; d. 1748.

WILLIAM ROBERTS, of near Bala, co. Mer. (bro. to Ellis Roberts, tailor). Rmd. to Gwynedd, Penna., abt. 1700. D. before 1748.

Wife, Mary, wid. of Ellis Pugh, jr., and dau. Owen Evans of Gwynedd. She d. 1748.

Children: 1. Ellis, and prob. others.

REES ROTHERS (*i.e.* Rees ap Rhydderch), of par. of Llanwenog, co. Card., yeoman. He had a deed, dated 1682, for 500 a. ld. in Penna.

JAMES ROWLAND, of Rhos y Bayvill, par. of Bayvill, co. Pemb., gentleman; s. William Rowland, of same place, gentleman. Rmd. to co. Chester, Penna., 1700. D.s.p.

JOHN ROWLAND, of Rhos y bayvill, par. of Bayvill, co. Pemb., gentleman; s. William Rowland, of same place, gentleman; descended in direct male line from Ednyfed Fychan, minister to Prince Llewelyn ap Iorwerth, and ancestor to the Royal House of Tudor. Rmd. to Whiteland, co. Chester, Penna., before 1715.

Wife, ——.

Children surname Rowland. (See Rowland Genealogy, compiled by Rev. Henry J. Rowland, of Philadelphia).

Among other descendants are James Day Rowland, Esq., of Ogontz, and Benjamin Rowland.

RICHARD AP THOMAS (otherwise Richard Thomas) of Whitford Garn, co. Flint, gentleman. Rmd. to Penna., 1682-3. He was a purchaser of a large tract of ld., most of which was surveyed in co. Chester, Penna. A genealogy of his descendants will be found in Furthey's Hist. of Chester Co., Pa. A pedigree, of Richard Thomas, in possession of the writer, traces his descent from several very ancient Welsh families of Flintshire.

—— THOMAS, of co. Mon. (bro. John, of same place). Rmd. to Philadelphia, Penna., abt. 1683.

Wife ——.

Children (surname Thomas): 1. Micah, m. his 1st cousin, Gwen Thomas (dau. John); 2. James, d. 1710; 3. Gabriel.

CECIL THOMAS, of near Treverig, co. Glam. Rmd. to Penna., 1707. Fd.

DANIEL THOMAS. Rmd. to Merion, Penna., before 1692.

DAVID THOMAS, of Machynlleth, co. Montg., bro. of William Thomas (2d) of Radnor. Rmd. to Radnor, Penna., about 1690. Fd. Freeholder in Radnor. D. 1737. He was then living in Gwynedd.

Wife, ——.

Children (surname Thomas): 1. Elizabeth, m. 1715, Ellis Roberts, of Gwynedd; 2. Rachel, m. —— Davis; 3. David; 4. Martha, m., 1719, Cadwalader Jones, of Gwynedd.

DAVID THOMAS, of co. Carm.; s. Thomas ap Lewis ap Philip ap Rhydderch. Rmd. to Radnor, Penna., prob. before 1700.

EDWARD THOMAS, of par. of Llanwddyn, co. Montg., yeoman; s. Thomas ap Howel, of same parish. Rmd. to Penna., prob. 1684. Fd. Freeholder of 312½ a. ld. (See ped. iv.).

Wife, ——.

Children (surname Edward or Edwards): 1. Thomas, liv. 1723; prob. others.

EVAN THOMAS, of near Dolobran, par. of Meivod, co. Montg., husbandman. Rmd. to Penna., 1718. Fd.

Wife, Katherine ——.

EVAN THOMAS, of par. of Llanykeaven, co. ——, yeoman. He had a deed, dated 1682, for 250 a. ld. in Penna., and prob. rmd. there, 1683.

HUGH JOHN THOMAS (*i.e.* Hugh ap John ap Thomas), of Nant-lleidiog, par. of Llanfor, co. Mer., yeoman; s. Thomas ap Hugh, of the same place. (Hugh John Thomas was also known as Hugh Jones). Rmd. to Merion, Penna, 1683. Fd. Freeholder of 156¼ a. ld., of which 76½ a. was surveyed to him in Merion. Rmd. from Merion to Plymouth, before 1703. D. 1727. (See ped. xviii.).

Wives: (1) ——, dau. William Pugh; d. in Wales; (2) Ann Williams, of Radnor; (3) Margaret Edwards, of Merion.

Children (surname Jones): 1. Hugh, d. 1719, unm.; 2. Joseph, b. 1697; 3. ——(dau.), m. Rowland Richard, before 1707; prob. others.

JAMES THOMAS, of par. of Llanboidy, co. Carm., yeoman. Rmd. to Merion, Penna., abt. 1686.

Wife, ———.

Children (surname Thomas): 1. James; prob. others.

JAMES THOMAS, of par. of Llanboidy, co. Carm., yeoman; s. James, of same place. Rmd. to Merion, Penna., with his parents, abt. 1686, and was then of age.

JANE THOMAS, dau. Thomas Morris, of par. of Llanwddyn, co. Montg. Rmd. to Penna., abt. 1708. Fd.

JOHN THOMAS, of par. of Llanwddyn, co. Montg.; s. Thomas Morris, of same place. Rmd. to Penna., abt. 1708. Liv. 1723.

Wife, ———.

Children probably assumed the surname of Jones.

JOHN THOMAS (called also John ap Thomas, and John Thomas ap Hugh), of Llaithgwm, par. of Llandderfel (now in Llanfor), co. Mer., gentleman (also designated yeoman); s. Thomas ap Hugh, of Wern Fawr, par. Llandderfel. John Thomas was deputy collector (for Penllyn Isavon) of Subsidy of 15 Car. II. (1663-4), and churchwarden for Llandderfel, 1666, some time after which he joined Friends. Afterwards constable for Penllyn. An original purchaser of Penna. lands, 1682. D. 1683, on the eve of embarkation for Penna. His 2d wife and children rmd. to Penna. same year. (See ped. i.).

Wives: (1) Anne, dau. John Lloyd; bur. Llandderfel, 1695; (2) Katherine Robert (1st wf. was sister to Dr. Edward Jones).

Children (surname Jones): 1. Thomas (by 1st wf.); 2. Robert (by 2d wf.); 3. Evan; 4. Cadwalader; 5. Elizabeth (by 1st wf.), m. Rees Evan, of Penmaen; 6. Katherine; 7. Mary (d. at sea); 8. Sidney (d. at sea).

JOHN THOMAS, of co. Mon. Rmd. to Penna., 1683. Ch. E. D. at Philadelphia, 1713.

Wife, Sarah ———.

Children (surname Thomas): 1. Gwen, m., 1689, Micah Thomas (her cousin); 2. Mary, m. William Snead; 3. Rachel, b. 1664; m. 1688-9, Thomas Wharton.

JOHN THOMAS, of co. Glam. ; s. Thomas Thomas, of same place. Rmd. to Penna., after 1700.

Wife, Esther, dau. John Pugh, of White Marsh; m. 1731.

MARGARET THOMAS, dau. of Thomas Morris, of par. of Llanwddyn, co. Montg. Rmd. to Penna., abt. 1708. Fd.

MORRIS THOMAS, of par. of Llanwddyn, co. Montg., yeoman ; s. Thomas Morris, of same place. Rmd. to Penna., 1708. Liv. 1723. Fd.

Wife ———.

Children prob. assumed the surname of Morris.

OWEN THOMAS, of co. Pemb. He came on a visit to Penna., 1719, and supposedly remained. Fd.

ROBERT THOMAS, b. abt. 1688-90; of Tyddyn Mawr, near Cefn Amwlch, on the seashore, co. Carn.; s. Thomas Evan, of same place, husbandman. Rmd. to Merion, Penna., before 1708. Ch. E. Living as a servant with Thomas Jones, of Merion, s. of John Thomas, of Llaithgwm, 1708. (See ped. vii.)

ROBERT THOMAS, of near Bala, co. Mer., husbandman ; s. Thomas James, of same place, gentleman. Rmd. to Merion, Penna., abt. 1700. Living there 1708. Fd.

SIMEON THOMAS, of co. Pemb., husbandman. Rmd. to Penna., 1708. Fd.

THOMAS JOHN THOMAS ; see Thomas Jones.

WILLIAM THOMAS, of Isygarreg, par. of Machynlleth, co. Montg., planter. Rmd. to Radnor, Penna., before 1686. Fd. Freeholder of 100 a. ld. in Radnor. D. 1689. No issue. He was related to several of the name in Penna.

Wife, Ann David, of Machynlleth ; sister to David David, of the same par.

WILLIAM THOMAS, of Machynlleth, co. Montg., yeoman ; nephew of William Thomas, of Radnor, who d. 1689 (see latter's will). Rmd. to Penna., about 1690. Fd. Freeholder of 100 a. ld. in Radnor. D. 1726.

Wife, Margaret ———.

Children (surname Thomas): 1. John, m. Mary Orme; 2. Ann, m. Evan Robert; s. Robert Ellis, of Radnor; 3. Thomas Thomas, m., 1708, Thamar, dau. Samuel Miles.

MARY TUDOR, of par. of Machynlleth, co. Montg., spinster; dau. Tudor ——, and Katherine David (or Davis). Rmd. to Penna., 1884. She m., 1686, Richard Orme.

HUGH SAMUEL (or Samuels), prob. of near Bala, co. Mer.; s. Samuel ——. Rmd. to Haverford. Penna., before 1692. Had bro. in Penna.

Wife ——.

Descendants surnamed Samuel, and Samuels.

JOHN SCOURFIELD, of par. of Narberth, co. Pemb., gentleman; s. and h. of Morris Scourfield, late of same place, gentleman (one of the first purchasers of land in Pennsylvania). Fd. Deed from John Scourfield to Owen Thomas, of Haverford, Penna., before 1703. The Scourfields are supposed not to have remained in the Province.

WILLIAM SMITH, of par. of Nantmell, co. Rad. Rmd. to Penna., 1698. Fd.

Wife, Elenor ——.

LEWIS WALKER, of co. Mer. Rmd. to Penna., 1687. Fd. Freeholder of 300 a. ld. in Radnor, Penna.

Wife, Mary Morris.

For descendants, see "Walker Genealogy," and Glenn's "Merion," 287.

RICHARD WALTER, of co. Brecon. Rmd. to Penna., before 1694, when he had a deed from Robert David for 101 a. ld. in Merion. Fd.

Wife, ——, dau. Henry Lewis, of Haverford.

Children (surname Walter): 1. William, liv. 1717; and probably others.

JOHN WATKIN, of Gwernevel (or Gwernefel), par of Llanycil, co. Mer., yeoman; s. Watkin ap ——; a kinsman of John ap Edward. He had a deed executed in Wales, in 1682, for $156\frac{1}{2}$ a. ld. in Penna., of which $76\frac{1}{2}$ a. were surveyed to him in Merion. If he rmd. to Penna., he soon returned to Wales, and he sold his Merion and Goshen ld. (the latter the balance of his original purchase), to Hugh Roberts, in 1684.

Some of the Founders

ISAAC WHELAN (or Wheeldon), of Llanrwst. co., Denb., purchaser, 1682, from John ap John, of land in Penna. Fd. He prob. rmd. to Penna., and was ancestor to a family of Whelan, or else a near kinsman of his.

DAVID WILLIAM (or Williams), of par. of Llanddeilo Vawr, co. Carm., gentleman (descended from Princes of South Wales). Rmd. to Penna. (with family), 1693.

EVAN JOHN WILLIAM (alias Evan Jones), of par. of Llangelynin, co. Mer., husbandman; s. John William (or John ap William), of same place, husbandman. Rmd. to Merion, Penna., 1683. Fd. D. soon after his arrival in Penna., sup. without issue.

EVAN JOHN WILLIAM (or Jones), of par. of Llanvachreth, co. Mer., gentleman; s. John William, of same place. Rmd. to Penna., 1684. Fd. D.s.p. (See ped. ix.).

HUMPHREY WILLIAM, of near Bala, co. Mer.; s. William ap David John. Rmd. to Gwynedd, Penna., before 1708, having then been living for some time with the family of Griffith John, then residing in Gwynedd, but late of Merion, G. J. having died the previous year. William David John, the father, was presumed to be alive in Wales, 1708. Descendants supposed to have assumed the surname of Humphreys.

MARGARET JOHN WILLIAM, of the par. of Llangelynin, co. Mer., sup. wid. Rmd. to Merion, Penna., 1683. She was sister of Rees John William, of Merion. The father, John William, of Llangelynin, was born about 1590. Fd. She was also called Margaret Jones.

REES JOHN WILLIAM, see Jones.

ROBERT WILLIAM (or Williams). Rmd. to Penna. before 1691. Ch. E. He had a deed, 21 Jan., 1703, from William Edward (William ap Edward), for 75 a. ld. in Goshen, and in 1707, he purchased 300 a. in the same township from Edward Jones, surgeon.

Wives: (1) —— ; (2) Gwen Cadwalader, m. 1691.

WILLIAMS, see Powel.

ELIZABETH WILLIAMS, of Llyndedwydd, near Bala, co. Mer., wid. of Robert ap Hugh (or Pugh); dau. William Owen (or William ap Owen), of par. of

Llanfor (Admon, 8 Sept., 1640), a freeholder, and Agnes verch Edward. Rmd. to Merion, Penna., with her s. Hugh Roberts. Fd. D. in Merion, 1699.

Children (surname Roberts) : 1. Hugh ; 2. Gainor.

ELLIS WILLIAMS (bro. Robert, of Goshen). Rmd. to Penna., prob. about 1700. He purchased lands in Goshen. from Edward Jones, surgeon, 1720.

HUGH WILLIAMS, of near Bala, co. Mer., yeoman, b. about 1660 ; s. William Pugh. Rmd. to Radnor, Penna., before 1700. Freeholder in Radnor. Liv. 1708. (See Pugh).

HUMPHREY WILLIAMS, of near Bala, co. Mer. Rmd. to Penna., supposedly in 1698.

JAMES WILLIAMS, of par. of Kilycwm, co. Carm., blacksmith. Rmd. to Penna., 1699. Ch. E. Freeholder in Cheltenham. D. 1707.

Wife, Ann Lewis of Haverford (m. 1699).

Children (surname Williams) : (mentioned, but not named in will).

JAMES WILLIAMS, of par. of Kilycwm, co. Carm., yeoman. Rmd. to Haverford, Penna., before 1699. Fd.

Wife, Ann Lewis ; m. 1699.

LUMLEY WILLIAMS, of town of Radnor, bachelor. Rmd. to near Philadelphia, Penna., 1698. He was prob. desct. of Lumley Williams. of Ystym-Colwyn (which estate the latter got by marriage with Dorothy, dau. and h. of Thomas ap Rhys) ; but in what way is uncertain, as a number of descts. bore the name of Lumley. Fd. Prob. Freeholder in Radnor. D.s.p.

THOMAS WILLIAMS, b. St. Austell, Cornwall, 1697; s. Andrew, of same place, of Welsh descent. Rmd. to Philadelphia, Penna., 1733. D. 1734-5. Fd.

Wife, Mary Reed, b. 1694, near Menheniot, Liscard.

Children : 1. Elizabeth, b. 1723 ; d. ; 2. Thomas, b. 1724 ; m. Rachel Warner ; 3. Joseph, b. 1725 ; d. ; 4. Joseph, b. 1728 ; d. ; 5. Samuel, b. 1729 ; m. Ann Thomas ; 6. Andrew, b. 1732. (For descts. see Gen. Notes of the late Howard Williams Lloyd).

MARTHA WISDOM, of par. of Malpas, co. Mon., spinster: dau. Thomas Wisdom of same place, yeoman. Rmd. to Penna., 1699.

SARAH WISDOM, of par. of Malpas, co. Mon., spinster, dau. Thomas Wisdom, of same place, yeoman. Rmd. to Penna., 1699.

JOHN WYNN, of Ruthin, co. Denb., bound for 5 years' servitude. Sailed "for Virginia," 1698, 19 Oct.

ROBERT WYNN (or Wynne), of Bryn yr Owen, co. Denb., gentleman : s. Gruffydd Wynne, of same place. Rmd. to Penna., or nearly, abt. 1682. (See ped. xvi.).

THOMAS WYNN (or Wynne) of Bryn yr Owen, co. Denb., gentleman ; s. Gruffydd Wynn, of same place. Rmd. to Maryland, before 1671. Descendants rmd. to Penna. (See ped. xvi.).

JOHN WYNNE, of Bron Fadog (or Vadog), or Bron Vadog, near Caerwys, co. Flint, gentleman ; s. Thomas ap John Wynne, of same place, gentleman. B. 1625. Rmd. to Penna., abt. 1682, or perhaps later. (See ped. xiv.).

THOMAS WYNNE, of Bron Fadog (or Vadog) or Bronvadog, near Caerwys, co. Flint, physician and surgeon ; s. Thomas ap John Wynne, of same place, gentleman. B. 1627. Rmd to Penna., 1682. (For ped. and sketch of him, see xvii.).

WILLIAM CORBET, from the Marches of Wales, was an early settler in Pennsylvania, and descended from a branch of the famous family of Corbet of Lee. Although originally Norman, and claiming descent in one line from the Plantagenets, the Corbets so frequently intermarried with the ancient Cymric Nobility as to be esteemed Welsh. F. T. Chandler and Percy M. Chandler, of Philadelphia, are descendants of William Corbet, as well as from Richard Hayes, of Ilmiston, co. Pembroke, and from Evan Powel, another of the early colonists, who claimed descent from the Princes of So. Wales.

PEDIGREE XXIV.

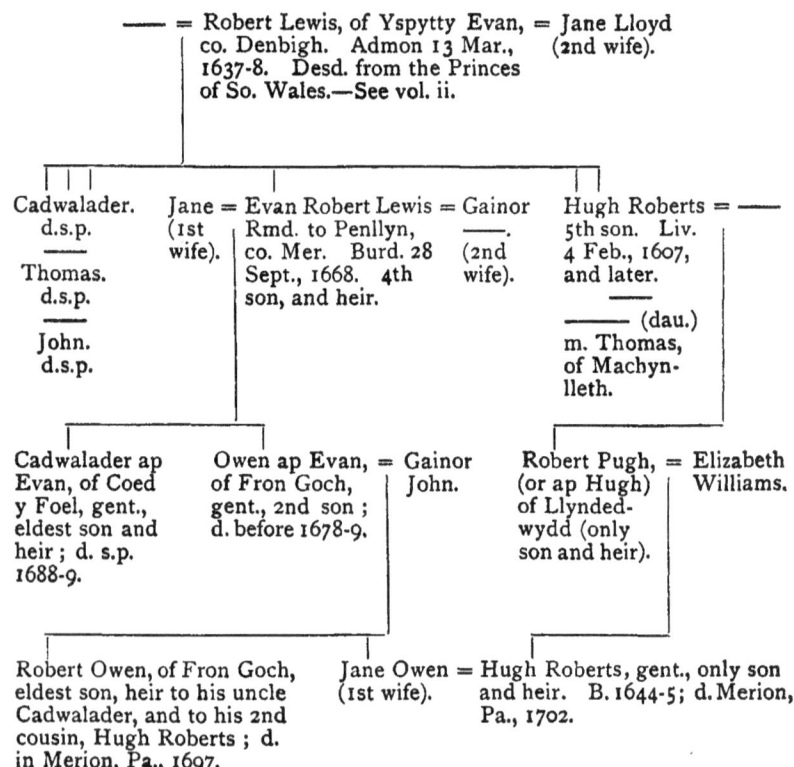

The above pedigree of Hugh Roberts is verified by the exemplification of a marriage settlement made 7 mo. 8, 1696, by Hugh Roberts in favour of Owen, his son, and Ann Bevan, wherein Robert Owen as one "of the other heirs" of the said Hugh Roberts releases any future claim he might have as next of kin to the freehold lands conveyed by the settlement. See also Exemplification Book, Vol. 7, 308, Phila., where transcript gives date, by error, as 1698.

PEDIGREE XXV.

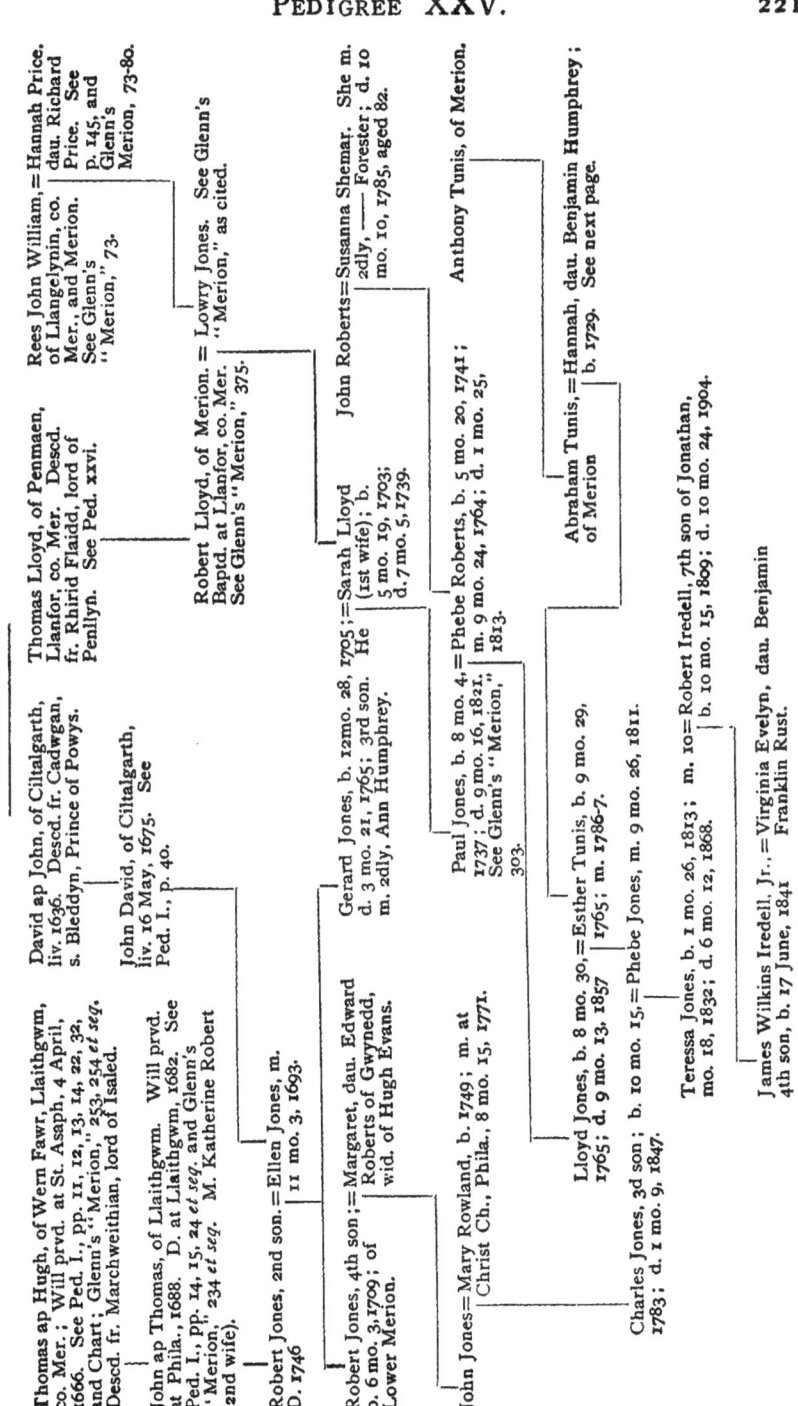

Thomas ap Hugh, of Wern Fawr, Llaithgwm, co. Mer.; Will prvd. at St. Asaph, 4 April, 1666. See Ped. I., pp. 11, 12, 13, 14, 22, 32, and Chart; Glenn's "Merion," 253, 254 *et seq.* Descd. fr. Marchweithian, lord of Isaled.

David ap John, of Ciltalgarth, liv. 1696. Descd. fr. Cadwgan, s. Bleddyn, Prince of Powys.

Thomas Lloyd, of Penmaen, Llanfor, co. Mer. Descd. fr. Rhirid Flaidd, lord of Penllyn. See Ped. xxvi.

Rees John William, = Hannah Price, of Llangelynin, co. Mer., and Merion. See Glenn's "Merion," 73. dau. Richard Price. See p. 145, and Glenn's Merion, 73-80.

John ap Thomas, of Llaithgwm. Will prvd. at Phila., 1688. D. at Llaithgwm, 1682. See Ped. I., pp. 14, 15, 24 *et seq.* and Glenn's "Merion," 334 *et seq.* M. Katherine Robert (2nd wife).

John David, of Ciltalgarth, liv. 16 May, 1675. See Ped. I., p. 40.

Robert Lloyd, of Merion. = Lowry Jones. See Glenn's Baptd. at Llanfor, co. Mer. See Glenn's "Merion," 375. "Merion," as cited.

Robert Jones, 2nd son. = Ellen Jones, m. D. 1746. 11 mo. 3, 1693.

Gerard Jones, b. 12mo. 28, 1705; = Sarah Lloyd d. 3 mo. 21, 1765; 3rd son. He (1st wife); b. m. 2dly, Ann Humphrey. 5 mo. 19, 1703; d. 7 mo. 5, 1739.

John Roberts = Susanna Shemar. She m. 2dly, —— Forester; d. 10 mo. 10, 1785, aged 82.

Anthony Tunis, of Merion.

Robert Jones, 4th son; = Margaret, dau. Edward b. 6 mo. 3, 1709; of Roberts of Gwynedd, Lower Merion. wid. of Hugh Evans.

Paul Jones, b. 8 mo. 4, = Phebe Roberts, b. 5 mo. 20, 1741; 1737; d. 9 mo. 16, 1821. m. 9 mo. 24, 1764; d. 1 mo. 25, See Glenn's "Merion," 1813. 303.

Abraham Tunis, = Hannah, dau. Benjamin Humphrey; of Merion b. 1729. See next page.

John Jones = Mary Rowland, b. 1749; m. at Christ Ch., Phila., 8 mo. 15, 1771.

Lloyd Jones, b. 8 mo. 30, = Esther Tunis, b. 9 mo. 29, 1765; d. 9 mo. 13, 1857 | 1765; m. 1786-7.

Phebe Jones, m. 9 mo. 26, 1811.

Charles Jones, 3d son; b. 10 mo. 15, = 1783; d. 1 mo. 9, 1847.

Teresa Jones, b. 1 mo. 26, 1813; m. 10 = Robert Iredell, 7th son of Jonathan, mo. 18, 1832; d. 6 mo. 12, 1868. b. 10 mo. 15, 1809; d. 10 mo. 24, 1904.

James Wilkins Iredell, Jr. = Virginia Evelyn, dau. Benjamin 4th son, b. 17 June, 1841 Franklin Rust.

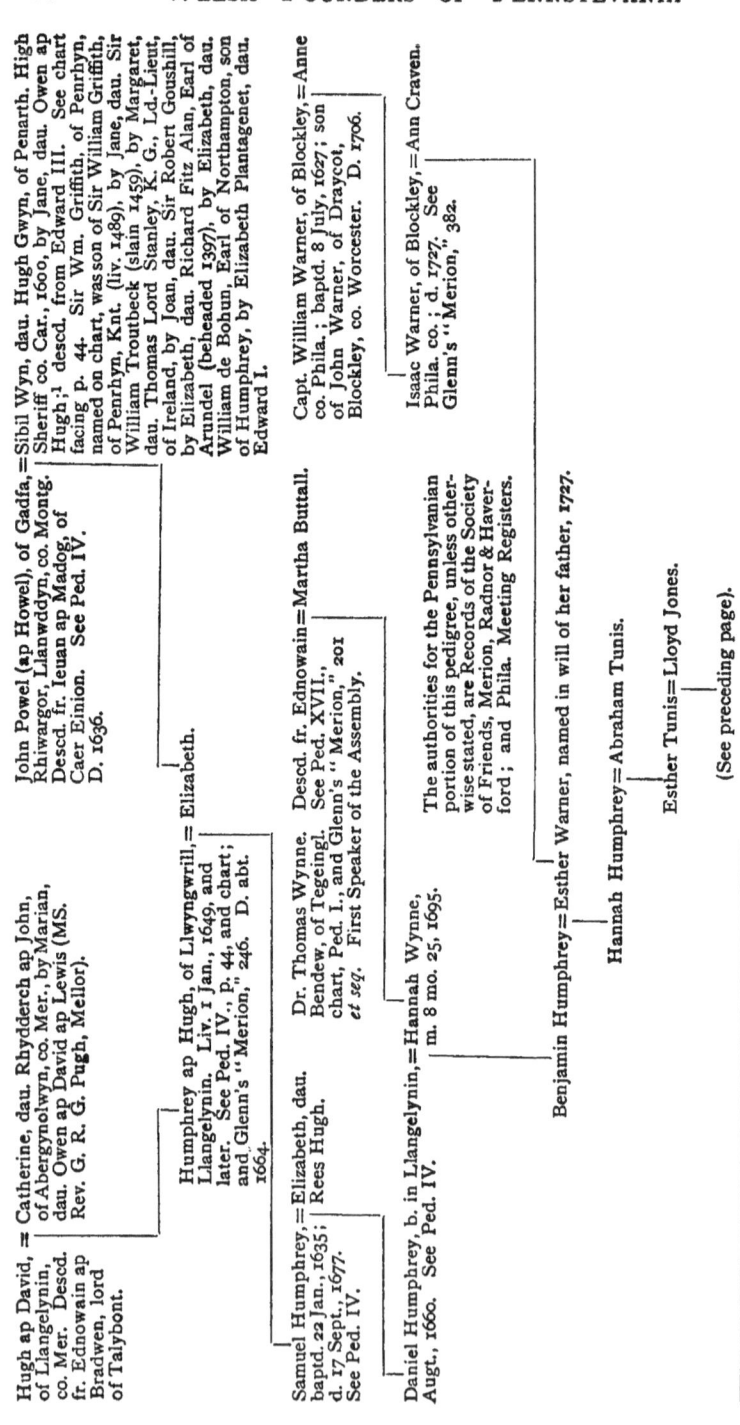

Hugh ap David, = Catherine, dau. Rhydderch ap John, of Llangelynin, of Abergynolwyn, co. Mer., by Marian, co. Mer. Descd. dau. Owen ap David ap Lewis (MS. fr. Ednowain ap Rev. G. R. G. Pugh, Mellor). Bradwen, lord of Talybont.

John Powel (ap Howel), of Gadfa, = Sibil Wyn, dau. Hugh Gwyn, of Penarth, High Rhiwargor, Llanwddyn, co. Montg. Sheriff co. Car., 1600, by Jane, dau. Owen ap Descd. fr. Ieuan ap Madog, of Hugh;[1] descd. from Edward III. See chart Caer Einion. See Ped. IV. facing p. 44. Sir Wm. Griffith, of Penrhyn, D. 1636. named on chart, was son of Sir William Griffith, of Penrhyn, Knt. (liv. 1489), by Jane, dau. Sir William Troutbeck (slain 1459), by Margaret, dau. Thomas Lord Stanley, K. G., Ld.-Lieut. of Ireland, by Joan, dau. Sir Robert Goushill, by Elizabeth, dau. Richard Fitz Alan, Earl of Arundel (beheaded 1397), by Elizabeth, dau. William de Bohun, Earl of Northampton, son of Humphrey, by Elizabeth Plantagenet, dau. Edward I.

Humphrey ap Hugh, of Llwyngwrill, = Elizabeth.
Llangelynin. Liv. 1 Jan., 1649, and
later. See Ped. IV., p. 44, and chart;
and Glenn's "Merion," 246. D. abt.
1664.

Dr. Thomas Wynne. Descd. fr. Ednowain = Martha Buttall.
Bendew, of Tegeingl. See Ped. XVII.,
chart, Ped. I., and Glenn's "Merion," 201
et seq. First Speaker of the Assembly.

Capt. William Warner, of Blockley, = Anne co. Phila.; baptd. 8 July, 1627; son of John Warner, of Draycot, Blockley, co. Worcester. D. 1706.

Samuel Humphrey, = Elizabeth, dau.
baptd. 22 Jan., 1635; Rees Hugh.
d. 17 Sept., 1677.
See Ped. IV.

Isaac Warner, of Blockley, = Ann Craven. Phila. co.; d. 1727. See Glenn's "Merion," 382.

Daniel Humphrey, b. in Llangelynin, = Hannah Wynne,
Augt., 1660. See Ped. IV. m. 8 mo. 25, 1695.

The authorities for the Pennsylvanian portion of this pedigree, unless otherwise stated, are Records of the Society of Friends, Merion, Radnor & Haverford; and Phila. Meeting Registers.

Benjamin Humphrey = Esther Warner, named in will of her father, 1727.

Hannah Humphrey = Abraham Tunis.

Esther Tunis = Lloyd Jones.

(See preceding page).

---

[1] Owen ap Hugh, of Bodeon, Esq., was High Sheriff of Anglesey, 1579-80; d. 1613, son of Hugh ap Owen ap Meyrick ap Llewelyn ap Halkyn, of Bodeon. Owen (or Owain) ap Meyrick, his father, and their wives, are represented in glass in Llangadwaladr Church, the portraits having been painted during life.

IREDELL-JONES.

James Wilkins Iredell, Jr., 4th son of Robert and Teressa (Jones) Iredell (see chart), was born in Norristown, Montgomery County, Pennsylvania, 17th June, 1841. In an ancient Norman MS. the first English ancestor of the Iredells is thus referred to : "Sir Pierre d'Ancome followed William the Norman and was present at the battle of Hastings; the king being pressed and in danger of his life Sir Pierre is stated to have rescued him by slaying those around, to whom the King said—"Sir Pierre thou hast given me Air (Eyre) to breathe. . . . The Conqueror subsequently gave him large tracts of land about Dale, or Dell," from which circumstances he is said to have assumed the surname of Eyredale, corrupted to Iredell ("Carews MSS., Bib : Coll.").[1]

Thomas Iredell, the great-great grandfather of James Wilkins Iredell, Jr., was son of Robert and Ellinore (Jackson) Iredell, and was born at Rigg Bank, in the County of Cumberland, England, 1676, baptized in December of the same year. He removed to the Province of Pennsylvania in 1700 (arriving at Philadelphia in the month of October), and brought with him this certificate which was presented for record to the Friends Meeting at Philadelphia.

From our monthly meeting upon Pardsay Cragg, in Cumberland, ye 27th of 6th month, 1700, to friends in Pennsilvania or other parts of America. Dear Friends and Brethren.—Ye tender salutations of our dearest love of truth always continues and reaches forth to you; the account we give you is in behalf of a young man ye bearer hereof, Thomas Iredell, who this day has laid before us ye transporting of himself into Pennsilvania requesting our certificate along with him.

We therefore certifie to all where he may come, that he has of late years come frequently among Friends, his carrage appears to be sober and truth like, those who know him best give no other account but well; he comes with consent of his mother, though no Friend; and inquiry hath been made as to his clearness in relation to marrage, but nothing appears to ye contrary. We need not further enlarge but subscribe ourselves your friends, and brethren in behalf of the aforesaid meeting.

Tho. Tiffin,	William Dixon.	Josias Ritson,
John Wilson,	John Nolson,	Tho. Watson,
John Burnyeat,	James Dickinson,	Wm. Bouch.

The last time Mr. James Wilkins Iredell was in England, he visited the Iredell home at Rigg Bank. The ancient mansion and the surrounding buildings, were in excellent repair. The date "1587" is cut in stone above one of the front windows of the house, and above

---

[1] According to the MS. quoted, which the writer has not seen, the crest of the Iredell family was a dexter arm embowed in armour ppr. tarnished, holding in the hand a sword. In connection with the traditions regarding the origin of the name, it should be borne in mind that the Conqueror would have spoken in French, and not in English.

the fireplace in the dining hall is carved "T.I. 1682." The property is now owned by John Iredell, who lives at Cokermouth. Thomas Iredell purchased land in the township of Horsham, county of Philadelphia, on which he erected a large stone house fronting on the York Road, on the hall door of which was an iron knocker, with "T.I. 1709," drilled in small holes. He married, 3 mo. 9, 1705, in the Friends Meeting House, Second and Market Streets, Philadelphia, Rebecca Williams, and had, besides other issue, Robert, born 1 mo. 4, 1721, of whom presently.

Mr. Iredell is also descended from Jan Lucken, as shewn in the Biographical Annals of Montgomery County, Pennsylvania.

"Jan Lucken and Mary Tyson, his wife, with thirteen other families, came from Crefeld, Germany; sailed from London on the ship *Concord*, arriving at Philadelphia, October 6, 1683, and settled at Germantown, now part of Philadelphia. They had eleven children." Peter Lucken, 7th son of Jan and Mary, was born 1 mo. 30, 1697, and married 1 mo., 28, 1719, Gainor Evans.

Robert Iredell, son of Thomas and Rebecca Iredell, was born 1 mo. 4, 1721; died 1779; he married 2 mo. 29, 1745, Hannah Lucken (born 8 mo. 21, 1727; died 1812), daughter of Peter and Gainor Lucken.

Jonathan Iredell, son of Robert and Hannah Iredell, was born 10 mo. 17, 1765, died 1850. He married, 10 mo. 1, 1798, Hannah Kirk, (born 9 mo. 26th, 1767; died in 1848), daughter of Rynear and Elizabeth Bliss Kirk.[1]

Robert Iredell, seventh son of Jonathan and Hannah Iredell, was born 10 mo. 15, 1809; died 10mo, 21, 1904; he married 10 mo. 18, 1832, Teressa Jones, born 1 mo. 23rd, 1813; died 6 mo. 12th, 1868, daughter of Charles and Phebe Jones (see chart).

James Wilkins Iredell's mother, on her father's side, was a descendant of John ap Thomas of Llaithgwm, near Bala; and on her mother's side, from Doctor Thomas Wynne of Bron Fadog, near Caerwys, North Wales. He sailed from London with William Penn in the ship "Welcome," and arrived in Philadelphia, October, 1682. Dr. Wynne was the Speaker of the First Pennsylvania Assembly 1682-1683; a member of the Assembly 1688, and Justice of the Peace for Sussex

---

[1] Mr. Iredell has the marriage certificate of his great grandfather, Rynear Kirk to Elizabeth Bliss Wilkins, widow, dated the first day of the fifth month 1766; and he has two pewter plates, marked "E.B." (Elizabeth Bliss), which are more than 150 years old. He also has the marriage certificate of his grandfather, Jonathan Iredell to Hannah Kirk, daughter of Rynear and Elizabeth Kirk, dated the fifth day of the tenth month 1792. Both certificates are beautifully written on parchment and are well preserved.

Pedigree XXV.—Iredell-Jones

County, 1689; he was also appointed Judge for the years 1690-1693 (see Chart, Pedigree I., and Pedigree XVII.)

Mr. Iredell was educated in the Public School, and at Tremont Seminary in Norristown, Pennsylvania. In August, 1861, he enlisted in the Fifty-first Pennsylvania Regiment of Infantry, commanded by Col. John F. Hartranft, and served until the end of the war. His first experience in the Army was with the Burnside expedition to North Carolina. Major General Ambrose E. Burnside commanded the Army, the Navy being under the command of Flag-Officer Commodore L. M. Goldsborough. After the battle of Newbern, the regiment was ordered to Washington, D.C., and became part of the Ninth Army Corps, under the command of Major General Burnside. December 10th, 1862, after the battle of Fredericksburg, General Burnside was appointed to command the Department of the Ohio, with headquarters at Cincinnati, at which place he arrived March 10th, 1863. After the siege of Knoxville, Tennessee, the Ninth Army Corps was ordered to return to the Army of the Potomac.

January 12th, 1867, Mr. Iredell was appointed General Agent for the Cincinnati Mutual Life for Southern Ohio. In 1870, he was elected Secretary of the Home Mutual Life Insurance Company of Cincinnati, which position he held until the Company re-insured in the Union Central.

October 6th, 1868, Mr. Iredell married Virginia Evelyn, daughter of Benjamin Franklin Rust of Kentucky. Their children were: Teressa J. Iredell, who married, 10th April, 1901, John Omwake,; Charles Jones Iredell, married, 20th November, 1900, Adelaide H. Monfort; Frank Rust Iredell, died in infancy; Virginia Rust Iredell, married, 6th October, 1908, John Tenney, Jr., of Plainfield, New Jersey. Benjamin Franklin Rust was born in Winchester, Virginia, November 28th, 1816; died March 16th, 1873. He married, 23rd January, 1838, Mary Theodosia Bradford. She was born in Lexington, Kentucky, August 13th, 1820; died in Cincinnati, December 26th, 1901. Mrs. Iredell's great great grandfathers, Rust and Bradford, served with credit during the War of the Revolution.

January 1st, 1872, Mr. Iredell was appointed Superintendent of Western Agencies by The Penn Mutual Life Insurance Company of Philadelphia, with headquarters in Cincinnati. February 3rd, 1887, he was appointed General Manager for Ohio, Kentucky and Tenessee. January 1st, 1910, he formed a partnership with his son, Charles Jones Iredell. At the second annual meeting of the National Association of Life Underwriters held in Detroit, 1891, he was elected a member of the Executive Committee and served in that position twenty years.

Mr. Iredell is a member of Avon Lodge, F. & A. M. No. 542, Cincinnati Chapter Royal Arch Masons, No. 2, Cincinnati Council of Royal and Select Master No. 1, Cincinnati Commandery of Knights Templars, No. 3, The Ancient Accepted Scottish Rite of Free Masonry of the Northern Jurisdiction of the United States. February 16th, 1881, he received the Thirty-third and last degree. October, 1888, 1889, and 1890, he was elected M. E. Grand High Priest of the Grand Chapter of Royal Arch Masons of the State of Ohio. He has been for many years President of the Board of Trustees of the Ohio Masonic Home at Springfield. He is a member of the Cincinnati Country Club; the Cincinnati Commercial Association; the Society of Colonial Wars, and the Grand Army of the Republic, Fred C. Jones No. 401.

PEDIGREE XXVI.

Robert, Thomas, and Gaynor Lloyd, were early in Merion. The latter m. Rowland —— who d. in Wales. Their child bur. at Merion. Gaynor m. 2dly, Robert Jones. According to custom she did not change her surname at marriage; but continued to subscribe herself *Gaynor Lloyd*. Robert Lloyd is supposed to have been in Penna. 1692. Perhaps he came with his mother, Lowry, 1686, leaving Thomas and Gaynor in Wales. If, however, Gaynor m. before 1686, Robert and Thomas may have remained with her. Such separation of families, incidental to emigration, was common. That Robert Lloyd was bro. to Thomas and Gaynor is proved by former's will of 1714, and by signatures to m. certifs. Gaynor Lloyd witnessed m. of Hugh Roberts and Elizabeth John, at Llwyn y Braner, Llanfor, 1689. Her identity is established by comparison of her sig. on this certif. with her subsequent sigs. Robert Lloyd was overseer to will of Robert Owen, b. at Fron Goch (adjoining Llwyn y Braner and Penmaen), 1697. Thomas Lloyd was at Penmaen 1691-2, and named in will of Ellis ap Hugh of

Pedigree XXVI.

Gwernefel, Llanycil (near above places), of 24 Feb., 1691; provd. at St. Asaph, 26 March, 1692. Evan Owen of Fron Goch, bro. to Robert, and Hugh Griffith, cousin to the Owens, witness this will.

Robert Lloyd, in will of 1714, appoints "my brethren Robert Jones, Richard Jones, Thomas Lloyd, John Jones," and certain "friends," overseers. H. W. Lloyd supposed John Jones identical with J. J. bro. of Richard, and of Lowry (Robert's wife). From other records it since appears that this J. J. was s. of Thomas John Evan of Radnor, by Lowry, wid. of Thomas Lloyd of Penmaen; therefore half bro. to Robert Lloyd. Robert Lloyd was baptd. at Llanfor, 14 Jan., 1667-8 (1668 N.S.): *Robertus fil. Tho: lloyd* (D.R.T.) Entries *in re* Thomas and Gaynor not surely identified. Thomas Lloyd, the father, was a tenant farmer, and also a poet of note. Traditionally, he was s. of Evan Lloyd ap Rhydderch, who held estates in Llanfor and Llanycil, which is confirmed by Evan's will of 29 Jan., 1671; provd. at St. Asaph, 20 Mch., 1672-3. Lowry, wife of Thomas, was, perhaps, sis. to Edward Foulke. From succession to lands held by Evan Lloyd, Llanycil Reg., wills and Admons. at St. Asaph, and visit. pedigrees:

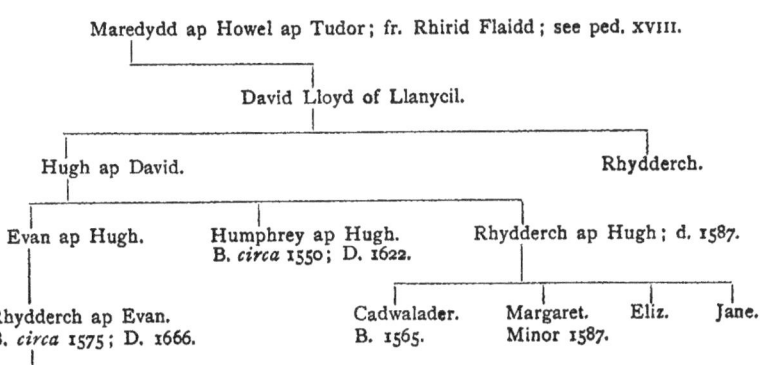

Robert Lloyd m. Llowry Jones, dau. Rees John William; for her ped. see Glenn's "Merion," pp. 73-81, 94-75; "Lloyd Manuscripts," ed. by T. A. Glenn, for Hist. Socty. of Penna., "Jones"; and pp. 145-6, 185 of this vol. Refs. to Robert Lloyd, his ancestry and descendants: Glenn's "Merion," 40-44 (as to his parents), 83-86, 375; "Lloyd Manuscripts," "Lloyd." Lloyd MSS., H.S. of Pa. (general); Pedigree XVIII., and pp. 191-2, this vol. Lowry Jones was a descendant of Tudor Vaughan, bro. of Owain Glyndwr (Glendower), and of Edward I.

Isaac Lloyd, b. 1739, s. Richard (by Hannah Sellers), s. Robert Lloyd and Lowry Jones, m., 1765, Ann Gibbons (fr. Ithel Fychan of Mostyn). Their s. Isaac, b. 1768, m. Elizabeth Gibbons (fr. Ithel Fychan); had: (a) Joseph, (b) Isaac, (c) Ann, m. Rowland Jones, (d) George, (e) John, *of whom presently*, (f), Sarah, (g) Richard, (h) Elizabeth, m. Robert Howell, (j) James, (k) Mary, (l) Hannah, m. James Neall, (m) William. John, 4th s. of Isaac and Elizabeth, b. 1805, m., 1837, Esther Barton Malcolm; had: (a) Malcolm, *of whom presently*, (b) Isaac, (c) Elizabeth, (d) Estelle, m. Henry T. Coates, *of whom presently*, (e) John, (f) Anne Morris, m. William M. Coates, *of whom presently*, (g) Laura, m. George M. Coates, *of whom presently*, (h) Emma Malcolm, m. Ashton Souder, (j) Mary Barcroft, m. Norman M. Jones; had Lloyd Peniston, Ethel Marriott, Edwin Olney. Malcolm, 1st s. of John, m. 1869, Annie, dau. Dr. S. B. Howell, s. Richard W. (by Mary T. Carpenter, a descendant of Thomas Lloyd of Dolobran, Lieut.-Governor of Pa., and of Edward I., and Henry IV., Kings of England); see Glenn's "Merion," 345-6; "Lloyd and Carpenter Families." Children of Malcolm Lloyd: (a) Howell, (b) Malcolm, (c) Stacy Barcroft, (d) Francis Vernon, (e) Anna Howell, (f) Esther, (g) Mary Carpenter.

Pedigree XXVI.

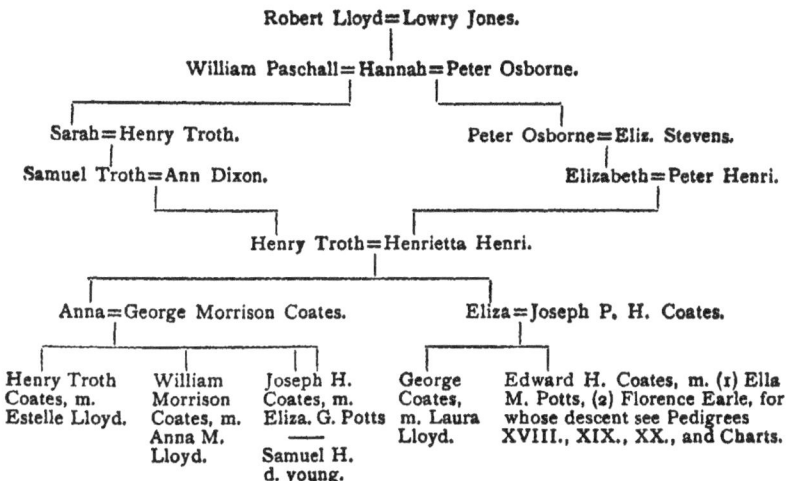

COATES.

Richard de Cotes.
1100 (*circa*). Chart. undated. [Woodcote deeds.] [Harl. MS. 1396, fo. 82b S. fo. 70b.-71b 83; Harl. MS. 1241, fo. 70b. S. ff. 70b.-71b.]

William de Cotes, s. Richard.

Hugh de Cotes, s. William.
Deed (undated). Adam de Monte to Hugh, son of William, son of Richard de Cotes, for lands at Eccleshall. [Woodcote deed.

Walter de Cotes, s. Hugh.
[Harl. MS. as above.]

Sir Robert de Cotes, Knight, s. Walter.
In Harl. ped., *Robertus de Cotes miles*. 1245-1257. Chart. of Sir James de Aldithle, to the Lord Bishop of Coventry and Lichfield, witd. by Robert de Cotes. [Woodcote deed.]

21 Edw. I. (1293). Deed, John de Aston (de Cotes), s. Robert de Cotes, confirming a grant which Robert (his father), son of Walter de Cotes made of lands in Cotes and Doddington. [Woodcote deed.]

John de Cotes, s. Robert, lord of Cotes, and *(jure uxoris)* of Aston, in Muckelston.
21 Edw. I. (1293). Deed, John de Aston (de Cotes), son of Robert and grandson of Walter as above.

Robert de Cotes ("19 Edw. II."), s. John. [Harl. ped.]

18 Edw. I. (1290). Johannis filius Rogeri le Child grants to Robert de Cotes and Alice his wife those lands which he (John) had of the gift of Roger his father, to the said Robert and Alice and their heirs; remainder to heirs of said Roger. [Woodcote deed.]

Robert m. Alice, dau. of Sir Richard Knightly, by Sibill, who had been 2nd wife of Roger lé Child. [Woodcote deed; "The Ancestor," vol. ii., 4.]

Robert de Cotes, of Cotes ("18 Edw. III."). [Harl. MS.; Woodcote deed.]

3 Edw. III. (1330). Robert Cotes a wit. to deeds *in. re* the Austin Priory of Trentham. [Salt. xi., 326-7.] 16 Edw. III. (1343). At the Pleas of Assize held at Stafford, before Royse Hillary *et al.* on the Feast of the Circumcision, Robert de Cotes, who bought an Assize of *novel disseisin* against John, son of John de Burgylin *et al. in. re* tenements in Knutton, did not appear. He and his sureties in *misericordia*. [Plea Roll, Staff., 16 Edw. III.]

21 Edw. III., Mich. De Banco. Robert de Cotes sued William de Eddesley and William de Holwebrok, in a plea that each should render an acct. for the time that they were receivers of his money. The defts. failed to appear, and the Sheriff returned that they had nothing attachable. He was ordered to produce them on the Quindene of St. Hilary. [Plea Roll, Staff., 21 Edw. III.] (Continued at Easter term, 22 Edw. III., to following Assize).

Robert m. Isabell, who by her first husband had Elford in dower. [Woodcote deed.]

Sir Thomas de Cotes, Kt., s. Robert. In Harl. ped. *Thomas de Cotes miles Dominus de Cotes.* He m. Elizabeth, dau. and h. of John ——.

10 Rich. II., Feast of St. Bernard the Apostle. Deed, *Johannis Spinke Cappelanius* [to] *Thomas filius Roberti de Cotes et Elizabeth uxor ejus*, for messuages in Cotes. [Woodcote deed.]

Humphrey Cotes, s. of Sir Thomas.

16 Hen. VI., a month fr. Easter Day. Fine (f.c.) Humphrey Cotes plt. William Pollesworth and Joan his wife, deforcs., touching 2 mess., 50 a. ld., 40 a. wood, and 10 a. pasture, in Alreston. Wm. and Joan remit rights to Humphrey and his heirs, for 20 m. sil. [Roll of Feet of Fine, Staff., 16 Hen. VI.]

19 Hen. VI., Octaves of St. Martin. Fine (f.c.), Humphrey Cotes Arm. and Roger Clerk, plts., William Bucknale and Margaret his wife, deforcs., touching ⅓ Flosbrooke. Wm. and Margaret remit rights to plts., and heirs of Humphrey, for 20 m. sil. [Roll of Feet of Fine Staff., 19 Hen. VI.]

22 Hen. VI., 6 June. Writ addressed to Humphrey Coates, one of His Majesty's Justices.

Humphrey m. Joanna Daventre.

Ellen Calvaley sometime wf. of John le Child, had ¼ of Enkerton in dower, and Agnes Knightley, sometime wf. of Robert de Falhurst gave her part of Enkerton to said Ellen 16 Rich. II. These two parts, being all Enkerton, came to Thomas, son of Robert, son of Robert de Cotes, father of Humphrey. [Woodcote deed.]

John Cotes of Cotes, High Sheriff of Stafford, 35 Hen. VI.; s. of Humphrey. [Harl. ped.] Lord of the manor of Cotes, and of Wilbrighton, Beffcote and Woodcote.

1472, 20 Augt. Will of John Cotes Esquire. To be burd. in chapel of St. Mary, Monastery of Lilleshall. Bequest for prayers for his soul, and for Elizabeth, testator's wife, and brothers and sisters. Bequest for effigies and arms on tomb. Exors., wife Elizabeth, and son Humphrey. A 2d will disposes of enfeoffed estates. Testator's "now wife" to have life interest in same, for her and "our children." Lands in Cotes, Wilbrighton and Beffcotes. Childn. be sent "to scole." Dowry for dau. Johane. Testator's brother Robert; "cozens," Sir Thomas Knightly and Humphrey Swinnerton. Wts: Thomas Acton, Humphrey Swinnerton, Humphrey Cotes, bro. of testator, *et al.* Provd. at Lichf., 6 Nov., 1472.

John Cotes m. 1st ——; 2dly, Elizabeth, dau. and co. h. of Thomas Dowaton, a descendant of (1) Ralph St. Owen, *temp.* William I., (2) of Walter, High Constable of England, *temp.* Hen. I., and, (3) of Bernard Newmarch of Brechnock, who m. Nest, dau. of Rhys ap Tudor, Prince of So. Wales (see vol. ii.)

ISSUE:

i. Humphrey, under 20 yrs., 147 —; slain at Bosworth Field, 1485. He m. Eleanor Blunt, and had: John, ancestor of Cotes of Woodcote, John (2d son of the name), Nicholas, and dau.

ii. John, *of whom presently.*

iii. Richard of Aylesbury.

iv. John, of Chrishall Abbey, Yorkshire, Steward.

v. Thomas, of Cristall Abbey, Yorkshire.

John Cotes, s. John Cotes. Died 1518.

"John Cotes, 2d son of John Cotes of Cotes com. Stafford and Woodcote, com. Salop, Esq.; died 1518." [From a deed; see ped. Leic. N. and Q., ii., 39.]

John Cotes, s. John, s. John de Cotes. Of Prestwood, Ellaston, near Norbury, Staffordshire.

1537, 16 Nov. Will of John Cootes of Prestwood. Testator mentions sons Alexander and Thomas; daus. Margaret and Joane; wife Elizabeth; brother Thomas; son-in-law Roger Byllynger. Provd. at Lich. 5 Feb., 1537-8.

Alexander Cotes, of Withington, Church Leigh, s. John.

"Alexander Cotes of Whittington (*sic*) co. Stafford [son of] John Cotes of Norbury, co. Stafford [son of] John Cotes, 2d son of John Cotes of Cotes, co. Stafford, and Woodcote, co. Salop, Esq." [Leic. N. and Q., ii., 39.]

1569-70, 4 Mar. Admon. estate of Alexander Cottes of Leigh, granted to Agnes relict, and Francis and John, sons. of decd. Inv., 13 Jan., 1569, accounts for monies due John Cotes, Thomas Cotes, Francis Cotes, and Frances Smyth (children of decd.), and others. The sums so owing appear to have been due fr. their mother's estate. The ch. of Robert Atkyns, decd., son-in-law, included. [Lich. Prob. Reg.]

Alexander Cotes m. 1st, Margaret, dau. and h. of John Justinian of Withington; m. 2dly, Agnes. [Visit. co. Staff.]

Thomas Cotes, 3d s. Alexander; of Sproxton, Bittersly, and Syston.

1569-70, 13 Jan. Named with his brothers and sister as creditor to his father. 14 Eliz., Easter. Fine, Thomas Cootes pltf., Gilbert Barye, *et al.*, deforcs., touching lands and tenements in Sproxton, Leicestershire. [Roll of Feet of Fine, Leicester, 14 Eliz.]

14-15 Eliz., Mich. Fine, Thomas Cotes *et al.*, pltfs., and George, Earl of Salop, *et al.*, deforcs. touching the manor and lordship of Bitteslye. (Roll of Feet of Fine, Leicest., 14-15 Eliz.]

1613, 27 Aug. Will (nunc.) of Everard Cotes of Sproxton "in presence of Thomas Cotes *senior et al.* Testator mentions sons John, Thomas, and Mark; Elizabeth, dau. of Thomas Caye, or Caue, and Agnes (Caue) wife of Richard Fealce *et al.*; and appoints Thomas Caye, Caue, or Coye,' exor. Provd. at Leicester, 8 Oct., 1613.

1615, 20 Feb. Admon. of estate of Thomas Cotes of Syston (near Sproxton), granted to Agnes, relict. Roger Cotes of Leicester, mercer, a surety. [Act Book, Leicester.] Roger Cotes was s. of John Cotes of Ayleston, s. Alexander; therefore nephew of decedent. Thomas Cotes m. Agnes, dau. [? Lawrence] Everard, and had (a) Lawrence, (b) Everard, d. 1613.

---

1 The will of John Cootes of Ayleston (father of Thomas Coats of same place), provd. at Leicester, 17 Dec., 1603, and to which Roger Cotes, surety for Admon. of Thomas Cotes of Syston is a witness, mentions his sister, Agnes Caue or Caye.

Pedigree XXVI.

Lawrence Cotes, s. Thomas of Sproxton and Syston.

> 1615, 22 Nov. Admon. of estate of Lawrence Coates of Sproxton, decd., granted to Thomas Coates, son of decd. Nathaniel, another son, surety. The index mentions a Henry Coates *in re* Admon. ; but as bond is missing, nothing else appears. [Act Book, Leicester.]

Thomas Cotes, s. Lawrence, of age 22 Nov., 1615. He m. Elizabeth —— (d. 1651), and was burd. at Sproxton, 27 Augt., 1635.

> 1615, 22 Nov. Thomas Cotes, son and Admon. of Thomas Cotes of Sproxton. [Act Book, Leicester.]

Henry Coates (or Cotes) of Sproxton, s. Thomas. Burd. at Sproxton, 2 Jan., 1671; m. Elizabeth ——; liv. 1679.

> 1671, 3 Jan. Admon. estate of Henry Cotes of Sproxton granted to Henry Cotes, eldest son and heir of decd. [Leicester Prob. Reg.] Henry, son of Henry Cotes was surety for his cousin, John, 1671. Henry Cotes was seized of certain tenements and lands in Sproxton which had belonged to Thomas, his father, and which were the same which Thomas Cotes of Sproxton and Syston acquired 14 Eliz.
>
> Issue of Henry and Elizabeth Cotes, or Coates, of Sproxton : (a) Henry, of age 1671, (b) Thomas, bapt. 27 Dec., 1649; burd. 1651, (c) William, bapt. 15 Dec., 1654, (d) Eleanor, bapt. 14 Apl., 1657 ; burd. 31 Jan., 1657, (e) Thomas, born 26 Sept., 1659 ; *of whom presently*. (f) Deborah, burd. 24 Apl., 1679.

Thomas Coates, s. Henry, removed to Philadelphia, Pennsylvania, 1683 ; m. Beulah Jaques of Philadelphia. He became a leading merchant of the Province, and was engaged in various other business enterprises. He made several voyages to England.

> "Thomas Coates of Sproxton, Leicestershire, England." [Town Records, Chester (now Delaware) co., Penna., origi. entry of his arrival in the Province.]
>
> "Thomas Coates son of Henry and Elizabeth of Sproxton, born September 26th, 1659." [Entry in family Bible by Samuel Coates, from orig. record ; transcribed by Dr. Coates. For descds. of Thomas Coates see "Thomas Coates," by the late Henry T. Coates, Esq., of Philadelphia.
>
> Name in Sproxton and Pennsylvania records, written Cotes, Cootes, Coats, Coates.

Welsh
Founders of Pennsylvania.

Welsh Founders of Pennsylvania.

BY

THOMAS ALLEN GLENN.

VOL. II.

Oxford

[Special edition of 100 copies privately printed at the request of Mrs. Charles Roberts of Haverford, Pennsylvania.]

Fox, Jones and Company, Kemp Hall, High Street

1913

THIS BOOK IS DEDICATED

TO

THE MEMORY OF

THE LATE

CHARLES ROBERTS,

OF PHILADELPHIA.

Preface.

THIS VOLUME embodies, in a condensed form, with other data, a portion of the genealogical notes of the late Charles Roberts, of Philadelphia.

Mr. Roberts' reputation as a collector of books and manuscripts illustrative of the history of his native State, and his services as a Councillor of The Historical Society of Pennsylvania are well known; but it is not, perhaps, so generally recognized that he was also an enthusiastic and pains-taking genealogist. He was, naturally, primarily interested in the far reaching ramifications of his own family, and, after a visit to Bala, Merionethshire, from whence his ancestor, Robert Cadwalader, removed to Gwynedd, Pennsylvania, carried his researches into that neighbourhood. After Mr. Roberts' death, his widow Mrs. Lucy Branson Roberts, now of Haverford, continued these investigations, and placed the results in the hands of the writer. As both Robert Cadwalader and his wife were related to almost all of the Welsh founders of Gwynedd, as well as to many of the first colonists in Merion, the data presented is of interest to a great many persons not directly connected with the Roberts family. For instance, Jane, wife of Robert Cadwalader, was the daughter of John Evan, of Ucheldre, near Bala, son of Evan Robert Lewis. She was, therefore, a sister of William John of Gwynedd, Griffith John of Merion, and Robert John (or *Jones*) of Abington. The children of William John also assumed the surname of *Jones*, but the descendants of Griffith John called themselves *Griffiths*. Jane was also first cousin to the Evan brothers of Gwynedd, to Robert Owen of Merion, Jane, wife of

Hugh Roberts of Merion, Ellen, mother of John Cadwalader of Merion, and others. Robert Cadwalader was remotely of the same male line of descent as John Cadwalader of Merion and John Thomas of Llaithgwm, and his children traced to Sir Robert ap Rhys, of Yspytty Evan, through both father and mother. The earlier portions of the pedigrees which appear in the following pages were complied by the undersigned, who assumes responsibility for their accuracy. The pedigree of Robert Cadwalader backward from Robert ap Howel of Llangower, is, however, contained in the Heraldic Visitations of North Wales. That of Jane, his wife, down to her grandfather, Evan Robert Lewis, who was born in the Parish of Yspytty Evan, is also so recorded. The authorities for the additions to the originals are sufficiently cited in the text.

The Genealogy of the descendants of Robert Cadwalader is from MS. of Mr. Charles Roberts. The statements therein have been carefully compared with the account of the family (also by Mr. Roberts) in Howard M. Jenkins' "Historical Collections of Gwynedd," with material collected subsequent to Mr. Robert's decease, and with communications from various members of the family. Where doubtful or conflicting statements have appeared the data has been entirely omitted. Because of lack of space it has been found necessary to also omit some branches of the family.

THOMAS ALLEN GLENN.

Meliden, Prestatyn,
    North Wales, Great Britain.
        July 1st, 1913.

Table of Contents.

Charles Roberts (1846-1902), p. x., Roberts, of Gwynedd (pedigree of Robert Cadwalader, who removed from Bala to Pennsylvania, 1698-1700), Price of Plâs Iolyn and Rhiwlas, pp. 1-46.

Owen, Evans, and Allied Families. Genealogy of the Princes of South Wales, Families of Cadwalader, Edward (Edwards), Foulke, George, Griffith of Cefn Amwlch, Hugh, John, Jones, Llewelyn, Lewis, Morgan, and others, pp. 47-108.

Roberts Genealogy (descendants of Robert Cadwalader of Gwynedd), pp. 109-123.

Illustrations.

Septimus Roberts (1786-1826), facing title page.

Elihu Roberts, facing p. 1.

Effigies of Rhys ap Maredydd (or Meredydd), his wife, and their son, Sir Robert ap Rhys, facing p. 19.

Plâs Iolyn, facing p. 23.

Dr. Ellis Price, facing p. 33.

Bala Lake, showing birthplace of Robert Cadwalader, facing p. 45.

Fron Goch, facing p. 85.

Cadwalader Roberts (1777-1871), facing p. 97.

Charles Roberts, (1784-1845), facing p. 109.

Solomon W. Roberts (1811-1882), facing p. 117.

Joseph Roberts, Jr., facing p. 120.

Charles Roberts (1846=1902).

CHARLES ROBERTS, the son of Elihu and Anne (Pettit) Roberts, was born in Philadelphia, August 21, 1846. He received his preparatory education at the Friends Select School, then on Cherry Street above Eighth Street, and in September, 1860, entered Haverford College, where he remained four years and was graduated with the degree of A.B., July, 1864. He always maintained a good rank in his class, and laid the foundation of those artistic, literary, and historic tastes which remained with him throughout life. At College, also, he formed warm and lifelong friendships. Not long after graduation he entered the employ of Whitall, Tatum and Co., of Philadelphia, large manufacturers of glassware, and became a member of the firm in 1869. He retired in 1885, and did not again enter into active business life, though always a busy man, giving much of his time to the service of others and of the community.

It would be impossible here to give in detail the various public and semi-public interests which claimed his wise and thoughtful care, and which benefited so much by his support. Whatever duty he undertook was faithfully performed. Always punctual to his appointments, he gave close attention to the business in hand, and by his unusual skill in matters of detail, was often able to point out flaws or errors, and to suggest valuable alterations and additions. He was a Manager of Haverford College (1872-1902), and Secretary of the Corporation (1883-1886), and always gave that institution his warmest support. There was scarcely a literary, scientific, or historical association in Philadelphia of which he was not a member, and to the interests of several he devoted much time and thought. He was member of the Council of the Historical Society of Pennsylvania, President of the Apprentices Library, Overseer of the William Penn Charter School, active member of the Academy of Natural Sciences, of the Fairmount Park Association, etc. He was also a member of several national associations, and of charitable associations in Philadelphia. It was, however, the part Charles Roberts took in public affairs which, perhaps, above others, deserves special mention.

In 1882 he was elected member of the Common Council of Philadelphia for the Ninth Ward, and held office two years. He at once took the stand of a conscientious servant of the public. In 1886 he was again elected, and afterwards continuously re-elected, and died while still a member, having had a continuous service of sixteen years. The character of this service is well stated in the memorial resolutions of the Council itself :— " An honest, upright citizen, and a conscientious, and faithful public officer." It was also truthfully said of him, by another pen :—" His eighteen years in the Common Council of Philadelphia was a record of absolute devotion to the good of the city, and of stainless and unambitious service. No bad measure escaped his adverse vote, and no good one failed to find him on record in its favor. He studied his subject and finally became so valuable for work no one else could or would do, that he was retained by the unanimous vote of his ward and the approbation of the whole city." For thirteen years he was a member of the Finance Committee, and for a large part of the time a member of the sub-committee on appropriations. "Although often an outspoken opponent of legislation that was supported by the majority of the Chamber, he retained the personal esteem and friendship of those whom he opposed." Everyone knew that he was absolutely incorruptible, and that all his actions were dictated solely by a desire to further the public good.

He was from early years a collector of autographs and historical papers, and later of objects of art. His collection of autographs was one of the largest private collections in America, numbering as it did over 10,000 items.* In this collection he showed his taste and judgment by always, when practicable, securing papers of literary, personal, or historic interest.

His collection of Quaker literature, prints, and manuscripts was large and comprehensive. It contained, among other things, the original manuscripts of William Penn's Travels in Holland and Germany, 1677, and also an autograph unpublished diary of Penn's tour in Ireland.

Charles Roberts was a lifelong member of the Society of Friends (Orthodox), and devoted much time and attention to its interests. In private life he was retiring, even diffident, and this gave rise to a manner which at times seemed to some brusque and even severe; but "to his friends he was always warm and tender, and to his opponents generous and fair." He was modest about his work and his benefactions, and few knew the extent of the latter.

He was married to Lucy Branson Longstreth, November 23, 1892.

He suffered from ill health for a number of months, and died shortly after a surgical operation, January 23, 1902.

---

*NOTE.—This valuable collection was given by his widow to Haverford College.

Welsh Founders of Pennsylvania.

Roberts of Gwynedd.

ROBERT CADWALADER, who, with his family, removed from near Bala, Merionethshire, to Gwynedd, Pennsylvania, between the years 1698 and 1700, and whose children assumed the surname of *Roberts*,[1] was a lineal descendant of Marchweithian of Isaled. This chieftain, according to accepted accounts, was head of the eleventh of the "Fifteen Tribes" of North Wales,[2] but the "Ancient Book of Madog ap Llewelyn ap Howel,"[3] mentions him as head of the tenth tribe. "Cambrian Biography" states that Marchweithian, who is there wrongly called of Isdulas, flourished in the beginning of the eighth century, but the dates at which his descendants are known to have lived proves this to be incorrect, and there is evidence to show that he was a contemporary of Gruffydd ap Cynan, who ruled in North Wales from 1080-1137, and that he fought beside that prince in the famous battle of Mynydd Carn. Authorities agree in stating that he was an *uchelwr* (nobleman), and *arglwydd*

---

[1] The Welsh people, as a rule, did not begin to assume fixed surnames until about the close of the seventeenth century : see preface.

[2] "Cambrian Register," 1796.

[3] "Hen Llyfr Madog ab Llewelyn ab Howel Esgᵉ yn dywedyd y 15 Llwyth," (Dwnn, ii., 83).

(lord) of the Cymwd (or commot) of Isaled.[1] The latter designation simply indicates that he had been appointed by his sovereign, or superior, ruler over that district, but, according to the ancient laws the authority of an *arglwydd* was not absolute, certain of his functions, according to custom, being delegated to others, for in every cymwd there was a *maer* and a *canghellor* "discharging prescribed governmental duties, and in each cymwd a court was held by them with the aid of other officers."[2] The lord received certain dues and services from the inhabitants of the cymwd, according to their rank, and an *ebediw* (relief) on the death of a free tribesman, but his rights over the land were not precisely analogous to those held by the lord of an English manor. He might be, and often was, a *penkenedl* (chief of the kindred) and the owner, subject to tribal customs, of *tir gwelyawg* (family land)—within the cymwd. The lands of Marchweithian, "were Carwedd Fynydd, Din Cadfael, Prees, Berain, Llyweni, Gwytherin, and many other townships in the Lordship of Isaled as appears by the extent of the Lordship and Honour of Denbigh, made in the time of Edward III."[3] at which time Cynwrig Fychan, the eighth in descent from Marchweithian, was living and in possession of a part of these estates.[4]

The ancient Cymwd (or commot) of Isaled, partly corresponding to the present hundred of the same name, situate in the cantref of Rhuvoniog, in Perfeddwlad, in Gwynedd (North Wales), consisted of a district lying east of the river Aled, and about sixteen miles in length and

---

[1] "History of Powys Fadog," iv., 101; Dwnn, ii., 83, 228, 332, 342; MS. pedigree in College of Arms; MS. pedigree of John Thomas of Llaithgwm, Penllyn, dated 1682; see "Merion in the Welsh Tract," Glenn, 253, and "The Pennsylvania Magazine of History and Biography," iv., 477, &c.

[2] "The Welsh People," Rhys and Brynmor-Jones, 4th Edition, 190.

[3] Dwnn's "Visitations," ii., 228, note 2; "Cambrian Register," 1796.

[4] "History of Powys Fadog," iv., 101.

nine or ten miles across in its widest part. It comprised the existant parishes of Llannefydd, Henllan, Llansannan, Nantglyn, Cerrig y Druidion, part of Yspytty Evan, Pentre Voelas, part of Llanrhaiadr, and Denbigh, including the above named townships.[1] The bounds of the original cymwd were, it would seem, roughly speaking, about as follows: Beginning at the confluence of the rivers Elwy and Aled, on the western boundary of the parish of Llannefydd, the line followed the course of the river Aled up to its source in Llyn Aled in Hiraethog, thence including a portion of Yspytty Evan, it touched what is now the northern county line between Denbighshire and Merionethshire, at a point near Cwm Maen in the parish of Llanfor and Cwm Pen Aner in the parish of Cerrig y Druidion, at the extreme southern part of the latter parish. From thence, following the eastern boundary of Cerrig y Druidion, the line ran in a north-easterly direction, passing near Caer Ddunod, and following the western boundaries of the parishes of Llanfihangel Llyn Myfyr and Cyffylliog and the eastern boundary of Nantglyn, to a point near Llanrhaiadr, and dividing that parish, touched the river Clwyd near Lleweni. Thence, skirting the southern line of Llanelwy, now St. Asaph, it followed the course of the river Elwy to the place of beginning. Several parishes appear to have been subsequently annexed to Isaled and are now included in the hundred of that name.

Isaled, which, as we have seen, includes a portion of the Vale of Clwyd, embraces a district of varied scenery. A tourist thus describes it as viewed from near Ruthin:[2] "The Clwydian mountains spring high upon our right, and roll away towards the sea, the peaks of Fenlli and Fammau and Arthur conspicuous above the rest. Upon our left the green slopes and winding glens lead upwards through

---

[1] William Owen's "Map of Wales according to the Ancient Divisions."
[2] "Highways and Byways in North Wales," By Arthur G. Bradley.

Cyffylliog and Clocaenog to the purple table-land, the silent wilderness of the Hiraethog, where fairies dance beside the banks of lonely lakes, and belated travellers see uncanny sights, and packs of white dogs with red ears go howling through the mist on the track of phantom deer, and relics of the prehistoric age lie strewn on every side." Further north, between Denbigh and St. Asaph, we reach the fertile plough lands of the " garden of North Wales." Westward from this part of the vale, stretching beyond Henllan and Llannefydd to Bangor, is vast upland intersected by winding valleys, and yet but little known to the outside world, and formerly with but a single road, and "so," writes the tourist we have quoted, " English captains, no matter what forces were behind them, trod this treacherous track with helmet on head, and hand fast gripped upon their sword-hilt, and a lively apprehension less each lateral glen and each bosky cliff might peradventure launch upon their long extended colums an avalanche of Merioneth spearmen and Carnarvon archers." Surely no other place in Wales, or anywhere else, has witnessed a tithe of the bloodshed which, since ages before the dawn of history, has stained the soil of Isaled and the adjacent country. It would seem, indeed, as if each field of waving grain, each pleasant meadow, each upland pasture, and each purple mountain had received its baptism amid the red desolation of forgotten wars. *The Hill of Slaughter, The Vale of Execution, The Mound of Strife, The Swamp of Sobs, The Mountain of Arrows, The Rock of Wailing, The Acre of Blood, The Hill of Einion's Death, The Bloody Slope*, are a few of many similar reminders, in daily use, of a grim, but silent past.

Some twenty-six or more centuries since on the gorse and heather clad hills to the northward and westward, which fall just short of dipping their feet into the Irish Sea, the rough stone axes of the Aborigines, they of Egyptian lineage, clashed with the polished weapons of the Goidels, the advance guard of the Aryan race, and here, perhaps six centuries later, Nativi and Goidels, now allied and kindred, together faced the Ordovices, Brythons of Gaul, of the second Celtic invasion. Here, also, below Morfa Rhuddlan, the ever victorious XXth Legion formed its battle line of brass and leather, and outposts of a cohort of the Nervii shivered on the wild Mynydd Hiraethog, whilst Varus, a Roman General, has left us his name at Bodfari (the dwelling of Varus) near Llyweni, although his villa has long since crumbled to dust. Toward the close of the fourth century the wild Irish Scotti overran Isaled with fire and sword, and advancing inland burned and sacked the rich and beautiful Roman-British city of Uriconium. We are credibly informed that these pirates held Gwynedd for a generation, in the end to be destroyed or driven out by Cunedda, who, about the time of the departure of the legions, commanded at the Roman Wall, and whose military authority extended over Wales, and so well did Cunedda do his work, that, as the chronicle informs us, the Scotti "never returned again to dwell there." Thrice the Saxons won this country by sheer slaughter, mowing the land stark bare before them, and thrice the Cymry hurled them headlong back across Offa's Dyke. But lamentable as it is, the Welsh themselves, by a long series of miserable tribal wars, contributed greatly, not only to their own misery, but also to the ultimate downfall of the independence of the Principality. At one time, we are told, much of the countryside near Isaled was a desert, and many of those few of the inhabitants who survived went to earn their bread in foreign countries, and few or none ever returned to their native land.

The Norman and Plantagenet kings made the Vale of Clwyd the base of their military operations against the Welsh, and in this way arose the castles of Ruthin, Denbigh, Rhuddlan, Dyserth and Prestatyn. The conquest of Wales by Edward I., the rising of Madog, in

1294, the Rebellion of Owain Glyndwr, who, among other things, burned St. Asaph Cathedral, the Wars of the Roses, and finally the Civil War, all left their mark on this part of Denbighshire, the last event during the latter conflict being the magnificent defence of Denbigh Castle by Sir William Salusbury, the royalist governor, who, by the way, was a descendant of Marchweithian. At the present day, despite the wars and conquests through which it has passed, Isaled is typically Welsh, and there are even some remote hamlets in which the English tongue is rarely heard. But this state of things is, after all, not so very surprising, for did not Taliesin centuries ago prophesy of the Cymry, that:

"Their Lord they shall praise,
Their language they shall keep,
Their land they shall lose,
Except wild Wales."

From the scant information extant, it would appear that Marchweithian had a grant of the government of the cymwd of Isaled from Gruffydd ap Cynan sometime after the battle of Mynydd Carn, which was fought 1079-80. He is stated to have left but one son, who, in turn, had but a single heir, whose only son, we are informed, was named Tagno, and each of these, we are led to infer, were successively lords of the same cymwd, and owners of the undivided possessions of Marchweithian. Tagno, however, left three sons, and with them, in accordance with the Welsh custom of gavelkind, commenced the partition of the Isaled lands, so that in process of time the posterity of Marchweithian held individually comparatively small areas. This subdivision of land was very much increased by one of the provisions of the Statute of Rhuddlan, which directed that in event of failure of heirs male, daughters should inherit, which had not before been the case. In the time of Edward III., we find that the only parts of the cymwd of Isaled which can be clearly identified as held by Marchweithian's descendants in the male line were the lands of Berain, Carwedd Fynydd, Llys Llywarch, and some others in the parish of Llannefydd, a part of Cerrig y Druidion, and perhaps a portion of Yspytty Evan. At this time Einion, the son of Cynwrig, appears to have been in possession of the Cerrig y Druidion estates, which continued to be subdivided among his posterity until the Act of 34 & 35, Henry VIII. c. 26, put a stop, generally, to the partition of land between all of the sons, although, in many cases the Act was evaded, and more or less division of estates and farms continued, either by feoffment of sons in the lifetime of their father, or by some other legal process. In some cases the law was simply disregarded by mutual consent, and in a number of districts this state of things continued down to the latter part of the seventeenth century. During the reign of Henry VIII., and succeeding reigns, it is sometimes difficult to identify landholders because of the custom of creating deeds of trust whereby lands, after the death of the grantor, were held for certain uses, such as the support of the widow, younger children, or relatives, with reversion to a grandson, or other kinsman, as the case might be, so that such lands frequently appear on the Lay Subsidy Rolls under the name of the trustee.

Marchweithian's court (*llys*) was at Llyweni, near the town of Denbigh, afterwards the seat of the Salusbury family. The residence of a Welsh chieftain in Marchweithian's time was built of timber roughly hewn from the forest, with a thatched roof, and consisted of one large hall partly partitioned by screens, and hung with skins and trophies of the chase. The shelter for domestic animals, the bake-house, baths, and sleeping-huts for the menial servants and bondsmen were detached. The court was fortified by stockades, ditches, and, in some cases, by rough stone fences, which served as the outer line of defence, as well as for cattle yards. There are various MS. pedigrees of Marchweithian extant, all of which have the merit of a very respectable antiquity. They agree in stating that his remote ancestor was Coŷl Hên (the old), who was a real personage, and flourished about the beginning of the fourth century. A portion of the pedigree from Coŷl down can be checked up from a manuscript of the eleventh century,[1] which is a copy of one composed in the last half of the tenth, but it is evident that several generations connecting Marchweithian with Urien Rheged, who also existed, have been accidentally omitted by some transcriber. There is no reason, however, to doubt that Marchweithian was the son of Tagno, who was the son of Llydd (or Llud), who was the son of one Llew, a descendant of Urien Rheged, a prince of Cumberland, whose pedigree from Coŷl is confirmed. The latter was supposedly of partly Roman blood, being the son of Tasciovanus, son of Tasciovanus, son of Telpuil [us] son of Urbanus, son of Gratian—the last two being Roman names. The pedigree traces Gratian to Beli (or Belinos) Mawr, who has been satisfactorily identified with Cunobelinos, son of Tasciovanus, a powerful over-king of the Brythons, who, during the lifetime of his father, resided at Camulodunon, whilst the latter occupied Verlamion, now Old Verulam near St Albans, as his headquarters. Cunobelinos died before 43 A.D., and was father of the celebrated Caratacos, of Togodumnos, of Amminios (or Adminios) who fled to Rome and surrendered himself to the mad emperor Caligula, and possibly others. Numbers of the coins of Cunobelinos and Tasciovanus, a few of those of Amminios, and one of Caratacos, have been found.[2] The family, which included Cassivellaunos who opposed the second landing of Cæsar, descended from Diviciacos the Gaul, who also ruled as over-king in Britain before Cæsar's time.

The principal thing known about Coŷl is that he was the grandfather of Cunedda, who was also partly of Roman blood, and who, holding the Roman office of *Dux Britan-*

---

[1] "Y Cymmrodor," ix., 174, &c.
[2] Evans's "Coins of the Ancient Britons."

niæ or *Dux Britanniarum* about the time of the departure of the legions, drove the Irish out of Wales, which they had overrun since the days of Maximus, established garrisons in that country under command of some of his sons (having first taken personal possession of considerable territory there) and, returning to the Roman Wall, at which by virtue of his office he held supreme command, fell in defending it against the northern barbarians and their Saxon allies.[1]

Marchweithian, as already noted, left an only son, Marchwystl, who, according to Dwnn[2] (ii., 228) and "History of Powys Fadog"[3] (iv., 59 ; note 1), was father of Ysdrwyth, father of Tagno (or Tangno). As no families seem to trace to Ysdrwyth through any son but Tagno, the latter is presumed to have been sole heir, and supposedly, also, lord of Isaled. "Tagno's house was on the top of Fron Fawr," a few miles from St. Asaph, on the road to Llannefydd, and some remains of entrenchments are yet visible. He had three sons. The eldest, Ithel, appears to have entered the Church, probably late in life,

---

[1] Considerable information concerning these remote ancestors of Marchweithian will be found in "The Welsh People," Rhys and Brynmor-Jones, and Rhys's, "Celtic Britain," and the authorities cited therein. Regarding the tenth century pedigrees appended to the MS. of the "Annales Cambriæ," one of which is Coŷl's, Sir John Rhys, Principal of Jesus College, Oxford, says that "it would be an excessive display of the sceptical spirit" to deny their accuracy "for many generations," especially as many of the individuals mentioned "really lived and played their parts among the Cymry in a sequence of events that is not inconsistent with the order of the names" in the pedigrees.

In the opinion of Mr. E. Phillimore "up to the date when all Welsh records necessarily become more or less fabulous, these genealogies have every claim to rank beside the 'Annales' and the 'Saxon Genealogies' as a valuable historical authority.", "Y Cymmrodor," ix., 149 (1888).

[2] "Heraldic Visitations of Wales and part of the Marches ; between the years 1586 and 1613, under the authority of Clarencieux and Norroy two Kings at Arms, by Lewys Dwnn, Deputy Herald at Arms ; transcribed from the original manuscripts, and edited, with numerous explanatory notes," by Sir Samuel Rush Meyrick, Knt., K.H., L.L.D., F.A.S. Published by the Welsh MSS. Society, Llandovery, 1846 (2 vols. fo.).

[3] "The History of the Princes, the Lords Marcher, and the Ancient Nobility of Powys Fadog, and the ancient Lords of Arwystli, Cedewen, and Meirionydd." By J. Y. W. Lloyd, of Clochfaen, Esq., M.A., K.S.G., London, 1881-1887 (6 vols., 8 vo.).

and founded Ithel's Chapel, now Llannefydd Parish Church, which he endowed with lands, and where he was buried under the High Altar. Elidr, the third son, was of Bryn y Neuadd.

Tyfod (or Tyfid)[1] Farfsych, the second son of Tagno, is described as of Carwedd Fynydd and Berain in the Parish of Llannefydd, Tywysog, and of other places in Henllan and neighbourhood, and the family appears to have still retained lands about Llyweni. Tyfod was succeeded by Heilin Gloff[2] (the lame), who is supposed to have been an only son. Heilin is likewise described as of Carwedd Fynydd and Berain, in Llannefydd, and was buried at the latter place. He married Nest, daughter of Cadwgan ap Llywarch (or Llowarch) ap Bran, of Porthamel, lord of Cymwd Menai, in Anglesey. Llywarch ap Bran was head of one of the "Fifteen Tribes" of North Wales, and a lineal descendant of Rhodri Mawr, over-king of all Wales, and lived towards the close of the reign of Gruffydd ap Cynan, but the above alliance places him in the same generation as Marchweithian's grandson. Supposing, however, that Nest was a younger daughter, born when her father was somewhat advanced in years, the generations agree, and this marriage, in any case, as well as those which follow, prove the correctness of the statement that Marchweithian was born about the middle of the eleventh century. Heilin Gloff was father of Llywarch ap Heilin, of Carwedd Fynydd and Berain, time of Henry III., who married Gwenllian, daughter of Madog ap Rhirid Flaidd. The latter was an *uchelwr* and chief proprietor of Pennant Melangell, Montgomeryshire, and is styled *arglwydd* (lord) of Penllyn, but his interests in that cymwd were probably merely governmental, for although his great

---

[1] This name appears also as Tivid, Tyvod, &c., in various MSS.
[2] Cae Cyriog MSS. ; " History of Powys Fadog." iv., 101, Dwnn, ii., 228, &c.

grandson had a grant of land there from Edward I., Rhirid's possessions were principally, if not altogether, elsewhere.

David, son of Urgeneth (or Gwrgene) Fleid (Flaidd) and brother of Rhirid Flaidd, is grantor in a deed to Baldwin (de Boulers), son of William, of Montgomery, dated between *circa* 1230-40, for certain parcels of land about Montgomery,[1] Rhirid dwelt at Llys Celynyn, in the parish of Pennant Melangell, and died soon after his brother Arthen, in the first quarter of the thirteenth century.[2] Einion, an uncle of Nest, fell at the seige of Dyserth Castle, in 1263,[3] and her nephew, Madog ap Iorwerth ap Madog ap Rhirid Flaidd, received from Edward I. a grant of the lands of Penanthlu (or Pennantlliw), a township in the parish of Llanuwchllyn, Penllyn, at the close of the thirteenth century.[4]

Llywarch ap Heilin had issue by Gwenllian his wife,[5] Cynwrig, of whom presently, and Einion. Cynwrig ap Llywarch held the lands of Carwedd Fynydd, Berain, and others in Llannefydd, and about Llyweni, as well as in Cerrig y Druidion. Cynwrig appears to have been a person of considerable standing in the community in which he lived, and seems to have held his lands partly from the king in *capite* and partly by knight's service from Henry de Lacy, who had been created lord of Rhuvoniog (including Isaled), thus supplanting Cynwrig's family. Under the designation of *Kenewvek Ab llawar* he is the fifth witness to the charter of " Henri de Lacy, Earl of Nicole, (Lincoln), Constable of Chester, and Lord of Rhos and Rhuvoniog," granted 3 Edward I. (1274-5) to Johan de la Chambre for two carucates of land in Llyweni, with

---

[1] Original among Myddelton deeds at Chirk Castle.
[2] Add. MS. 14,886, fo. 91, 14,869, fo. 81b, 14,869, fo 227b., Brit. Museum.
[3] " History of Powys Fadog."
[4] Extent of the " Commot of Penthlyn " (Penllyn), temp. Edward I.
[5] " History of Powys Fadog," iv., 101 ; Dwnn, ii., 228, &c.

liberties and freedom in the parts and forests adjacent,[1] and at a court held at Ruthin, on Tuesday, the Feast of St. Maur the Abbot, 25 Edward I. (15 January, 1296-7) he was one of the surities for Robert le Walker.[2]

Cynwrig ap Llywarch married Dyddgu, daughter of Cadwgan ap Ednyfed[3] ap Cadwgan Ddu ap Llywarch Goch[4] ap Llywarch of Llys Llywarch (or Llowarch), called Llywarch Holbwrch, Treasurer to Gruffydd ap Llewelyn ap Seisyllt, who was king of all Wales, and who died in 1063. The generations from Dyddgu to Llywarch Holbwrch, place the latter in the same generation as Marchweithian, thus further confirming the period at which the latter lived. Llys Llywarch (or Llowarch) (i.e. the court of Llywarch) was in the parish of Llannefydd, which formed part of Isaled, the cymwd over which Marchweithian was *arglwydd*, so it is necessary to explain that Llywarch was *arglwydd* of the cantref of Rhuvoniog (or Rhyfonioc), of which Isaled formed a part, prior, seemingly, to Marchweithian's appointment. The government of all Rhuvoniog, including Isaled, appears to have fallen into the hands of Henry de Lacy before the conquest of Wales by Edward I., but the titles of the descendants of the ancient free tribesmen were for the most part not disturbed.

Cynwrig ap Llywarch had at least two sons. The younger, Einion[5] ap Cynwrig, received for his share of his father's estates, lands in the parish of Cerrig y Druidion, in Denbighshire, and went there to live. His house is

---

[1] Chambers MSS. Transcription of the Norman French of the original by J. Y. W. Lloyd, of Clochfaen, Esq., M.A., K.S.G., made 1885.

[2] Ruthin Court Rolls, 25 Edw. I., No. 3, memb. 3, Public Record Office ; see also "The Court Rolls of the Lordship of Ruthin or Dyffryn=Clwyd, time of Edward I." in "Cymmrodorion Record Series," No. 2., 40-1.

[3] "History of Powys Fadog," iv., 101.

[4] Harl. MS. 1977, fo., 267.

[5] "History of Powys Fadog," iv., 101 ; Cae Cyriog MS. ; MS. pedigree of John Thomas of Llaithgwm, dated 1682, (Levick MSS.) now in Library of Historical Society of Pennsylvania, U.S.A.

supposed to have been Bryammer, in the township of Cwm Pen Aner, which was afterwards the home of one of his descendants, "Ieuan [or Evan] ap Goch." Among Einion's descendants were John Thomas, of Llaithgwm, whose sons (surnamed Jones) settled in Merion, Pennsylvania, in 1683, John Cadwalader, ancestor of the Cadwalader family of Pennsylvania and New Jersey, and other early colonists.[1]

Cynwrig Fychan (or Vychan), the eldest son[2] of Cynwrig ap Llywarch, inherited the lands of Carwedd Fynydd and Berain in the parish of Llannefydd, and others in Henllan, about Llyweni and elsewhere.[3] It is stated in one pedigree of this family that he lived at one time at Llys Llywarch (or Llowarch) in Llannefydd, which may have come to him from his mother's family, or have been acquired by purchase from her kinsfolk in the lifetime of his father. At a court held at Llannerch, near Denbigh, on Thursday in Whitsun-week, 22 Edward I., (June, 10th, 1294), Cynwrig Fychan, then a young man, under the designation of *Kenw' Vagh^{a}n*, was attached because he depastured the lord's land without leave. The damages amounted to 6d., and he was quit.[4] He was living 8 Edward III. (1334), when he is named as a landholder in the "Extent of the Lordship and Honour of Denbigh"[5]; he served with the English against the Scots, and was buried in Llannefydd Church, where his effigy in full armour remains.[6]

---

[1] See "Merion in the Welsh Tract," Glenn, 252, 78, 295, &c.

[2] Dwnn, ii., 228; "History of Powys Fadog," iv., 101-2.

[3] Extent of the Lordship and Honour of Denbigh, 8 Edw. III.

[4] Court of Llannerch, Ruthin Court Rolls, 22 Edw.I., Public Record Office; see also "Cymmrodorion Record Series," No. 2, 4. De Lacy's tenants holding by knights' fee, had usually rights of depasturage on the lord's land, for "all manner of beasts among all the glades of the forest," and "free pannage to all its swine of its own pale," likewise, "housebote and haybote in the forest of Llewenny," but leave must first be obtained.

[5] Dwnn, ii, 228, note 2.

[6] "History of Powys Fadog," iv., 101.

Cynwrig Fychan married Morfydd, daughter of Madog Ddu ap Madog Goch ap Ifor ap Gwgawn ap Cyfnerth ap Rhun ap Nefydd Hardd, and had issue: Heilin Frych, Howel ap Cynwrig Fychan, of whom presently, and Einion, ancestor of the Williamses of Hafod Garegog.

Heilin Frych, the eldest son, continued at Carwedd Fynydd and Berain, and was succeeded there by his son Gruffydd, ancestor to the celebrated Catherine of Berain, daughter and heiress of Tudor ap Robert, by Jane his wife, daughter and sole heiress of Sir Rowland Velville, Knt., Governor of Beaumaris Castle. Catherine Berain, who, because of the number of her descendants was called by the Welsh *Mam Cymru* (mother of Wales), is stated to have been the most beautiful as well as the wealthiest woman of her day, in the Principality. She was four times married, her first husband being John Salusbury of Llyweni, her second Sir Richard Clough of Bach y Graig, her third, Maurice Wynn of Gwydir, and her fourth, Edward Thelwall of Plâs y Ward. Thomas Salusbury, one of her sons, became implicated in the Babington Plot, and was with fourteen of his fellows brought to trial 13th September, 1586, charged, among other things, with attempting to raise a rebellion in the realm in favour of Mary Queen of Scots, then imprisoned at Chartley. Salusbury pleaded "Not Guilty," but was convicted on very questionable evidence, and beheaded. Sir John Salusbury, another son of Catherine, was Esquire of the Body to Queen Elizabeth, received the honour of knighthood, and represented Denbigh in Parliament. One of Catherine's descendants, says Bradley, in his "Highways and Byways in North Wales," "bore a name much more familiar to English ears than that of the illustrious Catherine herself, and this was Mrs. Thrale. Those who know their Johnson will remember how she brought the Doctor down to see the estate of Bachegraig [Bach y Graig], which had fallen to her through the Cloughs. The Doctor's mild adventures among the Denbigh squires, and his, with a few notable exceptions, affable behaviour as he rolled about their parlours, is of course, a matter of history." Sir Richard Clough, of Bach y Graig, Catherine's son, and Mrs. Thrale's ancestor, was a partner of the renowned Sir Thomas Gresham, and "was a sort of commercial ambassador for England in the Low Countries, and being a great builder in his native district, left the mark of his Flemish taste on many old buildings around Denbigh."

Catherine Beraine died 27 August, 1591, and was buried with her ancestors, in Llannefydd Church, on 1st September, following. An engraved portrait of her, from a painting formerly at Lluesog Lodge, may be found in Yorke's "Royal Tribes of Wales."

Howel ap Cynwrig Fychan is said to have espoused Margaret, daughter and co-heiress of Howel ap Ithel, lord of Rhos and Rhuvoniog,[1] but as this Howel ap Ithel was slain in 1115, and was, moreover, grandson to Rhirid ap Bleddyn ap Cynfyn, who was slain at battle of Llechryd in 1087, it is clear that some later Howel ap Ithel was originally intended to be meant. Howel ap Cynwrig's son, Tudor (or Tewdwr) ap Howel, took to wife Susanna, daughter and heiress of Maredydd[2] ap Madog descended from Jonas ap Hwfa ap Ithel Felyn of Iâl (now Yale) in Denbighshire, and had besides a younger son, David ap Tudor, of Gallt y Celyn, Maredydd[3] ap Tudor, whose wife was Efa, daughter of Ieuan ap Rhys Gwyn ap David Llwyd ap Goronwy Llwyd ap "Y Penwyn" of Melai.[3] This Goronwy Llwyd was grantee of the "raglorie" of Nantconwy and "avoterie" of Dolwyddelen and Mill of Penmachno, with their demesne lands, 1351, and is called "of Bettws". He was also one of the jury for taking the extent of Nantconwy on the next Monday after

---

[1] Dwnn, ii., 228, 343; Harl. MS. 2299.
[2] Dwnn, ii., 228.
[3] "Ibid."

the Festival of the Translation of St. Thomas the Martyr, 26 Edward III. (31 December, 1352), and was living 1356.[1] Goronwy's wife was Lleuci (some say Gwenhwyfar) daughter and heiress of Madog ap Elised (or Ellis), who, as a Baron of Edeyrnion, did homage to the Black Prince, 17 Edward III. (1344). Goronwy Llwyd's father, Iorwerth, surnamed "Y Penwyn" (white-headed), was an adherent of Edward I. in the war of 1282-3, and is supposed to have taken prisoner David, Prince Llewelyn's brother, who was subsequently tried by his peers as an English baron (which he certainly was), and condemned to be hanged, drawn and quartered, which sentence was literally carried out. Iorwerth's action in joining those Welshmen who went over to the king and his capture of David, led to the following lines, long preserved, and printed in the "Cambrian Quarterly" (iii., 460).

"Y Penwyn, pen hir arbennig—unben
Am un punt ar bymtheg,
Lloniad buartheg o wartheg
Newydd, a werth Ddavydd deg."

"The white-headed, long-headed, high-headed chief,
For fifteen pounds and one,
A new cow-yard full of cattle,
Sells David the beautiful."

Whatever Iorwerth's service may have been, it is certain that under the designation of *Yerward Penwyn* he had a grant from the crown of 30 shillings per annum, 18 Edward I. In 3 Edward II. he was Raglor of Nantconwy, where he resided, for which he had petitioned in 33 Edward I., an office which he continued to hold until his death, *circa* 1320. Ednyfed, the brother of David Llwyd ap Goronwy, is named in a rental of 6 Edward IV. (1467). Maredydd ap Tudor was of Plâs Iolyn, in the township of Trebrys, afterwards included in the parish of Yspytty Evan, Denbighshire, and was steward of the lands of the

---

[1] "Records of Caernarvon," 10; Hengwrt MS. 198, fo. 36; printed pedigree of Ffoulkes of Ereiviat, by William Wynne Ffoulkes, Esq.

Monastery of Aberconwy in Hiraethog, in 1450.[1] The immediate vicinity of Plâs Iolyn was neither a pleasant or safe neighbourhood in Maredydd's day. Sir John Wynn, in his history of "The Gwydir Family" speaks at some length of the condition of affairs existing before 1485, and later, near Yspytty Evan. He tells us that "from the town of Conway to Bala, and from Nant Conway to Denbigh there was continually fostered a wasp's nest which troubled the whole country, I mean a lordship belonging to St. John's of Jerusalem, called Spytty Jevan, a large thing (district), which had the privilege of Sanctuary. This peculiar jurisdiction, not governed by the king's laws, became a receptacle for thieves and murtherers whose safety being warranted them by law, made the place thoroughly peopled. Noe spot within twenty miles was safe from their incursions and roberies, and what they got within their limits was their owne." Maredydd (or Meredith) Wynn, the ancestor of Sir John, having removed from Lleyn, in Carnarvonshire to Dolwyddelen, near Plâs Iolyn, and purchased or leased from the Crown a great part of the lands adjacent to Yspytty Evan, proceeded to subdue these outlaws, saying, as an excuse for his removing into such a place, that it was better to kill thieves than one's own kindred, which, because of family feud, he would be forced to do if he remained in his old home. "To strengthen himself in the country, he provided out of all parts adjacent, the tallest and most able men he could heare of. Of these he placed colonists in the country, filling every empty tenement with a tenant or two, whereof most was on the king's land . . . within the space of certain years, he was able to make seven score tall bowmen of his followers, arrayed, as I have credibly heard, in this manner. Every one of them had a jacket or armorlett coate, a good Steele Cappe, a Short Sword and a Dagger, together with

---

[1] Records of the Abbey of Aberconwy, transcribed by J. Y. W. Lloyd, of Clochfaen, Esq., in "History of Powys Fadog," v., 406, *Tudor* by error being there printed *Thomas*.

his bow and arrowes; some of them alsoe had horses, and Chasing Staves which were to answer the crie upon all events. Whereby he grew soe strong that he began to put back and curb the Sanctuary of thieves and robbers, which at that time were wont to be above a hundred, well horsed and well appointed."

According to pedigrees extant Maredydd had issue, Robert[1] ap Maredydd and Rhys[2] ap Maredydd. The latter, who is also called Rhys Fawr ap Maredydd, was of Plâs Iolyn. He was one of the Lancastrian captains at the battle of Bosworth Field (1485) and was entrusted by Henry VII. with the Standard of England, after the former standard-bearer, Sir William Brandon, had been slain. He is supposed to have succeeded his father as steward of the lands of the Monastery of Aberconwy, as the position was hereditary, being afterwards held by Rhys's son, Maurice Gethin, who was appointed in 1501, which presumably is the date of Rhys ap Maredydd's death. Rhys was buried in Yspytty Evan Church, where alabaster effigies of himself and Lowry, his wife,[3] daughter of Howel ap Gruffydd Goch, of Rhos, may be seen. The children of Rhys ap Maredydd were: 1, Howel ap Rhys; 2, Sir (Rev.) Robert ap Rhys, of whom presently; 3, Maurice Gethin of Y Voelas, in Yspytty Evan, who, in 1501, was appointed steward for life of the lands of the Monastery of Aberconwy in Hiraethog. In 1545, 16 March, the Crown granted to Cadwaladr ap Maurice Gethin and Robert Wyn Gethin, sons of Maurice, and their heirs, the lands of Y Voelas, Cerniogau, and others, to hold of the manor of Hiraethog, in free soccage, by fealty only, and not in *capite*. By deed of partition dated 8 February, 1546, one of the brothers took

---

[1] " History of Powys Fadog," iv., 102.

[2] Harl. MS. 1977, fos. 64, 65 ; Harl MS. 1971 ; Hengwrt MS. 324 ; Dwnn, ii., 228 ; " History of Powys Fadog," iv., 102.

[3] Dwnn, ii., 343, note 2, by Sir Samuel Rush Meyrick, Knt., K.H., LL.D., F.A.S., who identifies the effigies.

Photo. by Miss S. Price.

Effigies of Rhys ap Meredydd, his Wife, and their Son, Sir Robert ap Rhys.

[Reproduced from "The Heart of Northern Wales," by kind permission of the Author, Mr. W. Bezant Lowe, M.A., F.C.S., Cae Carw, Llanfairfechan.]

Voelas and the other Cerniogau; 4, David ap Rhys; 5, Cadwaladr ap Rhys; 6, Sir Richard Pryse, Abbot of Aberconwy; 7, Hugh Pryse, also Abbot of Aberconwy (d. 8 July, 1528); 8, Efa, wife of David ap Gwilym ap David of Llwydiarth, in Môn, and afterwards wife of Maredydd ap Thomas of Porthamel; 9, Gwenhwyfar, wife of David ap Howel ap Gruffydd ap Jenkin of Llwydiarth, in Powys, and afterwards wife of Tudor Fychan ap Tudor ap Gruffydd ap Einion of Edeyrnion; 10, Margaret, wife of Gruffydd ap Llewelyn Fychan of Iâl; 11, Annest, wife of John ap William ap Maurice of Garth Eryr, and afterwards wife of John ap Jenkin Howel of Penllyn; 12, Elizabeth wife of Ellissau ap Howel ap Rhys of Edeyrnion.

A footnote to Dwnn (ii., 343, note 10) informs us that Robert ap Rhys, second son of Rhys ap Maredydd, "was cross-bearer and chaplain to Cardinal Wolsey; he was buried in Yspytty [Yspytty Evan] Church, where his effigy, in canonical robes, is still preserved." Note 2, page 228 of the same volume says that he is party to a deed dated 8th November, 1525. In "The History of Powys Fadog" (iv., 103), and elsewhere, he is called "Sir Robert ap Rhys," the "Sir," being the then equivalent of "Reverend," and was in common use both before and after the Reformation. Authorities agree that the mother of his children was a daughter of Rhys Lloyd, of Cydros (or Gydros), in Penllyn, but Dwnn in one pedigree calls her Mawd, and in another, Margaret. The children are given by Dwnn as follows :—
1, David Prys; 2, Elis Prys; 3, Kadwaladr ap Robert; 4, Richard abad (i.e., Richard the Abbot, which is an error, as the Abbot was this Richard's uncle); 5, John ap Robert; 6, Harri ap Robert; 7, Robert Wyn; 8, Thomas (Vaughan); 9, William (twin to Thomas); 10, Owein ap Robert; 11, Arthyr ap Robert, 12, Hyw ap Robert; 13, Hyw Abad (i.e., Hugh the Abbot, which is an error, as the Abbot was this Hugh's uncle); 14, Katrin Lloid, wife of William Salsbri (Salusbury); 15, Marged Wen, wife of William ap

Reinallt; 16, Lowri, wife of Robert Salsbri ; 17, ——, wife of Robert ap David Anwyl.[1] These children, it is evident from various circumstances, were born between about 1495 and 1520, that is to say prior to the Reformation.

The following notes afford us additional information regarding Sir Robert's relations with the Church in the neighbourhood of his home.

"Rob'to ap Ris (Robert ap Rhys) held a lease under the conventual seal of Strata Marcella, dated 20 February, 1527, for 59 years, for a tenement afterward in the possession of Ieu'n ap Hoell Vaughan (of Llwydiarth), who paid 13s. 4d. rent for it."[2] In Minister's Accounts, for 32-33 Henry VIII., Robert ap Rhys (or Rees) is called "Rob'ti ap Ris *custod' boscor'*, or forester of the lands of the Abbey of Strata Marcella, an office which was to be held by him or by deputy for life, by grant under the conventual seal, dated 8 October, 1528. He, under the designation of "Robertus ap Res, *clericus*" seems to have farmed Tirymynerch under the Abbey. In Minister's Accounts for Strata Marcella, 34 Henry VIII., he is called "Rob't. ap Rees *custod' Mon ib'm*," and[3] is mentioned in the same accounts at least as late as 1558, at which time he must have been quite advanced in years, and there is a tradition that he lived to a great age; but it is possible that the lands remained in his name on the rolls

---

[1] There is considerable contradiction in the various pedigrees of the family, regarding the order of birth of these children, and Dwnn confuses two of them Richard and Hugh, with their uncles of the same name (see "Montg. Colls.," v. 133). Ellis Price could not have been the second son. In a pedigree of "Vaughan of Pant Glas, in the Parish of Yspytty," in "History of Powys Fadog," v., 382, Thomas Vaughan, stated by Dwnn to have been the eighth son, is given as the second, but the same pedigree by mistake makes this Thomas Vaughan, High Sheriff of Merionethshire, in 1604, at which time he would have been upwards of ninety years of age. Thomas Vaughan, the son, is evidently intended to be meant. Reference should be made to Harl. MS. 1971, Hengwrt MS. 324, Harl. MS. ; 1977, fo. 64, 65; Cae Cyriog MS. ; Dwnn ii., 344 ; and pedigree in the College of Arms.

[2] "Montgomeryshire Collections," v., 402.

[3] Ibid, v., 402, vi., 381.

for some years after his decease. The Tirymynerch, or Tir y Mynach (the monk's land), above named, now a township in the parish of Llanbrynmair, in Montgomeryshire, belonged to the Monastery of Strata Marcella, but is *not* now, and probably never was comprised in the estates of Rhiwlas and Cwm Maen, Penllyn, as stated in "The History of Powys Fadog" (vi., 133). There is, however, a vale called Cwm Tir Mynarch beyond Fron Goch farm, near Bala, which is presumed to have formed part of the "Grange of Penllyn." Other lands in Penllyn which had belonged to the Abbey of Dinas Basing, in 26 Henry VIII., according to "Valor Ecclesiasticus," were leased to Sir Robert ap Rhys, and afterwards held by the descendants of his son Cadwaladr ap Robert, of Rhiwlas, but the latter, as we shall see, by virtue of a lease to him in person, held the "Grange of Penllyn." Sir Robert ap Rhys is called, in various pedigrees, "of Plas Iolyn," which was also the residence of his father, but his name is not mentioned as a landholder under the parish of Yspytty Evan in the Lay Subsidy Roll of 34-35 Henry VIII.,[1] although David ap Robert ap Rhys, his eldest son, is taxed in land and tenements there to the value of £50, presumably the Plâs Iolyn estate. This place may have been, and probably was, acquired by David either during the lifetime of his father, or by a settlement of his grandfather. The same property, it is said, afterwards belonged to Ellis Pryse, brother of David, who with Thomas Vaughan, (another brother) had a grant of the whole manor of Yspytty Evan, in 1568. Thomas Price (or Pryse), son of Ellis, is taxed under the parish of Yspytty Evan, in Lay Subsidy Roll of 39-40 Elizabeth.[2] The fact that the effigy of Sir Robert ap Rhys represents him in canonical robes indicates that he died a

---

[1] Lay Subsidy Roll for Denbighshire, 34-35 Hen. VIII., under "Sputty," No. $\frac{220}{188}$; Public Record Office, London.

[2] Lay Subsidy Roll for Denbighshire, 39-40 Elizabeth, under "Sputty" (Yspytty Evan), Hundred of "Islaet" (Isaled). No. $\frac{220}{188}$, Public Record Office, London.

churchman, and the *clericus* appended to his name, as well as the definite statement that he was chaplain and cross-bearer to Cardinal Wolsey, makes it certain that he was a priest prior to the Reformation, and in addition to his office of forester for Strata Marcella he was probably rector of Llandyssil in Montgomeryshire.[1] There can be no doubt, however, that Sir Robert conformed to the reformed Church, and it seems most probable, seeing that he was buried therein, that he became rector of Yspytty Evan.[2]

It seems certain, from the foregoing, that Sir Robert, like many others of his day, entered the Church after the death of his wife, which event probably occurred about 1520 to 1525. She was certainly not an heiress, as stated in " Montgomeryshire Collections " (v., 112).

David, the eldest son of Sir Robert ap Rhys, probably sold Plâs Iolyn to his brother Ellis. At any rate Ellis, who is stated in the pedigree by Dwnn to have been the second son,[3] but who certainly was much younger than Cadwaladr, the third son, and was most likely one of the youngest of Sir Robert's children, is also called of Plâs Iolyn, which, there seems to be no doubt, he actually owned, and, like other members of the family, he assumed the surname of Pryse, (or Price), the Welsh contraction of *ap Rhys*, thus perpetuating his grandfather's baptismal name. Ellis Pryse was generally known during his lifetime as the " Doctor Goch " (red doctor). He was educated at Cambridge, where he is stated to have taken the degree of L.L.D., and " was eminent for his powers of disputation, being one of those chosen by his College, in 1532, to

---

[1] Book of Corrodies, or " Queen Mary's Book," containing an account of the pensions, fees, and annuities which were liable, at the date of that Queen's accession, to be paid by the Crown to persons who had been inmates of religious houses at the time of the dissolution.

[2] It should be noted that there was another Robert ap Rhys, rector of Yspytty Evan, at the close of the sixteenth century, usually called Robert ap Rhys ap Sion.

[3] According to some pedigrees, Thomas Vaughan was the second son, although Dwnn calls him the eighth. See *Supra*.

Photo. by. A H. Hughes.

PLAS IOLYN.

[Reproduced from "The Heart of Northern Wales," by kind permission of the Author, Mr. W. Bezant Lowe, M.A., F.C.S., Cae Carw, Llanfairfechan.]

dispute against the representatives of Oxford ; when he got the best of it." He represented the county of Merioneth in the parliament of Queen Mary, and the first and second parliaments of Queen Elizabeth. He was High Sheriff of Merionethshire in the years 1552, 1556, 1564, 1568, 1574, 1579, 1584, and according to one account in 1598, in which year he must have been upwards of eighty years of age. He was also High Sheriff of Carnarvonshire in 1558, and served in the same office for Anglesey in 1578 and 1586, and for his own county, Denbigh, in the years 1550, 1557, 1559, and 1573, and was one of the Council of the Court of the Marches. He is ranked by the author of " Heraldry Displayed " among those fifteen gentlemen (five being of this family) "who fostered the literature of Wales during those years of its depression which followed the insurrection of Owain Glyndyfrdwy," and was of the first named of the gentlemen directed by Queen Elizabeth to hold the Royal Eisteddfod at Caerwys in 1568, being described in the Commission as "docto^r in Cyvill Lawe, and one of our Counsaill in our Marches of Wales." In 1576, he obtained the appointment of *Custos Rotulorum* for Merionethshire, and, in 1560, he, with Thomas Vaughan of Pant Glas (his brother), had a grant in fee from Queen Elizabeth of the manors and lands of Yspytty and Tir Ieuan, and the rectory of Yspytty and chapel of Penmachno, which had formed parcel of the commandry of the Knights' Hospitallers of St. John of Jerusalem, dissolved at the time of the Reformation. Dr. Pryse retained Tir Ieuan (St. John's land) for his share, and Thomas Vaughan took Eidda.[1]

Dr. Pryse was, for a time, the agent of Dudley, Earl of Leicester, who, because of his exactions, which in time became greatly magnified, acquired an unenviable reputation. The Doctor was also an advocate of religious

---

[1] "History of Powys Fadog," iv., 104-5 ; v., 407 ; Pennant, iii., 140.

tolerance, and succeeded in making a great many enemies among the clergy, and for these reasons, as well as his interest in science and literature, was supposed to have "had dealings with the Evil One," and Pennant, who was always ready to believe anything told him, calls Pryse "the most dreaded oppressor in his neighbourhood," a reputation not borne out by the many benefits he bestowed upon his countrymen and tenants. Dr. Ellis Pryse married Erllyw, daughter of Sir Owain Pool, vicar of Llandecwyn, near Harlech. His eldest son, Captain Thomas Pryse, who was High Sheriff of Denbighshire in 1599, fitted out and commanded a privateer against the Spaniards, and afterwards served in the land service at Tilbury in 1588.[1] He is ranked with his father as promoting the literature of Wales, and was himself no mean poet. Many of his verses are still preserved in MS., and some of them were published in the "Cylchgrawn" (Llandovery, 1834).

Cadwaladr ap Robert,[2] the third son of Sir Robert ap Rhys, had a lease under the conventual seal of Strata Marcella, dated 22 Henry VIII.,[3] (1530), for the "Grange of Penllyn," consisting of Rhiwlas and other lands, near Bala, and is mentioned in Minister's Accounts of the Abbey, as holding the same 27-32 Henry VIII., 32-33 Henry VIII., and in the years following, to 4-5 Philip and Mary inclusive. Cadwaladr's name does not appear 6 Philip and Mary, about which time he probably died. Edward VI., by patent 23 January, in the sixth year of his reign had leased the site of the Monastery of Strata Marcella and the "Grange of Penllyn" which had formerly been demised

---

[1] "History of Powys Fadog," iv., 105.

[2] Dwnn, ii., 228.

[3] He appears under the designation of *Kydwelly ap Ro'bt, Kidwellidar ap Rob't, Kidwellider ap Robt*, &c., in Minister's Accounts of the Abbey of Strata Marcella, 27-32 Hen. VIII. No. 209; 32-33 Hen. VIII. No. 164; 38 Hen. VIII. to 1 Edw. VI.; 2 Edw. VI., No. 83; 3 and 4 Edw. VI. (No. 152); 5 Edw. VI., No. 164, 5 and 6 Edw. VI., No, 177; Edw. VI. No. 62; 1 Mary, No. 200; 1 and 4 Philip and Mary, No. 213; 2 and 3 Philip and Mary, No. 225; 4 and 5 Philip and Mary, No. 249.

to Lord Powys, to Robert Trentham (subject of course to the rights of the tenants who held under grants under the seal of Strata Marcella), and 8 Elizabeth (1565-6), the Crown granted the reversion and reversions of the said lands and "Grange of Penllyn," with other lands, &c., to Rowland Heyward, Alderman of London, and Thomas Dyxon, clothworker, of the same place.[1] The heirs of Cadwaladr ap Robert thus became tenants of Dyxon and Heyward, and finally freeholders. The annual rental of the grange 5 Philip and Mary, was £16 13s. 4d.

Cadwaladr ap Robert, called of Plâs yn Rhiwlas which formed a part of the "Grange of Penllyn," married[2] Jane, daughter of Maredydd Wynn ap Ieuan ap Robert of Gwydir, by whom he had six sons and seven daughters. John, the eldest son, assumed the surname of Wynn. He inherited Plâs yn Rhiwlas, and was High Sheriff of Merionethshire, in 1577 and 1588. His eldest son, Cadwaladr, assumed the surname of Pryse, or Price, which was retained by his descendants, and the family still own and reside at Plâs yn Rhiwlas, which, by reason of additions made by succeeding generations is now of much greater extent than in the sixteenth century. Thomas, the second son of Cadwaladr ap Robert, was called Fychan, (or Vychan) probably because of his small stature, and was of Cerrig Hwfa. Pyers, the third son, settled in the parish of Llanycil, very near Bala. Humphrey and Robert, the fourth and fifth sons, acquired lands in Llanfor (then written Llanvawr), adjacent to Rhiwlas. The sixth son was Howel, of whom presently. Lowry, the eldest daughter, married Pyers ap Robert, of Maesmor, in Dinmael. The others were: Elliw, wife of Robert Wynn of Cerrig y Druidion; Catherine, wife of Richard ap Gruffydd; Sibil, wife of Rowland Vychan of Caer Gai;

---

[1] Patent Rolls, 8 Elizabeth, memb. 14.
[2] Dwnn, ii., 228.

Elin, wife of Maredydd ap Ieuan ap Robert of Llanfor (by whom she was mother of Cadwaladr ap Maredydd of Coed y Foel in Llanfor); Gwen, wife of David Lloyd of Ar Ddwyvaen, in Dinmael, and Grace, wife of Watkyn ap Edward of Garth Llwyd, Llandderfel, who was buried in Llandderfel Church, 22 February, 1610-11.[1]

Howel Fychan (or Vychan, the little), the sixth and youngest son of Cadwaladr ap Robert of Plâs yn Rhiwlas, acquired lands in the parish of Llangower,[2] part of which were adjacent to and extending into the adjoining parish of Llanuwchllyn, in Penllyn.

We have now followed the varying fortunes of this branch of the posterity of Marchweithian, from the fertile Vale of Clwyd, over the desolate solitude of the Hiraethog, to the sheep-ranges of Yspytty Evan; across Cerrig y Druidion to Rhiwlas, near Bala, and thence by way of Bala Lake (Lyn Tegid) to the pleasant pasture lands lying along the borders of Llangower and Llanuwchllyn, two of the five parishes (Llanfor, Llandderfel, and Llanycil being the others) included in the cymwd (now hundred) of Penllyn. As Penllyn was the birthplace not only of four generations of the family we are tracing, but also of a goodly number of those who, about the close of the seventeenth century, preceded, accompanied, or followed Robert Cadwalader (or Cadwaladr) and his family to the Province of Pennsylvania, the following notes may not be out of place.

In the list of the ancient divisions of Wales in Sir John Price's account of the Principality, the oldest known MS. of which is dated 1559, Penllyn is described as a "cantref" containing the "commots" of Uwchmeloch, Ismeloch, and

---

[1] Llandderfel Parish Register.

[2] Dwnn, ii., 229; "History of Powys Fadog," vi., 149. Llangower was sometimes formerly written Llangywair and Llangowair. Lay Subsidy Rolls, and other records cited *infra*.

Michaint.[1]   The oldest lists of cantrefs and cymwds[2] (or commots) of Wales, one of which is a copy of a lost eleventh century MS.,[3] agree with Sir John's, and a recent paper in "Montgomeryshire Collections," also speaks of "The Lordship of Penllyn, formerly a Province in the Principality of Powys Wenwynwyn," as a *cantref*.

In the so called Statute of Rhuddlan (1284),[4] which is the first official information we possess on the subject, Penllyn is called a *commot*, and the county of Merioneth is formed by uniting "Cantreda de Merioneth, Commotum de Ardudo et *Commotum* de Penthlin et Commotum de Dereynan." It will thus be seen that although Merioneth is referred to as a *cantref*, Penllyn was, at that time, clearly understood to be a *cymwd*. There is no evidence to show that Edward I. made any changes whatever in the sub-divisions recognized by the Welsh prior to the conquest of the Principality, and from the fact that Welshmen were largely employed by the king in the work of territorial survey, and almost exclusively in local government, it is exceedingly unlikely that an error in description occurred.

The extent of the newly-formed county of Merioneth, made shortly after the date of the Statute of Rhuddlan,[5] also designates Penllyn a "commot," and Ismeloch, which is there written "Isbelon," is only incidentally mentioned. The principal other sub-divisions are given as Bala, Artenllyn and Land Vaylo (Llandderfel), Penanthlu (in the present parish of Llanuwchllyn), Penmayn (now Penmaen, in Llanfor), Mochrader, and Penaran. At about the time this extent was made, Madog ap Iorwerth, a great-

---

[1] Sir John Price's "Description of Wales," Caligula A, vi., Cott. MS.

[2] The *cymwd*, usually written in English *commot*, contained twelve maenolydd and fifty trefydd (vills) and two cymwds were nominally equal to one cantref.

[3] Printed in Leland's "Itinerary," vol. v.

[4] Mid-Lent, 12 Edw. I., Record Com., pub. 1810, vol. i., 55.

[5] "Extenta Commoti de Penthlyn" (in Extent of Merioneth, temp. Edw. I., see "Arch. Camb.," 1867, 187); "History of Powys Fadog," vi., 140.

grandson of Rhirid Flaidd, was granted among other things the government of the balliwick of a "cantref," to be formed by uniting Penllyn and Ardudwy.¹ In a subsequent Extent and in various deeds, down to two centuries ago, some of which are in the possession of the writer, Penllyn is uniformly described as a commot or hundred. Robert Vaughan of Hengwrt informs us that "the cantred [cantref] of Penllyn *sometime* had it in three comots, Uwch Meloch, Is Meloch, and Migneint, but now all these three make but one comot [*i.e.*, Penllyn], which is divided in the balliwick's of Uwch Trewerin and Is Trewerin."² In a charter to the Abbey of Strata Marcella, Penllyn is designated a "province," which might mean anything.

It seems certain from the above that Penllyn was reckoned a cymwd long before the conquest of Wales by Edward I. On the other hand we have the evidence of the eleventh century account that it then constituted a cantref in Gwynedd. It seems probable, therefore, that Penllyn was reduced to the status of a cymwd by Prince Llewelyn ap Iorwerth sometime in the first quarter of the thirteenth century, probably directly after he deprived Gwenwynwyn of Powys of his government and lands, in 1216.³ The latter sub-divisions of Penllyn are not, owing to frequent changes, at first sight very easy to determine. At the present time there are five parishes,⁴ *viz.*, Llanfor, Llandderfel, Llanycil, Llanuwchllyn, and Llangower; but the bounds of these parishes have always varied considerably, and several of their townships

---

¹ Petition presented by this Madog to the Prince of Wales at Kensington, 33 Edw. I.

² Evans's MS.

³ "The Welsh People," Rhys and Brynmor-Jones, 318.

⁴ Under the most ancient divisions, Uwch Meloch contained the parish (formerly township) of Llangower only, Is Meloch, Llanfor and Llandderfel, and Mignant, Llanuwchllyn and Llanvihangel, the latter being now largely included in Llanycil. Penllyn was afterwards divided into Uwch Tryweryn and Is Tryweryn, which divisions, in records of the seventeenth century, are usually called Isavon and Uwchavon (*i.e.*, above and below the river—Tryweryn).

are at the same time described as of one parish or another. The parish of Llanfor,[1] according to an old description, contained the townships of Tre'r Llan (now Tre'r-llan), Rhiwaedog Uwch Avon, Rhiwaedog Is Avon, Pen Maen (now Penmaen), Cil Talgarth[2] (now Ciltalgarth), Llawr y Bettws, Ucheldrev (now Ucheldre), Garth, and Nant Lleidiog, (now Nant-lleidiog). The adjoining parish of Llandderfel, is stated to have included the townships of Trev Llan (now Tre'rllan), Nant Ffreiar (now Nant Ffrauar), Trev (Tref) Gynlas (now Cynlas), Selwern (now Selwrn), Crogen, Dol-Drewyn, and Llaethgwm (now Llaithgwm). Cynlas and Llaithgwm, however, are now locally in the parish of Llanfor, but, for ecclesiastical purposes, probably yet partly in Llandderfel. The present parish of Llanycil was formerly a township in the parish of Llanfihangel, which contained the townships of Cyffty, Gwernevel, Bedwarien, Llan-y-cil, Bala, Dwygraig and Llangywair (now written Llangower), and at present included in the parish of that name, which, as well as Llanycil, was formed out of part of Llanfihangel. Robert Vaughan of Hengwrt, writing about 1650, speaks of Llangower as in Llanfihangel,[3] but the official records of an earlier date refer to it as a parish. The same antiquarian mentions the additional townships of Cymysgadwy and Hengair as belonging at that time to Llanfor or Llandderfel (it is not clear which), and there may have been, and doubtless were, others.[4] The townships of Llanuwchlyn, according to Vaughan's account, were (*circa* 1650) Pen Aran, Trev Pris (Tref Brysg), Pennanlliw, (or Pennant Lliw), and Trev Castell. Another account adds Cynllwyd.

[1] In old records, and even down to the middle of the Nineteenth Century, Llanfor was most frequently written Llanvawr, and occasionally, also, Llanvor, Llanvour, Llanfaur, etc. The church is dedicated to St. Mor.

[2] Anciently sometimes written *Kiltalgarth* and *Giltalgarth*.

[3] "Merionethshire," MS. of Robert Vaughan of Hengwrt; Evans Collection.

[4] "Another MS. gives Caer Ceiliog as an additional township of Llandderfel.

Penllyn, at the time of the Roman invasion, was within the territory of the Ordovices. This warlike tribe is supposed to have been Brythonic,[1] and to have conquered this part of the country not so very long before the Roman occupation, the vanquished inhabitants, who were probably partly Aborigines of Egyptian origin and partly Goidels,[2] being enslaved. By the year 50 the Romans had advanced to the borders of this district, and it was probably soon after that the city of Uriconium near Shrewsbury was built. Ostorious Scapula was now in command of the Roman forces. This general was soon opposed by the Ordovices, and probably part of the Silures, under the leadership of the renowned Caratacos, son of Cunobelinos, who had led his own people, the Catuvellauni, against the invaders. Caratacos, however, was finally signally defeated near the Breidin Hills in the neighbourhood of Welshpool, and fled for protection to the Brigantes, whose queen surrendered him to the Romans. The Ordovices, however, were not completely subdued until 78 or 79, when Julius Agricola crushed them. Troops were immediately thrown into Penllyn, and a permanent station established at a place since called Caer Gai, on the margin of Bala lake. Caer is the Welsh for camp,

---

[1] The Brythons invaded Britain some time after the visit of Pytheas, in the fourthcentury B.C., and continued to come until the middle of the first. In the time of Cæsar men were still alive who remembered Diviciacos, the great Gaul, who ruled as over-king in Britain, as well as on the continent, and who was the ancestor of the earlier Brython over-kings, including Cunobelinos, and supposedly of Cassivellaunos, who opposed Cæsar.

[2] "That the pre-Celtic inhabitants of Britain were an off-shoot of the North African race," writes Prof. J. Morris Jones, "is shown by the cranial and physical similarity between the long-barrow men and the Berbers and Egyptians, and by the line of megalithic monuments which stretches from North Africa, through Spain and the west of France to Britain, marking the route of tribes in their migration." Additional evidence of an Egyptian origin has been discovered in the Welsh language, for the Goidels, forerunners of the Aryan race, landing in Britain not later than 600 B.C., conquered a great part of the Aborigines, destroying a large portion of the male population, but taking possession of their wives and daughters. The result of this was a mixed race speaking the Aryan tongue, but with non-Aryan modes of expression, and this pre-Aryan syntax, conforming to the Egyptian, remains in insular Celtic.

or fort, or city. Gai, however, is probably not identical with the Welsh *gai*, spray or foam, but a mere corruption of *Caius*, who, doubtless, was the general first in command of this station. About the year 105, this post was garrisoned by a cohort of a legion of the Nervii, and it is presumed that this detachment, in conformity with the military system of Rome, was quartered here for a long time. As a cohort was one-tenth of a legion, and normally consisted of 420 to 600 men, the position, from a stragetic point of view, must have been considered exceedingly important. The legion was recruited in Gaul, the Nervii being a Belgic people, and, strange to say, nearly related in blood to the Brythons themselves, but the commanding officers, the six centurians and their subordinate officers, would, at this period, be Romans. The station occupied the crest of a slope to the right of the road from Bala, about three-quarters of a mile beyond Glan y Llyn (or Glanllyn). The fosse and vallum are well preserved, and near the centre of the square stands the old mansion of Caer Gai, now occupied as a farm house. An outer dyke encloses a circuit of six or eight acres, and on one side boulders are so disposed as to give the impression of being the foundations of primitive buildings. Some years since (in 1885) there was unearthed in a field adjacent to the camp a Roman monument of red sandstone, with the remains of carving in base-relief, and an inscription stating that Julius, son of Gaveronis, a soldier of a cohort of the Nervii, had erected it. Fragments of pottery (one the remains of a mortuary urn), charred bone, charcoal, and pieces of metal were also found within the trenches which enclosed the monument. These trenches were 18 inches wide, 2½ feet deep, and 3 yards long, and were filled with black earth, entirely foreign to the soil, in which charcoal was found. This was probably an altar erected by an officer to the memory of the dead of the cohort, who, of course, would be cremated. An inscribed stone indicating the grave of a certain Saluianus, was previously found here, and also numbers of Roman bricks.

One of the first operations of the Romans in and near Penllyn was the construction by their engineers of the great military roads which met at Heriri Mons (also a Roman station) one of which passed Caer Gai, and at the south-eastern end of the town of Bala is an artificial mound, upon which, it is supposed, fortifications were erected to protect the pass to the sea. A detachment of the XXth Legion, long stationed at Chester, was for some time in this neighbourhood, and in Montgomeryshire, and one of their ensigns, a bronze bear, was found not long since adjacent to Penllyn. About the last quarter of the fourth century the Scotti from Ireland commenced to ravage the Welsh coast, but the discovery at Caer Gai, and other places, of coins of the Emperor Gratian, seems to prove that the Roman garrisons at this period still barred the passes to the inland towns. Exactly when the Irish forced their way through Penllyn and Powys is uncertain, but there is reason to suppose that it was about the end of the reign of Maximus, probably during the years 380-82, at which time the legions were withdrawn entirely, or almost entirely, from this portion of Britain, leaving the country practically defenceless. As we have already noted, Cunedda, who afterwards commanded at the Wall, drove the Scotti out and regained all of Gwynedd, which he restored to order and re-garrisoned.[1]

---

[1] See "The Welsh People," and authorities there cited. Cunedda placed some of his sons in command, and appears to have acquired possession of very extensive territories in Gwynedd, *viz.*, in Anglesey, in the Vale of the Clwyd, and in Merionethshire. It is conceivable that the original possessors of these lands had long since been slain, and that Cunedda, presuming his Welsh campaign to have taken place just prior to the fall of Roman rule (which is the most probable date), had no difficulty in obtaining a grant of them, probably in lieu of arrears of pay. No greater mistake can be made than to suppose that Cunedda was simply at the head of Brythonic tribesmen from the North, who seized Gwynedd without warrant. Although he opened the way to a re-population by the Brythonic people, a large nnmber of whom were, doubtless, from the North, yet his expedition against the Scotti must have been organized on purely military lines, and to have consisted of at least two legions (with cavalry auxiliaries) of disciplined troops, with adequate commissary and baggage trains, and, doubtless, the usual camp-following. It does not appear that all of these troops, the larger portion of which were probably recruited abroad, remained in Gwynedd, Cunedda himself, as stated, fell at the Wall, where a part of the cavalry force alone, at that time, consisted of nine hundred horse.

Photo. by A. H. Hughes.

DR. ELLIS PRICE.

[Reproduced from "The Heart of Northern Wales,"
by kind permission of the Author, Mr. W. Bezant
Lowe, M.A., F.C.S., Cae Carw, Llanfairfechan.]

From the date of Cunedda's re-occupation down to about the first quarter of the seventh century we have no authentic information whatever regarding Penllyn. All we know is that it formed a portion of the kingdom of Gwynedd and was ruled by a line of princes descended from Cunedda, who seem to have acquired their authority in the first instance by reason of having succeeded their ancestor as *Dux Britanniæ*, an office created by the Romans, and including command of the Wall, as well as over Wales, and which was retained under the government organized in Britain after the island was abandoned by Rome. It may be supposed that the rulers of Gwynedd, at least for several generations, continued to command at the Wall, and this supposition seems borne out by the fact that both Maelgwn, who is stated to have died in 547, and his son, Rhun, both descended from Cunedda, gained their reputation, not so much from their government of Gwynedd, as from their military achievements in the North. There is every reason for assuming that these early rulers of Gwynedd, holding also the office of *Dux Britanniæ* (which they undoubtedly did), were for some time after Roman rule in Britain had ceased, subject to an emperor, or dictator, or over-king, of all Britain. In addition, there is very respectable evidence, traceable to the middle of the tenth century, that the seat of government of this post-Roman British dynasty was at first established in London,[1] and that subsequently, as the Saxons began to win that portion of the island, the court was moved further and further north, until at last it established itself in the district called Manau, in the territory of the Guotodin, adjacent to the Wall, and under the protection of the Wall's defenders. It is

---

[1] In the laws of Howel Dda, the land measurements are said to have been originally compiled by Dyfnwal Moelmud, who was king "before the crown of London and the supremacy of this island were seized by the Saxons, and who first established good laws in this island." "Ancient Laws and Institutions of Wales," i., 182-5 (1841, Rolls ed., A. Owen).

likewise certain that, when the Saxons pushed the Cymry hard from the north as well as from the south, and neither the Wall nor the surrounding country was any longer tenable, several chieftains claiming descent from these post-Roman over-kings, with their people, withdrew into Wales, and one of them, Llywarch Hên, is identified with the legendary history of Penllyn.

According to the generally accepted legend, Llywarch met the Saxons in battle at Rhiwaedog (the bloody slope), some time in the seventh century, and defeated them, the youngest and last remaining of his twenty-four sons falling in the engagement.

> "To me there have been (because they were generous,
> It is mournful for the world to be without them),
> Many children fair and cheerful,
> But to-night I am all alone."[1]

Llywarch is stated to have continued to reside in the neighbourhood, some say at Rhos y Gwaliau, in the parish of Llanfor, until his death, at the age of 150 years in 660, and to have been buried in Llanfor church, where a stone, now built into one of the church walls, and bearing an inscription which has been variously rendered, is supposed to have originally marked his grave. The legend of Llywarch Hên, and biographical sketches of him by late Welsh writers, are founded largely upon the poems attributed to him, of which there are a great many extant, for it appears that the prince was a prolific poet as well as a warrior, and the verses give us a very realistic picture of the age in which he lived. Although there can be no doubt that Llywarch was a real person, and that the verses claimed for him not only preserve many incidents in his career, but also, for the most part, were, in their primary form, his own composition, yet it is equally certain that, by reason of

---

[1] Attributed to Llywarch Hên, and presumed to have been composed on the night after the battle of Rhiwaedog.

three or four centuries of partial oral transmission, and the evident introduction by late fourteenth century bards of situations incompatible with the probable date of the original, the statements which these poems contain must be accepted with great caution. The remainder of the exploits with which this prince is credited, are, for the most part, fabulous. Fortunately, however, we have some really trustworthy information regarding Llywarch Hên and the period in which he lived. He was the son of Elidr,[1] called in a very ancient genealogy "Brenin Gwynedd," but "over-king" must be intended, for Elidr appears to have been contemporary with Maelgwn, who was certainly sole ruler of Gwynedd.[2] Elidr was nephew to Elidr Gosgordd Vawr[3] or Elidr "of the great retinue," evidently a prince of considerable importance, if not actually an over-king of the post-Roman dynasty. Following Elidr's genealogy still further back we find that his great grandfather was first cousin to that same Dyfnwal Moelmud,[4] who is mentioned in the laws of Howel Dda as being king of Britain (after Roman rule), and as having held his court at London "before the crown . . . and the supremacy of this island was seized by the Saxons," and Dyfnwal was the grandson of Coÿl,[5] who, as well as Urien Rheged, Llywarch Hên's cousin, was, as we have seen, an ancestor of Marchweithian of Isaled. The most probable date which can be assigned for Llywarch's birth is *circa* 490 to 525, and bearing in mind the great age attained in later times by a number of those who claimed him as an ancestor, and many overlapped 100 years, we may,

---

[1] Pedigree transcribed by Dwnn from a MS. traceable to about the fourteenth century.

[2] Maelgwn was contemporary with Gildas, who calls him *Insularis Draco*. Gildas lived 516-570.

[3] Pedigree transcribed by Dwnn; MS. pedigree of eleventh century transcribed from one of the tenth, appended to the earliest MS. of the "Annales Cambriæ" (Harl. MS. 3859).

[4] "Ibid."

[5] "Ibid."

without any great stretch of imagination, concede that the poet-prince actually lived to the age of 117 years, which is the span of life assigned him by more modest antiquarians. Supposing this to be true, he may have survived the battle of Chester (*circa* 616),[1] without reaching an extraordinary age, and as the Saxons were now in the immediate neighbourhood of Penllyn, there seems to be no reason to doubt that a battle in which Llywarch took part was fought at Rhiwaedog about the first quarter of the seventh century. A circumstance which goes far to confirm the evidence derived from these genealogies, is that many of the earlier, and most of the latter, Welsh historians speak of Llywarch Hên's family as associated with the government of the Isle of Man, whereas what little we know from a reliable source concerning the early history of that island does not seem to connect it at all with Llywarch's descendants or ancestors. Now, the older Welsh genealogies, those which seem, upon critical examination, to have been transcribed from genuinely ancient compilations, and are, in all probability, as trustworthy as those of the tenth century appended to the "Annales Cambriæ," with which, so far as they duplicate, they agree, speak of Llywarch's descendants as kings of *Manaw*, which, of course, is the present Welsh for Man, but it is suggested that it was originally intended for the *Manaw* of the Gudodin of Welsh poetry, and the *Manau* of the Guotodin of Harl. MS. 3859, from which district, adjacent to the Roman Wall, Llywarch Hên undoubtedly came. It is, indeed, conceivable that the title of King of Manaw, which appears to have been the last remnant of England over which the post-Roman dynasty held sway, may have remained to the heirs of the last Roman-Brython over-kings, long after Manau

---

[1] The Annals of Tighernach put the battle under 613, but 616 is supposedly the correct date.

itself had fallen finally into Saxon hands. It is probable, considering the antiquity of the tradition, that Llywarch Hên was really buried at Llanfor, but the stone said to have marked his grave may have served quite another purpose.

Penllyn was again threatened, and possibly invaded, by the Saxons at various times down to the tenth century, but the details are meagre. From the grants of lands in Penllyn to the Abbies of Strata Marcella and Basingwerk, or Dinas Basing, and from the Extent of Edward I., and other sources of information, it is possible to form a very clear idea of the ownership of the cymwd from quite an early period. There seems to be no doubt that Penllyn originally formed a part of the personal estates of Bleddyn ap Cynfyn, who was Prince of Powys from about 1062 to 1072. Bleddyn's sons, Maredydd and Cadwgan, divided their father's lands between them. Cadwgan, who was also lord of Nannau, in Merionethshire, got Penllyn as part of his share. According to the Welsh account, which is confirmed by subsequent events, Cadwgan, shortly before his death, which occurred in 1110, granted Penllyn, together with Cyfeiliog and other lands, to Uchtrud, his third wife's uncle. Uchtrud having revolted against the house of Cadwgan, Einion ap Cadwgan and his cousin, Gruffydd ap Maredydd ap Bleddyn (with their kinsmen), in 1113, attacked Uchtrud, defeated his forces and dispossessed him of Penllyn, Cyfeiliog, and his other lands, which the conquerors divided between them. In this division, according to the same account, Gruffydd obtained Cyfeiliog, Mawddwy, and half of Penllyn; Einion ap Cadwgan and his brother got the other half of Penllyn and the cantref of Meirionydd. We should add that Madog, the brother of Einion, certainly acquired the latter's share upon his (Einion's) death without issue, in 1121, and that Gruffydd divided his share of the cantref with his brother, Madog ap Maredydd.

Madog ap Cadwgan's portion of Penllyn descended to his son, Einion ap Madog, commonly called "lord of Ciltalgarth," from whom it came undivided to the latter's son, Madog ap Einion, or as he was usually designated, Madog Hyddgam of Ciltalgarth, and with this personage we reach somewhat surer ground. Madog Hyddgam lived at a place yet called Cae Fadog (Madog's field), and his lands included a very large portion of the northern part of Penllyn. By a charter undated, but *circa* 1200, cited in a later, and "inspeximus charter,"[1] he sold a great part of the Penllyn lands to the Abbey of Strata Marcella. The territory conveyed has been aptly described as "lying between Bala, Ffestiniog, Yspytty Ieuan [Evan], Pentre Voelas, Cerrig y Druidion, and Llangwm, but falling more or less short of those places," and there is evidence amounting almost to a certainty that this sale to the Abbey was followed, or perhaps preceded, by others by Madog Hyddgam, and that the total of the lands conveyed amounted to a very large proportion of the present parishes of Llanfor and Llandderfel. It would seem that Madog reserved very little land for himself, and his descendants, for the most part, became tenants and vassals of the Abbey. The family, however, continued to reside at Cae Fadog, which apparently was reserved, for several centuries, and held this and other lands in Ciltalgarth until late in the seventeenth century. The last owner of Cae Fadog of whom we have been able to find a satisfactory account was Ellis William ap Hugh, of Cae Fadog, gentleman, letters of administration upon whose estate were granted 26 February, 1645 (1645-46) to Marrett verch John, his widow.[2] An old MS. pedigree of the Owen and Evans

---

[1] "Montgomeryshire Collections," v., 100.
[2] Act Book 1087/1875, Probate Registry St. Asaph

families, of Merion and Gwynedd,[1] states that Ellis, there called "Ellis Williams of Cai Fadog," had four daughters, Margaret, Douse, Gwenn and Ellin, of whom Ellin (or Eleanor) married John Morris "of Brin Gwin" [Bryn Gwyn] in Denbighshire "and had one daughter Ellin, who married Cadwalader Ab Evan [Cadwaladr, or Cadwalader, Evans] late of Gwynedd [Pennsylvania] deceased."

"Gwenn, another daughter of the said Ellis Williams had three children who came to Pennsylvania, vizt. 1 [John, father of] Ellis Pugh late of Gwynedd deceased 2 Ellin married to Edward Foulke late of Gwynedd dec^d. 3 Jane, married to Wm John of Gwynedd, also deceased."

Edward Foulke, who removed from Penllyn to Gwynedd, Pennsylvania in 1698, and whose descendants intermarried frequently with the Roberts' family, in an account of his own and his wife's ancestry, originally written in Welsh and dated 1702,[2] gives the pedigree of his wife's mother thus:—

"Gwen, the daughter of Ellis ap William ap Hugh ap Thomas ap David ap Madoc ap Evan ap Cott ap Evan ap Griffith ap Madoc ap Einion ap Meredith of Cai [Cae]—Fadog; and [she] was born in the same parish [Llanfor] and shire [Merioneth] with her husband."

A pedigree of William ap Hugh of Cae Fadog in Ciltalgarth (the father of Ellis Williams) in Harl. MS. 1969, however, whilst agreeing with Edward Foulke's pedigree as far back as "Madoc ap Evan," states that the

---

[1] Original in Historical Society of Pennsylvania, bound with "Some Records relating to Radnor and Merion Meeting." MS. Colls. of the Genealogical Society of Pa.

[2] "Historical Collections of Gwynedd," 32. There are a number of copies of Edward Foulke's original MS. extant in Pennsylvania. See also pedigree of Edward Foulke by T. A. Glenn, edited by Charles Mather Foulke, in the Library of the Historical Society of Pennsylvania, and a chart pedigree by E. Booth, in same Library, but the latter contains some errors, although the descent from Rhirid Flaidd is correctly given.

former (Madog) was son of Ieuan (Evan) Fychan ap Ieuan Y Cott ap Gruffydd ap Madog ap *Cadwgan*, of Ciltalgarth, ap Madog Hyddgam."

Ellis Williams, under the designation of "Elliseus ap W^{m.} ap Hughe," appears as a landholder in Penllyn, in the Lay Subsidy Roll for Merionethshire of 3 Charles I.,[1] and as "Elliseij ap William ap Hugh," under the parish of Llanfor, in Penllyn, in that of 1636.[2] In the Rolls of the Feet of Fine for Merionethshire, 14 September, 16 Charles I. (1640), we find Eliceus Willms, gentleman, plaintiff, and William Kyffyn, gentleman, and Gwen his wife, deforciants, in *re* three messuages, and lands in the township of Penmaen (adjoining Ciltalgarth) in Llanfor.[3]

We have seen that Gruffydd ap Maredydd and Madog ap Maredydd divided their share of Penllyn between them. Gruffydd's lands lay partly about Bala, whilst Madog's portion included pasture along the lake, and the lake itself. Roughly speaking, these brothers held the southern part of the then cantref. That part of Penllyn which was retained by Gruffydd ap Maredydd descended to his son Owain Cyfeliog, from whom it came to Gwenwynwyn the son of Owain. Much of this land, especially about Bala, was granted to the Abbey of Strata Marcella. In 1216, however, Prince Gwenwynwyn went over from Llewelyn to King John, and Llewelyn seized his territory. A compromise, however, was affected, and when Gwenwynwyn died in 1218, his lands were ceded to Llewelyn by the king during the minority of his (Gwenwynwyn's) heirs; but what remained of his Penllyn estates was evidently retained in the prince's hands and passed to the latter's heirs, for Prince Llewelyn ap Gruffydd and his brother David held Penmaen between them, and after their deaths,

---

[1] Lay Subsidy Roll, Merionethshire, No. $\frac{220}{886}$, 3 Car. I., Public Record Office, London.

[2] "Cambrian Quarterly," vii., 449 (1831).

[3] Rolls of the Feet of Fine, 16 Car. I., Autumn Bdle., Public Record Office.

in 1282 and 1283, respectively, it passed by forfeiture to the Crown, and the tenants became Crown tenants. It seems probable, also, that the same brothers also held the lands of Pennantlliw, in Llanwchllyn, which also fell to the Crown, and at the time of the Extent of Edward I. are described as *vasta* (waste),[1] but which, soon after were granted by the king to Madog ap Iorwerth ap Madog ap Rhirid Flaidd. The grant included Glanyllyn, and Castle Carn Dochan, on the south side of the river Lliw, was, doubtless, the residence of this Madog ap Iorwerth, who was the ancestor in direct line of the Edward Foulke, above mentioned, and through alliances, of the Roberts' family.

Madog ap Maredydd's quarter of Penllyn fell to his sons Elised (or Ellis) ap Madog and Owain Brogyntyn, probably share and share alike. Ellis seems to have granted all of his inheritance to Strata Marcella, and afterwards confirmed the same, which appears to have been a sale and not a free gift. Owain Brogyntyn, the half brother of Ellis, granted (probably sold) his share to the Abbey of Basingwerk, or Dinas Basing, by a charter dated between 1186 and 1224. This grant included "all the pasture land of Penthlin," as well as the fishings of the lake itself, and is said to have comprised a large portion of Llangower and Llanuwchllyn. These lands of Basingwerk, or Dinas Basing, Abbey, were as already noted, leased in 26 Henry VIII. to Sir Robert ap Rhys, father of Cadwaladr ap Robert, and grandfather of Howel, ancestor of the Roberts' family.

It will thus be seen that before the conquest of Wales by Edward I., most of the cymwd of Penllyn had passed into the possession of the Church, but, for one reason or another, some of it was afterwards not retained.

---

[1] "Arch., Camb.," 1867, 187.

There is, somewhere, a statement to the effect that King Edward refused to confirm all of the grants which had been made to the Church under the plea that the monks had sided with Prince Llewelyn, and there is probably some truth in this assertion, for we find that an inquisition was held at Bala, before Thomas de Wynnesburgh, on the day of March next after the Feast of the Holy Trinity, 17 Edward II., regarding the rights of the Monastery of Strata Marcella to a dairy called Pennantigȝ and one plot of land called Kymman, which Edward I. had seized, because of the disloyalty and violence of the monks during the late war.[1]

The conquest of Wales must have almost depopulated this cymwd. Under Penmayn (Penmaen), for instance, the Extent informs us that according to the testimony of Jeveni ab Howel, who had been Sheriff of Merionethshire, Llewelyn, Prince of Wales, and David ab Gruffydd (his brother), had held the ville of Penmayn equally between them, and that their land is waste. And concerning the men of Penmayn (Penmaen) . . . "they are dead and the lands are waste," and the same story, almost, is told of all the lands of Penllyn not then held by the Church. Near Bala, the estate of Ririd (Rhirid) ap Einion Goch Wreyk, being two ploughlands (and pasturage), which was probably at Rhiwaedog, now in Llanfor, had escheated to the Crown. Eynoun (Einion) ab Yerworth (Iorwerth) held here 2 shillings of land; Howel ab Ellisse was dead (value of his holding 20d. per annum) and a son of Philip ab Kenewryk (Cynwrig), evidently a minor, held here to the extent of 12d. per year.

From the time of Edward I. to the Reformation, Penllyn was largely under the domination of the monks and the tribe of Rhirid Flaidd, the most powerful branch

---

[1] "Abbey of Ystrad Marchell," in "Montg. Colls." v., 135-6.

of which latter continued at Llanuwchllyn; other septs seating themselves at Rhiwaedog, Bala and adjacent places.

Howel, ancestor of the *Roberts*' family, was, as we have seen, the sixth son, and among the youngest of the thirteen children of Cadwaladr ap Robert of Rhiwlas, lessee of the "Grange of Penllyn."[1] The precise date of his birth is unknown. The pedigree drawn up by Lewys Dwnn, and dated 21 July, 1588,[2] describes this Howel ap Cadwaladr (otherwise Howel Fychan) as "O Lan Gowair" (Llangower), and he appears to have then been alive, but was dead before 3 Charles I. (1627-8), the Lay Subsidy Roll[3] for that year naming him as father of Robert ap Howel, also then deceased, and as grandfather of Cadwaladr, son of Robert ap Howel, who was at that time seized of the lands of his father and grandfather aforesaid, which were then rated XX^s. iiij^d. per annum.

How Howel ap Cadwaladr acquired his Llangower and adjacent lands is not clear, but he was very probably enfeoffed therein by his father, Cadwaladr ap Robert, according to the custom of that period; at any rate it is certain that farms held by Howel's descendants down to the time of Robert Cadwalader (or Cadwaladr), who removed to Pennsylvania, had formed part of the estates which Howel's grandfather, Sir Robert ap Rhys, held under the Abbey of Basingwerk. There is evidence to show that Howel, or his grandson, Cadwaladr, secured other lands in Llanycil, probably leasehold, afterwards held by the family. The name of Howel's wife has not been ascertained, but it is evident that, as was then common, he was married when young, an example not

---

[1] See *supra*.
[2] Dwnn, i., 228.
[3] Lay Subsidy Roll for Merionethshire, 3 Car. I., under "Penllyn, No. 220/335, Public Record Office, London.

followed by several of his descendants.[1] His son and heir, then a mere youth, appears to be identical with Robert ap Howel, named in connection with a debt for a trifling sum, in the will of John ap Lewis of Llangower, dated 24 March, 1572 (1572-3).[2] Robert ap Howel, as noted, died prior to 3 Charles I. (1627-28), leaving a son and heir, Cadwaladr, who, under the designation of "Cadwaller ap Robert ap Ho^{ll}" is named as a landholder in the Lay Subsidy Roll of 3 Charles I.,[3] and, as "Cadd^r ap Robert" (his grandfather's name being omitted), under the parish of Llangower, in that of 1636.[4]. The precise date of the death of Cadwaladr ap Robert is not certain. He was father of Robert Cadwaladr (or Cadwalader) of Llangower, who, with his family, removed to Gwynedd, Pennsylvania, and whose children and descendants assumed the surname of *Roberts*.

---

[1] Robert ap Howel was over 30 years of age when his heir Cadwaladr was born, but daughters, or sons who died in infancy, may have intervened. His son, Cadwaladr Robert, must have been close to 40 years old when his son Robert Cadwalader was born. The latter is supposed to have been about 41 or 42 years of age at the time of his marriage in 1672, which would make his age about 68 or 70 at the time of his removal to Pennsylvania, which agrees with the statement in the family MSS. that he was then an old man ; but his wife was younger, and it is supposed that he had been married before (*i.e.*, before 1672), but either had no children, or else they died in infancy. Cadwalader Roberts, born 1673, married at the age of 41, and his brother Morris at the same age.

It should be noted here that there were others bearing the name Robert Cadwaladr (or Cadwalader) living in the same neighbourhood at about this period and considerable research has been found necessary in order to distinguish between them. Robert Cadwaladr of Nant y yddalid, Llanuwchllyn, had a son Cadwaladr (or Cadwalader), baptized 15 May, 1663. This Robert Cadwaladr, of Nant y yddalid (or Nant y derlie), was buried at Llanuwchllyn, 6 May, 1683. His pedigree is known. On 8 Sept., 1672, a Robert Cadwalader and Jane Griffith were married at Llanuwchllyn Church. He was buried at Llangower, 10 March, 1684, and his widow, Jane Griffith, was buried at the same place, 1688. Still another Robert Cadwaladr (or Cadwalader), was living in Llanuwchllyn, 1686 ; his wife was named Catherine. They were parents of a Cadwalader Roberts, baptized 6 April, 1677, and of Edward Roberts, baptized 1 Oct., 1677, and of a daughter Elizabeth, buried at Llanuwchllyn, Feb. 1686, and others.

[2] Probate Registry, St. Asaph.

[3] Lay Subsidy Roll for Merionethshire, 3 Car. I., under "Penllyn," No. 2̶4̶8̶/3̶3̶8̶, Public Record Office, London.

[4] "Cambrian Quarterly," iii. (1831), 449.

BALA LAKE.

SHOWING BIRTHPLACE OF ROBERT CADWALADER.

Robert Calwalader (or Cadwaladr), in conjunction with his brother, Evan Cadwalader, held an interest in a farm called Penbryn in the adjoining parish of Llanycil, where, at intervals, he resided. Like his father, grandfather, and great-grandfather, he was a farmer. In or before the year 1672, he married Jane, an elder daughter of John ap Evan (or John Evan) of Penmaen, in the parish of Llanfor, Merionethshire.[1] Their eldest son, Cadwaladr (or Cadwalader), was baptized at Llanuwchllyn Church, 1 June, 1673;[2] their first daughter, Margaret, was baptized in the same Church, 27 June, 1675[3] (d. young); their second son, Morris, was baptized in Llangower Church, 9 May, 1677.[4] The following year Robert Cadwalader removed temporarily to Llanycil, and John "ye son of Robt Cadwaladr & Jane his wif" was baptized there 7 January, 1678[5] (*i.e.* 1678-79). The family did not remain long in Llanycil at this time, for on 1 November, 1679, Robert Cadwalader is described as of Llangower,[6]

---

[1] See reference to will of John Evan, *infra*.

[2] Anno 1673. *Cadd^r son of Robert Cadwalader and Jane his wife*, baptized 1 June [Llanuwchllyn Parish Register Transcripts, Diocesan Registry. St. Asaph.] The Roberts MS. states that he was born 1673; see "Historical Collections of Gwynedd," 1st ed.

[3] Llanuwchllyn Parish Register Transcripts, Diocesan Registry, St. Asaph.

[4] Anno 1677. *Moriceus filius Roberti Cadd^r & Janæ uxoris eius baptizatus fuit nono die May.* [Llangower Parish Register Transcripts, Diocesan Registry, St. Asaph.]

[5] Llanycil Parish Register Transcripts, Diocesan Registry, St. Asaph. He died an infant.

[6] Bond dated 1 Nov., 1679. Gainor Jones of Llangower in the County of Merioneth, widow and executrix of the will of Humphrey Jones of Llangower, deceased, Robert Cadwalader of Llangower, yeoman, and Evan Cadwalader of Llanyckill, in the said County, yeoman. Witnesses: Cadwalader Jones, Robert Vaughan, Lewis Williams. This document was taken to Gwynedd, Pennsylvania, by Robert Cadwalader, and passed into the hands of Griffith John, brother-in-law of the latter, and thence into the possession of Griffith John's son-in-law and executor Thomas Jones of Merion, from whose descendants it was secured by the late James J. Levick, M.D., of Philadelphia, and is now (1910) among the Levick MSS. in the possession of that family. Humphrey Jones (or Humphrey ap John) was buried at Llangower, 1 February, 1678 (1678-79), but his will was not proved at St. Asaph, as no reference to it appears in the Act Book under the year named.

but, in the Autumn of 1681 (11 September)[1] a second John (the fourth son), was baptized in Llanycil Church. Rowland the fifth son of Robert and Jane, was baptized 29 March, 1685,[2] and Elizabeth, their second daughter, 9 December, 1688 ;[3] both at Llanycil. Nicholas, the sixth son, was, it is reasonable to suppose, younger than Elizabeth, but the record of his baptism, owing to the condition of the records, has not been found.

The family returned to their old home about 1694, and in the will of John Evan (or John ap Evan) of Penmaen, dated 4 August, 1696, Robert is described as "my son-in-law Robert Cadwalader of the parish of Llanuwllyn [Llanuwchllyn] in the County of Merioneth."[4]

We will now take up the pedigree of Jane, daughter of John ap Evan (or John Evan) of Penmaen, in the parish of Llanfor, which is also that of a number of the early settlers of Gwynedd and Merion, in Pennsylvania.

---

[1] Anno 1681. *Johannis filius Roberti Cadd^r de Penbryn et uxoris ejus bap^{tus} fuit undecimo die Septembris*, [Llanycil Parish Register Transcipts, Diocesan Registry, St. Asaph.]

"Historical Collections of Gwynedd," 1st. ed., p. 190, states that John was born about 1680, but the 2nd. ed. gives the date as "about 1677." If the latter date is from a statement of his age at the time of his decease, such statement was most probably wrongly taken from a family record of the birth of the first John.

[2] Anno 1685. *Rolandus filius Roberti Cadd de Penbryn et uxoris eius baptizatus fuit vigintinono die Martij 1685*, [Llanycil Parish Register Transcripts, Diocesan Registry, St. Asaph.]

"Historical Collections of Gwynedd," 1st. ed., p.191, states that Rowland was born 1685. The 2nd. ed., says "at Bala," but should read "near Bala."

[3] Anno 1688. *Elizab : filia Rob'ti Cadd^r and Janna^e ux : ejus bap^{ta.} fuit 9no. die Decemb : 1688.*

[4] The will of John Evan of the Township of Penmaen in the parish of Llanfor, Merionethshire, was proved at St. Asaph. 24 April, 1697 [" Copies of wills " 1824/1885, folio 165, &c. ; Probate Registry, St. Asaph. Original in Bdle. for 1697.] The testator also mentions his sons Cadwalader John, Griffith John (or Jones) who removed to Merion, Pennsylvania in 1690, but afterwards settled at Gwynedd ; William John, who removed to Gwynedd in 1698, and Rowland. Another son, Robert, who also went to Pennsylvania is not mentioned. The testator also mentions daughters, Margaret John, who died at sea on the voyage to Pennsylvania, Gwen John, widow, who died at Gwynedd, and Catherine John. For particulars see *infra*, where this will, and a detailed account of John Evans' children are given more at large

Owen, Evans, and Allied Families.

Rhodri Mawr, son of Merfyn[1] (Mermin) Frych (or Vrych). [Ped. appended to the "Annales Cambriæ," Harl. MS. 3859; "Y Cymmrodor," ix., 169, 170; Powel; Dwnn, ii., 99; Bridgeman; Rhys and Brynmor-Jones, 139.]

"By the death of Merfyn he [Rhodri] had become head of the line of Gwynedd. Afterwards, by his marriage with a daughter of Meurig ab Dyfnwallon, he became lord of Ceredigion and Ystrad Towi on the death of her brother Gwgan." [Jesus Coll. MS. 20; "Y Cymmrodor," viii., 87; Harl. MS. 3859; "Y Cymmrodor," ix., 180, ped. xxvi.; see Rhys and Brynmor-Jones, 143.]

According to Rhys and Brynmor-Jones (143), who follow Powel and other Welsh historians, Rhodri probably also became the ruler of Powys, through his "grandmother" Nest, "sister and heiress of Congen ab Cadell, king of Powys." Rhodri's dominions included "the remainder of Wales, except Dyfed, Morgannwg [Glamorgan] and those principalities roughly corresponding to the modern Brecknockshire and Radnor," and it is claimed, and admitted as possible by Rhys and Brynmor-Jones, that he exercised an over-lordship "even over these territories."

Rhodri "had continual conflicts with the Mercians and Danes."

855. Slays the Danish chief Horm in single combat.

876. Defeated by the Saxons, and obliged to flee to Ireland. [Rhys and Brynmor-Jones, 144.]

877. Returns to Wales, and is slain in battle with the Saxons, together with his brother Gwriad, being aged 89 years. [Rhys and Brynmor-Jones, 144; "Brut y Tywysogion"; Bridgeman; "Hist. Powys Fadog," Lloyd.]

Rhodri Mawr is stated to have divided his kingdom into three parts, Gwynedd (North Wales), Powys, and Deheubarth (South Wales), to the government of which he nominated his three eldest sons; but this has been doubted, and it seems more probable that after Rhodri's death these sons divided the country themselves.

ISSUE:

i. Anarawd, Prince of North Wales; he defeated the Saxons in 880, near Conway, in a battle called "Rhodri's Revenge," and died 915. [Rhys and Brynmor-Jones, 144-5, 147-9.]

---

[1] Spelled Mervyn in old Welsh Genealogies, and Mermin in Harl. MS. 3859, the oldest original MS. on the subject extant.

ii. Merfyn, Prince of Powys; defeated by his brother Cadell, who deprived him of Powys, 887; slain in 900. [See authorities cited.]
iii. Cadell, Prince of South Wales; *of whom presently.*
iv. Tudwal, King of Dyfed; he was wounded in the knee by the Saxon king Ædwal, at the battle of " Rhodri's Revenge," and afterwards became Chief Justice of Gwynedd. [Dwnn.]
v. Meurig, who is said to have been *arglwydd* (lord) of Ystrad Meurig. [Dwnn, ii., 98.]
vi. Gwriad, Prince of Tegeingl. [Dwnn, ii., 98.]
vii. Gwyddelig, who is said to have been *arglwydd* of Gwyddelwern. [Dwnn, ii., 98.]
viii. Angharad, married the "Lord of Clorghargws." [Dwnn, ii., 98.]

Cadell ap Rhodri Mawr, Prince of South Wales. [Ped. appended to " Annales Cambriæ," " Y Cymmrodor," ix., 149; Aneurin Owen's " Welsh Laws," &c., I., preface xiv.; Giraldus; Powel; Dwnn, I., 98, &c.; Bridgeman, 2, 4; Rhys and Brynmor-Jones, 143, 149, &c.; " Brut y Tywysogion."]

880. Cadell is said to have taken part in the battle of Conway, called "Rhodri's Revenge," when his brother Anarawd, prince of North Wales, defeated the Saxons.

893. The Saxons, under Ælfred, having invaded Cadell's territory, Cadell and Anarawd abandon the relation which they had established with the Northumbrians, and seek the friendship of Ælfred, probably 897. [Asser, M. H. B., 488.]

The residence and seat of government of the princes of South Wales was at Dinefwr (Dynevor, Dinevawr, or Dinas Vawr), the great palace, on the bank of the river Towi, in what is now Carmarthenshire. Here a castle which, after the custom of the time, was, doubtless of timber, had been erected by Rhodri Mawr. This structure was replaced by a stronghold built of stone and mortar by the Lord Rhys, which, in subsequent wars was repeatedly captured and retaken, and the ruins of which are now (1911) still to be seen.

The territory over which the princes of South Wales ruled as overlords, or as their individual possessions, varied considerably at different periods, according to the fortunes of war. It is commonly supposed to have corresponded nearly to the present counties of Cardigan, Carmarthen, Pembroke, Glamorgan, Monmouth, Brecknock, Radnor and part of Hereford, but within this territory were several separate governments, such as Glamorgan, Dyfed, and others, ruled by their own lords, or, as they early called themselves, kings, and over these petty governments, the princes of South Wales ruled, for most of the time, but not always, as over-lords only.

Owen, Evans, and Allied Families

The princes, after Rhodri's time, seem to have always held the "Kingdom of Ceredigion" and Ystrad Towi as their individual possessions. This district roughly corresponded to the present Cardiganshire and the greater part of the modern Carmarthenshire, and it was within these counties that the descendants of the Lord Rhys continned to hold vast possessions until conquered by Edward I. in 1282-3.

Cadell, Prince of South Wales; died 907, having some years before seized the government of Powys, and slain his brother Merfyn in battle, in 900. [Bridgeman, 4.] The name of his wife is uncertain.

ISSUE.

i. Howel Dda, *of whom presently*.
ii. Meurig; living 917.
iii. Clydawc, wounded in personal combat with his brother Meurig, 917. ["Brut y Tywysogion"; "Annales Cambriæ".] In 922, when Eadward the Elder had subdued all Mercia, Idwal, then prince of Gwynedd, together with Howel Dda and a Welsh prince named Clydawc, received him as their lord. ["Eng. Chron.," s. a. 922.] The "Brut" states that Clydawc (Clydog) died 917, but the date may be wrong. [See also Rhys and Brynmor-Jones, 151, and note 2.]

Howel Dda, eldest son of Cadell, succeeded to his father's government in South Wales and Powys, and, on the death of his cousin, Idwal Voel, in 943, he acquired that of North Wales, so that at first he is called " King of Deheubarth," and afterwards " King of the Welsh." ["Saxon Chron."; Bridgeman, 4; Rhys and Brynmor-Jones, 149, 156; ped. appended to "Annales Cambriæ"; "Y Cymmrodor," ix., 169, 170; "Welsh Laws," Aneurin Owen, i; Pref. xiv., note; "Brut y Tywysogion."]

Howel was over-lord of the smaller principalities, or as they were called, "kingdoms" of Gwent Dyfed, Breicheiniog, Buallt, Gleguising, and probably others. He does not appear, however, to have retained Glamorgan, although he attempted to do so ["Liber Landavensis."] He was under-king to the Saxon monarchs.

922. Howel does homage to Eadward the Elder. ["Saxon Chron."; Rhys and Brynmor-Jones, 151.]

926. Does homage to Æthelstan, at Hereford. ["Saxon Chron."; Rhys and Brynmor-Jones, 151.]

926-8. Makes a pilgrimage to Rome. ["Brut y Tywysogion"; "Annales Cambriæ"; Rhys and Brynmor-Jones, 153.]

Attends various Witenagemots, or Parliaments of his English overlords, 936-949. ["Saxon Chron."; Rhys and Brynmor-Jones, 153.]

Howel attested the following charters whilst in attendance at the several Witenagemots:

21 July, 931 ("Cod. Dipl." v., 199).
12 Nov., 931 („   „   ii., 173).
30 Aug., 932 („   „   v., 208).
15 Dec., 933 („   „   ii., 194).
28 May, 934 („   „   ii., 196).
16 Dec., 934 („   „   v., 217).
          937 („   „   ii., 203).
          946 („   „   ii., 269).
          949 („   „   ii., 292, 296).

His name is subscribed to these doubtful charters:

17 June, 930 ("Cod. Dipl." ii., 170).
1 Jan., 935 („   „   v., 222).
21 Dec., 935 („   „   ii., 203).

In the earlier charters he attests as *sub-regulus*, and in the later ones as *regulus*.

Howel and Morgan, the latter called "King" of Glamorgan, are parties to an Arbitration before Eadward the Elder (incorrectly transcribed Eadgar) concerning the districts of Ystradyew and Ewyas, and decided against Howel. ["Book of Llan Dâv," Oxford, 1893, 248; "Liber Landavensis," Llandovery, 1870, 237; Pelgrave, "English Commonwealth," v., 2, ccxliv.]

After North Wales came under his rule, in 943, Howel called together the chief men of Wales and formulated new laws for the government of the country, known as the "Laws of Howel Dda," and which, with some slight changes, continued partly in force until 34 Hen. VIII. ["Ancient Laws and Institutions of Wales," Aneurin Owen, Lond. Record Commissioners, 1841, fo., another ed. 2 vols., 8vo., 1841.]

Howel, "for his godlie behaviour, discreet and just rule" was "beloved of men." [Quoted by Rhys and Brynmor-Jones, 155; see Powel, and authorities elsewhere cited.]

950. Howel dies. His death, says Powel, "was sore bewailed of all men, for he was a prince that loved peace and good order, and that feared God."

Howel Dda is said to have married, first, Sain, daughter of "the Duke of Cornwall." [Dwnn, ii., 99.] He is stated to have married, secondly, Afandreg, daughter of Cynyr Fychan ap Cynyr Fawr (or Vawr) of Arfon. [Dwnn, ii., 99.] He married, also, Elen (died 943), daughter of Loumarch (Llywarch) ap Hymeid, King of Dyfed. This Hymeid, "with all the inhabitants of Demetia, compelled by the violence of Rhodri's six sons, submitted to Ælfred." [Asser's "Life of

Ælfred." But the genuineness of Asser's "Life" has been questioned.] As to Howel's marriage to Elen, see Anc. ped., appended to "Annales Cambriæ," "Y Cymmrodor," ix., 171.]

There is some uncertainty, from conflicting statements, as to the maternity of Howel Dda's children, and the following order is simply an arbitrary one, except that Owain was certainly the eldest, and it appears that his mother was Elen, seemingly the third wife of Howel. If, therefore, any of Howel's children, as enumerated, were by the two first women named, they were, doubtless, by marriages disallowed.

ISSUE:

i. Owain, *of whom presently.*
ii. Maredydd. [Dwnn, ii., 99; Bridgeman, 61.]
iii. Rhodri. [Dwnn, ii., 99; Bridgeman, 6; Rhys and Brynmor-Jones; Powel.] He was slain at the battle of Llanrwst, 951.
iv. Gwenllian. [Dwnn, ii., 99.]
v. Rhun. [Powel; Bridgeman, 6.] Slain before 948.
vi. Dyfnwal, slain 951 at the battle of Llanrwst. ["Brut y Tywysogion".]
vii. Eadwyne. Slain 951-2. ["Brut y Tywysogion"; Bridgeman, 6; Rhys and Brynmor-Jones.]
viii. Cynan, called "Conan y Gwyn." ["Brut y Tywysogion"; Bridgeman, 6.]
ix. Einion. [Bridgeman, 6.]

Owain ap Howel, eldest son of Howel Dda. [Ped. appended to "Annales Cambriæ," "Y Cymmrodor," ix., 169-70; "Gwentian Chronicles," 25; Dwnn, ii., 99; Bridgeman, 6; Rhys and Brynmor-Jones, 158; Aneurin Owen's "Welsh Laws," i., Pref. xiv.]

Owain and three of his brothers, Dyfnwal, Rhodri, and Eadwyne, succeeded jointly to the over-lordship of Deheubarth, or South Wales (excepting Glamorgan) upon the death of Howel Dda their father. [Rhys and Brynmor-Jones, 158.] But Ieuaf and Iago, sons of Idwal Voel, seized the government of Gwynedd, or North Wales. [Rhys and Brynmor-Jones, 155.]

950. Ieuaf and Iago attack Owain and his brothers and defeat them.

950. Ieuaf and Iago again attack Owain, but "Owen, Prince of Ceredigion (Cardigan) collected an army against them, and followed them back to Gwynedd so closely that many of them were drowned in the river Dyvi." ["Gwentian Chronicles".]

951. "Owen ap Howel Dda led an army into Gwynedd, and then the action of Aberconwy took place, in which such a slaughter was made, that both parties were obliged to retreat from losses they sustained in that battle." ["Gwentian Chronicles".] This was the battle of Llanrwst,

951-2. Dyfnwal, Rhodri, and Eadwyne, brothers of Owain, die, and Owain becomes sole prince of South Wales.

953. Owain is again attacked by Ieuaf and Idwal, but defeats them with fearful loss. ["Gwentian Chronicles."]

954-5. Owain defeated and driven from his government. Ieuaf and Idwal "held the kingdom of Dinefwr for several years." [Bridgeman.]

955. The Saxons, under Alvryd, invade North Wales, and Iago seizes his brother Ieuaf and pulls out his eyes. [Rhys and Brynmor-Jones, 156.] Owain, taking advantage of the opportunity, recovers his territory. [Bridgeman, 7.]

962. Pays a tribute of 300 wolves' heads to Eadgar, King of England. [Bridgeman, 7.]

987. Owain, Prince of South Wales dies. ["Brut y Tywysogion"; Rhys and Brynmor-Jones, 158.]

The name of Owain's first wife is unknown. He married, secondly, Angharad, daughter and heiress of Llewelyn ap Merfyn ap Rhodri Mawr. [Dwnn, ii., 99; "Hist. Powys Fadog," Lloyd, 65.]

ISSUE by first wife:
i. Einion, *of whom presently*.
ii. Cadwallon, died 961 (or 964). ["Gwentian Chronicles."]

ISSUE by second wife:
iii. Maredydd. He became king or prince of all Wales, and died a natural death, a thing unusual in this family, 998-9. [Dwnn, ii., 99; Bridgeman, 8; "Brut y Tywysogion"; Caradog; Rhys and Brynmor-Jones, 159-60.]
iv. Llywarch; his eyes were pulled out by Godfrey son of Harold, 986. [Powel.]
v. Iestyn. [Dwnn, ii., 99.]
vi. Siwauna. [„   „ „ .]
vii. Lleuku. [„   „ „ .]
viii. Ardden. [„   „ „ .]
ix. Marred. [„   „ „ .]
x. Gwerfyl. [„   „ „ .]
xi. Gwenllian. [„   „ „ .]

Einion ap Owain, eldest son of Owain ap Howel Dda, by his first wife. [Dwnn, ii., 99; "Brut y Tywysogion; Bridgeman, 7-8; Rhys and Brynmor-Jones, 159; Giraldus.] Einion commanded his father's troops.

967. Places Gower under tribute to his father.

981. Defeats the Danes under the famous Godrid, at Caer Faes, in

the parish of Llanwenog,[1] Cardiganshire. [Jones's "Hist. of Wales."] Meyrick confuses this with a battle fought with Howel ap Ieuan in the same year.

981-2. Defeats the English. ["Brut y Tywysogion."] Slain at the battle of Pen Coed Colwyn, 982-3. ["Hist. of Powys Fadog," 1-65.]

982. "The gentleman of Gwentland rebelled against their prince, and cruelly slew Einion, the son of Owen, which came thither to appease them." [Powel.] The "Brutt" places his death in 983.

Einion is spoken of as "a young man of high promise and a leader of great judgment and personal bravery." [Bridgeman, 7.] "A worthie and noble gentleman, who did manie notable acts in his father's time." [Powel.] Einion is said to have married Nest, daughter of the (Saxon) Earl of Devonshire. [Dwnn, ii., 99.]

ISSUE:

i. Eadwyn. [Powel; Giraldus.] Slain 993 in the battle of Clunog, where his tomb is said to exist with this inscription : EDWINI OCCISIO (the slaughter of Edwin). [Bridgeman, 9, 10; "Hist. Powys Fadog," Lloyd, i., 67.]
ii. Tewdwr. [Dwnn, ii., 99; Powel; Giraldus.] Slain at the battle of Llangwm, 993. ["Bruty Tywysogion"; Bridgeman, 10.]
iii. Cadell, *of whom presently.*
iv. Gwladys. [Dwnn, ii., 99.]
v. Gwenllian. [Dwnn, ii., 99.]
vi. Marred. [Dwnn, ii., 99.]

Cadell ap Einion, second son of Einion ap Owain, ap Howel Dda. [Leland, iii., 74; "Ex libro Giraldi Episco. Lincoln"; Bridgeman, 8, 11; "Hist. of Powys Fadog," i., 65.]

Cadell was at the battle of Llangwm, 993, and was probably there slain with his brother. This battle was fought in Denbighshire, six miles from Corwen (in Merionethshire) between Maredydd ap Owain ap Howel Dda, and the rebel chieftain, Idwal ap Meurig.

[Giraldus de Barri, from whose writings we correct a later and erroneous statement, but who, in one paragraph makes Tewdwr, father of Rhys ap Tewdwr, son, instead of grandson, of Einion ap Owain, was the fourth son of William de Barri, by his second wife, daughter of Nest, daughter of Rhys ap Tewdwr, and was, therefore, great great grandson to Tewdwr ap Cadell ap Einion ap Owain ap Howel Dda, whose birth and ancestry, from actual records which he examined, he carefully records. Giraldus was born in 1147, one hundred and fifty four years after the probable date of Cadell's death. He was made Archdeacon of Brecknock, in 1175. In 1188 he accompanied Archbishop Baldwin, who came into South Wales to preach a crusade. The Archbishop and Giraldus were entertained by the "Lord" Rhys, Prince

---

[1] Caer Faes, is an entrenched field on Ty Cam farm, in the parish of Llanwenog.

of South Wales and cousin to the latter. Whilst the guest of Rhys, Giraldus examined, it appears, the ancient archives relating to the family history of the princes of South Wales, and copied therefrom much information which he records. Among other things, he says that the genealogy of the princes was preserved in books, and that they traced their descent from "B.M." (i.e., Beli Mawr, otherwise Cunobelinos). But he adds that, as long pedigrees may appear trifling, they are omitted.

ISSUE:
i. Tewdwr, *of whom presently*.

Tewdwr ap Cadell ap Einion, is sometimes called Tewdwr Mawr; but the epithet "Mawr" (great) may have also been applied to his uncle, Tewdwr ap Einion, who was slain 993. [Bridgeman, 8, 11; "Hist. of Powys Fadog," Lloyd, i, 65.]

Tewdwr ap Cadell was living about the year 997, and is said to have been slain soon after that date, apparently in Brittany, where he probably married, and where his son, Rhys, is traditionally said to have lived almost all of his life.

ISSUE:
i. Rhys, *of whom presently*.
ii. Maredydd. [Dwnn, ii., 99.]
iii. Gwyn. [Dwnn, ii., 99.]
iv. Rhydderch. [Dwnn, ii., 99.]
v. Gwladys. [Dwnn, ii., 99.] Married Caradog ap Iestyn, Prince of Glamoran [Giraldus.][1]
vi. Angharad. [Dwnn, ii., 99.]
vii. Nest, married Sutrig, son of Alured, Danish King of Dublin. [Dwnn, i., 224.]
viii. Gwerfyl. [Dwnn, ii., 99.]
ix. Marred. [Dwnn, ii., 99.]

Rhys ap Tewdwr, eldest son of Tewdwr ap Cadell. [Giraldus; Dwnn, ii., 99; Bridgeman, ii.; Powel; "Brut y Tywysogion," and authorities cited elsewhere.] He was born in 997, and is stated to have been a mere child at the time of his father's death, and to have been brought up in Brittany, to which place his father had probably fled, to escape the violence of his kinsmen. Some accounts state, however, that his father fell in

---

[1] Bridgeman is in error here, as the language of Giraldus is unmistakable, and he should be good authority as to his great aunt.

Wales, and that Rhys was sent to Brittany for safety, where he remained for many years until he returned to claim the sovereignty of South Wales, which was not, by all accounts, until he was seventy-nine or eighty years old.

"Rees the sonn of Theodor as right inheritour to the kingdome of South Wales claimed the same, and the people received him with much joie, and made him their Prince." [Powel.]

"In him the legal succession was restored; he was moreover the choice of the people." [Yorke.]

"Upon the overthrow of this Rhys (ap Owain), his kinsman Rhys ab Tewdwr, a lineal descendant of Rhodri Mawr, succeeded to Deheubarth (South Wales) without any opposition of which evidence is handed down." [Rhys and Brynmor-Jones, 272.]

"According to Robert Vaughan of Hengwrt the immediate territories of this prince . . . . consisted only of the present counties of Cardigan and Caermarthen: as Pembroke, Breicheiniog, Gwent, and Gleguising (or Herefordshire) were governed by their several reguli. There can be but little doubt, however, that all these acknowledged the sovereign authority of the superior prince of South Wales." [Bridgeman, 11.]

1080. Rhys joins Gruffydd ap Cynan, at St. Davids, and they defeat Trahaiain, Prince of North Wales and his allies at the battle of Mynydd Carn. The biographer of Gruffydd says that Rhys did homage to Gruffydd on this occasion, and that Rhys promised him half of his dominions, but this is questionable. Rhys after the battle, withdrew, fearing treachery from his ally, and Gruffydd sent his Danish and Irish mercenaries to ravish his territory. After which Gruffydd marched to Powys, where he slaughtered all of the male inhabitants he encountered and carried their wives and the maidens into captivity. Mynydd Carn is in South Cardiganshire. [Bridgeman, 13; "Montg. Colls."; Rhys and Brynmor-Jones, 273.]

For his Herefordshire lands in the province of Arcenefelde, Rhys, under the designation of "Riset de Wales," paid William the Conqueror an annual tribute of £40. ["Herefordshire Domesday".]

1081. Rhys does homage to King William, at St. Davids. [Bridgeman, 12.]

1087. Attacked by the sons of Bleddyn ap Cynfyn, Prince of Powys, defeated and escapes to Ireland. [Bridgeman, 13.]

1089. Rhys recruits an army of Irish mercenaries, returns to South Wales, defeats the enemy at Llych Crei, and recovers his country. [Bridgeman, 13; Rhys and Brynmor-Jones, 277.]

"Rhys was evidently a wealthy chieftain, for the gifts he gave to his Irish mercenaries were so large as to attract special attention.." [Rhys and Brynmor-Jones, 277.]

Rhys ap Tewdwr was slain in battle (supposedly with the Normans) near the Castle of Brecknock, *in ipsa hebdomada Paschali*, 1093. [Florence of Worcester, ii., 31.] He was, most historians agree, about 96 years of age at the time of his death.

Rhys married several times; his last wife, to whom he was wedded when he was about 65 to 70 years old or more, being Gwladys, daughter and heiress of Rhiwallon ap Cynfyn of Powys. [Powel; Dwnn, ii., 99; " Hist. of Powys Fadog," i., 109.] Rhiwallon was slain at Mechain, 1068. [" Hist. Powys Fadog," Lloyd, i., 71.]

ISSUE by early alliances:
i. Goronwy, (Grono); he was in the king's prison, 1102; died in the Tower of London, 1103. [" Brut y Tywysogion"; " Gwentian Chronicles"; Powel.]
ii. Howel; he was in the prison of Ernulph [de Montgomery] son of Roger, lord of Castle Baldwin, "when King William had given (to Ernulph) a part of the territory of Res ap Tudor"; but he subsequently escaped "in a mained state with broken limbs." [" Brut y Tywysogion."]
iii. Owain. [Dwnn, i., 246.]

ISSUE by last wife:
iv. Gruffydd, *of whom presently.*
v. Gwenllian. [Dwnn, ii., 99.]
vi. Nest. [Dwnn, ii., 99.] Married, 1st, Gerald de Windsor; 2ndly, Stephen, Constable of Cardigan, she was the grandmother of Giraldus.
vii. Efa. [Dwnn, ii., 99.]
viii. Ardden. [Dwnn, ii., 99.]

Gruffydd ap Rhys, Prince of South Wales, eldest surviving son of Rhys ap Tewdwr. [Giraldus; " Brut y Tywysogion"; Powel; Dwnn, ii., 99; Bridgeman, 14, Chaps. ii., iii., &c.; Rhys and Brynmor-Jones, 300.] Unless otherwise noted the statements which follow are from Bridgeman.

Rhys ap Tewdwr, says Powel, had "a sonne called Gruffyth, who at his father's death was a verie child." He was, probably, about 12 years old in 1093, and doubtless, the youngest of the children of Rhys's last wife.

1115. Gruffydd having been sent to Ireland, was recalled by his brother-in-law, Gerald, husband of his sister Nest.

Being accused to the King of England of trying to stir up a revolt, he seeks the aid of Gruffydd ap Cynan, Prince of North Wales, who receives him kindly, but arranges to murder him, in order to obtain a reward from the king. Warned by his sister Nest, however, he escapes to Lleyn, where he takes sanctuary in the church of Aberdaron.[1] Gruffydd ap Cynan's men pursue him, and attempt to drag him from the sanctuary; but the clergy interfere, and Gruffydd escapes in a fishing boat.

1115. Rebels against the English, and, with a handful of followers, attacks the English outposts, ravaging the borders of Dyfed and Ceredigion.

1116. Sacks and burns the castle near Abberth, (Narberth). Attacks the castle of Llanymddyfri[2]; but is defeated. Destroys the outer works of the castle of Swansea, and takes Carmarthen Castle; also a castle in Gower, to the garrison of which he gives no quarter. Captures the castle of Kidwelli from de Londres, its governor.

The leading chieftains of Ceredigion now do homage to Gruffydd, as prince of South Wales. "And, with their assistance, Griffith not only demolished many castles and took great spoils, but also regained a portion of the lands and possessions of his father in these parts."

Gruffydd retreats to the wilds of Ystrad Towi, from which place he continues his attacks upon the English; but, in 1122, concludes a peace with King Henry, by which the latter cedes to Gruffydd much of his father's territory, to be held free, by homage and fealty, only.

1135-6. King Stephen summons Gruffydd to London to answer charges against the king's peace; but Gruffydd treats the summons with contempt, and proceeds to North Wales to procure assistance from Gruffydd ap Cynan, to whom he has now become reconciled, and whose daughter he has married.

Gwenllian, wife of Gruffydd and daughter of Gruffydd ap Cynan, during the prince's absence, leading her husband's troops against one Gruffydd ap Llewelyn, commanding for Maurice de Londres, is defeated, captured, and beheaded on the field of battle. Morgan, one of Prince Gruffydd sons, is slain, and Maelgwn, another son, made prisoner. On both sides 516 men were slain, and their bodies left on the field to be devoured by wolves. [Florence of Worcester.]

1136. Prince Gruffydd and the other chieftains now attack the Lords Marchers and the English and Fleming residents so that the execution of Gwenllian "was followed with a vast destruction of churches, towns, growing crops, and cattle, the burning of castles and other fortified places, and the slaughter, dispersion, and sale into foreign parts, of innumerable men, both rich and poor." March and April, 1136. Soon after this Gruffydd, assisted by the brothers of Gwenllian, and a majority of the chieftains of South Wales, subdued the entire country (part of South Wales) as far as Cardigan, driving out the English and Flemings; and replaced the old inhabitants on their lands, 1136.

---

[1] The church of Aberdaron stands on the sea coast almost at the extreme end of Lleyn, and is probably not much altered, so far as the walls are concerned, since Gruffydd took refuge therein. The doorway is early Norman.

[2] Llandovery.

1136. Gruffydd fights the battle of Cardigan, in the second week in October, and defeats the entire combined forces of the English and Flemings in Wales and on the Marches, commanded by Stephen, Constable of Cardigan, Robert Fitz-Martyn, Pain Fitz-John, and the sons of Gerald. "The slaughter of human life was so great that, besides the men who were led away into captivity, there remained 10,000 captured women, whose husbands and little ones had been partly drowned in the water, partly consumed in the flames, partly slain with the sword." The English indeed were utterly routed, and Gruffydd immediately pursued his advantage by conquering all of Pembrokeshire.

Prince Gruffydd ap Rhys, having completed the conquest of Cardigan, and thus regained most of the ancient possessions of his ancestors, gave a grand festival at his "palace" in Ystrad Towi (Dinefwr, or Dynevor, Castle) to which he invited all the princes and nobles of Wales and the Marches.

"For the entertainment of the guests he assembled the sages of the country, whom he appointed to hold disputations; and he brought together the chief bards and musicians of every district to display their skill in vocal and instrumental music. To these were added scenic representations, feats of skill, and athletic sports. This festival continued forty days, after which the guests were dismissed and the bards and players liberally rewarded according to their deserts." This was about the beginning of the year 1137. Gruffydd, after this, applied himself to new regulations of government, and the revision of the laws.

Prince Gruffydd ap Rhys died about April or May, 1137, having, according to Florence of Worcester, been murdered by his (second) wife. He married, first, Gwenllian, daughter of Gruffydd ap Cynan.

ISSUE by Gwenllian:

i. Morgan, born 1116-17; slain at the battle of Maes Gwenllian, 1136. [Bridgeman, 36.]
ii. Maelgwn, taken prisoner at the battle of Maes Gwenllian, 1136; supposed to have died in captivity. [Bridgeman, 36.]
iii. Anarawd, murdered by his father-in-law, Cadwaladr ap Gruffydd ap Cynan, 1142-3, leaving a son Einion, murdered in his bed, 1163. [Powel's continuation of "Welsh Chron."; Bridgeman, 36.]
iv. Cadell, wounded by the English whilst hunting in Dyfed, 1151-2. His wounds incapacitating him for further active service in the field, he went on a pilgrimage to Rome, 1156; died 1175. [Bridgeman, 40.]
v. Maredydd, born 1128; died 1154. ["Brut y Tywysogion".]
vi. Rhys, *of whom presently.*
vii. Gwenllian. [Dwnn, ii., 99.]
viii. Sioniad. [Dwnn, ii., 99.]
ix. Ales. [Dwnn, ii., 99.]
x. Marred. [Dwnn, ii., 99.]
xi. Ardden. [Dwnn, ii., 99.]
xii. Gwladys. [Dwnn, ii., 99.]

OTHER ISSUE:
xiii. Owain. [MS. ped.]
xiv. Rhys. [MS. ped.]
xv. Arod. [Dwnn, i., 225.]

Rhys ap Gruffydd, Prince of South Wales, called the "Lord Rhys" (or Res). He succeeded his father, Gruffydd ap Rhys, in 1137. ["Brut y Tywysogion"; Powel; Bridgeman; "Gwentian Chronicles".] The following notes are from the above authorities except when otherwise noted:

1145. Rhys rebels against the English, re-takes Dinefwr Castle which they had seized, and the castles of Carmarthen and Llanstephen.

1147. Takes the Castle of Gwys.

1150. Takes the castle of Llanrhystyd (Dinerth) by storm, and puts the garrison to death; seizes the Castles of Ystrad Meurig and others, and retires to the Vale of Towi, having won all of Ceredigion.

1153. Takes the castle of Aberllychwyr, in Gower, and demolishes it, burns that of Penwedig, called Castle Gwalter, at Llanfihangel Genau'r Glyn, that of Llanfihangel, in Pengwern, and that of Tenby, in Dyfed, by a night assault.

1154-5. Takes and demolishes Aberafon Castle, called Castle Humphrey, and those of Aberdyfi, Dineir (Dinerth?), and Llanrhystyd[1] (for the second time).

1155. Rebuilds Aberdyfi Castle, and others; storms and captures the very strong castle of Llanymddyfri.[2]

1157. Again takes the castle of Llanymddyfri.

1158. Rhys does homage at Woodstock to King Henry, who compels him to give 25 hostages, including two of his own sons.

1159. Rhys besieges Carmarthen, but unsuccessfully.

1161. Henry II. marches against Rhys, in person, and the latter surrenders, and is sent to prison in England.

1163-4. Released from prison, upon which he does homage to the king and gives hostages [Bartholomæi Cotton "Historia Anglicana".] After this Rhys again attacked the English, and re-captured all of Ceredigion (Cardiganshire), 1164; and in the same year attacks Dyfed and murders all the Flemings found there.

---

[1] The foundations of two castles, within a short distance of each other. One of these appears to have been known as Llanrhystyd and the other Dinerth.
[2] Llandovery.

1164. Rhys founds the Abbey of Strata Florida (Ystrad Fflur) for the monks of the Cistercian order, in Cardiganshire. ["Brut y Tywysogion," Bridgeman, 47.]

1164. Henry II. attacks Owain Gwynedd, Prince of Gwynedd and Rhys becomes Owain's ally. Henry, defeated, causes the male hostages, sons of Rhys and others, with 300 prisoners of war, to be mutilated, their eyes pulled out, their noses slit, and their ears cut off, and of those hostages who were maidens, he ordered their ears "stuffed."

1165, Nov. 5th. Rhys takes the castle of Aberteifi, or Cardigan, and re-takes the most part of Caerdigion.

1165-6. Captures Cilgerran Castle.

1166. Defeats the English and Flemings, near Cilgerran.

1167. Rhys, and the prince of North Wales, capture the castle of Rhuddlan, which they demolish, but afterwards rebuilt, and also take the castle of Prestatyn, and burn it.

1167-8. Builds the castle of Aberlynaun.

1168-9. Rhys concludes a peace with the king of England.

1171. Engages in other attacks upon the English, and attacks Gwynedd and Powysland.

1171, 8 Sept. Surrenders, upon summons, to Henry, II., at Cardiff, does homage, and is released, after promising the king 300 horses, 4,000 oxen, and 24 hostages.

1171, 11 Oct. The king enters Pembrokeshire, and grants Rhys Ceredigion (Cardigan), Ystrad Towi, Arwystli, and Elvael. Rhys rebuilds the castle of Cardigan, and about this time is appointed the king's Justiciary for South Wales.

1173, 12 Calds. of Oct. Confers with Hen. II. at Pembroke Castle, returns to Cardigan to collect horses for the king, and has another interview with him the following Easter. He supports the king against Prince Henry.

1174. Summoned to serve in England against the Earl of Derby. At the seige of Tutbury, in the king's service, 1175.

1175, 29 July. A commissioner for a peace between England and Wales.

1176. Prince Rhys ap Gruffydd holds a great festival at his castle of Cardigan, at Christmas.

1177. Summoned to attend the Parliament held at Oxford.

1177. Attacks the Normans in Maelienydd,[1] and builds the castle of Rhaiadr Gwy.

1178. Rhys is attacked by the sons of Gruffydd ap Cynan, of North Wales, but defeats them with great slaughter.

---

[1] Or Melenyeth.

1181-2. Engages in various quarrels with his English neighbours.

1184. Rhys grants a charter to Strata Florida Abbey, which is witnessed in the Church of St. Bridget at Rhaiadr, Radnor, by Gruffydd, Rhys, and Maredydd, sons of Rhys. [Cart. 10 Edw. III., *m*.6, *n*.9, *per inspeximus;* Bridgeman, 55, 56.]

Founds the Abbey of Tallagh, or Talley, in Carmarthenshire[1] (date uncertain). [Tanner's "*Not. Monastica*,"] benefactor to the Slebech Commandry (date uncertain) [Fenton's "Pembrokeshire," Appendix 4, 64.] Rhys was also benefactor and patron to several other religious Houses and Churches, including the Cathedral of St. Davids.

1184. Rhys again revolts against the English ; but has a truce with the king, and a conference at Worcester, under safe conduct. Peace is concluded, 1185, and Rhys raises a body of Welsh infantry for the king for service in the French Wars, 1185.

1188. Archbishop Baldwin and Giraldus, the Archdeacon, preach a crusade in South Wales, and are magnificently entertained by the "Lord Rhys," at Cardigan, and other places. [Giraldus.]

1189. Rhys does homage to Richard I., at Oxford, and considering himself insulted because the king did not receive him personally, revolts, and takes Carnwyllion, and several castles in Dyfed.

1189, Dec. Besieges Carmarthen, at Christmas, and captures the castles of St. Clare, Abercoran and Llanstephen.

1190. Rebuilds Kidwelly Castle.

1191, 15 Augt. (The day of the Assumption of St. Mary). Rhys retakes Dinefwr Castle.

1194-5. Taken prisoner by his sons, Howel and Maelgwn, but escaping soon afterward re-takes the castle of Dinefwr (Dynvor) which Maelgwn has seized. Upon his release Rhys again makes war upon the English, 1195 ; but De Broase wins the castle of St. Clare, held by Howel Sais ap Rhys, and in the same year, Rhys and Meredydd, sons of Rhys, revolt against their father and take the castle of Llanynddyfri.

1196. Rhys now musters a great army and wins the castle and town of Carmarthen, and subdues his rebellious sons.

1196-7. Captures Clun and Radnor Castles, and defeats Roger de Mortimer and Hugh de Saye ; storms and takes Payne Castle, in Elvael, but restores it to Willlam de Broase, whose daughter has married his son Gruffydd ap Rhys.

1197. Rhys, having ordered his sons to drag Peter de Leia, Bishop of St. Davids, out of bed and march him half clothed through the woods at night to Dinefwr (Dynevor) as a punishment for some insolence shown him, and refusing any apology or satisfaction to the bishop, is excommunicated.

---

[1] Tal y Llychu, now Talley.

1197, 24 April. Rhys dies shortly after, of the pleague, whilst still under the ban of excommunication ; but, through the entreaty of some of his sons who suffered penance for him, this was removed, although not before his decomposed body had been scourged, and he was buried in St. David's Cathedral Church. ["Annales de Wintonia"; Bridgeman, 66, 67.]

Notwithstanding his continuous military operations, Rhys was much concerned with the revision of the laws of Wales, and "the thirteenth century MS. of the Demetian Code makes mention of alterations and additions by Lord Rhys ab Gruffydd, who flourished from 1137 to 1197." [Rhys and Brynmor-Jones, 185.]

"Lord Rhys" is said to have possessed an exceedingly violent temper, and when angry beat his servants (bondsmen) and "hung his dogs," indiscriminately.

Rhys ap Gruffydd married Gwenllian, daughter of Madog ap Maredydd, Prince of Powys. [Giraldus Cambrensis ; Bridgeman, 68 ; Powel ; "Brut y Tywysogion" ; Dwnn, ii., 99, &c.,] He also, at various times, formed other alliances under the laws and customs of Wales, the children by such unions being, according to the said written laws, heirs equally with the other children, not only to their father's lands, but also, in some cases, to his title. The legitimacy of the issue of such alliances for purposes of inheritance from the father, was acknowledged by the Church of Wales, and when judged by the Welsh law, by the Crown of England, until the statute of Rhuddlan disinherited children so born after the date thereof.

ISSUE by Gwenllian :

i. Gruffydd, *de jure*, Prince of South Wales ; married Maud, daughter of William de Broase, a Norman lord of Brecheiniog (now Brecknock). She died 29 Dec., 1210. Gruffydd, having assumed the religious habit, and retired to Strata Florida, died 25 July, 1201. [Dwnn, ii., 90; Bridgeman, 56-69, 73-8, 210, 249.]

ii. Cadwgan. [Dwnn, ii., 90.]

iii. Rhys Gryg (or Grig) *of whom presently.*

iv. Maredydd, "gethin," called lord of Llanymddyfri ; "slain by the Englishmen of Kidwelly" at "Carnwyllaon" (Carnnyllion), 2 July, 1201 (St. Swithin's Day), and was buried in St. Mary's Church, Kydwelly. ["Annales Cambriæ"; Bridgeman, 77.]

v. Gwenllian, married Ednyfed Fychan, chief Counsellor to Llewelyn ap Iorwerth, Prince of North Wales, and also to his son Prince David. In letters patent dated at Shrewsbury, 17 Dec., 17 Hen. III., (1232), Ednyfed is styled *Idnevet Seneschallo ipsius Lewelini;* named as one of the arbitrators in a convention between Hen. III., and Prince David, at Gloucester, on the next Tuesday before the Feast of

Owen, Evans, and Allied Families

St. Dunstan, 24 Hen. III   Ednyved Fychan was ancestor to the *Royal House of Tudor.* [Dwnn, ii., 81, and note 1, Patent Rolls, 17 Hen. III.; Pennant's "Wales," ii., 268-70, Ed., 1784; Bridgeman; Powel.]

vi. Nest (called also Annes, i.e., An*nest*, and Gwenllian) confused in some pedigrees with her sister, wife of Ednyved Fychan (or Vychan); she married Rhodri, younger son of Owain Gwynedd, prince of North Wales. Rhodri was living 1176, and was ancestor to the Wynns of Gwydir and Anwyl families. [Dwnn, ii., 69; Powel; "History of the Gwydir Family," Wynn; Bridgeman, 69.]

vii. Gwenllian, died unmarried, 1190. [Bridgeman, 62.]

viii. Catherine, married Kydifor ap Dyfnwal, *arglwydd* (lord) of Castle Hywel (Cardiganshire).

OTHER ISSUE:

ix. Maelgwn (by Gwerfyl, daughter of Llewelyn ap Rhys ap Wardaf Frych) [Dwnn, ii., 90.] Confirmation charter to the Abbey of Strata Florida by *Mailgun fil. Resi principis South Wall*, 11 Kl' Feb., 1198. [Harl. MS. 6068, fo. 10.] Maelgwn acquired a considerable portion of his father's possessions, and became a renowned soldier. For particulars concerning his life, see Bridgeman's "Princes of South Wales."

x. Morgan (by Nest, daughter of Caradog Fychan ap Caradog). [Dwnn, ii., 90.] He was one of the witnesses to the confirmation charter of Maelgwn ap Rhys to the Abbey of Strata Florida, 11 Kl' Feb., 1198, and that of Maelgwn Vychan [Harl. MS. 6068, fo. 10.] Died 1251, being very aged, and having assumed the monastic habit, at Strata Florida, where he was buried.

xi. Morgan. [Golden Grove MS., Pub. Record Office, Lond.]

xii. Cynwrig (by Nest, daughter of Gruffydd Wynn ap Gwalchmai); he was one of the hostages given to Hen. II., 1164-5; being then aged about 10 or 12 years, and died in Whiteland Abbey, 1237, having survived his mutilation 72 years. [Dwnn, ii., 90; Bridgeman.]

xiii. Cynwrig (or Cyneuric). On the morning of leaving Strata Florida, the archbishop and Giraldus were met by this Cynwrig at the head of a body of light-armed youths. "This young man," writes Giraldus, "was of a fair complexion, with curled hair, tall and handsome, clothed only according to the custom of his country, with a thin cloak and inner garment, his legs and feet, regardless of thorns and thistles, were bare; a man not adorned by art but by nature; bearing in his presence an inate not acquired, dignity of manners," ["Itin." ii.]

xiv. Howel,[1] called *iddall*, the blind, to distinguish him from his brothers of the same name; he is said to have been a hostage, and was blinded, but whether he was one of those delivered in 1164-5, to Hen. II., in addition to Cynwrig and Maredydd, is uncertain. He may, like other of his kinsmen, had his eyes pulled out by some other chieftain, as this mode of punishment, or revenge, was then very popular in Wales. He was, however, certainly blind, and this precludes the notion that he could have been confused with either of his brothers of the same name, who it is evident must have been possessed of their eyesight. Howel "the blind" was living 1194, when, it is recorded, he was instrumental in obtaining the release of his father, who had been imprisoned by Howel's brothers, Maelgwn and Howel Sais. [Bridgeman; authorities cited.]

xv. Howel Sais (by Ysteder, daughter of Caradog ap Llowrodd). He had also been a hostage, probably one of the 24 given to Hen. II., in 1171, and remained so long in England that he acquired the epithet of *Sais*, and he is stated to have held the lordship of St. Clare. Some military operations are credited to him in 1173, and later, 1189, was in command of St. Clair (or Clare); he joined Maelgwn, his brother, against his father, in 1194; but afterwards falling out with Maelgwn, the latter's men fell upon him and stabbed him at Cemes. He was conveyed to Strata Florida, and assumed the habit of a monk, and dying of his wounds soon after, was there buried, 1204. ["Brut y Tywysogion"; Bridgeman.]

xvi. Howel, died 1199, at Stinguil, on his return from the court of King John, of England. ["Annales Cambriæ"; Bridgeman, 52.]

xvii. Cadwaladr, (by Gwenllian, daughter of Maredydd ap Gruffydd ap Tewdwr); murdered in Dyfed, 1186, and buried in Whiteland Abbey. ["Brut y Tywysogion"; Bridgeman, 58.]

xviii. Maredydd (by Efa, daughter of David Fras (Vras) ap Rhydderch); he was Archdeacon of Cardigan, and died at the Church of Llanbedr Tal Pont Stephan (now called Lampeter) and his body conveyed to St. Davids and buried by Iorwerth, the Bishop, near the grave of his father Rhys. ["Brut y Tywysogion"; Bridgeman, 108.]

xix. Maredydd "Iddall," the blind (by Gwyndyth, daughter of Cynddelw ap Brochmail, of Llangiwg, in Emlyn); one of the hostages delivered to Hen. II., in 1164, and, as well as his, brother, Cynwrig, was mutilated, his eyes pulled out, his nose slit, and his ears cut off by order of that king. He became a monk, and died 1239, at Whiteland Abbey, where he was buried. [Dwnn, ii., 90; Bridgeman, 70, 113.]

---

[1] It was at this time, and as late as the latter part of the reign of Queen Elizabeth, a very usual thing for parents to give two or more children the same name.

xx. Owain Caerwedros (by Sabel, daughter of Ieuan Hir), of Caerwedros; he died at Strata Florida, and there buried 1191. [Dwnn, ii., 90; "Brut y Tywysogion."] He held the lordship of Caerwedros, Ceredigion.
xxi. Tanglwyst (by Gwendyth, above named). [Dwnn, ii., 90.]
xxii. Gwladys, married Maredydd ap Rhydderch. [Dwnn.]
xxiii. Anarawd, living 1192. ["Brut y Tywysogion"; Bridgeman, 63.]
xxiv. Madog, living 1192. ["Brut y Tywysogion"]; his eyes were pulled out by his brother Anarawd.
xxv. —— (daughter), married Einion Clyd, who held the lordship of Elvael; he and his brother Cadwallon, who was lord of Maelienydd, attended the "Lord Rhys," in 1174, when he went to serve the King of England against the rebellious Earl of Derby. [Bridgeman; Lyttleton's "Hist. Hen. II.," iii., 178.] Their son, Einion, took the Cross in 1188. [Giraldus.]
xxvi. —— (daughter) married Einion ap Rhys, called lord of Gwrthrynion in Powysland. [Bridgeman.]
xxvii. —— (daughter), married William Martyn, of Cemes (Kemes). [Bridgeman.]
xxviii. Angharad, married Bledri, of Dyfed. [Dwnn.]
xxix. Elen, married Gruffydd ap Ifor "Bach."

Rhys Gryg, third son, by Gwenllian, of Rhys ap Gruffydd, was born *circa* 1150. According to the custom of gavelkind he succeeded to a large portion of his father's dominions, including the castle of Dinefwr; but his elder brother, Gruffydd, assumed the title of Prince of South Wales. ["Brut y Tywysogion"; Powel; Bridgeman, and authorities hereafter cited.]

The following particulars concerning him, unless otherwise specified, are from the authorities cited *in re* his father. Rhys Gryg (or Grig) is variously styled Rhys Grug, and Rhys Vychan (or Fychan) (*i.e.* junior).

1184. Rhys witnesses his father's Charter to Strata Florida. [Cart. 10 Edw. III. *m.* 6. *n.* 9. *per inspeximus.*]

1195. Revolts against his father, but captured and imprisoned.

1198. Takes Dinefwr (Dynevor) Castle, which had fallen into the hands of the English.

Storms and takes Llychwein (Llychwyr) Castle, with the assistance of the English, and puts the garrison to the sword, 1205, and, in 1207, takes Llangadoc[1] Castle. He also reduced Llanymddyfri, about this time.

---

[1] Llangadock, 21 miles E.N.E. from Carmarthen.

1209. Gruffydd opposes the King of England (John), who advances against him in person, and Rhys surrenders in the following year (1210) ["Annales of Waverley".] Is released.

1210. Defeats his brother, Maelgwn, in battle, and in the same year is summoned by King John to serve against Prince Llewelyn. In the following year joins the king in another expedition against the same prince (1211).

1212-13. Writ of King John to Foulk, Steward of Cardiff, Warden of the Marches, and to the Steward of Hereford, commanding them to take away from Res (Rhys) Fychan, "by some called Res Grug," all of "Ystradtywy." Dinefwr (Dynevor) Castle was captured by his nephew, Rhys ap Gruffydd, with the aid of the English, the same year.

1214. Rhys Gryg takes the Castle of Llanymddfri ; is taken prisoner at Carmarthen ; but escapes.

1214. Joins in an assault on Caerfyrddin Castle, which he destroys ; takes others on Christmas Eve, and on St. Stephen's Day captures Aberteifi and Cilgerran.

1216. Arbitration before Prince Llewelyn at Aberteifi, regarding a partition of lands. Rhys Gryg gets the castle of Dinefwr, and three cantrefs.

1217. Demolishes Gower Castle.

1219. Rhys Gryg marries Joane, daughter of Richard de Clare, ["Brut y Tywysogion".]

1220-1. Maredydd, son of Rhys Gryg and Joane de Clare, his wife, is born.

1221. Rhys Gryg joins the Earl of Pembroke against Prince Llewelyn; but is defeated, and again compelled to do homage to that prince.

1222. Composition of claim of Gervase, Bishop of St. David's, against Res ap Res (i.e. Rhys Gryg, for certain lands, by which the said Res and Mareduch (i.e. Maredydd), his *son and heir* (then an infant) acknowledge the right of the Bishop and the Church of St. David's to all of the lands claimed, and the said Res and his *sons* (i.e. by former wives) surrender all the said lands to the bishop, receiving them back again to hold as vassals of the Bishop of St. David's at an annual rent of one lance on the Feast of St. John the Baptist, and military service in the bishop's army in time of war, at the summons of the said bishop. ["Statuta Ecclesiæ Menevensis" (St. David's), Harl. MS. 1249 ; Bridgeman, 102, 103.]

1223, 21 Sept. Rhys Gryg does homage to Hen. III., and the king restores to him those lands which had been taken from him. [Rot. Lit., Claus., 7 Hen. III., *memb.* 1.]

1227.—Rhys Gryg is taken prisoner by his son Rhys Vychan, *alias* Rhys Mechyll, at Llanarth, and forced to surrender Llanymddfri Castle, and the lands appertinant thereto, to the said Rhys Vychan (or Fychan).

[From the above notes (under 1219 to 1227, inclusive) it is clear either that Joane was the first "wedded wife" of Rhys Gryg, or that an earlier marriage had been disallowed by the Pope, in order that the eldest son of Joane de Clare might inherit the entire vast estate. The evidence is in favour of the latter supposition. It appears that Rhys Gryg, having, at about the age of 70 years, married the daughter of a Norman earl, is persuaded to ignore the rights of his elder sons, and to make his youngest, and, according to English law, only legitimate son, Maredydd, his sole heir. To strengthen his position Rhys makes a peace with Henry III., and does homage to him as a baron of England, thus endeavouring to place himself under English law. It will be noted that in the composition with the Bishop of St. David's, above cited, Maredydd is named as "son and heir," but as the other "sons" are also included, it is plain that the bishop was protecting himself under both English and Welsh laws. Rhys Vychan (or Mechyll), eldest son of Rhys Gryg, and at this time about 50 or more years old, learning of his father's intention to repudiate the ancient laws of Wales, and annul the rights of his (Rhys Vychan's) brothers and himself under an earlier alliance, seizes him, and compels him to settle certain estates upon them.

1231, 30 Nov. Rhys Gryg is included in a temporary peace between England and Wales, being on the side of Llewelyn, so that prior to this he had again been in arms against the English. [Rymer.]

1233. Rhys joins the rebel barons Richard Marshall, Earl of Pembroke, and Hubert de Burgh, and takes the castles of Cardiff, Abergavenny, Pencelly, Blaenfyni, and Bwlch y Dinas.

1233. Rhys Gryg is wounded at the seige of Carmarthen and taken to his Castle of Dinefwr (Dynevor) in Llandeilo Vawr, where, shortly after, he dies of his wounds and is buried at St. David's, 1233. ["Brut y Tywysogion."]

>ISSUE[1] by Elliw, daughter of Thomas ap Gwgawn ap Bleddyn, who is said to have been a lord of Brecheiniog. [Salusbury Pedigrees.]
>i. Rhys Mechyll, *of whom presently*.
>ii. Iorwerth. [Dwnn, i., 50; ii., 99.]
>iii. Llewelyn. [Dwnn, ii., 99.]
>iv. Caradog. [Dwnn, ii., 99; Bridgeman, 111.]
>v. Sionedd (Jonet), married Sir John Marbury, Knt. [Dwnn, ii., 100.]
>vi. Angharad.
>vii. Ardden, married Einion ap Gwalter ap Trahaiarn, of Ystrad Gwalter. [Dwnn, ii., 100.]
>viii. Sionedd, married Gruffydd ap Cadwgan.
>ix. Gwenllian, married Sir Gruffydd ap Elidur, Kt. of the Holy Sepulchre, ancestor to Sir Rhys ap Thomas, K.G., who is

---

[1] It is conceivable that some of these children may have been by some other women as in nearly all cases the name of the mother is omitted,

credited by some Welsh historians with having slain Richard III., on Bosworth Field. A MS. at Rhiwlas, however, states that Richard was slain by Rhys ap Maredydd, of Plâs Iolyn.

x. Jane, married Gwgawn ap Hoedlin. [Dwnn, i., 271.]
xi. Gwenllian Gethin, married Howel ap Goronwy. [Dwnn i., 144.]
xii. Ardden, married Gwgawn ap Llewelyn, of Llangathen. [Dwnn, i., 139.]

ISSUE by Joane de Clare:

xiii. Maredydd, born *circa* 1220-1; named as *son and heir*, 122. [Harl. MS. 1249; "Statuta Ecclesiæ Minevensis"; Bridgeman, 102, 103.] He was of Drosslwyn [Dryslwyn], and died in that castle, 27 July, 1271. ["Brut y Tywysogion".]
xiv. Howel, pardoned, 7 Jan., 1278, for attacks on the English. [Rot. Wall., 9 Edw. I., *m.* 12, *de anno sexto.*] Again revolts, and "Ohelo ap Res Crek" and his men declared felons and outlaws, and Howel's lands forfeited, 10 June, 1280. [Rot. Wall., 6-9 Edw. I., *m.* 7 *de anno Octavo.*] Ancestor to a family in South Wales. [Dwnn, i., 236.]

Rhys Mechyll, eldest son of Rhys Gryg, called also Rhys Vychan, or junior, as in the case of his father. ["Brut y Tywysogion"; Powel; Bridgeman; Dwnn; and other authorities cited *infra.*] He was born, doubtless, when his father was quite young,[1] so that there is a great difference between his age and that of his half-brothers Maredydd and Howel, who were born when Rhys Gryg was about 70 years old.

Rhys Mechyll inherited, as his portion of his father's estates, Dinefwr (or Dynevor) Castle and the greater part of the Cantref Mawr, and he also appears to have continued to hold Llanymddyfri Castle, which, in 1227, he had forced his father to cede to him. [Bridgeman, 175, 176.]

1227. Rhys Mechyll takes his father prisoner at Llanarth, and compels him to grant him the Castle of Llanymddyfri and land appertinant thereto. ["Brut y Tywysogion."]

7 Hen. III. The king sends his letter to Res Vychan (Mechyll), son of Res Grig, advising him that Res Grig (the father) having done homage to him, must not be molested. [Rot. Lit. Claus., 7 Hen. III., *m.* 1.]

Rhys Mechyll died 1244. ["Brut y Tywysogion"; Bridgeman, 121.] He married a daughter of Lord Croft, of Croft Castle, Herefordshire. [Dwnn.]

---

[1] At this time, both in England and Wales, youths were married when only fourteen years old, or before. In Wales a son came of age, under the ancient laws, at fourteen years.

ISSUE:
i. Rhys Vychan, *of whom presently.*
ii. ——— (a son), living 20 Aug., 1246. [Bridgeman, 186.]
iii. ——— (a son), living 20 Aug., 1246. [Bridgeman, 186.]
iv. Gwenllian, married Gilbert Talbot. [Bridgeman, 186, and authorities hereafter cited.]

Rhys Vychan (or Fychan), eldest son of Rhys Mechyll (alias Vychan), lord of Dinefwr (Dynevor). [Bridgeman; Powel; "Brut y Tywysogion," and authorities hereafter cited.]

1244. Rhys Vychan attacks the English.

1245, 6 Jan. The *sons* of Res Wachan (*viz.*, Rhys Vychan or Mechyll) were summoned by King Hen. III., with the other barons of South Wales, to appear at the Court of Westminster on the morrow of Ash Wednesday, to answer for their transgressions against the king's peace. [Rymer]; and, on 20 August following the king took the homage of Res, the son of Res Wahan, at Woodstock, and because the said Res *and his brothers* had returned to the king's peace, the king's lieges are commanded to suffer the said Res and his brothers to pase hither and thither freely at their will. [Rot. Pat. 30 Hen. III., *m.* 2.]

1245. Rhys Vychan captures the Castle of Carregcennan (Caercynan) which his mother had surrendered to the English, out of the ill-will she bore her son. ["Brut y Tywysogion."]

Takes possession of the lands of Iscennen, which would seem to have been the inheritance of his uncle, Maredydd ap Rhys Gryg.

1252. Res (Rhys), Junior (Vychan), son of Res Vaphan, gives the king 20 marks to hold the same liberties and customs for his lands in Keyrmardin, as he and his ancestors had held in the time of Llewelyn, formerly Prince of Wales. [Rot. Fin., 34 Hen. III., *m.* 1.]

1256. Ejected from his lands by Llewelyn ap Gruffydd, Prince of Wales, and goes over to the English, on that account; but, soon after again joins Llewelyn. [Bridgeman, 176.] In the same year (1256), Maredydd ap Rhys Gryg breaks faith with Prince Llewelyn and goes over to the king, who concedes him all the lands which he then held, as well as the lands of his nephew, Rhys Vychan, namely Mabuderith (Meynaur), Mabelneu, Meynau Teylau, Ketheynauth and Meynaur filiorum Seysild (Widigadaf) with the Castles of Dinefwr and Karrekemien, with all their appurtenances for ever. [Charter 41 Hen. III., (18 Oct. 1257), Cal. Rot. Pat., 41 Hen. III., *m.* 1.]

But the lands of Rhys Vychan, which were thus granted by the king to Maredydd as escheats to the Crown, nevertheless remained in Rhys Vychan's possession, and were, at his death, transmitted to his sons. After the peace of 1267, a settlement as to the above lands was effected between Rhys Vychan and Maredydd. [Bridgeman, 177, and authorities there cited.]

1258, 8 March. Rhys Vychan is named in a compact with the Scots. [Rymer.]

1271. "On Octave of the Feast of St. Lawrence (17 Aug., 1271) died Res Vychan ap Res Mechyll ap Res Grig in his Castle of Dynevor, and was buried at Tal y Lychau." ["Brut y Tywysogion."]

He was buried at the Abbey of Tal y Llychau (now Talley), 7½ miles from Llandeilo Vawr, which was founded by his ancestor, Rhys ap Gruffydd, in 1197, and to which he was a benefactor. The remains of this Abbey, although partly demolished to rebuild the Church (St. Michael's) in 1773, are still considerable. [Lewis's "Top. Dic., Wales."]

It would appear that Rhys Vychan was twice married, *viz.*, first to Margaret, daughter of Gruffydd, and secondly, to Gwladys, daughter of Gruffydd ap Llewelyn, and sister to Llewelyn ap Gruffydd, Prince of Wales. The latter wife died 1261. Both of his wives, doubtless, were buried at Tal y Llychau Abbey. It is uncertain which wife was the mother of his children.

ISSUE:
i. Rhys Wendot, or Gloff, *of whom presently*.
ii. Llewelyn, lord of Iscennen (or Isgenen); imprisoned in the Tower of London, 1277; released before 1285. He is named as witness to a deed of Rhys ap Maredydd, 1285. [Rot. Wall., 13 Edw. I., *m*. 3.] Inq. P.M. held at Landow juxta Bregheynok (Brecknock), 8 April, 10 Edw. III. (1336). [Extracts from Coram Rege Roll, Trin., 12 Edw. III., Ro. 23] He died, according to this Inquisition, without legitimate issue surviving.
iii. Howel died 1282. [Bridgeman.]
iv. Gruffydd, joint lord of Iscennen (Isgenen), 1282. In the king's prison, 1283. ["Annales Cambriæ"; Bridgeman, 180.]
v. Margaret, married Madog ap Gruffydd Vychan, lord of Dinas Bran and Bromfield, by right, Prince of Powys Fadog. [Dwnn, i., 122.] She was living 4 and 12 Jan., 1278-9. [Rot. Wall., 6 Edw. I., *m*. 12 *dorso*.]

[There were, doubtless, other children who died in infancy.]

Rhys Wendot, or Gloff (the lame), called also Rhys Vychan (or Fychan), eldest son of Rhys Vychan. ["Brut y Tywysogion"; Powel; Bridgeman, 156, 174, 175, 177, 181, 183, 186; Dwnn.] He is designated lord of Dinefwr, Llandeilo Vawr and Ystrad Towi, and is stated to have also held the lordship of Cymytmaen, in Lleyn, Carnarvonshire, where his son was certainly seized of certain lands which Rhys Vychan, father of Rhys Wendot (or Gloft) seems to have held in right of one of his wives.

Rhys Wendot (or Gloff) divided his father's estates in South Wales with his brother, Llewelyn. [Inq. ad q. dam., 1 May, 11 Edw. II. (1318), No. 102.]

1277. Rhys joins Llewelyn against the king. [Bridgeman.]

1277. Deserts Llewelyn and offers to do homage to Edw. I.; but the king declines to accept his homage and retains him a prisoner, upon his surrender. [Bridgeman.]

5 Edw. I., 5 June (1277). Mandate to Payn de Cadurcis, Captain of the king's munitions in West Wales, to retain intire in the king's hands the Castles Dinnevor, Karekenye and Lanedevery, but to permit the men of Rhys Vaghan to hold their lands and tenements as before. Dated at Windsor. [Patent Rolls, 5 Edw. I., *memb.* 13; Cal. Pat. Rolls.]

1277, 1 July. The king receives the homage of Rhys at Worcester, and Rhys returns to South Wales on 10 October, following. [" Brut y Tywysogion"; Bridgeman, 156.]

5 Edw. I., 7 Oct. (1277). Safe conduct, until All Saint's Day, for Res Vaghan and Kanaan (Cynan) son of Mereduc (Maredydd), going with their horses, harness and men to their own parts. Given at Rhuddlan. [Patent Rolls, 5 Edw. I., *memb.* 5; Cal. Patent Rolls.]

1278, 10 Jan. Named by the king as "Res Vaghan of Dehuberd" (i.e., South Wales), in a letter to the King's Justices. [Rot. Wall., 6-9 Edw. I., *m.* 12, *de anno sexto.*]

1279, 11 Jan. Rhys (Res) Vychan, or Wendot, receives the king's pardon to him and to his men, for transgressions of the king's peace. [Rot. Wall., 6-9 Edw. I., *m.* 9, *de anno septimo.*] At this time he was reinstated in a portion of his inheritance, which the king had taken from him; but Dinefwr had been ceded to the Crown, and granted to Rhys ap Maredydd.

1282. Rhys joins the revolt of Llewelyn ap Gruffydd. [Bridgeman, 165.] Sends a memorial to the king through Llewelyn, of injuries done him by the king's subjects, 11 Nov., 1282.

[Prince Llewelyn is slain near Pont Orewyn, in Buallt, 10 Dec., 1282, and Prince David, Llewelyn's brother, is taken prisoner, 21 June, 1283.]

1283. Rhys holds out against the king. [Bridgeman, 174.] This " Res a Vawhan, the richest and most powerful of the Welsh chieftains, who had opposed the King during the whole period of the war, and who, moving from province to province, had committed great slaughter and ferociously devastated the King's lands, being discouraged in spirit when he heard of the death of Llewelyn and the capture of David, and being himself closely pursued by the King's forces, at length repaired with his accomplices to Humfrey de Bohun, Earl of Hereford, and surrendered to him." [Powel.] He was sent to London in fetters, and confined in the Tower, where he afterwards died (the date unknown) and his lands were forfeited to the Crown. [Inq. ad q. damnum, 11, Edw. II., No. 102.]

Rhys Vychan (otherwise Rhys Gloff) is stated by Dwnn to have married Gwervyl (Gwerfyl) v. *Maelgwn ab Cadwall^n ab Madg ab Ierwth a Cadw^n ab Elystan Glodryth.* "Ierwth" is a mistake for Idnerth. Elystan Glodryth was a chieftain, or prince, of Fferllys, a district in Herefordshire. He is the reputed founder of the Abbey of St. Mary's, at Cwm Hir, Radnorshire, and of three Churches dedicated to St. Michael, viz. in Kerry, Kenennllys and Builth. According to credible authority he died in 1067, and was buried at Hereford. ["Montgomeryshire Collections," i., 236.] Madog ap Idnerth, a lord of Maelienydd, was one of those who, in 1136, took part with Prince Gruffydd ap Rhys and the sons of Prince Gruffydd ap Cynan, in the attack upon the English in Cardiganshire, in which the latter were defeated with terrible slaughter. [" Brut y Tywysogion."] Madog died about 1141. [Powel; "Brut y Tywysogion;" "Gesta Stephani."] He married Reinalt, daughter of Gruffydd ap Cynan, Prince of North Wales, and was, therefore, brother-in-law to Gruffydd ap Rhys, Prince of South Wales, his superior lord.

Cadwallon ap Madog, of Maelienydd, was a benefactor to the Abbey of Cwm Hir, in 1143. He opposed Henry II., and was present at the battle of Crogen, in 1165. According to Powel, the cantrefs of Arwystli and Elvael, with other districts, were granted by the king to Rhys ap Gruffydd, the "Lord Rhys," in 1171. In this case Cadwallon would continue to hold under Rhys, and, accordingly, we find him doing homage with that prince, to the king, at Gloucester, in 1175.

On 22 Sept., 1179, Cadwallon ap Madog was waylaid and murdered by retainers of Roger de Mortimer, in returning from the king's court, and whilst under the king's safe-conduct. [Montgomeryshire Collections," i., 239.]

Cadwallon left two sons, Maelgwn and Cadwallon. [Montgomeryshire Collections," i., 240.] In 1193-4, these sons were acting in conjunction with the "Lord Rhys" against the English. ["'Brut y Tywysogion".] Maelgwn died 1197. His brother, Cadwallon, died after 1193-4, leaving two sons, Cadwallon and Maelgwn, who, having been taken in rebellion, were both hanged by King John, at Bridgenorth, supposedly in 1212. ["Montgomeryshire Collections," i., 241; Inq. 34 Hen. III., No. 29; Inq. 33 Hen. III., No. 84.]

From the above it is certain that Rhys Vychan IV., *alias* Rhys Gloff, could not have married a daughter of Maelgwn ap Cadwallon, who was, as we have seen, hanged by King John, supposedly in 1212, unless, indeed, she was an infant at the time of her father's death. It is much more probable, in fact quite certain, that Gwerfyl was not the daughter, but the *grand-daughter* of Maelgwn ap Cadwallon, and daughter of Maelgwn ap Maelgwn, *alias* Maelgwn Vychan.

This Maelgwn ap Maelgwn was a very important personage, holding extensive territories in Radnor, and was one of those Welsh lords who, on the morrow of the Assumption of the Blessed Virgin Mary, 25 Hen. III. (16 August, 1241) bound themselves by oath to be of the king's fealty. [Appendix to Powel's " History," 8vo. ed. 356-7.]

ISSUE:[1]
  i. Madog Goch, *of whom presently*.
  ii. Maredydd Goch. [Hengwrt MS. No. 70; Dwnn, i., 261.]
  iii. Rhys Abernig. [Hengwrt MS. No. 70; Dwnn, i.]

Madog Goch, son of Rhys Wendot, otherwise Rhys Gloff and Rhys Vychan.

Madog ap Res (Gloff) ap Res Vychan ap Res Mechyll ap Res Gryg, is named in MS. pedigree by Robert Vaughan of Hengwrt. [Peniarth MS. No. 70; see also Bridgeman, 181.]

Madoc ap Rhys Gloff ap Rhys Vaughan ap Rhys Mechyllt ap Rhys Grug, is named in MS. pedigree brought from Wales, in 1698, by the Evans brothers of Gwynedd, Pennsylvania. [Evans MSS.; Parker Foulke MSS.;" Historical Collections of Gwynedd," H. M. Jenkins 1st. ed., 214-15.] Named as above in Tai Croeswn MS. cited in " History of Powys Fadog," vi., 232-4. As Madog ab Res Gloff, he is mentioned in the pedigree under " Cevn Amwlch," in Visitations of North Wales, Dwnn (Deputy Herald), dated 22 Sept., 30 Elizabeth (1588), and in pedigree under " Graianog,' dated 1602. In the two last pedigrees, however, the descent from the " Lord Rhys" is tentatively and incorrectly given.

Madog became seized, perhaps by enfeoffment by his father, of certain lands in the cymwd (or commot) of Cymytmaen, in Lleyn. These lands comprised parts of the present parishes of Penllech, Aberdaron, and neighbourhood. It is claimed that he held the lordship of Cymytmaen, which statement seems borne out by various circumstances. That these lands had been part of the possessions of one Gruffydd, father of one of the wives of Rhys Vaughan, Madog's grandfather, seems certain.

Madog, according to tradition, fought under his father, in 1282, and it is conceivable that Edward I. followed, in this instance, the same policy which he pursued in others, *viz.*, although punishing the great chieftains by death or imprisonment, and confiscation of their vast estates, yet, at the same time, he permitted their sons, upon their submission, to retain for their support inconsiderable properties which they had acquired previous to the war.

29 Edw. I., 28 April (1292). Madog Goch does homage and fealty for his lands to the king, at Carnarvon. [Cited in Patent Rolls, 18 Edw. III., Cal. Patent Rolls, vi., 231.][2]

Madog[3] married Tanglwyst, daughter of Goronwy ap Einion ap

---

[1] A Madog Goch, and Nynnaw his brother, were in rebellion against the king in 1294, and ravaged the king's manor of Overton, and there is a grant to these brothers of their lives and limbs, " the forfeiture whereof belongs to the king," dated at Conway, 3 Jan., 23 Edw. I. (1294-5) [Cal. Patent Rolls, ii., 128.] I am inclined to suppose that this was the same Madog, and perhaps identical with that Madog, said to have been kinsman of Llewelyn, who was in arms against the king at this time.

[2] There was probably another son. See *infra*.

[3] From the " Records of Caernarvon," it appears that Madog " Coch" held all of the vill of Penllech, which, in 1352, was held by his descendants.

Goronwy ap Rhys ap Caradog ap Iestyn ap Gwrgant, Prince of Glamorgan. [Dwnn, ii., 175, 180 ; History of Powys Fadog," vi., 283.]

Issue.

i. Trahaiarn Goch, *of whom presently*.

Trahaiarn Goch, son of Madog Goch (or Madog ap Rhys). [Dwnn, ii., 175, 278, 280, 281 ; Peniarth MS. ; Evans MS. ped. ; " History of Powys Fadog," vi., 232-4 ; Bridgeman, 181.]

Trahaiarn (Trahairn, Trahearn, &c.) Goch is called in some pedigrees lord of Cymytmaen, in Lleyn, Carnarvonshire, and in others simply designated as "of Lleyn." It is evident from a survey made by the Crown in 1352 that he held considerable land in Cymytmaen, which, in the latter year was in the possession of his descendants. ["Records of Caernarvon," 37-38, &c.]

He succeeded to his lands after 28 April, 21 Edw. I. (1292), in which year his father was alive. [Cal. Patent Rolls, vi., 231.]

29 Edw. I., 28 Jan. (1301). Trahaiarn appears as father of Llewelyn ap Trahaiarn, pardoned with others, for outlawry (they were then in arms against the king) on condition that he surrender to Clifford goal before Easter. [Cal. Patent Rolls, ii., 565.]

18 Edw. III. (1325). Named as father of David Goch of Cymytmaen, and then dead. [Transcript of Ministers' Accounts of Wales ; Harl. MS. (B.M.) 1974.]

Trahaiarn Goch married Gwerfyl, daughter of Madog ap Meurig, descended from Elystan Glodryth, or Glodrudd. [Dwnn, ii., 175.]

ISSUE :

i. Llewelyn.[1] Pardon to Llewelyn ap Trahaiarn *et al.* for outlawry, for non-appearance before the king to answer a plea of trespass of Roger de Mortuo Mari, on condition that they surrender to Clifford goal before Easter, and take their trial. Dated 28 Jan., 29 Edw. I. (1301). [Patent Rolls, 29 Edw. I., *memb.* 30 ; Cal. Patent Rolls, ii., 565.] David ap Llewelyn, the 2d son of Llewelyn ap Trahaiarn, was 10th man on the jury for taking the extent of the hundred of Cymytmaen, at Nevyn, on the next Thursday after the Festival of St. James the Apostle,

---

[1] Ieuan ap Llewelyn, the eldest son of Llewelyn ap Trahaiarn, was probably the father of Walter ap Ieuan ap Llewelyn, named as one of the grantors in a deed dated at Westminster, 1 August, 1362, Sir Gilbert Talbot *et al.* to John, Earl of Lancaster, *et ux.*, whereby the grantors, heirs of Llewelyn ap Rhys Vychan ap Rhys Mechyll ap Rhys Gryg, cede to the said Earl and Blanche his wife, the Castle of Carreckemyn, and comot of Iskennyn (Isgenen) together with the mills, parks . . . and "natives and their services." [Rot. Claus., 36 Edw. III. *m.*, 18 *dorso*.]

26 Edw. III. (1352) ["Records of Caernarvon."], and was ancestor to a family living at Llandygwydd. [Dwnn, i., 33.]

ii. David Goch, *of whom presently*.
iii. Trahaiarn Gam. [Dwnn.]
v. Ithel Talfrith ; he is, doubtless, identical with Ithell Duy, Foreman of the Jury for taking the extent of Cymytmaen, 26 Edw. III. (1352). [Dwnn ; "Records of Caernarvon."]
v. Madog, his son, Iorwerth, is the 3d man, sons Griffuth and Kenrick Nos. 7 and 8, and son Madog, the 11th man on the Jury for taking the extent of Cymytmaen, 26 Edw. III. (1352). ["Records of Caernarvon."]
vi. Maredydd. [Dwnn.]
vii. Iorwerth Vychan ; his son, David, living 1352.
viii. Llywarch ; his son, Ieuan, living 1352.

David Goch, second son of Trahaiarn Goch. [Evans MS. ped. ; Dwnn, ii., 175, 278, &c. ; Tai Croeswn MS. ; "History of Powys Fadog," vi., 232, 234; Ministers' Accounts relating to Wales ; Harl. MS. 1974.]

David Goch, under the law of gavelkind, inherited one eighth part of his father's lands in Cymytmaen, *viz.,* parts of Bodreith (called Tref Baythain), Penllech, the Mills of Bodwda, Newith, and Vagheys, lands in Aberdaron and elsewhere.

12 Edw. II., 6 June (1319). Grant to David Goch, for life, on account of his good services to the late king (Edw. I.) of 60 shillings per annum, to be received at the hands of the Chamberlain at Kaernarvon (Carnarvon). [Patent Rolls, 12 Edw. II., *memb.* 7 ; Cal. Patent Rolls, iii., 344.]

18 Edw. II. (1325). Under the designation of "David Goch ap Trah'rn" he is called "firmar man ii Neugolf," *viz.,* farmer, or lessee, of the Crown manor of Neugolf in the hundred of Cymytmaen, in this year, and is mentioned as being alive on Friday, 9 Nov., 1329. [Transcript of Ministers' Accounts relating to Wales.]

David Goch appears to have acquired the lands of Graianog, Uwch Gwafi, an estate at Novem Burgum, on the coast of Anglesey, and a mansion and lands in the vill of Rungdewar, in Efidnydd.

18 Edw. III. (1344). David Goch does homage and fealty for his lands to the king at Carnarvon. [Cal. Patent Rolls, vi., 231.]

Towards the close of his life David Goch entered the Monastery of St. Mary, on Ynys Enlli, or Bardsey Isle, adjacent to his home, and, assuming the religious habit, became Abbot of that House, where before 26 Edw. III. (1352), he died, and was buried. [Dwnn, ii., 119 ; "Records of Caernarvon."]

The Monastery of St. Mary, Ynys Enlli, "from the remotest period of antiquity, appears to have been the resort of devotees, who, retiring from the cares of this world sought an asylum here, where they passed the remainder of their lives."

David Goch married Mawd, daughter of David Lloyd, son of Llewelyn. The latter was son of David ap Llewelyn, Prince of Wales. David's mother was Joanna (or Joan), daughter of John, King of England. [Dwnn, ii., 175.]

ISSUE:

i. David Vaughan. He held, in or before 1352, 6 bovats of land in the vill of Bodreeth, and four bondsmen (there would be lands allotted to them) in the same vill, 1 bovat of land in the vill of Penthlagh (Penllech), one sixteenth of the mill of Bodreeth, and one third part of a messuage and lands in the vill of Rungdewar, in the comotte [cymwd] of Enyonnedd (Evionydd or Efionydd) concerning the value of which last, the jury say they know nothing.[1]

David Vaughan had four sons in the vill of Bodreeth, *viz.* Griffuth (Gruffydd), Duy, Ieuan Seys, Hoell (Howel) ap David and David Meryn; of whom the latter was dead in 1352, leaving two (infant) sons. Gruffydd Duy aud Ieuan Seys were felons, and their interest in their father's lands and in the mill of Bodreeth had been forfeited for treason, and were in the hands of the Prince in the above year.[2] [" Records of Caernarvon," 37 ; folio 24 of orig. MS.]

ii. Ieuan Goch, *of whom presently.*

iii. Gruffydd (?)[3]

Ieuan Goch, second son of David Goch, called of Penllech and Graianog. [Evans MS. ped.; Dwnn, ii., 175, 278; Tai Croeswn MS.; " Records of Caernarvon," 37 ; " History of Powys Fadog," vi., 232, 234.]

26 Edw. III., on the next Thursday after the Festival of St. James the Apostle (1352). Ieuᵃn ap David Gogh is named as the second man on the jury for taking the extent of the hundred of Cymytmaen, at Nevyn.

---

[1] This is an illustration of the results of the custom of gavel kind. It appears that David Vaughan, who must have been dead by 1352, held less than 100 acres of free land in Cymytmaen, four slaves, part of a mill and one third of a messuage and lands in Efionydd.

[2] They appear to have been leaders in one of the insurrections of Owain Lawgoch, who set himself up as Prince of Wales on the strength of his descent from Owain Gwynedd.

[3] I am inclined to suppose that David Goch's third son was identical with that Gruffydd ap David Goch who acquired lands in Penmachno, and whose effigy remains in Bettws y Coed Church, and that the latter, therefore, is not the same person as David, said to be illegitimate son of David, Prince of Wales, who was executed 1283, as generally supposed, and so stated in several pedigrees, but identical with David Goch of Penllech. See a future page.

26 Edw. III. (1352). Ieuᵃn ap David Gogh and others were owners of the Wele Res ap Seisilth in the vill of Bodreeth ("called Trefa Baythain"), and parts of the mills of Bodwrda (in Aberdaron), Newith and Vagheys. He was also one of the heirs to the vill of Tyndowet (Tydweiliog), in Cymytmaen, and it would appear that he held land in Penllech, and was one-third owner of a mansion and lands (in common with his brothers) in the vill of Rungdewar, in Efionydd. ["Records of Caernarvon," 37-38. Reference to original MS., E͒ Codice MS. to Harl. 696 et 4776, folio 24.]

There are conflicting statements regarding the wife of Ieuan Goch, but there can be no doubt that she was Efa, daughter of Einion ap Celynin, of Llwydiarth, in Montgomeryshire. This Einion, under the designation of "Anian ap Celynin" had a grant from John de Charleton, of Weston, in the villᵃ of Pennayrth, in Glasmeynoc, on the Thursday after the Decollation of St. John the Baptist, 14 Edw. III. (1340). ["Montgomeryshire Collections," v., 400.]

ISSUE:
i. Madog, *of whom presently*.
ii. Maredydd, of Penllech. [Dwnn, ii., 175, &c.; "History of Powys Fadog," vi., 233.] His son, Ieuan, of Penllech, had David Vaughan, of Penllech, who had Gruffydd ap David Vaughan, living at Michaelmas, 1481, ancestor of the Griffiths of Cevn (Cefn), Amwlch, in Lleyn, Carnarvonshire. [Dwnn, ii., 176, *note* 1.] Griffith (or Gruffydd) ap Sion (John) Griffith, grandson of the above, was living 1 June, 1510. John Gruffydd (or Griffith), his son, died 1585, and *his* son, Gruffydd ap Sion (John) Gruffydd, was High Sheriff of Carnarvonshire, 1590, dying at Oxford, in 1599. John Griffith, son of the preceding, was High Sheriff of Carnarvonshire, 1604, and was living 1618, in which year his son, John Griffith, "junior," was Sheriff. The latter represented his county in Parliaments of 1620-1, 1625-6, 1627-8. [Dwnn, ii., 176, *ns*. 2-4.]
iii. John Carrog Bach, of Carrog,[1] ancestor to the Carrogs of Lleyn. [Tai Croeswn MS.]
iv. Howel. [Dwnn, ii., 260.]
v. Morfydd, married Maredydd ap Howel, of Efionydd; he is mentioned 26 Edw. III. (1352). [Dwnn, ii.; "Records of Caernarvon"], and held the lordship of Gest, 6 Rich. II. ["Montgomeryshire Collections".] Morfydd's will was proved 1416.

Madog (otherwise Madog ap Ieuan Goch, Madog Goch, &c.), eldest son of Ieuan Goch. [Evans MS. ped.; Dwnn, ii., 175, 278.]

Named in the "Cevn Amwlch" pedigree as *Madg̃ hynav gwyr yr Ysbyty*; *viz.*, "ancestor to the men of Yspytty (Yspytty Ieuan, or Evan)." [Dwnn, ii., 175.]

---

[1] Carrog is in the parish of Aberdaron. I think that a number of the family were buried in this Church.

26 Edw. III. The next Thursday after the Festival of St. James the Apostle (1352). Madog Goch is the ninth man on the jury (of which his father is the second) for taking the extent of the hundred of Cymytmaen. ["Records of Caernarvon."] At this time he was a very young man.

Named in a deed of Iorwerth ab Ithel Vychan for certain lands near Penllech (undated). Dwnn's original MS. has this entry opposite his definite statement that Madog was son of "Ivan gôch o Benllach" (*viz.* Ieuan Goch of Penllech). *Not* [NOTE]: *o weithred Ierwth. ab Ithel Vy^n yn gwerthu tir*; *i.e.*, "Out of a deed of Ierwerth ab Ithel Vychan for the sale of land." [Dwnn, ii., 175; marginal note by Lewys Dwnn.]

The name of Madog's wife is not given in any pedigree of this family we have examined. It is most probable, however, that she was Alex, or Ales, one of the daughters of Ieuan ap Madog Gwenwys, of Guilsfield, or Beechfield. Madog Gwenwys, otherwise Madog de Beechfield, was in the garrison of Caus Castle, Oct., 1266, and a juror of Worthyn Liberty, 1274, and first juror at the Assize of 1292. His son, Ieuan, married Gwenhwyfar verch Gruffydd ap Alo, which Gruffydd was living 10 August, 1309, at which time he was aged about 40 years, or under. ["Montgomeryshire Collections," vi., 84, 86.]

 ISSUE:[1]
  i. Deikws Ddu, *of whom presently.*

Deikws Ddu ap Madog. [Evans MS. ped.; Dwnn, ii., 278.]

22 Rich. II. (1398). Diekws Ddu, one of the Captains of Henry of Bolingbroke, Duke of Lancaster, endicted as a felon and traitor, and his lands forfeited.

Deikws Ddu married Gwen, daughter of Ieuan Ddu ap Meurig ap Madog ap Gwilym ap Madog Vychan ap Madog ap Maelog Crwm, who is said to have been *arglwydd* (lord) of the cymwd of Llechwedd Isaf, and of Creuddyn, the Promontory of the Great and Little Orme's Head. Maelog lived *circa* 1175 "as Sir Thomas Williams' Book avereth." ["Llyfr William Cynwal," Dwnn, ii., 278.]

 ISSUE:
  i. Einion, *of whom presently.*
  [He was probably a younger son.]

Einion ap Deikws Ddu. [Evans MS. ped.; Dwnn, ii., 278.]

Einion's sons, Howel, Ieuan, and David, are stated in the R. E. Evans MS. to have been alive 6 Hen. VIII. (1514), and if so, must have been well advanced in years. Einion's paternal second cousin, Gruffydd ap

---

[1] There were, doubtless, several other children, and it is by no means certain that Deikws Ddu was the eldest child or even the eldest son.

David Vaughan (or Vychan), of Penllech, was alive at Michaelmas, 1481. [Ministers' Accounts ; Dwnn, ii., 176, *note* 1.], and his second cousin, Ieuan ap Robert, grandson of Morfydd verch Ieuan Goch, of Penllech, was living 4 Nov., 1468.

Einion (being then long since dead) is named in the Lay Subsidy Roll of 34-35 Hen. VIII. as grandfather of "Gruff ap howell ap Engion" (Einion), and "Ieuⁿ lloid ap Ieuⁿ ap Engion," both of the parish of "Sputty" (Yspytty Evan), Denbighshire. [L. S. Denbighshire, No. $\frac{220}{188}$, Public Record Office, London.]

The wife of Einion ap Deikws Ddu was Morfydd, daughter of Matw ap Llywarch ap Gwyn ap Llewelyn ap Maredydd ap Llewelyn ap Llywarch ap Urien ap Tegwared, from Collwyn "Lord of Lleyn."

ISSUE:
i. Howel, *of whom presently*.
ii. Ieuan, living 6 Hen. VIII. ; he had Ieuan Lloyd ap Ieuan ap Einion, of Yspytty Evan, who was living 34-35 Hen. VIII.
iii. David, living 6 Hen. VIII. [Dwnn, ii., 278.]

Howel ap Einion, eldest son of Einion ap Deikws Ddu. [Evans MS, ped.;[1] Dwnn, ii., 278.] According to tradition he was at the battle of Bosworth Field, in 1485, and there is some evidence to show that he served as an archer, or man at arms, under his cousin, Maredydd ap Ieuan ap Robert. This Maredydd, in 1485, removed from Eifonydd, Lleyn, to Nantconwy, adjacent to Yspytty Evan, in Denbighshire, where he purchased and leased large estates, and "to strengthen himself in the country" against the robbers who at that time made their home within the Sanctuary of Yspytty Evan, then belonging to the Knights of St. John of Jerusalem, and who numbered "above a hundred, well horsed and well appointed," he "provided out of all parts adjacent, the tallest and most able men he could hear of. Of these he placed colonists in the country filling every empty tenement with a tenant or two, whereof most was on the king's land," and within the space of a few years "was able to make seven score tall bowmen of his followers," who were armed thus : Each

---

[1] In one copy of the Evans MS. pedigree he is called Howel Goch.

man had an "armorlett coate," a steel-cap, short sword and dagger, with bow and arrows, most of them being mounted, and having "chasing staves" (hunting spears, or lances), and they were bond "to answer the crie (summons to arms) upon all events." As the home of Maredydd was only about fifteen miles from Penllech, it is reasonable to suppose, taking their relationship into consideration, that Howel and his brother, Ieuan ap Einion, accompanied him to the neighbourhood of Yspytty Evan. At any rate, the sons of both brothers were living in the latter place in 1543.

6 Hen. VIII. (1514). The MS. of R. E. Evans. Esq., states that Howel, and his brothers, Ieuan and David, were alive in this year. Probably from a deed, but not *cited*.

Howel (being long since dead) is named in Lay Subsidy Roll of 34-35 Hen. VIII., as father of " Gruff [Gruffydd] ap howell ap Engion" (Einion), " Res ap Howell ap Engion," " Robt. ap howell," and " Edward ap howell ap Engion," all of " Sputty" (Yspytty Evan), and in that of 35 Hen. VIII., 12 Nov. (1543), as father of " Benet ap Howell ap Engion," and " David ap Howell ap Engion," of the adjoining parish of " Kerykedrudyon" (Cerrig y Druidion).

The wife of Howel ap Einion was Mali, daughter of Llewelyn ap Ieuan ap Iolyn, descended from Llewelyn Eurdorchog of Iâl; but the pedigree given of her omits generations. [Dwnn, ii., 278.] The mother of Mali was Dyddgu, daughter of Einion Llydan of Voelas, ap Tudor ap Howel ap Cynwrig ap Cynwrig Fychan of Llannefydd, from Marchweithian (see *Roberts'* pedigree, and chart *infra*). In one pedigree *Howel* is omitted, and *Cynwrig* is by error written *Cadwgan*, probably from mistaking the contraction *Cwg*.

ISSUE:

i. Gruffydd, *of whom presently*.

ii. David ap Howel. [Dwnn, ii., 278.] He was of the parish of Cerrig y Druidion, dead 12 Nov., 35 Hen. VIII. (1543), and had issue, Rees, living 1543, and John ap David, who had William Cynwal, the eminent poet and antiquarian, who wrote between 1560-1600 (lived at Penmachno and buried in Yspytty Evan Church). Sir (Rev.) Rhys Cynwal, collated to the Vicarage of Llangwm, Denbighshire, in 1591, Thomas Cynwal, and Catherine. [Dwnn, ii., 278.]

iii. Robert ap Howel ap Einion, of the parish of Yspytty Evan. Named in Lay Subsidy Roll for Denbighshire, (under parish of "Sputty") 34-35 Hen. VIII. (1543-4).

iv. Rhys (Res) ap Howel ap Einion, of the parish of Yspytty Evan; living 34-35 Hen. VIII. (1543-4).

v. Edward ap Howel ap Einion,[1] of the parish of Yspytty Evan; living 34-35 Hen. VIII. (1543-4).

vi. Benet ap Howel ap Einion, of the parish of Cerrig y Druidion, living 12 Nov., 35 Hen. VIII. (1543). [Lay Subsidy Roll for Denbighshire; 35 Hen. VIII., under "Kerykedrudyon," No. $\frac{220}{166}$, Public Record Office, London.][1]

Gruffydd ap Howel[2] ap Einion, of the parish of Yspytty Evan, Denbighshire. [Evans MS. ped.; Dwnn, ii., 278.]

34-35 Hen. VIII. (1543). Gruffydd, under the designation of "Gruff ap howell ap Engion," is assessed in the parish of "Sputty" (Yspytty Evan), "in bonis xx^s." [Lay Subsidy Roll for Denbighshire, 34-35 Hen. VIII., No. $\frac{220}{166}$, Public Record Office, London.][3]

Gruffydd married Gwenllian, daughter of Einion ap Ieuan Lloyd, of Llansannan, ap Madog ap Iorwerth[4] ap Llewelyn Chwith, of Chwibren, in the parish of Llansannan, ap Cynwrig[5] ap Bleddyn Lloyd of Hafodunos, in the parish of Llangerniw, in the lordship of Rhyfioniog [or Rhuvoniog] Denbighshire, ap Bleddyn Vychan ap Bleddyn ap y Gwion[6] ap Rhaidr Vach, from Hedd Moelwynog, head of the 9th Noble Tribe of Wales. [Dwnn, ii., 278; Hengwrt MS. 384.]

---

[1] None of the brothers residing in Yspytty Evan or Cerrig y Druidion are taxed in land, but in goods only. Robert ap Howel ap Einion, who appears under the designation "Robt ap howell ap Engion," is rated at £18, there being only three others, including his son and two freeholders, of an equal rate, the majority of the residents being set down at from 20 shillings to £8. The total rating of the different members of this family in Yspytty Evan, 34-35 Hen. VIII., amounted to £61, whilst the wealthiest landowner is only rated in lands, tenements, goods and cattle, at £50.

[2] Otherwise Griffith ap Howel Goch.

[3] Gruffydd is not mentioned in the assessment for the 2d. payment of a Subsidy granted 37 Henry VIII. under "Spitty," 1 Edw. VI. No. $\frac{220}{189}$, Pub. Rec. Office, London.

[4] Ieuan ap Llewelyn, the brother of Iorwerth, of Chwibren, died on the Feast of St. Stephen, 1435. [Hengwrt MS. 384.] Rhys, son of Ieuan, of Chwibren, was esquire of the Body to Edward IV., and was "very unruly in the Lancastrian wars."

[5] Meurig Lloyd, the brother of Cynwrig ap Bleddyn Lloyd "finding himself and his tenants much oppressed by the English laws, did kill one of the judges, and hang divers other officers on oak trees in Uwch Dulas; on which account his lands and inheritance in Rhuvoniog escheated to the Crown, and so still remain, for the most part, to this day, and are known by the name of Tir Meurig Llwyd; whereupon he withdrew for his safety to the Sanctuary of Halston, and then put himself under the protection of John Fitz Alan . . . . afterwards Earl of Arundel," who died 52nd Henry III., (1268).

[6] Y Gwion's mother was daughter to Y Gwion ap Hwva of Iâl, who was brother to Caswallon, lord of Llysycil, in Iâl, whose son Iorwerth was one of the witnesses to a grant of lands by Prince Madog ap Gruffydd Maelor to the Abbey of Valle Crucis, in 1202. This Iorwerth was the direct male ancestor of Gwenhwyfar, mother of Gwenllian, wife of Gruffydd ap Howel ap Einion.

The mother of Gwenllian, daughter of Einion ap Ieuan Lloyd, was Gwenhwyfar, daughter of Goronwy ap David ap Gruffydd, descended from Iorwerth ap Caswallon ap Hwva (or Hwfa), who was witness to a grant to Valle Crucis Abbey, in 1202. Caswallon was lord of Llysycil, in Iâl (Yale), Denbighshire. The mother of Gwenhwyfar was Anne, daughter of Gruffydd ap Llewelyn ap Ieuan ap Rhys Gethin [1] ap Gruffydd Vychan ap Gruffydd [2] of Llanrwst ap David Goch.

ISSUE:

i. David ap Gruffydd (or Griffith), married Elizabeth verch Rhys, of the adjoining parish of Cerrig y Druidion. [Dwnn, ii., 278.] He probably removed to the latter parish.

ii. Edward ap Gruffydd (Griffith) of the parish of Yspytty Evan [Dwnn, ii., 278.] He is assessed in goods in the parish of "Sputty," 34-35 Hen. VIII. (1543), and under "Spitty" 1 Ed. VI, (1547-8). [Lay Subsidy Rolls, Denbighshire, 34-35 Hen. VIII. No. $\frac{220}{168}$; 1 Edw. VI., No. $\frac{220}{169}$, Pub. Rec. Office, London.] The will of his eldest son, Evan Lloyd ap Edward, of Yspytty Evan, was proved at St. Asaph, 1592. [Act Book $\frac{1584}{1593}$, Probate Registry, St. Asaph.]

iii. Lewis ap Gruffydd, *of whom presently.*

iv. Robert ap Gruffydd ap Howel, named in will of Jenkin ap Res of "Spytty," dated 10 April, 1570.

v. Catherine, married Sir (Rev.) Robert ap Rhys ap Sion (John) vicar of Yspytty Evan. [Dwnn, ii., 278.]

---

[1] Rhys Gethin was a brother of Howel Coetmore of Castle Cefel Ynghoedmor, one of the Captains at Agincourt and owner of Gwydir, which estate, his son, David ap Howel, sold to Maredydd ap Ieuan ap Robert, ancestor to the Wynns of Gwydir, before 1525. Rhys Gethin, who is also said to have been at Agincourt, was of Fedw Deg and Hendref Rhys Gethin, in the parish of Bettws y Coed. Howel Coetmore was buried at Llanrwst, where his effigy remains.

[2] Gruffydd ap David Goch was of the parish of Llanwrst, and was foreman of the jury for taking the extent of Nant Conwy, on the next Monday after the Translation of St. Thomas of Canterbury, 26 Edw. III. (1352). He was buried in the Church of Bettws y Coed where his effigy still remains bearing this inscription: HIC IACET GRUFUD AP DAVID GOCH. AGNUS DEI MISERERE MEI. [Description in "Arch. Cambr.," 1874, 128.] David Goch is stated to have been an illegitimate son of David, Prince of Wales, who was executed by Edward I. in 1283; but I think that this is an error.

Rhys Gethin's wife was Morfydd, daughter of Howel Sele, lord of Nannau, near Dolgelley, who was slain in single combat by Owain Glyndwr and his body hidden in a hollow oak tree in Nannau Park, where the skeleton, still grasping a rusted sword, was long afterwards discovered. Howel's grandfather, Meurig (Meuric) ap Ynyr Vychan, living 21 Edw. III. (1347-8), was buried in Dolgelley Church, where his effigy remains. Ynyr Vychan of Nannau was charged with others in Parliament of 15 & 16 Edw. II. (1322-3) with attacking, on the next Wednesday after the Feast of St. Gregory, in the 15th of Edw. II., the castle of John Grey, at Ruthin, setting fire to the town, and killing two men. [Rolls of Parl. i., 397.]

Lewis ap Gruffydd (or Griffith), of the parish of Yspytty Evan, third son of Gruffydd ap Howel ap Einion. [Evans MS. pedigree; Dwnn, ii., 278-9.]

34-35 Hen. VIII. (1543). Lewis ap Gruffydd, under the designation of *lewes ap Gruff*, is assessed in the parish of "Sputty" (hundred of "Islaet,") (Yspytty Evan) "in bonis" vij ^{li} (£7), it being an assessment for the first payment of a Subsidy. [Lay·Subsidy Roll for Denbighshire, 34-35 Hen. VIII., No. $\frac{220}{186}$ Public Record Office, London.]

He died prior 43 Eliz. (1601), [Dwnn, ii., 279], and was buried at Yspytty Evan Church.

Lewis ap Gruffydd married Ellen, daughter of Edward ap Evan of the parish of Llanwddyn, Montgomeryshire,[1] ap Tudor ap David ap Evan Ddu. The mother of Ellen was Catherine, daughter of Gruffydd ap Llewelyn ap Einion. This Einion was the son of David ap Ieuan ap Einion, the celebrated constable of Harlech Castle.[2]

ISSUE:

i. David Lewis, married Marsley, daughter of David ap Rhys, of "Llanuvydd." [Dwnn, ii., 278.]

ii. William Lewis,[3] died before 1601 (supposedly); married Margaret, daughter of Lewis David of Duffryn Clwyd; and had issue, Sir (Rev.) Evan Lloyd of "Llandav" (Llandaf),[4] living in 1601. He was then married, and had Edward and Margaret. [Dwnn, ii., 278.]

iii. Evan Lewis, married Gwen verch William, sister to Edward ap Hugh Prydydd. [Dwnn, ii., 278.]

iv. Robert Lewis, *of whom presently*.

v. John Lewis, died young. [Dwnn, ii., 278.]

vi. Cadwaladr Lewis. [Dwnn, ii., 278.]

---

[1] I can find no trace of Edward ap Evan in those records of Llanwddyn so far searched. Llanwddyn belonged to the Knights of St John of Jerusalem, and the family of Edward were probably tenants of the knights prior to the Reformation.

[2] The following is from a note by Sir Samuel R. Meyrick, Dwnn, ii., 216: "David ap Ievan ap Einion was constable of the Castle of Harlech, and held it for several years for king Henry VI. against the hostile faction of the Yorkists. It was during his custody of that fortress, that the unfortunate monarch, accompanied by his intrepid Queen, found a refuge within its walls, in 1463. An account of David's gallant bearing, when constable of Harlech, will be found in the Autobiography of Lord Herbert, of Cherbury; and a petition, and other proceedings consequent upon his refusal to surrender the Castle, in the Rolls of Parliament for the first and fourth years of King Edward IV.

[3] In one place in the transcript of the Dwnn pedigree he is called William Cadwaladr, and in another, William ap Rhys, although William Lewis is clearly intended in each instance.

[4] Probably Llandaff, near Cardiff.

Robert Lewis, fourth son of Lewis ap Gruffydd (Griffith), of the parish of Yspytty Evan. [Evans MS. ped.; Dwnn, ii., 278-9.]

> 39-40 Eliz. (1596-7). Robert Lewis, of the parish of "Sputty" (Yspytty Evan) is assessed in the roll of the second payment of a Subsidy granted 39 Eliz., on freehold land, to the value of 20 shillings.[1] [Lay Subsidy Roll for Denbighshire, under "Sputty" (hundred of "Islaet")[2] 39-40 Eliz., No. 220/188 [Pub. Rec. Office, London.]
>
> 43 Eliz. "1601." Named in a pedigree by Lewys Dwnn, Deputy Herald; certified by Rev. Evan Lloyd, the nephew of Robert Lewis, 1601. [Dwnn, ii., 278-9.]
>
> 1637, 13 March. Administration of the goods and credits of Robert Lewis, late of the parish of Spytty (Yspytty Evan, Denbighshire), deceased, granted to Jane Lloyd, the relict of the deceased. [Act Book 1637/1638, Probate Registry, St. Asaph.]

Robert Lewis married, first, Gwerfyl, daughter of Llewelyn ap David, of Llanrwst, Denbighshire. [Dwnn, ii., 278-9.] He married, secondly, after 1601, Jane Lloyd, who was living 24 April, 1638.

> ISSUE (by 1st wife):
>
> i. Cadwaladr. [Dwnn, ii., 278.]
>
> ii. Thomas. [Dwnn, ii., 278.]
>
> iii. John. [Dwnn., ii., 278.]
>
> iv. Evan, *of whom presently*.
>
> v. Hugh. [Dwnn, ii., 278.] Witness to the will of Thomas ap Ieuan ap Robert of "Spytty" (Yspytty Evan), 4 Feb., 1606. [Probate Registry, St. Asaph. Filed will.]
>
> vi. Humphrey. [Dwnn, ii., 278.]
>
> vii. Lowry. [Dwnn, ii., 278.]
>
> viii. Margaret. [Dwnn, ii., 278.]
>
> ix. Jane. [Dwnn, ii., 278.]
>
> x. Catherine. [Dwnn, ii., 278.]
>
> xi. Ellen. [Dwnn, ii., 278.]
>
> xii. Margaret. [Dwnn, ii., 278.]

---

[1] The highest ratings in this Roll are that of Thomas Price, Esq., and Robert Wynne ap Cadwalader, Esq., who are assessed at only £5, and £4, respectively. The former was lord of the manor.

[2] Isaled. These assessments were nominal.

FRON GOCH.

Evan Robert Lewis, fourth son of Robert Lewis, was born in the parish of Yspytty Evan, Denbighshire. [Evans MS. ped.; Dwnn, ii., 278.] He appears to have acquired or assumed the epithet of Llwyd (or Lloyd), by which he was occasionally designated, and which his son, Evan Lloyd Evan (otherwise Evan ap Evan), adopted as a surname.

43 Eliz. (1601). Named as fourth son of Robert Lewis in the pedigree by Lewys Dwnn, Deputy Herald, and certified by the Rev. Evan Lloyd [ap William Lewis] 43 Eliz. (1601). [Dwnn, ii., 278-9.]

"Evan Robert Lewis was an honest sober Man, lived in Fron Goch." [Owen and Evans MS. genealogy of *circa* 1797.]

"Evan Robert Lewis, an honest sober man, born near the end of the reign of Queen Elizabeth." [Owen MS. genealogy in possession of the late George S. Conarroe, Esq., of Philadelphia; see "Historical Collections of Gwynedd," H. M. Jenkins, 1st ed., 144-5.]

"Ieuan, known as Evan Robert Lewis. . . . He removed from Rhiwlas (or its neighbourhood), in Merionethshire to Vron Goch (probably in Denbighshire) [Merionethshire], and there passed the remainder of his life. He had five sons, all taking for themselves, in the Welsh manner, the surname ap Evan." ["Historical Collections of Gwynedd," H. M. Jenkins, 1st ed., 144; from Evans MSS.]

Fron Goch, which gave its name to the present ecclesiastical district of the same name, is a large farm partly in the parish of Llandderfel, to which it still pays tithes, but mostly in the township of Ucheldre, in the parish of Llanfor, Merionethshire. It was formerly of much greater extent than at the present time, several parcels of land having been cut out of it, and appears to have extended into the township of Cynlas, formerly part of Llandderfel, but now locally in Llanfor. The principal residence was in Llanfor, near the present Fron Goch Station, but there were other tenements, some of them on detached parcels, belonging to Fron Goch. The tenants have of late times always baptized and buried at Llanfor Church, but in earlier days they occasionally buried at Llandderfel, especially if residing at the time in any of those tenements belonging to Fron Goch which lay within the latter parish. There is evidence to show that Fron Goch was sometimes considered to be a township of itself.

Evan Robert Lewis's daughter, and presumably eldest child, Alice, was married in 1624, so that if she was then aged about 16 years, her father's birth can be placed not much later than 1586-7. The visitation pedigree dated 1601, gives him as the fourth son among twelve children (there were also six daughters) of Robert Lewis, all born before the above date, so that if he was, say, the seventh child, and the youngest of the twelve was an infant in 1601, which seems to have been the case, the approximate date of Evan's birth would be *circa* 1684.

Rhiwlas is an estate, with the mansion house near Bala, about one and a half miles from Fron Goch, which now forms part of the Rhiwlas property. Evan Robert Lewis, may, upon his removal from Yspytty Evan, have lived for a time very near Rhiwlas and subsequently gone to Fron Goch, but it seems more probable that the original MS. from which R. E. Evans acquired his data referred to a Rhiwlas in Yspytty Evan, in Denbighshire, and that he accidentally reversed the names of the counties. Fron Goch is about three miles from the border of Yspytty Evan parish. Rhiwlas (the green slope), is a very common name, and scores of farms were formerly so called, some of which are now known by other names.

1606-7, 4 Feb. Named as a creditor in the will of Thomas ap Evan ap Robert, of " Sputty " (Yspytty Evan), Denbighshire (to which his brother, Hugh Robert, and his kinsman, John Griffith ap Edward were witnesses), proved Feb., 1606-7. [Probate Registry, St. Asaph ; filed will.]

Evan Robert Lewis, removed to Penllyn before 8 Dec., 1624, and on that date is described as of the parish of "Llanvawr" (Llanfor). [Llandderfel Parish Register, anno 1624.]

Evan Robert Lewis, after his second marriage and at the time of his death, if we are right in supposing that the following refers to him, lived in the township of Cynlas, about one mile from Fron Goch House, and probably on land then included in the farm of Fron Goch.[1]

1668, 28 Sept. "Evan ap Robt. [Lewis] de Kynlas sepultus est vicesimo octavo die Septembris." [Llandderfel Parish Register, anno 1668.]

1668, 12 Nov. "Robert filius Evani ap Robt. Lewis ex ijus uxore Gaynor sepultus fuit duodecimo die Novembris." [Llandderfel Parish Register, anno 1668.] As no reference to the will or an administration of Evan Robert Lewis can be found in the Act Book $\frac{1637}{1670}$ at St. Asaph, or at London, it is presumed that, as was then frequently the case, he had some time before his decease vested any property he may have owned in trustees for the use of himself during life, and for the benefit of his widow and children after his decease.

The name of the first wife of Evan Robert Lewis is given in one of the Evans MSS. as Jane, and there is no doubt, although not proven, that she was one of the daughters and eventual co-heiresses of Cadwaladr ap Maredydd, of Coed y Foel, in the township of Penmaen, Llanfor. At any rate, Cadwaladr (or Cadwalader) ap Evan, eldest son of Evan Robert Lewis, and heir to his mother, acquired, apparently by inheritance, one half of Coed y Foel, and John Wynne, the grandson of Thomas Wynne [2]

---

[1] Cynlas was formerly considered a part of Llandderfel, but is now, locally, in Llanfor.
[2] Thomas Wynne was the second son of Robert Wynne of Garth Meilio. [Add. MS. 9864; will of Robert Wynne of Garth Meilio, dated Sept., 1619, Reg. $\frac{1620}{1623}$, folio 6, Probate Registry, St. Asaph.]

who is proved to have married the other daughter of Cadwaladr ap Maredydd, held the other half, in 1698,[1] hence the place, so divided, was afterwards known as Coed y Foel isaf and Coed y Foel uchaf (*viz.*, lowest and uppermost). Coed y Foel adjoins Fron Goch. The mother of Cadwaladr ap Maredydd was Elin, daughter of Cadwaladr ap Robert, of Rhiwlas, son of Sir Robert ap Rhys of Yspytty Evan (see *Roberts* pedigree). [Add. MS. 9864, British Mus. ; Dwnn, ii., 228.]

Evan Robert Lewis married, secondly, Gainor ——.[2]

ISSUE:

i. Cadwalader[3] ap Evan, "of Coed y Voel [now Coed y Foel] in the County of M'ioneth.... gen." (gentleman). D. s. p. Will dated 25 Dec., 4 Jac. II., 1688 ; proved "ultimo die January," 1688 (1688-9). [Register "Testamenta Reg'rata," "Copies of Wills" $\frac{1684}{1690}$, folos 228-30, Probate Registry, St. Asaph ; original in Bundle for 1688.]

The testator "being ould and sick in body," mentions a deed of trust made by him, the said Cadwaladr ap Evan of Coed y Voel, gentleman, to Andrew Jones, of Llanycill, in the said county, gentleman, dated 28 May, 4 Jac. II., whereby he had enfeoffed the said Andrew Jones in all of his said lands of Coed y Foel, in trust, for purposes named in deed, including the support of his wife Grace, reserving the right to charge the said lands by will or otherwise, to the extent of £40, which he does, disposing of said sum partly as follows :

To nephew Griffith John, £10 " in lieu of a promise made him."

To "my two nieces Ellin vch Evan and her sister Marget vch. Evan *or their Ex^{ts}. or Administrat^s*,"[4] 50 shillings each.

To "my brother John Evan," 20 shillings.

To "nephew Wm Jo^n Evan [5] [William John Evan] £5 "upon condition y^t his father in law Hugh Cadd [Cadwaladr] shall likewise give him the sd.... five pounds."

To niece Gwen Jo^n Evan, £4.

---

[1] The will of John Wynne of Coed y Foel in Penmaen, in the parish of Llanvawr (Llanfor), dated 20 March, (1697-8) was proved 1698. [Probate Registry of St. Asaph, Bundle for 1698.] The testator bequeaths his half of Coed the Foel in trust for his son John Wynne.

[2] Proved by record of burial of Robert, son of Evan Robert Lewis, 1668. The fact that her name is mentioned in this entry in the Register does not, however, necessarily prove that she was then alive, or that he had not been married a third time, after her decease.

[3] Or Cadwaladr. His name is abbreviated "Cadder," in original will. About this time the termination *dr* in this name began to give way to *der*.

[4] The words in italics interlined and noted; see *infra*.

[5] Afterwards known as William John.

To niece Catherine Jon Evan 20 shillings.

To niece Jane vch. Evan ¹ 20 shillings.

To "con" [cousin] Maurice Humphrey, 10 shillings.

To "con" Marget Humphrey, 5 shillings.

To nephew Rowland Thomas Jon,² 5 shillings.

To "con" Morgan Robt., 5 shillings.

To testator's old servant David Rowland, 5 shillings, and to present servants, Wm Hugh Read, and Evan Robert Evan, 5 shillings each.

To nephew Evan Owen,³ 20 shillings.

To niece Elizabeth Owen, 20 shillings.

The testator appoints "my well beloved brother Evan Lloyd Evan⁴ of Ucheldre in the sd county, [and] my well beloved brother Gruffuth ap Evan of Uchelldre [sic] aforesd in the sd County yeomen and Cadder. [Cadwaladr] Jon Evan nephew," to be joint executors. Witnesses: Edward Foulke,⁵ Dafudd Gruffudd, [the mark of] Robt. Jon , Maurice Davies.

Proved 31 Jan., 1688 (viz. 1688-9),⁶ by Evan Lloyd Evan, Griffith ap Evan, and Cadwalader Jon· Evan, the executors named in the will. The Inventory of the personal estate of Cadder [Cadwalader or Cadwaladr] ap Evan, late of Coed y voel, in the County of M'ioneth, gent" deceased, was taken 28 Jan., 1688, by John Thomas, David Gruffuth, Robt. Wm., and Tho: Evan.

Several apparent discrepancies between this will and other records need explanation.

(a) Margaret, daughter of Evan Lloyd Evan, of Ucheldre, viz., the Margaret or Marget, vch. [daughter of] Evan, named in

---

¹ Jane vch. [daughter of] Evan seems to be a clerical error for Jane Jon Evan; see infra.

² Rowland was son of Thomas John of Llandderfel and Alice, Cadwalader ap Evan's sister.

³ Son of Owen ap Evan of Fron Goch.

⁴ Otherwise Evan ap Evan.

⁵ This was the Edward Foulke who removed to Gwynedd, Pennsylvania, in 1698, as proved by his signature.

The Coed y Foel farm upon which he lived was that part of the original estate of Coed y Foel owned, in 1688, by Cadwalader ap Evan, whose manager, no doubt, he was. Grace, the widow of Cadwalader ap Evan, appears not to have survived very long, and the place thus fell to the next heir of Cadwalader named in the deed of trust, presumably Robert Owen, eldest son of Cadwalader's brother, Owen ap Evan, of Fron Goch, deceased. Robert Owen removed to Pennsylvania in 1690, and he, or whoever was the tail heir, must have sold the property to Roger Price, Esq., of Rhiwlas, who was Edward Foulke's landlord in 1698.

⁶ The year then commenced in March.

the above will, was buried at Llanfor 21 Augt., 1688, four months before the date of the will. The entry in transcript of Llanfor Parish Register reads, under anno 1688 : " Margareta fili Evani Lloyd Evan de Ucheldre sepulta fuit vicesimo primo die Augst."[1]

(b) " Jane vch Evan." Evan Lloyd Evan is not known to have had a daughter Jane, nor is Cadwalader ap Evan known to have had a sister who married Evan ——.

(c) The transcripts of Llanfor Register contains the following entry under anno 1688 : " Cadd^r ab Evan de Penmen [Penmaen] sepultus fuit secundo die Feb." If this is correct, the will was proved before Cadwalader was buried, and, as the Inventory was taken 28 Jan., he was not buried until five or six days after his death.

Regarding (a), the explanation is that a rough draft of this will must have been made by Cadwalader ap Evan's solicitor, shortly after the execution of the deed of trust, 28 May, 1688, and prior to Margaret's death, and left with the testator, who neglected to have a fair copy of it executed. He was evidently taken suddenly worse 25 Dec., for no other explanation can be given for making a will on Christmas Day. Maurice Davies, a neighbour, engrossed the will, doubtless from the original draft, and very hurriedly, hence the inclusion of Margaret, whose name appeared in the draft. After the will was engrossed, however, the mistake was discovered, and the words "*or their Ex. or Administrat^s*" interlined, and noted in presence of the witnesses (see original will). The words do not occur in connection with any other bequest.

As to (b). Jane vch Evan seems to be a mere clerical error for Jane Jo^n Evan, and the person intended was, doubtless, Jane John Evan, or Jane vch John Evan, (otherwise Jane John), daughter of John Evan and wife of Robert Cadwalader.

In re (c), there is no doubt, in the opinion of officials, that there is an error in the transcript of the Parish Register, or perhaps the error was in the original, and that the correct date of the burial was 2 *Jan.*, and not 2 *Feb.*, 1688 (1688-9). Such errors in the returns, and even in the originals, are frequently noted, and arose from the clergymen making loose notes and entering them in the register at some future time. This view accords well with the fact that Cadwalader was evidently very ill 25 Dec. He died, doubtless, two or three days after. However, cases in which wills were proved before burial have occurred, especially in Wales.

---

[1] Diocesan Registry, St. Asaph.

ii. John ap Evan,[1] commonly called John Evan. [Evans MSS.; will of his brother Cadwalader.]

At the time of his decease he was a freeholder in the township of Penmaen, in the parish of Llanfor (adjoining Fron Goch), and had been twice married. His second wife was Margaret verch [daughter of] John, usually called Margaret John. She became convinced of the principles of the Society of Friends, which, in addition to the nonconformity of several of his children, caused John ap Evan much anxiety. He died about the month of April, 1697, and having previously provided for most of his children by various settlements, he, under the designation of "John Evan of Penmaen, in the parish of Llanfawr [Llanfor], in the County of Merioneth, yeoman," executed a last will and testament, dated 4 Augt., 1696; proved 24 April, 1697. [Reg. $\frac{1696}{1699}$, folio 165, Probate Registry, St. Asaph; original in bundle for 1697.] This will seems to have been made mainly for the purpose of barring his wife's right of dower, and cutting off those of his children already fully provided for. The residue of his personal estate would thus go to those children not named.

The testator bequeaths as follows:

To son Cadwaladr (or Cadwalader) John, 10 shillings.
To son Griffith John, 10 shillings.
To daughter Margaret John, 10 shillings.
To daughter Gwen John, £10.
To son William John, 10 shillings.
To son Rowland John, 10 shillings.
To daughter Catherine John, £5.

Item, "whereas I see the condition of Margarett John my wife to be Reasonable and good, having a competency of a joynture for her subsistence, I give and bequeath unto the said Margarett my wife in lieu and in barr of the moiety of my Personal estate the summ of ten shillings, her Dissent from the Communion of ye Church of England and vaine opinion having occasioned my frequent Disturbances and trouble."[2]

"I appoint my daughter, Gwen John, widow, and my son-in-law, Robert Cadwalader of the parish of Llanuwllyn [Llanuwchllyn] in the County of Merioneth to be joint executors."

Witnesses: John Owen [+] Mark, John Jones [+] Mark, Margarett William [+] Mark, Row. Price.

---

[1] He is stated in the Evans MS. genealogies to have been the eldest son, but this is wrong as Cadwalader was certainly the eldest. My own opinion is that John was the *third* son, and Owen the second; but from the data at hand this is uncertain.

[2] Margaret John, of Penmaen, was one of those fined for being present at a meeting at Llwyn y Braner, in Llanfor, 16 May, 1675, and she was subsequently frequently prosecuted.

The children omitted from the will are, Robert John, the second son, Jane, eldest daughter, wife of Robert Cadwalader (the executor), and Gainor (by second wife).

John ap Evan left issue by his first wife as follows :

(a) Cadwaladr, living 4 Augt., 1696.

(b) Robert John (or Jones); removed to Pennsylvania, 1696, and settled at Abington.[1]

(c) Griffith John ; removed to Pennsylvania, 1690, and settled in Merion.[2]

(d) *Jane,* married *Robert Cadwaladr* (or Cadwalader), and removed to Gwynedd, Pennsylvania, 1700 (*circa*). Their children assumed the surname of *Roberts*.

(e) Margaret, married David Evans ;[3] she died during the voyage to Pennsylvania, 1698, leaving daughters, Gwen, married to Thomas Foulke, son of Edward, of Gwynedd, and Margaret,[4] who married 9 month 1, 1705, Robert Humphrey, of Gwynedd. He was probably brother of John Humphrey, of Gwynedd, and son of Humphrey Jones, and Gainor his wife, of Llangower.

(f) Gwen, married, first, John ———; she was a widow 4 Augt., 1696 ; married, secondly, as his second wife, John Humphrey, late of Llangower. She had a daughter, Jane Jones, who married 3 month, 29, 1707, her first cousin, Evan Griffith, then of Merion, afterwards of Gwynedd.

(g) Catherine, living unmarried, 4 Augt., 1696.

John ap Evan had issue by Margaret John, his second wife :

---

[1] Robert John, or Robert Jones, as he afterwards wrote his name, removed to Pennsylvania in 1696, and brought a certificate from the Meeting at Hendre Mawr dated 12 month 10, 1696. He settled at Abington, near Philadelphia, and became a prosperous man in the province. He is named as a trustee in the will of his cousin, Robert Owen, of Merion, 1697, and was one of the witnesses to the will of his half-brother, William John, of Gwynedd, in 1712.

[2] Griffith John, sometimes called Griffith Jones, removed to Pennsylvania in 1690. His certificate of Removal was given him from Hendre Mawr, 6 month 8, 1690, the same date as that of his cousin Robert Owen, so that they doubtless crossed the sea in the same ship. He settled in Merion, having purchased land there from Evan Rees of Penmaen, Llanfor, Merionethshire, as early as 28 July, 1683, and subsequently from one John Roberts, nephew of Thomas Lloyd of Llangower. He is mentioned as " my cousin Griffith John " in will of Robert Owen, of Merion, 1697. Griffith John died in Merion, 1707-8. His will bears date 26 June, 1707, and was proved at Philadelphia, 31 Jan., 1707-8. [Will Book C, 69.] He had issue : John Griffith, who married, 3 month 6, 1707, Grace, daughter of Edward Foulke, of Gwynedd, Evan Griffith, who married 3 month, 29, 1707, Jane Jones, step daughter of John Humphrey of Gwynedd, and went there to live, and Ann Griffith, who married Thomas Jones (son of John Thomas of Llaithgwm), of Merion.

[3] David Evans settled in the township of Radnor, and his daughter Gwen married Thomas Foulke, son of Edward and Eleanor, of Gwynedd, 4 month 27, 1706. She died 12 month, 1760, at Gwynedd.

[4] An Evans MS. Genealogy of 1797 calls her Gainor, but Margaret is right; there was, it appears, another daughter called Gainor.

(h) William John, who removed to Gwynedd, Pennsylvania, 1698.[1]
(i) Rowland John.
(k) Gainor.

iii. Owen ap Evan, of Fron Goch.[2] He married Gainor John who was living 11 March, 1678-9. He died at Fron Goch about the year 1671. [Owen and Evans MS. Genealogies of 1797; endorsement on writ of 20 May, 1675, Levick MSS.; Bond for performance of marriage settlement of Robert Owen, 6 March, 1678-9; Marriage Certificate of R. O., 11 March, 1678-9; "Merion in the Welsh Tract," Glenn; "Historical Collections of Gwynedd," Jenkins.] Owen ap Evan had issue:

(a) Robert Owen, born *circa* 1552;[3] removed to Merion, Pennsylvania, 1690; died 1697; married 11 March, 1678-9, Rebecca, daughter of Owen Humphrey, of Llwyndu, Esq., and had issue: 1 Gainor, 2 Evan, 3 Jane, 4 Elizabeth, 5 Owen, 6 John, 7 Robert, 8 Rebecca (died inft.). [See "Merion," Glenn.]

---

[1] William John is, I believe, identical with the William John son of a John Evan, who was baptized at Llanfor Church, 10 Augt., 1673, and that he was then several years old. John Evan was a staunch Church-man, whilst his second wife, Margaret John, early joined the Society of Friends, and as early as 1675, she with her step-son, Robert Jones, both described as of Penmaen in Llanfor, were fined for attending a Meeting, and there is evidence to show that she became associated with the Society before that year. It appears that on this account she finally separated from her husband. This difference in religious belief would account for the delay of a few years in the baptism of William. Numerous other cases of the kind occur about this time in the Llanfor Register, where baptisms are recorded which were delayed because of religious controversy, in some instances for a number of years. About 1690 the returns to the Diocesan Registry show the baptisms of many children aged several years, of youths and maidens, and even of adults, indicating a reaction against Quakerism. William John is named in the will of his uncle, Cadwalader Evan of Coed y Voel, dated 25 Dec., 1688, as follows: To my "nephew Wm. Jon. Evan" £5 "upon condition yt his father in law Hugh Cadder shall likewise give him" £5. He had, apparently, been but recently married. His father, John Evan of Penmaen, in his will dated 4 Augt., 1696, which was executed for legal purposes, he is cut off with a triffling bequest, but his father, according to the then custom, had, doubtless, provided for him at his marriage.

William John married Jane, daughter of Hugh ap Cadwalader ap Rhys, of the parish of Yspytty Evan, Denbighshire, and removed to Pennsylvania in 1698. He settled at Gwynedd, where he died in 1712. His will is dated 11 Augt., 1712, and was proved at Philadelphia, 1 Nov., 1712. [Will Book C, 321, Philadelphia.] The children of William John were: John Williams, to whom his father bequeathed 1400 acres of land, Gainor, Ellin, and Katherine. He owned 322 acres of land in Gwynedd, and 1400 acres elsewhere. One of his daughters married William Lewis of Haverford, and another married David Llewelyn of the same place. He does not appear to have been a member of the Society of Friends at the time of his removal to Pennsylvania. His wife survived him and is mentioned in his will, the witnesses to which were: Robert Jones, supposedly his brother, but perhaps his great nephew, Edward Foulke, his brother-in-law (they having married sisters), Thomas Jones, Robert Jones, and Evan Griffith, his nephew (son of Griffith John of Merion).

[2] I am inclined to suppose that whatever title this family had to Fron Goch was derived from Gainor John's family and that Evan Robert Lewis had been only a tenant of it, or of a portion of it.

[3] The approximate date of his birth is given in "Merion," from an MS. pedigree, as *circa* 1657—for which read *circa* 1652, which is approximately correct.

OWEN, EVANS, AND ALLIED FAMILIES 93

(b) Rowland Owen, of the parish of Llanfawr (Llanfor) "yeoman"; party to a bond 9 Nov., 1680, *in re* estate of his brother-in-law, Cadwalader Thomas ap Hugh (cited *infra*). Will of Rowland Owen "of Vrongoch in the p'ish of Llanvawr in the County of M'ioneth and Dioc'e of Sct. Asaph, gen." (gentleman) is dated 5 Oct., 1717; proved 7 Nov., 1717. [Bundle for 1717, Probate Registry, St. Asaph.] The testator names wife Dorothy (Jones), and children: Robert, Owen, John, Sarah, Ann, Mary and Jane; descendants assumed the surname of Owen.

(c) John Owen, Administrator of estate of Cadwalader Thomas ap Hugh, husband of his sister, Ellen Owen, 9 Nov., 1680, he being then of Bala; as per Bond of said John Owen, "brother of Ellen Owen widow and Relict of Cadwalader Thomas ap Hugh," Robert Vaughan of Llanyckill, "gentleman," and Rowland Owen of Llanfawr, "yeoman," appears. [Filed Admon. Bond, Bundle for 1680, Probate Registry, St. Asaph.][1]

(d) Owen Owen. [Owen and Evans MSS.]

(e) Evan Owen [Owen MS. ped.; Evans MS.] Named in will of his uncle, Cadwalader ap Evan, of Coed y Foel, 25 Dec., 1688; convicted of being present at a Meeting of Friends, before 20 May, 1675 (see *supra.*). He had a bequest under will of William Prichard (William Richard ap David) of Llanfawr (Llanfor), proved 4 May, 1687. [Filed will, Bundle for 1687, Probate Reg. St. Asaph.]

(f) Jane [Owen and Evans MS.], married Hugh Roberts, (as his first wife) "gentleman" of Llanfor. He married, secondly, 1689, in Wales, Elizabeth John. Jane died in Merion, Pennsylvania, 7 month 1, 1686.

Hugh Roberts was one of the overseers of the will of Robert Owen. He died at Merion 18th of 6 mo., 1702. Will dated 25th of 5 mo., 1702; proved 7 Dec., 1702. [Will Book B, p. 265, Off. Reg. of Wills, Philadelphia, Pennsylvania. See "Merion," Glenn, 323 *et seq.*] His second son, Owen Roberts, Esq., was High Sheriff of Philadelphia, 1716, 1723, having been Treasurer of Philadelphia County, from 22 July, 1712 to 1716. Member of the Common Council, 1711.

---

[1] Rowland Owen and John Owen are omitted in the Owen and Evans MS. Pedigrees. Neither of them appear to have joined the Society of Friends. As Robert Owen, the eldest brother of Ellen, wife of Cadwalader Thomas ap Hugh, as well as the brothers of Cadwalader himself were Quakers, they could not take the oath required, hence we find John Owen, the younger brother of Ellen, administering.

Member of the Provincial Assembly, 1711, and was Collector of Imposts, 1716-1723. Edward Roberts, Esq., third son of Hugh, was Mayor of Philadelphia, from 2 Oct., 1739, having been a Justice of the City and Orphans' Courts, member of the Common Council, and Alderman.

(g) Ellin Owen [Owen and Evans MS. Genealogies.] She married Cadwalader Thomas, otherwise Cadwalader Thomas ap Hugh, of Ciltalgarth, in the parish of Llanvawr (now Llanfor), who died in Llandrillo, in 1680.

1680, 9 Nov. Bond. John Owen of Bala, Robert Vaughan of Llanyckill, and Rowland Owen of Llanfawr (Llanfor), in the County of Merioneth, to the Bishop of St. Asaph, for the good administration by the said John Owen, brother of Ellen Owen, widow, and relict of Cadwalader Thomas ap Hugh, late of Llandrillo, decd., of the goods, &c., of the said Cadwalader Thomas ap Hugh, to the use of the said Ellen Owen, and Thomas Cadwalader, Jane Cadwalader, Catherine Cadwalader, John Cadwalader, and Elizabeth Cadwalader, children of the said deceased. [Bundle for 1680, Probate Registry, St. Asaph.] John Cadwalader, son of Ellin, removed to Pennsylvania in 1699, and was father of Dr. Thomas Cadwalader, whose sons, General John Cadwalader and General Lambert Cadwalader were distinguished officers. Frances, daughter of the former, married Thomas, Lord Erskine.

(h) Elizabeth Owen, named in will of her uncle, Cadwalader ap Evan, of Coed y Voel, dated 25 Dec., 1688 [cited *supra*.] She appears to have been living 1 March, 1678-9, and to have signed, as a witness, marriage certificate of her brother, Robert Owen.

iv. Griffith ap Evan, living 31 Jan., 1688, and then of the township of Ucheldre, in the parish of Llanfor. Fron Goch is partly in Ucheldre, so that the lands of these brothers adjoined. He had issue :

(a) Hugh Griffith.[1] [will of C. ap E., 1688 ; Evans MS.] He

---

[1] Hugh Griffith is called " of Gwerevol," [Gwernevel] in 1681, and had then joined the Society of Friends, and a writ for his arrest had been issued. Hugh Griffith and Evan Owen, his cousin, witnessed the will of Ellis ap Hugh of Gwernefel, in the parish of Llanykill (Llanycil), 24 Feb., 1691 ; will proved at St. Asaph, 26 March, 1692. In his certificate of Removal, dated from Hendre Mawr Mtg., 12 month 10, 1696, it is stated that he had been a widower for these many years. He had sons, Evan and Hugh, who lived in Gwynedd, the former called himself Evan Hughes ——, or Hugh.

OWEN, EVANS, AND ALLIED FAMILIES 95

married Mary ——, and removed to Pennsylvania, 1696.

(b) Edward Griffith.[1] [Evans MS.] Died in Llanycil, Wales, leaving issue, *viz.*, Griffith Edward, who probably married Lowry, daughter of Evan Morris, of Kefn (Cefn) Dwy graige, Llanfor [will of E. M. proved 31 July, 1695, Reg. $\frac{1624}{1695}$, folio 63, Probate Registry, St. Asaph], and removed to Pennsylvania, Jane, removed to Pennsylvania, married 4 mo., 9, 1713, John Jones, of Montgomery (son of Rees Jones of Merion), and Margaret, who also removed to Pennsylvania, and married David George, of Blockley,

(c) Robert Griffith, died at sea on the voyage to Pennsylvania, in 1698, and left issue : Catherine, who married William Morgan, of Montgomery ; a daughter, who died unmarried, and perhaps others.

(d) David Griffith.

(e) Catherine, married John Williams, of Montgomery, near Gwynedd, Pennsylvania.

v. Evan Lloyd Evan, also known as Evan ap Evan, and Evan Evans. In the Evans MSS. he is designated as "of Fron Goch," and may have lived there for a time with his brother Owen ap Evan. In or about 1671, however, he was joint tenant, with his brother John Evan, of the adjacent farm of Tyddyn y bedw, belonging to Evan Lloyd ap Rhydderch, of Garn, Llanfor, as appears by the latter's will dated 29 Jan., 1671 ; proved at St. Asaph, 20 March, 1672. In the will of his brother, Cadwalader Evan of Coed y Foel, dated 25 Dec., 1688, he is described as Evan Lloyd Evan, of the township of Ucheldre. [Reg. $\frac{1684}{1690}$, folios 228-230, Probate Registry, St. Asaph.] He was buried at Llanvawr (Llanfor) Church, 25 April, 1690.[2] [Transcript Llanfor Reg. Diocesan Registry, St. Asaph.] He was twice married.

Evan Lloyd had issue by his first wife :

(a) Margaret, buried at Llanfor, 21 Augt., 1688.

(b) Ellin, married John ——; she had by him : Robert John, who assumed the surname of Jones, and became prominent in Gwynedd, Pennsylvania, to which place

---

[1] Edward Griffith was of the township of Llaithgwm, 16 May, 1675, and was then a Friend.

[2] Anno 1690 "*Evan Lloyd Evon de Ucheldre sepult fuit vicesimo quinto die Apr.*"

he removed in 1698 ; Cadwalader Jones, who died at sea, 1698, leaving children surnamed Jones, or Cadwalader who were brought up in Gwynedd.

Evan Lloyd Evan had issue by his second wife:

(c) Thomas ap Evan (called Thomas Evans), who removed to Gwynedd, 1698.

(d) Robert ap Evan (called Robert Evans), who removed to Gwynedd, 1698.

(e) Owen ap Evans (called Owen Evans), who removed to Gwynedd, 1698.

(f) Cadwaladr (or Cadwalader) ap Evan (called Cadwalader Evans), who removed to Gwynedd, 1698.

(g) Sarah, married Evan Pugh[1] (ap Hugh). They removed to Gwynedd, 1698.

[For descendants of the Evans brothers of Gwynedd, see " Historical Collections of Gwynedd."]

---

[1] H. M. Jenkins, following another, but later, MS. says *Robert* Pugh, see *infra*.

CADWALADER ROBERTS.
Nat. 1777 – Ob. 1871.

CHART A.

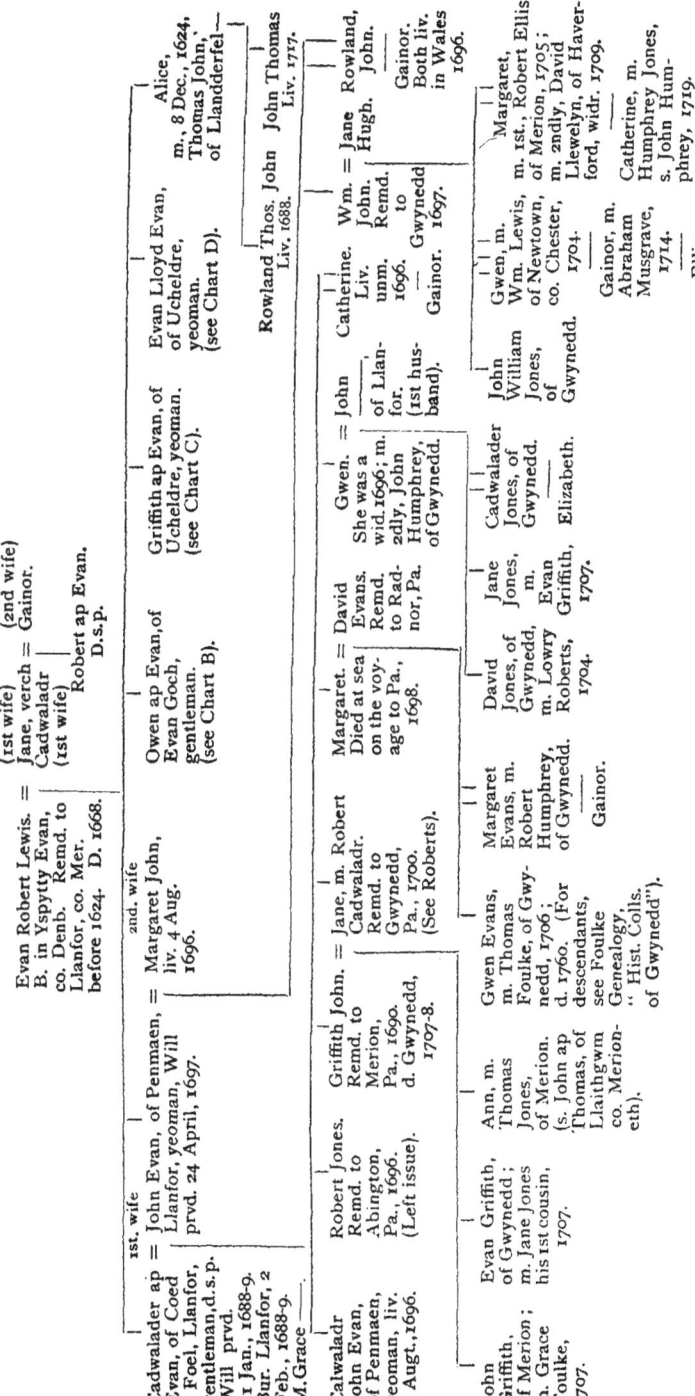

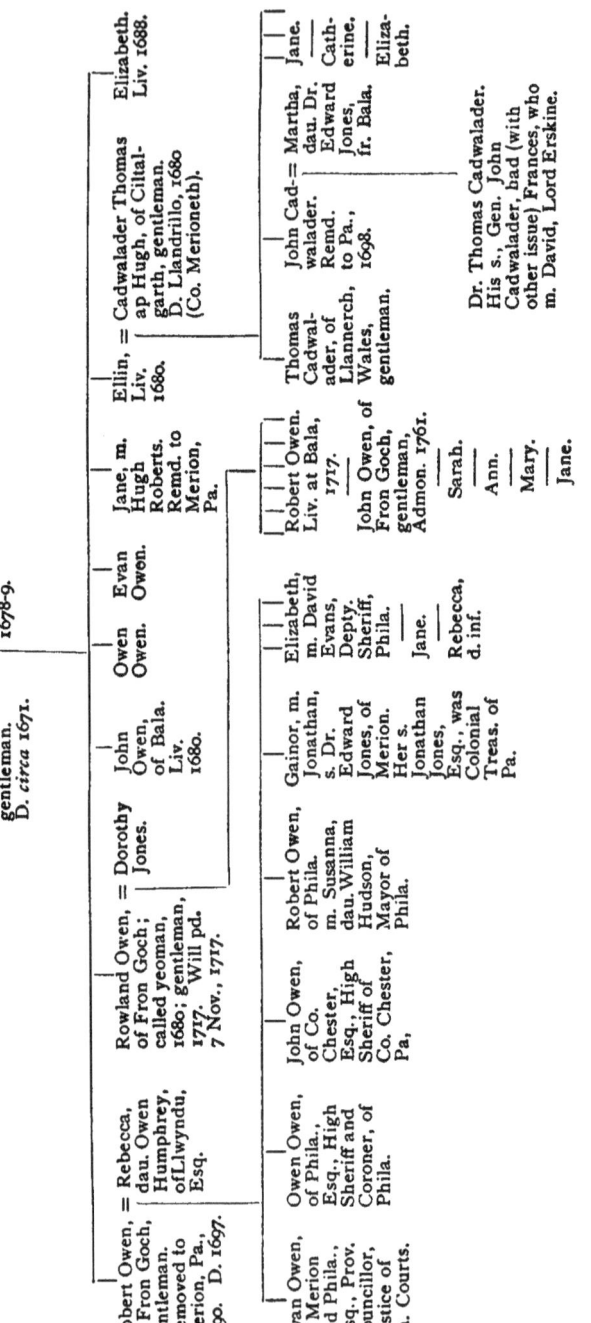

CHART C.

Griffith ap Evan, = ———
of Ucheldre,
Llanfor, co.
Mer., yeoman.
Liv. Dec., 1688.

Children:

- **Hugh Griffith,** of Gwernefel, Llanycil, yeoman. Remd. to Pa. 1696; setd. at Gwynedd, 1698. = **Mary** ———
- **Edward Griffith,** of Llaithgwn 16 May, 1675; d. in Llanycil, before 1713. "Husbandman." = ———
- **Robert Griffith.** = ——— D. at sea on voyage to Pa., 1698.
- **David Griffith.** D. in Wales.
- **Catherine.** Remd. to Gwynedd, 1698; m. John Williams, of Montgomery.

Children of Hugh Griffith and Mary:

- **Griffith Hugh,** of Gwynedd; m. Jane, dau. Robert Ellis, of Radnor, 1718.
- **Evan Hugh,** of Gwynedd, (alias Evan Griffith); m. Bridget Jones, of Radnor, 1705.
- **Robert Hugh,** of Gwynedd; m. Catherine, d. Evan Pugh, 1717.
  - Edward.
  - David.
  - Ellin.

Children of Edward Griffith:

- **Griffith Edward.** Remd. to Gwynedd, Pa.
- **Jane.** Remd. to Gwynedd, Pa.; m. John Jones, of Montgomery, 1713.
- **Margaret.** Remd. to Gwynedd, Pa.; m. David George, of Blockley.

Children of Robert Griffith:

- **Catherine,** m. William Morgan, of Montgomery.
-  dau. d. umn.
- Perhaps other issue, who took the surname of *Roberts*.

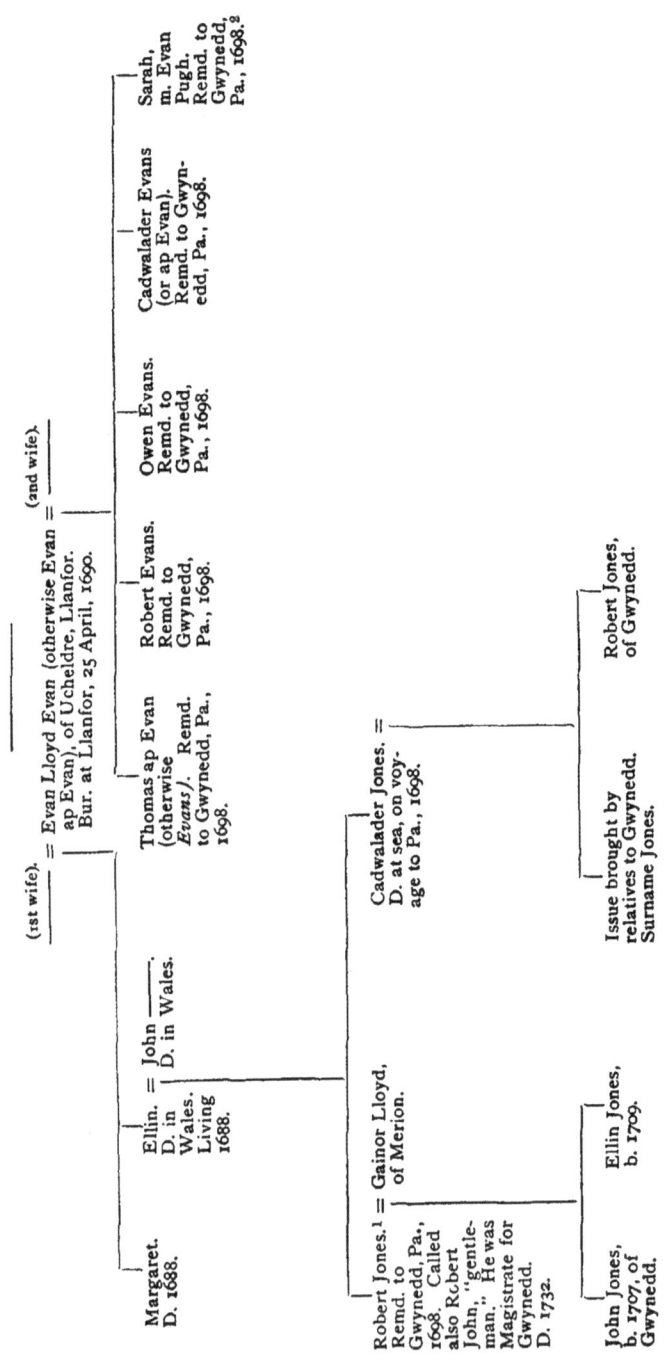

ADDENDA.

Here follow copies of the two original family documents upon which the foregoing pedigree is primarily based, *viz.* (a) MS. pedigree brought to Gwynedd, Pennsylvania, in 1698, by the sons of Evan ap Evan, otherwise Evan Lloyd Evan, and (b) MS. genealogy of the descendants of Evan Robert Lewis, compiled 1797.

(a) MS. pedigree brought from Wales.

In or before 1797, Cadwalader Evans, of Philadelphia (born 1749), son of Rowland (b. 1718), became interested in the genealogy of his family, and, in October, 1797, John Evans, sen. (son of John; grandson of Cadwalader, son of Evan Lloyd Evan of Ucheldre), and his sister Elizabeth· (aged 67 and 71 years), furnished Cadwalader with materials (family documents, &c.) for a record of the family. Among the MS. handed him was the pedigree brought from Wales in 1698. Cadwalader drew up several genealogies of the descendants of Evan Robert Lewis, principally of the Evans branch, one of which, dated 1797, was largely utilized by Howard M. Jenkins in his "Evans Genealogy," but this copy had been added to as late as 1810, or later. The MSS. of Cadwalader Evans descended to Rowland E. Evans, who died 1866. A copy of the original MS., annotated and amplified by the latter from the visitation pedigree, remains in the hands of Rowland Evans, of Haverford, and was copied by the writer,[1] in 1895.[2] Mrs. William Parker Foulke, however, whose husband was a descendant of the Evans family, obtained from Rowland E.

---

[1] T. A. Glenn.

[2] The original document could not at that time be found, having been mislaid among other family MSS.

Evans a copy of the original pedigree, as well as one of his amplified genealogies. It is as follows :[1]

"Evan ap Robert ap Lewis ap Griffith ap Howel Goch ap Einion ap Deikws ddu ap Madoc ap Ievan Goch ap David Goch ap Trahnarn Goch ap Madoc ap Rhys Gloff ap Rhys Vaughan ap Rhys Mechyllt ap Rhys Grug ap Rhys ap Griffith ap Rhys ap Tewdur Mawr ap Einion ap Owen ap Howel ddu [dda] ap Cadelli ap Rodri Mawr ap Mervyn Vrych."

This pedigree bears the marks of having been originally compiled independently of that by Lewys Dwnn. For instance, the individual here called "Howel *Goch* (the red) ap Einion," is designated by Dwnn as "Holl ab Ein^n," (Howell ap Einion), the *Goch* being omitted. It is most probable that the original MS. had belonged to Cadwalader ap Evan of Coed y Foel, who was a man of literary inclinations, as indicated by the books mentioned in the inventory of his estate. The date of the compilation therefore can be placed in or before 1688.

(b) The genealogy here given of the descendants of Evan Robert Lewis is from one supposedly several years older than those by Cadwalader Evans (1797), and is in the possession of the Historical Society of Pennsylvania, bound in a MS. volume of the Genealogical Society's "Collections," marked "Some Records Relating to Radnor Meeting." It was probably prepared by John Evans, of Gwynedd, born 1730, who furnished the family data to his nephew, Cadwalader Evans, and the following is a verbatim copy.

Ellis Williams of Cai fadog[2] had four Daughters, vizt Margaret, Douse, Gwenn, & Ellin.

---

[1] Reference should be had to "Historical Collections of Gwynedd," H. M. Jenkins, pp. 58, 153, 214; note 3.

[2] Cae Fadog is a farm in the township of Ciltalgarth (anciently written Kiltalgarth), in the parish of Llanfor (otherwise Llanvawr) in the comot of Penllyn, near Bala, Merionethshire. Ciltalgarth is also the name of a farm in the same township.

Ellis Williams, alias Ellis William ap Hugh, "gentleman," is named as a principal freeholder in the Lay Subsidy Roll for Penllyn, 3 Car. I., and in 1636. He died 1645, and letters of admon. on his estate were granted that year to Marre vch. John, his widow.

Owen, Evans, and Allied Families—Addenda 103

The said Ellin married John Morris of Brin Gwin in Denbighshire, by her had one daughter named Ellin who married Cadwalader Ab Evan late of Gwynedd deceased.[1]

Gwenn, another daughter of the said Ellis Williams had three children [2] who came to Pennsylvania, *vizt*.

1 Ellis Pugh late of Gwynedd deceased.[3]

2 Ellin married to Edward Foulke late of Gwynedd dec^d.

3 Jane, married to Wm John of Gwynedd,[4] also deceased.

Hence it appears that Thomas Foulke & John Evans were second cousins, as being each of them great grand children of Ellis Williams abovenamed.

Evan Robert Lewis was an honest sober Man, lived in Fron Gooh,[5] he had five Sons, *vizt*.

1. John ab Evan,[6] 2. Cadw^r. ab Evan. 3. Owen ab Evan. 4. Griffith ab Evan and 5 Evan ab Evan.

1 *vizt*. John ab Evan [7] had three Sons and three

---

[1] Cadwalader ab Evan, otherwise Cadwalader Evan (or Evans) was the son of Evan Lloyd Evan (alias Evan ap Evan) one of the sons of Evan Robert Lewis. He removed to Gwynedd, Pennsylvania, 1698.

[2] Her husband was Hugh ap Cadwalader ap Rhys, of the parish of Yspytty, Evan, Denbighshire, who was living 25 Dec., 1688. She had brothers who settled in Gwynedd.

[3] This should read *John Pugh* [Hugh, or ap Hugh] *jather of Ellis Pugh* [or Hugh] *late of Gwynedd, deceased.*

[4] William John was son of John ap Evan of Penmaen.

[5] Evan Robert Lewis. He removed from the parish of Yspytty Ieuan (Evan) to that of Llanfor, before 1624.

[6] John appears to have been the *second*, or possibly the third son, and *Cadwalader* the first. Evan Robert Lewis had also a daughter, Alice, who married Thomas John, of Llanderfel, 8 Dec., 1624.

[7] John ap Evan (otherwise John Evan) was of the township of Penmaen, Llanfor. His will, dated 4 Augt., 1696, was proved at St. Asaph, 24 April, 1697.

daughters by his first Wife, *vizt*. (a) Cadwalader (b) Robert (c) Griffith (d) Margaret, (e) Gwen, (f) Catharine [1]

The Second son (b) Robert came to Pennsylvania [2] and settled at Abington and left Issue.

(c) Griffith, the youngest Son of the said John ab Evan came also to Pennsylvania,[3] had issue two Sons and one Daughter, *viz* Evan Griffith late of Gwynedd, dec^d. and John Griffith late of Merion, dec^d. their Sister married Thomas Jones [4] late of Merion deceased.

The said (1) John ab Evan had issue by a second Wife[5] *vizt*. . . . (g) William John,[6] (h) Rowland John and (i) Gainor John —— William the eldest Son settled in Gwynedd and left issue (d) Margaret their Sister died on Sea,[7] and left issue two daughters, *viz* Gwen who married Thomas Foulke of Gwynedd and Gainor who married Robert Humphrey also of Gwynedd.

Hence it appears that the said Gwen & Gainor were second cousins to John Evans of Gwynedd late deceased —as he was Grandson to Evan ab Evan (5) they grand daughters of John ab Evan (1) who was a Brother of the said Evan ab Evan (5)

---

[1] He had also, by his first wife, a daughter, Jane, married to Robert Cadwalader of Llanuwchllyn and Llangower, who removed to Gwynedd, Pennsylvania (see *Roberts* genealogy).

[2] Certificate of Removal from Hendre Mawr Mtg., 12 month 10, 1696.

[3] This was Griffith John, of Merion. Certificate from Hendre Mawr Mtg., 6 month 8, 1690.

[4] Son of John Thomas of Llaithgwm.

[5] Margaret John. She joined the Society of Friends, and because of quarrels on this account she left her husband, who remained a member of the Church of England.

[6] William John was baptized at Llanfor 10 Augt., 1673, he being then several years old. The ceremony had evidently been delayed owing to the disagreement of his parents on the question of religion. He died at Gwynedd, 1712.

[7] She was the wife of David Evans, afterwards of Radnor, Pennsylvania. Gainor is an error for Margaret, unless R. H. married twin sisters.

(2) Cadw^r ab Evan Son of the said Evan Robert Lewis, died without issue.¹

(3) Owen ab Evan had three Sons and two Daughters² vizt. $\overset{1}{\text{Robert}}$, $\overset{2}{\text{Owen}}$ & $\overset{3}{\text{Evan}}$, $\overset{4}{\text{Jane}}$ and $\overset{5}{\text{Ellin}}$.—$\overset{1}{\text{Robert}}$³ one of the Sons came to Pennsylvania and settled in Merion, and left Issue four Sons and two daughters, viz. Robert, Owen, Evan and John, Gainor and Elizabeth.⁴

$\overset{4}{\text{Jane}}$ one of the Daughters of the said Owen ab Evan came here married Hugh Roberts who had issue three sons vizt. Robert, Owen and Edward⁵—the two latter lived and died in Philad^a. Robert settled in Maryland— each of them left Issue. E$\overset{(5)}{\text{ll}}$in one of the Daughters of the said Owen ab Evan died in Wales, but her Son John Cadwalader lived and died in Philad^a.⁶—the late Doctor Cadwalader being his Son, and the present John Dickinson his Grandson.

(4) Griffith ab Evan⁷ had four Sons and one Daughter viz $\overset{1}{\text{Hugh}}$, $\overset{2}{\text{Edward}}$, $\overset{3}{\text{Robert}}$, $\overset{4}{\text{David}}$ & Catharine.

$\overset{1}{\text{Hugh}}$ one of the Sons came here, settled in Gwynedd,⁸ died there, left a numerous issue.

---

¹ Cadwalader ab Evan (otherwise Cadwalader Evans) of Coed y Foel, gentleman, was buried at Llanfor, 2 Feb., 1688. Will proved at St. Asaph 31 Jan., 1688.

² He had, however, also, sons Rowland and John, and a daughter Elizabeth.

³ Robert Owen of Merion, Pennsylvania, who arrived 1690.

⁴ The order of birth of Robert Owen's sons was—Evan, Owen, John, and Robert. He had two other daughters, Jane and Rebecca, the latter dying in infancy.

⁵ The children of Hugh Roberts and Jane Owen were: Robert, b. 1673; Ellin (or Ellen), b. 1675, Owen, b. 1677, Edward, b. 1680, William, b. 1682, Elizabeth, b. 1683. William died in 1697. Owen Roberts was High Sheriff of Philadelphia City and County. Edward Owen became Mayor of Philadelphia, 1739-40.

⁶ Ellin (or Ellen) Owen, married Cadwalader Thomas ab Hugh, of Ciltalgarth, who died in Llandrillo, 1680 (see pedigree ii.).

⁷ Griffith ap Evan was living in Ucheldre, Llanfor, 31 Jan., 1688.

⁸ The Certificate of Removal of Hugh Griffith was given him by Hendre Mawr Mtg., and dated 12 month 10, 1696.

Edward,[2] second son of the said Griffith ab Evan died in Wales, his Son Griffith Edward came here with two of his Sisters *viz.* Jane and Margaret.—Jane married to John Jones of Montgomery and Margaret to David George of Blockley.

Robert[3] another Son of the said Griffith ab Evan died at sea, two of his Daughters arrived here Catherine, one of them was married to William Morgan of Montgomery— the other sister died single.

Catharine[5] the only daughter of the said Griffith ab Evan came here, was married to Jnº. Williams of Montgomery, left issue, died at a very advanced age.

(5) Evan ab Evan[1] Youngest Son of the said Evan Robert Lewis had issue by his first Wife two Daughters, and by the latter Wife four Sons and one Daughter. *viz* Thomas,[1] Robert,[2] Owen,[3] Cadwalader[4] & Sarah[5] one of his Daughters[a] by the first wife had issue two Sons, Robert Jones one of the Sons settled in Gwynedd and was a County Magistrate many years and left issue, his Brother Cadr died at sea and left issue.

Thomas, eldest Son of the said Evan ab Evan arrived in Pennsylvania with his Brethren[2,3,4] & Sister[5] with many other of their Relations in July 1698, and settled in

---

[1] Evan ab Evan, or Evan Lloyd Evan, was of Ucheldre, parish of Llanfor. Cadwalader Evan of Coed y Voel, gentleman, in his will dated 25 Dec., 1688, appoints his "well-beloved brother, Evan Lloyd Evan, of Ucheldre in the sd County and well-beloved brother Gruffuth ap Evan of Uchelldre aforesd in the sd County yeomen and Cadder Joⁿ Evan [my] nephew to be Joint Executors." [Proved at St. Asaph, 31 Jan., 1688.]

Evan Lloyd Evan was buried at Llanfor, 25 April, 1690.

[2] Margaret, daughter of Evan Lloyd Evan of Ucheldre, was buried at Llanfor, 21 Augt., 1688.

Evan Lloyd Evan had two other daughters, Ellen and Jane, both of whom are supposed to have been by the first wife; Margaret, having died young, not having been included by the compiler of this genealogy.

Gwynedd, having taken up the whole Township between them. The said Thomas[1] lived to a very advanced Age, and left issue four Sons and two Daughters, *viz* Robert, Evan, Owen, & Hugh Lowry and Sarah.

Robert[2] the second Son of Evan ab Evan died in Gwynedd, had two Sons Evan and Hugh and three daughters *viz*. Lowry, Ann and Mary, who were all married and left issue.

Owen[3] ab Evan, third Son of Evan ab Evan, did not arrive to great Age, left issue: Evan, Robert, Thomas, John, Cad^r. and Elizabeth who have all left issue except John and Cad^r.

Cadwalader[4] ab Evan Youngest Son of the said Evan ab Evan arrived to great age and left issue one Son and one Daughter, *viz* John Evans, late of Gwynedd deceased, and Sarah married to John Hank.

Sarah[5] the Daughter of the said Evan ab Evan had issue by Evan Pugh [1] two Sons and four Daughters.

---

[1] The Evans MS. genealogy of 1797 (addition of about 1810 or later) followed by H. M. Jenkins in "Historical Collections of Gwynedd," states that she married *Robert* Pugh.

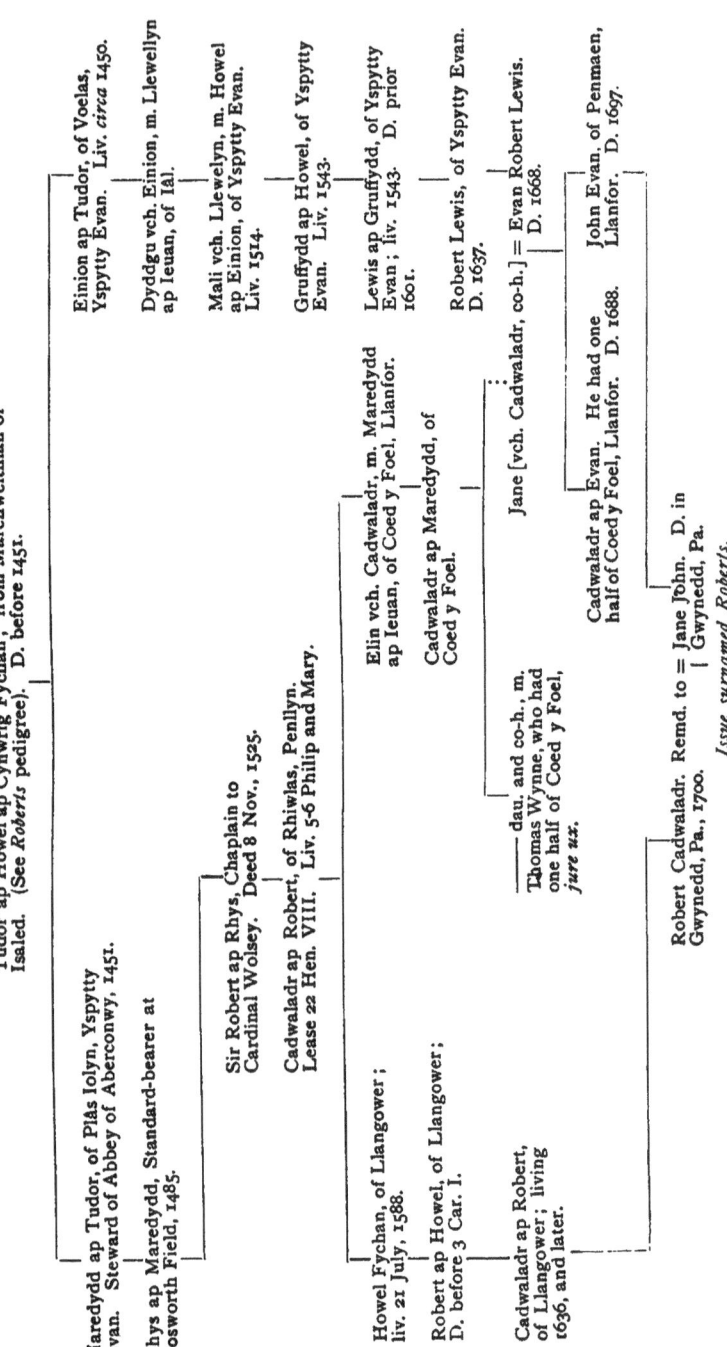

CHARLES ROBERTS,
Nat. 1784.- Ob. 1845.

Roberts Genealogy.

I. (1). ROBERT CADWALADER (see p. 44) m. Jane, dau. John Evan, of Penmaen (see p. 91). Both rmd. to Gwynedd, Penna.

II. ISSUE:

2. Cadwalader (Roberts),[1] bapt. 1 June, 1673.
3. Margaret, bapt. 27 June, 1675; d. young.
4. Morris, bapt. 9 May, 1677.
5. John, bapt. 7 Jan., 1678; d. inft.
6. John, bapt. 11 Sept., 1681.
7. Nicholas.[2]
8. Rowland, bapt. 29 Mch., 1685.
9. Elizabeth, bapt. 9 Dec., 1688; m. at Gwynedd, Pa., 9 mo. 21, 1718, Daniel Morgan (s. of Edward), who was b. 1691; d. 7 mo. 6, 1773. She d. 1777. Their children were: (a) Benjamin, b. 1719; m. Sarah Davis; (b) Ruth, b. 1721; m., 1st, Nathan, s. Evan Evans, of Gwynedd; m., 2dly, 1773, Moses Peters.

II. (2). CADWALADER ROBERTS, s. Robert Cadwalader, b. in Penllyn; bapt. at Llanuwchllyn, 1 June, 1673; rmd. to Gwynedd, Penna., 1698. Grantee, 1710, of 140 a. land from Robert John, on or near site of borough of North Wales. He m., 4 mo. 9, 1714, Eleanor Humphrey, dau. Humphrey Ellis and Jane his wife. She was b. 8 mo. 17, 1693; d. 1755, having m. 2dly, Rowland Hughes. Cadwalader d. 5 mo. 7, 1731, of small-pox, at Gwynedd. Admon. to his wid., Eleanor, 31 May, 1731. He was a man esteemed for his benevolence, and an elegy written at the time of his death is preserved in Jenkins's "Gwynedd," p. 188.

III. ISSUE:

10. Rebecca, b. 3 mo. 14, 1715; d. 12 mo., 1795; m., 11 mo. 3, 1735-6, William Erwin, of N. Wales.[3]
11. Robert, b. 10 mo. 18, 1719.

II. (4). MORRIS ROBERTS, s. Robert Cadwalader, b. in Penllyn; bapt. at Llangower, 9 May, 1677. Remd. to Gwynedd, Penna, 1698. He. m., 2 mo. 28, 1718, Elizabeth Robeson, of Abington. In 1734 he remd. to North Carolina.

---

[1] The children of Robert Cadwalader assumed the surname of *Roberts*.

[2] The date of baptism of Nicholas, owing to the condition of the records, cannot be precisely determined.

[3] William Erwin was bur. at Gwynedd, 11 mo. 12, 1793, having had by Rebecca Roberts, his wife, the following children: (a) Cadwalader, b. 1 mo. 25, 1737; (b) William, b. 10 mo. 23, 1738.; bur 11 mo. 12, 1738; (c) Ellin, b. 8 mo. 10, 1740; d. abt. 1800; m. (Lic. 7 Feb., 1774) Conrad Hoover, who d. 1793; (d) Sarah, b. 11 mo. 14, 1740; bur. at Gwynedd, 1 mo. 4, 1799, unm.; (e) Francis, b. 11 mo. 25, 1744; d.s.p.; (f) William, b. 7 mo. 6, 1746; d.s.p.; (g) Elizabeth, d. at Gwynedd, 1798, unm.; (h) Robert; (i) Jane, d. unm.; (k) John, d. 1810; m. Hannah Magargey.

III. ISSUE:

12. Susanna, m., 3 mo. 22, 1754, Zacob Zimerman (or Zimberman), of Worcester, and had: Jacob and Susanna.
13. Hannah, m. William Howe, and "removed to back country."
14. Sophia, m. 11 mo., 1753, John Cadwalader (b. 3 mo. 27, 1721), and had: John, b. 1755; Elizabeth, b. 1760; David and Morris. The family remd. to Olney, and John, Jr., remd. thence to Virginia.
15. Lydia, m. Joseph Jones.
16. Morris, d. young.
17. Nehemiah, bur. at Gwynedd 7 mo. 9, 1802; unm.

II. (6). JOHN ROBERTS, s. Robert Cadwalader, b. in Penllyn; baptd. at Llanycil, 11 Sept., 1681; remd. to Gwynedd, Penna., and m., 6 mo. 7, 1706, Elizabeth Edward, of Merion. He d. at Montgomery (having remd. there from Oxford) 1773. Will of 5 mo. 15, 1763, pvd. 30 Sept., 1773.

III. ISSUE:

18. Elizabeth, b. 6 mo. 15, 1707; m., 1st, 2 mo. 15, 1730-1, John Jones, by whom she had: Jane, John, Mordecai, Evan, Margaret, Ellen, Ann; and 2dly (abt. 1750), John Blair, by whom she had: Jonathan.
19. Mordecai, b. 1 mo. 22, 1709; d. 6 mo. 4, 1745.
20. Jane, d. unm.
21. John, b. 5 mo. 28, 1714; d. 10 mo. 4, 1801, at Gwynedd; m., 1st, 3 mo. 13, 1736, Jane, dau. John and Sarah Hank (b. 8 mo. 12, 1714; d. 10 mo. 7, 1762); m., 2dly, 10 mo. 11, 1764, Ellin, dau. Thomas Williams (b. 6 mo. 26, 1723; d. 12 mo. 12, 1796). John Roberts, d. 10 mo. 4, 1801.

II. (7). NICHOLAS ROBERTS, s. Robert Cadwalader, b. in Penllyn; remd. to Gwynedd, Penna, after 1698. He m., 1st, 3 mo. 23, 1717, Margaret, dau. Edward Foulke; m., 2dly, 9 mo. 7, 1728, Gaynor Bowen, of Willstown, wid.; and d. at Gwynedd, 1733. Admon to Evan Foulke and John Roberts, 14 April, 1733.

III. ISSUE:

22. Jane, b. 2 mo. 20, 1718; d. 3 mo. 23, 1790; m. 8 mo. 20, 1741, David Morris, s. Cadwalader, of Phila.[1]
23. Ellen, b. 11 mo. 6, 1720; m. 6 mo. 27, 1757, John Siddons.
24. Elizabeth, b. 6 mo. 11, 1723; d. 5 mo. 29, 1790; m., 1743, David Humphrey, of Gwynedd, s. Robert and Margaret.[2]

---

[1] Their children were: (a) Elizabeth, b. 1745; d. 1824; m., 1769, David Jackson, of Robeson (b. 1730; d. 1813), s. Ephraim and Mary; (b) Eleanor, b. 1746; d. 1808; m., 1779; Benjamin Worrall, of Caln (b. 1750; d. 1830); (c) Nicholas, b. 1749; d. 1807; m. Hannah Jackson; (d) Edward, m., 1778, Hannah Worrall; (e) Jane, b. 1760; d. 1834; m., 1785, Abiah Cope, of co. Chester, s. Samuel, and Deborah Parke.

[2] For descendants see a future page.

Roberts Genealogy

II. (8.) ROWLAND ROBERTS, s. Robert Cadwalader, b. in Penllyn; baptd. at Llanycil 29 Mch., 1685. Remd. to Gwynedd, Penna, and d. at Montgomery, 7 mo. 22, 1749. He m., 1st, 3 mo. 1, 1713, Mary Pugh, dau. of Robert and Sarah, of Gwynedd; and m., 2dly, Ann Bennett, of Abington, wid. Rowland Roberts was a minister among Friends. His will, of 7 mo. 12, 1749, was pvd. 10 Oct., 1749.

   III. ISSUE:
25. Eldad, b. 12 mo. 19, 1713.
26. Sarah, b. 11 mo. 13, 1715.

Eldad Roberts m. 1st, 1747, Elizabeth, dau. Richard Mitchell, of Wrightstown, co. Bucks, who d. 5 mo., 1760; he m. 2dly, 10 mo. 18, 1763, Jane, dau. Isaac Jones, of Montgomery. The will of Eldad Roberts, dated 1 mo. 29, 1789, was pvd. 26 Mch., 1789, at Norristown, Pa. He owned a plantation in Montgomery. ISSUE: (a) John, b. 1750; d. 1823, unm.; (b) Mordecai, of whom presently; (c) Elizabeth, b. 1764, m. Isaiah Mullen, by whom she had John; (d) Mary, b. 1766; d. 1 mo., 1859, at Gwynedd.

Mordecai Roberts, s. Eldad, b. 7 mo., 11, 1753; m. Ellen Decker. During the War of the Revolution he served with the American forces. For issue see *infra*.

   III. (11). ROBERT ROBERTS, of Gwynedd, s. Cadwalader, b. 10 mo. 18, 1719; d. 1760. Will dated 8 mo. 14, 1760; pvd. 29 Dec., 1760. He m. at Gwynedd, 11 mo. 11, 1742, Sarah, dau. Joseph Ambler and Ann Williams, his wife.

   IV. ISSUE:
27. Cadwalader, b. 10 mo. 18, 1743.
28. Ann, b. 1745; d. 1823; m. Hugh Foulke.
29. Joseph, b. 8 mo. 27, 1847.
30. Ellen, b. 1 mo. 15, 1749; d. unm., 2 mo. 25, 1827.
31. Rebecca, b. 1752; d. inft.
32. Mary, b. 1753; d. 1825; m. Jacob Albertson, of Cheltenham.
33. Hannah, b. 4 mo. 5, 1756; d. 9 mo. 27, 1825; m. Samuel Thomas, s. of John; d.s.p.

   III. (21). JOHN ROBERTS of Whitpain, s. John, b. 5 mo. 28, 1714, d. 10 4, 1801; m., 1st, 3 mo., 13, 1736, Jane, dau. John and Sarah Hank; m., 2dly, 10 mo. 11, 1764, Ellin, dau. Thomas Williams. (Jane b. 1714, d. 1762; Eleanor d. 1769).

   IV. ISSUE:
34. Cadwalader, b. 1737; d. 1748.
35. John, b. 9 mo. 30, 1738.
36. Elizabeth, b. 1740; d. 1794; m. Thomas Evans, of Gwynedd. (For descendants see "Evans Genealogy," H. M. Jenkins).
37. Ruth, b. 3 mo., 1743; d. 12 mo., 1820, m. Nathan Cleaver, s. Peter and Elizabeth, of Upper Dublin.
38. Sarah, b. 5 mo., 1745; d. 1 mo., 1837, unm.
39. Ann, b. 1748; d. 1808; m. Morgan Morgan.
40. Jane, b. 3 mo., 1751; d. 11 mo. 1, 1821; m., 10 mo. 22, 1778, David Shoemaker.

41. Mary, b. 11 mo. 5, 1753; d. 9 mo. 23, 1786, m., 6 mo., 1777, William Hallowell, s. Joseph, of Whitemarsh.
42. Job, b. 3 mo. 23, 1757.
43. Jonah, b. 1760 ; d. 1761.
44. Eleanor, b. 1768 ; m. Richard Shoemaker.

IV. (27). CADWALADER ROBERTS, of Montgomery, s. Robert, b. 10 mo., 18, 1743 ; d. 2 mo. 7, 1816. He m., 5 mo. 24, 1768, Mary, dau. Richard and Ann Shoemaker, She was b. 3 mo. 14, 1744 ; d. 12 mo. 23, 1795.

V. ISSUE:

45. Edward, b. 3 mo. 9, 1771.
46. Ezekial, b. 12 mo. 19, 1775.
47. Cadwalader, b. 11 mo. 3, 1777.
48. Joseph, b. 11 mo. 2, 1779.
49. Richard, b. 1 mo. 1, 1782.
50. Agnes, b. 1783 ; d. 1872 ; m. Caleb Evans. (For descendants see "Evans Genealogy," H. M. Jenkins).
51. Mary, b. 1786 ; d. 1830 ; m., 1808, Edward Spencer, s. Job and Hannah of Horsham.[1]

IV. (29). JOSEPH ROBERTS, of Montgomery, s, Robert, b. 8 mo. 27, 1747 ; d. 1 mo. 12, 1799. In 1769, he purchased of Henry McQuoin "White Cottage Farm," on the Horsham Road, in Montgomery. He was a man of unusual physical strength. He m., 1st, 5 mo. 22, 1770, Sarah (b. 1748), dau. Richard and Agnes Shoemaker ; and, 2dly, 5 mo. 11, 1774, Mercy, dau. Isaac and Sarah Pickering, of Solebury, co. Bucks. Mercy was b. 8 mo. 27, 1745 ; d. 2 mo. 14, 1829.

V. ISSUE:

52. Sarah, b. 8 mo. 27, 1771 ; d. 10 mo. 31, 1854 ; m., 1st, Paul Conrad; m., 2dly, at Valley Mtg., 10 mo. 25, 1815, Isaac Walker, of Tredyffrin, s. Joseph and Sarah, by whom she had one child, Isaac R. Walker.
53. Isaac, b. 4 mo. 27, 1775.
54. Jonathan, b. 4 mo. 19, 1777 ; d. 8 mo. 25, 1832, unm.
55. Hugh, b. 3 mo. 28, 1779 ; d. 3 mo. 18, 1848, unm.
56. George, b. 3 mo. 10, 1781.
57. John, b. 1783 ; d. inft.
58. Charles, b. 7 mo. 26, 1784.
59. Septimus, b. 9 mo. 30, 1786 ; d. 1 mo. 6, 1826, unm. He was one of the earliest students at Westtown, his name being on the roll 6 mo., 1803. From 1809 to 1812 he was a teacher there. Previous to 1809 he was teacher of the Friends' School for coloured children in Philadelphia, and a portrait of him, by one of his pupils, is extant. He afterwards was appointed to a position in the Offices of the Lehigh Coal and Navigation Co. at Mauch Chunk, where he died.
60. Mercy, b. 9 mo. 14, 1789 ; d. 1 mo. 26, 1870, unm.
61. Joseph, b. 3 mo. 22, 1793 ; d. 8 mo. 25, 1835, unm. For a sketch of him see "Hist. Colls. of Gwynedd."

Roberts Genealogy

IV. (35). JOHN ROBERTS, s. John, b. 9 mo. 30, 1738 ; d. 8 mo. 11, 1824. He m., 1772, Elizabeth, dau. Peter Cleaver, of Upper Dublin. She was b. 5 mo. 24, 1808.

V. ISSUE :

62. Peter, b. 4 mo, 7, 1773 ; d.s.p. 2 mo. 2, 1801 ; m., 1800, Elizabeth Comfort. She m., 2dly, Benjamin White.
63. Ruth, b. 8 mo. 28, 1775 ; d. 9 mo., 1857 ; m., 1803, Jesse Ambler, s. John and Anne. No issue. Jesse d. 1851, aged 75.

IV. (42). JOB ROBERTS, of Whitpain, s. John, b. 3 mo, 23, 1757 ; d. 8 mo. 20, 1851. He m. 1st, 1781, Mary Naylor (b. 1758 ; d. 1816) ; 2dly, Sarah, dau. Joseph Williams, and wid. of —— Thomas. For biographical sketch see " Hist. Collections of Gwynedd," p. 387.

V. ISSUE :

64. Hannah, b. 1783 ; d. 1785.
65. Jane, b. 3 mo. 1, 1785 ; d. 2 mo. 1, 1847 ; m. 5 mo. 12, 1807, Charles Mather, s. Isaac and Mary. Issue : (a) Job R. ; (b) Mary Morris ; (c) Hannah B., m. John C. Lester, of Richland ; (d) Jane, m. Benjamin G. Foulke, of Richland ; (e) Susanna M., m. Samuel J. Levick ; (f) Letitia, m. William Walmsley ; (g) Charles ; (h) Lydia T.

V. (45). EDWARD ROBERTS, s. Cadwalader, b. 3 mo. 9, 1771 ; d. 10 mo. 25, 1850. He m., 1796, Rebecca, dau. David Philips. He was a farmer and settled, about 1795, at Catawissa, near where many of his descendants live.

VI. ISSUE :

66. Cadwalader, b. 1 mo. 12, 1800.
67. Hannah, b. 1802 ; d. inft.
68. William. b. 1804.
69. Hannah, b. 1806, m. Edward Shay, of Horsham, and had John, b. 1835, m. Hannah Haupt.
70. Edward, b. 12 mo. 29, 1808.
71. David, b. 8 mo. 19, 1811.
72. Stephen, b. 7 mo. 10, 1814 ; m. Margaret George, and had : (a) Eli W., m. Kate Marchimer ; (b) George E., m. Ella M. Jacobs.
73. Josiah A., b. 2 Feb., 1820.

V. (46). EZEKIEL ROBERTS, s. Cadwalader, b. 12 mo. 19, 1775 ; d. 2 mo. 13, 1856. He was a farmer and remd. first to near Toronto, Canada, and later to Ohio. He was bur. at Belmont, O. He m. Anne Doyle (b. 8 mo. 28, 1777 ; d. 2 mo. 2, 1827).

VI. ISSUE :

74. Joseph, b. 1799 ; d. 1830 ; m. Esther Scott ; b. 1809 ; d. 1883. Issue : (a) Amanda, m. Jeptha Kinsey.

75. Mary, b. 1801 ; d. 1856 ; m. Abraham Griffith, and had : (a) Elma, m. John Cooper, of Cedar Falls, Ia. ; (b) Anna R., m. Wm. Giffen, of Newport, Ohio ; (c) Rees, L., m. Catharine Seal, of Morning View, Ohio ; (d) Charles, m. Sarah J. Peck, of New Jersey ; (e) Ruth, m. Reuben Creighton, of Mt. Horeb, Ohio.
76. Agnes, b. 1803 ; m. Rees Larkin, and had issue.
77. George, b. 1805 ; d. 1827.
78. Charles, b. 1808.
79. John, b. 1810.
80. Nancy, b. 1812 ; m. John Taggart, of St. Clavisrille, Ohio.
81. Esther, b. 1815 ; d. 1878 ; m. David Smith.

V. (47). CADWALADER ROBERTS, of Gwynedd, s. Cadwalader, b. 11 mo. 3, 1777 ; d. 2 mo. 19, 1871. He m., 12 mo. 14, 1802, Elizabeth (b. 1781, d. 1842), dau. Thomas and Elizabeth.

VI. ISSUE :
82. Job, b. 1814 (and 2 other children who d. in infancy).

V. (48). JOSEPH ROBERTS, s. Cadwalader, b. 11 mo. 2, 1779 ; d. 4 mo. 11, 1859 ; m. Elizabeth Rubencamp (d. 1840). He was a farmer ; bur. at Horsham.

VI. ISSUE :
83. Agnes, b. 1804 ; d. 1882 ; m. Jonathan Jarrett, and had : (a) J. Roberts ; (b) Elizabeth ; (c) Mary ; (d) Tacy A., m. Jesse Ambler.
84. Charles, b. 1807.
85. Mary, b. 1810, m. Henry Magee, and had : (a) Martha W. ; (b) Charles R. ; (c) Elizabeth ; (d) Agnes J., m. Charles H. Kehr ; (e) J. Roberts ; (f) Henry.
86. Jesse, b. 1812 ; d. 1819.

V. (49). RICHARD ROBERTS, s. Cadwalader, b. 1 mo. 1, 1782 ; d. 9 mo. 17, 1860 ; m. 1805, Mary, dau. Alexander Scott. She d. 1828 ; bur. at Horsham. Richard was of Ohio ; bur. at Emerson.

VI. ISSUE :
87. Israel, b. 1806.
88. Alexander S., b. 1809.
89. Mary, b. 1811.
90. Ezekiel, b. 1813.
91. John C., b. 1815.
92. Rowland, b. 1817.
93. Phebe, b. 1820 ; d. 1879 ; m. William Waterman, and had : (a) George (Ohio) ; (b) Israel R. (W. Va.) ; (c) Charles R. (Ohio).

V. (53). ISAAC ROBERTS, of Whitemarsh, s. Joseph, b. 4 mo. 27, 1775 ; d. 8 mo. 13, 1851 ; m. 3 mo. 13, 1800, Alice, dau. Ezra Comfort. She was b. 4 mo. 23, 1779 ; d. 2 mo. 22, 1841. Both bur. at Plymouth.

Roberts Genealogy

VI. Issue:
94. Mercy, b. 6 mo. 3, 1801 ; d. 4 mo. 26, 1873.
95. Elizabeth, b. 7 mo. 10, 1803 ; d. 12 mo. 23, 1825.
96. Ezra, b. 1805.
97. Charles W., b. 1807.
98. Joseph V., b. 6 mo. 16, 1810 ; d. 3 mo. 12, 1834.
99. Jacob, b. 1810.
100. Isaac, b. 2 mo. 1, 1814 ; m., 1850, Mary H. Bacon, dau. John, d.s.p.
101. Hiram, b. 8 mo. 28, 1816 ; unm.
102. Hannah, b. 4 mo. 30, 1819; d. 6 mo. 16, 1882.

V. (56). GEORGE ROBERTS, of Gwynedd, s. Joseph, b. 3 mo. 10, 1781 ; d. 6 mo. 16, 1851 ; m., 12 mo. 16, 1806, Phebe, dau. Alexander Scott, and Jane his wife. She was b. 1 mo. 12, 1783 ; d. 8 mo. 16, 1860. Both were bur. near Penllyn.

VI. Issue:
103. Jane, b. 6 mo. 23, 1809 ; m. 12 mo. 18, 1832, Jacob T. Lukens, s. William and Martha, and had : (a) Phebe ; (b) Willet ; (c) Martha T., m. Richard T. Shoemaker ; (d) George R. ; (e) Jonathan R. ; (f) Elizabeth L., m. Jonathan P. Iredell ; (g) Joseph R. ; (h) Hannah W. ; (i) Mary ; (k) Anna.
104. Jonathan, b. 4 mo. 9, 1811; d. unm.
105. Elizabeth, b. 12 mo. 21, 1817.
106. Joseph, b. 5 mo. 12, 1820, m. 3 mo. 10, 1859, Alice P. Hallowell; d.s.p.
107. Septimus, b. 1826.

V. (58). CHARLES ROBERTS, of Philadelphia, s. Joseph, b. at Montgomery, 7 mo. 26, 1784 ; d. 7 mo. 9, 1845 ; m., 1st, 11 mo. 1, 1810, Hannah, dau. Solomon White, of Philadelphia. She was b. 8 mo. 17, 1789 ; d. 12 mo. 4, 1830. He m., 2dly, 10 mo. 16, 1834, Anna Maria, dau. Richard Hoskins. She was b. 7 mo. 11, 1794 ; d. 12 mo. 5, 1869.

VI. Issue:
108. Solomon W., b. 8 mo. 3, 1811.
109. Elihu, b. 10 mo. 2, 1813.
110. Samuel A., b. 1816 ; d. 1817.
111. Caleb C, b. 1821.
112. Henrietta, b. 1 mo. 26, 1824 ; d. 1 mo. 17, 1877 ; m. 1 mo. 9, 1854, Dr. Richard J. Levis, of Philadelphia, and had : (a) Anna R. (d.); (b) Louise, m. John Thompson ; (c) Mary H. (d.); (d) Henrietta R. (d) ; (e) Minford ; (f) Alice.

VI. (66). CADWALADER ROBERTS, s. of Edward, b. 1 mo. 12, 1800 ; d. 5 mo. 20, 1876 ; m. 10 mo. 25, 1842, Ann Phillips. She was b. 3 mo. 14, 1819 ; d. 8 mo. 22, 1864. Cadwalader was born at Catawissa, Pa.

VII. Issue:
113. Rececca, b. 10 mo. 16, 1845 ; d. 6 mo. 9, 1859.
114. Edward C., b. 5 mo. 19, 1848 ; d. 2 mo. 4, 1866.

115. David B., b. 1 mo. 26, 1850 ; d. 2 mo. 22, 1877.
116. Ruth H., b. 9 mo. 24, 1853 ; d. 7 mo. 5, 1879 ; m. William U. John, of Bear's Gap, and had : (a) Mary A. ; (b) Rebecca A. ; (c) Rachel E. ; (d) Ruth H.
117. Sarah E., b. 1858 ; m., 1880, James Crawford.
118. Rachel A., b. 1860.

VI. (70). EDWARD ROBERTS, of Bloomfield, Ind., physician, s. Edward, b. 12 mo. 29, 1808 ; m. Annie Bartholomew.

 VII. ISSUE :

  119. Josiah ; 120. Petrican ; 121. Charles H. ; 122. Caroline ; 123. Rebecca ; 124. Cordelia ; 125. Agnes ; 126. Edward ; 127. Josephine ; 128. Hannah ; 129. Vilaria.

VI. (71). DAVID ROBERTS, s. Edward, b. 8 m. 19, 1811 ; m., 1835, Frances Saunders (b. 1817).

 VII. ISSUE :

  130. Alfred, b. 1837 ; m. Eliz. R. Richel.
  131. Rebecca R., b. 1839 ; m., 1865, Aaron Sechler.
  132. Hannah, b. 1842 ; m. George W. Mowrer.
  133. Josiah R., b. 1844 ; m. Eliz. J. Clawson.
  134. John E., b. 1847 ; m. Laura Derling.
  135. Margaret, b. 1851 ; m. Peter A. Richel.
  136. Fannie, b. 1854 ; m. Theodore C. Reese.
  137. Sarah, b. 1857.

VI. (72). STEPHEN F. ROBERTS, s. Edward, b. 7 mo. 10, 1814 ; m. Margaret George.

 VII. ISSUE :

  138. Eli W., m. Kate Machimer.
  139. George E., m. Ella M. Jacobs.

VI. (73). JOSIAH A. ROBERTS, of Columbia, co. Pa., s. Edward, b. 2 Feb., 1820 ; m., 1845, Anna M. Clewell.

 VII. ISSUE :

  140. William H., b. 1846 ; m. Ellen Barndt.
  141. Harvey, b. 1848 ; m. Maria S. Fenstermacher.
  142. Arthur, b. 1850 ; m. Mary E. Rauch.
  143. Sarah A., b. 1852 ; m. Charles Decker.
  144. Edward, b. 1854 ; m. Rettie Lewis.
  145. Anna M., b. 1857. }
  146. David, b. 1857. }
  147. Clarence, b. 1860.
  148. Clay, b. 1860 ; d. inft. }
  149. Clara, b. 1860 ; d. inft. }
  150. Joseph, b. 1862.

SOLOMON W. ROBERTS.
Nat. 1811,—Ob. 1882.

VI. (74). JOSEPH ROBERTS, of Ohio, s. Ezekiel and Anne, b. 1799; d. 1830; m. Esther Scott (b. 1809, d. 1883).

VII. ISSUE:
151. Amanda, b. 1830 ; m. Jeptha Kinsey.

VI. (78). CHARLES ROBERTS, of Iowa, farmer, s. Ezekiel and Anne, b. 1808 ; d. 1875 ; m. Sarah Harris.

VII. ISSUE:
152. John, m. Mary Barrett, 2dly, Sarah A. McKee. 153. Martha A., m. James H. Lounsberry. 154. Levi, m. Mary J. Rogers. 155. Ezekiel, m. Samantha Jackson. 156. Theudas, m. Mary A. Noe. 157. Wright, m. Samantha Severe. 158. Frances M., d. unm. 159. Emanuel N., m. Eleanor Frazier. 160. Charles H., m. Mary J. Hagan. 161. Amanda, m. John D. Oden. 162. Sarah J., m. Anthony M. James. [These families of Iowa and Missouri, 1883.]

VI. (82). JOB ROBERTS, farmer, s. Cadwalader, b. at Gwynedd, 4 mo. 1, 1814 ; d. 8 mo. 31, 1858, in co. Harford, Md. He m. Hannah, dau. Yeomans Pickering, of co. Bucks, Pa. She was b. 7 mo. 23, 1811.

VII. ISSUE:
163. William P., b. 6 mo. 16, 1845.
164. Ellwood P., b. 9 mo. 30, 1847. He served with the 195th Regt. Pa. V. Infantry, and d. 23 Nov., 1864, in U.S. Military Hospital, Philadelphia. Bu. at Gwynedd.
165. Horace Wills, b. 12 mo. 5, 1850 ; m. Edith R. Hooper.
166. Richard Job., b. 11 mo. 5, 1854 ; m. Martha C. Shoemaker.

VI. (84). CHARLES ROBERTS, of Upper Dublin, farmer, s. Joseph, b. 1807 ; d. 1866 ; m. Sarah A. Kenderdine (b. 1807, d. 1871).

VII. ISSUE:
167. Elizabeth, b. 1832 ; d. unm., 1862.
168. Gulielma, b. 1834 ; d. 1865, s.p. ; m. Edwin Thomas.
169. Jesse, b. 1837 ; m. Sarah E. Skirving.
170. George K., b. 1840 ; m. Elizabeth E. Shay.
171. Richard K., b. 1843 ; m. Ruth A. Michener.
172. Anna J., b. 1845 ; d. unm., 1866.
173. Joseph, b. 1848 ; m. Mary W. Evans (see Evans Gen., Jenkins, No. 242).

VI. (87). ISRAEL ROBERTS, of Ohio, merchant, s. Richard, b. 1806 ; d. 1849 ; m. Sarah T. Ward (b. 1809, d. 1880).

VII. ISSUE:
174. Frances L., Chicago, Ill., b. 1834. 175. Josephine, b. 1838, m. Capt. Eber B. Ward, 34th Regt. Ill. V. Infantry. He d. 1863. 176. Mary A., b. 1842 ; d. 1855.

VI. (88). ALEXANDER S. ROBERTS, s. Richard, b. 1809; d. in Texas, 1850. Captain of Ill. Regt. in service of U.S.A. during the Black Hawk Indian War. He m. Mary Fort.

VII. ISSUE:
177. Amanda, of Liberty, Texas.

VI. (90). EZEKIEL ROBERTS, of Ohio, s. Richard, b. 1813. A minister of the Society of Friends. He m., 1st, Eliza Ann Griffith (b. 1817, d. 1867), and 2dly, 1876, Elizabeth P. Harrison.

VII. ISSUE (by 1st wf.):
178. Richard E., m. Mira G. Smith.

VI. (92). ROWLAND ROBERTS, of Short Creek, Ohio, miller, s. Richard, b. 1817; m., 1843, Mary Ann Humphreys (b. 1819).

VII. ISSUE:
179. Charles H. (lawyer, Chicago). 180. Sarah Irene. 181. Richard A., m. Catharine P. Barnes. 182. Mary Elizabeth. 183. Agnes E.

VI. (97). CHARLES W. ROBERTS, of West Chester, Pa., s. Isaac, b. 1807; m. Martha W. Walker (b. 1808, d. 1877), wid., dau. James Cresson.

VII. ISSUE:
184. Martha C. 185. James C., m. Elizabeth L. Garrett. 186. Mercy Anna.

VI. (99). JACOB ROBERTS, of co. Chester, Pa., s. Isaac, b. 1810; m., 1837, Phebe Williams (b. 1810).

VII. ISSUE:
187. Josiah A. 188. Joseph. 189. Hannah W. 190. Alice, d. inft. 191. Sarah W.

VI. (107). SEPTIMUS ROBERTS, of Worcester, s. George, b. 7 mo. 15, 1826; m. Ellen H., dau. David and Margaret Ambler.

VII. ISSUE:
192. Phebe A. 193. Margaret A. 194. Elizabeth. 195. Sue. 196. Jane.

VI. (108). SOLOMON W. ROBERTS, of Philadelphia, civil engineer, s. Charles and Hannah, b. 8 mo. 3, 1811; d. 3 mo. 20, 1882; m., 1st, 1851, Anna S. Rickey (b. 1827, d. 1858), dau. Randal H.; m., 2dly, 1865, Jane E. Shannon (b. 1834, d. 1869), dau. Ellwood. For an extended biographical sketch of Solomon W. Roberts see "Historical Colls. of Gwynedd," Jenkins, pp. 207-9.

VII. ISSUE (by 1st wf.):
197. Anna H. 198. Alfred R., m. Emily I. Lewis, and had Sydney L., b. 1881. 199. Elizabeth W., d. 200. Edith C., d. 201. Arthur W., d.

ISSUE (by 2d wf.):
202. Ellwood S., d. 203. Mary E.

Roberts Genealogy

VI. (109). ELIHU ROBERTS, of Philadelphia, s. Charles, b. 10 mo. 2, 1813; m., 1838, Anne, dau. Woodnutt Petit, of Salem, N.J. She was b. 3 mo. 11, 1817.

VII. ISSUE:
204. Charles E., b. 1841; d. inft.
205. Woodnutt P., b. 1845; d. inft.
206. Charles, b. 8 mo. 21, 1846 (see biographical sketch); m. Lucy Branson Longstreth.
207. Hannah White, b. 11 mo. 30, 1848; m., 1880, Charles E. Hopkins.

VI. (111). CALEB C. ROBERTS, of Philadelphia, s. Charles, b. 1821; m., 1849, Helen S., dau. Col. John Bingham.

VII. ISSUE:
208. John B., physician, b. 1852.
209. Mary B., m. Theodore Kitchen.

VII. (152). JOHN ROBERTS, of Nebraska, a pioneer of that State, s. Charles, b. 1831; m. Mary Barrett (d. 1853), and m., 2dly, Sarah A. McKee.

VIII. ISSUE:
210. Mary, b. 1853; m. Charles Martley. 211. Charles H. 212. Sarah Elizabeth, m. Charles S. Wright, and 2dly, Geo. O. Hoffman. 213. I. Frances, m. Henry Christie. 214. E. Dell. 215. Eda B. (twin with preceding), m. Chas. W. Fleming. 216. John. 217. Dwight J.

IV. MORDECAI ROBERTS, b. 7 mo. 11, 1753, s. Eldad (25); m. Ellen Decker.

V. ISSUE:
218. Eleanor. 219. John. 220. Eldad. 221. Charles, b. 1 mo. 14, 1798. 222. Mordecai, b. 5 mo. 27, 1795. 223. Martha, b. 1 mo. 14, 1798; d. 1 mo. 15, 1852; m., 2 mo. 8, 1816, Benjamin Barns (b. 8 mo. 17, 1798), d. 8 mo. 31, 1876. 224. James. 225. Mary, m. Frederick Wonerly. 226. Ann, m. James Bumbaugh, 227. Jane, b. 5 mo. 9, 1809; d. 3 mo. 5, 1879; m. Davis Penegar, of Chester (d. 12 mo. 9, 1882). 228. ——.

V. (220). ELDAD ROBERTS, d. 1843, s. Mordecai; m. Elizabeth Waters (d. 6 mo. 25, 1847).

VI. ISSUE:
229. Ellen, m. George Brookman, Thomas Waters. 230. Mary, d. 4 mo. 14, 1851; m. Henry Townsley. 231. Rebecca, m. Levi Townsley. 232. Joanna, m. —— Mason. 233. Enos.

V. (221). CHARLES ROBERTS, b. 1 mo. 14, 1798; d. at Alleghney City, 3 mo. 26, 1868; s. Mordecai; m. 3 mo. 31, 1822, Mary E. Harrison (b. 7 mo. 17, 1804; d. 7 mo. 21, 1889, in Mercer, co. Pa.)

VI. ISSUE:
234. John W., b. 9 mo. 18, 1823. 235. Joseph L., b. 3 mo. 8, 1825. 236. Caroline H., b. 10 mo. 12, 1832.

V. (222). MORDECAI ROBERTS, b. 5 mo. 27, 1795 ; d. 4 mo. 6, 1848 ; s. Mordecai. He m., 8 mo. 7, 1819, Rebecca Srope (d. 3 mo. 7, 1857).

VI. ISSUE:
237. Charles, b. 4 mo. 21, 1820. 238. Sarah S., b. 1 mo. 29, 1822 ; d. 1853. 239. John H., b. 1 mo. 3, 1625. 240. David L., b. 5 mo. 2, 1827 ; d. 1833. 241. Mary C., b. 9 mo. 18, 1829 ; d. 1832. 242. Samuel S., b. 9 mo. 14, 1832 ; d. 1865. 243. Rebecca E., b. 8 mo. 25, 1837 ; m. Harrison Carver.

VII. (163). WILLIAM P. ROBERTS, s. Job, b. 6 mo. 16, 1845 ; m. 4 mo. 12, 1869, Anna Mary (b. 2 mo. 23, 1846), dau. Abner Pugh, of Oxford, Pa. She d. 10 mo. 20, 1870, and he m., 2dly, 9 mo. 26, 1876, Agnes Doyle, dau. John Taggert, of St. Clairville, Ohio. She was b. 3 mo. 1, 1854 ; d. 8 mo. 14, 1895.

WILLIAM P. ROBERTS, grad. 1869 from Law Dept. Univ. of Michigan. Served in Am. Civil War, in 47th Regt. Penna. V. Infantry, and as an officer of 45th Regt U.S. Col. troops. Now of Minneapolis, Minn.

VIII. ISSUE:
244. Horace Wills, Jr., b. 7 mo. 8, 1877.
245. Roy Goodwin, b. 1 mo. 29, 1880.

III. (15) LYDIA ROBERTS, d. Morris, m. abt. 1750, Joseph Jones, of Pikeland (d. 1793).

IV. ISSUE:
246. John, b. 10 mo. 28, 1751 ; d. 10 mo. 23, 1802 ; m, Mary Stall. 247. Joseph, b. 3 mo. 11, 1753 ; d. 8 mo. 25, 1836 ; m. Ann Flynn. 248. Samuel, m. Rachel Davis. 249. Isaac, m. May Dugan. 250. Jonathan, b. 1764 ; d. 1832. 250a. Elizabeth, m. Amos Packer. 251. Jesse.

IV. (250). JONATHAN JONES, s. Joseph and Lydia (Roberts), b. 1764 ; d. 1832 ; m. Jennie Beatty.

V. ISSUE:
252. Jonathan, b. 7 mo. 26, 1804 ; d. 11 mo. 10, 1848 ; m. Sophia Christman. 253. David, b. 2 mo. 9, 1808 ; d. 1838. 254. Jesse, b. 5 mo. 27, 1809 ; d. 8 mo. 12, 1869 ; m. Amelia J. Mitchell. 255. Isaiah, b. 6 mo. 10, 1810. 256. Betsey, b. 4 mo. 2, 1799 ; d. 2 mo. 26, 1840. 257. Mary B., b. 9 mo. 11, 1800 ; d. 6 mo. 3, 1884 ; m. Jesse Dickinson.

V. (255). ISAIAH JONES, s. Jonathan, b. 6 mo. 10, 1810 ; d. 8 mo. 23, 1881 ; m., 6 mo. 11, 1842, Berthenna Wilton.

VI. Issue:
258. Jesse, b. 2 mo. 27, 1845 ; d. 1 mo. 9, 1883 ; m. Lydia J. Millard.
259. Charles, b. 4 mo. 23, 1849.   259. Bartlet, b. 5 mo. 13, 1854.
260. George, b. 2 mo. 6, 1847 ; d. 1850. 261. Mary J., b. 11 mo. 6, 1851 ; d. 8 mo. 24, 1853. 262. John Wilton, b. 10 mo. 23, 1856. Jennie, m. Hubert Yard. 263. Samuel D., b. 10 mo. 5, 1864.[1]

VI. (262). JOHN WILTON JONES, s. Isaiah, b. 10 mo. 23, 1856 ; m., 18 Sept., 1888, at Marineth, Wis., Virginia, dau. of Stephen Bougie and Ozilda Berthrand, his wife, of Marineth. Rmd. from Albany, Ind., to New Orleans, La., 1893.

VII. Issue:
264. Viola Virginia.   265. Berthrand Wilton.   266. Eva Bethena.

IV. (250a). ELIZABETH JONES, dau. Joseph and Lydia Roberts, m. Amos Packer, and had (with other issue) a dau. (277) Hannah, who m. John Wentz, by whom she had issue. 278. Hezikiah Wentz, b. 12 mo. 22, 1823; m. Joanna Davids. She d. 7 mo. 7, 1895.

Issue (surname Wentz):
279. John, b. 1851. 280. Hannah J., b. 1849. 281. Charles, b. 1853 ; m. Carrie Dock. 282. Samuel, b. 1855 ; m. Bella Smith. 283. Rowland, b 1859 ; m. Edith Britton. 284. Clara Iola, b. 1862, m. J. J. Key. Hannah J. Wentz, b. 7 mo. 22, 1849 (280) ; dau. of Hezikiah, m., 9 May, 1867; Abraham Dickey, b. at Buffalo Run, Pa., 22 Augt., 1844, s. William.

Issue (surname Dickey):
281. Jennie May, b. 1868 ; m. Fred. Schwab, of Cameron, Pa. 282. Johanna S., b. 1870 ; d. inft. 283. Harry Ellsworth, b. 1872 ; m. Anna Leahy. 284. Charles A., b. 1875 ; m. Maud Sprague. 285. William Thomas, b. 1878. 286. Samuel M., b. 1881 ; d. young. 287. Olive Belle, b. 1886. 288. Lollo Elizabeth, b. 1890.

III. (22). JANE ROBERTS, b. 2 mo. 20, 1718 ; d. 3 mo. 23, 1790 ; dau. of Nicholas. She m. 8 mo. 20, 1741, David Morris, s. Cadwalader (see p. 110).

IV. Issue:
289. Elizabeth, b. 1745 ; d. 1824 ; m., 1769, David Jackson. 290. Eleanor, b. 1746 ; d. 1808 ; m., 1779, Benjamin Worrall. 291. Nicholas, b. 1749 ; d. 1807 ; m. Hannah Jackson. 292. Edward, m., 1778, Hannah Worrall. 293. Jane, b. 1760.

IV. (293). JANE MORRIS, b. 1760, dau. of David and Jane Roberts. She m., 1785, Abiah Cope, of Co. Chester, and d. 1834.

---

[1] Samuel D. Jones (263) m. Lucy Oraline Mangham, widow, dau. of William S. Burton and Mary Lindsay, his wife, of Point Cooper Parish, La. They had : Samuel Burton. b. 27 Augt., 1891, d. inft. ; Lucy Oraline, b. 7 Augt., 1894 ; Lewis Jerome, b. 15 May, 1896. Residence, Winona, Miss.

V. Issue:

294. David, b. 1787. 295. Samuel, b. 1789, m. (1) Mary Ann Pusey; (2) Ann Williams. 296. Abiah, b. 1791, m. Mary Hannum. 297. Deborah, b. 1793. 298. Morris, m. Ann Swayne.

V. (294). DAVID COPE, b. 1787; d. at Whiteland, 1864; m. Deborah Phillips Cope.

VI. Issue:

299. Jane M., b. 1827. 300. Mary Phillips, b. 1830. 301. Deborah Evans, b. 1833. 302. Elizabeth, b, 1836, m. Joseph Scattergood. 303. Caroline, b. 1839, m. George J. Scattergood. 304. ——.

VI. (300). MARY PHILLIPS COPE, b. 1830; d. 1862; m., 1853, Benjamin W. Passmore, who d. 12 mo. 20, 1897 (of Concord, Pa.).

VII. Issue:

305. Sarah W., b. 1854. 306. Elizabeth S., b. 1856; d. inft. 307. Deborah C., b. 1858.

VII. (305). SARAH W. PASSMORE, b. 11 mo. 3, 1854; d. Benjamin and Mary Phillips Cope. She m., 6 mo. 11, 1884, at Concordville, Pa., Joseph Elkinton Jr., s. Joseph and Malinda Patterson, of Phila.

VIII. Issue:

308. Joseph Passmore, b. 1887. 309. Mary Cope, b. 1888. 310. Rebecca, b. 1890. 311. Howard West, b. 1892. 312. Frances D., b. 1894.

IV. (40). JANE ROBERTS, b. 3 mo., 1751; d. 11 mo. 1, 1821; dau. of John. She m., 10 mo. 22, 1778, David Shoemaker, and had (313) Margaret Shoemaker, who m. Ezra Comfort, and had (314) Sarah Comfort, who m. Hughes Bell, and had (315) Chalkley Bell, who m. Mary Emlen, and had (316) Sarah Emlen Bell, who m. Isaac Price Garrett, of Lansdowne, Del., Co. Pa. Their only dau., Anne Emlen Garrett, (317) m., 6 mo. 11, 1903, at Lansdown, James Alexander Kell, b. 1866, at York, Pa. (son of James Kell and Jane Elizabeth Fischer, his wife), of West Rittenhouse St., Gmt.

IV. (41). MARY ROBERTS, b. 1753; d. 1786; dau of John. She m., 1777, William Hallowell (see p. 112).

V. Issue:

318. John, b. 1778; m. Alice Potts. 319. Job, b. 1780, m. Hannah Thomas. 320. Sarah, b. 1782.

V. (320). SARAH HALLOWELL, b. 3 mo. 17, 1782; d. 7 mo. 14, 1835; dau. of William and Mary Roberts. She m., 11 mo. 17, 1807, Samuel Conrad, b. 7 mo. 4, 1780; d. 11 mo. 17, 1827, at Upper Dublin, Pa.

VI. Issue:

321. Asenath, b. 1808; m. Amos Lukens. 322. Job, b. 1810; m. Ann Sill. 323. Ephraim, b. 1813; d. unm. 324. Ruth Ann, b. 1815.

Roberts Genealogy

VI. (324). RUTH ANN CONRAD, b. 10 mo. 5, 1815; d. 11 mo. 12, 1089; dau. of Samuel and Sarah. She m., 3 mo. 23, 1837, Isaac Roberts, s. John and Rachel (b. 6 mo. 26, 1814; d. 7 mo. 13, 1866 at Plymouth). They had (with other issue) a son (325) Isaac Roberts, of Swarthmore, b. at Norristown, Pa., 2 mo. 1, 1854; m., 6 mo. 12, 1894, Ruth Kirk, dau. of Joseph W. Thomas and Mary P. Williams, his wife, of Chester Valley, and had : (326) Mary Thomas, b. Conshohocken, 4 mo. 23, 1897.

IV. (32). MARY ROBERTS, b. 1753 ; dau. of Robert ; m. Jacob Albertson.

V. ISSUE:

327. Hannah, b. 1784. 328. Rebecca, b. 1787. 329. Josiah, b. 1788 ; m. Alice T. Maulsby. 330. Jacob, b. 1790; m. Martha Livezey. 331. Benjamin, b. 1790; m. Amy Haines. 331. Rebecca, b. 1793 ; m. George Shoemaker, of Whitemarsh. The above Hannah Albertson (327), b. 1784 ; m., 11 mo. 12, 1807, Jesse Williams, s. Richard and Sarah (b. 1780; d. 1814), of Plymouth, and had (with other issue), a son (332) Jesse Williams, who m. Frances C. Stokes, and had (333) Henry Stokes Williams, of Rosemont, Pa., b. 1853 ; m., 10 mo. 18, 1900, at Haverford, Mary Rhoads, dau. of John B. Garrett and Hannah Rhoads Haines, his wife.

ISSUE :

334. Elizabeth Garrett. 335. Margaret Rhoads.

www.ingramcontent.com/pod-product-compliance
Lightning Source LLC
Chambersburg PA
CBHW071226290426
44108CB00013B/1300